Fodor's 2011

NEW YORK CITY

D0172298

Fodor's Travel Publications   New York, Toronto, London, Sydney, Auckland
www.fodors.com

Be a Fodor's Correspondent

Your opinion matters. It matters to us. It matters to your fellow Fodor's travelers, too. And we'd like to hear it. In fact, we need to hear it.

When you share your experiences and opinions, you become an active member of the Fodor's community. That means we'll not only use your feedback to make our books better, but we'll publish your names and comments whenever possible. Throughout our guides, look for "Word of Mouth," excerpts of your unvarnished feedback.

Here's how you can help improve Fodor's for all of us.

Tell us when we're right. We rely on local writers to give you an insider's perspective. But our writers and staff editors—who are the best in the business—depend on you. Your positive feedback is a vote to renew our recommendations for the next edition.

Tell us when we're wrong. We're proud that we update most of our guides every year. But we're not perfect. Things change. Hotels cut services. Museums change hours. Charming cafés lose charm. If our writer didn't quite capture the essence of a place, tell us how you'd do it differently. If any of our descriptions are inaccurate or inadequate, we'll incorporate your changes in the next edition and will correct factual errors at fodors.com immediately.

Tell us what to include. You probably have had fantastic travel experiences that aren't yet in Fodor's. Why not share them with a community of like-minded travelers? Maybe you chanced upon a beach or bistro or B&B that you don't want to keep to yourself. Tell us why we should include it. And share your discoveries and experiences with everyone directly at fodors.com. Your input may lead us to add a new listing or highlight a place we cover with a "Highly Recommended" star or with our highest rating, "Fodor's Choice."

Give us your opinion instantly at our feedback center at www.fodors.com/feedback. You may also e-mail editors@fodors.com with the subject line "New York City Editor." Or send your nominations, comments, and complaints by mail to New York City Editor, Fodor's, 1745 Broadway, New York, NY 10019.

You and travelers like you are the heart of the Fodor's community. Make our community richer by sharing your experiences. Be a Fodor's correspondent.

Tim Jarrell, Publisher

FODOR'S NEW YORK CITY 2011

Editors: Maria Teresa Hart (lead editor), Jess Moss, John Rambow

Editorial Contributors: Lynne Arany, Alexander Basek, Joanna Cantor, Nicole Crane, Gary Lippman, Meryl Pearlstein, Adeena Sussman, Jacqueline Terrebonne

Production Editors: Astrid deRidder, Carolyn Roth
Maps & Illustrations: David Lindroth; Mark Stroud and Henry Colomb, Moon Street Cartography, *cartographers;* Bob Blake, Rebecca Baer, *map editors;* William Wu, *information graphics*
Design: Fabrizio La Rocca, *creative director;* Guido Caroti, Siobhan O'Hare, *art directors;* Tina Malaney, Chie Ushio, Ann McBride, Jessica Walsh, *designers;* Melanie Marin, *senior picture editor*
Cover Photo: (Aerial view of Wall Street): Cameron Davidson/Corbis
Production Manager: Amanda Bullock

ISBN 978-1-4000-0458-4

ISSN 0736-9395

SPECIAL SALES
This book is available at special discounts for bulk purchases for sales promotions or premiums. Special editions, including personalized covers, excerpts of existing books, and corporate imprints, can be created in large quantities for special needs. For more information, write to Special Markets/Premium Sales, 1745 Broadway, MD 6-2, New York, New York 10019, or e-mail specialmarkets@randomhouse.com.

AN IMPORTANT TIP & AN INVITATION
Although all prices, opening times, and other details in this book are based on information supplied to us at press time, changes occur all the time in the travel world, and Fodor's cannot accept responsibility for facts that become outdated or for inadvertent errors or omissions. So **always confirm information when it matters,** especially if you're making a detour to visit a specific place. Your experiences—positive and negative— matter to us. If we have missed or misstated something, **please write to us.** We follow up on all suggestions. Contact the New York City editor at editors@fodors.com or c/o Fodor's at 1745 Broadway, New York, NY 10019.

PRINTED IN SINGAPORE

10 9 8 7 6 5 4 3 2 1

CONTENTS

Fodor's Features

CONTENTS

MAPS

ABOUT
THIS BOOK

Our Ratings

Sometimes you find terrific travel experiences and sometimes they just find you. But usually the burden is on you to select the right combination of experiences. That's where our ratings come in.

As travelers we've all discovered a place so wonderful that its worthiness is obvious. And sometimes that place is so unique that superlatives don't do it justice: you just have to be there to know. These sights, properties, and experiences get our highest rating, **Fodor's Choice,** indicated by orange stars throughout this book.

Black stars highlight sights and properties we deem **Highly Recommended,** places that our writers, editors, and readers praise again and again for consistency and excellence.

By default, there's another category: any place we include in this book is by definition worth your time, unless we say otherwise. And we will.

Disagree with any of our choices? Care to nominate a place or suggest that we rate one more highly? Visit our feedback center at www.fodors.com/feedback.

Budget Well

Hotel and restaurant price categories from ¢ to $$$$ are defined in the opening pages of the respective chapters. For attractions, we always give standard adult admission fees; reductions are usually available for children, students, and senior citizens. Want to pay with plastic? **AE, D, DC, MC, V** following restaurant and hotel listings indicate if American Express, Discover, Diners Club, MasterCard, and Visa are accepted.

Restaurants

Unless we state otherwise, restaurants are open for lunch and dinner daily. We mention dress only when there's a specific requirement and reservations only when they're essential or not accepted—it's always best to book ahead.

Hotels

Hotels have private bath, phone, TV, and air-conditioning and operate on the European Plan (aka EP, meaning without meals), unless we specify that they use the Continental Plan (CP, with a Continental breakfast), Breakfast Plan (BP, with a full breakfast), or Modified American Plan (MAP, with breakfast and dinner) or are all-inclusive (including all meals

and most activities). We always list facilities but not whether you'll be charged an extra fee to use them.

Listings

★ Fodor's Choice
★ Highly recommended
✉ Physical address
✛ Directions or Map coordinates
🕮 Mailing address
☎ Telephone
🖷 Fax
⊕ On the Web
✍ E-mail
🖃 Admission fee
☉ Open/closed times
Ⓜ Metro stations
▭ Credit cards

Hotels & Restaurants

🏨 Hotel
🛏 Number of rooms
⚴ Facilities
🍽 Meal plans
✕ Restaurant
⚱ Reservations
🏛 Dress code
⚲ Smoking
🆇 BYOB

Outdoors

⛳ Golf
⛺ Camping

Other

☾ Family-friendly
⇨ See also
✉ Branch address
☞ Take note

Experience
New York City

NEW YORK CITY TODAY

New York, New York. It's hard living here when the economy's up, and it's even harder when the economy is going down. New Yorkers are trying to make do with a new normal that includes a financial sector just getting back on its feet and a cooling real-estate market. So please excuse us if we're gruff—or make that even gruffer than normal.

Those anxieties go all the way to the top: like many of us, Mayor Michael Bloomberg barely survived 2009 with his job intact. After successfully campaigning to extend the term limits for mayor and city council, allowing him to run a third time, he pushed hard to convince New Yorkers he was still the best man for the job. Some criticized, finding his third term hubristic. But ultimately Bloomberg avoided unemployment and returned to the office of mayor.

It won't be an easy third term with MTA budget shortfalls and a shrinking tax base. Many of the city's linchpin industries, including finance, real estate, hospitality, and the arts are in financial recovery. Difficulties in the finance sector in particular ripple through the city. But slowly people are returning to their pre-recession ways, eating out, hitting Broadway shows, and shopping down Fifth Avenue—at least while there are bargains to be had.

A spotlight continues to shine on real estate here. In Manhattan rents have fallen from their 2007 peaks. Condo buildings conceived during the boom are coming to completion in a completely different market. The Williamsburg and Greenpoint waterfront in Brooklyn is still full of half-empty or half-finished projects. Citywide, pioneering gentrifiers worry that their neighborhoods might not stay so nice while recovering from a downturn. Despite the doom and gloom, prices here still outstrip most U.S. cities: Manhattan apartment prices are "down" to an average of $810,000.

No matter the economy, people still get hungry, so locals are still eating out, and chefs are quick to cater to the budget conscious. Heck, you can even have an eight-course meal with Tom Colicchio, Mr. Top Chef himself, at his restaurant Craft as part of his recent "Tom Tuesday Dinner" promotion. More cheaply, you can try to spot David Chang while slurping from a bowl of noodles at the Momofuku Noodle Bar or simply eat your weight in

WHAT WE'RE TALKING ABOUT

Several things in this economy have slowed to a crawl, but the gourmet/specialty food trucks hitting the streets keep taking off. Now meals-on-wheel covers everything from French bistro to authentic ramen noodles. And don't forget dessert: Treat Truck, Street

Sweets, even the Big Gay Ice Cream Truck (yes, that's its name) can provide the suitable post-meal sugar buzz.

Don't cry for them, Argentina—Broadway has seen quite a few shows drop the curtain for good, including *Gypsy*, *Spamalot*, *Spring Awakening*,

Hairspray, *Young Frankenstein*, and *Grease*. But ever the comeback kid, musical theater bounced back with *Hair*, *Billy Elliot*, and *Promises*, *Promises*.

Real estate is an obsession in New York City, even more so when the market is down and deals can be made.

french fries at Pommes Frites. There's something for everyone to eat, and plenty of restaurants have promotions, inexpensive lunches, and prix-fixe menus to lure diners on slower nights, so keep an eye out for those. Since strong cocktails are a necessity during these trying times, New York's bars have risen to the task by serving delicious, complex drinks at bars like Death & Co. and the Clover Club.

Meanwhile, in the world of the performing arts, long-running shows are closing, but things aren't totally dire. There are bargain tickets galore to the surviving plays and musicals, and Off-Broadway shows are ascendant in popularity and quality. Plus, we still have *Law & Order* (filming just about everywhere in the city on any given day) as well as *Gossip Girl* and *30 Rock* at the Silvercup Studios in Queens. Musically, there's everything from indie troubadour Beirut at the Brooklyn Academy of Music to Billy Joel playing the last concert at Shea Stadium. And if those don't appeal, there are countless other venues from Red Hook to Morningside Heights.

They say that if you can make it here you can make it anywhere. In a New York that's in flux between identifying as a "luxury city" (as Mayor Bloomberg called it) and becoming a town with the same struggles as the rest of America, "making it" feels like an even bigger accomplishment. Luckily, New Yorkers are a proud bunch, and we're happy to share all the tips and tricks we've learned. Welcome.

Several neighborhoods were pinned as "up and coming" before the housing bubble popped, including Inwood in the far north and outer borough spots Sunset Park, Jackson Heights, and SoBro (aka South Bronx). Will they gain momentum again, or remain in housing limbo? We'll see in 2011.

Move over, Magnolia. What's the next cupcake craze? It could be the whoopee pie. *The New York Times* anointed this sweet treat as the successor, and its less-decorative, modest "cake-sandwich" style seems to be a sign of the times.

New Yorkers love a good parade, especially when it's to welcome home their victorious Yankees after winning the World Series in 2009. But can that momentum move forward in a new decade? That depends on how the Bronx Bombers play.

NEW YORK CITY PLANNER

Weather This

New York City weather, like its people, is a study in extremes. Much of winter brings bone-chilling winds and an occasional traffic-snarling snowfall, but you're just as likely to experience mild afternoons sandwiched by cool temperatures.

In late spring and early summer, streets fill with parades and sidewalk concerts and Central Park has free performances. Late August temperatures sometimes claw skyward, giving many subway stations the feel and bouquet of dingy saunas (no wonder the Hamptons are so crowded). This is why September brings palpable excitement, with stunning yellow-and-bronze foliage complementing the dawn of a new cultural season. Between October and May, museums mount major exhibitions, most Broadway shows open, and formal opera, ballet, and concert seasons begin.

Getting Around

Without a doubt, the best way to explore New York is on foot. No matter what neighborhood you're headed to, you'll get a better sense of it by wandering around; you can check out the architecture, pop into cool-looking shops and cafés, and observe the walk-and-talk of the locals. Our easy grid pattern makes it hard to get lost for more than a few blocks—and if you do, you'll find New Yorkers are surprisingly helpful with directions.

The days when New York's subways were dangerous are long gone. Now the city's network of underground trains is the most efficient way to get around. (City buses are equally cheap, but can take forever to navigate through traffic, especially crosstown.) The subway is by no means flawless: good luck understanding loudspeaker announcements on all but the newest trains; the floors are sticky; stations are sweltering in summer; and platforms are grimy year-round. In other words, it's quite obvious that the subway is over 100 years old. Still, for now $2.25 gets you to almost any neighborhood in Manhattan or the outer boroughs, and lines that service the most popular destinations are generally clean, with maps and signs that clearly state where you're going. It gets crowded during rush hours, when you'll likely find that all the subway car seats are taken—and have to join your fellow riders in the particular New York sport of "strap-hanging."

If you've got a long way to go and would rather be comfortable than thrifty, hail one of the ubiquitous yellow cabs that troll New York's streets around the clock. A December 2006 hike in taxi fares means that a 20-minute ride can now set you back more than $15. But you'll get to look at the scenery as you go and talk to the driver (who might be from as far away as Bangladesh or Ukraine). Avoid trying to hail a cab between 4 and 4:30 PM, unless you want to do a lot of futile street-side arm waving; it's when the drivers change shifts.

°F   °C

68   20

50   10

32   0

14   -10

J F M A M J J A S O N D

1

Our Streets

The map of Manhattan is, for the most part, easy to follow: north of 14th Street, streets are laid out in a numbered grid pattern. Numbered streets run east and west (crosstown), and broad avenues, most of them also numbered, run north (uptown) and south (downtown). The main exception is Broadway, which runs the entire length of Manhattan on a diagonal. Below 14th Street, street patterns get chaotic. In the West Village, West 4th Street intersects West 11th Street, Greenwich Street runs roughly parallel to Greenwich Avenue, and Leroy Street turns into St. Luke's Place for one block and then becomes Leroy again. There's an East Broadway and a West Broadway, both of which run north–south, and neither of which is an extension of Broadway, leaving even locals scratching their heads.

Street Smarts

Avoid deserted blocks in unfamiliar neighborhoods. A brisk, purposeful pace helps deter trouble wherever you go. New York City is a safe city, but it's still a city, so keep jewelry out of sight on the street; better yet, leave valuables at home. Don't wear gold chains or large jewelry, even if it's fake.

When in bars or restaurants, never hang your purse or bag on the back of a chair or put it underneath the table.

Never leave any bags unattended, and expect to have yourself and your possessions inspected thoroughly in such places as airports, sports stadiums, museums, and city buildings. Police officers stationed by subway token booths also reserve the right to check your bags before you pass through the turnstile to enter the platform.

Politely ignore panhandlers on the streets and subways; people who offer to hail you a cab (they often appear at Penn Station, the Port Authority, or the airport), and limousine and gypsy cab drivers who (illegally) offer rides priced according to how desperate you look.

Knockoff wristwatches will keep excellent time until you're about an hour away from the vendor, so don't bother with them; ditto for pirated DVDs. Trust us, they work poorly and, not for nothing, their sale is highly illegal.

If you wander into a cold snap, do as the locals do and buy an inexpensive hat or scarf from a sidewalk vendor. Similarly, if it rains, scan the mouths of subway stairwells for umbrella salesmen who materialize so quickly you'll think the raindrops hydrated them into existence.

Our Hours

Subways and buses run around the clock, and so do plenty of businesses—including restaurants, pharmacies, copy shops, and even fitness clubs (there's no wait for a treadmill at 4 AM). Other shops and services have more extensive hours than you'll find elsewhere in the United States; for example, there are quite a few places where you can get groceries—or get your hair and nails done—at 11 PM. In general, though, you can safely assume that most shops are open seven days a week, from about 10 to 7 Monday Saturday and from noon to 6 on Sunday. Bars generally close at 4 AM, though some after-hours clubs are open later.

Two Ways to Save

Consider buying a CityPass, a group of tickets to six top-notch attractions in New York: the Empire State Building, the Guggenheim Museum, the American Museum of Natural History, the Museum of Modern Art, the Metropolitan Museum of Art (including the Cloisters), and Circle Line Cruises or admission to Liberty and Ellis Island. The $74 pass, which saves you half the cost of each individual ticket, is good for nine days from first use.

Discount coupons are available at the city's official tourism marketing bureau, **NYC & Company** (⊕ www.nycvisit. com), near Times Square.

WHAT'S WHERE

1 Lower Manhattan. Heavy-duty landmarks anchor the southern tip: Wall Street and the Financial District; the breezy waterfront parks of Battery Park City and historic South Street Seaport; ferry terminals dispatching boats out to Ellis Island and the Statue of Liberty; and the gradually evolving construction site at Ground Zero, where thousands flock daily to pay their respects.

2 Chinatown and Little Italy. Between Broome Street and Columbus Park (to the north and south) and the Bowery and Broadway (to the east and west), these touristy areas teem with street vendors selling knockoff handbags and "Faux-lex" watches. Brave the crowds, and explore some of the less traveled streets to find vestiges of what makes these neighborhoods special: Chinese herb shops, exceptional noodle joints, Italian cafés, and gelaterias.

3 SoHo, NoLita, and TriBeCa. The only struggling creative types in SoHo these days are sidewalk merchants hawking canvases, handmade jewelry, and T-shirts; the superluxe shops dominate here. To the east, NoLita has more tiny boutiques and restaurants. South and west of SoHo are the streets of TriBeCa, broader and also quieter, because hardly anyone can afford to live here.

4 The East Village and the Lower East Side. Once an edgy neighborhood of artists and punks, now filled with combination of artists, fashionable lawyers, and students, the East Village centers around the scruffy but beloved Tompkins Square Park. The neighborhood is one of the city's best for eating, both in terms of variety and quality. To the south, the rapidly gentrifying Lower East Side (bounded by the Bowery, Clinton, Houston, and Delancey streets) draws hipsters with live-music clubs, independent clothing shops, wine-and-tapas bars, and health-food joints.

5 Greenwich Village and the Meatpacking District. Happily, artists with rent-controlled apartments, out-and-proud gays, and university students are still in the Village today, but because those quaint town houses have become so expensive, residents also include wealthy media moguls, celebrities, and socialites. From 14th Street south to Houston and from the Hudson River east to 5th Avenue, the blocks are a jumble of jazz clubs, posh restaurants, former speakeasies, and rainbow flags. Farther west, the once blue-collar Meatpacking District has evolved into a swanky clubbing and late-night restaurant scene for the young and scantily clad.

6 Chelsea. Like its namesake London district, our Chelsea has a small-town personality, albeit with big-city prices. Its leafy streets (which stretch from 14th to the upper 20s) are lined with renovated brownstones and spacious art galleries; its avenues (from 6th to the Hudson) brim with restaurants, bakeries, bodegas, and men's clothing stores. Chelsea has supplanted the Village as the center of gay life in the city.

7 Union Square, Murray Hill, and Gramercy. Bustling Union Square Park, bounded by 14th and 17th streets, Broadway, and Park Avenue, hosts the city's best green-market four times a week. On the 14th-Street edge are broad stone steps where break-dancers and other performers busk for onlookers. North, up Broadway, is Madison Square Park, beloved for its outdoor summer jazz concerts. Nearby are the preening mansions and town houses of Gramercy in the East 20s, and of Murray Hill in the East 30s.

WHAT'S WHERE

8 Times Square and Midtown West. Once profoundly seedy, Times Square today is homogenous, over-the-top razzle-dazzle. Neon, scrolling tickers, and massive TV screens coat building facades, and street preachers and musicians man the corners. Towering office buildings continue to line Broadway going north, ending at Columbus Circle at the edge of Central Park.

9 Rockefeller Center and Midtown East. Near Rockefeller Center, justly famous for its tree and rink, are ultraswank Saks, Tiffany & Co., Henri Bendel, and Bergdorf Goodman, among others. St. Patrick's Cathedral, on 5th Avenue, is a key landmark. Heading south will bring you to the stately New York Public Library (and the adjacent Bryant Park), Grand Central Terminal, and the Chrysler Building.

10 The Upper East Side. North of 59th Street, between 5th and Park avenues, the Upper East Side is home to more millionaires than any other part of the city. Historic-district designation has kept the tony mansions and apartment buildings intact and largely uninterrupted by "plebeian" structures. Tucked into this stretch of 5th are the Museum Mile and, a block east, Madison Avenue's haute boutiques.

11 The Upper West Side. In the shadow of ornate prewar buildings, sidewalks burst with stroller-pushing caregivers, dog-walkers, joggers, and students. By day the dominant draw is the American Museum of Natural History; by night, Lincoln Center. Way north sit the eminently walkable Columbia University campus and the grounds of the Cathedral Church of St. John the Divine, with catacombs and wandering peacocks.

12 Harlem. A hotbed of African-American and Hispanic-American culture for almost a century, Harlem still sizzles today. The brownstone-lined blocks between about 110th and 145th streets—many of which languished in the '70s and '80s—are being refurbished: Bill Clinton moved his post-presidency offices here in 2001. Chic boutiques and restaurants are popping up, while music venues from the 1920s and '30s are still in full swing.

13 Brooklyn and the Outer Boroughs. Brooklyn, our largest borough, counts among its stars Coney Island, Prospect Park, and the Brooklyn Botanic Gardens. Its ultra-distinct neighborhoods include the hipster Neverland Williamsburg and the Italian-American Carroll Gardens. Staten Island harbors a commuter-transporting ferry, and Queens has pocket communities of Greeks, Indians, and Dominicans (among others), as well as Flushing Meadows and Citi Field. The Bronx was best known for the old Yankee Stadium—it's likely the new one will remain famous, too—but Arthur Avenue's Italian restaurants, the New York Botanical Garden, and the Bronx Zoo are no slouches.

NEW YORK CITY TOP ATTRACTIONS

Metropolitan Museum of Art

(A) The largest art museum in the western hemisphere, the Met is—naturally—a mecca for art lovers of all stripes. Treasures from all over the world and every era of human creativity comprise its expansive collection. It's easy to get dizzy circling all the Dutch master canvases, bronze Rodins, and ancient Greek artifacts—but if you need a breather, you can always retire to the Temple of Dendur or the rooftop café.

Times Square

(B) Times Square is the most frenetic part of New York City: a cacophony of flashing lights and shoulder-to-shoulder crowds that many New Yorkers studiously avoid. But if you like sensory overload, the chaotic mix of huge underwear billboards, flashing digital displays, on-location television broadcasts, and outré street performers will give you your fix. In an effort to make this headache-inducing mecca more traversable, Mayor Bloomberg banned cars on Broadway between 42nd and 49th streets in 2009, creating a pedestrian mall.

Empire State Building

(C) From the 86th-floor observatory, which towers 1,050 feet above the city, you can see up to 80 mi away on a clear day (and it's heated and air-conditioned, unlike the deck 16 stories farther up). The views at night are equally stunning, with the glittering city lights French architect Le Corbusier once called "a Milky Way come down to earth." If you're afraid of heights, gazing at the building from afar will still deliver a dose of dazzle—especially after dark, when it's illuminated by colored lights that correspond to different holidays and events.

Museum of Modern Art

(D) Described as a "modernist dream world" after its $425 million face-lift in 2004, MoMA has since become as famous for its architecture as for its collections. Yoshio Taniguchi, the Japanese architect responsible for the redesign, created newly spacious, soaring-ceiling galleries suffused with natural light, where masterpieces like Monet's *Water Lilies,* Picasso's *Les Demoiselles d'Avignon,* and van Gogh's *Starry Night* can get the oohs and aahs they deserve. The museum's restaurant next door, the Modern, is nearly as breathtaking.

Brooklyn Bridge

(E) "A drive-through cathedral" is how critic James Wolcott described this, one of New York's noblest and most recognized landmarks. Spanning the East River, the Brooklyn Bridge connects the island of Manhattan to the borough of Brooklyn (once an independent city, and still worth a visit in its own right). A leisurely hour's stroll on the pedestrian walkway (which you'll share with bicyclists and in-line skaters) is an essential New York experience. Traffic is beneath you, and the views along the East River and of Manhattan's Financial District are some of the best anywhere.

Statue of Liberty

(F) Presented to the United States in 1886 as a gift from France, Lady Liberty is a near-universal symbol of freedom and democracy, standing 152 feet high atop an 89-foot pedestal on Liberty Island. You can get a taste of the thrill millions of immigrants must have experienced as you approach Liberty Island on the ferry from Battery Park. The statue's crown was closed to visitors for almost eight years following the September 11 attacks, but reopened on July 4, 2009.

American Museum of Natural History

(G) The towering, spectacularly reassembled dinosaur skeletons that greet you when you enter this museum are practically worth the (suggested) price of admission. But there's tons more, including exhibits of ancient civilizations, animals both stuffed and living (don't miss the live Butterfly Conservatory October–May), a hall of oceanic creatures overlooked by a 94-foot model of a blue whale, and space shows at the adjoining Rose Center for Earth and Space.

Central Park

(H) The literal and spiritual center of Manhattan, Central Park has 843 acres of meandering paths, tranquil lakes, ponds, and open meadows. For equestrians, softball and soccer players, strollers, ice- and roller-skaters, rock climbers, bird-watchers, boaters, picnickers, and outdoor performers, it's an oasis of fresh air and greenery that lets them forget—at least for a little while—the hustle and congestion of the city.

Bronx Zoo

(I) One urban jungle deserves another. Only at the world's largest urban zoo is there room for gorillas to lumber around a 6.5-acre simulated rain forest, or tigers and lions to roam nearly 40 acres of open meadows.

SoHo

(J) The elegant cast-iron buildings, cobblestone streets, art galleries, chic boutiques, and swanky hotels make this a wonderful area in which to shop, drink, and dream of a more glamorous life.

NEW YORK CITY WITH KIDS

Though much of New York revolves around the distinctly adult pursuits of making and spending money, it's also a great city for kids. Our top activities include:

American Museum of Natural History. The hands-down favorite for both visiting and local kids, this museum's many exhibits could entertain most children for a week. The dinosaurs alone are worth the trip, as is the live Butterfly Conservatory that runs each year from October to May. There are also an IMAX theater, ancient-culture displays, and wildlife dioramas with taxidermied creatures that hit the right mix of fascinating and creepy.

Bronx Zoo. The country's largest metropolitan wildlife park is home to more than 4,000 animals, including endangered and threatened species. Plan to spend a whole day here, so your kids don't have to choose between Congo Gorilla Forest and the Siberian cats at Tiger Mountain. Be sure to check out the World of Darkness, a black-lighted indoor exhibit of nocturnal creatures. On Tuesday from April through October the zoo runs special tours for young children.

Central Park Zoo. Three climatic regions—Rain Forest, Temperate Territory, and Polar Circle—are represented at this bite-size zoo. The rain-forest frogs, red pandas, and performing sea lions are all nifty—but the winner is the underwater viewing window into the polar bear pool.

Children's Museum of Manhattan. Interactive exhibits in this five-floor museum change frequently—but they're always fun. As well as visiting with TV friends like Dora the Explorer, your little ones can build castles in the sand laboratory, and—in warm weather—race boats on a zigzagging outdoor watercourse.

New York Aquarium. Alongside the creaky amusements of Coney Island, this aquarium is home to more than 10,000 marine species, including walrus, giant sea turtles, sand-tiger sharks, and sea otters.

New York Botanical Garden. Fifty gardens and plant collections fill this gorgeous 250-acre space; there are flowering rose and water-lily gardens in the warm months, and hothouses full of tropical flowers in winter. Don't miss the Children's Adventure Garden and its boulder maze.

Rose Center for Earth and Space. The appropriately space-age design of the new Hayden Planetarium (and its accompanying cosmos museum) has made waves among architects—but the thrilling daily space shows inside are a big bang with kids. The complex is part of the American Museum of Natural History, though planetarium tickets are sold separately.

Sony Wonder Technology Lab. The line to get into this futuristic fantasy world might be long (as well as having great interactive exhibits, the museum has free entry). But don't worry—a slightly freaky talking robot will keep your kids entertained while they wait. Inside, there are more robots and image and sound labs where kids can record their own digital music, movies, and games.

South Street Seaport Museum. The fleet of historic square-riggers with looming masts might be the first thing to catch your children's eyes—but there's much more going on here, including weekend concerts, performances by storytellers and shanty-singers, and special guided tours for families.

NEW YORK CITY LIKE A LOCAL

The phrase "in a New York minute" is clichéd for a reason: in this wonderful, frenetic, and overwhelming city, things really do change in a flash. Even for those of us who live here, keeping up with the latest trends in fashion, art, music, food, and nightlife can be exhausting.

Thankfully, there are a few tricks to navigating this city—unspoken, hard-won bits of knowledge that help us locals get the most out of our hometown without driving ourselves crazy. And at the risk of compromising our New York credibility (after all, we consider ourselves members of an exclusive club, and guard our secrets accordingly), we've decided to share those tricks here. Just don't tell anyone we told you.

Getting Around Like a Local

First, when distance is involved, take the subway. Skip the horse-drawn carriages that wait for fares around Central Park; a jaunt in one will leave you exposed to the elements; stalled in exhaust-filled traffic; guilt-ridden about the poor, plodding horse; and broke. Pedicabs aren't of much use either, except for the novelty value.

When hailing a taxi, recognize which cabs to avoid flagging down. Don't wave at cars whose rooftop lights aren't illuminated; these already have passengers inside. Taxis whose roof lights are only lighted at the edges—not the center— are off-duty, and will rarely pick you up unless your destination is on their way to the garage.

Think twice about getting into a cab whose driver has cut across three lanes of traffic to get to you; if he's willing to risk his life and the lives of others just to pick you up, he might not suddenly morph into a model of safe driving once you're inside. Then again, he might be the only sure bet to get you to the airport when you're running late.

Once you're in a cab, know your passenger rights. Although your driver will likely career at high speeds while simultaneously cursing, leaning on his horn, and chattering into his cell-phone headset, you're entitled to ask him to slow down. You're also allowed to ask him to turn off his phone or blaring car radio, and if he doesn't comply, refrain from tipping him. Cabbies make almost nothing aside from tips, so tack 15% to 20% onto your fare after any satisfactory ride.

Lastly, hailing a cab between the hours of 4 and 6 PM is near impossible. It's rush hour, when every workaday New Yorker is trying to get home, and available taxis are very scarce, and they're all but nonexistent between 4 and 4:30 when the driver shifts change, so don't even waste your time trying to find one—head right for the subway or else hoof it.

Speaking of walking, it's crucial that you be aware of the implicit rules of the New York City sidewalk. Most importantly, when walking here, move quickly. Realize that New Yorkers are like sharks: if they stop moving forward, they die (and if you stop moving, one might bite your head off). Unless you're holding the hand of a small child, single file is the rule; walking two or three abreast will cause locals to jostle, sideswipe, and growl at you. Stopping on the sidewalk to take pictures of each other or consult your guidebook will also put you at risk for being hip-checked. If you need a moment to consult your map or text-message a friend, make like you're on the highway: pull over and get out of the way.

Dining Like a Local

The first rule of New York eating is, forget the heavy breakfast—at least on weekdays. Although weekend brunches are popular—as the lines in front of morning restaurants on Saturday and Sunday attest—when the rest of the city is on the clock, it's better to get up and go. Grab a cup of joe and a muffin from a café, a deli, or one of the ubiquitous sidewalk carts (they're passably good), and walk around while you eat. This will give you more valuable exploring time (trust us, there's too much to see to waste the whole morning lingering over omelets), and will also help you save money for the most important meal of the day: dinner.

While we're on the subject, you should plan to eat dinner later than you ordinarily would—if you want to experience the real New York dining scene, that is. Most New York restaurants are empty at around 6 PM and don't fill up until at least 7:30 or 8, so if you eat early, you'll have your pick of tables. Prime-time dinner reservations—between 8 and 10 o'clock—are the hardest to score, but will ensure that you're surrounded by chic dining companions.

Of course, if you can't get a good reservation (and you don't have young kids in tow), you can always do what many savvy locals do: eat at the bar. You'll get the same great food and people-watching, plus you'll get to feel like an insider while other folks are still waiting for a table.

Going Out Like a Local

There's one major rule New Yorkers abide by when hitting the nightspots: avoid, avoid, avoid the big clubs on Friday and Saturday nights. The only people you're likely to see then are other visitors, the pickup artists trying to scam them, and kids too young to know better. Locals and A-listers go clubbing on Tuesday, Wednesday, and Thursday—on weekends you'll either find them at smaller, low-key bars and lounges or huddled in their apartments with Netflix and take-out Chinese.

When you do hit one of the superswanky spots in Chelsea or the Meatpacking District, don't over- or underdress. If you're female, don't confuse "dressy" with "formal"; leave the cocktail dress at home and go for something casually sexy: tight, dark jeans, a classy-yet-revealing top, a fabulous handbag, and heels are almost always a safe bet, as is the classic NYC black. If you're a guy, don't imagine that you can dress like the hip-hop artists you see on MTV; Pharrell may get past the doormen wearing slouchy jeans, sneakers, and a hoodie, but he's Pharrell. You—and pardon us for making assumptions here, it's what we exclusive-club types tend to do—are not.

SITTING IN A TV AUDIENCE

Tickets to tapings of TV shows are free, but can be very hard to come by on short notice. Most shows accept advance requests by e-mail, phone, or online— but for the most popular shows, like *The Daily Show with Jon Stewart*, the request backlog is so deep you might even have to wait a few months before they'll accept any new ones. Same-day standby tickets are often available—but be prepared to wait in line for several hours, sometimes starting at 5 or 6 AM, depending on how hot the show is, or the wattage of that day's celebrity guests.

The Shows

The Daily Show with Jon Stewart. The smirking, amiable, and incisive Jon Stewart pokes fun at news headlines on this half-hour cable show. The program tapes from Monday through Thursday; you can request advance tickets by e-mailing the studio or by checking the calendar on the Web site. For standby tickets, show up well before the 5:45 PM doors-open time. Audience members must be 18 or older. ⊠ *733 11th Ave., between W. 51st and W. 52nd Sts., Midtown West* ☎ *212/586-2477* ⊕ *www.thedailyshow.com* ✎ *requesttickets@thedailyshow.com* Ⓜ *C, E to 50th St.*

The Martha Stewart Show. Master baker, craft-maker, and champion of all "good things," Martha Stewart hosts her show with a live studio audience and various celebrity guests. The program generally tapes weekdays at both 10 AM and 2 PM. You can only request tickets through the Martha Stewart Web site. Often, show producers are recruiting for groups of people (like nurses, new moms, or brides-to-be), and if you fit that category, your chances of scoring tickets increase. Occasionally standby tickets are given out.

two hours prior to showtime. Audience members must be at least 10 years old. ⊠ *221 W. 26th St., between 7th and 8th Aves., Chelsea* ☎ *212/727-1234* ⊕ *www.marthastewart.com/get-tickets* Ⓜ *C or 1 to 23rd St.*

Good Morning America. Robin Roberts and George Stephanopoulos host this early-morning news and entertainment standby. *GMA* airs live, weekdays from 7 AM to 9 AM, and ticket requests (online only) should be sent four to six months in advance. ⊠ *7 Times Sq., at W. 44th St. and Broadway, Midtown West* ☎ *212/930-7855* ⊕ *abcnews.go.com/GMA/tickets-good-morning-america-audience/story?id=144752* Ⓜ *1, 2, 3, 7, N, Q, R, W, S to 42nd St./Times Sq.*

Late Night with Jimmy Fallon. We still miss Conan O'Brien, lost in the late-night NBC shuffle, but Jimmy Fallon has a few things going for him, namely his house band, the Roots. For tickets, call the Ticket Information Line for a maximum of four tickets in advance. Single standby tickets are available on taping days—Monday through Friday—at the West 49th Street side of 30 Rockefeller Plaza; arrive before 9 AM. You must be 17 years or older. ⊠ *30 Rockefeller Plaza, Midtown West* ☎ *212/664-3056 ticket information line* ⊕ *www.latenightwithjimmyfallon.com* Ⓜ *B, D, F, V to 47th–50th Rockefeller Center.*

The Late Show with David Letterman. Letterman's famously offbeat humor and wacky top-10 lists have had fans giggling for more than two decades. Call 212/247-6497 starting at 11 AM on tape days— Monday through Thursday—for standby tickets. For advance tickets (two maximum), you can submit a request online or fill out an application in person at the theater. You must be 18 or older to sit in the audience. ✉ *Ed Sullivan Theater, 1697 Broadway, between W. 53rd and W. 54th Sts., Midtown West* ☎ *212/975–5853* ⊕ *www.lateshowaudience.com* Ⓜ *1, C, E to 50th St.; B, D, E to 7th Ave.*

Live! with Regis and Kelly. The sparks fly on this morning program, which books an eclectic roster of guests. **Standby tickets become available weekdays at 7** AM **at the ABC Studios** (✉ *7 Lincoln Sq., corner of W. 67th St. and Columbus Ave., Upper West Side*). Otherwise, write for tickets (four tickets maximum) a full year in advance or fill out a form online. Children under 10 aren't allowed in the audience. ⓘ *Live Tickets, Ansonia Station, Box 230-777, 10023* ☎ *212/456–3054* Ⓜ *1 to 66th St./Lincoln Center.*

Saturday Night Live. Influential from the start, *SNL* continues to captivate audiences. Standby tickets—only one per person—are distributed at 7 AM on the day of the show at the West 49th Street entrance to 30 Rockefeller Plaza. You may ask for a ticket for either the dress rehearsal (8 PM) or the live show (11:30 PM). Requests for advance tickets (two per applicant) must be submitted by e-mail only in August to snltickets@nbcuni.com; recipients are determined by lottery. You must be 16 or older to sit in the audience. ✉ *NBC Studios, Saturday Night Live, 30 Rockefeller Plaza, between W. 49th and W. 50th Sts., Midtown West* ☎ *212/664–3056* Ⓜ *B, D, F, V to 47th–50th Sts./ Rockefeller Center.*

Today. America's first morning talk–news show airs weekdays from 7 AM to 10 AM in the glass-enclosed, ground-level NBC studio across from its original home at 30 Rockefeller Plaza. You may well be spotted on TV by friends back home while you're standing behind anchors Meredith Vieira

and Matt Lauer (if you bring a funny sign, you're more likely to catch the cameraman's attention). ✉ *Rockefeller Plaza at W. 49th St., Midtown West* Ⓜ *B, D, F, V to 47th–50th Sts./Rockefeller Center.*

NEW YORK CITY FOR FREE

If you think everything in New York costs too much, well, you're right—almost. In fact, the city has tons of free attractions and activities; you just need to know where to look for them. *Choose from our list of favorite freebies, below.*

Outdoor Fun

Walk across the Brooklyn Bridge for a spectacular view of the Financial District, Brooklyn, the seaport, and Manhattan.

Ride the Staten Island ferry to see the Statue of Liberty, Ellis Island, and the southern tip of Manhattan from the water. Check out the spiffy Whitehall terminal in Manhattan, completed in 2005 after a $200 million renovation. The ferry is popular as an inexpensive date spot—the cafeteria onboard is a surprisingly inexpensive place to buy beer and snacks. M *1 to South Ferry; 4, 5 to Bowling Green.*

Catch a free movie screening in Bryant Park in summertime. A tradition since 1992, watching films alfresco surrounded by tall Midtown buildings is a summertime rite of passage for New Yorkers. Bring a blanket and a picnic basket, and be prepared to stake out a good spot on the lawn well in advance. The park runs from 40th to 42nd streets between 5th and 6th avenues; movie schedules are posted on ⊕ *www. bryantpark.org* M *B, D, F, V to 42nd St.*

Wander Battery Park City's waterfront promenade; the breeze and passing boats will make you forget you're in the gritty city, though the view of the Statue of Liberty will remind you that you couldn't be anywhere but New York. M *4, 5 to Bowling Green; 1 to South Ferry.*

Kayak on the Hudson; the Downtown Boathouse gives free lessons and paddling tours. There's even an indoor-swimming-pool program to hone kayaking skills in winter months. The boats are distributed on a first-come, first-served basis, so cloudy days and early mornings are the best times to avoid the crowds. ⊠ *Pier 40 at Houston St.* ⊕ *www. downtownboathouse.org* M *B, D, F, V to 47th–50th Sts./Rockefeller Center.*

Watch wannabe trapeze artists swing and soar at the Trapeze School New York (as shown on *Sex and the City*). They've helped locals and visitors alike make leaps of faith since 2002. ⊠ *Pier 40 at Houston St.* ⊕ *www.trapezeschool.com* M *A, C, E to Canal St.*

Taste the goods at the Union Square greenmarket (on Monday, Wednesday, Friday, and Saturday), where farmers offer samples of their organically grown produce, artisanal cheeses, and fresh bread. The greenmarket, a hip outing for all, is often filled with families shopping for dinner, famous chefs choosing ingredients, and foodies stalking Food Network hosts.

Stroll the Coney Island boardwalk for some old-school kitsch (before it's redeveloped into swanky condos). There are also plenty of annual events for free here, including the outrageous Mermaid Parade and the Fourth of July hot-dog-eating contest. M *B, F, N, Q to Stillwell Ave.*

Check out the street performers around New York's parks: break-dancing crews in Union Square, ragtime duets in Central Park, nutty unicyclists in Washington Square. Buskers in the subway are better than you'd expect—the MTA has a committee that vets official performers, with the top performers assigned to the busiest subway stops.

Smell the cherry blossoms in spring at the Central Park Conservatory; the pathways beneath the blossoming trees are gorgeous, and much closer than the botanical gardens in the outer boroughs. ⊠ *5th Ave. at 105th St.* Ⓜ *6 to 103rd.*

Music, Theater, and Dance

Watch tango dancers and jazz musicians *outside* Lincoln Center at the annual month-long Out of Doors festival, held in August. It includes more than 100 performances of spoken word, beat boxing, and bigwigs like Dave Brubeck and Arlo Guthrie. Ⓜ *1 to 66th St./Lincoln Center.*

Hit Central Park Summerstage for big-name performers like Afrobeat bandleader Seun Kuti and Columbia's own Vampire Weekend.

Catch rising stars in classical music, drama, and dance at the Juilliard School's free student concerts (check ⊕ *www.juilliard. edu* for a calendar of events). Free tickets are available at the Juilliard box office for theater performances; there's also a line for standby an hour before the show. Smaller acts don't require tickets beforehand. ⊠ *144 W. 65th St.* Ⓜ *1 to 66th St./ Lincoln Center.*

Entertain thyself at Shakespeare in the Park, one of New York City's most beloved events—80,000 watch each year. It's been going strong since 1962, and shows usually feature celebrities earning their olde English acting chops. Get in line early at the Public Theater for a shot at tickets, or head to the Delacorte Theater in Central Park. ⊠ *425 Lafayette St.* Ⓜ *6 to Astor Pl.*

Get gratis giggles at the Upright Citizens Brigade Theatre's comedy shows. The theater has moved a few times since 1999, but the improv comedy, inspired by Chicago's Second City, remains sharp regardless of location. Professional comedians, including UCB cofounder and Saturday Night Live alumna Amy Poehler, are sprinkled in with amateurs during the shows. ⊠ *307 W. 26th St.* ⊕ *www.ucbtheatre.com* Ⓜ *A, C, E to 23rd St.*

Art, Lit, and Architecture

Visit the Metropolitan Museum of Art; if you'll believe it, the $20 entry fee is really a suggested donation. You can pay as much, or as little, as you wish. Smaller donations may get some eye-rolling from the cashier, but it's a small price to pay for access to world-famous works. ⊠ *1000 5th Ave. at 80th St.* ⊕ *www.metmuseum. org* Ⓜ *6 to 86th St.*

Browse through the galleries scattered throughout the city. Chelsea's full of expensive galleries with superstar artists, though things get edgier the closer you get to the West Side Highway; you'll also find a trendy art scene in Williamsburg, Brooklyn.

Marvel at Grand Central Terminal's spectacular main concourse; the ceiling painted with the constellations of the zodiac is one of the city's treasures. Ⓜ *4, 5, 6 to Grand Central/42nd St.*

Attend a reading at one of the city's hundreds of bookstores. Night owls shouldn't feel left out—they can attend readings of their own at bars like the Half King in Chelsea or Pete's Candy Store in Brooklyn.

Explore the new MoMA on Friday between 4 and 8 PM, when the $20 entry fee is waived during Target Free Friday Nights. Tickets are not available in advance, so plan to wait in line. ⊠ *11 W. 53rd St., between 5th and 6th Aves.* ⊕ *www.moma.org* Ⓜ *E, V to 5th Ave./53rd St.; B, D, F to 47–50th St./Rockefeller Center.*

CHOW DOWN CHINATOWN WALK

The knockoffs lining Canal Street only represent the surface of Chinatown, but many New Yorkers rarely venture past this; cultural differences and the language barrier can be intimidating to the uninitiated. Thankfully, the language of food is universal, so spend the day strolling while partaking of local snacks. By the end of this walk you'll be both a confident Chinatown explorer and blissfully sated!

Classic Chinatown: Canal Street, Tai Chi, and Bubble Tea

Start out at Canal Street, the most bustling strip in Chinatown. After running this gauntlet of knockoff handbags and perfumes, head one block south to the tidy, English-labeled **Dragon Land Bakery** (125 Walker St.) to indulge in Chinese baked goods such as a brioche-like sweet bean bun. Pastry in-hand, turn right at Mulberry St. to stroll past produce carts piled high. At the corner of Bayard Street you'll find **Columbus Park,** where you can spot people warming up with tai chi or playing "Chinese chess." Cross down on Mott Street and take a left on Pell. To the right is Doyers Street, a dogleg dubbed "the Bloody Angle" because of gang warfare at the beginning of the 20th Century. It's home to the neighborhood's oldest dim sum restaurant, **Nam Wah Tea Parlor** (13 Doyers). Loop around on Bowery. At Bayard there's usually a small stand selling Hong Kong cakes: light, sweet balls that taste like mini pancakes. They're irresistible at 15 for a dollar. If you need something to wash them down with, head back half a block on Bayard to **Vivi Bubble Tea** (49 Bayard St.), a cheerful storefront selling bubble tea (tea or fruit drinks with tapioca balls) and popcorn chicken dusted with flavorings like basil or curry. Fortified, cross up north onto Elizabeth Street ,where you'll continue to spot seafood markets crowding the sidewalks; weave around the buckets of twitchy crabs.

Sweet and Sour Strolling

On Hester, just off Elizabeth, you'll find **Munchies Paradise** candy store (167 Hester). Help yourself to samples from dried squid to a dozen kinds of fermented plums, then get a bag of your favorites for on-the-go snacking. Continue north on Mott to the **Banh Mi Saigon Bakery** (138-01 Mott St.). Inside, it's a classic Chinatown mashup: jewelry store up front/lunch counter at the back selling Banh Mi Vietnamese sandwiches—baguettes with pickled vegetables, cilantro, and assorted meats. On Grand, you may smell the **Kam Wo** tea store (211 Grand St.) before you even set foot inside. The medicinal loose teas and soups stocked here are prescribed to improve vision or soothe aching joints.

The Sights—and Smells— of Chinatown

On the corner of Grand and the Bowery is the **Tu Quyn Pharmacy** (230 Grand), displaying an impressive selection of durian, a spiky fruit with a strong odor, available for the adventurous to sample. Continuing on Grand you'll pass the **Ocean Star** (250 Grand St.), a slightly more spacious seafood market to explore if you're traveling in a group. Finally, cross Chrystie Street and rest your feet at **Vanessa's Dumpling House** (118A Eldridge), with ample seating and inexpensive options like sesame fried bread stuffed with Peking duck for less than $3.

—Alexander Basek

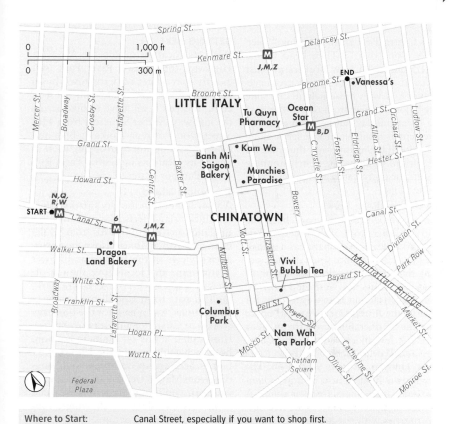

Where to Start:	Canal Street, especially if you want to shop first.
Length:	2 mi (about 3 hours with lots of stops for nibbling)
Where to Stop:	Columbus Park is nice for sitting if the weather is good; Nam Wah is worth seeing if the weather is not.
Best Time to Go:	Noon on the dot, when the foods are fresh and the lines are shortest.
Worst Time to Go:	Sunday afternoons, when the crowds are oppressive, or on hot days, when the asphalt and fish markets are odiferous.
Highlights:	Munchies Paradise, Banh Mi Saigon Bakery, Columbus Park

NYC'S WATERFRONT PARKS

Does Central Park make you think: "Been there. Done that."? Then head to the waterfront. Even New Yorkers are just discovering some of these new green getaways. And with those helpful city bike lanes, doing a tour from one to the next is a great full-day outing, with one-way bike rentals available at key spots along the route. If biking isn't your thing just hit the park to walk, kayak, watch stunning sunsets, or try to catch a free event from spring to fall.

The Hudson River Park

This five-mile greenway park hugs the Hudson River from 59th Street to Battery Park. Although the park has a unified design, it's divided into seven distinct sections that reflect the different neighborhood just across the Westside Highway. The star attraction here—especially for kids—is the Intrepid Sea, Air, and Space Museum at Pier 86 across from 46th Street. A few blocks south, The Circle Line and World Yacht offer boat tours of the Hudson. At piers 96 and 40, The Downtown Boat House (⊕ *downtownboathouse.org*) offers free kayaking. A classic summer experience is the free outdoor movies with popcorn are shown on Wednesday and Friday nights at Pier 54. Chelsea Piers, the mammoth sports center between piers 59 and 61 offers bowling, a driving range, ice skating, even trapeze classes. At Pier 66 Boathouse, you can take a two-hour $60 introductory sailing course with Hudson River Community Sailing (⊕ *hudsonsailing.org*) The park also sponsors free tours and classes including free fishing. (Yes, fishing in NYC.) For a calendar of events and activities, go to ⊕ *hudsonriverpark.org*.

GETTING HERE

With its location across the Westside Highway, the Hudson River Park isn't exactly easy to get to. Crosstown buses at 14th, 23rd, and 42nd will get you close, but you'll still have to hike across the highway. At Pier 84 across from 44th Street, you can rent a bike at Bike and Roll with an option of dropping it off at any of its locations in Central Park, Riverside Park, or Battery Park.

Governors Island

A new addition to the city's parks scene, this little island feels like a small New England town just 800 yards from NYC's financial district. Tourists love the unparalleled views of the Harbor and Lower Manhattan, and locals love the out-of-the-city experience. The 172-acre park, built in part from landfill from subway excavations, was a base for the US Army and Coast Guard for almost two centuries. Until 2003, it was off limits to the public, which could be why the 19th-century homes here are so well-preserved. Anytime from May to October (when the park is open), you'll find numerous weekend programs including art showings, concerts, and family programs. Bikers take a bike over on the ferry or rent one on the island. It's ideal biking conditions with five miles of car-free lanes (although you will have to watch for people-movers!). For more information including updated ferry schedules and a calendar of activities, go to ⊕ *govisland.org*.

GETTING HERE

Governors Island is accessible by a pleasant seven-minute ferry ride that leaves from a dock at 10 South Street, next to the Staten Island Ferry. (Don't expect to get a seat for the trip!) By Subway: 1 to South Ferry Station; 4, 5 to Bowling Green; or

R, W to Whitehall St. Station. By bus: M1 (weekdays only), M6, M9, and M15.

The High Line

Another new attraction, the High Line was once an elevated railroad track that serviced the long ago factories along the lower west side. Neglected and forgotten, it went through a dramatic conversion into to a highly acclaimed park that integrates landscaping with witty rail-inspired design. Vegetation here includes 210 species of plants, trees, and shrubs intended to reflect the wild plants that flourished for decades after the tracks were abandoned in 1980. The park—30 feet above street level—is open between Gansevoort Street in the Meatpacking District to 20th Street with another section extending up to 30th street expected to open in 2010. The viaduct runs alongside and sometimes through buildings including Chelsea Market. Wonderful sweeping views of the Hudson River and an extended sightline of the Meatpacking district are the highlights, but some visitors also report getting an eyeful of uninhibited couples at the nearby Standard Hotel. On Sundays at 2 PM during warm-weather months, the park offers guided tours. For more information and a calendar, go to ⊕ *thehighline.org* or call 212/500–6035.

GETTING HERE

The High Line is accessible at Gansevoort, 14th, 16th, 18th, and 20th streets with elevator access at 14th and 16th. Sorry, the elevated route is strictly for pedestrians, so park that bike and walk. The High Line is two block west of the subway station at 14th Street and 8th Avenue which is served by the L/A/C/E. You can also take the C/E to 23rd street and walk two blocks west. The 1/2/3 stops at 14th Street and 7th Avenue, three blocks away. By Bus: M11 to Washington Street, M11 to 9th Avenue, M14 to 9th Avenue, M23 to 10th Avenue, M34 to 10th Avenue.

Battery Park City

Built over the past 30 years on landfill jutting out into the Hudson River, Battery Park City is a high-rise residential neighborhood split in two by the World Financial Center and its marina. Although the Hudson River Park promenade borders BPC alongside the Westside Highway, locals prefer the route that follows the river's edge through BPC—it's the more scenic path heading to the World Trade Center site from Battery Park. In South Battery Park City, you'll pass by the Museum of Jewish Heritage, 36 Battery Place. Nearby are several reasonably priced outdoor restaurants with stunning views of the Statue of Liberty. **Gigino of Wagner Park** (✉ *20 Battery Pl.* ☎ *212/528–2228*) offers Italian cuisine and reservations for the outside patio are a must. Or skip the food in favor of high art, public exhibits are scattered throughout BPC. In Wagner Park, Louise Bourgeois has created "Eyes," two large balls that represent oversized, ahem, body parts. At Vesey Street is the Irish Hunger Memorial by artist Brian Tolle, which includes an Irish cottage dismantled stone by stone and reassembled here. And in Rockefeller Park at Chambers Street, Tom Otterness has created "The Real World" a popular collection of whimsical—and dark—bronze sculptures, including tiny workers rolling giant pennies.

GETTING HERE

Subway: South Battery Park: 1, W, R to Rector Place, 4, 5 to Wall Street. North Battery Park: 1, 2, 3, A, C to Chambers Street, E to World Trade Center. Bus: M9, M20, M22.

SIGHTSEEING NEW YORK CITY

Taking a guided tour is a good idea, even if you prefer flying solo. For one thing, it will help you get your bearings in this city; for another, it's a great way to investigate out-of-the-way areas, or learn about a particular facet of the city's history, inhabitants, or architecture.

Boat Tours

In good weather a **Circle Line Cruise** (✉ *Pier 83 at W. 42nd St., Midtown West* ☎ *212/563–3200* ⊕ *www.circleline42. com*) around Manhattan Island is one of the best ways to get oriented in the city. The three-hour, 35-mi circumnavigation gives a good sense of where things are. The cruises run at least once daily; the cost is $34 per person (there's also a shorter "semi-Circle" option available for $30).

Looking for a more historical experience? The **Shearwater** (✉ *North Cove Marina, Lower Manhattan* ☎ *212/619– 0885* ⊕ *www.shearwatersailing.com*), an 82-foot yacht dating from the 1920s, sails from the North Cove Marina at the World Financial Center and makes daily 90-minute public sails and Sunday brunch sails from mid-April through mid-October. Shearwater also offers two-hour sunset sails in June, July, and August. Reservations are advised, though they can only be made a maximum of two weeks in advance for sunset sails. Fares start at $45.

Bus Tours

Gray Line New York (✉ *777 8th Ave., between 47th and 48th Sts., Midtown West* ☎ *800/669–0051* ⊕ *www. graylinenewyork.com*) runs a number of "hop-on, hop-off" double-decker bus tours in various languages, including a downtown Manhattan loop, upper Manhattan loop, a Brooklyn loop, and evening tours of the city. Packages include entrance fees to attractions.

Walking Tours

The wisecracking PhD candidates of **Big Onion Walking Tours** (☎ *212/439–1090* ⊕ *www.bigonion.com*) lead themed tours such as "Irish New York" and "Jewish Lower East Side," as well as famous multiethnic eating tours and guided walks through every neighborhood from Harlem to the Financial District and Brooklyn. Tours run daily and cost $15; there's an additional $5 fee for the eating tours.

The knowledgeable **Joyce Gold** (☎ *212/ 242–5762* ⊕ *www.nyctours.com*) has been conducting neighborhood walking tours since 1976. Her theme walks like "Gangs of New York and the Bloody Five Points," and "Hell Ain't Hot: This Here's Hell's Kitchen," run on weekends and cost $15.

The **Municipal Art Society** (☎ *212/935– 3960; 212/439–1049 recorded information* ⊕ *www.mas.org*) conducts a series of walking tours, which emphasize the architecture and history of particular neighborhoods. The cost is $15 per person. MAS also runs two weekly tours: Downtown Manhattan on Tuesdays, and Grand Central Station on Wednesdays. Both weekly tours begin at 12:30, and there's a $10 suggested donation.

New York City Cultural Walking Tours (☎ *212/979–2388* ⊕ *www.nycwalk.com*) have covered such topics as buildings' gargoyles and the Millionaire's Mile of 5th Avenue. Two-hour public tours run on some Sundays from March to December, and are $15 per person (no reservations needed); private tours can be scheduled throughout the week at $60 per hour (most tours run about three hours).

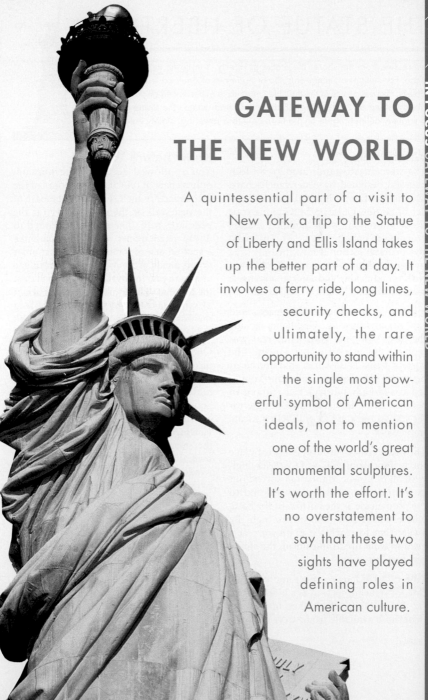

GATEWAY TO THE NEW WORLD

A quintessential part of a visit to New York, a trip to the Statue of Liberty and Ellis Island takes up the better part of a day. It involves a ferry ride, long lines, security checks, and ultimately, the rare opportunity to stand within the single most powerful symbol of American ideals, not to mention one of the world's great monumental sculptures. It's worth the effort. It's no overstatement to say that these two sights have played defining roles in American culture.

THE STATUE OF LIBERTY

Impressive from the shore, the Statue of Liberty is majestic in person and up close. For millions of immigrants, the first glimpse of America was the Statue of Liberty. You get a taste of the thrill they must have experienced as you approach Liberty Island on the ferry from Battery Park and witness the statue grow from a vaguely defined figure on the horizon into a towering, stately colossus.

What's Here

The statue itself stands atop an 89-foot pedestal designed by American Richard Morris Hunt, with Emma Lazarus's sonnet "The New Colossus" ("Give me your tired, your poor, your huddled masses yearning to breathe free . . ."). This massive pedestal section is now the only area to which visitors have access, and only with timed tickets and after an extensive security check.

Inside the pedestal is an informative and entertaining museum. Highlights include the torch's original glass flame that was replaced because of water damage (the current flame is 24-karat gold and lit at night by floodlights), full-scale copper replicas of Lady Liberty's face and one of her feet, Bartholdi's alternative designs for the statue, and a model of Eiffel's intricate framework.

The observatory platform is a great place for a photo op; you're 16 stories high with all of Lower Manhattan spread out in front of you. You'll then descend to the promenade at the bottom of the base, where you're still four stories high. Be aware that to reach the platform you'll need to walk up 26 steps from the elevator drop-off point.

Liberty Island has a pleasant outdoor café for refueling as well as a large cafeteria. The gift shop sells trinkets little better than those available from street vendors.

Know Before You Go

You're allowed access to the museum only as part of one of the free tours of the promenade (which surrounds the base of the pedestal) or the observatory (at the pedestal's top). The tours are limited to 3,000 participants a day. To guarantee a spot on one of the tours, you must order tickets ahead of time—they can be reserved up to one year in advance, by phone or over the Internet. There are a limited amount of same-day standby tickets available at the Castle Clinton and Liberty State Park ticket offices.

Once you reach the island, there are no tickets available. And without a ticket, there is absolutely no admittance into the museum or observatory. You can get a good look at the statue's inner structure on the observatory tour through glass viewing windows that look straight into the statue. Be sure to try the view from several different viewing spots to get the whole interior. There has been no access to the torch since 1916, however the park service now offers limited access to the statue's crown.

Liberty Highlights

■The surreal chance to stand next to, and be dwarfed by, the original glass torch and the copper cast of Lady Liberty's foot.

■The vistas of New York from the observatory platform.

■The rare opportunity to look up the skirt of a national monument.

Statue Basics

- 📠 212/363–3200; 877/523–9849 ticket reservations
- 🌐 www.statuecruises.com
- 🎟 Free; ferry $12.00 round-trip; crown tickets $3
- 🕐 Daily 9:30 AM–5:00; extended hours in summer.

Liberty helicopters

VIEWS OF THE CROWN

Some unique ways to see Lady Liberty:

Rise in the Ritz-Carlton New York Battery Park: A swank cocktail lounge 14 stories high with straight sight lines to the statue.
Liberty Helicopter: Sightseeing tours that fly over the crown and torch (⇨ Chapter 1, Sightseeing Tours).
Kayak: Free kayak tours of the harbor depart from the NYC Downtown Boathouse (See Smart Travel Tips, Sports & the Outdoors).

FAST FACT: To move the Statue of Liberty from its initial home on a Paris rooftop to its final home in the New York Harbor, the statue was broken down into 350 individual pieces and packed in 214 crates. It took four months to reassemble it.

FAST FACT: The face of Lady Liberty is actually a likeness of sculptor Frederic-Auguste Bartholdi's mother—quite a tribute.

FAST FACT: *Liberty Enlightening the World*, as the statue is officially named, was presented to the United States in 1886 as a gift from France to celebrate the centennial of the United States, a symbol of unity and friendship between the two countries. The 152-foot-tall figure was sculpted by Frederic-Auguste Bartholdi and erected around an iron skeleton engineered by Gustav Eiffel (the same Eiffel who would later create the Eiffel Tower).

Foundation of the pedestal to torch: 305'6"

Heel to top head: 111'6"

ELLIS ISLAND

Chances are you'll be with a crowd of international tourists as you disembark at Ellis Island. Close your eyes for a moment and imagine the jostling crowd 100 times larger. Now picture that your journey has lasted weeks at sea and that your daypack contains all your worldly possessions, including all your money. You're hungry, tired, jobless, and homeless. This scenario just begins to set the stage for the story of the millions of poor immigrants who passed through Ellis Island at the turn of the 20th century. Between 1892 and 1924, approximately 12 million men, women, and children first set foot on U.S. soil at the Ellis Island federal immigration facility. By the time the facility closed in 1954, it had processed ancestors of more than 40% of Americans living today.

What's Here

The island's main building, now a national monument, reopened in 1990 as the Ellis Island Immigration Museum, containing more than 30 galleries of artifacts, photographs, and taped oral histories. The centerpiece of the museum is the white-tile Registry Room (also known as the Great Hall). It feels dignified and cavernous today, but photographs show that it took on a multitude of configurations through the years, always packed with humanity undergoing one form of screening or another. While you're there, take a look out the Registry Room's tall, arched windows and try to imagine what passed through immigrants' minds as they viewed lower Manhattan's skyline to one side and the Statue of Liberty to the other.

Along with the Registry Room, the museum's features include the ground-level Railroad Ticket Office, which has several interactive exhibits and a three-dimensional graphic representation of American immigration patterns; the American Family Immigration Center, where for a fee you can search Ellis Island's records for your own ancestors; and, outside, the American Immigrant Wall of Honor, where the names of more than 700,000 immigrant Americans are inscribed along a promenade facing the Manhattan skyline.

The gift shop has a selection of international dolls, candies, and crafts. You can also personalize a number of registry items here as well.

Making the Most of Your Visit

Because there's so much to take in, it's a good idea to make use of the museum's interpretive tools. Check at the visitor desk for free film tickets, ranger tour times, and special programs.

Consider starting your visit with a viewing of the free film *Island of Hope, Island of Tears*. A park ranger starts off with a short introduction, then the 25-minute film takes you through an immigrant's journey from the troubled conditions of European life (especially true for ethnic and religious minorities), to their nervous arrival at Ellis Island, and their introduction into American cities. The film is a primer into all the exhibits and will deeply enhance your experience.

The audio tour ($8) is also worthwhile: it takes you through the exhibits, providing thorough, engaging commentary interspersed with recordings of immigrants themselves recalling their experiences.

Ellis Island Highlights

■Surveying the Great Hall.

■The moving film *Island of Hope, Island of Tears*.

■Listening to the voices of actual immigrants who risked their lives to come to America.

■Reading the names on the American Immigrant Wall of Honor.

■Researching your own family's history.

Ellis Island Basics

- ☎ 212/363–3200 Ellis Island; 212/561–4500 Wall of Honor information
- ⊕ www.ellisisland.org
- 🎫 Free; ferry $12.00 round-trip
- ⊙ Daily 9:30–5:00; extended hours in summer.

IMMIGRANT HISTORY TIMELINE

Starting in the 1880s, troubled conditions throughout Europe persuaded both the poor and the persecuted to leave their family and homes to embark on what were often gruesome journeys to come to the golden shores of America.

1880s 5.7 million immigrants arrive in U.S.

1892 Federal immigration station opens on Ellis Island in January.

1901–1910 8.8 million immigrants arrive in U.S.; 6 million processed at Ellis Island.

1907 Highest number of immigrants (860,000) arrives in one year, including a record 11,747 on April 17.

1910 75% of the residents of New York, Chicago, Detroit, Cleveland, and Boston are now immigrants or children of immigrants.

1920s Federal laws set immigration quotas based on national origin.

1954 Ellis Island immigration station is closed.

Ellis Island: New arrivals line up to have their papers examined. ca. 1880 – 1910.

FAST FACT: Some immigrants who passed through Ellis Island later became household names. A few include Charles Atlas (1903, Italy); Irving Berlin (1893, Russia); Frank Capra (1903, Italy); Bob Hope (1908, England); Knute Rockne (1893, Norway); and Baron Von Trapp and his family (1938, Germany).

FAST FACT: In 1897, a fire destroyed the original pine immigration structure on Ellis Island, including all immigration records dating back to 1855.

FAST FACT: Only third-class, or "steerage," passengers were sent to Ellis Island. Affluent first- and second-class passengers, who were less likely to be ill or become wards of the state, were processed on board and allowed to disembark in Manhattan.

Four immigrants and their belongings, on a dock, look out over the water; view from behind.

PLANNING

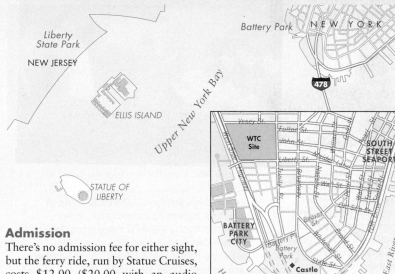

Admission

There's no admission fee for either sight, but the ferry ride, run by Statue Cruises, costs $12.00 ($20.00 with an audio tour). Ferries leaving from **Battery Park** (See Chapter 2) every half hour take you to both islands. (Note that large packages and oversize bags and backpacks aren't permitted on board.) Reserve tickets in advance online—you'll still have to wait in line, both to pick up the tickets and to board the ferry, but you'll be able to pick up a Monument Pass allowing you access to the pedestal of the statue, the museum, and the statue's interior structure. There is no fee for the Monument Pass and you cannot enter inside the statue without it.

Where to Catch the Ferry

Broadway and Battery Pl., Lower Manhattan Ⓜ Subway: 4, 5 to Bowling Green.

When in New Jersey

Directly on the other side of the Hudson River from Battery Park, Liberty State Park is an impressive stretch of green with ample parking and quick ferries to the monuments. Lines are almost never an issue here, something that can't be said about the New York side.

Planning Tips

Buy tickets in advance. This is the only way to assure that you'll have tickets to actually enter the Statue of Liberty museum and observatory platform.

Be prepared for intense security. At the ferry security check, you will need to remove your coat; at the statue, you will need to remove your coat as well as your belt, watch, and any metal accessories. At this writing, no strollers, large umbrellas, or backpacks are allowed in the statue.

Check ferry schedules in advance. Before you go, check www.statuecruises.com.

Keep in mind that even though the last entry time for the monument is at 4:30 PM, **the last ferry to the Statue of Liberty and Ellis Island is at 3:30 PM.** You need to arrive by at least 3 PM (to allow for security checks and lines) if you want to make the last ferry of the day.

Lower Manhattan

WITH CHINATOWN AND TRIBECA

WORD OF MOUTH

"[I'd] like to visit Ground Zero with my 17 year old daughter . . . Any information will be appreciated."

—sailingsailing

"Visit the Winter Garden . . . Inside, there are some dioramas and a display of what [Ground Zero] will look like when completed."

—Emily C

GETTING ORIENTED

0   1/8 mi
0   200 meters

TRIBECA

CHINATOWN

Ericsson Pl.

Canal St.

Walker St.

White St.

N,R,Q,W

6

J,M,Z

Mahayana
Buddhist
Temple

Museum of
Chinese in
the Americas

Edward
Moose
House

Bayard St.

Columbus
Park

Criminal Courts
Building

Kim Lau
Square

Doyers St.

Pell St.

Leonard St.

Worth St.

Thomas St.

Washington
Market Park

New York State
Supreme Court

Federal Plaza

Hogan St.

Hayes St.

Duane St.

Independence
Plaza

Reade St.

Foley Square

Chambers St.

1,2,3   A,C

J,M,Z
4,5,6

Warren St.

Warren St.

City
Hall

Brooklyn
Bridge
Walkway

Brooklyn Bridge

Park Pl. W.

Park Pl.

Murray St.

Murray St.

Woolworth
Building

R,W

Peck Slip

Park Row

Beekman St.

Spruce St.

Barclay St.

Vesey St.

2,3

St. Paul's Chapel

M
E

Fulton St.

Ann St.

J,M,Z

4,5

2,3

South Street Seaport
Historic District

New York
Mercantile
Exchange

World
Financial
Center

World Trade
Center Site

R,W

Cortlandt St.

Dey St.

John St.

John St.

SOUTH STREET SEAPORT

North Cove
Yacht
Harbor

Liberty St.

Federal Reserve
Bank of New York

Maiden Lane

**BATTERY
PARK
CITY**

Cedar St.

Albany St.

Thames St.

Federal Hall
National Memorial

Cedar St.

Pine St.

Esplanade

Carlisle St.

Trinity
Church

Exchange Pl.

Museum of
American Finance

Rector St.

4,5

NYSE

2,3 Wall St.

J,M,Z

New York City
Police Museum

W Thames St.

R,W

Hanover Sq.

Third Pl.

Second Pl.

Bowling Green

Beaver St.

Fraunces
Tavern

Vietnam Veterans
Memorial

South
Cove

4,5

First Pl.

Alexander
Hamilton
Custom House

Jeanette
Park

Museum
of Jewish
Heritage

Skyscraper
Museum

R,W

Pier A

**LOWER
MANHATTAN**

Battery
Park

Castle Clinton
National Monument

1

Staten Island
Ferry

Statue of
Liberty

Brooklyn-
Battery
Tunnel

Hudson River

East River

West St.

Greenwich St.

Hudson St.

West Broadway

Broadway

Church St.

Lafayette St.

Centre St.

Mulberry St.

Mott St.

Elizabeth St.

Bowery

Chrystie St.

Canal St.

Mulberry St.

Pearl St.

William St.

Nassau St.

FDR Drive

Water St.

Front St.

South St.

Battery Pl.

State St.

Whitehall St.

Broad St.

Stone St.

Pearl St.

Water St.

MAKING THE MOST OF YOUR TIME

Visit Lower Manhattan during business hours on a weekday to capture the district's true vitality—but expect to be jostled on the crowded sidewalks if you stand still too long—or walk too slowly. On weekends you could feel like a lone explorer in a canyon of buildings in the Financial District. The neighborhood all but shuts down in the evening; conclude your visit by watching the sunset on the Hudson River. Chinatown is a live wire pretty much any time of day, but even more so on the weekends.

GETTING HERE

Many subway lines service this area. The Fulton Street/Broadway–Nassau station, serviced by nine different subway lines, puts you within walking distance of City Hall, South Street Seaport, and the World Trade Center site (⇨ *Ground Zero essay in this chapter*).

If Chinatown is your downtown destination, don't even think of driving here—the area's cramped streets and heavy congestion make this an exceptionally tough place to navigate. The subway is a better idea, with the J, M, N, R, Q, W, Z, and 6 (Canal Street) and the B and D (Grand Street) all serving the area. The 1 subway line stops in the heart of TriBeCa (Franklin Street).

WORD OF MOUTH (WWW.FODORS.COM/FORUMS)

"Ground Zero is what you expect. A large building site surrounded by hawkers and gawkers. I didn't want to go there. Much more moving is St. Paul's [Chapel]. Firefighters and rescue workers used it as a base in the tragic days after 9/11 and there are small memorials and exhibits inside. It's extremely heart wrenching but I would advise people to visit there to get an uplifting example of what the human spirit can achieve and rescue from utter tragedy. We were all moved to tears by it." —MacSporran

2

FODOR'S CHOICE

Brooklyn Bridge

South Street Seaport

TOP ATTRACTIONS

Kim Lau Square

New York Stock Exchange

Staten Island Ferry

TOP EXPERIENCES

Visiting Ground Zero

Taste-testing Chinatown's dim sum

Touring Ellis Island (⇨ *Ch. 1*)

Strolling TriBeCa's Harrison Street

Relaxing on Pier 17's deck at South Street Seaport

BEST FOR KIDS

Castle Clinton

Seaport Museum

Washington Market Park

NEARBY MUSEUMS (⇨ *CH. 14*)

Museum of American Finance

Museum of Jewish Heritage

Museum of Chinese in the Americas

New York City Police Museum

Skyscraper Museum

Sightseeing
★★★★★

Nightlife
★★

Dining
★★★★

Lodging
★★

Shopping
★★

Pirates, rogue politicians, upwardly mobile go-getters, robber barons, scrappy entrepreneurs, and roaming packs of pigs scouring the streets for garbage: what does this motley crew have in common? They're the citizenry that built and inhabited the southern tip of Manhattan in various eras, and in varying combinations.

Updated by
Joanna G.
Cantor

Lower Manhattan, or in the parlance of New Yorkers emphatically giving directions to tourists, "all the way downtown," has long been where the action—or transaction—is. Back when the neighborhood was the village of New Amsterdam (1626–47), its roguish director-general, Peter Minuit, did the quintessential deal on behalf of the Dutch, trading knives, tools, and cloth to an Algonquian tribe, the Canarsees, for all of Manhattan (the old saw of $24 is more or less an urban myth). In 1789, a year before New York City would lose its title as America's capital, George Washington was sworn in as the nation's first president at Federal Hall, where, two years later, Congress would ratify the Bill of Rights.

Little is left from Manhattan's colonial era, however: apart from a precious few structures built in the 1700s, the 19th-century brick facades of South Street Seaport are about as old as it gets here. As you'll notice immediately, the neighborhood has largely given way to the sometimes intimidating (and on weekends, seemingly deserted) skyscraper-lined canyons of Wall Street and lower Broadway. Bounded by the East and Hudson rivers to the east and west, respectively, and by Chambers Street and Battery Park to the north and south, this is an area you can fully and best appreciate by walking its streets.

You'll want to see what's here, but above all you'll want to see what's not, most notably in that empty but evolving gulf among skyscrapers: Ground Zero. *As you tour the area, refer to our feature in this chapter to deepen your understanding of the devastation of the 9/11 attacks and the effort to rebuild.*

The southern tip has often served as a microcosm for a city that offers as many first shots as it does second chances, so it's appropriate that it's the key point of departure for the Statue of Liberty and Ellis Island (⇨ *Our feature in Chapter 1*). This experience should never be dismissed as too touristy. Like nothing else, the excursion will remind you that we're a city of immigrants and survivors.

The city's downtown neighborhoods give you a close-up view of some of the many cultures of Manhattan. Tucked to the west, south of Canal Street, residential TriBeCa has a quieter vibe and still owes much of its cred to Robert De Niro, whose investments in the area include the TriBeCa Grill and the nonprofit TriBeCa Film Center. Unlike nearby SoHo and NoLita's in-your-face commercial presence, TriBeCa keeps more to itself, with self-assurance and urban grace. And although TriBe-Ca's money is hidden away behind grand industrial facades, you can get a taste of it at one of the posh neighborhood restaurants or when the stars turn out for the annual TriBeCa Film Festival in spring.

Chinatown, by contrast, is a living, breathing, anything-but-quiet ethnic enclave: a quarter of the city's 400,000 Chinese residents live here above storefronts crammed with souvenir shops and restaurants serving every imaginable regional Chinese cuisine, from modest dumplings to sumptuous Hong Kong feasts. What started as a 7-block area has morphed into more than 40 blocks above and below Canal Street with tea shops, restaurants, Buddhist temples, herbalists, acupuncturists, and pungent open-air markets.

THE FINANCIAL DISTRICT, THE SEAPORT, AND THE WORLD TRADE CENTER AREA

THREE WAYS TO EXPLORE

THE BATTERY'S DOWN

The best piece of navigational advice about the city still resides in the tune, "New York, New York" (the one from the musical *On the Town*): "The Bronx is up and the Battery's down." But once you head down (take the 4 or 5 train to the Bowling Green stop at Broadway and Battery Place; the 1 train to South Ferry, or the R or W train to Whitehall), you'll want a clue about what's actually down here.

Perhaps mercifully, after all your walking as well as standing on buses and trains with no available seats, Battery Park has plenty of places to sit, including two tiers of wood benches that line the promenade facing New York Harbor. On a reasonably clear day you'll be able to see Governors Island, a former Coast Guard installation now managed by the National Park Service; a hilly Staten Island in the distance; the Statue of Liberty; Ellis Island; and the old railway terminal in Liberty State Park, on the mainland in Jersey City, New Jersey.

Your key point of interest within the park is **Castle Clinton National Monument,** once a fort intended as a defense against the British, though the castle's cannons were never fired in war. The building saw far more action in later centuries as an opera house, an aquarium, and a processing center for immigrants. In 2005 the Bosque gardens by landscape

Where can I find ... ?

COFFEE	Financier Patisserie 62 Stone St. Swell joe, pastries, and soups.	La Colombe Torrefaction 319 Church St. Upscale coffee for TriBeCa's discerning café crowd.
A QUICK BITE	Adrienne's Pizza Bar 54 Stone St. Quality slices, right in the Financial District.	Chinatown Ice Cream Factory 65 Bayard St. Sample almond cookie, green tea, or mango flavors.
COCKTAILS	Church Lounge 2 6th Ave., near White St. Attracts a celeb crowd with 30+ signature cocktails.	Brandy Library 25 North Moore St. The name says it all.

artist Piet Oudulf were opened, as was the Spiral Fountain, with 35 illuminated and interactive jets. Adjoining Battery Park on this western side is Robert F. Wagner Jr. Park, which has public bathrooms and a restaurant-café.

Perhaps most relevant for your purposes, within Castle Clinton is the ticket office for ferries to the Statue of Liberty and Ellis Island; catch the ferries to both at the west end of the park.

The northern tip of Battery Park skims **Bowling Green,** New York's first public park. In the 18th century New Yorkers rioted periodically in the park. The most notable brouhaha involved the toppling and beheading of a statue of King George III that was once the park's centerpiece. The statue was melted into bullets used in the Revolutionary War. But you can still see traces of the riot; every 12th post on the fence that surrounds the park is a bit mangled. These spikes were once surmounted by gold crowns, which the mob gleefully wrenched off during the riot. On Bowling Green's south side a warren of blocks contain additional remnants of New York's colonial history, including **Fraunces Tavern,** established in 1762 and still serving meals (try the apple pie). George Washington was fond of the tavern, and the American Revolution was in part planned here. History buffs will want to view the American Revolution/early New York City collections in the Fraunces Tavern Museum, which includes four 19th-century buildings in addition to the 18th-century Fraunces Tavern building. *See the listing below for details.*

SHOW ME THE MONEY

Late in the evening of December 15, 1989, sculptor Arturo Di Modica left a 7,000-pound surprise gift for NYC under the Christmas tree in front of the New York Stock Exchange—his bronze *Charging Bull* statue. The bull quickly became the icon of Wall Street. Ask New Yorkers who don't frequent the downtown area where the statue is and they'll usually tell you it's somewhere on Wall Street near the stock exchange. But the statue actually resides in **Bowling Green,** where it was moved after police complained it was blocking traffic in its original location. Since the city never commissioned it, the bull is still officially dubbed a "temporary installation."

After you pose for snapshots with the bull, head northeast to **Wall Street,** one of the most famous thoroughfares in the world. The epicenter of Wall Street is—you guessed it—the **New York Stock Exchange,** at the intersection of Wall and Broad streets. The stock exchange traces its beginnings back to a group of brokers who, in 1792, shortly after Alexander Hamilton issued the first bonds in an attempt to raise money to cover Revolution-caused debt,

> ### BROOKLYN BRIDGE FACTS
>
> ■ Overall length: 6,016 feet
>
> ■ Span of twin Gothic-arch towers: 1,595½ feet
>
> ■ Distance from top of towers to East River: 272 feet
>
> ■ Distance from roadway to the water: 133 feet
>
> ■ Number of times the line "If you believe that, I've got a bridge to sell you" is used referring to the Brooklyn Bridge: Infinite

were in the habit of meeting under a buttonwood tree that once grew on Wall Street. The exchange itself isn't open to visitors, but there is a related museum at the **Federal Hall National Memorial.**

Look at the facade of 23 Wall Street, just across from the exchange. The deep pockmarks and craters were created on September 16, 1920, when, at noon, a horse-drawn wagon packed with explosives detonated in front of the building, killing 33 people and injuring 400. Those responsible were never apprehended and no one ever claimed credit for what was the worst terrorist attack on American soil until the Oklahoma City bombing and later 9/11.

Marking Wall Street's far west end is **Trinity Church,** whose parish was founded by King William III of England in 1697. Trinity's burial ground serves as a resting place for a half-dozen notables, including Alexander Hamilton.

If you get tuckered out, do as the locals do and hit the spa. The **Wall Street Bath & Spa** (88 Fulton St., 212/766–8600) offers old-school saunas and plunging pools for $32.50 a day. Those with bigger bonuses should snag an appointment at **The Setai Spa** (40 Broad St., 3rd floor above SHO restaurant, 212/363–5418). The luxurious massages and facials make for excellent top-tier pampering.

THE STREET OF SHIPS

It's hard to see history in Lower Manhattan's rebuilt and bustling streets. But at **South Street Seaport** history is right in your face. The seaport was created to time-warp visitors back to the days when NYC was a bustling nautical town, and it succeeds in part. Its spiffy little fleet does bring you back to the 19th century, when tall ships sailed from South Street, a time when pirates—Captain Kidd had a house near the wharves—and merchants walked the cobblestone streets and warehouses held treasures from exotic ports. What the seaport, in all its scrubbed tourist beauty, does not include among its careful restorations are the gambling houses, brothels, and saloons that were once so common in this area.

A mix of old and new: Lower Manhattan's bright lights combine with the seaport's historic ships.

TOP ATTRACTIONS

Fodor's Choice
★
Brooklyn Bridge. "A drive-through cathedral" is how the critic James Wolcott describes one of New York's noblest and most recognized landmarks, which spans the East River and connects Manhattan to Brooklyn. A walk across the bridge's promenade—a boardwalk elevated above the roadway and shared by pedestrians, in-line skaters, and bicyclists—takes about 40 minutes from the heart of Brooklyn Heights to Manhattan's civic center. It's well worth traversing for the astounding views. (The bridge's mid-point is a popular spot for proposals.) A web of steel cables, hung from the towers and attached to block-long anchorages on either shore support the roadway. Ⓜ *4, 5, 6 to Brooklyn Bridge/City Hall; J, M, Z to Chambers St.; A, C to High St.-Brooklyn Bridge.*

Federal Hall National Memorial. It's a museum now, but this site has a most notable claim: George Washington was sworn in here as the first president of the United States in 1789, when the building was Federal Hall of the new nation. When we lost capital rights to Philadelphia in 1790, Federal Hall reverted to New York's City Hall, then was demolished in 1812 when the present City Hall was completed. The museum within covers 400 years of New York City's history, with a focus on the life and times of what is now the city's Financial District. You can spot this building easily—it was modeled on the Parthenon, and a statue of George Washington is planted quite obtrusively on the steps. ⊠ *26 Wall St., at Nassau St., Lower Manhattan* 🕾 *212/825–6990* ⊕ *www.nps.gov/feha.index.htm* 📧 *Free* ⊘ *Weekdays 9–5* Ⓜ *2, 3, 4, 5 to Wall St.; A, C to Broadway-Nassau; J, M, Z to Broad St.*

New York Stock Exchange (NYSE). Unfortunately you can't tour it, but it's certainly worth ogling. At the intersection of Wall and Broad streets, the exchange is impossible to miss. The neoclassical building, designed by architect George B. Post. opened on April 22, 1903. It has six Corinthian columns supporting a pediment with a sculpture titled *Integrity Protecting the Works of Man,* featuring a tribute to the then-sources of American prosperity: Agriculture and Mining to the left of Integrity; Science, Industry, and Invention to the right. The Exchange was one of the world's first air-conditioned buildings. ⊠ *11 Wall St. Lower Manhattan* Ⓜ *2, 3, 4, 5 to Wall St.; J, M, Z to Broad St.*

Fodor's Choice **South Street Seaport Historic District.** Had this charming cobblestone cor-
★ ner of the city not been declared a historic district in 1977, we have no doubt you'd be glancing indifferently at yet more hyperdeveloped skyscrapers in this spot rather than at the city's largest concentration of early-19th-century commercial buildings. If you've been to either Boston's Quincy Market or Baltimore's Harborplace, you may feel a flash of déjà vu—the same company leased, restored, and adapted the existing buildings, preserving the commercial feel of centuries past. The result blends a quasi-authentic historic district with a homogenous shopping mall.

At the intersection of Fulton and Water streets, the gateway to the seaport, is the *Titanic* **Memorial,** a small white lighthouse that commemorates the sinking of the RMS *Titanic* in 1912. Beyond the lighthouse, Fulton Street turns into a busy pedestrian mall. On the south side of Fulton is the seaport's architectural centerpiece, **Schermerhorn Row,** a redbrick terrace of Georgian- and Federal-style warehouses and countinghouses built from 1811 to 1812. Some upper floors house gallery space, and the ground floors are occupied by upscale shops, bars, and restaurants.

☺ Also at 12 Fulton Street is the main lobby of the **South Street Seaport Museum** (☎ *212/748–8600* ⊕ *www.southstseaport.org* � *Apr.–Dec., Tues.–Sun. 10–6; Jan.–Mar., Fri.–Mon. 10–5 [only Schermerhorn Row Galleries open Mon.; ships open 12–4, weather permitting]*), which hosts walking tours, hands-on exhibits, and fantastic creative programs for children, all with a nautical theme. You can purchase tickets ($10) at either 12 Fulton Street or Pier 16 Visitors Center.

Cross South Street, once known as the Street of Ships, under an elevated stretch of the FDR Drive to **Pier 16,** where historic ships are docked, including the *Pioneer,* a 102-foot schooner built in 1885; the *Peking,* the second-largest sailing bark in existence; the iron-hulled *Wavertree;* and the lightship *Ambrose.* The Pier 16 ticket booth provides information and sells tickets to the museum, ships, tours, and exhibits. Pier 16 is the departure point for various seasonal cruises.

To the north is **Pier 17,** a multilevel dockside shopping mall with national chain retailers such as Express and Victoria's Secret, among others. Weathered-wood decks at the rear of the pier make a splendid spot from which to contemplate the river, with views as far north as Midtown Manhattan and as far south as the Verrazano–Narrows Bridge. ⊠ *South Street Seaport, Lower Manhattan* ☎ *212/732–7678* *events and shopping information* ⊕ *www.southstreetseaport.com* ⊠ *free; $5 to ships, galleries, walking tours, Maritime Crafts Center, films, and other seaport events* Ⓜ *2, 3, 4, 5, A, C, J, M, Z to Fulton St./ Broadway-Nassau.*

Staten Island Ferry. About 70,000 people ride the ferry every day, and you should be one of them. Without having to pay a cent, you get great views of the Statue of Liberty, Ellis Island, and the southern tip of Manhattan. You'll pass tugboats, freighters, and cruise ships—a reminder that this is still a working harbor. The boat embarks from the Whitehall Terminal at Whitehall and South streets, near the east end of Battery Park. The ferry provides transport to Staten Island, one of the city's boroughs. But if you don't want to visit Staten Island you can usually remain onboard for the return trip. Occasionally a boat is taken out of service for a while; if you're told to disembark, walk down the main gangplank (the same one you used when you came aboard), enter the terminal, and catch the next boat back to the city. ⊕ *www.siferry.com* Ⓜ *1 to South Ferry; R, W to Whitehall St.; 4, 5 to Bowling Green.*

WORTH NOTING

City Hall. You just might spot news crews jockeying on the front steps as they attempt to interview city officials, which is perhaps all you want to know about City Hall. But if the history of local politics is truly your thing, the hall is open for tours. Among the highlights within are the Victorian-style **City Council Chamber,** the **Board of Estimate Chamber,** with colonial paintings and church-pew-style seating; and the **Governor's Room,** which includes a writing table that George Washington used in 1789 when New York was the U.S. capital. If nothing else, take a moment to snap a photo of the austere columned exterior. ⊠ *City Hall Park, Lower Manhattan* ☎ *212/788–2656* ⊕ *www.nyc.gov/html/ tours/city_hall.shtml for tours* ⊠ *Free* ☉ *Tours weekdays; reservations required* Ⓜ *R, W to City Hall; 4, 5, 6 to Brooklyn Bridge/City Hall; J, M, Z to Chambers St.*

Federal Reserve Bank of New York. With its imposing mix of sandstone, limestone, and ironwork, the reserve looks the way a bank ought to: strong and impregnable. The gold ingots in the subterranean vaults here are worth roughly $140 billion—reputedly a third of the world's gold reserves. Hour-long tours (conducted six times a day and requiring reservations made at least five days in advance) include a visit to the gold vault, the trading desk, and "FedWorks," a multimedia exhibit center where you can track hypothetical trades. Visitors must show an officially issued photo ID, such as a driver's license or passport, and will pass through scanning equipment to enter the building; the Fed advises showing up 20 minutes before your tour to accommodate security screening. Photography is not permitted. ⊠ *33 Liberty St., between William and Nassau Sts., Lower Manhattan* ☎ *212/720–6130* ⊕ *www.newyorkfed. org* ⊠ *Free* ☉ *1-hr tour by advance reservation, weekdays 9:30–3:30* Ⓜ *A, C to Broadway/Nassau; J, M, Z, 2, 3, 4, 5 to Fulton St.*

St. Paul's Chapel. For more than a year after the World Trade Center attacks, the chapel's fence served as a shrine for visitors seeking solace.

People from around the world left tokens of grief and support, or signed one of the large drop cloths that hung from the fence. After having served as a 24-hour refuge where rescue and recovery workers could eat, pray, rest, and receive counseling, the chapel, which amazingly suffered no damage, reopened to the public in fall 2002. The ongoing exhibit, titled "Unwavering Spirit: Hope & Healing at Ground Zero," honors the efforts of rescue workers in the months following September 11. Open since 1766, St. Paul's is the oldest public building in continuous use in Manhattan. ⊠ *209 Broadway, at Fulton St., Lower Manhattan* ☎ *212/233–4164* ⊕ *www.saintpaulschapel.org* ⊗ *Mon.–Sat. 10–5:45, Sun. 8–3:45* Ⓜ *2, 3, 4, 5, A, C, J, M, Z to Fulton St.*

Trinity Church. Alexander Hamilton is buried under a white-stone pyramid in the church's graveyard, not far from a monument commemorating steamboat inventor Robert Fulton (buried in the Livingston family vault with his wife). The church (the third on this site) was designed in 1846 by Richard Upjohn. Its most notable feature is the set of enormous bronze doors designed by Richard Morris Hunt to recall Lorenzo Ghiberti's doors for the Baptistery in Florence, Italy. *Trinity Root*, a 12½-foot-high, 3-ton sculpture by Steven Tobin cast from the sycamore tree struck by debris on 9/11 behind St. Paul's Chapel, was installed in front of the church in 2005. A museum outlines the church's history; a daily tour is given at 2. ⊠ *74 Trinity Pl., entrance at Broadway and the head of Wall St., Lower Manhattan* ☎ *212/602–0800* ⊕ *www. trinitywallstreet.org* ⊗ *Weekdays 7–6, Sat. 8–4, Sun. 7–4; churchyard Nov.–Apr., daily 7–4; May–Oct., weekdays 7–5, Sat. 8–4, Sun. 7–3* Ⓜ *4, 5 to Wall St.; R, W to Rector St.*

Vietnam Veterans Memorial. At the center of a triangular plaza sits this 14-foot-high, 70-foot-long rectangular memorial. Passages from news dispatches from the wartime period and the letters of military service people are etched into its wall of greenish glass. The Walk of Honor memorializes 1,741 New Yorkers who lost their lives in the war. ⊠ *End of Coenties Slip between Water and South Sts., adjacent to 125 Broad St., Lower Manhattan* ⊕ *www.nyvietnamveteransmemorial.org* Ⓜ *1 to South Ferry; R, W to Whitehall St.; J, M, Z to Broad St.*

Woolworth Building. Until 40 Wall Street stole the title in 1930, the 792-foot Woolworth Building, opened in 1913, was the world's tallest building. Make a quick stop in the lobby to check out the stained-glass skylight and sculptures set into the portals to the left and right: one represents an elderly F. W. Woolworth counting his nickels and dimes, another depicts the architect, Cass Gilbert, cradling in his arms a model of his creation. ⊠ *233 Broadway, between Park Pl. and Barclay St., Lower Manhattan* Ⓜ *2, 3 to Park Pl.; R, W to City Hall.*

Battery Park. Jutting out at the southernmost point of Manhattan, leafy Battery Park provides plenty of places to sit and rest, including two tiers of wood benches that line the promenade facing New York Harbor. From here you can see Governors Island, a former Coast Guard installation now managed by the National Park Service; a hilly Staten Island in the distance; the Statue of Liberty; Ellis Island; and the old railway terminal in Liberty State Park, on the mainland in Jersey City, New

Continued on page 58

A GLIMPSE OF THE FUTURE

An illuminated **antenna** will reach to 1,776 feet to commemorate America's founding.

Tower 2
Designed by Norman Foster.
Finish date unknown.

One World Trade Center
Designed by David Childs.
The roof will be 1,368 feet tall—identical to that of the tallest twin tower.
Tentative finish: 2013.

Tower 3
Designed by Richard Rogers.
Finish date unknown.

7 World Trade Center
Designed by David Childs.
Opened in 2006.

Transportation Hub
Designed by Santiago Calatrava.
Finish date unknown.

9/11 Museum
Tentative finish: 9/11/11.

Tower 4
Designed by Fumihiko Maki.
Finish date unknown.

National September 11 Memorial
Entitled *Reflecting Absence*, this will feature 30-foot-tall waterfalls.

GROUND ZERO
THE WORLD TRADE CENTER SITE

A decade after September 11, 2001, Ground Zero still attracts thousands of visitors who come to connect with the events that unfolded here. At first, though, a visit here may feel like just gazing at a large construction site. (The space remains encircled by fencing.) But with a bit of knowledge you can appreciate places touched by that day. Many of the sites nearby, such as St. Paul's Chapel and the "10 House" firehouse on Liberty Street, are as essential to understanding the complete story as Ground Zero itself.

(above) Ground Zero view from the Winter Garden; (below) 9/11 memorial wall; (opposite) A rendition of the future World Trade Center site

THE TOWERS

The World Trade Towers, each 110 stories tall, were an impressive feat of engineering. Construction began in 1968, and the Twin Towers officially opened in 1973. Avoiding the typical construction used at the time, the architects gave each building an exterior skeleton made up of 244 slim steel columns and an inner "core" tube that supported the weight of the tower.

Approximately 50,000 people worked in the north tower (1 World Trade Center) and south tower (2 World Trade Center), and another 40,000 people visited the 16-acre complex every day. Beneath the towers was a multi-level mall with nearly 100 stores and restaurants.

The Twin Towers prior to 9/11

EVENTS OF THE DAY On September 11, 2001, terrorist hijackers steered two jets into the World Trade Center's Twin Towers, demolishing them and five outlying buildings.

■ The first hijacked jet, American Airlines Flight 11, crashed into the north tower, 1 World Trade Center, at 8:46 AM, cutting through floors 93 to 99. The tower collapsed at 10:28 AM. Cantor Fitzgerald, a brokerage firm headquartered between the 101st and 105th floors, lost 658 of its 1,050 employees. At the Windows on the World restaurant (floors 106 and 107), 100 patrons and 72 staff members died.

■ The second hijacked jet, United Airlines Flight 175, hit the south tower, 2 World Trade Center, at 9:03 AM, crashing through the 77th to 85th floors. The plane banked as it hit, so portions of the building remained undamaged on impact floors. Consequently, one stairwell initially remained passable from at least the 91st floor down. The tower collapsed at 9:58 AM.

■ The attack killed 2,752 people. (Deaths are still being counted; the most recent casualty, Leon Heyward, died in fall 2008 from lymphoma caused by exposure to the toxic atmosphere that formed after the towers' collapse.) The fenced-in 16-acre work site that emerged from the rubble, almost immediately dubbed Ground Zero, has come to symbolize the personal and historical impact of September 11.

(above) Towers burning after attack; Pedestrians flee as the south tower falls

THE DAMAGE

Why *did* the towers fall? A three-year federal study revealed several reasons. The two airplanes used in the attack, both Boeing 767s, hit their respective towers at roughly 500 mph. They both damaged the exterior columns, destroying core supports for at least three of the north tower's floors and up to six of the south tower's floors. Ensuing fires, fed by tens of thousands of gallons of jet fuel, further weakened the buildings. The collapse of the most heavily damaged floors then triggered a domino effect, causing the towers to crumple at an estimated speed of about 125 mph.

Many other area buildings suffered collateral damage. The World Financial Center office complex, to the west of Ground Zero, has as its centerpiece the 10-story glass-domed Winter Garden. After having nearly all its glass blown out in the attacks, the atrium reopened in September 2002 after repairs that included the installation of 2,000 windows and 1.2 million pounds of stone.

The 47-story 7 World Trade Center, to the north of Ground Zero, was struck by large chunks of falling debris from the north and south towers. The building remained standing at first, but subsequent fires caused it to collapse later that afternoon. A new 52-story 7 World Trade Center opened in May 2006 with a much smaller footprint than its predecessor.

St. Paul's Chapel, across the street from Ground Zero, sustained no major damage; staff there credit a huge sycamore

that toppled over during the attack. Its gigantic root system, now above ground, helped to shield the building and the headstones in its attached cemetery from falling debris.

Although the New York Stock Exchange's building wasn't physically harmed during the attacks, the market remained closed for six days (including 9/11). When trading resumed on September 17, the Dow Jones industrial average dropped 684.81 points, or 7.13 percent. The American Stock Exchange (Amex), however, sustained some damage on 9/11, and for two weeks Amex stocks and exchange-traded funds were traded on the NYSE floor.

A LOOK TO THE FUTURE

A vision of the future Manhattan skyline

After years of delays, the process of filling the massive void at Ground Zero is well under way. The World Trade Center Memorial and Museum is within a year of completion. One World Trade Center, the tallest of the new office towers, is also moving along, and so, to varying degrees, are Santiago Calatrava's soaring, controversial new transportation hub and three other distinctive towers, each to be built by a notable architect. In addition, the portion of Greenwich Street that was paved over in 1966 in preparation for the building of the World Trade Center is likely to be reinstated, meaning that traffic will now cut through Ground Zero. The hope is that restoring the street grid will help revitalize nearby businesses and neighborhoods, which are now isolated by the site.

Future downtown skyline at dusk

NATIONAL SEPTEMBER 11 MEMORIAL AND MUSEUM AT THE WORLD TRADE CENTER

No building will occupy the exact space where the Twin Towers once stood. In their place, as part of the memorial titled "Reflecting Absence," will be recessed, thirty-foot-tall waterfalls. After the water cascades down into the two subterranean reflecting pools outlining the Twin Towers' original footprints, it will then tumble down into smaller square holes at the center of each pool. Surrounding each waterfall on the plaza level will be a low bronze wall with the names of the approximately 2,752 victims of 9/11 cut into it, so that the water and light can be seen through them. The work, designed by the architects Michael Arad and Peter Walker, will be set in a plaza filled with sugar gum and white oak trees.

The museum is to be built below the plaza surface, with just a small visitor center at plaza level. Visitors will walk down a long, twisting ramp that will take them all the way to the bedrock the towers were built on, 71 feet below. One exhibit here will be the "last column," the last piece of steel to be removed from the site, which was covered with slogans and memorials from rescue crews and others. The museum will also incorporate a 65-foot-high section of the original foundation, the so-called slurry wall that prevented the Hudson River from swamping the grounds after the attacks. Although the museum is on target to be finished by the tenth anniversary of 9/11, nearby construction is likely to keep it closed to the public until 2012. Authorities hope to have the memorial plaza itself open to the public by 9/11/11, however.

1 World Trade Center 1/1/2010

Fumihiko Maki, Larry Silverstein, and Norman Foster

ONE WORLD TRADE CENTER

Previously known as the Freedom Tower, One World Trade Center will occupy the northwest corner of Ground Zero. The largest building on the site will have a roof that's 1,368 feet tall—identical to that of the taller of the Twin Towers. An illuminated antenna will further increase the building's total height to 1,776 feet to commemorate America's founding. An observation deck is planned for the 100th and 101st floors, 1,265 feet from street level, and a restaurant will be on the floor above. Designed by David Childs of Skidmore, Owings & Merrill, the new 1 WTC is on schedule to reach its roof level by early 2011 and to be finished by the end of 2013. The three other office buildings on the site (at this writing all at various stages of construction) are each by a different prominent architect: Fumihiko Maki, Richard Rogers, and Norman Foster.

TRANSPORTATION HUB

About 1,000 feet of subway tunnels collapsed after the towers fell, closing the Cortlandt Street station across the street from Ground Zero. The Port Authority of New York and New Jersey's World Trade Center PATH train station was also damaged in the attacks, and its temporary train station is due to be replaced by a transportation hub designed by Spanish architect and engineer Santiago Calatrava. Inspired by the image of a child releasing a dove, the massive glass-roofed building will be larger than Grand Central Terminal, with many shops besides connections to the Hudson ferries and all nearby subway stations. It's currently on schedule for completion in late 2013, although that date may change.

For more information on the new structures, visit ⊕ *www.lowermanhattan.info* and ⊕ *www.buildthememorial.org*.

A GROUND ZERO WALK

A woman watches the Ground Zero construction site

1 Begin your walk in front of the **Ground Zero construction site** (20 Vesey St.), where maps and a scale model help visitors picture both the original World Trade Center as well as what the site will look like once all the construction is over.
☞ Across the street is **St. Paul's,** the Episcopal chapel that became a dormitory, mess hall, and medical center in the months after 9/11. Even George Washington's pew was called back into service for the exhausted rescue workers.

Inspired by the giant sycamore that fell under the rubble and helped protect old headstones in St. Paul's graveyard, the *Trinity Root* sculpture, a 9/11 memorial pictured here, can be seen at Trinity Church

2 After exiting the chapel, head back to Vesey Street, keeping the chapel on your left. Continue west to reach the pedestrian bridge over the West Side Highway; the bridge takes you to the World Financial Center and its palm-tree-filled atrium, **the Winter Garden.**
☞ From its second floor you can see nearly all of Ground Zero.

The Winter Garden Atrium

3 Exit the World Financial Center and head to the Hudson River. From the ferry terminal here, many people fled on 9/11 on boats commanded by volunteer captains. The well-to-do neighborhood here, **Battery Park City,** is partially built on landfill excavated during the building of the World Trade Center. After 9/11, many of the community's 9,000 residents were unable to return to their apartments for months.

Re-enter the World Financial Center complex and find your way to the southern pedestrian bridge, which leads to Liberty Street.

The firefighters' memorial

4 Once you reach street level, you'll be near the former **Deutsche Bank building,** at 130 Liberty. Severely damaged and filled with toxic dust from the south tower's collapse, the building is still being "deconstructed." Across Greenwich Street, at 124 Liberty, is **10 House,** a fire station nearly destroyed on 9/11. Now the station's restored exterior is covered with a 56-foot bronze bas-relief "dedicated to those who fell and to those who carry on." **The Tribute WTC Visitor Center,** a project of the September 11th Families' Association, is next-door. Its exhibits give a heartbreaking picture of the many lives lost on that day.

The Tribute WTC Visitor Center

WHEN TO GO

There are no special viewing hours, and the site seldom feels crowded. Early weekday mornings, when many tourists and locals are still working on their first cups of coffee, are good times to go.

TIMING

Allow half a day to linger at all these sites.

INFORMATION AND VISITOR CENTERS

Stop at the information booth at Vesey Street, near the temporary PATH station, for maps of the area (as well as a free Wi-Fi hotspot). The **9/11 Memorial Preview Site** (20 Vesey St., 212/267–2047, ⊕ www. national911memorial.org, free) is open from 10-7 from Monday to Wednesday, Friday, and Saturday, from 10-9 on Thursday, and 10-6 on Sunday. **The Tribute WTC Visitor Center** (120 Liberty St., 866/737–1184, ⊕ www. tributewtc.org, $10) is open from 10-6 on Monday and Wednesday through Saturday, noon-6 on Tuesday, and noon-5 on Sunday.

TOURS

The Tribute Center leads walking tours of Ground Zero several times daily. New York City Vacation Packages (877/692–8747, ⊕ www.nycvp.com, from $19) conducts guided tours of lower Manhattan and World Trade Center sites.

GETTING THERE

Subway:

❶, **ℝ**, **Ⓦ** to Rector St.;

❷,**❸**,**④**,**⑤**,**Ⓐ**,**Ⓒ**,**Ⓙ**,**Ⓜ**,**Ⓩ** to Fulton St./Broadway-Nassau;

Ⓔ to World Trade Center/Church St.

PATH:
Any line to World Trade Center stop.

Jersey. On crystal-clear days you can see all the way to Port Elizabeth's cranes, which seem to mimic Lady Liberty's stance.

The park's main structure is **Castle Clinton National Monument,** the ticket office site and takeoff point for ferries to the Statue of Liberty and Ellis Island. The monument was once known as Castle Garden, when from 1855 to 1890 it served as America's first official immigration center (Ellis Island opened in 1892). The interior of the park is loaded with monuments and statues, including *The Sphere,* which for three decades stood on the plaza at the World Trade Center as a symbol of peace. Damaged but still intact after the collapse of the towers, it serves as a temporary memorial to those who lost their lives the year before. In 2005 the Bosque gardens by landscape artist Piet Oudulf were opened, as was the Spiral Fountain, with 35 illuminated and interactive jets. Adjoining Battery Park on this western side is Robert F. Wagner Jr. Park, which has public bathrooms and a restaurant-café.

The southern link in a chain of parks connecting Battery Park north to Chambers Street, **Robert F. Wagner Jr. Park** has a flat, tidy lawn and wide benches from which to view the harbor or the stream of runners and in-line skaters on the promenade. A brick structure that holds public bathrooms and a restaurant provides additional views from its flat roof. *For more information on Battery Park, see the* NYC's Waterfront Parks *feature in the Experience chapter.* ⊠ *Broadway and Battery Pl., Lower Manhattan* Ⓜ *4, 5 to Bowling Green.*

CHINATOWN AND TRIBECA

THREE WAYS TO EXPLORE

A STREET THAT DEFINES THE COMMUNITY

For a quick taste of Chinatown, head to Mott Street, Chinatown's main thoroughfare. This is where the first Chinese immigrants (mostly men) settled in tenements in the late 1880s. Today the street is dense with restaurants, hair salons and barbershops, bakeries, tea parlors, and souvenir shops, most of them lying below Canal Street. If you plan it right, you can create a movable feast, starting with soup dumplings, a specialty from Shanghai, and continuing with Peking duck, a yellow custard cake, and a jasmine bubble tea, each at a different place. Or, you can have it all come to you at **Ping's Seafood,** with dim sum for lunch. The few blocks above Canal overflow with food markets selling vegetables and fish (some still alive and squirming). Walk carefully, as the sidewalks can be slick from the ice underneath the eels, blue crabs, snapper, and shrimp that seem to look back at you as you pass by. A good place to get oriented or arrange a walking tour is the **Museum of Chinese in the Americas.**

MOVIE-PERFECT BUT WITH A SHADY PAST

To the right off restaurant-lined Pell Street is alley-size **Doyers Street,** the site of early-20th-century gang wars and today a favorite location for film shoots. Tobey McGuire and Kirsten Dunst had a heart-to-heart talk in *Spider-Man 2,* and Woody Allen used it in two of his films, *Alice* and

Small Time Crooks. Quirky, angled and authentic, this curving road-way is where you can find Chinatown's oldest teahouse, dating from 1920, **Nom Wah Tea Parlor.** There's also a relatively hidden and grungy underground passage, formerly a storage place for liquor and now lined with Chinese travel agencies and other very low-tech businesses (don't expect to see signs in English). The street makes a sharp angle (according to legend, it was built this way by Chinatown merchants to thwart straight-flying ghosts who brought bad luck; history says it's because the street was once the entryway to brewer Heinreich Doyers's elegant home) before it reaches the **Bowery,** a point known as "Bloody Angle" because of the visibility-challenged victims' inability to anticipate a gang's attacks from the corner. The Bowery itself was once lined with theaters and taverns, but earned a reputation well into the late 20th century as the city's skid row. Today it's a busy commercial thoroughfare. The oldest row building in New York City, the **Edward Mooney House,** is located on 18 Bowery on the corner of Pell Street. Erected in 1785 by Edward Mooney, the house was a residence until the 1820s, and was at one time or another a hotel, tavern, pool hall, restaurant, and bank. Today, it's a historic landmark and is open to the public.

STAR POWER AND STELLAR LOOKS

Walking the photogenic streets of TriBeCa, full of cast-iron factories as well as a time-defying stretch of Federal row houses on Harrison Street, you can understand why everyone from Robert De Niro to J.F.K. Jr have bought apartments here. The two-block-long Staple Street, with its connecting overhead walkway, is a favorite of urban cinematographers. At 60 Hudson Street is the art-deco Western Union Building—try to sneak a peek at its magnificent lobby.

TOP ATTRACTIONS

Columbus Park. People-watching is the thing in this park. If you swing by in the morning, you'll see men and women practicing tai chi; the afternoons bring intense games of mah-jongg. In the mid-19th century the park was known as Five Points—the point where Mulberry Street, Anthony (now Worth) Street, Cross (now Park) Street, Orange (now Baxter) Street, and Little Water Street (no longer in existence) intersected—and was notoriously ruled by dangerous Irish gangs. In the 1880s a neighborhood-improvement campaign brought about the park's creation. Ⓜ *N, Q, R, W, 6 to Canal St.*

Kim Lau Square. Ten streets converge at this labyrinthine intersection crisscrossed at odd angles by pedestrian walkways. Standing on an island in this busy area is the **Kim Lau Arch,** honoring Chinese casualties in American wars. A statue on the square's eastern edge pays tribute to a Quin Dynasty official named Lin Ze Xu, the Fujianese minister who sparked the Opium War by banning the drug. Ⓜ *4, 5, 6 to Brooklyn Bridge/City Hall.*

Washington Market Park. This landscaped recreation space with a gazebo and playground—ideal for permitting the kids to blow off steam—was named after the great food market that once sprawled over the area. Across the street at the elementary school are a stout red tower

Getting decked out for the carnival of colors and sounds that is the Chinese New Year's parade in Chinatown.

resembling a lighthouse and a fence with iron ship figures—reminders of the neighborhood's dockside past. There's a small greenmarket here on Wednesday and Saturday. ⊠ *Greenwich St. between Chambers and Duane Sts., TriBeCa* Ⓜ *1, 2, 3 to Chambers St.*

WORTH NOTING

Mahayana Buddhist Temple. You'll be able to say you saw New York's largest Buddha here at the largest Buddhist temple in Chinatown; it's at the foot of the Manhattan Bridge Arch on the Bowery. A donation of $2 is requested. There's a great gift shop on the second floor. Before its incarnation as a place of worship in 1997, this was the Rosemary, an adult-movie theater. ⊠ *133 Canal St., at the Bowery, Chinatown* ☎ *212/343–9592* ⊙ *Daily 8 AM–7 PM* Ⓜ *4, 5, 6 to Brooklyn Bridge/ City Hall.*

SoHo and Little Italy

WORD OF MOUTH

"I took the subway to SoHo and had a great breakfast at Balthazar. It was just eggs, sausage, and toast, but just the atmosphere alone made it just seem better. The waitress was very nice and sent the maitre'd over to give me directions. He had it all—he was handsome and French!"

—MichelleY

GETTING ORIENTED

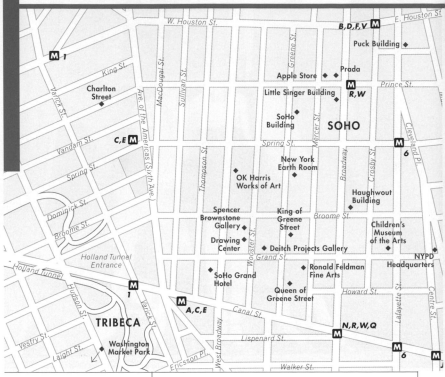

FODOR'S CHOICE

Greene Street

St. Patrick's Old Cathedral

TOP ATTRACTIONS

Apple Store (⇨ Ch. 17)

Pearl River Mart (⇨ Ch. 17)

San Gennaro Shrine

TOP EXPERIENCES

Browsing SoHo's boutiques

Architecture-ogling along
Greene Street

Grazing Little Italy's Grand
Street grocers

Doing brunch at Balthazar

MAKING THE MOST OF YOUR TIME

If you're coming to shop in SoHo and NoLita, plan to arrive after 11 AM, as most shops open late and stay open until early evening. If art is your thing, avoid Sunday, because most galleries are closed. SoHo is almost always a madhouse (unless it's raining), but weekdays are somewhat less frenetic. NoLita is calmer and less crowded. Little Italy represents a very small area nowadays—just four blocks. You can see it all in a half-hour, or you can spend an afternoon exploring the grocers and the stores hawking touristy Italian-theme T-shirts, bumper stickers, and assorted tchotchkes, capped off with a meal at one of Mulberry Street's almost-authentic Italian-American restaurants. If you come in mid-September during the San Gennaro festival (a huge street fair in honor of the patron saint of Naples) you—along with thousands upon thousands of other people—can easily spend an entire day and night exploring the many food and souvenir booths and playing games of chance.

St. Patrick's
Old Cathedral

NOLITA

J,M,Z Ⓜ

Umberto's
Clam House

DiPalo's
Fine Foods   Ⓜ B,D

Alleva

E. Rossi & Co.

Piemonte
Ravioli

Hester St.

**LITTLE
ITALY**

National Shrine
of San Gennaro

I,M,Z

NEARBY MUSEUMS (⇨ CH. 14)
Children's Museum of the Arts
New York City Fire Museum

AREA SHOPS (⇨ CH. 17)
Agent Provocateur
Bellora
De Vera
Kirna Zabête
Les Petits Chapelais
Marc Jacobs
MarieBelle
Marni
McNally Jackson
Moss
Pearl River Mart
Prada
Pylones
R by 45rpm
Santa Maria Novella
Stuart Moore

GETTING HERE

SoHo is roughly bounded by Houston Street, Canal Street, 6th Avenue, and Lafayette Street. To the east, NoLita grows daily, but lies pretty much between Houston, the Bowery, Kenmare, and Lafayette. There are plenty of subways that service the area; take the 6 or A, C, E to Spring Street; the R, W to Prince Street; or the B, D, F, V to Broadway-Lafayette.

WORD OF MOUTH

"Sunday. Our Soho day. Based largely on Fodorite advice, we [had] brunch at Balthazar. The decor is perfect—it really did feel as if we were in a classic French brasserie. Much cheaper than going to Paris, and no jet lag. Well fortified, we head out to Spring Street for a spot of shopping/browsing through Kate's Paperie, Sur la Table, down to Pearl River, and then (more walking) past enticing windows." —*SB_Travlr*

Sightseeing ★★★	SoHo (South of Houston) and NoLita (North of Little Italy) are shopper's paradises, supertrendy, painfully overcrowded on weekends, often overpriced, and undeniably glamorous. Not too long ago, though, these neighborhoods were quiet warrens of artists' lofts and galleries, and the only reason to visit was to go gallery hopping.
Nightlife ★★★	
Dining ★★★	
Lodging ★★	
Shopping ★★★★★	

Updated by Joanna G. Cantor

Checking out the art is still a big reason to come to SoHo, but shopping has for the most part supplanted the quest for visual stimulation. In between whipping your credit card out of your wallet and feverishly searching for a café with empty seats, do take a few seconds to savor what other passersby may miss: the neighborhood's Belgian brick cobblestones and turn-of-the-20th-century lampposts.

And then—just east of Broadway—you'll find the remains of what once was a thriving, lively community of Italian Americans: the tangle of streets that make up Little Italy. A few nostalgic blocks surrounding Mulberry Street between NoLita and ultrabusy Canal Street are all that remain of the vast community that once dominated the area, but what remains is still a cheerful salute to all things Italian, with red-green-and-white street decorations on permanent display and specialty grocers and cannelloni makers dishing up delights. If you want to see a current, thriving, and far less symbolic Little Italy, head up to Arthur Avenue in the Bronx (⇨ Ch. 13) and you'll find a cornucopia of authentic Italian goods marketed to local families rather than tourists.

SOHO

THREE WAYS TO EXPLORE

SHOP 'TIL YOU DROP

The stretch of Broadway between Houston and Broome streets is a flurry of pedestrian traffic with retail giants like H&M, Banana Republic, and Victoria's Secret, as well as smaller city favorites like **Scoop NYC** and **Zara.** ■TIP➔ Unless you're in dire need of something specific, skip the mass marketers and check out the stores that may be less familiar to you—they offer some of the city's most elegant and singular fashions. To the west or east in SoHo are boutiques from established contemporary designers like **Vivienne Tam, Nanette Lepore, Nicole Miller,** and **Barbara Bui.** In NoLita, on Elizabeth, Mulberry, and Mott streets, you'll mix with models and magazine editors at one-off shops by young

> ### SOHO WAS HELL
>
> SoHo once had the less trendy moniker "Hell's Hundred Acres," so named because the crowded slums were repeatedly beset by frequent fires, but it boomed after the Civil War, when the neighborhood came to be known simply as the Eighth Ward.

3

designers just starting to make their marks. There, amid lingering remnants of the neighborhood's immigrant past, custom-designed jewelry, hand-sewn dresses, trendy home furnishings, and high-concept lighting fill the storefronts. When you're ready to "drop" you can hit **Bliss SoHo Spa** (568 Broadway, 2nd Fl., between Prince and Houston Sts.) for a muscle-soothing Ginger Rub massage. Just be warned, this type of pampering isn't the "walk in" variety, so book at least a month ahead on ⊕ *www.blissworld.com*, or you can just enjoy the spa store with its lotions and potions to cart back to your hotel.

THE ARTS SCENE AND DESIGN: A LEGACY

Even if you're not in the market for a $1,000 skirt, the 23,000-square-foot **Prada** design store is worth a stop to check out the Rem Koolhaas design. ■TIP➔ Try something on just to experience the drama of the dressing room, just as hyperdesigned as the rest of the space. A showcase of everything wired, the **Apple Store** is a tech-head's Nirvana. Showcasing new Mac products, it's a place to learn about everything from photography to the care of your PowerBook or iPod. Edgy in the '70s and '80s, SoHo still retains some of the artists' galleries that brought the neighborhood to the forefront of the city's art scene at the time. Several of SoHo's better exhibition spaces, including **Deitch Projects,** the **Drawing Center,** and **Spencer Brownstone,** are clustered in the vicinity of Greene and Wooster streets near Grand and Canal. Many a rainy day can be spent enjoying the often outré collections showcased inside, no purchase necessary.

CAST IRON, COBBLESTONES, AND ARCHITECTURAL MASTERPIECES

SoHo has the world's greatest concentration of cast-iron buildings, built in response to fires that wiped out much of lower Manhattan in the mid-18th century. Although it's hard to single out any one block, as almost all have gorgeous examples of the various cast-iron styles (Italianate, Victorian Gothic, Greek Revival), Greene Street has two standouts, the **Queen of Greene Street** and the **King of Greene Street.** Even the lampposts in this neighborhood are architectural gems, with their turn-of-the-20th-century bishop's-crook style, adorned with cast-iron curlicues from their bases to their curved tops; they're the perfect complement to the paving stones below. Other notable buildings are the Beaux-Arts **Little Singer Building** and the **Haughwout Building** on Broadway, and the 1885 Romanesque Revival **Puck Building,** a former magazine headquarters and now a busy event space.

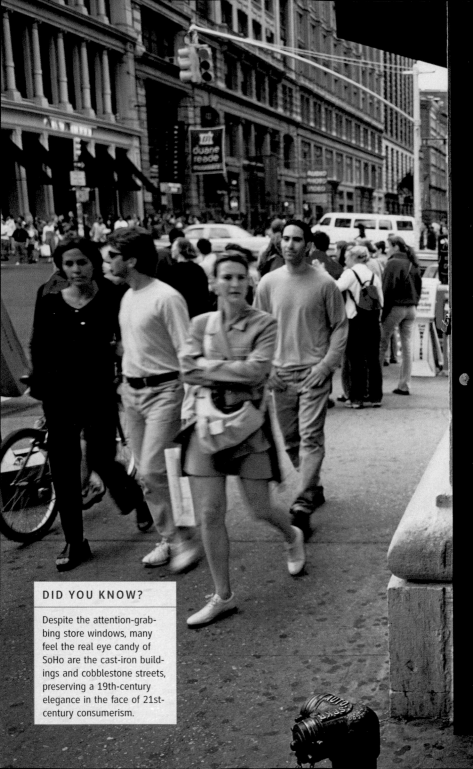

DID YOU KNOW?

Despite the attention-grab-
bing store windows, many
feel the real eye candy of
SoHo are the cast-iron buildings and cobblestone streets,
preserving a 19th-century
elegance in the face of 21st-
century consumerism.

TOP ATTRACTIONS

Fodor's Choice
★

King of Greene Street. This five-story Renaissance-style 1873 building has a magnificent projecting porch of Corinthian columns and pilasters. Today the King is painted a brilliant shade of ivory and houses a boutique on the ground floor with an array of fashion-forward international labels. ⊠ *72–76 Greene St., between Spring and Broome Sts., SoHo* Ⓜ *R, W to Prince St.*

Queen of Greene Street. The regal grace of this 1873 cast-iron beauty is exemplified by its dormers, columns, window arches, projecting central bays, and Second Empire–style roof. ⊠ *28–30 Greene St., between Grand and Canal Sts., SoHo* Ⓜ *J, M, N, Q, R, W, Z, 6 to Canal St.*

> **KIDS IN SOHO AND LITTLE ITALY**
>
> This is primarily a grown-up section of town, unless you're raising dedicated shoppers, but there are things for the kids to do here. Check out the programs and events at SoHo's Children's Museum of the Arts (⇨ *Chapter 14*) and the interactive if overtly commercial Scholastic Store (also in SoHo at 557 Broadway). Steam can be blown off at Little Italy's DeSalvio Playground at the corner of Spring and Mulberry streets— it's far from fancy, but the kids may enjoy clambering on red, white, and green equipment.

WORTH NOTING

Charlton Street. The city's longest stretch of Federal-style redbrick row houses from the 1820s and '30s runs along the north side of this street, which is west of 6th Avenue and south of West Houston Street. The high stoops, paneled front doors, leaded-glass windows, and narrow dormer windows are all intact. Nearby King and Vandam streets have more historic houses. Much of this area was once the site of a mansion called Richmond Hill; in the late 18th century Richmond Hill was set in what is described as a beautiful wild meadow with glimpses of the nearby city and the "hamlet" of Greenwich Village, which served variously as George Washington's headquarters and the home of Abigail Adams and Aaron Burr. Ⓜ *1 to Houston St; C, E to Spring St.*

Haughwout Building. Perhaps best known for what's no longer inside—the world's first commercial passenger elevator, invented by Elisha Graves Otis—the building's exterior is still well worth a long look. Nicknamed the Parthenon of Cast Iron, this five-story, Venetian palazzo–style structure was built in 1857 to house department-store merchant E. V. Haughwout's china, silver, and glassware store. Each window is framed by Corinthian columns and rounded arches. ⊠ *488–492 Broadway, at Broome St., SoHo* Ⓜ *6 to Spring St.; R, W to Prince St.*

Little Singer Building. Ernest Flagg's 1904 masterpiece reveals the final flower of the cast-iron style with a delicate facade covered with curlicues of wrought iron. The central bay windows are recessed, allowing the top floor to arch over like a proscenium. The L-shaped building's second facade is around the corner on Prince Street. ⊠ *561 Broadway, SoHo* Ⓜ *R, W to Prince St.*

Where can I find . . . ?

COFFEE	Aroma Espresso Bar 145 Greene St. Find out why locals skip Starbucks to come here.	Once Upon a Tart 135 Sullivan St. Great name with the goods to back it up.
A QUICK BITE	Lombardi's 32 Spring St. Killer pizza. Take a leap of faith with the clam pie.	Ceci-Cela 55 Spring St. Éclairs, crèmes brûlées, and truffles? Oui.
COCKTAILS	Fanelli's 94 Prince St. A true neighborhood bar.	MercBar 151 Mercer St. Chic locals, excellent martinis.

3

LITTLE ITALY

TWO WAYS TO EXPLORE

HOUSEWARES, FOOD SHOPS, AND THE MOB

Around Grand Street near Mulberry and Mott are a number of fine family run Italian grocers, including the fifth-generation **DiPalo's Fine Foods** (amazing cheese and cured meats—don't just stand there salivating, ask for a sample!), fourth-generation **Alleva** (the mozzarella and the fried rice balls are among the best eats in NYC), and **Piemonte Ravioli** (pick up some dried pasta to make at home). Try to avoid visiting just before dinner, when the locals all seem to shop—you'll have a much less frenzied experience and more chance to taste the goods. (DiPalo's in particular has long lines most days.) Established in 1910, **E. Rossi & Co.** sells music, espresso makers, and other essential items for Italian homes, and they're always happy to talk about the neighborhood. At the corner of Hester and Mulberry streets stands what was once **Umberto's Clam House** (now Ristorante Da Gennaro), where in 1972 mobster Joey Gallo was gunned down by mob hit men during dinner. Although this was Little Italy's most notorious whack job, there are less well-known mob spots here, like John "The Dapper Don" Gotti's former Manhattan headquarters at 247 Mulberry Street in NoLita.

THE HEART OF LITTLE ITALY

St. Patrick's Old Cathedral (263 Mulberry St.) was established in 1809, and described by the *New York Gazette* as "a grand and beautiful church, which may justly be considered one of the greatest ornaments of our city." Step inside this Gothic Revival church, once the scene of race riots, vehement anti-Catholic protests, and other less savory bits of NYC history, and you'll see a peaceful space which has a grandeur that far exceeds what you might expect to find in this neighborhood.

TOP ATTRACTIONS

National Shrine of San Gennaro. A replica of the grotto at Lourdes is the high point of this church's richly painted interior. The church becomes a focal point during the annual San Gennaro festival. ✉ *113 Baxter St., near Canal St., Little Italy* ☎ *212/226–6427* ☉ *Masses Sat. noon, 5:30; Sun. 9, noon, 2 (Vietnamese)* Ⓜ *N, Q, R, W, 6 to Canal St.; J, M, Z to Canal St.*

Fodor's Choice
★

St. Patrick's Old Cathedral. If you've watched The Godfather, you've peeked inside St. Patrick's Old Cathedral—the interior shots of the infamous baptism scene were filmed here. The unadorned exterior of the cathedral gives no hint to the splendors within, including an 1868 Henry Erben pipe organ. The enormous marble altar surrounded by hand-carved niches (reredos) house an extraordinary collection of sacred statuary and other Gothic exuberance. There's a maze of mortuary vaults underneath the Cathedral (older residents of Little Italy recall playing hide and seek in the vaults), and the outdoor cemetery is the final resting place for notable New Yorkers including the Venerable Pierre Toussaint, an African-American who was born a slave in Haiti, made his fortune as a New York hairdresser, and whose many charitable works have resulted in his consideration for sainthood. Also interred here is Bishop Hughes—better known during his time as "Dagger John," a nickname he earned for his fiery temperament and the distinctive pointed cross he always scrawled after signing his name. ✉ *263 Mulberry St., corner of Mott and Prince Sts., Little Italy* ☎ *212/226–8075* ☉ *Hours may vary, usually open 8 AM–5 PM; Masses Mon.–Fri. 9 and 12:10, Sat. 9, 12:10, and 5:30, Sunday 9:15, 10:15 (Chinese), 11:30 (Spanish), 12:45, and 7 PM* Ⓜ *N, R to Prince St.; 6 to Bleecker St.*

> ## MULBERRY SIZZLES
>
> Crowded with restaurants, cafés, bakeries, imported-food shops, and souvenir stores, the few blocks of Mulberry Street between Canal and Broome streets are where Little Italy still lives. Although the waiters inviting you to dine are mostly Albanian and not Italian, there's still a festive air about; try to snag an outdoor table. In September Mulberry Street becomes the giant Feast of San Gennaro, a crowded 11-day festival that sizzles with the smell of sausages and onions. This is by far the city's most extensive annual street fair. For festival information, call 212/768–9320.

WORTH NOTING

New York City Police Headquarters. Seen in Martin Scorsese's *Gangs of New York*, this magnificent 1909 Edwardian baroque structure with a striking copper dome served as the headquarters of the New York City Police Department until 1973. Designed to "impress both the officer and the prisoner with the majesty of the law," it was converted into luxury condos in 1988 and is known today as the Police Building Apartments. Big-name residents have included Cindy Crawford, Winona Ryder, and Steffi Graf. ✉ *240 Centre St., between Broome and Grand Sts., Little Italy* Ⓜ *6 to Spring St.; J, M, Z to Bowery.*

The stark, simple interior of OK Harris Works of Art illustrates the typical gallery space in SoHo.

GALLERIES

Deitch Projects. This energetic enterprise composed of two gallery spaces shows works from the global art scene, as well as performance groups such as the Citizens Band. Artists on view have included Swoon, Ryan McGinness, and Kihinde Wiley. ⊠ *76 Grand St., between Greene and Wooster Sts., SoHo* ☎ *212/343–7300* ⊕ *www.deitch.com* Ⓜ *C, E to Spring St.* ⊠ *18 Wooster St., between Grand and Canal Sts., SoHo* ☎ *212/343–7300* Ⓜ *A, C, E to Canal St.*

Drawing Center. At this nonprofit organization the focus is on contemporary and historical drawings seen nowhere else. Works often push the envelope on what's considered drawing; many projects are commissioned especially by the center. A second gallery is across the street at 40 Wooster Street. ⊠ *35 Wooster St., between Broome and Grand Sts., SoHo* ☎ *212/219–2166* ⊕ *www.drawingcenter.org* Ⓜ *A, C, E to Canal St.*

New York Earth Room. Walter de Maria's 1977 avant-garde work consists of 140 tons of gently sculpted soil (22 inches deep) filling 3,600 square feet of space of a second-floor gallery maintained by the Dia Art Foundation. You cannot touch, tread on, tease, or otherwise molest the dirt, nor can you take its photo. If you like the work, check out de Maria's *Broken Kilometer*, a few blocks away at 393 West Broadway. ⊠ *141 Wooster St., between W. Houston and Prince Sts., SoHo* ☎ *212/ 989–5566* ⊕ *www.earthroom.org* ⊠ *Free* ☉ *Wed.–Sun. noon–6* PM *(closed 3–3:30 and during the summer)* Ⓜ *R, W to Prince St.; B, D, F, V to Broadway-Lafayette.*

OK Harris Works of Art. This SoHo stalwart hosts a wide range of visual arts: paintings, digitally enhanced photographs, trompe-l'oeil reliefs, and sculptures. The gallery closes from mid-July to early September. ✉ *383 West Broadway, between Spring and Broome Sts., SoHo* ☎ *212/431–3600* ⊕ *www.okharris.com* Ⓜ *C, E to Spring St.*

Ronald Feldman Fine Arts. Founded in 1971, this gallery represents more than 30 international contemporary artists. It has a large selection of Andy Warhol prints, paintings, and drawings. ✉ *31 Mercer St., between Grand and Canal Sts., SoHo* ☎ *212/226–3232* ⊕ *www.feldmangallery. com* Ⓜ *J, M, N, Q, R, W, Z, 6 to Canal St.*

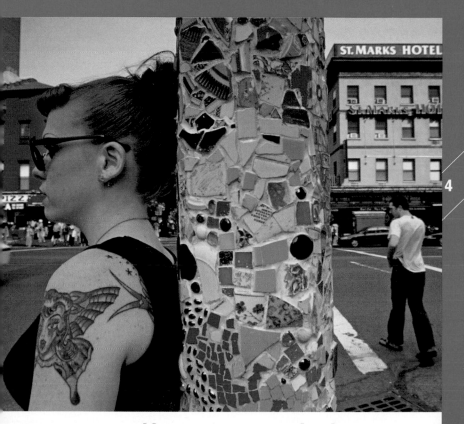

East Village and the Lower East Side

WORD OF MOUTH

"We thought the Tenement Museum was one of the best 'museums' we've been to in a long time. The Tenement Museum, a walk around the Lower East Side, and lunch at Katz's Deli—a perfect morning/afternoon!"

—sf3707

GETTING ORIENTED

E. 14th St.

M 4,5,6, L, N,Q,R,W

M L

E. 13th St.

The Strand Book Store

E. 12th St.

Third Ave.

Second Ave.

First Ave.

Broadway

Fourth Ave.

E. 11th St.

St. Mark's Church-in-the-Bowery

E. 10th St.

Russian & Turkish Baths

Stuyvesant St.

Stuyvesant St.

E. 9th St.

P.S. 122

Astor Place Subway Station

Tompkins Square Park

Sculpture for the Living

Cooper Union Foundation Building

St. Marks Place

M R,W

St. Marks Pl.

Fourth Ave.

McSorley's Old Ale House

Astor Pl.

M 6

E. 7th St.

Taras Shevchenko Pl.

St. George's Ukranian Catholic Church

Ave. A

Ave. B

Colonnade Row

Joseph Papp Public Theater

Third Ave.

E. 6th St.

EAST VILLAGE

Merchant's House Museum

E. 5th St.

Cooper Square

ALPHABET CITY

Lafayette St.

Gt. Jones St.

E. 4th St.

E. 3rd St.

Nuyorican Poets Café

E. 2nd St.

6 M

Bleecker St.

E. 1st St.

Angel Orensanz Center for the Arts

F,V M

B,D,F,V M

E. Houston St.

Mulberry St.

Mott St.

Elizabeth St.

Bowery

Chrystie St.

Eldridge St.

Forsyth St.

Allen St.

Orchard St.

Ludlow St.

Essex St.

Norfolk St.

Suffolk St.

Stanton St.

Prince St.

Rivington St.

LOWER EAST SIDE

Babeland

Gallery Onetwentyeight

Economy Candy

Hotel on Rivington

Essex Street Market

Bialystoker Synagogue

Spring St.

M 6

Blue Moon Hotel

M J,M,Z,F

Delancey St.

J,M,Z M

Lower East Side Tenement Museum

Kehila Kedosha Janina

Broome St.

0   1/8 mile

0   200 meters

Eldridge St. Synagogue

Jewish Daily Forward

MAKING THE MOST OF YOUR TIME

Houston Street, which runs the entire width of this part of Manhattan, somewhat neatly divides the area south of 14th Street and east of 4th Avenue and the Bowery into the East Village (above) and the Lower East Side (below). So many communities converge in these neighborhoods that each block seems like a new neighborhood unto itself.

The East Village lets loose on weekend nights, when reservations fill up and bar-hoppers converge. Visiting on weekdays makes for a more low-key experience, when establishments attract mostly locals shuffling on errands and visitors enjoying the mellow shopping and café vibe. Weekend days see the street life at its most vibrant, with brunch spots like Prune and Back Forty filled with lingering patrons, and boutiques shoppers trying on vintage dresses.

The Lower East Side is not an early riser any day of the week. Although there's plenty to see during the day, nightfall offers a different vision: blocks that were previously empty rows of pulled-down gratings transform into clusters of throbbing bars. When shopping, be aware that a number of traditional food and clothing establishments close on Saturday to observe the Jewish Sabbath, and on Sunday Orchard Street below Houston becomes a pedestrian-only strip where street vendors set up their stands outside the many "bargain district" clothing and specialty shops. On the increasingly trendy streets around Rivington and Stanton, stores, bars, and cafés buzz all week but are less crowded by day.

GETTING HERE

Take the R or W subway line to 8th Street or the 6 to Astor Place. To reach Alphabet City, take the L to 1st Avenue or the F or V to 2nd Avenue. Head southeast from the same stop on the F or V; or take the F to Delancey or the J, M, Z to Essex Street. Driving is not recommended, as parking here is very difficult.

4

Sightseeing
★★
Nightlife
★★★★★
Dining
★★★★★
Lodging
★★
Shopping
★★★★

The high concept of "La Bohème meets hipsters in vintage clothing," better known as the musical *Rent,* accurately pegs the East Village as a community of artists, activists, and other social dissenters. Spend some time wandering these bohemian side streets, and you'll be struck by the funky pastiche of ethnicities whose imprints are visible in the neighborhood's restaurants, shops, and, of course, people.

Updated by
Meryl D.
Pearlstein

Another defining point in the neighborhood's history, American punk was born here at the now-defunct CBGB; the punk rock/indie scene is kept alive at the many small music venues both here and on the Lower East Side. A walk along the lively but somewhat homogenized St. Mark's Place will evoke this once-gritty and counter-culture scene. But the arrival of a Trader Joe's and glass-and-chrome condos signal that a tamer neighborhood has taken hold.

The Lower East Side, the historic "Gateway to America" for many seeking a better life, has seen waves of Irish, German, Jewish, Hispanic, and Chinese immigrants: a legacy of tough times and survival instincts that has been movingly captured in the Lower East Side Tenement Museum (⇨ *Chapter 14*). Today a cool arts and nighttime scene, some distinctively modern high-rises, and the ultracontemporary New Museum exist alongside buildings and cultural centers staunchly rooted in the past.

EAST VILLAGE

THREE WAYS TO EXPLORE

ASTOR PLACE: ANCHORED IN TIME

Stop a moment at Astor Place, the triangle formed by the intersections of East 8th Street, Lafayette Street, Astor Place, and 4th Avenue. The area seems frozen in time, in a way, with both a university and an arts community holding on to the idealism of the neighborhood's past. On any given day you can see students from NYU or Cooper

Union shooting a film or sketching a scene; political groups soliciting signatures; and punks and rockers boldly evincing the city's bohemian subculture.

Distinctive architecture and design are also part of this area's legacy. On East 4th Street off Lafayette is the **Merchant's House Museum,** an example of upscale residential Manhattan life in the 19th century, and open for a self-guided tour. Although now in a sorry state, **Colonnade Row,** around the corner along Lafayette Street, is marked by marble Corinthian columns in front of a sweep of Greek Revival mansions once home to millionaires John Jacob Astor and Cornelius Vanderbilt. You'll have to look closely to see them, through the soot and above the mix of theaters and restaurants and other retail that now fill their lower levels.

New design-forward buildings are also popping up in the area. **Cooper Union's Science and Art Building,** opened September 2009, is an exciting new landmark in the neighborhood. The **Sculpture for Living** building, a much-maligned glass-and-steel tower of million-dollar apartments, sits smack in the middle of numerous low-rises in jarring contrast. The building's name and shape seem to ironically reference what had previously been Astor Place's focal point, **the Alamo,** a giant spinning cube on the central traffic island. At the entrance to the **Astor Place Subway Station** is a cast-iron replica of the Beaux-Arts kiosks that covered most subway entrances in the early 20th century.

STREETS WITH A CHARACTER OF THEIR OWN

The East Village is an area of nonconformity, and its streets are no different. East 6th Street between 2nd and 3rd avenues is known as Little India. Spilling around the corners to each of the avenues, Bangladeshi and Indian restaurants offer inexpensive, authentic dining choices. Two blocks east, the strip between Avenues A and B has an eclectic assortment of South American and other international (and generally affordable) restaurants.

East 7th Street between 2nd and 3rd avenues is dominated by **St. George's Ukrainian Catholic Church,** the meeting place for the local Ukrainian community and the site of an annual Ukrainian folk festival in spring. Incongruously, the block also has an odd assortment of brewpubs, including the grizzly **McSorley's Old Ale House,** which has remained unchanged in both menu and decor over its 100-plus-year-old history, but it now allows women to partake in the revelry.

One block north is **St. Marks Place,** aka 8th Street between 3rd Avenue and Avenue A. Over the years, beatniks, artists, and punk rockers have congregated at this hub of the East Village scene. Today the block between 2nd and 3rd avenues feels like a shopping arcade for the vinyl-pants set. It's crammed with body-piercing and tattoo salons; shops selling cheap jewelry, sunglasses, incense, and caustic T-shirts; and restaurants and bars. And if you're craving Asian food, there seems to be a new restaurant opening here every day. ■TIP➜ Many claim that the egg cream was hatched at Gem Spa (✉ *131 2nd Ave.* ☎ *212/995–1866)* , a 24-hour newsstand at the corner of St. Marks and 2nd Avenue. Cold milk, seltzer, and chocolate or vanilla syrup combine to make this peculiarly New York drink, which comes in two sizes: $2 for a small, $2.50 for a large.

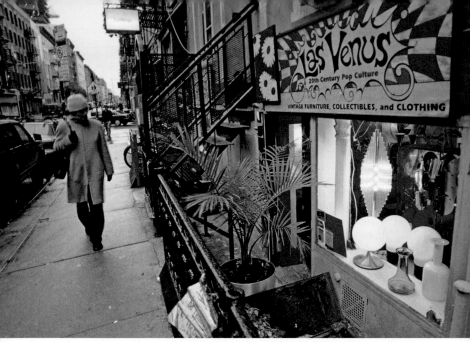

Vibrant vintage clothing boutiques and pop culture shops display the funky, freewheeling vibe of the East Village.

One block north and a proverbial world away in look and feel is Stuyvesant Street, a strip of historic redbrick row houses and the oldest street in Manhattan, laid out along a precise east–west axis (other streets in the city follow the island's geographic orientation). Fitting in perfectly is **St. Mark's-in-the-Bowery Church,** a charming 1799 fieldstone country church that occupies the former site of Dutch governor Peter Stuyvesant's family chapel.

THE CITY'S BOHEMIA

East of 1st Avenue is nicknamed **Alphabet City,** with avenues designated by letters instead of numbers. Alphabet City was once a burned-out area of slums and drug haunts, but has gentrified somewhat and is pretty safe today. The area still has a young, artistic rawness about it, especially in the late hours in the tiny bars and innovative restaurants around Avenues A, B, and C. At the center of the crowded tenements is **Tompkins Square Park,** a popular hangout with playgrounds, green expanses, and active dog runs. The Avenue A side has one of the city's most interesting arrays of inexpensive ethnic restaurants, Internet cafés, collectibles shops, and low-rent bars. Contributing to the artistic bent is popular Friday-night poetry slam at the **Nuyorican Poets Café** on East 3rd Street between Avenues B and C. At 151 Avenue B, on the west side of the park, stands a brownstone where jazz saxophonist Charlie Parker lived in the '50s.

TOP ATTRACTIONS

Alphabet City. The north–south avenues east of 1st Avenue, from Houston Street to 14th Street, are all labeled with letters, not numbers, which gives this area its nickname, Alphabet City. With the exception of Avenue D, it is now fairly gentrified, with colorful community gardens dotting the area. The many reasonably priced restaurants with their bohemian atmosphere on Avenues A, B, and C, and the cross streets in between, attract all kinds. A close-knit Puerto Rican community makes its home around Avenue C, with predominantly Latino shops and bodegas, plus a "Nuyorican" café and music venue. Avenue A along the park has a wide variety of ethnic cafés and bars, and Avenue B likewise has a growing restaurant scene. Also called Loisaida Avenue (a Spanglish creation meaning Lower East Side), Avenue C has a few fun spots like **Sunburnt Cow** and **Esperanto.** ⊠ *East Village* Ⓜ *6 to Astor Pl.; L to 1st Ave.; F, V to 2nd Ave.*

Astor Place Subway Station. At the beginning of the 20th century almost every Interborough Rapid Transit (IRT) subway entrance resembled the ornate cast-iron replica of a Beaux-Arts kiosk that covers the stairway leading to the uptown No. 6 train here. Inside, plaques of beaver emblems line the tiled station walls, a reference to the fur trade that contributed to John Jacob Astor's fortune. Milton Glaser, a Cooper Union graduate, designed the station's murals. ⊠ *On traffic island at E. 8th St. and 4th Ave., East Village* Ⓜ *6 to Astor Pl.*

McSorley's Old Ale House. Joseph Mitchell immortalized this spot, which claims to be one of the city's oldest, in *The New Yorker.* Opened in 1854, it didn't admit women until 1970. Fortunately, it now offers separate restrooms. The mahogany bar, gas lamps, potbelly stove, and yellowing newspaper clips are originals. Try to visit on a weekday before 7 PM so you can enjoy one of the two McSorley's ales and a cheese plate with onions in relative peace. Be warned: on weekends this place is a zoo, and there can be a line to get in day or night. ⊠ *15 E. 7th St., between 2nd and 3rd Aves., East Village* ☎ *212/473–9148* Ⓜ *6 to Astor Pl.*

Russian and Turkish Baths. It's clear from the older Soviet types devouring blintzes and Baltika beer served in the lobby that this is no cushy, uptown spa. But the three-story public bathhouse, which dates to 1892, isn't about pampering as much as hearty, Slavic-style cleansing. There's a eucalyptus steam room, a Finnish sauna, pull-chain showers, and an ice-cold plunge pool (45°F), and you're encouraged to alternate cooking in the hot rooms with plunges in the cold pool to stimulate circulation, a bathing cultures staple. Traditional massages and scrubs are offered without appointment. Except for a few single-sex hours per week on Wednesday, Thursday, and Sunday, the baths are coed, with bathing suits or shorts worn, and felt hats (alleged to decrease lightheadedness) for the seriously old-school. ⊠ *268 E. 10th St., between 1st Ave. and Ave. A, East Village* ☎ *212/674–9250* ⊕ *www.russianturkishbaths.com* ⊠ *$30* ⊙ *Weekdays noon–10, Sat. 9 AM–10 PM, Sun. 8 AM–10 PM* Ⓜ *L to 1st Ave.*

Fodor's Choice ★ **St. Marks Place.** The longtime hub of the edgy East Village, St. Marks Place is the name given to idiosyncratic East 8th Street between 3rd Avenue and Avenue A. During the 1950s, beatniks Allen Ginsberg and Jack Kerouac lived and wrote in the area; the 1960s brought Bill Graham's Fillmore East, Andy Warhol's the Dom, the Electric Circus nightclub, and hallucinogenic drugs. The studded, pink-haired and shaved-head punk scene followed, continuing today, although a little more diluted, with pierced rockers and teenage Goths. The blocks between 2nd and 3rd avenues have time-tested alternative-clothing boutiques and Asian restaurants galore. At 80 St. Marks Place, near 1st Avenue, is the Pearl Theatre Company, which performs classic plays from around the world. The handprints, footprints, and autographs of such past screen luminaries as Joan Crawford, Ruby Keeler, Joan Blondell, and Myrna Loy lie in its sidewalk. At 96–98 St. Marks Place (between 1st Avenue and Avenue A) stands the building that was photographed for the cover of Led Zeppelin's *Physical Graffiti* album. The cafés between 2nd Avenue and Avenue A attract customers late into the night. Ⓜ *6 to Astor Pl.*

Ⓒ **Tompkins Square Park.** This leafy spot amid the East Village's crowded tenements is a release valve. The park fills up with locals year-round, partaking in picnics, drum circles, the playground, and two dog runs. The Charlie Parker Jazz Festival, honoring the former park-side resident and noted jazz saxophonist, packs the park in late August. But it wasn't always so rosy. In 1988 police followed then-mayor David Dinkins's orders to clear the many homeless who had set up makeshift homes here, and homeless rights and anti-gentrification activists fought back with sticks and bottles. The park was reclaimed and reopened in 1992 with a midnight curfew, still in effect today. ⊠ *Bordered by Aves. A and B and E. 7th and E. 10th Sts., East Village* Ⓜ *6 to Astor Pl.; L to 1st Ave.*

WORTH NOTING

St. Mark's Church in-the-Bowery. This charming 1799 fieldstone country church stands on what was once Governor Peter Stuyvesant's *bouwerie*, or farm. St. Mark's is Manhattan's oldest continually used Christian site, and both Stuyvesant and Commodore Perry are buried here in vaults. Be sure to check out the gorgeous modern stained-glass windows on the balcony, which replaced the more traditional windows like those on the ground level after a fire in the late '70s. Over the years St. Mark's has hosted many progressive arts events including readings by poet Carl Sandburg and dance performances by Martha Graham and Merce Cunningham. The tradition has continued with Danspace, the Poetry Project, and the Ontological Hysteric-Theater, which give performances throughout the year. ⊠ *131 E. 10th St., at 2nd Ave., East Village* ☎ *212/674–6377* Ⓜ *6 to Astor Pl.; L to 3rd Ave.*

Stuyvesant Street. This diagonal slicing through the block bounded by 2nd and 3rd avenues and East 9th and 10th streets is unique in Manhattan: it's the oldest street laid out precisely along an east–west axis. Among the handsome 19th-century redbrick row houses are the Federal-style **Stuyvesant-Fish House** (⊠ *21 Stuyvesant St., East Village*), built as a wedding gift for a great-great-granddaughter of the Dutch governor Peter Stuyvesant, and **Renwick Triangle,** an attractive group

Where can I find . . . ?

COFFEE	Black Hound New York 170 2nd Ave. Coffee and "Busy Bee Cake" in a New York minute.	D'espresso 100 Stanton St. Italian-style coffee, plus the pastries to match.
A QUICK BITE	Katz's Delicatessen 205 E. Houston St. Yes, yes, yes, Meg Ryan had her big scene right here.	Il Laboratorio del Gelato 95 Orchard St. Seasonal flavors make this gelato la crème de la crème.
COCKTAILS	Cake Shop 152 Ludlow St. A kickin' blend of music, cock- tails, and coffee.	McSorley's Old Ale House 15 E. 7th St. "McSurly" service? Who cares? It's about the beer.

of Anglo-Italianate brick and brownstone residences, which face Stuyvesant and East 10th streets. Ⓜ *6 to Astor Pl.*

LOWER EAST SIDE

THREE WAYS TO EXPLORE

THE HISTORIC LOWER EAST SIDE: GATEWAY TO AMERICA

Directly south of the East Village, on the other side of Houston Street, is the traditional Lower East Side, a juxtaposition of old and new worlds, where a hot nightlife scene is growing amid aged businesses that hark back to the area's immigrant heritage. The historic heart of the Lower East Side is Orchard Street, the center of New York's fabric and garment district at the turn of the 20th century. At the **Lower East Side Tenement Museum** (⇨ *Chapter 14*) different tours draw you into Irish, German, Polish, Jewish, and Sicilian family life of the period. Some of the old building fronts remain, as do dated clothing shops (the so-called Bargain District), but younger fashion-furious boutiques and other cool shops have moved in as well.

THE REMNANTS OF THE FIRST JEWISH IMMIGRANT COMMUNITY IN THE CITY

Several historic synagogues, their gorgeous facades squeezed among the tenements, are still in use. The **Eldridge Street Synagogue** was the first Orthodox synagogue erected by the large number of Eastern European Jews who settled on the Lower East Side in the late 1880s. Its main sanctuary has just completed a glorious restoration, allowing the synagogue to become a permanent museum and home to its practicing orthodox congregation. The only Romaniote (Greek Jewish) synagogue in the western hemisphere, **Kehila Kedosha Janina** also functions as a museum to this obscure branch of Judaism. The city's oldest synagogue, dating to 1850, is now the funky **Angel Orensanz Center for the Arts,** named for the sculptor who purchased the synagogue when it fell into disrepair. This originally German synagogue was modeled after the Cathedral of Cologne and now hosts exhibits and dramatically lighted events such as the wedding of Sarah Jessica Parker and Matthew Broderick. The busiest of the Lower East Side synagogues today is the orthodox **Bialystoker Synagogue,** with its dramatic blue-sky-clouds-and-stars ceiling; scenes from the zodiac; and "hidden" balcony door (you can open it), which was once used by the Underground Railroad to hide slaves during the synagogue's former days as a Methodist church.

Starting on Houston Street and heading south along Essex, Allen, and Orchard streets, you can munch on traditional pickles, bialys, knishes, and strudel as you walk by buildings with Hebrew letters and antique Jewish books in the windows. The indoor **Essex Street Market** took the place of the pushcarts that once dominated Hester Street, and has a colorful assortment of fish markets, butchers, and Latino shops. (Note that it's not open on Sunday.)

CENTER FOR THE CULTURALLY HIP

The epicenter of the trendy, gentrified Lower East Side falls along parallel Rivington and Stanton streets, between Orchard and Essex streets, and the section of Ludlow Street that crosses them. Among the restaurants, boutiques, and bars are stores that fluctuate from hip to historic, like **Babeland,** a women-oriented sex shop, and **Economy Candy,** every kids' fantasy and a pseudo-general store literally crammed to the rafters with barrels of nuts and shelves of old-time and current candy favorites.

TOP ATTRACTIONS

Eldridge Street Synagogue. This was the first Orthodox synagogue erected by the large number of Eastern European Jews who settled in the Lower East Side in the late 19th century. The exterior is a striking mix of Romanesque, Gothic, and Moorish motifs. Inside is an exceptional hand-carved ark of mahogany and walnut, a sculptured wooden balcony, jewel-tone stained-glass windows, stenciled walls, and an enormous brass chandelier. The synagogue can be viewed as part of a tour, and begins at the small museum downstairs where interactive "touch tables" teach all ages about Eldridge Street and the Lower East Side. Family programs add to the community experience. ⊠ *12 Eldridge St., between Canal and Division Sts., Lower East Side* ☎ *212/219–0888* ⊕ *www.eldridgestreet.org* ✉ *$10* ☉ *Sun.–Thurs. 10–5; tours on the half hr* Ⓜ *F to E. Broadway; B, D to Grand St.*

★   **Gallery Onetwentyeight.** Inside the jewel-box space, artist Kazuko Miyamoto directs crisp and provocative group shows. ⊠ *128 Rivington St., between Essex and Norfolk Sts., Lower East Side* ☎ *212/674–0244* ⊕ *www.galleryonetwentyeight.org* Ⓜ *F to Delancey St.; J, M, Z to Essex St.*

Greenwich Village and Chelsea

WORD OF MOUTH

"We enjoyed the Chelsea Market tour very much. It's a fun place to shop but the tour adds history plus the yummy tastings. Also, don't miss walking on the High Line."

—dfrostnh

GETTING ORIENTED

0 — 1/4 mile
0 — 400 meters

W. 34th St.

A,C,E   1,2,3   N,Q,R,W,
B,D,F,V

W. 32nd St.

Madison Square Garden
/Penn Station

W. 31st St.

W. 30th St.

W. 29th St.

W. 28th St.

W. 27th St.

R,W

W. 26th St.

CHELSEA

W. 25th St.

Matthew
Marks
Gallery

Gagosian
Gallery

Andrea
Rosen
Gallery

London
Terrace

W. 24th St.

Madison
Square

Chelsea Art
Museum

W. 23rd St.   C,E   F,V

W. 22nd St.   Chelsea
Hotel   R,W

Matthew
Marks
Gallery

Paula Cooper
Gallery

W. 21st St.

Cushman
Row

St. Peter's
Episcopal Church   W. 20th St.

David
Zwirner
Gallery

W. 19th St.

Joyce
Theater   W. 18th St.

Chelsea
Piers

W. 17th St.

W. 16th St.

Chelsea
Market

W. 15th St.

A,C,E,L   1,2,3   F,V,L

MEATPACKING
DISTRICT   W. 14th St.

W. 13th St.

Little W. 12th St.

W. 12th St.

GREENWICH
VILLAGE

W. 11th St.

Ganservoort St.

Horatio St.

Jane St.

Abingdon
Square

W.10th St.

W. 9th St.

W. 8th St.

W. 12th St.

Bethune St.

Bank St.

Perry St.

Charles St.

Waverly Pl.

Wash. Pl.

Christopher St.

W. 4th

Washington Sq. S.

A,B,C,D,E,F,V

W. 3rd

WEST
VILLAGE

Bedford St.

Leroy St.

Father
Demo Sq.

Bleecker St.

Barrow

Morton St.

Carmine St.

MacDougal St.

Sullivan St.

Thompson St.

La Guardia Pl.

Leroy St.

Downing St.

Clark St.

W. Houston St.   See Greenwich Village map

MAKING THE MOST OF YOUR TIME

Weekday afternoons the streets of the West Village are nearly empty. Because of the many artists, students, and writers who live here, you'll have just enough company at the cafés and shops to make you feel like an insider instead of a tourist. To truly appreciate the Meatpacking District, make a 9 PM or later dinner reservation at a hot restaurant, then hit the bars to see where the glitterati are this week. If shopping is your pleasure, weekdays are great; come after noon, though, or you'll find most spots shuttered.

Chelsea has a dual life: typical gallery hours are Tuesday–Saturday 10–6, but at night the neighborhood changes into a party town, with gay bars and difficult-to-enter clubs that don't rev up until after 11.

GETTING HERE

The West 4th Street subway stop—serviced by the A, B, C, D, E, F, and V—puts you in the center of Greenwich Village. Farther west, the 1 train has stops on West Houston Street and Christopher Street/Sheridan Square. The A, C, E, 1, 2, 3, and L trains stop at 14th Street for both the Meatpacking District and Chelsea. The latter is further served by the C, E, 1, F, and V lines at the 23rd Street stop and the 1 stop at 28th Street. The L train connects Union Square on 14th Street to the Meatpacking District at 8th Avenue and 14th Street. 14th Street and 23rd Street are both also served by the PATH trains.

WORD OF MOUTH (WWW.FODORS.COM/FORUMS)

"Weave your way through the West Village and definitely go down Bleecker Street (all the way down) for amazing bakeries and cheese shops, and grab a slice of cake at Amy's or a dessert and coffee/hot chocolate with homemade whipped cream at Rocco's." —amanda amanda

FODOR'S CHOICE
Chelsea Market
Washington Square Park

TOP ATTRACTIONS
Chelsea Hotel
Cushman Row
Gay Street
Patchin Place
75½ Bedford Street

TOP EXPERIENCES
Gallery-hopping in Chelsea
Wandering along Bedford, Barrow, Grove, and Commerce streets
Clubbing in the Meatpacking District

BEST FOR KIDS
Chelsea Piers
The High Line
Hudson River Park

NEARBY MUSEUMS (⇨ CH. 14)
Chelsea Art Museum
Forbes Galleries
Rubin Museum of Art

AREA SHOPS (⇨ CH. 17)
Aedes De Venustas
Books of Wonder
Bottle Rocket
Fisch for the Hip
Flight 001
Loehmann's
Mxyplyzyk

5

Sightseeing
★★★

Nightlife
★★★★★

Dining
★★★★★

Lodging
★★★

Shopping
★★★★

Long the home of writers, artists, bohemians, and bon vivants, the West Village is a singular section of the city. High-rises and office towers have no business among the small curving streets, peculiar alleys, and historic town houses here, although a new boom in distinctive apartment living by designer architects has emerged around the west edges of the Village north to Chelsea. Primarily residential, the area also has many specialty restaurants, cafés, and boutiques with a warm and charming neighborhood vibe. Tiny as they might be, restaurants like The Little Owl and 'ino invite you to linger, as do larger restaurants with outside dining areas.

Updated by
Meryl D.
Pearlstein

Fertile doesn't even begin to describe the West Village's yield of creative genius. In the late 1940s and early 1950s abstract expressionist painters Franz Kline, Jackson Pollock, Mark Rothko, and Willem de Kooning congregated here, as did Beat writers Jack Kerouac, Allen Ginsberg, and Lawrence Ferlinghetti. The '60s brought folk musicians and poets, notably Bob Dylan. NYU students keep the idealistic spirit of the neighborhood alive, but polished professionals have also moved into the high-rent town houses. The Meatpacking District, in the far northwest part of the Village, has cobblestone streets whose original meatpacking tenants are being replaced by a different kind of meat-market life: velvet-rope clubs, trendy restaurants, and trendy-chic shops.

Overlapping the Meatpacking District to the north, stylish Chelsea has usurped SoHo as the world's contemporary-art-gallery headquarters *(an extensive gallery list and map at the end of this chapter will help you find your way)*. The west edge of the neighborhood has high-profile galleries housed in cavernous converted warehouses that are easily identified by their ultracool, glass-and-stainless-steel doors. Other former warehouses, unremarkable by day, pulsate through the night as the city's hottest nightclubs. Chelsea has also replaced the West Village as the heart of the city's gay community. One-of-a-kind boutiques and gay-friendly shops are scattered among unassuming grocery stores and other remnants of Chelsea's immigrant past.

GREENWICH VILLAGE AND THE MEATPACKING DISTRICT

FIVE WAYS TO EXPLORE

PARKS, STATELY LIVING, AND ARCHITECTURAL NOTABLES

At **Washington Square Park** the city's central business artery, 5th Avenue, ends, and the student-bohemian feel of the Village begins. Circle the recently spruced-up open square, but don't expect to find a bench or fountain-side seat not occupied by New York University students, professors, pigeon-feeders, or idlers of all sorts. On the park's north side is the grand **Washington Memorial Arch,** which looks upon the **Row,** two blocks of lovingly preserved Greek Revival and Federal-style town houses.

Residences are sometimes tucked away in little enclaves in the Village. **Washington Mews** and **MacDougal Alley** are two cobblestone private streets just above the park. **Grove Court,** a cluster of brick-front homes, seems like a precursor to today's gated communities. West of 6th Avenue on 10th Street is the wrought-iron gateway to a tiny courtyard called **Patchin Place.** Around the corner is another alley filled with homes, **Milligan Place.**

The beautiful blocks of 19th-century redbrick town houses that predominate in the Village are occasionally marked by attempts at nonconformity. At **18 West 11th Street** sits a home with a modern, angled bay window, a building erected to replace the town house inadvertently blown up by the antiwar group the Weathermen in 1970. The triangle formed by West 10th Street, 6th Avenue, and Greenwich Avenue originally held a market, a jail, and the magnificent towered courthouse that is now the **Jefferson Market Library.** Where Christopher Street crosses Waverly Place is the triangular 1831 brick **Northern Dispensary building.**

A SINGULAR STREET

Christopher Street has long been the symbolic heart of New York's gay and lesbian community. On this street, among cafés, lifestyle boutiques, and clothing shops, is one of the city's most acclaimed off-Broadway theaters, the **Lucille Lortel,** where major off-Broadway playwrights like David Mamet, Eugene Ionesco, and Edward Albee have their own markers in the sidewalk. There's also an active nightlife scene, anchored by the **Duplex** piano bar and cabaret at the corner of 7th Avenue. At **51–53 Christopher Street** the historic Stonewall riots marked the beginning of the gay rights movement. Across the street is a green triangle named **Christopher Park,** where commemorative statues of gay and lesbian companions mingle with real-live visitors. Far west, where Christopher Street continues to the river, a fountain and a landscaped pier with benches mark a stop in **Hudson River Park,** part of the city's greenway.

YOU'RE GUARANTEED TO GET LOST HERE

West of 7th Avenue South the Village turns into a picture-book town of twisting tree-lined streets, quaint houses, and tiny restaurants. Streets cross back and forth, and Greenwich Street and Greenwich Avenue bear no relation to each other. In a seemingly random way, West 4th inexplicably crosses West 10th and West 11th streets.

The area where Grove and Bedford streets intersect is among the most beautiful in the Village. These streets still feel like 19th-century New York, with simple redbrick homes from the early part of the century as well as a clapboard home and even a home built to resemble a Swiss chalet. Commerce Street, the location of the historic **Cherry Lane Theatre,** is undoubtedly one of the city's most romantic lanes. Minetta Lane, a "hidden" alley dating from the city's speakeasy history, lies between Washington Square Park and 6th Avenue, and is now home to the innovative **Minetta Lane Theatre** and **Minetta Tavern.**

A STREET THAT DEFINES A NEIGHBORHOOD

If you walk from one end of Bleecker Street to another you can pass through a smattering of everything Village: NYU buildings, used-record stores, Italian cafés and food shops, charming restaurants and bakeries, and funky boutiques, plus a park with a playground and tables and benches. On this extended block you can grab an espresso, check out century-old butcher shops, and sample some of the city's best thin-crust pizza. West of 7th Avenue you can also find fashion and home-furnishings boutiques featuring antiques, eyeglasses, shoes, and designer clothing.

To absorb some of the area's idealism and spirituality, stop at **Our Lady of Pompeii Church** at Bleecker and Carmine, where Mother Cabrini, a naturalized Italian immigrant who became the first American saint, often prayed. At 119 MacDougal Street is **Caffe Reggio,** one of the Village's first coffeehouses, pretty much unchanged since it opened in 1927. Partly because of the proximity of NYU, the streets in the area also attract a young crowd to its theaters, cabarets, and jazz clubs. Two of the best for getting your jazz on are the **Blue Note** at West 3rd near 6th Avenue and the **Village Vanguard** on 7th Avenue South just below West 11th Street, considered by many to be "the Carnegie Hall of jazz."

GLAM, NIGHTLIFE, AND THE CITY THAT NEVER SLEEPS

The **Meatpacking District** is concentrated in a few blocks of the West Village, between the Hudson River and 9th Avenue, from Little West 12th Street to West 14th Street, with some fringe activity heading toward West 16th Street. This burgeoning cobblestoned area is a meat market by morning, and a metaphorical one at night, when the city's trendiest frequent the equally trendy restaurants and bars here. Attracting a late-day shopping crowd, affluent-angled retailers and services line West 14th Street and include hair-cutting extortionist **Sally Hershberger** (whose cuts cost about $800) and the boutiques of fashion designers **Alexander McQueen** and **Stella McCartney.** For one of the city's most extensive and expensive shoe departments, visit **Jeffrey,** the district's pioneer retailer.

The nabe's newest attraction, **the High Line,** is a formerly abandoned railroad track-turned-promenade and park, is becoming a runway of sorts for fashionistas as they strut past the gleaming windows of the new über-chic hotel **The Standard.**

The city's recent crop of slick mega-restaurants seem to have found their homes in the streets between Little West 12th and West 16th, with huge Asian-food and -style "temples" like **Buddakan** (16th Street and 9th Avenue), **Morimoto** (16th Street and 10th Avenue), **Matsuri** (16th Street and 9th Avenue), and **Ajna Bar,** formerly Buddha Bar (Little West 12th between 9th Avenue and Washington Street). Equally sexy but somewhat smaller, **Spice Market** has a rich Southeast Asian design, **Tanuki Tavern** dishes up Japanese tapas, and late-night hot spot **Pastis** is a wall-to-wall version French bistro scene. The scene-y **Hotel Gansevoort** is brilliant purple at night and has a rooftop pool and bar. From the top you can look down at the pool at the private SoHo House, used in *Sex and the City.* A notable exception among all the glitz is the rough-and-tumble **Hogs and Heifers,** a neighborhood drinking hole infamous for its bra-covered bar and the movie *Coyote Ugly,* based on it.

CLOSE UP

Bleecker Street's

Little Italy can be besieged by slow-moving crowds, touristy shops, and desperate restaurant owners who call at you like shooting-gallery barkers at Coney Island. With its crowded cafés, bakeries, pizza parlors, and old-world merchants, Bleecker Street between 6th and 7th avenues seems more vital as a true Italian neighborhood.

For an authentic Italian bakery experience, step into **Rocco's** (No. 243) for wonderful cannoli, cream puffs, and cookies packed up or order an espresso to linger over the treats.

Step into the past at the old-style butcher shops, such as **Ottomanelli & Sons** (No. 285) and **Faicco's Sausage Store** (No. 260), where Italian locals have gotten their pork custom cut since 1900.

The sweet (or stinky) smell of success seems nowhere more evident than at **Murray's Cheese** (No. 254), at Cornelia Street. The original shop, opened in 1940 by Murray Greenberg (not Italian), was not much larger than the display case that stocked the stuff. Now it's a fromage fiend's emporium, with everything from imported crackers to bamboo cutting boards. Samples of cheese, gelato, salami, and other goodies are frequently offered.

In a town that's fierce about its pizza, some New Yorkers swear by **John's Pizzeria** (No. 278). But be forewarned: they don't deal in individual slices—whole thin-crust pies only. Got diet-breaking guilt? Head east to Carmine Street and Our Lady of Pompeii Church, where Mother Cabrini, a naturalized Italian immigrant and the first American saint, often prayed.

TOP ATTRACTIONS

Gay Street. A curved, one-block lane lined with small row houses, Gay Street is named after Sydney Howard Gay, managing editor of the long-defunct *New York Tribune,* who lived here during the Civil War with his wife and fellow abolitionist Lucretia Mott. In the 1930s this darling thoroughfare and nearby Christopher Street became famous nationwide when, from No. 14, Ruth McKenney wrote her somewhat zany autobiographical stories published in *The New Yorker* and later in *My Sister Eileen,* based on what happened when she and her sister moved to Greenwich Village from Ohio. Also on Gay Street, Howdy Doody was designed in the basement of No. 12. ⊠ *Between Christopher St. and Waverly Pl., Greenwich Village* Ⓜ *1 to Christopher St./Sheridan Sq.; A, B, C, D, E, F, V to W. 4th St.*

Patchin Place. This little cul-de-sac off West 10th Street between Greenwich and 6th avenues has 10 diminutive 1848 row houses. Around the corner on 6th Avenue is a similar dead-end street, **Milligan Place,** with five small homes completed in 1852. The houses in both quiet enclaves were originally built for waiters who worked at 5th Avenue's high-society Brevoort Hotel, long since demolished. Later Patchin Place residents included writers Theodore Dreiser, e.e. cummings, Jane Bowles, and Djuna Barnes. Milligan Place became popular among playwrights, including Eugene O'Neill. Ⓜ *A, B, C, D, E, F, V to W. 4th St.*

So Much Fun It's Scary!

All things weird and wonderful, all creatures great and squall, all things witty and fantastical, New York City has them all—and on All Hallows' Eve they freak through the streets in New York's Halloween parade. White-sheeted ghouls feel dull compared to fishnets and leathers, sequins and feathers posing and prancing along 6th Avenue in this vibrant display of vanity and insanity.

In 1973 mask maker and puppeteer Ralph Lee paraded his puppets from house to house visiting friends and family along the winding streets of his Greenwich Village neighborhood. His merry march quickly outgrew its origi-nal, intimate route and now, decades later, it parades up 6th Avenue, from Spring Street to 21st Street, attracting 50,000 creatively costumed exhibition-ists, artists, dancers, musicians, hun-dreds of enormous puppets, scores of bands, and more than 2 million spectators. Anyone with a costume can join in, no advance registration

required, although the enthusiastic interaction between participants and spectators makes it just as much fun to watch. It's a safe "street event" for families and singles alike, and a joyful night unlike any other.

The parade lines up on 6th Avenue between Canal and Spring streets from 6:30 PM to 8:30 PM. The walk actually starts at 7 PM, but it takes about two hours to leave the staging area. It's best to arrive from the south to avoid the crush of strollers and participants. Get there a few hours early if you can. Costumes are usually handmade, clever, and outrageous, and revelers are happy to strike a pose. The streets are crowded along the route, with the most congestion below 14th Street. Of course the best way to truly experience the parade is to march—if you're not feeling the face paint, you can volunteer to help carry the puppets. For information, contact ⊕ www.halloween-nyc.com.

—Jacinta O'Halloran

75½ Bedford Street. Rising real-estate rates inspired the construction of New York City's narrowest house—just 9½ feet wide—in 1873. Built on a lot that was originally a carriage entrance of the Isaacs-Hendricks House next door, this sliver of a building was home to actor John Bar-rymore and poet Edna St. Vincent Millay. ⊠ 75½ Bedford St., between Commerce and Morton Sts., Greenwich Village Ⓜ A, B, C, D, E, F, V to W. 4th St.

Fodor's Choice
★
Ⓒ

Washington Square Park. NYU students, street musicians, skateboarders, jugglers, chess players, and those just watching the grand opera of it all generate a maelstrom of activity in this physical and spiritual heart of the Village. The newly restored 9½-acre park had inauspicious begin-nings as a cemetery, principally for yellow fever victims—an estimated 10,000–22,000 bodies lie below. (A headstone was actually unearthed in 2009.) At one time, plans to renovate the park called for the removal of the bodies; however, local resistance prevented this from happening. In the early 1800s the park was a parade ground and the site of public executions; bodies dangled from a conspicuous Hanging Elm that still stands at the northwest corner of the square. Today that gruesome past is all but forgotten, as playgrounds attract parents with tots in tow, dogs go leash-free inside the popular dog runs, and everyone else seems drawn toward the large central fountain.

The triumphal European-style **Washington Memorial Arch** stands at the square's north end, marking the start of 5th Avenue. In 1889 Stanford White designed a wood-and-papier-mâché arch, originally situated a half block north, to commemorate the 100th anniversary of George Washington's presidential inauguration. The arch was reproduced in Tuckahoe marble in 1892, and the statues—*Washington as General Accompanied by Fame and Valor* on the left, and *Washington as Statesman Accompanied by Wisdom and Justice* on the right—were added in 1916 and 1918, respectively. ⊠ *5th Ave. between Waverly Pl. and 4th St., Greenwich Village* Ⓜ *A, B, C, D, E, F, V to W. 4th St.*

ALSO WORTH SEEING

Chumley's. A speakeasy during the Prohibition era, this still-secret tavern behind an unmarked door on Bedford Street has been closed for structural reasons for a few years. Inside, however, it retains its original ambience, with oak booths, a fireplace once used by a blacksmith, and a sawdust-strewn floor. For years Chumley's attracted a literary clientele (John Steinbeck, Ernest Hemingway, Edna Ferber, Simone de Beauvoir, and Jack Kerouac), and the book covers of their publications still proudly adorn the walls. There's another "secret" entrance in Pamela Court, accessed at 58 Barrow Street around the corner. Watch for the bar's reopening this year; it's one-of-a-kind. ⊠ *86 Bedford St., near Barrow St., Greenwich Village* ☎ *212/675–4449 (currently not in service)* Ⓜ *A, B, C, D, E, F, V to W. 4th St.*

Northern Dispensary. Edgar Allan Poe was a frequent patient at the triangular dispensary, built in 1831 as a private medical clinic for indigent Villagers. The weird Georgian brick building has *one* side on *two* streets (Grove and Christopher streets where they meet) and *two* sides facing *one* street—Waverly Place, which splits in two directions. Sadly, you can't visit the interior. ⊠ *165 Waverly Pl., Greenwich Village* Ⓜ *A, B, C, D, E, F, V to W. 4th St.*

St. Luke's Place. Steeped in New York City history and shaded by graceful gingko trees, this street officially called Leroy Street has 15 classic Italianate brownstone and brick town houses (1851–54). Novelist Theodore Dreiser wrote *An American Tragedy* at No. 16, and poet Marianne Moore resided at No. 14. Mayor Jimmy Walker (first elected in 1926) lived at No. 6; the lampposts in front are "mayor's lamps," which were sometimes placed in front of the residences of New York mayors. This block is often used as a film location: No. 12 was shown as the Huxtables' home on *The Cosby Show* (although on the show it was in Brooklyn), and No. 4 was the setting of the Audrey Hepburn movie *Wait Until Dark*. Before 1890 the playground on the south side of the street near Hudson was a graveyard where, according to legend, the dauphin of France—the lost son of Louis XVI and Marie Antoinette— is buried. ⊠ *Between Hudson St. and 7th Ave. S, Greenwich Village* Ⓜ *1 to Houston St.*

Washington Mews. A rarity in Manhattan, this private gated picturesque street is lined on one side with the former stables of the houses on the Row on Washington Square North. ⊠ *Between 8th St. and Washington Sq. N, between 5th Ave. and University Pl., Greenwich Village* Ⓜ *A, B, C, D, E, F, V to W. 4th St.*

IF THERE'S STILL TIME

Christopher Park. You might have to share a bench in this tiny park with George Segal's life-size sculptures of a lesbian couple. A gay male couple is also captured in mid-chat nearby. The park was a punchline in the 90's gay comedy *Jeffrey*. ⊠ *Bordered by W. 4th, Grove, and Christopher Sts., Greenwich Village* Ⓜ *1 to Christopher St./Sheridan Sq.*

Jefferson Market Library. After Frederick Clarke Withers and Calvert Vaux's towered Third Judicial Courthouse was constructed in 1877, critics variously termed its hodgepodge of styles Venetian, Victorian, or Italian. Villagers, noting the alternating wide bands of red brick and narrow strips of granite, dubbed it the "lean bacon style." Now a library, the veritable Victorian Gothic castle was the site of the murder trial of architect Stanford White at the beginning of the 20th century. ⊠ *425 6th Ave., at 10th St., Greenwich Village* ☎ *212/243–4334* Ⓜ *A, B, C, D, E, F, V to W. 4th St./Washington Sq.; 1 to Christopher St.*

> ### THE CUPCAKE CRAZE
>
> **Magnolia Bakery** (⊠ *401 Bleecker St., at W. 11th St.* ☎ *212/462–2572*), made famous by a scene in *Sex and the City*, kicked off an urbanite hunger for buttercream that still hasn't been sated more than 10 years, and two more locations, later. The bakeries that followed in its success, Buttercup Bakeshop, Billy's, and Sugar Sweet Sunshine, have been bringing a sugar buzz to other neighborhoods, and that cupcake colony continues to expand throughout the Upper East Side, Upper West Side, Midtown, Chelsea, and the Lower East Side with mobile vendors like the Cupcake Stop joining in the sweet success.

The Row. Built from 1833 through 1837, this series of beautifully preserved Greek Revival row houses along Washington Square North, between University Place and MacDougal Street, once belonged to merchants and bankers, then writers and artists such as John Dos Passos and Edward Hopper. ⊠ *1–13 and 19–26 Washington Sq. N, between University Pl. and MacDougal St., Greenwich Village* Ⓜ *A, B, C, D, E, F, V to W. 4th St./Washington Sq.*

Twin Peaks. In 1925 financier Otto Kahn gave money to a Village eccentric named Clifford Daily to remodel an 1835 house for artists' use. The building was whimsically altered with stucco, half-timbers, and the addition of a pair of steep roof peaks. The result: an imitation Swiss chalet. ⊠ *102 Bedford St., between Grove and Christopher Sts., Greenwich Village* Ⓜ *1 to Christopher St./Sheridan Sq.*

CHELSEA

TWO WAYS TO EXPLORE

THE CONTEMPORARY ARTS

North of the Meatpacking District, Chelsea is the nexus of the American art scene, with a thriving gallery culture that spans from 20th to 27th streets, primarily between 10th and 11th avenues. The range of contemporary art on display includes almost every imaginable medium and style; if it's going on in the art world, it'll be in one of the 300 or so galleries here. Standouts include the enormous **David Zwirner Gallery** on West 19th Street, across from the amazing Frank Gehry–designed IAC office building; the **Robert Miller Gallery** on West 26th Street, whose proprietor is a titan in the New York art world and represents the estate of Diane Arbus among others; and the galleries of **Gagosian** and **Matthew Marks**, both showing the latest in painting, photography, and sculpture. For a taste of the artistic past, there's the **Chelsea Art Museum** on West 22nd Street, housed in a former Christmas ornament factory. If it's performing arts that you're more interested in, the **Joyce Theater** on 8th Avenue and 19th Street showcases modern dance troupes like Pilobolus, Elisa Monte Dance, and Momix.

ARCHITECTURAL ICONS

The neighborhood's history is on display a few blocks east on West 23rd Street at the legendary **Chelsea Hotel,** one of the best-known reminders of the street's heyday as a gathering point for the literati and creatures of counterculture. Equally distinguished long-term digs can be found on West 20th Street in the **Cushman Row** town houses, dating from the 1820s, and at **London Terrace** on West 23rd Street, home to such notables as Isaac Mizrahi and Annie Leibovitz. Regardless of whether they rent or own, nearly all neighborhood residents make frequent pilgrimages to block-long **Chelsea Market** at 15th Street between 9th and 10th avenues, the former National Biscuit Company Building, now filled with gourmet and specialty stores, restaurants, bakeries, florists, and the headquarters of the Food Network.

TOP ATTRACTIONS

Chelsea Hotel. The shabby aura of the hotel is part of its bohemian allure. This 12-story Queen Anne–style neighborhood landmark (1884) became a hotel in 1905, although it has always catered to long-term tenants with a tradition of broad-mindedness and creativity. Its literary roll call of live-ins is legendary: Mark Twain, Eugene O'Neill, O. Henry, Thomas Wolfe, Tennessee Williams, Vladimir Nabokov, Mary McCarthy, Brendan Behan, Arthur Miller, Dylan Thomas, and William S. Burroughs. In 1966 Andy Warhol filmed a group of fellow artists in eight rooms; the footage was included in *The Chelsea Girls* (1967). The hotel was also seen on-screen in *I Shot Andy Warhol* (1996) and in *Sid and Nancy* (1986), a dramatization of the real-life murder of Nancy Spungen, stabbed to death here by her Sex Pistols bassist boyfriend Sid Vicious. Read the commemorative plaques outside, then check out

Out and On Display: George Segal's sculptures of two gay couples in Christopher Park illustrate gay pride in Greenwich Village.

the eclectic collection of art in the lobby, some donated in lieu of rent. ✉ *222 W. 23rd St., between 7th and 8th Aves., Chelsea* ☎ *212/243-3700* ⊕ *www.hotelchelsea.com* Ⓜ *1, C, E to 23rd St.*

Fodor'sChoice ★ ☖ **Chelsea Market**. In the former Nabisco plant, where the first Oreos were baked in 1912, nearly two-dozen food wholesalers flank what is possibly the city's longest interior walkway in a single building—from 9th to 10th avenues. You can snack your way from one end to the other, nibbling Fat Witch brownies, Ronnybrook farmer's cheese, Amy's Bread sourdough, or just watch the bread being made as it perfumes the halls. The market's funky industrial design—a tangle of glass and metal creates the awning and art, artifacts, and a factory pipe converted into an indoor waterfall—complements the eclectic assortment of bakers, butchers, florists, grocers, cafés, and wine merchants inside. ✉ *75 9th Ave., between W. 15th and W. 16th Sts., Chelsea* ☎ *212/243-6005* ⊕ *www.chelseamarket.com* ☽ *Mon.–Sat. 7–10, Sun. 8–8* Ⓜ *A, C, E, L to 14th St.*

☖ **Chelsea Piers**. A phenomenal example of adaptive reuse, this sports-and-entertainment complex along the Hudson River between 17th and 23rd streets (entrance on 23rd) is the size of four 80-story buildings lying flat. There's pretty much every kind of sports activity going on inside and out from golf to ice-skating, rock climbing, soccer, bowling, gymnastics, and basketball. Plus there's a spa, elite sport-specific training, film studios, and a brewery. It's the jumping-off point for some of the city's varied water tours and dinner cruises. Trips on the river via private yacht can be arranged by **Surfside 3 Marinemax Marina** (☎ 212/336–7873). Lunch cruises, dinner cruises, and cabaret sails can

Contemporary art finds a home in the Pace Wildenstein Gallery, one of many such spaces in Chelsea.

be reserved on *Bateaux New York* or *Spirit of New York*, which both leave from **Pier 61** (☎ 866/211–3805). Sophisticated themed cruises on the retro-designed *Imagine* and *Adirondack* schooners leave from Pier 59 through **Classic Harbor Line** (☎ 646/336–5270). ⊠ *Piers 59–62 on Hudson River from 17th to 23rd Sts.; entrance at 23rd St., Chelsea* ☎ *212/336–6666* ⊕ *www.chelseapiers.com* Ⓜ *C, E to 23rd St.*

The *Titanic* was scheduled to arrive at Chelsea Piers on April 16, 1912. Fate intervened and the "unsinkable" ship struck an iceberg on April 14 and went down. Of the 2,200 passengers aboard, 675 were rescued by the Cunard liner *Carpathia*, which arrived at Chelsea Piers eight days later. Check out Chelsea Piers' historical photos on the wall between piers 60 and 61.

Cushman Row. Built in 1840, this string of homes between 9th and 10th avenues represents some of the country's most perfect examples of Greek Revival row houses. Original details include small wreath-encircled attic windows, deeply recessed doorways with brownstone frames, and striking iron balustrades and fences. Note the pineapples, a traditional symbol of welcome, on top of the black iron newels in front of No. 416. ⊠ *406–418 W. 20th St., between 9th and 10th Aves., Chelsea* Ⓜ *C, E to 23rd St.*

The High Line. Once a 1.5-mi elevated railroad track carrying freight trains, this space is now being transformed into Manhattan's newest green retreat in the spirit of Paris's Promenade Plantée. A long "walking park" with occasional benches, art installations, and views of the Hudson River and the Manhattan skyline, the High Line is set above the west end of the Village. Reclining chairs that roll along the track give it a playful air. The first section from Gansevoort to 20th streets opened in 2009, and in its final stage it will reach up to 30th Street, with scattered access points. Future plans include water features, children's attractions, viewing platforms, sundecks, and performance areas. Check the Web site for announcements and openings. ⊠ *10th Ave. from Gansevoort St. to 30th St., Greenwich Village and Chelsea* ⊕ *www. thehighline.org* Ⓜ *L to 8th Ave.*

GALLERIES

Alan Klotz Gallery. Fine 19th- and 20th-century and contemporary photography is the focus of the exhibitions here. Shows range from the modern photo-realistic domestic scenes by Melissa Ann Pinney to the more playful portraits of photojournalist Jonathan Torgovnik. Also here are extensive collections from some of history's most important photographers, including Josef Sudek, Berenice Abbott, and Eugene de Salignac. ⊠ *511 W. 25th St., Suite 701, between 10th and 11th Aves., Chelsea* ☏ *212/741–4764* ⊕ *www.klotzgallery.com* Ⓜ *C, E to 23rd St.*

Andrea Rosen. The gallery showcases artists on the cutting edge, such as sculptor Andrea Zittel, Felix Gonzalez-Torres, and painter and installation artist Matthew Ritchie. ⊠ *525 W. 24th St., between 10th and 11th Aves., Chelsea* ☏ *212/627–6000* ⊕ *www.andrearosengallery.com* Ⓜ *C, E to 23rd St.*

ATM Gallery. On an industrial cobblestone block just off the West Side Highway, this gallery is now located in a larger space. Eleven artists, six from Japan, are represented here in a gallery that began in the East Village in 2002. ⊠ *621 W. 27th St., between 11th and 12th Aves., Chelsea* ☏ *212/375–0349* ⊕ *www.atmgallery.com* Ⓜ *C, E to 23rd St.*

Casey Kaplan. Founded in 1995, this gallery represents 17 contemporary artists from Europe and the Americas. Casey Kaplan showcases sophisticated and ambitious exhibitions of works by such artists as Liam Gillick, Trisha Connelly, Carsten Höllen, and Brian Jungen. ⊠ *525 W. 21st St., between 10th and 11th Aves., Chelsea* ☏ *212/645–7335* ⊕ *www. caseykaplangallery.com* Ⓜ *C, E to 23rd St.*

Cheim & Read. This prestigious gallery represents artists such as Louise Bourgeois, William Eggleston, Joan Mitchell, Jenny Holzer, Donald Baechler, and Jack Pierson. ⊠ *547 W. 25th St., between 10th and 11th Aves., Chelsea* ☏ *212/242–7727* ⊕ *www.cheimread.com* Ⓜ *C, E to 23rd St.*

David Zwirner. Proving his finger is on the pulse of contemporary art, Zwirner shows works in all mediums by such emerging artists as Luc Tuymans, Stan Douglas, Thomas Ruff, Diana Thater, and Yutaka Sone. ⊠ *525 W. 19th St., between 10th and 11th Aves., Chelsea* ☏ *212/727–2070* ⊕ *www.davidzwirner.com* Ⓜ *C, E to 23rd St.*

Gagosian. This enterprising modern gallery has two large Chelsea branches and a third on the Upper East Side, one in Beverly Hills, plus one in London. All present works by heavy hitters, such as sculptor Richard Serra, the late pop-art icon Roy Lichtenstein, and Willem

Chelsea Galleries

de Kooning. ⊠ *555 W. 24th St., at 11th Ave., Chelsea* ☎ *212/741–1111*⊠*522 W. 21st St., between 10th and 11th Aves., Chelsea* ☎ *212/741–1717* ⊕ *www.gagosian.com* Ⓜ *C, E to 23rd St.*

Galerie Lelong. This large gallery presents challenging installations and art, as well as many Latin American artists. Look for Alfredo Jaar, Andy Goldsworthy, Cildo Meireles, Ana Mendieta, Hélio Oiticica, Sean Scully, and Petah Coyne. ⊠ *528 W. 26th St., between 10th and 11th Aves., Chelsea* ☎ *212/315–0470* ⊕ *www.galerielelong.com* Ⓜ *C, E to 23rd St.*

Gladstone Gallery. The international roster of artists in this gallery's two locations includes sculptor Anish Kapoor, photographer Sharon Lockhart, and multimedia artists Matthew Barney and Richard Prince. ⊠ *515 W. 24th St., between 10th and 11th Aves., Chelsea* ☎ *212/206–9300* ⊠ *530 W. 21st St., between 10th and 11th Aves., Chelsea* ☎ *212/206–7606* ⊕ *www.gladstonegallery.com* Ⓜ *C, E to 23rd St.*

Jack Shainman. Both emerging and established artists are shown here, such as Subodh Gupta, a young sculptor from India, and Kerry James Marshall, who deals with African-American issues. You might find works by Phil Frost, whose imagery is derived from graffiti, or Zwelethu Mthethwa, a South African photographer. ⊠ *513 W. 20th St., between 10th and 11th Aves., Chelsea* ☎ *212/645–1701* ⊕ *www.jackshainman. com* Ⓜ *C, E to 23rd St.*

Chelsea Galleries 101

Good art, bad art, edgy art, downright disturbing art—it's all here waiting to please and provoke in the contemporary art capital of the world. For the uninitiated, the concentration of nearly 300 galleries within a seven-block radius can be overwhelming, and the sometimes cool receptions upon entering and deafening silence, intimidating. Art galleries are not exactly famous for their customer-service skills, but they're free, and you don't need a degree in art appreciation to stare at a canvas or any installation.

There's no required code of conduct, although most galleries are library-quiet and cell phones are seriously frowned upon. Don't worry, you won't be pressured to buy anything; staff will probably be doing their best to ignore you.

Galleries are generally open Tuesday through Saturday from 10 AM to 6 PM.

Gallery-hop on a Saturday afternoon—the highest traffic day—if you want company. You can usually find a binder with the artist's résumé, examples of previous work, and exhibit details (usually including prices) at the front desk. If not, ask. You can also ask if there's information you can take with you.

You can't see everything in one afternoon, so if you have specific interests, plan ahead. Find gallery information and current exhibit details at ⊕ www.galleryguide.org (you can pick up a free print copy of the publication at any gallery desk). Sift further through your choices by checking the "Art Guide" in Friday's "Weekend" section of the New York Times. You can also learn more about the galleries and the genres and artists they represent at ⊕ www.artincontext.org.

—Jacinta O'Halloran

Luhring Augustine. Since 1985 owners Lawrence Luhring and Roland Augustine have worked with established and emerging artists from Europe, Japan, and America. ⊠ 531 W. 24th St., between 10th and 11th Aves., Chelsea ☎ 212/206–9100 ⊕ www.luhringaugustine.com Ⓜ C, E to 23rd St.

Marlborough. With galleries in London, Monaco, and Madrid, the Marlborough empire also operates two of the largest and most influential galleries in New York City. The Chelsea location (the other's in Midtown) shows the latest work of modern artists, with a special interest in sculptural forms, such as the large-scale work of Michele Oka Doner. Red Grooms, Richard Estes, and Fernando Botero are just a few of the 20th-century luminaries represented. ⊠ 545 W. 25th St., between 10th and 11th Aves., Chelsea ☎ 212/463–8634 ⊕ www.marlboroughgallery.com Ⓜ C, E to 23rd St.

Mary Boone. A hot SoHo gallery during the 1980s, this venue now resides both in Midtown and in the newer flash point of Chelsea. Boone continues to show established artists such as Barbara Kruger and Eric Fischl, as well as newcomers. ⊠ 541 W. 24th St., between 10th and 11th Aves., Chelsea ☎ 212/752–2929 ⊕ www.maryboonegallery.com Ⓜ C, E to 23rd St.

Where can I find . . . ?

COFFEE	Donut Pub 203 W. 14th St. Care for an apple fritter with your coffee? Pull up a stool.	Joe the Art of Coffee 141 Waverly Pl. Java with swirled milk almost too beautiful to gulp down.
A QUICK BITE	Three Tarts 164 9th Ave. Artisanal sweets in pocket-sized portions.	Peanut Butter & Co 240 Sullivan St. From smooth to crunchy to superfunky.
COCKTAILS	Velour Lounge 297 10th Ave. Galleryqoers winding down and nightclubbers warming up.	Flatiron Lounge 37 W. 19th St. Art deco hangout, mini-martini flights.

Matthew Marks. A white-hot venue for both the New York and international art crowd, openings at any of the three Matthew Marks galleries are always an interesting scene. Swiss artist Ugo Rondinone made his U.S. debut here, as did Andreas Gursky. Nan Goldin, Ellsworth Kelly, Brice Marden, Katharina Fritsch, and a cast of illustrious others also show here. ⊠ *523 W. 24th St., between 10th and 11th Aves., Chelsea* 📞 *212/243–0200* Ⓜ *C, E to 23rd St.* ⊠ *522 W. 22nd St., between 10th and 11th Aves., Chelsea* 📞 *212/243–0200* ⊕ *www.matthewmarks.com* Ⓜ *C, E to 23rd St.* ⊠ *526 W. 22nd St., between 10th and 11th Aves., Chelsea* 📞 *212/243–0200* Ⓜ *C, E to 23rd St.*

Nancy Hoffman. Contemporary painting, sculpture, drawing, prints, and photographic works by an impressive array of international artists are on display here. Gallery artists range from Rupert Deese, known for his conceptual shaped canvases, to Michael Gregory, whose muted oil landscapes reference Americana. ⊠ *520 W. 27th St., between 10th and 11th Aves., Chelsea* 📞 *212/966–6676* ⊕ *www.nancyhoffmangallery. com* Ⓜ *C, E to 23rd St.*

Metro Pictures. The hottest talents in contemporary art shown here include Cindy Sherman, whose provocative photographs have brought her international prominence. ⊠ *519 W. 24th St., between 10th and 11th Aves., Chelsea* 📞 *212/206–7100* ⊕ *www.metropicturesgallery.com* Ⓜ *C, E to 23rd St.*

Pace Wildenstein. The Midtown specialist in 20th- and 21st-century art now has two spaces in Chelsea. The West 25th Street location can fit the largest sculpture and installations. Their roster concentrates on upper-echelon artists, sculptors, and photographers, including Elizabeth Murray, Chuck Close, Sol LeWitt, and Robert Rauschenberg. ⊠ *534 W. 25th St., between 10th and 11th Aves., Chelsea* 📞 *212/929–7000* Ⓜ *C, E to 23rd St.* ⊠ *545 W. 22nd St., between 10th and 11th Aves., Chelsea* 📞 *212/989–4258* ⊕ *www.pacewildenstein.com* Ⓜ *C, E to 23rd St.*

Paula Cooper. SoHo pioneer Paula Cooper moved to Chelsea in 1996, and enlisted architect Richard Gluckman to transform a warehouse into a dramatic space with tall ceilings and handsome skylights. Now she has three galleries that showcase the minimalist sculptures of Carl André, the dot paintings of Yayoi Kusama, and the provocative photos of Andres Serrano, among other works. ✉ *534 W. 21st St., between 10th and 11th Aves., Chelsea* ☎ *212/255–1105* ⊕ *www.paulacoopergallery. com* Ⓜ *C, E to 23rd St.* ✉ *521 W. 21st St., 2nd fl., between 10th and 11th Aves., Chelsea* ☎ *212/255–5247* Ⓜ *C, E to 23rd St.* ✉ *465 W. 23rd St., at 10th Ave., Chelsea* ☎ *212/255–4499* Ⓜ *C, E to 23rd St.*

Postmasters. Postmasters shows new and established conceptual artists, with one room devoted to multimedia shows. Recent exhibits have included Claude Wampler's *Pomerania*—a series of photographs, sculptures, video, and drawings examining the artist's relationship with her pet Pomeranian. ✉ *459 W. 19th St., between 9th and 10th Aves., Chelsea* ☎ *212/727–3323* ⊕ *www.postmastersart.com* Ⓜ *C, E to 23rd St.*

Robert Miller. Miller, a titan of the New York art world, represents some of the biggest names in modern painting and photography, including Diane Arbus and the estates of Lee Krasner and Alice Neel. ✉ *524 W. 26th St., between 10th and 11th Aves., Chelsea* ☎ *212/366–4774* ⊕ *www.robertmillergallery.com* Ⓜ *C, E to 23rd St.*

Sean Kelly. Drop in to this large space for works by top contemporary American and European artists including Marina Abramovic, Robert Mapplethorpe, Antony Gormley, Joseph Kosuth, and James Casebere. ✉ *528 W. 29th St., between 10th and 11th Aves., Chelsea* ☎ *212/239– 1181* ⊕ *www.skny.com* Ⓜ *1 to 28th St.; C, E to 23rd St.*

Sonnabend. This pioneer of the SoHo art scene continues to show important contemporary artists in its Chelsea space, including Jeff Koons, Ashley Bickerton, and British art duo Gilbert & George. ✉ *536 W. 22nd St., between 10th and 11th Aves., Chelsea* ☎ *212/627–1018* Ⓜ *C, E to 23rd St.*

Tanya Bonakdar. This gallery presents such contemporary artists as Uta Barth, whose blurry photos challenge ideas about perception, and Ernesto Neto, a Brazilian artist who has made stunning room-size installations of large nylon sacks filled with spices. ✉ *521 W. 21st St., between 10th and 11th Aves., Chelsea* ☎ *212/414–4144* ⊕ *www. tanyabonakdargallery.com* Ⓜ *C, E to 23rd St.*

303. International cutting-edge artists shown here include photographers Doug Aitken and Thomas Demand and installation artist–painter Karen Kilimnik. 303 is closed in August and weekends between July 5 and Labor Day. ✉ *547 W. 21st St., between 10th and 11th Aves., Chelsea* ☎ *212/255–1121* ⊕ *www.303gallery.com* Ⓜ *C, E to 23rd St.*

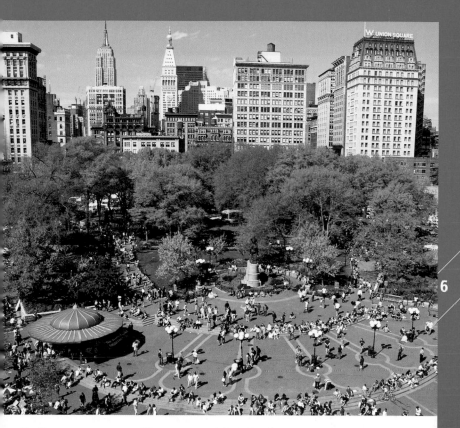

Union Square to Murray Hill

WORD OF MOUTH

"Union Square is very lively and very busy . . . on any given day there is a protest or a commercial filming or a news crew grabbing 'man on the street' interviews . . . and 2 blocks south is one of the best bookstores in the US—the Strand."

—mp

GETTING ORIENTED

W. 37th St.

E. 37th St.

W. 36th St.

E. 36th St.

♦ Morgan Library

♦ Sniffen Court

♦ Church of the Incarnation ♦

E. 35th St.

♦ Macy's

N,R,Q,W
Ⓜ **B,D,F,V**
Herald Square

B. Altman Building/ New York Public Library Science, Industry, and Business Library (SIBL)

E. 34th St.

Empire State Building

E. 33rd St.

Ⓜ 6

W. 32nd St.

E. 32nd St.

Fifth Ave.

E. 31st St.

Madison Ave.

E. 30th St.

Park Ave. S.

Lexington Ave.

Marble Collegiate Church ♦

Broadway

♦ Church of the Transfiguration

E. 29th St.

MURRAY HILL

R,W
Ⓜ

6
Ⓜ

W. 28th St.

E. 28th St.

W. 27th St.

♦ Museum of Sex

E. 27th St.

♦ New York Life Insurance Building ♦

W. 26th St.

E. 26th St.

(Sixth Ave.)

W. 25th St.

♦ Appellate Division, New York State Supreme Court

E. 25th St.

Third Ave.

Second Ave.

Madison Square Park

W. 24th St.

E. 24th St.

R,W
Ⓜ

♦ Metropolitan Life Insurance Tower

F,V
Ⓜ

W. 23rd St.

6
Ⓜ

E. 23rd St.

♦ Flatiron Building

W. 22nd St.

E. 22nd St.

FLATIRON DISTRICT

E. 21st St.

♦ Gramercy Park

Avenue of the Americas

W. 20th St.

Fifth Ave.

National Arts Club ♦ ♦ Players Club

E. 20th St.

W. 19th St.

E. 19th St.

GRAMERCY

W. 18th St.

Broadway

E. 18th St.

W. 17th St.

Union Square Theater ♦

Union Square W. S.

Park Ave. S.

Lexington Ave.

E. 17th St.

W. 16th St.

♦ Union Square West

Stuyvesant Square

♦ Union Square

Daryl Roth Theater ♦

W. 15th St.

F,L,V
Ⓜ

University Pl.

L,N,Q,R,W, 4,5,6
Ⓜ

L
Ⓜ

W. 14th St.

E. 14th St.

Third Ave.

0   1/8 mile

W. 13th St.

Broadway

0   200 meters

♦ The Strand

W. 12th St.

MAKING THE MOST OF YOUR TIME

Union Square is lively round-the-clock. Many establishments in the area are open late, and everyone seems to hang out on wide, concrete steps on the south end of the park. During warmer months student protests, dance troupes, and the fabulous greenmarket add to the electricity. Walking north into the Flatiron District and toward the Empire State Building in the 30s, the atmosphere changes from a younger, more casual vibe to one of skyscrapers and big-city hustle.

GETTING HERE

Both Union Square/14th Street and Herald Square/34th Street are major subway hubs, connected by the N, Q, R, and W lines. Any of these trains can bring you right to the center of the action. For Madison Square Park, take the local R or W to 23rd Street. You can reach the Empire State Building via the B, D, F, N, Q, R, V, or W line to 34th Street or the 6 to 33rd Street. The 6 also has stops at 23rd and 28th streets.

WORD OF MOUTH (WWW.FODORS.COM/FORUMS)

"Does anyone have suggestions for the best way/place to view the [Macy's] parade (other than in front of the TV!!). Best place to park (if driving), best place to watch, time to arrive, etc. Thanks for any advice." —peterl43

"Best time to arrive is early—at least 2 hours before the parade starts to get a decent spot. The farther uptown you go the less crowded it will be—but that is only relative. Once you've decided where you want to stand, go to iconparking. com to see garages in the area—but do be aware that rates are much higher on holidays and parade days if you're anywhere near the route of march." —nytraveler

FODOR'S CHOICE

Empire State Building

The Strand

TOP ATTRACTIONS

Flatiron Building

Macy's

TOP EXPERIENCES

People-watching around Union Square

Browsing the piles of books in the Strand

Strolling among the rare books at the Morgan Library (⇨ Ch. 14)

Shopping on lower 5th Avenue

BEST FOR KIDS

Empire State Building

Madison Square Park

NEARBY MUSEUMS (⇨ CH. 14)

Morgan Library

Museum of Sex

AREA SHOPS (⇨ CH. 17)

ABC Carpet & Home

Beads of Paradise

Compleat Strategist

The Complete Traveller Antiquarian Bookstore

Fresh

Jo Malone

Kidding Around

Space Kiddets

6

Sightseeing
★★★★

Nightlife
★

Dining
★★★★

Lodging
★★★

Shopping
★★★★

Union Square refers to an area of the city anchored by Union Square Park, which resides between 14th and 17th streets and Broadway and Park Avenue South. If you're in this area on a Tuesday, Thursday, or Sunday, you've missed one of the best parts of being here, the expansive and colorful farmers' market. But don't despair if you're here on a nonmarket day: skateboarders keep the pace moving and vendors of all kinds lobby for your attention. NYU students, nannies with their charges, chess players, visitors, and locals all gather in this open space.

Updated by
Joanna G.
Cantor

The haste and hullabaloo of the city calms considerably as you stroll through the mostly residential neighborhoods of Murray Hill and Gramercy Park to the east. Just above Union Square and to the west, the Flatiron District and the remnants of Ladies' Mile (as it was known in the late 1880s) continue the shopping and commercial buzz.

Murray Hill stretches from 30th to 40th streets between 5th and 3rd avenues. The residential side streets are tree-lined and town-house filled with some high-profile haunts: the Morgan Library and Museum with its vast book stacks and rare manuscripts, and King Kong's favorite hangout, the Empire State Building, where the hustle of the big city picks up again.

Dignified Gramercy Park, named for its 1831 gated garden square ringed by historic buildings and private clubs, is an early example of the city's creative urban planning. Even though you can't unpack your picnic in the exclusive residents-only park, you can bask in its historic surroundings and artistic significance. Beautiful Greek Revival, Italianate, Gothic Revival, and Victorian Gothic buildings flank its sides. Off its southern edge is a small street honoring Washington Irving, where you can find one of the city's most charming inns, the Inn at Irving Place, and a number of casual restaurants. Just north of the park is Ian

Schrager's cooler-than-cool reincarnation of the Gramercy Park Hotel on Lexington Avenue.

The Flatiron District—anchored by Madison Square Park on the north and Union Square to the south—is one of the city's busiest neighborhoods, particularly along 5th Avenue and Park Avenue South. In some ways it should still be called Ladies' Mile: the area is a favorite for spotting models because of the number of agencies and photography studios here. You can also see charming shops, some of the city's coolest hotels and trendiest restaurants, and an elegant turn-of-the-20th-century skyline that's brilliantly lighted at night.

TWO WAYS TO EXPLORE

PARK LIFE AND A TASTE OF CULTURE

The energy of **Union Square** reaches its peak during its greenmarket on Monday, Wednesday, Friday, and Saturday, when more than 25 farms and food purveyors set up shop on the square's north and west sides to peddle everything from produce to meat, fresh fish to baked goods; all of it makes for great grazing. For those who prefer a sit-down environment, the area also offers up some intriguing restaurants, including Danny Meyer's **Union Square Café** and the spicy **Mesa Grill.** On nearby Irving Place, **Pete's Tavern,** dating from 1864, maintains its claim as the oldest original bar in the city. Two famous writers, O. Henry (*Gift of the Magi*) and Ludwig Bemelmans (*Madeline*), were "inspired" here, probably from the amazing eggnog or Pete's House Ale.

Although Union Square is a "passive park," meaning there are no sports, there are playgrounds and a dog run. It's also a great place for music and off-off-Broadway theater. One block to the east, on Irving Place, **The Fillmore New York at Irving Plaza** posts a list of upcoming concerts under its marquee, spanning the likes of Tom Jones and Willie Nelson to DJ Shadow. The **Vineyard Theatre,** where *Avenue Q* began, is here, as well as the **Daryl Roth Theatre** and the **Union Square Theatre,** both offering innovative and sometimes participatory theater. Union Square's most love-it-or-hate-it feature is the *Metronome* art sculpture with its bank of cascading numbers. Half art installation, half timepiece, it sits above the former Virgin Megastore, and is actually a clock that counts both time elapsed and time remaining in the day. At noon and midnight huge bursts of steam emerge, turning into trickles throughout the day. The birthplace of some more venerated 20th-century art, **33 Union Square West,** now occupied by the new Puma concept store, once held Andy Warhol's Factory.

A few blocks north of Union Square along Irving Place, the hustle and flow fades into serenity with the look-but-don't touch primness of **Gramercy Park.** The park oozes urbane theatrical and artistic ambience, surrounded by the tony likes of the **Players Club** (technically just called "The Players") and the **National Arts Club,** both established to indulge and encourage a passion for the arts.

6

ARCHITECTURE AT ITS MOST ELABORATE

Rimming **Madison Square Park** is some of Manhattan's most impressive skyline. In the northeast corner, the gold-top **New York Life Insurance** building was the tallest in the city when it opened in 1903. The elaborately carved Beaux-Arts structure one block down at East 25th Street, is the **Appellate Division, New York State Supreme Court,** with its main entrance tucked onto the side street. The imposing **Metropolitan Life Insurance Tower,** between East 23rd and 24th streets, is another classically inspired spire. One of the buildings most emblematic of New York City, the charming and historic **Flatiron Building** is a limestone-and-terra-cotta vessel sailing its prowlike shape uptown from its berth on 23rd Street. With the surrounding towers lighted in various colors, Madison Square Park positively glows at night. The park has been recently flanked with triangular concrete "parks" with flowers and outdoor seating. It's a great place to spend some time and enjoy a burger or frozen custard from the wonderful **Shake Shack**, where there's usually a queue that wraps around the tree-lined path.

At the edge of Murray Hill, at 33rd Street and 5th Avenue, looms the inimitable **Empire State Building.** Canonized in postcards, books, and on film, the building reaches toward the sky with its majestic spire, which is lighted up at night according to an elaborate calendar of dates and corresponding colors. An excellent view can be had from the steps of the Italian-Renaissance-style **B. Altman Building** one block north. From there it's a quick walk up Madison Avenue to the **Morgan Library and Museum** (⇨ *Ch. 14*), with its impressive collection of rare books and manuscripts. Down 5th Avenue at 27th Street, the **Museum of Sex** (⇨ *Ch. 14*) sits behind an unassuming facade, giving little hint of its salacious interior.

TOP ATTRACTIONS

Fodor'sChoice **Empire State Building.** Bittersweet though it is, this landmark is once again
★ the city's tallest building. Its pencil-slim silhouette, recognizable virtu-
☾ ally worldwide, is an Art Deco monument to progress, a symbol for New York City, and a star in some great romantic scenes, on- and off-screen. Its cinematic résumé—the building has appeared in more than 200 movies—means that it remains a fixture of popular imagination, and many visitors come to relive favorite movie scenes. You might just find yourself at the top of the building with *Sleepless in Seattle* look-alikes or even the building's own *King Kong* impersonator.

Built in 1931 at the peak of the skyscraper craze, this 103-story limestone giant opened after a mere 13 months of construction. The framework rose at an astonishing rate of 4½ stories per week, making the Empire State Building the fastest-rising skyscraper ever built. Many floors were left completely unfinished so tenants could have them custom designed.

■ **TIP➔** Thanks to advance ticketing on the Internet ($2 extra), you can speed your way to the observatory on the 86th floor. If this is your first visit, rent a headset with an audio tour from Tony, a fictional but "authentic" native New Yorker, available in eight languages. The 86th-floor

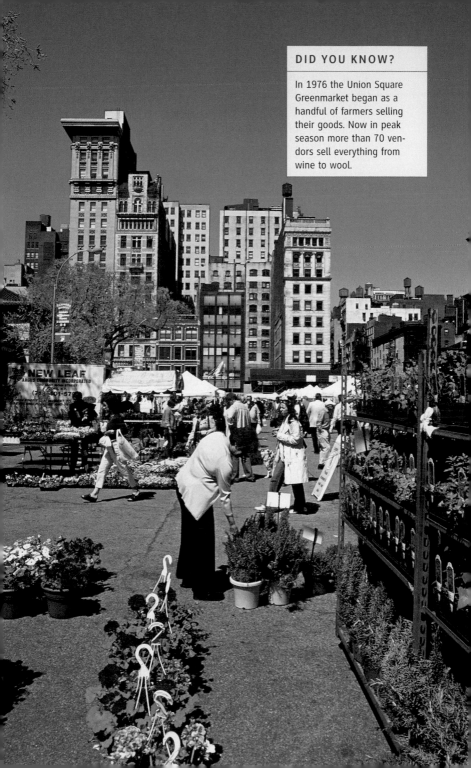

observatory (1,050 feet high) is outdoors and spans the building's circumference. This is the deck to go to to truly see the city. Don't be shy about going outside into the wind (even in winter) or you'll miss half the experience. Bring quarters for the high-powered binoculars: on clear days you can see up to 80 mi. If it rains, you can view the city between the clouds and watch the rain travel sideways around the building from the shelter of the enclosed walkway. The advantage of paying the extra $15 to go to the indoor 102nd floor is that this observatory affords an easy and less-crowded circular walk-around from which to view the city. It also feels more removed and quieter. Express tickets can be purchased for front-of-the-line admission for an extra $45.

Time your visit for early or late in the day—morning is the least crowded time, and at night the city lights are dazzling. A good strategy is to go up just before dusk and witness nightfall. ■**TIP→** Be aware that at busy hours visitors can experience long waits and feel rushed through their tour by the staff. As an alternative, consider the Top of the Rock (⇨ *Ch. 7*) for an equally stunning panorama.

Even if you skip the view from up top, be sure to step into the lobby and take in the ceilings, beautifully restored in 2009. The gilded gears and sweeping Art Deco lines are a romantic tribute to the machine age and part of the original vision for the building, lost, painted over, and covered with a drop ceiling until now.

Although some parents blanch when they discover both how much it costs and how it lurches, the second-floor **NY SKYRIDE** is a favorite of the 7- and 8-year-old set. The ride presents a movie, motion, and sights, rolled up into New York's only aerial virtual-tour simulator. ☎ *212/279–9777 or 888/759–7433 ⊕ www.nyskyride.com ✆ $36; $47 combo SKYRIDE and observatory (discounts are available on their Web site) ۩ Daily 8–10* .

✉ *350 5th Ave., at E. 34th St., Murray Hill ☎ 212/736–3100 or 877/692–8439 ⊕ www.esbnyc.com ✆ $20 ۩ Daily 8 AM–2 AM; last elevator up leaves at 1:15AM* Ⓜ *B, D, F, N, Q, R, V, W to 34th St./ Herald Sq.; 6 to 33rd St.*

Flatiron Building. When completed in 1902, the Fuller Building, as it was originally known, caused a sensation. Architect Daniel Burnham made ingenious use of the triangular wedge of land at 23rd Street, 5th Avenue, and Broadway, employing a revolutionary steel frame, which allowed for the building's 22-story, 286-foot height. Covered with a limestone and white terra-cotta skin in the Italian Renaissance style, the building's shape resembled a clothing iron, hence its nickname. When it became apparent that the building generated strong winds, gawkers would loiter at 23rd Street hoping to catch sight of ladies' billowing skirts. Local traffic cops had to shoo away the male peepers—one purported origin of the phrase "23 skidoo." There is a small display of historic building and area photos in the lobby. ✉ *175 5th Ave., bordered by E. 22nd and E. 23rd Sts., 5th Ave., and Broadway, Flatiron District* Ⓜ *R, W to 23rd St.*

Macy's. Sure, you can shop in Macy's in other cities, but there's a say-you-did-it appeal to walking that indoor city block between 6th Avenue

Where can I find . . . ?

COFFEE	71 Irving Pl. Coffee & Tea Bar 71 Irving Pl. Owners roast their own beans—always a good sign.	Spoon 17 W. 20th St. Caterers who also know a thing or two about coffee.
A QUICK BITE	City Bakery 3 W. 18th St. Signature "pretzel croissants" and super-thick hot chocolate.	Shake Shack in Madison Square Park A true contender for New York's best burger.
COCKTAILS	Cibar 56 Irving Pl. Martinis, quiet, candlelit basement.	Molly's Pub and Shebeen 287 3rd Ave. Superfriendly, super Irish, and amazing pints.

(where it meets Broadway) to 7th Avenue, from 34th to 35th streets, verifying that yes, it is indeed the world's largest store (11 floors, 2 million square feet of selling space). In that spirit, chance a ride on one of the narrow wooden escalators you can find tucked among its metallic brethren: installed in 1902, they were the first escalators ever used in an American store. ■**TIP➔** If you're in town in April, visit Macy's during its flower show, when the store is blanketed with banks of tulips, sprouting orchids, and more than 30,000 varieties of flowers and plants. At Thanksgiving, Macy's world-famous balloons float down the avenue, stopping in front of the store for performances by a variety of celebs, bands, and dancers. The store's Christmastime windows are a must-see, sparking a *Miracle on 34th Street* spirit. ✉ *W. 34th St. between Broadway at 6th and 7th Aves., Murray Hill* ☎ *212/695–4400* ⊕ *www.macys.com* ☾ *Hrs vary seasonally; Mon.–Sat. 10–9:30, Sun. 11–8* Ⓜ *B, D, F, N, Q, R, V, W to 34th St./Herald Sq.; 1, 2, 3 to 33rd St.*

DID YOU KNOW?

The first Macy's Thanksgiving Day Parade in 1924 was called "Macy's Christmas Day Parade" although it took place on Thanksgiving. It included camels, goats, elephants, and donkeys. The parade is the world's second-largest consumer of helium after the U.S. government. Each year balloons are floated through the parade. Due to a helium shortage in 1958, however, the balloons were brought down Broadway on cranes.

Fodor's Choice
★

The Strand. Serious bibliophiles flock to this monstrous book emporium with some 2 million volumes (the store's slogan is "18 Miles of Books"). The stock includes both new and secondhand books, plus thousands of collector's items. A separate rare-book room is on the third floor at 826 Broadway (accessible through the main store). Check out the basement, with discounted, barely touched reviewers' copies of new books, organized by author. ■**TIP➔** Don't be too goal oriented or you might end up frustrated. The beauty of the Strand is that you'll never quite leave with what you came for, and treasures will essentially find you. ✉ *828*

CLOSE UP

Empire State Building

At night the Empire State Building illuminates the Manhattan skyline with a colorful view as awe-inspiring from a distance as the view from the top. The colors at the top of the building are changed regularly to reflect seasons, events, and holidays, so New Yorkers and visitors from around the world always have a reason to look at this icon in a new light.

The building's first light show was in November 1932, when a simple searchlight was used to spread the news that New York–born Franklin Delano Roosevelt had been elected president of the United States. Douglas Leigh, sign designer and mastermind of Times Square's kinetic billboard ads, tried to brighten up prospects at the "Empty State Building" after the Depression by negotiating with the Coca-Cola Company to occupy the top floors. He proposed that Coca-Cola could change the lights of the building to serve as a weather forecast and then publish a small guide on its bottles to decipher the colors. Coca-Cola loved this idea, but the deal fell through due to Pearl Harbor, when the U.S. government needed office space in the building.

In 1956 the revolving "freedom lights" were installed to welcome people to America; then in 1964 the top 30 floors of the building were illuminated to mark the New York World's Fair. Douglas Leigh revisited the lights of the ESB in 1976, when he was made chairman of City Decor to welcome the Democratic Convention. He introduced the idea of color lighting, and so the building's tower was ablaze in red, white, and blue to welcome the convention and to mark the celebration of the American Bicentennial. The color lights were a huge success, and they remained red, white, and blue for the rest of the year.

Leigh's next suggestion of tying the lights to different holidays, a variation on his weather theme for Coca-Cola, is the basic scheme still used today. In 1977 the lighting system was updated to comply with energy conservation programs and to allow for a wider range of colors. Leigh further improved this new system in 1984 by designing an automated color-changing system so vertical fluorescents in the mast could be changed with the flick of a switch, the only automated portion of the building's lighting system to date. With a schedule that changes each year, the lights honor national holidays, the multiethnic population of New York, special local and national events, and charitable causes. The city's greatest night-light dims respectfully, however, to allow for migrating birds that could otherwise be distracted. For a full lighting schedule, click on ⊕ *www.esbnyc.com.*

—Jacinta O'Halloran

Broadway, at E. 12th St., Union Square ☏ *212/473–1452* ⊘ *Mon.–Sat. 9:30* AM*–10:30* PM*, Sun. 11–10:30* Ⓜ *L, N, Q, R, W, 4, 5, 6 to Union Sq./14th St.*

Union Square. A park, farmers' market, meeting place, and site of rallies and demonstrations, this pocket of green space sits in the center of a bustling residential and commercial neighborhood. The name "Union" originally signified that two main roads—Broadway and 4th Avenue—crossed here, but it took on a different meaning in the late 19th and early 20th centuries, when the square became a rallying spot for labor protests; many unions, as well as fringe political parties, moved their headquarters nearby. Since 9/11, antiwar groups have led their public campaigns here. Statues in the park include George Washington, Abraham Lincoln, Gandhi (often wreathed in flowers), and the Marquis de Lafayette sculpted by Frederic Auguste Bartholdi, creator of the Statue of Liberty. Plaques in the sidewalk on the southeast and southwest sides chronicle the park's history from the 1600s to 1800s.

Union Square is at its best on Monday, Wednesday, Friday, and Saturday (8–6), when the largest of the city's **greenmarkets** brings farmers and food purveyors from the tri-state area. Browse the stands of fruit and vegetables, flowers, plants, fresh-baked pies and breads, cheeses, cider, New York State wines, fish, and meat. Between Thanksgiving and Christmas, artisans sell gift items in candy-cane-stripe booths at the square's southwest end.

New York University dormitories, theaters, and cavernous commercial spaces occupy the handsomely restored 19th-century commercial buildings that surround the park. The run of diverse architectural styles on the building at 33 Union Square West, the **Decker Building,** is as imaginative as its former contents: this was once home to Andy Warhol's studio. The redbrick-and-white-stone **Century Building** (✉ *33 E. 17th St., Flatiron District*), built in 1881, on the square's north side, is now a Barnes & Noble bookstore, with original cast-iron columns. The building at 17th Street and Union Square East, now housing the New York Film Academy and the Union Square Theater, was the final home of **Tammany Hall,** an organization famous in its day as a corrupt and powerful political machine. Two blocks south at Union Square East and 15th Street is the former U.S. Savings Bank, now the Daryl Roth Theatre. ✉ *E. 14th to E. 17th Sts., between Broadway and Park Ave. S, Flatiron District* Ⓜ *L, N, Q, R, W, 4, 5, 6 to Union Sq./14th St.*

WORTH NOTING

♻ **B. Altman Building/New York Public Library–Science, Industry, and Business Library (SIBL).** In 1906 department-store magnate Benjamin Altman gambled that his fashionable patrons would follow him uptown from his popular store in the area now known as the Ladies' Mile Historic District. His new store, one of the first of the grand department stores on 5th Avenue, was designed to blend with the mansions nearby. Note in particular the beautiful entrance on 5th Avenue. In 1996 the New York Public Library set up a high-tech library here. A 33-foot-high atrium unites the building's two floors, the lending library off the lobby and the research collections below. Downstairs a wall of electronic ticker tapes and TVs tuned to business-news stations beams information and instructions to patrons. Tours are offered Tuesday and Thursday at 2. ✉ *188 Madison Ave., between E. 34th and E. 35th Sts., Murray Hill* ☎ *212/592–7000* ⊕ *www.nypl. org* ☽ *Mon. 11–6, Tues.–Thurs. 10–8, Fri. and Sat. 11–6* Ⓜ *6 to 33rd St.*

Madison Square Park. The benches of this elegant tree-filled park afford great views of some of the city's oldest and most charming skyscrapers (the Flatiron Building, the Metropolitan Life Insurance Tower, the New York Life Insurance Building, and the Empire State Building) and serve as a perfect vantage point for people-, pigeon-, dog-, or squirrel-watching. Baseball was invented across the Hudson in Hoboken, New Jersey, but the city's first baseball games were played in this 7-acre park in 1845. On the north end an imposing 1881 statue by Augustus Saint-Gaudens memorializes Civil War naval hero Admiral Farragut. An 1876 statue of Secretary of State William Henry Seward (the Seward of the term "Seward's folly"—as Alaska was originally known) sits in the park's southwest corner, though it's rumored that the sculptor placed a reproduction of the statesman's head on a statue of Abraham Lincoln's body. ✉ *E. 23rd to E. 26th Sts., between 5th and Madison Aves., Flatiron District* Ⓜ *R, W to 23rd St.*

> ### LABOR DAY IS BORN
>
> On September 5, 1882, more than 10,000 New York City union workers took an unpaid day off to march from City Hall to Union Square in the city's first Labor Day parade. The day was celebrated with picnics, speeches, and concerts. Twelve years later Congress passed an act making the first Monday in September a legal holiday to celebrate workers.

IF THERE'S STILL TIME

Appellate Division Courthouse. Sculpted by Frederick Ruckstuhl, figures representing Wisdom and Force flank the main portal of this imposing Beaux-Arts courthouse, built in 1899. Melding the structure's purpose with artistic symbolism, statues of great lawmakers line the roof balustrade, including Moses, Justinian, and Confucius. In total, sculptures by 16 artists adorn the ornate building, a showcase of themes relating to the law. This is one of the most important appellate courts in the country: it hears more than 3,000 appeals and 6,000 motions a year, and also admits approximately 3,000 new attorneys to the bar each year. Inside the courtroom is a stunning stained-glass dome set into a gilt ceiling. All sessions, which are generally held Tuesday to Friday afternoons, are open to the public. (Visitors can call the main number ahead of time to be sure court is in session.) ✉ *27 Madison Ave., entrance on E. 25th St., Flatiron District* ☎ *212/340–0400* ☽ *Weekdays 9–5* Ⓜ *R, W, 6 to 23rd St.*

Metropolitan Life Insurance Company Tower. When it was added in 1909, the 700-foot tower resembling the campanile of St. Mark's in Venice made this 1893 building the world's tallest. The clock's four faces are each three stories high, and their minute hands weigh half a ton each.

CLOSE UP

Gramercy Park

Only residents with keys can enter this private park, but a look through the bars in the wrought-iron fence that encloses it is well worth your time. The beautifully planted 2-acre park, designed by developer Samuel B. Ruggles, dates from 1831, and is flanked by grand examples of early-19th-century architecture and permeated with the character of its many celebrated occupants.

When Ruggles bought the property it was known as "Krom Moerasje" (little crooked swamp) named by the Dutch settlers. He drained the swamp and set aside 42 lots for a park to be accessible exclusively to those who bought the surrounding lots in his planned London-style residential square. The park is still owned by residents of buildings in the surrounding square, although neighbors from the area can now buy visiting privileges.

In 1966 the New York City Landmarks Preservation Commission designated Gramercy Park a historic district. Notable buildings are:

No. 2, the redbrick house at the corner of Gramercy Park West and 20th Street, dates to 1843 and is an example of the earliest houses built here. The original house would have also included a wrought-iron veranda like that of its 1847 neighbors, **Nos. 3 and 4.** James Harper, founder of Harper Publishing House and former mayor of New York, lived at No. 4 from 1847 to 1869.

No. 15 was once home to Samuel Tilden, governor of New York. It was designed by Calvert Vaux in Gothic Revival brownstone with black granite trim and included a secret passageway to 19th Street so Tilden could escape his political enemies. It is now home to the 100-year-old National Arts Club.

Next door at **No. 16** Gramercy Park South lived the actor Edwin Booth, perhaps most famous for being the brother of Lincoln's assassin. In 1888 he turned his Gothic-trim home into the Players, a clubhouse for actors and theatrical types who were not welcome in regular society. A bronze statue of Edwin Booth as Hamlet has pride of place inside the park.

Other notables include the School of Visual Arts' women's residence at **No. 17,** which contains the former home of Joseph Pulitzer, and the mock-Tudor at **No. 38,** home to John Steinbeck from 1925 to 1926 when he struggled as a reporter for a New York newspaper.

The clock chimes on the quarter hour. The building and its Art Deco loggias have appeared in such films as *Radio Days* and *The Fisher King.* ✉ *1 Madison Ave., between E. 23rd and E. 24th Sts., Flatiron District* Ⓜ *R, W, 6 to 23rd St.*

Midtown

INCLUDING TIMES SQUARE AND ROCKEFELLER CENTER

WORD OF MOUTH

"We allowed ourselves a quick look into St Patrick's Cathedral . . . and continued walking heading toward Times Square. Despite the reputation, I loved it. There's nothing like it anywhere—it really is like the throbbing heart of New York. I know, I know only a tourist would see it like that. So full of people, color, and movement."

—mazj

GETTING ORIENTED

FODOR'S CHOICE	MAKING THE MOST OF YOUR TIME
Grand Central Terminal Top of the Rock	If you're staying in Midtown, take advantage of your prime location: rise early and be first in line at landmarks and museums. To avoid the crowd while shopping or sightseeing, hit the streets at midday on weekdays or early on weekends. (Alternatively, to experience the thrill of thousands of racing workaday suits, visit Grand Central Terminal or Rockefeller Center at rush hour.) At night, stroll through Rockefeller Plaza or gaze up at the Chrysler Building shimmering in the dark. You'll see Midtown at its quieter moments, when the romance of the city washes over you.
TOP ATTRACTIONS	
Bryant Park Rockefeller Center	
TOP EXPERIENCES	
Elbowing through Times Square	**GETTING HERE**
Watching ice-skaters at Rock-efeller Center Window shopping Fifth Avenue	You can get to Midtown via (almost) all the subways; many make numerous stops throughout the area. The B, D, F, and V trains serve Rockefeller Center and 42nd Street at 6th Avenue. The 1, 2, 3, 7, A, C, E, N, Q, R, S, and W serve Times Square and West 42nd Street. The 4, 5, 6, 7, and S take you to Grand Central.

CENTRAL PARK

Central Park South — N,R,W

The Plaza ◆   ◆ Grand Army Plaza

Avenue of the Americas (Sixth Ave.)

Marian — W. 58th St. — Edwynn Houk Gallery
Goodman Gallery   Greenberg Van Doren Gallery

F — W. 57th St. — ◆ Tiffany & Co.

Marlborough Gallery ◆

W. 56th St. — Tibor de Nagy Gallery   Trump Tower

W. 55th St.

American Folk Art Museum ◆   Museum of Modern Art (MoMA) ◆   ◆ University Club

W. 53rd St.

E,V M

Museum of Arts and Design   ◆ The Paley Center for Media

W. 51st St.   St Patrick's ◆ Cathedral

Radio City Music Hall   GE Building, Top of the Rock   W. 50th St.

Lower Plaza ◆   ◆ Saks Fifth Avenue
W. 49th St. — Rockefeller Center

Christie's ◆   Today Show Studios   W. 48th St.

B,D,F,V M

W. 47th St.

Queens-Midtown Tunnel

W. 46th St.

E. 56th St.
E. 55th St.
E. 54th St.

First Ave.

◆ Beekman Place

Japan Society ◆

United Nations ◆

Ford Foundation Building ◆

FDR Drive

Fifth Ave.

mi

NEARBY MUSEUMS (⇨ CH. 14)

American Folk Art Museum

International Center of Photography

Japan Society

Museum of Arts and Design

Museum of Modern Art

The Paley Center for Media

AREA SHOPS (⇨ CH. 17)

American Girl Place

Apple Store

Bergdorf Goodman

Bloomingdale's

Chanel

Christian Dior

F.A.O. Schwarz

Gucci

Louis Vuitton

Prada

Saks Fifth Avenue

Toys "R" Us

7

WORD OF MOUTH (WWW.FODORS.COM/FORUMS)

"How would I get from Times Square to the Fifth Avenue Shopping District?" —Nick

"You're better off walking. Be prepared to jostle and be jostled" —greg

"Unless you're a 5 pack a day smoker … WALK from Times Square to 5th and make a left. When you get to Saks, look across the street [at Rockefeller Center]. Stop in St. Patrick's Cathedral. If you're exhausted when you get to 59th Street, take a subway back to Times Square." —al

BEST FOR KIDS

Bryant Park

Times Square

Sony Building

United Nations

Sightseeing
★★★★★
*Nightlife
★★
Dining
★★★★
Lodging
★★★★★
Shopping
★★★★★

Washington D.C.'s got its Mall chockablock with landmarks, and we've got ours: Midtown, mobbed with more massive urban monuments—Rockefeller Center, Times Square, and Grand Central Terminal among them—than any other part of the city. This is the New York City people picture when they think of the Big Apple.

Updated by
Meryl D.
Pearlstein

The funny thing is that most locals come to think of Midtown as simply the end point for their workaday commute; they often forget the wonder its skyscrapers elicit, the magic of the department store windows decked out in razzle-dazzle display. When movies need a big-city backdrop, they come to Midtown and get close-ups of Rockefeller Center, Grand Central Terminal, and the Empire State Building; their majestic architecture never fails to impress. Even the small screen seems focused here, as *Today* show early-risers know. But while Midtown's attractions seem obvious, there are gems less familiar to visitors, like Rockefeller Center's Top of the Rock or St. Bartholomew's, that are every bit as show-stopping.

And who could forget the origin of that phrase "bright lights, big city": Times Square. The shopping here may be ordinary and the restaurants average, but the amazing theaters of the Great White Way still have a gravitational pull. Seeing a show can be pricey, but join the line at the TKTS booth (⇨ *Ch. 15*) and suddenly orchestra tickets don't seem out of the question.

TWO WAYS TO EXPLORE

MIDTOWN'S ARCHITECTURE
Soaring skyscrapers frame an architectural playground, a mind-boggling patchwork of styles spanning two centuries that coalesce into one of the world's great urban landscapes. No painting or sculpture compares with the artistic beauty of Midtown itself. Modern glass towers coexist with 19th-century limestone mansions; pocket-size parks and peaceful plazas provide sanctuary amid steel towers that climb high into the clouds.

Art Deco is perhaps Midtown's most distinctive style. Its principles of symmetry and geometric angularity, coupled with Machine Age materials steel and aluminum, governed such mega-achievements of the 1920s and '30s as the **Chrysler Building** (considered one of the great Art Deco masterpieces) and **Rockefeller Center,** and decorated such Jazz Age landmarks as the **Waldorf=Astoria Hotel** and **Beekman Tower,** all located in the 40s east of 6th Avenue. Should you be continuing up 6th, you'll hit a landmark piece of Art Deco architecture, **Radio City Music Hall,** with its distinctive pink-and-blue neon sign. If you're continuing downtown, get a taste of Greco-Roman 20th-century neoclassicism and walk along East 42nd Street to the Beaux-Arts masterpieces **Grand Central Terminal** and nearby **New York Public Library,** two brilliantly designed public spaces as beautiful as they are functional.

A great place to see the coexistence of New York's old and new is on Park Avenue, where the Byzantine dome of **St. Bartholomew's Church** reclines two blocks south of the bronze-and-glass **Seagram Building,** designed by modernist innovator Mies van der Rohe. For an even sharper contrast, try to glimpse two remaining 19th-century mansions (at No. 9 11 and No. 13–15 West 54th Street) from the upper levels of the **Museum of Modern Art;** in fact, all of the museum's cleverly placed windows frame similar juxtapositions of urban settings.

Moving north, relive the 1980s at the dark-glass **Trump Tower** (✉ *725 5th Ave., at E. 56th St.*). Its ostentatious atrium flaunts that decade's unbridled luxury, with expensive boutiques and gaudy brass everywhere. The "Donald" resides above in a penthouse (with an elevator that famously descends from his bedroom to his office), and the famous boardroom from the TV show *The Apprentice* is also above. Step into the '90s at the flagship **Louis Vuitton–Moët Hennessy Tower,** an arced glass skyscraper that's both conspicuous and elegant, just like the handbags sold by the resident French luxury-goods giant. Finally, return to the 21st century with the glitzy display that is **Times Square:** its blend of culture and consumerism, architecture and advertising, makes it a glittering high-tech lasso looping in gawking tourists and theatergoers into one giant bottlenecked bundle.

CULTURE HIGH AND LOW

Whether you want to see a Broadway show, visit world-class museums, or tour a television studio, Midtown is the place to be. You can score good seats to some of the hottest Broadway and off-Broadway shows for half the going rate at the TKTS booth in Duffy Square at 47th Street and Broadway. Although people think of Broadway as the heart of the theater scene, few theaters actually line the thoroughfare. To see some of Broadway's grande dames, head west on 45th Street. Here you can see a bevy of Broadway beauties, including the **Booth,** the **Schoenfeld,** the **Jacobs,** the **Music Box,** and the **Imperial.** On the southern side of 45th Street you can find the pedestrians-only **Shubert Alley,** distinguished by colorful posters advertising the latest hit plays and musicals, and the **Shubert Theatre,** one of Broadway's most lustrous gems. Head west along 44th Street to see its neighbors, the **Helen Hayes,** the **Broadhurst,** the **Majestic,** and the **St. James.** Tucked among them, at No. 243, is **Sardi's,** the legendary Broadway watering hole, and nearby is the former speakeasy

Where can I find . . . ?

COFFEE	Fika 41 W. 58th St. Coffee break with a Swedish twist.	Macchiato Espresso Bar 141 E. 44th St. Popular for morning cups, light lunches.
A QUICK BITE	Kati Roll Company 49 W. 39th St. Indian food wrapped up burrito-style.	John's Pizzeria 260 W. 44th St. Best pizza in nabe. Try the "essence of garlic" on your pie.
COCKTAILS	Bann 350 W. 50th St. A sleek oasis in the Theater District with upscale Korean choices.	P. J. Clarke's 915 3rd Ave. New York's most famous Irish bar, and for good reason.

'21' Club with its row of jockeys out front, once the ultimate retreat for New York high society.

Also in Times Square are the **MTV Studios** at Broadway and 45th Street. Upstairs is the MTV TRL studio, and if you're there around 3 PM you'll see the barricades go up to impose some structure on the hordes of excited teenagers who gather here hoping to catch a glimpse of their favorite singer.

Music lovers can also get their fix. In the West 40s–50s area are the jazz venues **Birdland** and **Iridium.** Continue farther north to 57th Street to **Carnegie Hall,** the world-famous performance venue for classical music and other showstoppers.

TOP ATTRACTIONS

🄲 **Bryant Park.** A lovely green space amid skyscrapers, this is one of Manhattan's most popular parks. Lining the perimeter of the sunny central lawn, tall London plane trees cast welcome shade over stone terraces, formal flower beds, gravel pathways, and a smattering of kiosks selling everything from sandwiches to egg creams. In the afternoon the garden tables scattered about fill with lunching office workers and folk enjoying the park's free Wi-Fi (signs show you how to log on). In summer you can check out live jazz and comedy concerts and free outdoor film screenings on Monday at dusk. At the east side of the park, near a squatting bronze cast of Gertrude Stein, is the stylish Bryant Park Grill, which has a rooftop garden, and the adjacent open-air Bryant Park Café, open seasonally. Twice a year the park becomes the site for the city's famous fashion shows, with giant white tents and red carpets springing up. On the south side of the park is an old-fashioned **carousel** (⛄ $2) where kids can ride fanciful rabbits and frogs instead of horses. Come late October the park rolls out the artificial frozen **"pond"** (◷ *Nov.–mid-Jan., Sun–Thurs. 8 AM–10 PM, Fri. and Sat. 8 AM–midnight*) for ice-skating. Rental for skates and locker will run you $12 for skates and $9 for a lock to use with a "free" locker). Surrounding the ice rink are the Christmas market–like stalls of the **Holiday Shops** (♥ *Late Nov.–Jan. 1*), selling handcrafted and designer goods from around the world. ⊠ *6th Ave. between W. 40th and W. 42nd Sts., Midtown West* ☎ *212/768–4242* ⊕ *www.bryantpark.org* ♥ *Hours vary by month. See Web site for exact times* Ⓜ *B, D, F, V to 42nd St.; 7 to 5th Ave.*

★ **Chrysler Building.** A monument to modern times and the mighty auto-motive industry, the former Chrysler headquarters wins many a New Yorker's vote for the city's most iconic and beloved skyscraper (the world's tallest for 40 days until the Empire State Building stole the honor). Architect William Van Alen, who designed this 1930 Art Deco masterpiece, incorporated car details into its form: American eagle gargoyles sprout from the 61st floor, resembling car-hood ornaments used on 1920s Chryslers; winged urns festooning the 31st floor refer-ence the car's radiator caps. Most breathtaking is the pinnacle, whose tiered crescents and spiked windows radiate out like a magnificent steel sunburst. View it at sunset to catch the light gleaming off the tip. Even better, observe it at night, when its peak illuminates the sky like the backdrop to a Busby Berkeley musical. The inside is off limits apart from the amazing time-capsule lobby replete with chrome "grillwork," intricately patterned wood elevator doors, marble walls and floors, and an enormous ceiling mural saluting transportation and the human endeavor. ⊠ *405 Lexington Ave., at E. 42nd St., Midtown East* Ⓜ *4, 5, 6, 7, S to 42nd St./Grand Central.*

Fodor's Choice ★ **Grand Central Terminal.** Grand Central is not only the world's largest (76 acres) and the nation's busiest (500,000 commuters and subway riders use it daily) railway station, but also one of the world's greatest public spaces ("justly famous," as critic Tony Hiss noted, "as a crossroads, a noble building, and an ingenious piece of engineering"). A massive four-year renovation completed in October 1998 restored the 1913 landmark to its original splendor—and then some.

You can best admire Grand Central's exquisite Beaux-Arts architec-ture from its ornate south face on East 42nd Street, modeled after a Roman triumphal arch. Crowning the facade's Corinthian columns and 75-foot-high arched windows, a graceful clock keeps time for hur-ried commuters. In the central window stands an 1869 bronze statue of Cornelius Vanderbilt, who built the station to house his railroad empire. Step inside past the glimmering chandeliers of the waiting room to the majestic **main concourse**, 200 feet long, 120 feet wide, and 120 feet (roughly 12 stories) high, modeled after a Roman bath. Overhead, a celestial map of the twinkling fiber-optic constellations covers the robin's egg–blue ceiling. During rush hour you'll be swept into the tides and eddies of human traffic, which swirl around the central informa-tion kiosk, a popular meeting place. Experience the thrill, then escape up the sweeping staircases at either end, where balconies house three upscale restaurants. Any would make an enjoyable perch from which to survey the concourse, but for a real taste of the station's early years, head beyond the western staircase to the **Campbell Apartment,** a clubby

7

Grand Meals

If you're looking for a great meal around Grand Central, head to one of these go-to restaurants.

Amid the hustle and bustle of Grand Central Station is the elegant **Grand Central Oyster Bar & Restaurant** (⊠ 89 E. 42nd St., at Vanderbilt Ave. ☎ 212/490–6650). This sprawling space, with a tiled-vaulted ceiling, brings a sense of grandeur to a chaotic transportation hub. Famous for its architecture and decor—the Oyster Bar's impressive raw bar and fresh seafood are the real reason customers have been returning for the past 90 years.

If you want to indulge yourself, stop at the stylish **Michael Jordan's The**

Steakhouse (⊠ Grand Central Terminal, 23 Vanderbilt Ave. ☎ 212/655–2300) located on the balcony of Grand Central Station. The prime dry-aged rib eye or the succulent 2½-pound lobster are reason enough to dine here. But if you don't have time to sit for a meal, pull up a stool at the restaurant's bustling bar and have a drink off the impressive wine list.

For classic Italian cuisine, head to **Naples 45** (⊠ 200 Park Ave., at 45th St. ☎ 212/972–7001). This spacious restaurant with an open kitchen feels friendly and casual. The comforting menu of pizzas and pastas will please any and all palates. Breakfast is also served.

---

cocktail lounge housed in the restored private offices and salon of 1920s tycoon John W. Campbell.

Despite its grandeur, Grand Central still functions primarily as a railroad station. Underground, more than 60 ingeniously integrated railroad tracks lead trains upstate and to Connecticut via Metro-North Commuter Rail. The subway connects here as well. The **Municipal Art Society** (⊠ 457 Madison Ave., between 50th and 51st Sts., Midtown East ☎ 212/935–3960 ⊕ www.mas.org) leads architectural tours of the terminal that begin here on Wednesday at 12:30. Reservations are not required, and a $10 donation is suggested. Meet at the information booth, Main Concourse. Main entrance ⊠ E. 42nd St. at Park Ave., Midtown East ☎ 212/935–3960 ⊕ www.grandcentralterminal.com Ⓜ 4, 5, 6, 7, S to 42nd St./Grand Central.

Radio City Music Hall. This icon of New York City was built to enchant everyone who stepped inside its doors. Shortly after the stock market crash of 1929, John D. Rockefeller wanted to create a symbol of hope in what was a sad, broke city. He selected a piece of real estate in an area of Manhattan then known as "the speakeasy belt," and partnered with the Radio Corporation of America to build a grand theater, a place where everyday people could see the finest entertainment at sensible prices. Every inch of the interior was designed to be extraordinary. RCA head David Sarnoff named their creation "Radio City Music Hall." When it opened, some said it was so grand there was no need for performances, people would get more than their money's worth by simply by sitting there and enjoying the space. Despite being the largest indoor theater in the world with its city-block long marquee, it feels warm and intimate.

And although there are performances and media events here year-round, most people (more than a million visitors every year, in fact) want to attend the Radio City Christmas Spectacular. Make reservations as early as possible, especially if you want to attend near the Christmas holidays or on weekends. The shows tend to sell out, but you can usually find tickets up until at least mid-October. Happily, there are no bad seats at Radio City Music Hall, so if you are booking late, grab what you can get. Tickets—about $42–$100 per person for the 90-minute show—can be purchased at the Radio City Music Hall, Madison Square Garden, or the Beacon Theatre Box Offices; on the Web; by phone on the Christmas Spectacular hot line (☎ 212/307–1000); or at Ticketmaster. ⊠ 1260 6th Ave., at W. 51st St., Midtown ☎ 212/307–7171 ⊕ www.radiocity.com Ⓜ B, D, F, V to 47th–50th St./Rockefeller Center; N, R to 49th St.

Rockefeller Center. If Times Square is New York's crossroads, Rockefeller Center is its communal gathering place, where the entire world converges to snap pictures, skate on the ice rink, peek in on a taping of the *Today* show (or—with luck—NBC's *30 Rock*), shop, eat, and take in the monumental Art Deco structures and public sculptures from the past century. Totaling 49 shops, 28 restaurants (1.4 million square feet in all), the complex runs from 47th to 52nd streets between 5th and 7th avenues. Special events and huge pieces of art dominate the central plazas in summer, and in December an enormous twinkling tree towers above (visit ⊕ www.rockefellercenter.com for a schedule).

At the complex's center is the sunken **Lower Plaza**, site of the world's most famous ice-skating rink October through April (it's a café in summer). Skaters swoop or stumble across the ice while crowds gather above on the Esplanade to watch the spins and spills. Hovering above, the gold-leaf statue of the fire-stealing Greek hero **Prometheus**—Rockefeller Center's most famous sculpture—forms the backdrop to zillions of photos. Carved into the wall behind it, a quotation from Aeschylus reads PROMETHEUS, TEACHER IN EVERY ART, BROUGHT THE FIRE THAT HATH PROVED TO MORTALS A MEANS TO MIGHTY ENDS. The Lower Plaza provides access to the marble-lined corridors underneath Rockefeller Center, which house restaurants (everything from the high-end Sea Grill to pizza parlors), a post office, and clean public restrooms—a rarity in Midtown. ⊠ Between 5th and 6th Aves. and W. 49th and W. 50th Sts., Midtown West ☎ 212/332–7654 for the rink Ⓜ B, D, F, V to 47th–50th Sts./Rockefeller Center.

Rising up on the Lower Plaza's west side is the 70-story (850-foot-tall) Art Deco **GE Building** (☎ 212/332–6868), a testament to modern urban development. Here Rockefeller commissioned and then destroyed a mural by Diego Rivera upon learning that it featured Vladimir Lenin. He replaced it with the monumental *American Progress* by José María Sert, still on view in the lobby, flanked by additional murals by Sert and English artist Frank Brangwyn. While in the lobby, pick up a free "Rockefeller Center Visitor's Guide" at the **information desk**. Up on the 65th floor sits the now shuttered **Rainbow Room**, a glittering big-band ballroom from 1934 through 2009. The GE Building also houses **NBC Studios**, whose news tapings, visible at street level, attract gawking crowds. For ticket information for NBC shows or the 70-minute studio

7

The high-steppin' Rockettes show off their signature moves at Radio City Music Hall.

tour, visit the NBC Experience Store at the building's southeast corner. ✉ *30 Rockefeller Plaza, between 5th and 6th Aves. at 49th St., Midtown West* ☎ *212/664–7174* ✆ *NBC Studio Tour $18.50* ☞ *Children under 6 not permitted* ⊙ *Tours depart every 30 mins Mon.–Sat. 8:30–5:30, Sun. 9:30–4:30* Ⓜ *B, D, F, V to 47th–50th Sts./Rockefeller Center.*

Fodor's Choice
★
Top of the Rock. Rockefeller Center's multifloor observation deck, first opened in 1933 and closed in the early 1980s, reopened in 2005 to be embraced by visitors and locals alike. Arriving just before sunset affords a view of the city that morphs before your eyes into a dazzling wash of colors, with a bird's-eye view of the tops of the Empire State Building, the Citicorp Building, and the Chrysler Building, and sweeping views northward to Central Park and south to the Statue of Liberty. Transparent elevators lift you to the 67th-floor interior viewing area, then an escalator leads to the outdoor deck on the 69th floor for sightseeing through nonreflective glass safety panels. Then, take another elevator or stairs to the 70th floor for a 360-degree outdoor panorama of New York City on a deck that is only 20 feet wide and nearly 200 feet long. Reserved-time ticketing eliminates long lines.

ABOUT THE TREE

A holiday tradition began in 1931 when workers clearing away the rubble for Rockefeller Center erected a 20-foot-tall balsam. It was two years into the Great Depression, and the 4,000 men employed at the site were grateful to finally be away from the unemployment lines. The first official tree-lighting ceremony was held in 1933.

Ice-skating under the sculpture of Prometheus is a winter ritual for many local and visiting families.

Indoor exhibits include films of Rockefeller Center's history and a model of the building. Especially interesting is a Plexiglas screen on the floor with footage showing Rock Center construction workers dangling on beams high above the streets; the brave can even "walk" across a beam to get a sense of what it might have been like to erect this skyscraper. ■ TIP→ The local consensus is that the views from the Top of the Rock are better than those from the Empire State Building, in part because the Empire State is part of the skyline here. ⊠ *Entrance on 50th St., between 5th and 6th Aves., Midtown West* ☎ *877/692–7625 or 212/698–2000* ⊕ *www.topoftherocknyc.com* 🎟 *$20* ⊙ *Daily 8–midnight; last elevator at 11 PM* Ⓜ *B, D, F, V to 47th–50th Sts./Rockefeller Center.*

WORTH NOTING

New York Public Library (NYPL) Humanities and Social Sciences Library. The "Library with the Lions" is a 1911 masterpiece of Beaux-Arts design and one of the great research institutions in the world, with 6 million books, 12 million manuscripts, and 2.8 million pictures. But you don't have to crack a book to make it worth visiting: an hour or so at this National Historic Landmark is a peaceful (and free!) alternative to Midtown's bustle, along with some pretty incredible architecture, especially when combined with a stroll through adjacent **Bryant Park.** Buy a drink at a park kiosk, then head to the library's grand 5th Avenue entrance to people-watch from the block-long marble staircase, then check out the opulent interior.

The library's bronze front doors open into **Astor Hall,** which leads to several special exhibit galleries and, to the left, a stunning periodicals

Keeping It Real in Times Square

How to act like a local in Times Square? Look as if you want to leave. The local art of walking in Times Square involves zigzagging around the slow crowds that gather like obstacles. Avoid looking overtly at the billboards, and whatever you do, don't snap pictures. Display an ironic detachment: you're just passing through.

Why the snide comments? Consider the noise and billboards from a New Yorker's perspective. The chains that dominate here from Applebee's to M&M's World to Toys "R" Us with its Ferris wheel make some locals mourn the old "naughty, bawdy, gaudy" Times Square portrayed in the musical *42nd Street*. It's true we like to reminisce about the Times Square where glitz and grime converged, rich and poor shimmied together on the dance floor, sailors chased after chorus girls, and young men and women from Small-town, USA, arrived with a suitcase full of dreams.

Times Square's status as the city's nightlife playground began in 1895, when Oscar Hammerstein opened the Olympia Theatre (an over-the-top folly that closed in 1898), the first of many entertainment venues, from theaters and movie palaces to porn cinemas and strip clubs, for which the thoroughfare would grow notorious. Its fate as Manhattan's entertainment capital was sealed on October 27, 1904, with the opening of the city's first subway line, which included a station at 42nd Street: people from all walks of life had easy access to its risqué brand of entertainment.

Over the next century Times Square rose and fell with the times, functioning like a circus mirror in which New York saw itself exaggerated. During the Roaring Twenties its Roseland Ballroom introduced many New Yorkers to Ella Fitzgerald, Duke Ellington, and Benny Goodman, while hundreds of speakeasies opened on Broadway in the wake of Prohibition. During the Depression the great theaters converted into cheaper burlesques, movie houses, and peep shows.

The mostly harmless street hustlers and peep shows, which coexisted in relative peace with the swank restaurants and remaining legitimate theaters through the post–WWII era and into the 1960s, grew more insidious in the 1970s as urban flight to the suburbs left behind a breeding ground for crime. Magnifying the general plight of New York, Times Square descended into a dark stage of prostitution and drug dealing, whose raffish denizens were portrayed in Martin Scorsese's 1976 film *Taxi Driver*. When Robert De Niro's character Travis Bickle talks of wanting to wash away the scum and lowlifes of the city, he echoed most New Yorkers' sentiments.

After a Herculean cleanup begun in the 1980s and 1990s, Bickle got his wish, to an extent he could not ever have imagined. The 49-story Marriott Marquis hotel trampled five historic theaters. Viacom brought the MTV and Nickelodeon television networks to Broadway. Times Square today is a family-friendly, open-air promenade of familiar brand names in theme park–like settings, from ESPN Zone to the world's largest McDonald's. But not all change is bad; we also have a new pedestrian-friendly stretch of Broadway and the stadium seating behind TKTS. And, of course, we never lost the rich theater scene itself, which locals DO frequent along with visitors.

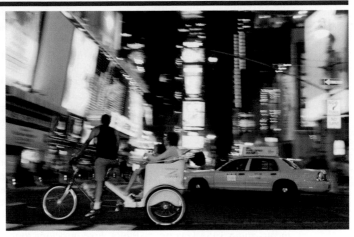

In truth, it can be great fun, particularly when the lights stand out at nighttime—especially if you're with kids (whose hands you must *never* release because of the undertow-like crowds)—just try to focus on the flashing walls of neon colors and not the overwhelming corporate advertising.

While nobody's really nostalgic (no matter what they may say) for the derelict Times Square of the '70s and '80s, at least that Times Square reflected (however grotesquely) the challenges all the city's residents were facing. New Yorkers pride themselves on their survivor's ability to tough out the harshness of city living. For decades Times Square embodied that toughness ("if I can make it here, I can make it anywhere"). The thoroughfare reflected everything that was wonderful about New York: freedom of expression, progressive ideas, live-and-let-live attitude, the ability of a world of cultures and classes to coexist on top of each other, and—more than anything—the triumph of great ideas, talent, and the almighty dollar. Out in the open, underneath the bright-lighted billboards, it was clear as day what New York City had to offer newcomers, take it or leave it. Today the authenticity of that moment is missing, but don't let the locals make you jaded, this spot still has some of its old show-time charm.

Times Square Visitors Center. Newly reopened after a $1.8 million renovation, this visitor center is a savvy place to take shelter and get your bearings when the crowds threaten to suck you into an undertow. Stop by for multilingual kiosks, MetroCards, interactive Google Earth map tables, sightseeing and theater tickets, and (most important!) free restrooms. ✉ *1560 Broadway, between 46th and 47th Sts., Midtown West* ☏ *212/869–1890* ⊕ *www.timessqarenyc.org* ⊗ *Mon.–Fri. 8–7, Sat.–Sun. 8–8* Ⓜ *1, 2, 3, 7, N, Q, R, W, S to 42nd St./Times Sq.*

7

room with wall paintings of New York publishing houses. Walk up the sweeping double staircase to a second-floor balconied corridor overlooking the hall, with panels highlighting the library's development. Make sure to continue up to the magisterial **Rose Main Reading Room**—297 feet long (almost two full north–south city blocks), 78 feet wide, and just over 51 feet high; walk through to best appreciate the rows of oak tables and the extraordinary ceiling of this space. Several additional third-floor galleries show rotating exhibits on typography, literature, bookmaking, and maps (past exhibits have included old New York restaurant

> ### THE NAME GAME
>
> Thanks to a donation of a cool $100 million from Wall Street financier Stephen A. Schwarzman, the New York Public Library will likely be sporting a new name. The ample gift is set to kick off a billion-dollar renovation, which is projected to be complete in 2014, after which it'll be christened the Stephen A. Schwarzman Building. Assuming that the city's Landmarks Preservation Commission doesn't object, the new name will be discreetly carved into the building facade near the main entrance.

menus and a 1455 Gutenberg Bible). Free one-hour tours leave Tuesday–Saturday at 11 and 2 from Astor Hall. There are women's rooms on the ground floor and third floor, and a men's room on the third floor. ⊠ *5th Ave. between E. 40th and E. 42nd Sts., Midtown West* ☎ *212/930–0800 for exhibit information* ⊕ *www.nypl.org* ⊙ *Mon. and Thurs.–Sat. 10–6, Sun. 1–5, Tues. and Wed. 10–7:30; exhibitions until 6* Ⓜ *B, D, F, V to 42nd St.; 7 to 5th Ave.*

★ **United Nations Headquarters.** Officially an "international zone" and not
Ⓒ part of the United States, the U.N. Headquarters is a working symbol of global cooperation. Built between 1947 and 1961, the headquarters sit on a lushly landscaped, 18-acre tract on the East River, fronted by flags of member nations.

The main reason to visit is the 45-minute guided tour (given in 20 languages), which includes the **General Assembly** and major council chambers, though some rooms may be closed on any given day. The tour includes displays on war, nuclear energy, and refugees, and passes corridors overflowing with imaginatively diverse artwork. Free tickets to assemblies are sometimes available on a first-come, first-served basis before sessions begin; pick them up in the General Assembly lobby. If you just want to wander around, the grounds include a beautiful riverside promenade, a rose garden with 1,400 specimens, and sculptures donated by member nations. The complex's buildings (the slim, 505-foot-tall green-glass **Secretariat Building**; the much smaller, domed **General Assembly Building**; and the **Dag Hammarskjöld Library**) evoke the influential French modernist Le Corbusier (who was on the team of architects that designed the complex) and the surrounding park and plaza remain visionary. Inside, the **Delegates Dining Room** (☎ *212/963–7625*) is open for an international buffet lunch weekdays ($25; jackets required for men, no jeans or sneakers; reservations required at least one day in advance, no children under 12 years old). The public concourse, beneath the visitor entrance, has a coffee shop, gift shops, a bookstore,

CLOSE UP

Art for Art's Sake

The mosaics, murals, and sculptures that grace Rockefeller Center—many of them considered Art Deco masterpieces—were all part of the plan of John D. Rockefeller Jr. In 1932, as the steel girders on the first of the buildings were heading heavenward, Rockefeller put together a team of advisers to find artists who could make the project "as beautiful as possible." More than 50 artists were commissioned for 200 individual works.

Some artists scoffed at the idea of decorating an office building. Picasso declined to meet with Rockefeller to discuss the project, and Matisse replied that busy business executives would not be in the "quiet and reflective state of mind" necessary to appreciate his art. And some of those who agreed to contribute, including muralists Diego Rivera and José María Sert, were not popular with the public. A group of American artists protested Rockefeller's decision to hire these "alien" artists.

The largest of the original artworks installed at Rockefeller Center, Lee Lawrie's two-ton sculpture *Atlas,* was controversial because it was said to resemble Italy's fascist dictator, Benito Mussolini. The sculpture, depicting a muscle-bound man holding up the world, drew protests in 1936. Some even derided Paul Manship's golden *Prometheus,* which soars over the ice-skating rink, when it was unveiled the same year. Both are now considered to be among the best public artworks of the 20th century.

Lawrie's sculpture *Wisdom,* perched over the main entrance of 20 Rockefeller Plaza, is another of the gems of Rockefeller Center. Also look for Isamu Noguchi's stainless-steel plaque *News* over the entrance of the Bank of America Building at 50 Rockefeller Plaza and Attilio Piccirilli's two-ton glass-block panel called *Youth Leading Industry* over the entrance of the International Building. René Chambellan's bronze dolphins in the fountains of the Channel Gardens are also crowd-pleasers.

and a post office where you can mail letters with U.N. stamps. If you want to have a meal in the Delegates Dining Room, be sure to bring a photo ID and make a reservation as far in advance as possible. *Visitor entrance* ✉ *1st Ave. at E. 46th St., Midtown East* ☎ *212/963–8687* ⊕ *www.un.org* ✆ *Tour $12.50* ☞ *Children under 5 not admitted* ☉ *Tours weekdays 9:30–4:45; tours in English leave General Assembly lobby every 30 mins; Delegates Dining Room, 11:30–2:30* Ⓜ *4, 5, 6, 7, S to 42nd St./Grand Central.*

IF THERE'S STILL TIME

☺ **Daily News Building.** One of the city's most unusual lobbies resides in Raymond Hood's Art Deco and modernist tower. An illuminated 12-foot globe revolves beneath a black glass dome. Around it, spreading across the floor like a giant compass and literally positioning New York at the center of the world, bronze lines indicate mileage to various

A statue of Atlas stands across the street from the looming Gothic St. Patrick's Cathedral.

international destinations. ✉ *220 E. 42nd St., between 2nd and 3rd Aves., Midtown East* Ⓜ *4, 5, 6, 7, S to 42nd St./Grand Central.*

The Plaza. With two sides of Central Park *and* 5th Avenue at its doorstep, this world-famous 19-story 1907 building claims one of Manhattan's prize real-estate corners. Henry Hardenbergh, who built the Dakota on Central Park West, here concocted a birthday-cake effect of highly ornamented white-glazed brick topped with a copper-and-slate French mansard roof. The original hotel was home to Eloise, the fictional star of Kay Thompson's children's books, and has appeared in many movies, including Alfred Hitchcock's *North by Northwest, Plaza Suite,* and *Home Alone 2.* After a $400 million renovation, the Plaza reopened in early 2008. The legendary Oak Room, Oak Bar, and Grand Ballroom are all back, as are new high-end shops (including an Eloise-themed mecca), luxury hotel rooms, and condo hotel units. ✉ *5th Ave. at W. 59th St., Midtown West* ☎ *212/759–3000* Ⓜ *N, R, W to 5th Ave./59th St.*

St. Bartholomew's Church. Known to locals as St. Bart's, this handsome 1919 limestone-and-salmon-color brick church represents a generation of Midtown Park Avenue buildings long since replaced by modernist behemoths and contemporary glass-and-steel towers. It's a pleasant surprise to stumble upon its triple-arched Romanesque

BART ON SCREEN

St. Bart's should have a SAG card: it has had roles in the movies *Arthur* and *Maid in Manhattan,* among others, and has also showed up on episodes of *Sex and the City* and *Law & Order.*

Irish pride takes to the streets and sweeps up Fifth Avenue in the annual St. Patrick's Day Parade.

portal and see the intricately tiled Byzantine dome set against the sky-scrapers, then have a bite at its popular outdoor café open in good weather. St. Bart's also sponsors major music events throughout the year, including the summer's Festival of Sacred Music, with full-length masses and other choral works; an annual Christmas concert; and an occasional organ recital series that showcases the church's 12,422-pipe organ, the city's largest. The church has been associated with VIPs in many capacities, including weddings. ⊠ *324 Park Ave., at 51st St., Midtown East* ☎ *212/378–0222; 212/378–0248 for concert information* ⊕ *www.stbarts.org* ⊙ *Mon., Tues., Thurs., Fri., Sat. 9–6, Sun. 7:45–6, Wed. 9–8:30* Ⓜ *6 to 51st St./Lexington Ave.; E, V to Lexington–3rd Aves./53rd St.*

St. Patrick's Cathedral. The country's largest Catholic cathedral (seating approximately 2,400) this 1859–79 Gothic edifice is among New York's most striking churches (note the 330-foot spires). Among the statues in the alcoves around the nave is a modern depiction of the first American-born saint, Mother Elizabeth Ann Seton. The 5th Avenue steps are a convenient, scenic rendezvous spot. Sunday Masses can overflow with tourists; off-hours are significantly more peaceful. Many of the funerals for fallen New York City police and firefighters after 9/11 were held here. ⊠ *5th Ave. between E. 50th and E. 51st Sts., Midtown East* ☎ *212/753–2261 rectory* ⊕ *www.ny-archdiocese.org* ⊙ *Daily 6:30 AM–8 PM* Ⓜ *E, V to 5th Ave./53rd St.*

Seagram Building. Ludwig Mies van der Rohe, a pioneer of modern architecture, built this boxlike bronze-and-glass tower in 1958. The austere facade belies its wit: I-beams, used to hold buildings up, here

The view of Midtown from across the Hudson River shows the skyline punctuated by the Empire State Building.

are merely attached to the surface, representing the *idea* of support. The Seagram Building's innovative ground-level plaza, extending out to the sidewalk, has since become a common element in urban skyscraper design. ⊠ *375 Park Ave., between E. 52nd and E. 53rd Sts., Midtown East* ⛟ *Free* ⏱ *Tours Tues. at 3* Ⓜ *6 to 51st St./Lexington Ave.; E, V to Lexington–3rd Aves./53rd St.*

☾ **Sony Building.** Designed by Philip Johnson in 1984, the Sony Building's rose-granite columns and its giant-size Chippendale-style pediment made the skyscraper an instant landmark. The first-floor public arcade includes electronics stores, an upscale kosher restaurant, a café, and an atrium filled with children and adults playing chess. ⊠ *550 Madison Ave., between E. 55th and E. 56th Sts., Midtown East* ⏱ *Daily 7* AM–*11* PM Ⓜ *E, V to 5th Ave./53rd St.*

FRUGAL FUN

Have kids in tow? The free **Sony Wonder Technology Lab** (⊠ *550 Madison Ave., between E. 55th and E. 56th Sts., Midtown East* ☎ *212/833–8100* ⊕ *www.sonywondertechlab.com* ⏱ *Tues.–Sat. 10–5, Sun. noon–5; last entrance 30 mins before closing*) in the Sony Building lets them program robots, edit music videos, or take a peek inside the human body. Admission is free, but call at least seven days ahead for reservations, as it's very popular.

University Club. Among the best surviving works of McKim, Mead & White, New York's leading turn-of-the-20th-century architects, this 1899 pink Milford granite palace was built for an exclusive club of degree-holding men. (The crests of various prestigious universities hang above its windows.) The club's popularity declined as individual universities built their own clubs and as gentlemen's clubs became less important to the New York social scene. Still, the nine-story Italian High Renaissance Revival building (the facade looks as though it's three stories) stands out, grand as ever, among the shiny 5th Avenue shops. ✉ *1 W. 54th St., at 5th Ave., Midtown West* Ⓜ *E, V to 5th Ave./53rd St.*

GALLERIES

David Findlay Jr. Fine Art. This gallery concentrates on contemporary and 20th-century American painters from Winslow Homer to Robert Rauschenburg to op artist Richard Anuszkiewicz. ✉ *41 E. 57th St., 11th fl., at Madison Ave., Midtown East* ☎ *212/486–7660* ⊕ *www. davidfindlayjr.com* Ⓜ *N, R, W to 5th Ave.*

Edwynn Houk. The impressive stable of 20th-century photographers here includes Sally Mann, Lynn Davis, and Elliott Erwitt. The gallery also has prints by masters Edward Weston and Alfred Stieglitz. ✉ *745 5th Ave., between E. 57th and E. 58th Sts., Midtown East* ☎ *212/750–7070* ⊕ *www.houkgallery.com* Ⓜ *N, R, W to 5th Ave.*

Greenberg Van Doren. This gallery exhibits the works of young artists as well as retrospectives of established masters. You can purchase works here by Georgia O'Keeffe, Ed Ruscha, and Robert Motherwell, among others. ✉ *730 5th Ave., at E. 57th St., 7th fl., Midtown East* ☎ *212/445–0444* ⊕ *www.agvdgallery.com* Ⓜ *N, R, W to 5th Ave.*

Marian Goodman. The excellent contemporary art here includes Jeff Wall's staged photographs presented on light boxes, South African artist William Kentridge's video animations, and Gerhard Richter's paintings. ✉ *24 W. 57th St., between 5th and 6th Aves., Midtown West* ☎ *212/977–7160* ⊕ *www.mariangoodman.com* Ⓜ *F to 57th St.*

Marlborough. With its latest branch in Chelsea, Marlborough has raised its global visibility up yet another notch. The gallery represents modern artists such as Michele Oka Doner, Magdalena Abakanowicz, and Israel Hershberg. Look for sculptures by Tom Otterness—his whimsical bronzes are found in several subway stations. ✉ *40 W. 57th St., between 5th and 6th Aves., Midtown West* ☎ *212/541–4900* ⊕ *www. marlboroughgallery.com* Ⓜ *F to 57th St.*

Pace Wildenstein. The giant gallery—now in Chelsea as well—focuses on such modern and contemporary painters as Julian Schnabel, Mark Rothko, and New York School painter Ad Reinhardt. ✉ *32 E. 57th St., between Park and Madison Aves., 4th fl., Midtown East* ☎ *212/421–3292* ⊕ *www.pacewildenstein.com* Ⓜ *N, R, W to 5th Ave.*

Peter Findlay. Covering 19th- and 20th-century works by European artists, this gallery shows pieces by Mary Cassatt, Paul Klee, and Alberto Giacometti. ✉ *41 E. 57th St., 8th fl., at Madison Ave., Midtown East* ☎ *212/644–4433* ⊕ *www.findlay.com* Ⓜ *N, R, W to 5th Ave.*

Spanierman. This venerable gallery deals in 19th- and early-20th-century American painting and sculpture. Their inventory list and scholarship is amazing, and they frequently sell to museums looking to broaden their own collections. ✉ *45 E. 58th St., between Park and Madison*

7

Rockefeller vs. Rivera

As Rockefeller Center neared completion in 1932, John D. Rockefeller Jr. still needed a mural to grace the lobby of the main building. The industrialist's taste dictated that the subject of the 63-foot-by-17-foot mural was to be grandiose: "human intelligence in control of the forces of nature." He hired an artist known for his grand vision, Mexican painter Diego Rivera.

With its depiction of massive machinery moving mankind forward, Rivera's *Man at the Crossroads* seemed exactly what Rockefeller wanted. Everything was going fine until someone noticed that near the center of the mural was a portrait of Soviet Premier Vladimir Lenin surrounded by red-kerchiefed workers. Rockefeller, who was building what was essentially a monument to capitalism, was less than thrilled. When Rivera was accused of willful propagandizing, the artist famously replied, "All art is propaganda."

Rivera refused to remove the offending portrait (although, as an olive branch, he did offer to add an image of Abraham Lincoln). In early 1934, as Rivera was working on the unfinished work, representatives for Rockefeller informed him that his services were no longer required. Within a half hour, tar paper had been hung over the mural. Despite negotiations to move it to the Museum of Modern Art, Rockefeller was determined to get rid of the mural once and for all. Not content to have it painted over, he ordered ax-wielding workers to chip away the entire wall.

Rockefeller ordered the mural replaced by a less offensive one by José María Sert. (This one did include Lincoln.) But Rivera had the last word. He re-created the mural in the Palacio de Bellas Artes in Mexico City, adding a portrait of Rockefeller among the champagne-swilling swells ignoring the plight of the workers.

Aves., Midtown East ☎ 212/832–0208 ⊕ www.spanierman.com Ⓜ N, R, W to 5th Ave.

Tibor de Nagy. Founded in 1950, this gallery shows work by 20th-century artists such as Biala, Nell Blaine, Jane Freilicher, and Shirley Jaffee. Instrumental in bringing many of America's finest abstract expressionist artists to public attention in the mid-20th century, the gallery now shows abstract and realistic work. It's open Tuesday–Saturday, closed weekends June through mid-August, and closes up completely from mid-August to Labor Day. ✉ 724 5th Ave., between W. 56th and W. 57th Sts., Midtown West ☎ 212/262–5050 ⊕ www.tibordenagy.com Ⓜ N, R, W to 5th Ave.

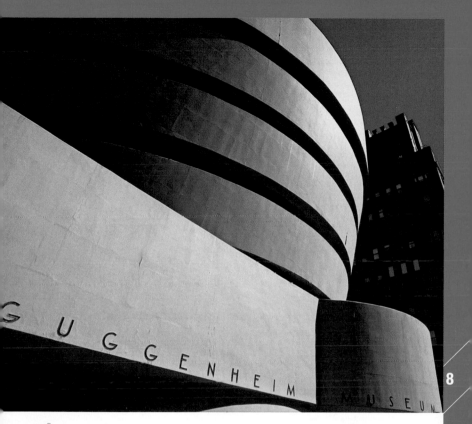

The Upper East Side

WORD OF MOUTH

"[Is the Upper East Side] worth a day of sightseeing?"
—Johnnyman7

"Honestly, it just depends what you are looking to do. I really would recommend the Met. I'm not a huge museum person, but I absolutely loved the Met."
—Lolly100

GETTING ORIENTED

St. Nicholas Russian Orthodox Cathedral

Museum of the City of New York

El Museo del Barrio

6

Jewish Museum

Cooper-Hewitt National Design Museum

Solomon R. Guggenheim Museum

CENTRAL PARK

Gracie Mansion

Henderson Place Historic District

4,5,6

Neue Galerie New York

Schaller & Weber

Carl Schurz Park

YORKVILLE

Metropolitan Museum of Art

Crawford Doyle

Mitchell-Innes & Nash Gallery

Maison du Chocolat

Leo Castelli Gallery

Gagosian Gallery

6

The Carlyle Hotel

Whitney Museum of American Art

Jane Kahan Gallery

Frick Collection

Hirschl & Adler Gallery

Asia Society and Museum

Sotheby's

Knoedler & Co. Gallery

Americas Society

6

Temple Emanu-El

China Institute Gallery

Wildenstein & Co. Gallery

B,Q

Mount Vernon Hotel Museum and Garden

Metropolitan Club

Serendipity 3

Roosevelt Island Tramway

Bloomingdale's

Queensboro Bridge

N,R,W

N,R,W, 4,5,6

East River

Roosevelt Island

East River

FDR Dr.

Park Ave.

Madison Ave.

Lexington Ave.

Fifth Ave.

Third Ave.

Second Ave.

First Ave.

York Ave.

East End Ave.

E. 97th St.
E. 96th St.
E. 95th St.
E. 94th St.
E. 93rd St.
E. 92nd St.
E. 91st St.
E. 90th St.
E. 89th St.
E. 88th St.
E. 87th St.
E. 86th St.
E. 85th St.
E. 84th St.
E. 83rd St.
E. 82nd St.
E. 81st St.
E. 80th St.
E. 79th St.
E. 78th St.
E. 77th St.
E. 76th St.
E. 75th St.
E. 74th St.
E. 73rd St.
E. 72nd St.
E. 71st St.
E. 70th St.
E. 69th St.
E. 68th St.
E. 67th St.
E. 64th St.
E. 63rd St.
E. 62nd St.
E. 61st St.
E. 60th St.
E. 59th St.
E. 58th St.

0   1/4 mile
0   400 meters

MAKING THE MOST OF YOUR TIME

The Upper East Side lends itself to a surprising variety of simple but distinct itineraries: Regimented hopping up and down Museum Mile; languorous gallery grazing (⇨ *gallery listings at the end of this chapter*); window-shopping on Madison Avenue; or bar-hopping for young twentysome-things on 2nd Avenue. But this area is also home to a variety of communities that are best explored on foot to weave around the town houses, boutiques, consignment stores, and hidden gardens.

If all that walking wears you out, you can always hit one of the nail salons and indulge in a neighborhood stereotype of the pampered Upper East Sider. A well-deserved post–Museum Mile foot rub and mani/pedi are surprisingly reasonably priced.

GETTING HERE

Take the Lexington Avenue 4 or 5 express trains to 59th or 86th Street. The 6 local train also stops at 59th, 68th, 77th, 86th, and 96th streets. If you're coming from Midtown, the F train will let you out at Lexington Avenue at 63rd Street, where you can connect to the 4, 5, and 6 after a short walk. From the Upper West Side, take one of the crosstown buses, the M66, M72, M79, M86, and M96. You can also take the N, R, or W train to 59th St. and Lexington Avenue.

WORD OF MOUTH (WWW.FODORS.COM/FORUMS)

"For the East Side, window shopping on Madison is always enjoyable. Just about every high end store you can think of has a shop there. One huge plus to the [Upper East Side] is that there are far fewer tourists around. I know that everyone likes to come here and see Times Square, and it is certainly something to see, but having to navigate through the ridiculous crowds becomes exhausting. I think you might enjoy coming uptown and just being able to walk leisurely without people bumping into you." —elysag

FODOR'S CHOICE

Gracie Mansion

TOP ATTRACTIONS

Metropolitan Museum of Art (⇨ *Ch. 14*)

Mount Vernon Hotel Museum and Garden

TOP EXPERIENCES

Lingering at the Carlyle

Window-shopping on Madison

NEARBY MUSEUMS (⇨ *CH. 14*)

Asia Society and Museum

Cooper-Hewitt National Design Museum

El Museo del Barrio

Frick Collection

Jewish Museum

Museum of American Illustration

Museum of the City of New York

National Academy

Neue Galerie New York

Solomon R. Guggenheim Museum

Whitney Museum

AREA SHOPS (⇨ *CH. 17*)

Calvin Klein

Giorgio Armani

Michael Kors

Oscar de la Renta

Vera Wang

8

Sightseeing
★★★
Nightlife
★★
Dining
★★★
Lodging
★★
Shopping
★★★★

To many New Yorkers the Upper East Side connotes old money and high society. Alongside Central Park, between 5th and Lexington avenues, up to East 96th Street, the trappings of wealth are everywhere apparent: posh buildings, Madison Avenue's flagship boutiques, and doormen in braided livery.

Updated
by Meryl
Pearlstein

Although a glance up and down the manicured grass meridian of Park Avenue may conjure scenes from *Bonfire of the Vanities* or *Gossip Girl*, there are more than palatial apartments, elite private schools, and highfalutin clubs up here—starting with world-class museums. The Metropolitan Museum of Art, the Guggenheim, and many others lie on and around "Museum Mile" (⇨ *Chapter 14*), as do a number of worthy art galleries (⇨ *list at the end of this chapter*). For a local taste of the luxe life, hit up the platinum-card corridor that is Madison Avenue for its lavish boutiques, marble-counter cafés, and the epitome of class, the **Carlyle Hotel**.

Venture east of Lexington Avenue and you encounter a less wealthy—and more diverse—Upper East Side, one inhabited by couples seeking some of the last affordable places to raise a family south of 100th Street, and recent college grads getting a foothold in the city (on weekend nights 2nd Avenue resembles a miles-long fraternity and sorority reunion). One neighborhood particularly worth exploring is northeast-lying Yorkville, especially between 78th and 86th streets east of 2nd Avenue. Once a remote hamlet with a large German population, its remaining ethnic food shops, 19th-century row houses, and, one of the city's best-kept secrets, Carl Schurz Park, make for a good half-day's exploration.

TWO WAYS TO EXPLORE

NEW YORK'S LAP OF LUXURY

Walking up Madison Avenue between East 60th and East 82nd Street is like stepping into the pages of a glossy magazine. Many fashion houses have their flagships here and showcase their lush threads in equally exquisite settings. Compared with the megastores of Midtown, Madison Avenue feels quieter; it's significantly less crowded and more conducive to leisurely shopping (window or otherwise). Beyond clothing, the boutiques here carry baubles to satisfy anyone's champagne wishes, whether it's a box of truffles at **La Maison du Chocolat,** an intriguing read at **Crawford Doyle Booksellers,** or a piece of contemporary silver tableware at **Christofle** (✉ *680 Madison Ave.* ☎*212/308–9390*). When your feet grow tired, grab a seat at a glitzy café and take in the fashion show on the sidewalk. End the day in style with dinner at **Café Boulud** or a drink at one of the neighborhood's sleek lounges or bars.

A NEIGHBORHOOD IN EVERY BLOCK

The Upper East Side is more than just an enclave for the wealthy. In fact, a great way to experience Manhattan's hodgepodge of communities is to walk east from 5th Avenue to the East River—zigzagging to include both avenues and side streets—and watch the neighborhoods change. One good place to start is along lavish East 65th Street, passing the Romanesque **Temple Emanu-El;** the double town house at No. 47 built for Sara Delano Roosevelt and her son, Franklin; and the acclaimed French restaurant **Daniel** across the street. End several blocks and a world away at the 18th-century **Mount Vernon Hotel Museum and Garden** on 61st Street between 1st and York Avenues. Another good route starts at 1040 5th Avenue, at East 85th Street, the former home of Jacqueline Kennedy Onassis, which overlooks the reservoir that now bears her name. Heading east beyond Park Avenue, the town houses and boutiques give way to the quaint secondhand stores and the residential high-rises of **Yorkville** (the one at 185 East 85th appeared in the opening credits of the TV show *The Jeffersons*). Few remaining shops recall the neighborhood's German and Hungarian immigrant past (which earned 2nd Avenue the nickname "Goulash Avenue"); one delicious reminder is the 1937 food shop **Schaller & Weber** (✉ *1654 2nd Ave., at East 86th St.*), where you can pick up homemade bratwurst or imported stollen, cookies, and other goodies. From here, continue east to see the official mayoral residence, **Gracie Mansion,** and the serene riverside **Carl Schurz Park.**

8

TOP ATTRACTIONS

☯ **Carl Schurz Park.** Above the East River, this park, named for a German immigrant who was a prominent newspaper editor in the 19th century, is so tranquil you'd never guess you're directly above FDR Drive. Walk along the promenade, where you can take in views of the river and the Roosevelt Island Lighthouse across the way; to the north are Randall's and Wards islands and newly renamed RFK Bridge (aka the Triborough Bridge)—as well as the more immediate sight of locals pushing strollers, riding bikes, or exercising their dogs. If you're visiting with kids, there's a very worthwhile playground at the 84th Street end with climbing

Where can I find . . . ?

COFFEE	Sant Ambroeus 1000 Madison Ave., by 77th St. The best cappuccino this side of Milan.	Two Little Red Hens 1652 2nd Ave., by 86th St. First-rate joe and the cupcakes to match.
A QUICK BITE	Le Pain Quotidien 1131 Madison Ave., 14 84th St. European open-face sand- wiches and salads.	Totonno's 1544 2nd Ave., by 80th St. No slices, but the best white pizza you'll ever eat.
COCKTAILS	Bemelmans Bar 35 E. 76th St., by Madison Ave. Classy but unpretentious.	Molly Pitcher's Ale House 1641 2nd Ave. by 85th St. A sports bar with 16 beers on tap.

equipment, swings, and other diversions for toddlers and older children. If you enter the park at its 86th Street entrance or you're exiting there, you'll find yourself approaching the grounds of a Federal-style wood-frame house that belies the grandeur of its name—Gracie Mansion.

Fodor's Choice The official mayor's residence, **Gracie Mansion** (⊠ *Carl Schurz Park, East End Ave. opposite 88th St., Upper East Side* ☎ *212/570–4751* 🎫 *$7* ⊙ *45-min guided tours by advance reservation only; Wed. 10–2* Ⓜ *4, 5, 6 to 86th St.*) was built in 1799 by shipping merchant Archibald Gracie, with an enlargement in 1966. Tours of the highly impressive interior—which must be scheduled in advance and take place under limited hours—take you through its history and colorful rooms furnished over centuries and packed with American objets d'art. Nine mayors have lived here since it became the official residence in 1942, but New York City's current mayor, Michael Bloomberg, broke with tradition; he chose to stay in his own 79th Street town house, though he uses this house for meetings and functions. ■**TIP→** If you exit the park at 86th Street, cross East End Avenue for a stroll through Henderson Place, a miniature historic district of 24 connected Queen Anne–style houses in a dead end. The small redbrick houses, built in 1881 "for persons of moderate means," have turrets marking the corner of each block and symmetrical roof gables, pediments, parapets, chimneys, and dormer windows. ⊠ *Carl Schurz Park spans East End Ave. to the East River, E. 84th to E. 90th Sts., Upper East Side* Ⓜ *4, 5, 6 to 86th St.*

ⓒ **Mount Vernon Hotel Museum and Garden.** Built in 1799, this former carriage house became a day hotel (a sort of country club) in 1826. Now restored and owned by the Colonial Dames of America, it provides a glimpse of the days when the city ended at 14th Street and this area was a country escape for New Yorkers. The 45-minute tour passes through the eight rooms that display furniture and artifacts of the Federal and Empire periods. Many rooms have real artifacts like clothes, hats, and fans that children can handle. There is a lovely adjoining garden, designed in an 18th-century style. ⊠ *421 E. 61st St., between York and 1st Aves., Upper East Side* ☎ *212/838–6878* ⊕ *www.mvhm. org* 🖻 *$8* ⊗ *Sept.–July, Tues.–Sun. 11–4* Ⓜ *4, 5, 6, F, N, R, W to 59th St./Lexington Ave.*

WORTH NOTING

Metropolitan Club. The grandest of the über-exclusive clubs abutting Central Park, this Italian Renaissance–style edifice was commissioned by J. P. Morgan in the 1890s when a friend was denied membership to the Union League Club (the "new money" of bankers was too vulgar for New York society at the time). Morgan's grandiose result outdid the other clubs in magnificence, with lordly gates and an ornate lounge overlooking Central Park. Today's members include leaders of foreign countries, presidents of major corporations, and former U.S. president Bill Clinton. ⊠ *1 E. 60th St., near 5th Ave., Upper East Side* Ⓜ *N, Q, R, W to 5th Ave.*

Although **Roosevelt Island** (the 2-mi-long East River slice of land that parallels Manhattan from East 48th to East 85th streets) is now a quasi-suburb of 10,000 people, the vestiges of its infamous asylums, hospitals, and prisons make this an offbeat trip for the historically curious. At the south tip is the **Renwick Ruin,** the eerie remains of a smallpox hospital built in the Gothic Revival style. On a small park at the island's north tip is a lighthouse built in 1872 by island convicts. Most of what's in between (new condominiums and a modern-day hospital) is fairly banal, but riverside esplanades provide nice panoramas of Manhattan. You can get here by subway, but more fun is the five-minute ride on the **Roosevelt Island Tramway,** the only commuter cable car in North America, which lifts you 250 feet in the air, with impressive views of Queens and Manhattan. A visitor center, made from an old trolley kiosk, stands to your left as you exit the tram. Red buses service the island, 25¢ a ride. ⊠ *Tramway entrance at 2nd Ave. and either 59th St. or 60th St., Upper East Side* ☎ *212/832–4555* ⊕ *www.rioc.com, island corporation, www.rihs.us, historical society* 🖻 *$2.25 (subway Metrocard accepted)* ⊗ *Sun.–Thurs. 6 AM–2 AM, Fri. and Sat. 6 AM–3:30 AM; leaves every 15 mins* Ⓜ *F to Roosevelt Island.*

GALLERIES

Many Upper East Side art galleries reside in town houses or upper stories on Madison Avenue. Although their often limited hours and location lend an exclusive air (sometimes they're identified only by the lettering near the buzzer—which you must ring to be let in), once inside, the atmosphere is generally welcoming, even if you're not in the market for a Pollock painting.

Gagosian Gallery. Nicknamed Mr. Go Go for his aggressive approach to art dealing, Larry Gagosian represents some of the most talked-about and playful of contemporary artists. Works by Damien Hirst, Andy Warhol, Tracey Emin, and Jeff Koons have all been exhibited in this massive, multi-level penthouse gallery, one of the three Gagosian spaces

8

in New York alone. ✉ *980 Madison Ave., at E. 77th St., Upper East Side* ☎ *212/744–2313* ⊕ *www.gagosian.com* Ⓜ *6 to 77th St.*

Hirschl & Adler. Although this town house has a selection of European works, it's best known for its American paintings, prints, and decorative arts. The celebrated 19th- and 20th-century artists whose works are featured include Stuart Davis, Childe Hassam, Camille Pissarro, and John Singleton Copley. ✉ *21 E. 70th St., between 5th and Madison Aves., Upper East Side* ☎ *212/535–8810* ⊕ *www.hirschlandadler.com* Ⓜ *6 to 68th St./Hunter College.*

Jane Kahan. This welcoming gallery represents very lofty works. Besides ceramics by Picasso and modern master tapestries, one of this gallery's specialties, you'll see works by late-19th- and early-20th-century modern artists such as Fernand Léger, Joan Miró, and Marc Chagall. ✉ *922 Madison Ave., 2nd fl., between E. 73rd and E. 74th Sts., Upper East Side* ☎ *212/744–1490* ⊕ *www.janekahan.com* Ⓜ *6 to 77th St.*

Knoedler & Company. Knoedler helped many great American collectors, including industrialist Henry Clay Frick, start their collections. Now it represents 20th-century painters such as Helen Frankenthaler, Frank Stella, and John Walker. ✉ *19 E. 70th St., between 5th and Madison Aves., Upper East Side* ☎ *212/794–0550* ⊕ *www.knoedlergallery.com* Ⓜ *6 to 68th St./Hunter College.*

Leo Castelli. Castelli was one of the most influential dealers of the 20th century. He helped foster the careers of many important artists, including one of his first discoveries, Jasper Johns. The gallery continues to show works by Roy Lichtenstein, Ed Ruscha, Jackson Pollock, and other heavies. ✉ *18 E. 77th St., between 5th and Madison Aves., Upper East Side* ☎ *212/249–4470* ⊕ *www.castelligallery.com* Ⓜ *6 to 77th St.*

Mitchell-Innes & Nash. This sleek spot represents the estates of Roy Lichtenstein and Jack Tworkov. ✉ *1018 Madison Ave., between 78th and 79th Sts., Upper East Side* ☎ *212/744–7400* ⊕ *www.miandn.com* Ⓜ *6 to 77th St.*

Sotheby's. Occupying its own 10-story building, this branch of the storied U.K. auction house puts on display many of the items it will be auctioning. A sizeable portion of these are extremely high-profile: a copy of the Magna Carta, Fabergé eggs, rare Tiffany lamps, and Norman Rockwell's 1943 painting *Rosie the Riveter* have all been sold through this Sotheby's. ✉ *1334 York Ave., at E. 72nd St., Upper East Side* ☎ *212/606–7000* ⊕ *www.sothebys.com* Ⓜ *6 to 77th St.*

Wildenstein & Co. This branch of the Wildenstein art empire was the first to take root in New York; its reputation for brilliant holdings was cemented by the acquisition of significant museum-quality collections. Look for French impressionist exhibitions. ✉ *19 E. 64th St., between 5th and Madison Aves., Upper East Side* ☎ *212/879–0500* ⊕ *www.wildenstein.com* Ⓜ *6 to 68th St./Hunter College; F to 63rd-Lexington Ave.*

Central Park

WORD OF MOUTH

"For anybody reading this who has never been to NYC before, listen carefully: get up early, and walk in Central Park on the weekend. Do it. As soon as you take two steps inside, you realize that you are going to LOVE New York with all your heart and soul, and that you want to have her babies."

— MacSporran

OUR BACKYARD

HOW A SWAMP BECAME AN OASIS

1855 Using eminent domain, New York City acquires 843 acres of undeveloped swamp for the then-obscene sum of $5 million, displacing 1,600 people living there.

1857 Frederick Law Olmsted becomes superintendent of a park that does not yet exist. He spends days clearing dirt and evicting squatters and evenings working with architect friend Calvert Vaux on what will become the Greensward plan. The plan is the winning entry in the city's competition to develop a design for the park.

The Panic of 1857 creates widespread unemployment. Thousands of workers begin the task of moving five million cubic yards of dirt and planting more than five mil-

lion trees, plants, and shrubs. Beleaguered by bureaucrats, Olmsted and Vaux unsuccessfully submit their resignations several times.

1873 The Greensward plan is completed. It has been the basic blueprint for Central Park ever since.

Twenty-five million people use Central Park each year; on an average spring weekend day, a quarter-million children and adults flood these precincts from all over Manhattan, frolicking in the 21 playgrounds, bellying up the 150 drinking fountains (water not guaranteed), and collapsing on more than 9,000 benches, which would span seven miles if you lined them up. There are more than 50 monuments and sculptures in the park, but many more ways to make your own fun.

30 ▷ THINGS WE LOVE TO DO IN CENTRAL PARK

1 Take a rowboat out on the Lake

2 Watch the sea lions play at feeding time

3 Walk around the Reservoir

4 Ice-skate at Wollman Rink

5 Watch rollerbladers show off

6 Go bird watching at the Ramble

7 Lie in the grass at Sheep Meadow

8 Rent a bike at the Boathouse

9 Sit on the hill behind the Met Museum

10 See a free concert or play

11 Catch a softball game

12 Clap for the jugglers

13 Remember John Lennon at Strawberry Fields

14 Run through an icy playground sprinkler

15 Rent a gondola and a gondolier

16 Cross the park on the bridle path

17 Stand under the gnarly 72nd Street pergola

18 Hear the Delacorte Clock's musical chimes

19 Crunch the snow before anyone else

20 Pilot a tiny boat at Conservatory Water

21 Stroll through Shakespeare Garden

22 Fish at Harlem Meer

23 Watch dogs play

24 Smell the Conservatory Garden tulips

25 Shoot photos from Bow Bridge

26 Ride the Carousel; wave at everyone

27 People-watch at Bethesda Fountain

28 Picnic on the Great Lawn

29 Pet the bronze Balto statue

30 Climb to the top of Belvedere Castle

(top left) Monarch butterfly pollinates at Conservatory Garden (top center) Hansom driver between fares (top right) Chrysanthemums near Sheep Meadow (center) The skyline with some of the park's 26,000 trees (bottom) Park skaters in the 1860s.

PARK BASICS

Several entrances lead into the park. You can enter from the east, west, south, and north by paved pedestrian walkways, just off Fifth Avenue, Central Park North (110th St.), Central Park West, and Central Park South.

Four roads, or transverses, cut through the park from east to west—66th, 79th, 86th, and 96th streets. The East and West drives are both along the north–south axis; Center Drive enters the south edge of the park at Sixth Avenue and connects with East Drive around 66th Street.

Three Visitor Centers—the Dairy (just south of the 66th St. transverse), Belvedere Castle (just north of the 79th Street transverse), and the Charles A. Dana Discovery Center (at the top of the park at Central Park North)—have directions, park maps, event calendars, and volunteers who can guide you.

TOURS

The **Central Park Conservancy** gives nine different free walking tours of the park on Wednesday, Saturday, and Sunday, based on the season. Most tours are 60 to 90 minutes, and custom tours are also available. If you'd rather go it alone, the Conservancy also offers an audio guide you can follow on your cell phone. Each description is read by a different celebrity or NYC VIP. Dial 646/862-0997 then the extension that corresponds to each landmark and hit pound. For more information, see centralparknyc.org

WHERE AM I?

Along the main loop and some smaller paths, lampposts are marked with location codes. Posts bear a letter—always "E" (for east) or "W" (for west)—followed by four numbers. The first two numbers tell you the nearest cross street. The second two tell you how far you are from either 5th Avenue or Central Park West (depending on whether it's an "E" or "W" post). So E7803 means you're near 78th Street, three posts in from 5th Avenue. For street numbers above 99, the initial "1" is omitted, for example, E0401 (near 104th Street, one post in from 5th Avenue).

PERFORMERS AND THE PARK: SOULMATES

It was inevitable that Central Park, conceived to give so much and ask little in return, would attract artists and arts lovers who feel the same way.

Be they superstars like Paul Simon, Diana Ross, or Barbra Streisand or one of the amateur musicians, animal handlers, or jugglers who delight passersby, they all share the urge to entertain and give back to the city, the park, and its visitors.

Information on scheduled events is provided, but if you can't catch one, don't fret: you'll be rewarded by the serendipitous, particularly on summer and autumn days. Just keep your ears peeled for the music, applause, and laughter. The Central Park Conservancy, in cooperation with other arts patrons, drives a series of free events, including the Harlem Meer Performance Festival and the Great Lawn performances by the Metropolitan Opera and New York Philharmonic. One standout is SummerStage, which yields a cornucopia of international performers.

Perhaps the brass ring of park performances is the more than four-decade-old Shakespeare in the Park, which wows about 80,000 New Yorkers and visitors during any given summer. Free tickets (two per person) are given out starting at 1 PM for the performance that evening, but you need to line up by midmorning or earlier depending on the show. The wait is worth it, though, as casts are often studded with the likes of Meryl Streep, Philip Seymour Hoffman, Natalie Portman, Morgan Freeman, Denzel Washington, and Kevin Kline.

GOINGS ON

Central Park Film Festival: Five nights at end of summer; Rumsey Playfield, near E. 72nd St. entrance.

Harlem Meer Performance Festival: Late June–early Sept., Sun.; at Dana Discovery Center, near Lenox Ave. entrance.

New York Grand Opera: Performances Aug.–Sept.; Naumburg Bandshell; mid-park near 72nd St.

New York Philharmonic: Two performances in June or July; Great Lawn.

Shakespeare in the Park: Late May–early Sept., Tues.–Sun. evenings.

Storytelling: June–Sept., Sat. 11 AM; Hans Christian Andersen Statue.

SummerStage: Late May or June–early Sept.; Rumsey Playfield. Big-name, up-and-coming, and international musicians perform here, mostly for free.

Swedish Cottage Marionette Theatre: Since 1947, puppeteers have entertained in this 1876 Swedish schoolhouse. $8 adults/$5 kids. Mon.–Sun. hours vary; reservations required.

(center) N.Y. Philharmonic associate conductor Xian Zhang (right) Shakespeare's *Much Ado About Nothing*

FROM 59TH TO 72ND ST.

  The busy southern section of Central Park is where most visitors get their first impression. Artists line the entrances off Central Park South, and drivers of horse carriages await passengers. But no matter how many people congregate in this area, you can always find a spot to picnic, ponder, or just take in the beauty, especially on a sunny day.

At the southeast corner of the park, you will come upon one of its prettiest areas, the **Pond**. Swans and ducks cruise on its calm waters, and if you follow the shore line to Gapstow Bridge and look southward, you'll see much of New York City's skyline: to the left (east) are the peak-roofed Sherry-Netherland Hotel, the black-and-white CBS Building, the Chippendale-style top of the Sony Building, and the black-glass Trump Tower. In front of you is the château-style Plaza Hotel.

Opening in late October, **Wollman Memorial Rink** sits inside the park against a backdrop of Central Park South skyscrapers. You can rent skates there, buy snacks, and have a perfect city-type outing. There's a lively feeling here with lots of great music playing and a

terrace so you can watch if you're not into skating.

The **Friedsam Memorial Carousel**, also known as the Central Park Carousel, was built in 1908. It has 58 nearly life-size hand-carved horses and remains a favorite among young and old. Its original Wurlitzer organ plays calliope waltzes, polkas, and standards. Even if you don't need visitor infomation, the **Dairy** is worth a stop for its Swiss-chalet exterior.

If you saw the film *Madagascar,* you may recognize the Central Park Zoo, officially known as the **Central Park Wildlife Center**. Here, the polar bears play at the Polar Circle, monkeys frolic in the open-air Temperate Territory, and the Rain Forest showcases flora and fauna that you wouldn't expect to see in Manhattan. An unusual exhibit is the ant colony—even New York City's zoo has a sense of humor. Stick around to see the sea lion feedings (call for times) and to watch the animal statues dance to a variety of nursery rhymes at the **Delacorte Musical Clock** just outside, on the hour and half-hour from 8 AM to 6 PM.

Wedged between the zoo and the clock is **The Arsenal**, the second-oldest building in the park. Inside

QUICK BITES

Zabar's, on 80th and Broadway, is a perennial pit stop for picnic fare, but you can avail yourself of many grab-and-go eateries and supermarkets on either side of the park. Your best bet for rations: west of Columbus Ave. and east of Park Ave.

If you prefer a more formal (and pricier) bite, **The Boathouse Restaurant** (Midpark at 74th St.) is an open-air restaurant and bar. An adjacent café dishes up good, cheap meals. The Moorish-style Mineral Springs Pavilion (Midpark at W. 69th St.) houses the **Sheep Meadow Café**, which serves sandwiches, salads, and grilled steak and fish.

are rotating exhibits that often cover park history and landscape art.

North of the clock is **Tisch Children's Zoo**, where kids can pet and feed sheep, goats, rabbits, cows, and pigs. Enter through the trunk of a make-believe tree and arrive at The Enchanted Forest, filled with huge "acorns," a climbable "spider web," and hoppable "lily pads."

Perhaps more pettable than any of the zoo's occupants is a decidedly more inert creature, perched on a rockpile at East Drive and 67th Street: **Balto**. Shiny in places from constant touching, this bronze statue commemorates a real-life sled dog who led a team of huskies that carried medicine for 674 mi across perilous ice to Nome, Alaska, during a 1925 diphtheria epidemic.

The Mall, at the intersection of Central Drive and East Drive, is arguably the most elegant area of Central Park. In the beginning of the 20th century, it was the place to see and be seen. Today, these formal walkways are still a wonderful place to stroll, meander, or sit and take in the "parade" under a canopy of the largest collection of American elms in North America. The mall's

southern end, known as **Literary Walk**, is lined with statues of authors and artists such as Robert Burns and William Shakespeare.

(from left to right) Riding on the outside track (recommended) of the Carousel; Getting in a workout on a park drive loop; The Mall, where Dustin Hoffman's character famously teaches his son to ride a bike in *Kramer vs. Kramer*.

The large expanse to the west of the Mall is known as **Sheep Meadow**, the only "beach" that some native New Yorkers have ever known. Join in on a Frisbee or football game, admire the tenacity of kite flyers, or indulge simultaneously in the three simplest meadow pleasures of them all—picnicking, sunbathing, and languorously consuming the newspaper.

There's a reason why the ornate **Bethesda Fountain**, off the 72nd Street transverse, shows up in so many movies set in New York City: the view from the staircase above is one of the most romantic in the city. The statue in the center of the fountain, The Angel of the Waters, designed by Emma Stebbins, is surrounded by four figures symbolizing Temperance, Purity,

Health, and Peace. There's a good amount of New York–style street entertainment here, too, with break dancers, acrobats, and singers all vying for your spare change. It's also a great place to meet, sit, and admire the beautiful lake with its swans For a glimpse of the West Side skyline, walk slightly west to **Cherry Hill**. Originally a watering area for horses, this circular plaza has a small

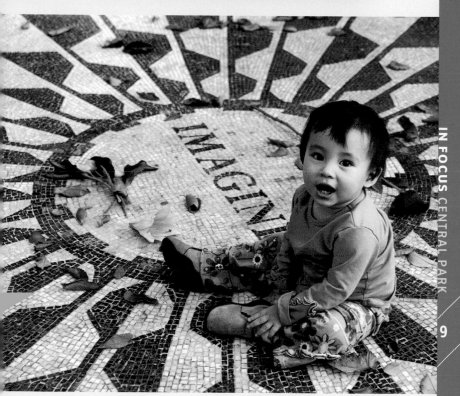

wrought-iron-and-gilt fountain. It's particularly beautiful in the spring when the cherry trees are in full pink-and-white bloom. Farther west are the newly rebuilt Oak Bridge and the lovely Ladies Pavilion, emblematic of the park's past.

Across from the Dakota apartment building on Central Park West is **Strawberry Fields**, named for the Beatles' 1967 classic, "Strawberry Fields Forever." Sometime called the "international garden of peace," this spot draws fans in pilgrimages who reflect among its shrubs, trees, and flower beds, and lay flowers on the black-and-white "Imagine" mosaic. On December 8, hundreds of Beatles fans mark the anniversary of Lennon's death by gathering here.

(top from left to right) Seals cavorting at the zoo; Artist painting the oft-rendered Gapstow bridge, which spans the northeast end of the Pond; Cutting through the park is a classic midday timesaver and post-work respite; Meeting up and chilling out at world-famous Bethesda Fountain (center left); Nighttime at Wollman Rink serves up twinkling skyscrapers and skaters of all abilities (center right); The late John Lennon and his widow, Yoko Ono, often visited the site of what would become Strawberry Fields.

FROM 72ND ST. TO THE RESERVOIR

Playgrounds, lawns, jogging and biking paths, and striking buildings populate the midsection of the park. You can soak up the sun, have a picnic, or even play in a pick-up basketball or baseball game by the Great Lawn; get your cultural fix at the Metropolitan Museum of Art; or train for the next New York City Marathon along the Reservoir.

A block from Fifth Avenue, just north of the 72nd Street entrance, is a peaceful section of the park where you'll find the **Conservatory Water**, named for a conservatory that was never built. Generations of New Yorkers have grown up racing radio-controlled model sailboats here. It's a tradition that happens each Saturday at 10 AM from spring through fall. Smaller boats are available for rent. At the north end is the **Alice in Won-**derland statue; on the west side of the pond, a bronze statue of **Hans Christian Andersen**, the Ugly Duckling at his feet, is the site of Saturday storytelling hours during summer.

At the brick neo-Victorian **Loeb Boathouse** on the park's 18-acre Lake, you can rent a rowboat, kayak, or a bicycle as well as ride in an authentic Venetian gondola. The attached café is a worthy pit stop.

Designed to resemble upstate New York's Adirondack Mountain region, the **Ramble** covers 38 acres and is laced with twisting, climbing paths. This is prime bird-watching territory, since it's a rest stop along a major migratory route and a shelter for many of the more than 230 species of birds that have been sighted in the park; bring your binoculars. Because the Ramble is so dense and isolated,

however, don't wander here alone, or after dark. Head south through the Ramble and you'll come to the beautiful cast-iron **Bow Bridge**, spanning part of the Lake between the Ramble and Bethesda Fountain. From the center of the bridge, you can get a sweeping view of the park as well as of the apartment buildings on both the East Side and the West Side.

North of the Ramble atop Vista Rock, **Belvedere Castle** is the second-highest natural point in the park. If you can't get tickets for Delacorte Theater, you can climb to one of the castle's

(from left to right) Belvedere means "beautiful view" in Italian, a clue to why we climb to the top of Belvedere Castle; Birders, photographers, and couples of all ages are drawn to Bow Bridge; Red-eared slider turtles frolic in Turtle Pond, at the base of Belvedere Castle.

three terraces and look down on the stage. You'll also get a fantastic view of the Great Lawn—it's particularly beautiful during the fall foliage months—and of the park's myriad bird visitors. Since 1919 the castle has served as a U.S. Weather Bureau station, and meteorological instruments are set on top of the tower. If you enter the Castle from the lower level, you can visit the Henry Luce Nature Observa-tory, which has nature exhibits, children's workshops, and educational programs.

Somewhat hidden behind Belvedere Castle, **Shakespeare Garden** is an informal jumble of flowers, trees, and pathways, inspired by the flora mentioned in Shakespeare's plays and poetry. Bronze plaques throughout the garden bear the bard's lines mentioning the plants.

The Great Lawn hums with action on weekends, on warm days, and on most summer evenings, when its baseball fields and picnic grounds fill with city folks and visitors alike. Its 13 acres have endured millions of footsteps, thousands of ball games, hundreds of downpours, dozens of concerts, fireworks displays, and even a papal mass. On a beautiful day, everyone seems to be here.

Chancing upon the 70-ft-tall **Cleopatra's Needle** always feels a bit serendipitous and delightfully jarring, even to the most cynical New Yorkers. This weathered hieroglyphic-covered obelisk began life in Heliopolis, Egypt, around 1500 BC, but has only a little to do with Cleopatra—it's just New York's nickname for the work. It was eventually carted off to Alexandria by the Romans in 12 BC, and

it landed here on January 22, 1881, when the khedive of Egypt made it a gift to the city.

At the southwest corner of the Great Lawn is the fan-shaped **Delacorte Theater,** home to the summer Shakespeare in the Park festival.

If you want to take in several sites in a single brisk jaunt, consider walking the **Naturalists' Walk.** On this path you can wind your way

toward the Swedish Cottage, the Shakespeare Garden, and Belvedere Castle on a landscaped nature

(top, from left to right) A female Canada goose and goslings on Turtle Pond; Cyclists make good use of the bike paths; Bikers as well as joggers boost their egos by outpacing the hansom carriages; Racing boats at Conservatory Water (center) In the 1930s, a flock of mutant sheep was evicted from what would later be known as Sheep Meadow.

walk with spectacular rock outcrops, a stream that attracts bird life, a woodland area with various native trees, stepping-stone trails, and, thankfully, benches.

North of the Great Lawn and the 86th Street transverse is a popular gathering place for New Yorkers and visitors alike, the **Jacqueline Kennedy Onassis Reservoir**. Rain or shine, you'll see runners of all ages and paces heading counterclockwise around the 1.58-mi cinder path that encircles the water. The path in turn is surrounded by hundreds of trees that burst into color in the spring and fall. The 106-acre reservoir, finished in 1862, was a source of fresh water for Manhattanites. It holds more than a billion gallons, but it's no longer used for drinking water; the city's main reservoirs are upstate. From the top of the stairs at 90th Street just off 5th Avenue you have a 360-degree panorama of the city's exciting skyscrapers and often-brilliant sunsets. On the south side, there are benches so you can rest and recharge.

FROM THE RESERVOIR TO 110TH ST.

 More locals than tourists know about the wilder-looking, less-crowded northern part of Central Park, and there are hidden gems lurking here that enable even the most tightly wound among us to decompress, at least for a short while.

Walking along Fifth Avenue to 105th Street, you'll see a magnificent wrought-iron gate—once part of the 5th Avenue mansion of Cornelius Vanderbilt II—that marks the entrance to the **Conservatory Garden**. As you walk through it, you enter a different world, a quiet place that's positively idyllic for reading and slowing down. The Italian-style Central Garden is a beauty, with an expansive lawn, a strikingly simple fountain, and a wisteria-draped pergola that just oozes romance.

The French-inspired **North Garden** is a colorful place with plants placed into elaborate patterns. Springtime is magical—thousands of tulips come to life in a circle around the garden's striking Untermyer Fountain and its three bronze dancers; in the fall, chrysanthemums take their place. The English-style **South Garden** conjures up images from the classic children's book *The Secret Garden*. The garden is

a beautiful hodgepodge of trees, bushes, and flowers that bloom year-round. A free tour is conducted on Saturday at 11 AM, from April through October.

Yes, there are fish in Central Park. At **Harlem Meer**, the third-largest body of water in Central Park, you can borrow fishing poles (identification required) from mid-April through October and try your hand at catching (and releasing) the large-mouth bass, catfish, golden shiners, and bluegills that are stocked in the water's 11 acres. You can also learn about the upper park's geography, ecology, and

history at the Victorian-style **Charles A. Dana Discovery Center**.

Although only a shell of this stone building remains, **Blockhouse #1** serves as a historical marker: the structure was built in 1814 as a cliffside fortification against the British. The area is deserted and dense with trees, so go as a group here.

(left) A pensive raccoon in the park's northern reaches (center); Indulging in a park favorite, soccer, near East Meadow (right); A jogger makes her counterclockwise progress along the Reservoir.

CONTACT INFORMATION

Central Park Conservancy
☎ 212/310–6600 (park events); 212/360–2726 (walking tours)
🌐 www.centralparknyc.org

Central Park SummerStage
☎ 212/360–2756
🌐 www.summerstage.org

Central Park Wildlife Center (Central Park Zoo)
☎ 212/439–6500
🌐 www.centralparkzoo.org

Central Park Visitor Centers
☎ 212/794–6564
🌐 www.nycgovparks.org
☎ 212/639–9675

Charles A. Dana Discovery Center
☎ 212/860–1370
Delacorte Theater
☎ 212/539–8500
🌐 www.publictheater.org

Loeb Boathouse, Boathouse Restaurant
☎ 212/517–2233
🌐 www.thecentral parkboathouse.com

Swedish Cottage Marionette Theatre
☎ 212/988–9093

Wollman Memorial Rink
☎ 212/439–6900
🌐 www.wollmanskating rink.com

PALE MALE: IF YOU CAN MAKE IT HERE . . .

Telescoping the nest from within the park; Pale Male returns home; watching the brood like a hawk; Pale Male's progeny.

Since 1993, the red-tailed hawk Pale Male has sired and raised 23 offspring in a nest on the 12th floor of 927 Fifth Avenue, near 74th St. and one of the city's toniest co-ops. Despite his upscale digs, life hasn't always been easy. He's lost mates (current partner Lola is his fourth), eggs, chicks, and even his home. In 2004, the co-op trashed Pale Male and Lola's nest and blocked their return. Under pressure from the news media and protesters (some holding signs that urged passing drivers to "Honk-4-Hawks"), the board relented less than a month later. A platform was installed to hold the nest, and Pale Male and Lola returned and began to rebuild. Today the hawks' numbers are growing—in 2005 Pale Male's son Junior and his mate, Charlotte, hatched two chicks in their nest at the Trump Parc building.

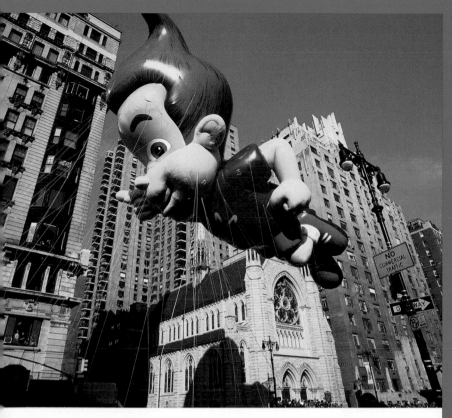

The Upper West Side

INCLUDING MORNINGSIDE HEIGHTS

WORD OF MOUTH

"The Upper West Side is more residential . . . there are of course a few stops that you might want to see and my best suggestions would be: NY Historical Society, Museum of Natural History, The Cloisters, St. John the Divine, Columbia University, and LOTS of good shopping on Broadway from 72nd to 90th Sts."

—travelbuff

GETTING ORIENTED

105th–123rd St.

59th–85th St.

Grant's Tomb
The Cloisters
Riverside Church
Barnard College
Columbia University
Cathedral Church of St. John the Divine
Riverside Park

W. 123rd St.
W. 121st St.
W. 120th St.
W. 119th St.
W. 118th St.
W. 117th St.
W. 116th St.
W. 115th St.
W. 114th St.
W. 113rd St.
W. 112nd St.
W. 111st St.
W. 109th St.
W. 108th St.
W. 107th St.
W. 106th St.
W. 105th St.

Amsterdam Ave.
Morningside Park
Morningside Dr.
Morningside Ave.
Broadway
Riverside Park
Henry Hudson Parkway
Cathedral Pkwy.

B,C
B,C
Central Park N.
St. Nicholas Ave.
CENTRAL PARK

W. 85th St.
W. 84th St.
W. 83rd St.
W. 82nd St.
W. 81st St.
W. 80th St.
W. 79th St.
W. 78th St.
W. 77th St.
W. 76th St.
W. 75th St.
W. 74th St.
W. 73rd St.
W. 72nd St.
W. 71st St.
W. 70th St.
W. 69th St.
W. 68th St.
W. 67th St.
W. 66th St.
W. 65th St.
W. 64th St.
W. 63rd St.
W. 62nd St.
W. 61st St.
W. 60th St.
W. 59th St.

Riverside Park
Zabar's
H&H
Flea Market
Fairway
Ansonia Hotel
Verdi Square
Lincoln Center
Metropolitan Opera House
Time Warner Center
Museum of Arts and Design

American Museum of Natural History
New-York Historical Society
The San Remo
The Dakota
Great Lawn
Belvedere Castle
The Lake
Sheep Meadow
Friedsam Memorial Carousel

Hudson River
Promenade
West Side Highway
Riverside Drive
West End Ave.
Broadway
Amsterdam Ave.
Columbus Ave.
Central Park West

1,2,3
1
1
A,B,C,D,1
Central Park South
Columbus Circle

0   1/4 mile
0   400 meters

MAKING THE MOST OF YOUR TIME

Broadway is hands down the most walkable and interesting thoroughfare on the Upper West Side, due largely to its broad sidewalks and aggressive mélange of retail stores, restaurants, and apartment buildings. If you head north from the Lincoln Center area until about 81st Street (about 0.75 mi) you'll get a feel for the neighborhood's local color, particularly above 72nd Street; up here you'll encounter residents of every conceivable age and ethnicity either shambling or sprinting (New Yorkers wouldn't know a medium pace if they tripped over it, quite literally), street vendors hawking used and newish books, and such beloved landmarks as the 72nd Street subway station, the Beacon Theater, the produce mecca Fairway (the cause of perhaps the most perpetually congested block), and Zabar's, a food spot that launches a memorable assault on all five of your senses—and your wallet.

Should you venture farther uptown you'll encounter a high concentration of apartments and the families that complain about outgrowing them, along with a smattering of decent and enduring restaurants. If you're intrigued by having the city's only Ivy League school close at hand, hop the 1 train to 116th Street and emerge on the east side of the street, which puts you smack in front of Columbia University and its Graduate School of Journalism. Pass through the gates and up the walk for a look at a cluster of buildings so elegant you'll understand why it's an iconic NYC setting.

GETTING HERE

The A, B, C, D, and 1 subway lines will take you to Columbus Circle. From there, the B and C lines run along Central Park, stopping at 72nd, 81st, 86th, 96th, 103rd, and 110th streets. The 1 train runs up Broadway, stopping at 66th, 72nd, 79th, 86th, 96th, 103rd, 110th, 116th, and 125th streets. The 2 and 3 trains, which also go along Broadway, stop at 72nd and 96th.

FODOR'S CHOICE

Columbia University

TOP ATTRACTIONS

American Museum of Natural History (⇨ *Ch. 14)*

Riverside Park

TOP EXPERIENCES

Walking Broadway

Grazing Zabar's

Strolling the Riverside Park boat basin

NEARBY MUSEUMS (⇨ *CH. 14)*

American Museum of Natural History

Museum of Art and Design

New-York Historical Society

AREA SHOPS (⇨ *CH. 17)*

Allan & Suzi

Betsey Johnson

Design Within Reach

Intermix

Kiehl's Since 1851

L'Artisan Parfumeur

Sean

Westsider Rare & Used Books

Z'Baby Company

10

Residents of the Upper West Side (which lies between West 59th and West 110th streets) will proudly tell you that they live in one of the last real neighborhoods in the city. That's highly debatable (as is most everything in NYC), but people actually do know their neighbors in this primarily residential section of Manhattan, and some small owner-operated businesses still flourish.

On weekends stroller-pushing parents cram the sidewalks and shoppers jam the gourmet food emporiums and eclectic stores that line Broadway and Columbus Avenue. Those who aren't shopping are likely to be found in Riverside Park, the neighborhood's communal backyard. Lively avenues, quiet tree-lined side streets, and terrific restaurants and museums, all in a relatively compact area, make this the perfect neighborhood in which to experience life the way the locals do.

Most people think the area north of 106th Street and south of 125th Street on the West Side is just an extension of the Upper West Side. But technically it's called Morningside Heights, and it's largely dominated by Columbia University, along with the cluster of academic and religious institutions—Barnard College, St. Luke's Hospital, and the Cathedral of St. John the Divine, to name a few. Within the gates of the Columbia or Barnard campuses or inside the hushed St. John the Divine, New York City takes on a different character. This is an *uptown* student neighborhood—less hip than the Village, but friendly, fun, and intellectual.

THREE WAYS TO EXPLORE

LIVE LIKE A NEW YORKER

The upper 70s and lower 80s of the Upper West Side depict a very livable, bourgeois New York. Families and young couples settled here, attracted to the peaceful streets combined with the best accessories of urban living: museums and performance centers, plentiful stores, restaurants, gourmet markets, and parks. You could shop and eat your way up and down this stretch of Broadway and Columbus Avenue for hours, turning along tree-lined side streets of gorgeous brownstones. Museum lovers should stroll right up Central Park West—passing the **Dakota** and other elegant residences—to reach the **American Museum of Natural History** and the **New-York Historical Society.** Need a rest? Go for a spot of tea at **Alice's Teacup** (⊠ *102 W. 73rd St.* ☎ *212/799–3006*) or assemble a picnic at **Zabar's** (⊠ *80th St. at Broadway*) and take it to nearby **Riverside Park.**

LIVE LIKE A COLUMBIA STUDENT

Feeling a world away (actually, only 50 blocks) from the hustle of Mid-

town, Morningside Heights moves at the scholarly pace of its many schools, including **Columbia University** and **Barnard College.** Both campuses have beautiful buildings, but the area's architectural winner is the **Cathedral Church of St. John the Divine,** the world's largest Gothic-style cathedral. And when you get hungry, well . . . with students come great cheap eats: you could root out some of the city's best bagels (plenty of candidates on Broadway), peruse a local newspaper at an old-school diner, or sample the authentic Mexican cooking on Amsterdam Avenue.

ENJOY A LITTLE NIGHT MUSIC

Have a night on the town without heading south of Central Park. The Upper West Side is New York's epicenter of the performing arts, especially classical music. Juilliard and other music schools reside here, but the acoustic star is **Lincoln Center** (⇨ *Chapter 15*), a 16-acre collective of concert halls that draws the world's greatest musicians, dancers, and other performers. In 2009 the Center finished major renovations to its Alice Tully Hall and to many of its exteriors, making the complex much more a part of the neighborhood. Its sparkling main plaza (⊠ *W. 63rd St. at Columbus Ave., Upper West Side*), with its gorgeously renovated fountain, is a thrilling place to wander through. You can snag same-day tickets at 25%–50% off at Lincoln Center's new TKTS-like booth, located in the David Rubenstein Atrium on Broadway between 62nd and 63rd streets. The Atrium is also the site for free performances every Thursday at 8:30 PM. Sharing the neighborhood's energetic vibe are busy **Columbus Circle, the new Museum of Art and Design** (⇨ *Chapter 14),* and the 55-story **Time Warner Center.** Locals sneer at the skyscraper complex's mall-like atmosphere, but it includes a great collection of shops, Jazz at Lincoln Center, and a blue-chip lineup of restaurants, including **Per Se, Masa,** and **Porter House New York.**

10

TOP ATTRACTIONS

Fodor's Choice ★   **Columbia University**. Wealthy, private, Ivy League, New York's first college has a pedigree that has always attracted students. But for a visitor, the why-go resides within its campus, bucolic and quietly energetic at once. The main entrance is at 116th Street and Broadway, site of the Columbia Graduate School of Journalism. After walking past the "J-School" on your right, follow the herringbone-patterned brick pathway of College Walk to the main quadrangle, the focal point for campus life. (When you eventually leave, exit through the quad's south gate to West 114th Street's Frat Row, where brownstones housing Columbia's frats display quirky signs of collegiate pride.) Dominating the quad's south side is **Butler Library** (1934), modeled after the Roman Pantheon, which holds the bulk of the university's 8 million books. Looking north, you'll see **Low Memorial Library,** its steps presided over by Daniel Chester French's statue *Alma Mater.* Low is one of the few buildings you can enter (on weekdays), either to check out the former Reading Room and marble rotunda or pick up a map or take a campus tour at the **visitor center.** (Alternatively, you can visit Columbia's Web site ahead of time for a podcast and map covering architectural highlights.) North of the quad (near a cast bronze of August Rodin's *Thinker*) is the interdenominational **St. Paul's Chapel,** an exquisite little Byzantine-style dome church with salmon-color Guastavino tile vaulting inside. (This same design can be seen in Grand Central Terminal and many other buildings throughout the city.) Right across Broadway from Columbia's main gate lies the brick-and-limestone campus of women-only **Barnard College** (212/854–2014), which also gives tours. ⊠ *Morningside Heights* ☎ *212/854–4900* ⊕ *www.columbia.edu* ☉ *Visitor center weekdays 9–5. Tours begin at 1 weekdays from Room 213, Low Library* Ⓜ *1 to 116th St./Columbia University.*

> ### MAN'S BEST FRIEND
>
> The ZIP code 10024—roughly the Upper West Side from West 77th to West 91st Street—has more dogs per capita than any other in the country. You can see dogs of all pedigrees being walked, but the best place to watch the pooches is the enclosed dog run in Theodore Roosevelt Park behind the Museum of Natural History. (In such dog runs everyone's best friends can play off leash.) Dog owners can pick up a gift for Fido around the corner at **Canine Ranch** (⊠ *452A Columbus Ave., between 81st and 82nd Sts.* ☎ *212/787-7387*), a doggie boutique and "barkery."

☺   **Riverside Park**. Walking around concrete and skyscrapers all day, you can easily miss the expansive waterfront park just blocks away. Riverside Park—bordering the Hudson from 58th to 156th streets—dishes out a dose of tranquillity. Its original sections, designed by Olmsted and Vaux of Central Park fame and laid out between 1873 and 1888, are often outshone by Olmsted's "other" park. But with its waterfront bike and walking paths and lighter crowds, Riverside Park holds its own.

One of the park's loveliest attributes is a half-mile waterfront **promenade,** a rare spot in Manhattan where you can walk right along the

Where can I find . . . ?

COFFEE	Hungarian Pastry Shop 1030 Amsterdam Ave. Encourages lingering over a Danish with the Columbia set.	Zabar's Café 2245 Broadway, at 80th St. Brewed with the beans from store next door.
A QUICK BITE	Bouchon Bakery 10 Columbus Circle, Time Warner Center Boulangerie sandwiches and macaroons.	Gray's Papaya 2090 Broadway, at 72nd St. Go to counter, say "two with everything, medium papaya."
COCKTAILS	Emerald Inn 205 Columbus Ave., at 69th St. Longtime neighborhood bar near Lincoln Center.	Hi-Life Bar and Grill 477 Amsterdam Ave., at 83rd St. 1940s movie decor.

river's edge. Reach it by heading through an underpass beneath the West Side Highway at the park's entrance at West 72nd Street and Riverside Drive (look for the **statue of Eleanor Roosevelt**). The promenade takes you past the **79th Street Boat Basin,** where you can watch a flotilla of houseboats bobbing in the water. Above it, a ramp leads to the **Rotunda,** home in summer to the Boat Basin Café, an open-air spot for a burger, a beer, and river views.

At the end of the promenade **and up** a staircase, a community garden explodes with flowers. Cresting a hill along Riverside Drive at West 89th Street stands the Civil War **Soldiers' and Sailors' Monument** (1902, designed by Paul M. Duboy), an imposing 96-foot-high circle of white-marble columns. ⊠ *W. 72nd to W. 156th Sts. between Riverside Dr. and Hudson River, Upper West Side* Ⓜ *1, 2, 3 to 72nd St.*

WORTH NOTING

10

Cathedral Church of St. John the Divine. The largest Gothic-style cathedral in the world, even with its towers and transepts still unfinished, this divine behemoth comfortably asserts its bulk in the country's most vertical city. Episcopal in denomination, it acts as a sanctuary for all, giving special services that include a celebration of New York's gay and lesbian community as well as the annual Blessing of the Bikes, when cyclists of all faiths bring their wheels for a holy-water benediction. The cathedral hosts **musical performances** (⊕ *www.stjohndivine.org*) and has held funerals and memorial services for such artists as Duke Ellington, Jim Henson, George Balanchine, James Baldwin, and Alvin Ailey. The 2009 renovation to fix damage from a 2001 fire left the church looking newly scrubbed and newly magnificent.

Built in two long spurts starting in 1892, the cathedral remains only two-thirds complete. What began as a Romanesque-Byzantine structure under the original architects George Heins and Christopher Grant

Lafarge shifted (upon Heins's death in 1911) to French Gothic under the direction of Gothic Revival purist Ralph Adams Cram. You can spot the juxtaposition of the two medieval styles by comparing the finished Gothic arches, which are pointed, with the still-uncovered arches, which are rounded in the Byzantine style.

To get the full effect of the cathedral's size, approach it from Broadway on West 112th Street. Above the 3-ton central bronze doors is the intricately carved **Portal of Paradise,** which depicts St. John witnessing the Transfiguration of Jesus, and 32 biblical characters. Then step inside to the cavernous nave. Over 600 feet long, it holds some 5,000 worshippers, while the

> ### HOLY HOUSE CATS
>
> On the first Sunday of October the Cathedral Church of St. John the Divine is truly a zoo. In honor of St. Francis, the patron saint of animals, the church holds its usual Sunday service with a twist: the service is attended by men, women, children, dogs, cats, rabbits, hamsters, and the occasional horse, sheep, or ant farm. In past years upward of 3,500 New Yorkers have shown up to have their pets blessed. A procession is led by such guest animals as elephants, camels, llamas, and golden eagles. Seats are first-come, first-served.

162-foot-tall dome crossing could comfortably contain the Statue of Liberty (minus its pedestal). Turn around to see the **Great Rose Window,** made from more than 10,000 pieces of colored glass, the largest stained-glass window in the United States.

At the end of the nave, surrounding the altar, are seven chapels expressing the cathedral's interfaith tradition and international mission—with menorahs, Shinto vases, and dedications to various ethnic groups. The **Saint Saviour Chapel** contains a three-panel bronze altar in white-gold leaf with religious scenes by artist Keith Haring (his last work before he died in 1990).

Outside in the cathedral's south grounds, don't miss the eye-catching **Peace Fountain.** It depicts the struggle of good and evil in the form of the archangel Michael decapitating Satan, whose head hangs from one side. Encircling it are whimsical animals cast in bronze from pieces sculpted by children. ⊠ *1047 Amsterdam Ave., at W. 112th St., Morningside Heights* ☎ *212/316–7540* ⊕ *www.stjohndivine.org* ⌑ *Tours $6* ⊙ *Mon.–Sat. 7–6, Sun. 7–7; tours Tues.–Sat. at 11 and 1, Sun. at 2. A vertical tour with a climb of 124 feet to top is given on Sat. at noon and 2 (reservations required; $15). Sun. services at 8, 9, 11, 1, and 4* Ⓜ *1 to 110th St./Cathedral Pkwy.*

Columbus Circle. This busy traffic circle at Central Park's southwest corner anchors the Upper West Side and makes a good starting place for exploring the neighborhood if you're coming from south of 59th Street. The central 700-ton granite monument (capped by a marble statue of Christopher Columbus) serves as a popular meeting place.

To the west looms the **Time Warner Center,** its 80-story twin glass towers designed by skyscraper architect David M. Childs. The concave front of its lower floors envelops Columbus Circle's curve, while the upper

Famous Film Sites

Breakfast at Tiffany's (1961): Holly Golightly's apartment is at 169 East 71st Street, between Lexington and 3rd avenues.

Ghostbusters (1984): Dana Barrett's apartment is at 55 Central Park West (between 65th and 66th streets). Movie magic made it appear taller than its 19 stories. The Columbia University campus appears near the beginning of the movie.

Hannah and Her Sisters (1986): Hannah lives at the Langham (135 Central Park West, between 73rd and 74th streets), which was Mia Farrow's own apartment.

Manhattan (1979): The film opens at Elaine's restaurant (2nd Avenue between East 88th and East 89th streets). Isaac meets his high-school-age girlfriend outside the Dalton School, at 108 East 89th Street.

Rosemary's Baby (1968): The movie was filmed at the Dakota Apartments (Central Park West, at 72nd Street).

West Side Story (1961): The tenements where the film was shot were later torn down to build Lincoln Center.

When Harry Met Sally (1989): The titular characters run into each other at the Shakespeare & Company bookstore (Lexington Avenue at 69th Street). Later they walk through the sunny modern-art wing at the Metropolitan Museum of Art.

You've Got Mail (1998): Kathleen's bookshop was Maya Schaper Cheese & Antiques (West 69th Street at Columbus Avenue). Joe stood her up at Café Lalo (West 83rd Street, between Amsterdam and Broadway) and rescued her at the checkout at Zabar's (Broadway at 80th Street). The final scene is at the Riverside Park 91st Street Garden.

towers mirror the angle of Broadway and the lines of the city's street grid. Its first three floors house stores that include Sephora, Williams-Sonoma, Borders, and Coach. The third and fourth floors have restaurants, including outrageously priced and acclaimed sushi restaurant Masa (a meal for two starts at $800), plus Thomas Keller's takeout-friendly Bouchon Bakery, and the new A Voce. Above are luxury condos, offices, Thomas Keller's somewhat less-accessible restaurant Per Se, and the Mandarin Oriental Hotel, whose restaurant and bar make a bird's-eye perch for surveying the city below. The performing arts center **Jazz at Lincoln Center** is also in the complex.

Just north of Columbus Circle, the **Trump International Hotel and Tower** fills the wedge of land between Central Park West and Broadway; it's home to the self-named Jean Georges restaurant, where the celebrity chef works his culinary magic. On the circle's south side, at 2 Columbus Circle, is the former Huntington Hartford building, built in 1964. In 2008 it reopened as the new home of the **Museum of Arts and Design** *(⇨ Chapter 14)* after extensive renovation that clad its exterior in lots of zigzags and narrow slits of glass. ☎ *212/258–9800* ⊕ *www.jalc.org* Ⓜ *A, B, C, D, 1 to 59 St./Columbus Circle.*

The Dakota. One of the first residences built on the Upper West Side, the château-style Dakota (1884) remains an architectural fixture with its picturesque gables, gaslights, copper turrets, and a central courtyard. Celebrity residents have included Boris Karloff, Rudolf Nureyev, José Ferrer, Rosemary Clooney, Lauren Bacall, Leonard Bernstein, Gilda Radner, and Connie Chung, but none more famous than John Lennon, who in 1980 was shot and killed at the Dakota's gate by a deranged fan. ✉ *1 W. 72nd St., at Central Park W, Upper West Side* Ⓜ *B, C to 72nd St.*

Grant's Tomb *(General Grant National Memorial).* Walk through upper Riverside Park and you're sure to notice this towering granite mausoleum (1897), the final

AT THE ANSONIA

You'd have to stare at the sidewalk to miss the turrets, sloped roof, and filigreed iron balconies of the Ansonia Hotel (Broadway between 73rd and 74th streets), a Beaux-Arts throwback famous for its many interesting residents. Babe Ruth, Igor Stravinsky, and Theodore Dreiser all lived there, and Bette Midler got her start singing in the gay Continental Baths that once occupied the basement. (Her accompanist was Barry Manilow.)

resting place of Civil War general and two-term president Ulysses S. Grant and his wife Julia Dent Grant. But who's buried here, as the old joke goes? Nobody—they're *entombed* in a crypt beneath a domed rotunda, surrounded by photographs and Grant memorabilia. Once a more popular sight than the Statue of Liberty, this pillared Classical Revival edifice feels more like a relic of yesteryear. The words engraved on the tomb, LET US HAVE PEACE, recall Grant's speech to the Republican convention upon his presidential nomination. Surrounding the memorial are swoopy benches covered with colorful mosaic tiles. Made in the 1970s as a public art project, they are now as beloved as they are incongruous with the grand memorial they surround. ✉ *Riverside Dr. at W. 122nd St., Morningside Heights* ☎ *212/666–1640* ⊕ *www.nps.gov/gegr* ✂ *Free* ☉ *Daily 9–5; 20-min tours at 10, noon, 2 and 4* Ⓜ *1 to 116th St. or 125th St.*

The San Remo. You're likely to notice its twin towers rising above the trees in Central Park, looking like the fairy-tale spires of some urban palace, which it more or less is. Rita Hayworth, Paul Simon, Diane Keaton, and Dustin Hoffman are among the celebrities who've resided in the 1930 building's giant apartments. At their peaks, the towers recede into circular columned Greek temples (modeled after the cathedral in Seville, Spain). They make a useful "compass" if you get disoriented in Central Park and want to know which way is west. ✉ *145 Central Park W, between W. 74th and W. 75th Sts., Upper West Side* Ⓜ *B, C to 72nd St.*

Harlem

WORD OF MOUTH

"When we were in NYC we tried to book a show at the Blue Note but couldn't get in so we tried the Lenox Lounge in Harlem instead. I thought it was great! Wonderful art deco interior, an intimate area, and the 4-piece band was terrific."

—baysidegirl

GETTING ORIENTED

Highbridge Park

C M   **B,D** M

W. 155th St.

Hispanic Society of America

409 Edgecombe Avenue

W. 163rd St.

Sugar Hill

W. 152nd St.

Dance Theatre of Harlem

W. 151st St.

W. 150th St.

W. 149th St.

W. 148th St.

M³

W. 147th St.

W. 146th St.

M **1** HAMILTON HEIGHTS

M **A,B,C,D**

³

W. 145th St.

THE BRONX

145 St. Bridge

Harlem River

Madison Ave. Bridge

W. 144th St.

W. 143rd St.

W. 142nd St.

W. 141st St.

W. 140th St.

Strivers' Row

W. 139th St.

City College

W. 138th St.

M **1**

ST. NICHOLAS HISTORIC DISTRICT

Abyssinian Baptist Church

W. 137th St.

W. 136th St.

M **2,3**

E. 135th St.

W. 135th St.

M **B,C**

W. 134th St.

W. 133rd St.

W. 132nd St.

E. 131st St.

W. 130th St.

Astor Row Houses

E. 129th St.

The Cotton Club

W. 129th St.

M **1**

W. 128th St.

Sylvia's Soul Food Restaurant

125th St. Metro North Station

W. 127th St.

W. 126th St.

Apollo Theatre

M **A,B,C,D**

African Sq.

M **2,3**

Dr. Martin Luther King Jr. Blvd. (125th St.)

Studio Museum in Harlem

W. 124th St.

Lenox Lounge

W. 123rd St.

W. 122nd St.

HARLEM

W. 121st St.

Marcus Garvey Park

W. 120th St.

E. 119th St.

Barnard College

Columbia University

W. 116th St.

Canaan Baptist Church of Christ

Minton's Play House

E. 117th St.

M **B,C**

M **2,3**

First Corinthian Baptist Church

W. 114th St.

Malcolm Shabazz Harlem Market

E. 115th St.

Masjid Malcolm Shabazz

W. 113th St.

W. 112th St.

W. 111th St.

M **1**

M **B,C**

M **2,3**

W. 109th St.

Central Park North

CENTRAL PARK

Harlem Meer

E. 110th St.

0   1/4 mile

0   400 meters

Riverside Dr.
Riverside Park
Henry Hudson Pkwy
Broadway
Amsterdam Ave.
Convent Ave.
St. Nicholas Ave.
Jackie Robinson Park
Frederick Douglass Blvd.
St. Nicholas Park
Adam Clayton Powell Jr. Blvd.
Lenox Ave./Malcolm X Blvd.
Fifth Ave.
Park Ave.
Madison Ave.
Mt. Morris Park West
Dr. Martin Luther King Jr. Blvd.
Morningside Park
(8th Ave.)
(7th Ave.)
Sixth Ave.
St. Nicholas Ave.
Central Park W.
Harlem River Dr.

11

MAKING THE MOST OF YOUR TIME

One underhyped simple pleasure in Harlem is shopping: you can make your way along 125th Street, where brands like H&M coexist with local favorites like Carol's Daughter. While you're at it, visit the Studio Museum in Harlem, which showcases contemporary works of Harlem's artist community.

GETTING HERE AND AROUND

The 2 and 3 subway lines stop on Lenox Avenue; the 1 goes along Broadway; and the A, B, C, and D trains travel along St. Nicholas and 8th avenues. And yes, as the song goes, the A train is still among the quickest ways to Harlem.

The city's north–south avenues take on different names in Harlem: 6th Avenue is called Malcolm X Boulevard *and* Lenox Avenue (its former name); 7th Avenue is Adam Clayton Powell Jr. Boulevard; and 8th Avenue is Frederick Douglass Boulevard. West 125th Street, the major east–west street, is sometimes called Dr. Martin Luther King Jr. Boulevard.

SAFETY

In the past two decades Harlem's crime rate has decreased far below the heights it reached in the 1980s. It is still advisable, however, to use common sense. Stay close to main commercial areas like 125th Street and Lenox Avenue if you visit at night.

WORD OF MOUTH (WWW.FODORS.COM/FORUMS)

"We are thinking of doing [a church gospel] tour. I have some misgivings about using a church service as entertainment. Anyone done this?" —susan4

"If it bothers you, there are plenty of other options . . . You can go by yourself to a gospel service, or BB King's in Times Square has a gospel brunch with the Harlem Gospel choir on Sundays." —mclaurie

TOP ATTRACTIONS

Abyssinian Baptist Church

Canaan Baptist Church of Christ

Strivers' Row

Sugar Hill

TOP EXPERIENCES

A jazz session at Lenox Lounge

Attending a gospel service

Walking 125th Street

Indulging in a soul-food lunch or dinner

BEST FOR KIDS

Marcus Garvey Park

NEARBY MUSEUMS (⇨ *CH. 14*)

Hispanic Society of America

Studio Museum in Harlem

AREA SHOPS (⇨ *CH. 17*)

H&M

M.A.C.

WHERE TO EAT (⇨ *CH. 18*)

Amy Ruth's

Miss Mamie's Spoonbread Too

Native

SNAPSHOT-WORTHY

Apollo Theatre

First Corinthian Baptist Church

Masjid Malcolm Shabazz

Strivers' Row

Sightseeing
★★
Nightlife
★★★★
Dining
★★★
Lodging
★★
Shopping
★

Harlem is known throughout the world as a center of culture, music, and African-American life. Today's Harlem, however, is a very different Harlem from that of 20 years ago, when many considered its attractions inaccessible or the location dangerous. Today more and more renovated and new buildings join such historic jewels as the Apollo Theatre, architecturally splendid churches, and cultural magnets like the Studio Museum in Harlem and the Schomburg Center for Research in Black Culture.

Updated
by Meryl
Pearlstein

As overcrowded apartments and expensive rents downtown make Harlem a more and more attractive area, black (and, increasingly, white) professionals and young families are restoring many of Harlem's classic brownstone and limestone buildings. This new growth has brought much new life and commerce to the community, but sadly it has also priced out some longtime residents.

Back in 2001, former president Bill Clinton's selection of 55 West 125th Street as the site of his New York office was an inspiration to businesses considering a move to Harlem; now the busy thoroughfare sprouts outposts of Starbucks, Old Navy, MAC Cosmetics, and H&M side-by-side with local shops like Carol's Daughter. Outside, the sidewalk is a continuous traffic jam of people, offering a concentrated glimpse of neighborhood life. Pedestrians compete with street-side hawkers selling bootleg CDs and DVDs, books, and homemade essential oils in nondescript bottles.

THREE WAYS TO EXPLORE

FIND RELIGION IN HARLEM
Some of Harlem's most interesting religious buildings—especially its Baptist churches—stand on 116th Street. You can admire the ornate theatrical facade of the giant **First Corinthian Baptist Church** or fill your

11

soul with the mellifluous gospel music of the **Canaan Baptist Church of Christ's** choir during a Sunday service. Take a hint from the parishioners and follow up with the smothered chicken and waffles at **Amy Ruth's**. After lunch, walk by the plain but colorful **Masjid Malcolm Shabazz**—a mosque primarily attended by West Africans and African-Americans. Finish at **Malcolm Shabazz Harlem Market,** where you can stock up on jewelry, African masks, and caftans at good prices.

RELIVE THE JAZZ AGE

Many of Harlem's historic jazz venues (mostly found on 125th Street) are still active, so you can pay respect to the legends like Duke Ellington and Louis Armstrong, then listen to a legend-in-the-making. A giant digital marquee announces the **Apollo Theatre,** where jazz and funk godfather James Brown debuted in 1956 and was laid out in splendor following his death in 2006. (Following this tradition, king of pop Michael Jackson was also given a final farewell here in 2009.) Around the corner, the **Lenox Lounge** buzzes with action; eat here and be transported back in time; or enjoy a swing concert or gospel brunch at the **Cotton Club** (⊠ *656 W. 125th St., off West Side Hwy.*), which continues the tradition of the celebrated original (closed in 1935). Continue the pilgrimage at the **Minton's Playhouse** (⊠ *206 W. 118th St.*), the birthplace of bebop, where Thelonious Monk was house pianist in the 1940s. It reopened in 2006 after being closed since 1974.

Do a little preconcert shopping along 125th Street for herbal pedicures at Carol's Daughter or snakeskin belts at Men's Walker Shoes. Or check out the exhibitions of contemporary African-American–oriented artworks at the **Studio Museum in Harlem.**

HUNT THE GHOSTS OF THE HARLEM RENAISSANCE

Take the subway up to the 140s and lower 150s (between Edgecombe and Convent avenues) and you can find yourself on a rocky bluff above lower Harlem. Here, in the enclaves of **Sugar Hill** and **Hamilton Heights,** the Harlem elite of the late 1800s and early 1900s could literally "look down on" their neighbors. Some blocks will require more imagination than others to re-create their former glory (especially Edgecombe Avenue, where many leaders of the Harlem Renaissance once resided), but the brownstones of Convent Avenue and adjacent **Hamilton Terrace** remain in mint condition. Finish your walk at **Strivers' Row,** a pair of posh blocks that have attracted well-to-do African-Americans since 1919.

TOP ATTRACTIONS

Abyssinian Baptist Church. This 1923 Gothic-style church holds one of Harlem's richest legacies, dating to 1808 when a group of parishioners defected from the segregated First Baptist Church of New York City and established the first African-American Baptist church in New York State. Among its legendary pastors was Adam Clayton Powell Jr., a powerful orator and civil rights leader and the first black U.S. congressman. Today sermons by pastor Calvin Butts III are fiery, and the seven choirs are excellent. Because of its services' popularity, the church maintains separate lines for parishioners and tourists. Dress

Where can I find . . . ?

COFFEE	Hue-Man Bookstore & Cafe 2319 Frederick Douglass Blvd., near 125th St. Good joe and fun bookstore.	Patisserie des Ambassades 2200 Frederick Douglass Blvd. Classic combo of pastries and java.
A QUICK BITE	Uptown Juice Bar 54 W. 125th St. Tasty veggie fare; snacks; "detoxifying" juices.	Make My Cake 121 St. Nicholas Ave., at 116th St. Calling all red velvet cake aficionados!
COCKTAILS	The Den 2150 5th Ave., near 132nd St. Hidden gem, specialty drinks.	Lenox Lounge 288 Lenox Ave., near 125th St. Quintessential Harlem jazz spot.

your best, and get there early on Sunday holidays. ✉ *132 Odell Clark Pl., W. 138th St., between Adam Clayton Powell Jr. Blvd., 7th Ave., and Malcolm X Blvd., Lenox Ave./6th Ave., Harlem* ☏ *212/862–7474* ⊕ *www.abyssinian.org* ☉ *Sun. services at 9 and 11* Ⓜ *2, 3 to 135th St.*

Canaan Baptist Church of Christ. The heavenly gospel music during Sunday-morning services makes up for this church's concrete-box-like exterior (visitors may enter once parishioners are seated). Pastor emeritus Wyatt Tee Walker worked with Dr. Martin Luther King Jr. (who delivered his famous "A Knock at Midnight" sermon here). ✉ *132 W. 116th St., between Malcolm X Blvd., Lenox Ave./6th Ave., and Adam Clayton Powell Jr. Blvd., 7th Ave., Harlem* ☏ *212/866–0301* ☉ *Services Sun. morning at 8 and 11* AM Ⓜ *2, 3 to 116th St.*

Hamilton Heights. To taste this neighborhood's Harlem Renaissance days, walk down tree-lined Convent Avenue, detouring onto adjacent **Hamilton Terrace,** and see a time capsule of elegant stone row houses in mint condition. (Until 2008 Hamilton Grange, founding father Alexander Hamilton's Federal-style mansion, stood at 287 Convent Avenue. The clapboard structure, owned by the National Park Service, has been moved around the corner to Saint Nicholas Park. At this writing it's closed for refurbishment and scheduled to reopen for tours in 2010: visit ⊕ *www.nps.gov/hagr* for updates). Continue down Convent Avenue and see the Gothic spires (1905) of **City College** loom seemingly out of nowhere. Meander through the Oxford-inspired campus (try to spot the rebellious sycamore that "ate" the KEEP OFF THE GRASS sign) before heading east through the park to Strivers' Row. ✉ *Convent Ave. between 138th and 150th Sts., Harlem* Ⓜ *A, B, C, D to 145th St.*

Strivers' Row. Some of the few remaining private service alleys that once ran behind the city's town houses (where deliveries would arrive via horse and cart) lie behind these elegant 1890s Georgian and neo-Italian homes, visible through iron gates. Note the gatepost between No. 251 and 253 on West 138th Street that says, "Private Road. Walk Your

Horses." When the houses failed to sell to whites, the properties on these blocks were sold to African-American doctors, lawyers, and other professionals. The Row earned its enduring nickname in the 1920s from less affluent Harlemites who felt its residents were "striving" to become well-to-do. ⊠ *W. 138th and W. 139th Sts. between Adam Clayton Powell Jr. and Frederick Douglass Blvds., Harlem* Ⓜ *B, C to 135th St.*

WORTH NOTING

First Corinthian Baptist Church. One of the most ornate structures in Harlem, this church kicked off its life in 1913 as the Regent Theatre, one of the country's early movie palaces that replaced the nickelodeons. Its elaborately columned and arched facade loosely resembles the Doges' Palace in Venice. The Regent was sold to the church in 1964. ⊠ *1912 Adam Clayton Powell Jr. Blvd., 7th Ave., Harlem* ☎ *212/864–5976* ☉ *Services Sun. at 8 and 10:45* Ⓜ *2, 3 to 116th St.*

☙ **Marcus Garvey Park**. At the center of this historic, tree-filled public square, atop a 70-foot-high outcrop of Manhattan schist (the same bedrock that anchors our skyscrapers) stands a 47-foot cast-iron **watchtower** (Julius Kroel, 1865), the last remnant of a citywide network used to spot and report fires in pre-telephone days. Around it, an **Acropolis** provides great views of Manhattan, and of the handsome neoclassical row houses of **Mount Morris Park Historic District,** which extends west from the park. ⊠ *Interrupts 5th Ave. between W. 120th and W. 124th Sts., Madison Ave. to Mt. Morris Park W, Harlem* ⊕ *www.east-harlem. com/parks_mg.htm* Ⓜ *2, 3 to 125th St.*

Masjid Malcolm Shabazz *(Mosque)*. Talk about religious conversions. In the mid-'60s the Lenox Casino was transformed into this house of worship and cultural center, and given bright yellow arches and a huge green onion dome that loudly proclaims its presence in a neighborhood of churches. Once functioning as Temple No. 7 under the Nation of Islam with a message of pro-black racism, the mosque was bombed after the assassination of Malcolm X, who had preached here. It was then rebuilt and renamed for the name Malcolm took at the end of his life, El-Hajj Malik Shabazz; its philosophy now is one of inclusion. These days the Sunni congregation has a large proportion of immigrants from Senegal, many of whom live in and around 116th Street. Next door is Graceline Court, a 16-story luxury condominium building that opened in 2008. Note how it cantilevers somewhat awkwardly over the mosque. ⊠ *102 W. 116th St., at Malcolm X Blvd., Lenox Ave./6th Ave., Harlem* ☎ *212/662–2200* Ⓜ *2, 3 to 116th St.*

Sugar Hill. Standing on the bluff of Sugar Hill overlooking Jackie Robinson Park, outside **409 Edgecombe Avenue,** you'd never guess that here resided such influential African-Americans as NAACP founder W.E.B. DuBois and Supreme Court Justice Thurgood Marshall, or that farther north at **555 Edgecombe,** writers Langston Hughes and Zora Neale Hurston and jazz musicians Duke Ellington, Count Basie, and others lived and played (unless you catch the Sunday jazz concerts here from 4 to 6:30 PM in Apartment 3F). Harlem's society hill from the 1920s to the 1950s is today another partly cleaned-up "evolving"

D.I.Y. Harlem Gospel Tours

The typical "gospel tour" includes only a 20-minute stop at a church to hear some of the sermon and the gospel music. Then you're off (via bus) to another Harlem sight or to a soul-food brunch. Prices range from $35 to $80. The tours are an expeditious, if not authentic, way to experience a bit of Harlem.

Tours garner mixed reactions from church officials and parishioners. Some see it as an opportunity to broaden horizons and encourage diversity. But others find tours disruptive and complain that tourists take seats away from regular parishioners (churches regularly fill to capacity). If you decide to go on one of these tours, remember that parishioners do not consider the service, or themselves, to be tourist attractions. Also, dress nicely. Harlem churchgoers take the term "Sunday best" to heart, and are impressively decked out. Be as quiet as possible and avoid taking photos or videos.

For a rich gospel-church experience, do your own tour. The following are some of the uptown churches with gospel choirs:

Abyssinian Baptist Church is one of the few churches that does not allow tour groups. Services are at 9 and 11. **Canaan Baptist Church of Christ** has services at 8 and 11. **Convent Avenue Baptist Church** (✉ *420 W. 145th St., between Convent and St. Nicholas Aves., Harlem* ☎ *212/234–6767* ⊕ *www.conventchurch.org*) has services at 8, 11, and 6. **First Corinthian Baptist Church** has services at 8 and 10:45.

Greater Refuge Temple (✉ *2081 Adam Clayton Powell Jr. Blvd., at 124th St., Harlem* ☎ *212/866–1700*) has services at and 11, 4, and 7. **Memorial Baptist Church** (✉ *141 W. 115th St., between Adam Clayton Powell Jr. and Malcolm X Blvds., Harlem* ☎ *212/663–8830* ⊕ *www. mbcvisionharlem.org*) has services at 8 and 11.

neighborhood, on its way to regentrification. Walk over to Hamilton Heights for a better-preserved taste of the Harlem Renaissance years. ■**TIP**➔ If you're here after 9:30 PM, drop by the basement jazz club St. Nick's Pub (✉ 773 St. Nicholas Ave., near 149th St. ☎ 212/283–9728), a laid-back local fixture that's been around for ages. Bring some bills to stuff into the tip jar that circulates, grab a drink, and enjoy the late-night jam sessions. ✉ *Bounded by 145th and 155th Sts. and Edgecombe and St. Nicholas Aves., Harlem* Ⓜ *A, B, C, D to 145th St.*

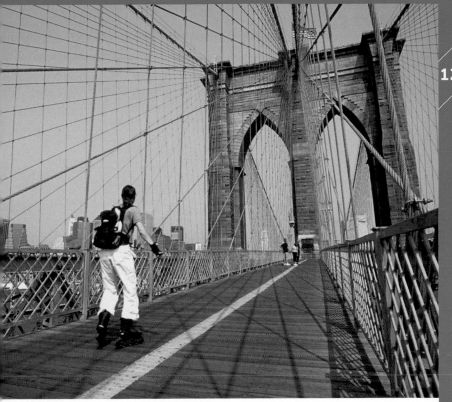

Brooklyn

WORD OF MOUTH

"Walking over the Brooklyn Bridge was a really neat experience; I liked being elevated above the bridge deck, with the traffic below us on both sides. . . . A word of caution . . . be sure to stay out of the bike lane, as the cyclists come whipping past you like they're being chased by the law."

—artstuff

GETTING ORIENTED

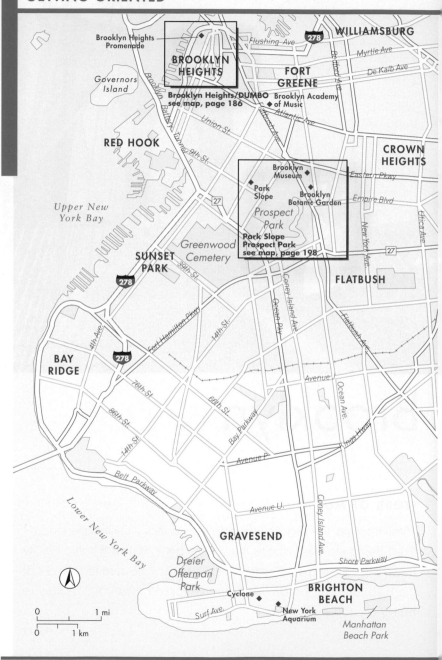

WILLIAMSBURG

Myrtle Ave

De Kalb Ave

Flushing Ave

Brooklyn Heights
Promenade

**BROOKLYN
HEIGHTS**

Governors
Island

**FORT
GREENE**

**Brooklyn Heights/DUMBO
see map, page 186**

Brooklyn Academy
of Music

Union St.

9th St.

Atlantic Ave.

RED HOOK

**CROWN
HEIGHTS**

*Upper New
York Bay*

Brooklyn
Museum

Eastern Pkwy

Park
Slope

Brooklyn
Botanic Garden

Empire Blvd

*Prospect
Park*

New York Ave.

27

Utica Ave.

**Park Slope
Prospect Park
see map, page 198**

*Greenwood
Cemetery*

**SUNSET
PARK**

39th St.

27

FLATBUSH

278

14th St.

Fort Hamilton Pkwy

Coney Island Ave.

Ocean Pky

Flatbush Ave.

**BAY
RIDGE**

278

76th St.

66th St.

Avenue H

Ocean Ave.

86th St.

14th St.

Bay Parkway

Avenue P

Belt Parkway

Avenue U.

Coney Island Ave.

Lower New York Bay

GRAVESEND

*Dreier
Offerman
Park*

Cyclone

Shore Parkway

**BRIGHTON
BEACH**

New York
Aquarium

Surf Ave.

*Manhattan
Beach Park*

0 ——— 1 mi

0 ——— 1 km

MAKING THE MOST OF YOUR TIME

The best way to enter this borough is by its most majestic bridge. Walking across the wooden pedestrian path of the Brooklyn Bridge—a classic New York experience—takes about 30 minutes, all worth it for the panoramic views of the sky-lines and the harbor. It's also a great way to transition from the bustle of Manhattan into Brooklyn's slower pace. After you exit onto Cadman Plaza, walk southwest to poke around Brooklyn Heights, a charming neighborhood of posh 19th-century brownstone homes, or walk north into the hip neigh-borhood of DUMBO to grab a slice at legendary Grimaldi's Pizza. To get to Brooklyn's sights more quickly, take the 2 or 3 train to the Eastern Parkway/Brooklyn Museum stop. The museum, the Botanic Garden, the Children's Museum, and Prospect Park are all close, and a weekend trolley makes it easy to combine attractions.

GETTING HERE

To get to Williamsburg, take the L train from any 14th Street station in Manhattan to Bedford Avenue, the first stop in Brooklyn. You can reach Brooklyn Heights by the 2 or 3 train to Clark Street, the M or R to Court Street, or the 4 or 5 to Borough Hall. To get to DUMBO, take the F train to York Street or walk from Brooklyn Heights. The F to 7th Avenue will take you to the center of Park Slope. From there, walk uphill to reach Prospect Park or walk north on 7th Avenue to sample the shops. The hipper boutiques and eateries are two long blocks west, on 5th Avenue. Closer subway stops to 5th Avenue include M or R to Union Street. To reach the Brooklyn Museum, Brooklyn Botanic Garden, and Prospect Park take the 2 or 3 train to Eastern Parkway/Brooklyn Museum. Coney Island is the last stop on the D, F, N, and Q trains, and the Q or B will take you to Brighton Beach. Allow a good part of the day for these trips, since it takes about an hour to reach the ocean from Manhattan.

FODOR'S CHOICE

The Brooklyn Bridge

Brooklyn Heights Promenade

Coney Island

TOP EXPERIENCES

Rocking out late at night in Williamsburg

Screaming at the top of the Cyclone roller coaster

Smelling the Roses at the Brooklyn Botanic Garden

BEST FOR KIDS

Brooklyn Children's Museum

Brooklyn Ice Cream Factory

Brooklyn Superhero Supply Co.

Keyspan Park

Lefferts Historic House

New York Aquarium

Transit Museum

NEARBY MUSEUMS

Brooklyn Children's Museum

Brooklyn Historical Society

Brooklyn Museum

Coney Island Museum

C.V. Starr Bonsai Museum at the Brooklyn Botanic Garden

Transit Museum

AREA SHOPS

Bird

Future Perfect

Jacques Torres Chocolate

Spring

Sightseeing
★★★
Nightlife
★★★★
Dining
★★★★
Lodging
★
Shopping
★★★

Updated by
Alexander
Basek

Hardly Manhattan's wimpy sidekick, Brooklyn is the largest and most populous of all the boroughs, with more than 2.5 million residents. If it were an independent city, it would be the fourth-largest in the country. Diverse neighborhoods share a down-to-earth character: neighborly chats take place on the steps of brownstones, family-owned businesses preserve their heritages, and patrons at restaurants and bars are happy to eat and drink rather than "see and be seen." It's largely Brooklyn that has lent New York its streetwise and sincere personality, famously captured in films such as *Do the Right Thing, Moonstruck,* and *Brighton Beach Memoirs.*

THREE WAYS TO EXPLORE

LOCAL LANDMARKS AND PERFECT PARKS

In the midst of urban bustle, Brooklyn is full of green getaways and natural attractions. Relax like real Brooklynites by packing a picnic lunch and heading to **Prospect Park**'s lush Long Meadow. Or find its hidden nooks and surprises, like the zoo, the ravine, and great summer concerts. Next door is the breathtaking **Brooklyn Botanic Garden**. Take an unexpected detour to **Green-Wood Cemetery**, where you can walk along its hills and lakes or hunt for the headstones of V.I.P.s among the R.I.P.s. And no tour of Brooklyn would be complete without a pilgrimage to **Coney Island**, where the boardwalk, hot dogs, and amusement parks have thrilled generations of New Yorkers.

BOUTIQUE BONANZA

Manhattan is slowly being taken over by chain stores, but Brooklyn's boutique scene is thriving. It's easy to spend an afternoon looking at ladylike knits or punchy, bright-color sundresses, chuckling at ironic home items (resin deer antlers, anyone?), or simply discovering new designers. Start off in Williamsburg at **Future Perfect**, a modern-home-decor lover's dream, then hop over to other Brooklyn spots like **Catbird, Mandate of Heaven,** or **Noisette.** In Park Slope, stroll down 5th and 7th avenues for a more sophisticated range. And over in Carroll Gardens, combine boutique hopping with lunch at one of the celebrated restaurants on **Smith Street.**

EPICURE'S PARADISE

Eating your way through Brooklyn is one of the best ways to experience the mix of old, new, and immigrant cultures that make the borough so vibrant. Carroll Gardens perhaps best epitomizes this mix; here 50 years of Italian heritage meet a more recent and highly acclaimed restaurant scene on Smith Street. Take the F train to Bergen and stroll south on Smith to standout eateries like **Char No. 4** or **Saul,** then walk off your meal along leafy Court Street, stopping at one of its bakeries for dessert. (Try **Sweet Melissa** for chocolate covered graham crackers.) For more international adventures, head to **Brighton Beach** for smoked fish at elaborate Russian palaces beneath the train tracks or browse the Central Asian eateries on Brighton Beach Avenue. (**Café Kashkar** is a local fave.) In Sunset Park, wallet-friendly fare from Latin America (clustered on 5th Avenue) and East Asia (on 8th Avenue) compete for your taste buds' time. **Ba Xuyen,** on 8th Avenue between 42nd and 43rd streets, vies for the title of New York's best bahn mi (Vietnamese hero sandwiches), while **Tacos Matamoros,** at 5th Avenue and 45th Street, is full of locals eating authentic and adventurous tacos and tortas.

WHAT IT COSTS					
	¢	$	$$	$$$	$$$$
AT DINNER	under $10	$10–$17	$18–$24	$25–$35	over $35

Price per person for a median main course or equivalent combination of smaller dishes. Note: if a restaurant offers only prix-fixe (set-price) meals, it has been given the price category that reflects the full prix-fixe price.

BROOKLYN HEIGHTS

Brooklyn's toniest neighborhood offers residents something wealthy Manhattanites will never have: a stunning view of the Manhattan skyline from the **Brooklyn Heights Promenade.** First developed in the mid-1800s as the business center of the then-independent city of Brooklyn, it boasts historic cobblestone streets of pristine brownstones.

In the early to mid-20th century the Heights was a bohemian haven, home to writers like Arthur Miller, Truman Capote, Alfred Kazin, Marianne Moore, Norman Mailer, and W.E.B. DuBois. In the '80s a new generation of gentrifiers moved in, and—even with a softening real estate market—homes here are still as pricey as their Manhattan counterparts.

Much of its early architecture has been preserved, thanks to its designation as New York's first historic district in the 1960s. Some 600 buildings built in the 19th century represent a wide range of American building styles. Many of the best line **Columbia Heights,** a residential street that runs parallel to the promenade, but any of its adjoining streets are also worth strolling. On **Willow Street** be sure to note No. 22, Henry Ward Beecher's prim Greek Revival brownstone, and Nos. 155–159. These three brick Federal row houses were alleged stops on the Underground Railroad. The skylight in the pavement by the gate to No. 157 provided the light for an underground tunnel leading to an 1880 carriage house. And for those more interested in pop culture, head to the corner of Willow and Cranberry streets, where you may recognize the Federal-style town house from the movie *Moonstruck.*

Brooklyn Borough Hall. Built in 1848 as Brooklyn's City Hall, this Greek Revival landmark is one of Brooklyn's handsomest buildings. Adorned with Tuckahoe marble, the building features a hammered square rotunda and a two-story Beaux-Arts courtroom. Today it serves as the office of Brooklyn's borough president and the home of the **Brooklyn Tourism & Visitors Center** (☎ *718/802–3846*), which has historical exhibits, a gift shop, and helpful information. It's open weekdays 10–6 and summer Saturdays from 10 to 4. On Tuesday and Saturday a green-market sets up on the flagstone plaza in front. ✉ *209 Joralemon St., between Court and Adams Sts., Brooklyn Heights* ☎ *718/802–3700* ⊕ *www.visitbrooklyn.org* 🚋 *Free* Ⓜ *2, 3, 4, 5 to Borough Hall; M, R to Court St.*

12

Fodor's Choice

★

☺

Brooklyn Heights Promenade. Stretching from Orange Street in the north to Remsen Street in the south, this esplanade provides enthralling views of Manhattan. Find a bench and take in the skyline, the Statue of Liberty, and the Brooklyn Bridge—an impressive 1883 steel suspension bridge designed by John Augustus Roebling. To your left is Governors Island, a former Coast Guard base that's now become a prime picnic destination for locals. Below you are the Brooklyn–Queens Expressway and Brooklyn's industrial waterfront of warehouses, piers, and parking lots. A greenway initiative is moving forward in a bid to replace all but the expressway. At the south end of the promenade, near Montague Street, is a small playground. Ⓜ *2, 3 to Clark St.; A, C to High St.*

Brooklyn Historical Society. Housed in an 1881 Queen Anne–style National Landmark building (one of the gems of the neighborhood), the Brooklyn Historical Society displays memorabilia, artifacts, art, and interactive exhibitions. Upstairs, an impressive library—which contains an original copy of the Emancipation Proclamation—is invaluable to researchers. ✉ *128 Pierrepont St., at Clinton St., Brooklyn Heights* ☎ *718/222–4111* ⊕ *www.brooklynhistory.org* 💲*$6* ☉ *Wed.–Fri. and Sun. noon–5, Sat. 10–5* Ⓜ *2, 3, 4, 5 to Borough Hall; A, C, F to Jay St.; M, R to Court St.*

☺

Transit Museum. Step down into a 1930's subway station, where you'll find more than 60,000 square feet devoted to the history of public transportation. Interact with the collection of vintage trains and turnstiles, sit behind the wheel of city buses, and laugh over old subway advertisements and signs. The gift store is a treasure trove of NYC-theme souvenirs to bring home. ✉ *Boerum Pl. at Schermerhorn St., Brooklyn Heights* ☎ *718/694–1600* ⊕ *www.mta.info/mta/museum/* 💲*$5* ☉ *Tues.–Fri. 10–4, weekends noon–5.*

Plymouth Church of the Pilgrims. Built in 1849, this Protestant Congregational church was a center of abolitionist sentiment, thanks to the stirring oratory of Brooklyn's most eminent theologian and the church's first minister, Henry Ward Beecher (brother of Harriet Beecher Stowe, who wrote *Uncle Tom's Cabin*). Because it provided refuge to slaves, the church was known to some as the Grand Central Depot of the Underground Railroad. Though the architecture of this brick building may seem simple, it was enormously influential on subsequent American Protestant churches. Three Louis C. Tiffany stained-glass windows were added in the 1930s. In the gated garden beside the church a statue of Beecher by Gutzon Borglum (who later sculpted Mount Rushmore) depicts one of the slave "auctions"—publicity stunts wherein church members purchased the slaves' freedom. A fragment of Plymouth Rock is in an adjoining arcade. ✉ *75 Hicks St., at Orange St., Brooklyn Heights* ☎ *718/624–4743* ⊕ *www.plymouthchurch.org* ☉ *Service Sun. at 11; tours by appointment* Ⓜ *2, 3 to Clark St.; A, C to High St.*

WHERE TO EAT

$$

AMERICAN

✕**Henry's End.** At this nearly 40-year-old neighborhood favorite, the casual decor belies the quality of the food and wines you'll find. Wild game such as elk, kangaroo, and ostrich take center stage during the "Wild Game Festival" in the winter months; seasonal seafood and foraged vegetables star in the springtime. ⊠ *44 Henry St., near Cranberry St., Brooklyn Heights* ☎ *718/834–1776* ☰ *AE, D, DC, MC, V* ☉ *No lunch* Ⓜ *2, 3 to Clark St.; A, C to High St.*

$ ✕ **Noodle Pudding.** The name is bad, but the food is great at this cozy
ITALIAN restaurant serving the best regional Italian fare in Brooklyn Heights. Locals especially rave about the osso buco served with goat-cheese polenta. It does get crowded, but that means it's noisy enough that you can bring the kids. ⊠ *38 Henry St., near Middagh St., Brooklyn Heights* ☎ *718/625–3737* ⚓ *Reservations not accepted* ☰ *No credit cards* ☉ *No lunch* Ⓜ *A, C to High St.*

$ ✕ **Teresa's.** This busy mom-and-pop coffee shop serves well-prepared
POLISH Polish and American food, including breakfast all day. Fill up on delicate orange ricotta pancakes, pierogi, and juicy kielbasa. ⊠ *80 Montague St., near Hicks St., Brooklyn Heights* ☎ *718/797–3996* ☰ *AE, D, MC, V* Ⓜ *2, 3 to Clark St.; M, R to Court St.*

DUMBO

A downhill walk from Brooklyn Heights is the area called DUMBO (*Down Under the Manhattan Bridge Overpass*). It was once known as Fulton Landing, after the inventor and engineer Robert Fulton, who introduced steamboat ferry service from Brooklyn to Manhattan in 1814. Factories and dry-goods warehouses thrived here until the Manhattan Bridge was completed in 1909. The area then fell on hard times, but since the 1970s artists have been drawn by the historic warehouses for use as spacious studios. Today the area is full of luxury condos, art galleries, and small businesses.

The **Fulton Ferry Landing**'s view of Manhattan and the Brooklyn Bridge makes it a favorite site for wedding photos; the New York Water Taxi stops here as well. When all that sightseeing makes you hungry, walk uphill to the always excellent, always crowded, **Grimaldi's Pizzeria,** and the **Brooklyn Ice Cream Factory.** Wander the empty, old cobblestone streets for photo ops (try to frame the Empire State Building within the anchorage of the Manhattan Bridge) and visit the galleries and new boutiques.

Ⓒ **Empire-Fulton Ferry State Park.** This charming 9-acre park is a great place for a riverside picnic or just enjoying the view. The large playground includes a replica of a boat for make-believe voyages across the East River. From April to October the park is home to a wide range of arts performances, and on Thursday nights in July and August Movies with a View projects New York classic films on an outdoor screen with no cover charge. ⊠ *New Dock St. at Water St., DUMBO* ☎ *718/858–4708* ⊕ *nysparks.state.ny.us* ✉ *Free* ☉ *Daily dawn–dusk* Ⓜ *A, C to High St.; F to York St.*

WHERE TO EAT

$$ ✕ **Five Front.** This cozy restaurant tucked into an old town house under-
AMERICAN neath the Brooklyn Bridge serves classic American fare. Beyond burgers and steaks, they also turn out seared sea scallops and salads with seasonal vegetables. The romantic back garden gets swarmed with couples in the summertime. ⊠ *5 Front St., near Cadman Plaza W, DUMBO*

12

☎ *718/625–5559* ☰ *AE, DC, MC, V* ☺ *Closed Mon.* Ⓜ *A, C to High St.; 2, 3 to Clark St.; F to York St.*

$ ✕ **Grimaldi's Pizzeria.** This classic New York–style parlor serves excellent
PIZZA pizza pies from its coal ovens. Although sometimes inconsistent, when they're good the thin crisp crust is slightly blackened, and the fresh mozzarella oozes satisfyingly. Grimaldi's popularity allows them to be picky: no slices, no reservations, no credit cards, and no empty tables (expect a wait). Impatient foodies have been known to phone in a to-go order, swoop past the lines, and then enjoy their pizza in the nearby Brooklyn Bridge Park. ✉ *19 Old Fulton St., between Front and Water Sts., DUMBO* ☎ *718/858–4300* ☝ *Reservations not accepted* ☰ *No credit cards* Ⓜ *A, C to High St.; 2, 3 to Clark St.; F to York St.*

$$$$ ✕ **River Café.** The River Café's incredible views of the waterfront, lush
NEW AMERICAN flowers, and live piano music make it a favorite for romantic meals, marriage proposals, fancy birthdays, and special celebrations. Alas, the food and service don't quite keep up with the views, so skip the dining room and have a drink at the bar, where you can still enjoy the amazing ambience. Gentlemen: coat and tie are required after 5 PM. ✉ *1 Water St., near Old Fulton St., DUMBO, Brooklyn* ☎ *718/522–5200* ⊕ *www. rivercafe.com* Ⓜ *F to York St.; A, C to High St.*

GALLERIES

No trip to DUMBO would be complete without some gallery hopping—most are open afternoons Thursday through Sunday. On the first Thursday of every month hours are extended until 8:30 PM, and there are often receptions and live music. The **DUMBO Arts Center** (*DAC* ✉ *30 Washington St., between Water and Plymouth Sts.* ☎ *718/694–0831* ⊕ *www. dumboartscenter.org*) exhibits contemporary art in a 3,000-square-foot gallery. Their popular fall Art Under the Bridge festival offers performances, special exhibits, and open studios throughout DUMBO. Inside a 6,000-square-foot restored boiler building, **Smack Mellon Studios** (✉ *92 Plymouth St., at Washington St.* ☎ *718/834–8761* ⊕ *www.smackmellon. org*) exhibits up-and-coming artists, and nurtures them with studio space and other support. At exhibition space and design shop **Spring** (✉ *126a Front St.* ☎ *718/222–1054*) you can view contemporary art, then satisfy your shopping urges with quirky home goods.

NIGHTLIFE

Galapagos Art Space. Performances here could almost take a backseat to the unique architecture of supper-club red banquettes floating above a huge lagoon of water. (Hold onto your purse!) Thankfully, the theater, music, and performance art is dynamic enough to grab your attention. ✉ *16 Main St., DUMBO* ☎ *718/222–8500* ⊕ *www.galapagosartspace. com* ☐ *Ticket prices vary* ☺ *Opening times vary* Ⓜ *F to York St.; A, C to High St.*

SHOPPING

At **Jacques Torres Chocolate** (✉ *66 Water St.* ☎ *718/875–9772* ⊕ *www. mrchocolate.com*), feel like Charlie getting a peek at the Oompa Loompas as you peer into the small factory while munching on a few unusual-flavored chocolate bonbons and sipping a thick, rich cup of hot

DID YOU KNOW?

The Brooklyn Heights Promenade is extra popular on the 4th of July, when the winding walkway offers excellent views of Macy's firework display over the New York skyline.

chocolate. (For the latter, try the "wicked" flavor, spiked with chilies and cinnamon.)

Forget the touristy "I Heart NY" shirts. Pick up souvenirs they'll actually wear at **Neighborhoodies** (✉ *26 Jay St.* ☎ *718/243–2265* ⊕ *www. neighborhoodies.com* ☉ *Weekdays 10–6, Sat. by appointment*), where locals swear allegiance by emblazoning sweatshirts and other clothing with their favorite nabe. The Brooklyn branch allows you to instantly create custom pieces.

WILLIAMSBURG

For much of the 20th century this industrial area on the East River was home to a mix of Latin Americans, Poles, Hasidic Jews, and factories. Then, as Manhattan rents rose in the 1990s, artists and indie rockers migrated across on the L train to transform the neighborhood into an artistic bohemian center.

Today Williamsburg's main drag of Bedford Avenue is a veritable catwalk of fabulously dressed starving artists and wealthy hipsters on their way from the L train to a range of stylish bars and clubs, artists' studios, vintage stores, and costly boutiques. Meanwhile, the area's young families and migrating Manhattanites head to one of the many posh restaurants near the Williamsburg Bridge. Note that the shops and attractions listed here are spread out, so be prepared to walk a few blocks on safe (though sometimes graffitied and abandoned) blocks filled with former factories.

WHERE TO EAT

$$
AMERICAN
Fodor'sChoice
★

✗**Dumont.** Slide into a candlelit leather booth and order what is perhaps the best mac and cheese in the city, served bubbling hot and punctuated with (optional) smoky bacon. The juicy burgers, which also have a large fan club, are best enjoyed at a table in the charming back garden. (Reservations only available online via opentable.com.) ✉ *432 Union Ave., between Metropolitan Ave. and Devoe St., Williamsburg* ☎ *718/486–7717* ▭ *MC, V* Ⓜ *L to Lorimer St.*

$
SOUTHERN

✗**Fette Sau.** It may surprise you to come to a former auto-body repair shop to eat meat, but the funky building and outside courtyard seem just right for some serious 'cue. Here a huge wood-and-gas smoker delivers well-smoked brisket, sausages, ribs, and even duck, ordered by the pound. Avoid the disappointing salads and sides, and instead order some of the more than 40 American whiskeys and 10 microbrews. Come early, as tables fill up, and even with 700 pounds of meat a night, the good stuff runs out by 9 PM. ✉ *354 Metropolitan Ave., near Havemeyer St., Williamsburg* ☎ *718/963–3404* ⚑ *Reservations not accepted* ▭ *MC, V* Ⓜ *L to Lorimer St.*

$$$
MEXICAN

✗**La Superior.** Serving some of Brooklyn's best Mexican grub this side of the Red Hook ball fields, La Superior melds Mexican street food with the Williamsburg ethic. The service is slapdash and the decor is unremarkable, but the food—from tongue tacos to Poblano quesadillas—is never a disappointment. Don't be surprised if your waiter has a seat at your table while discussing the menu. ✉ *295 Berry St., Williamsburg*

Where can I find . . . ?

COFFEE IN PARK SLOPE	Gorilla Coffee 97 5th Ave. Grab an expertly pulled shot.	Red Horse Café 497 6th Ave. Sip some micro-roast.
SWEETS NEAR THE BRIDGE	Brooklyn Ice Cream Factory 1 Water St. Superlative hot fudge.	Almondine Bakery 85 Water St. Awesome croissants and sandwiches are picnic-perfect.
COCKTAILS IN CARROLL GARDENS	Clover Club 210 Smith St. Swanky modern cocktails in a cozy atmosphere.	The Jake Walk 282 Smith St. Fifty wines, 130 whiskeys, and 40 artisanal cheeses.

12

☏ *718/388–5988* ⊕ *lasuperiornyc.com* ⌕ *No reservations* ▭ *No credit cards* Ⓜ *L to Bedford Ave.*

$$$$
STEAK
✗ **Peter Luger Steak House.** Long before Brooklyn was chic, even the snobbiest Manhattanites flocked to Luger's. Other steak houses have more elegant ambience, bigger wine lists, and less brusque service, but the steak makes the trip to this 122-year-old temple of red meat worth it. You may not see a menu, but here's all you need to know: sizzling Canadian bacon, crisp German-fried potatoes, creamed spinach, and the main event—precision-chosen, dry-aged porterhouse steak, dripping in juices and melted butter. Three tips: bring a buddy (individual steaks are available, but porterhouse is only served for two, three, or four), make a reservation (prime slots fill up more than a month in advance), and bring lots of cash—Luger's doesn't take plastic. The lunch-only burger is beloved among locals. ⊠ *178 Broadway, at Driggs Ave., Williamsburg* ☏ *718/387–7400* ⌕ *Reservations essential* ▭ *No credit cards* Ⓜ *J, M, Z to Marcy Ave.*

GALLERIES
Williamsburg's 70-plus galleries are distributed randomly, with no single main drag. Plan your trip ahead of time using the online **Williamsburg and Greenpoint Monthly Art Guide** at ⊕ *www.wagmag.org.* (You can also pick up a copy at neighborhood galleries and some cafés.) Hours vary widely, but almost all are open weekends. Call ahead.

Although serendipitous poking is the best way to sample the art, two longtime galleries are must-sees. **Pierogi** (⊠ *177 N. 9th St., between Bedford and Driggs Aves., Williamsburg* ☏ *718/599–2144*) remains hip yet cheerfully accessible. Be sure to check out the famous "Flat Files," a collection of the portfolios of more than 700 young contemporary artists. At **Sideshow Gallery** (⊠ *319 Bedford Ave., between S. 2nd and S. 3rd Sts., Williamsburg* ☏ *718/486–8180*) enjoy the diverse exhibitions as well as readings and concerts.

NIGHTLIFE

Barcade. Like Chuck E. Cheese for grown-ups, Barcade invites you to reminisce about your arcade-loving youth by playing one of more than 30 vintage arcade games for only a quarter. Casual players will love familiar favorites like "Ms. Pacman," while serious video gamers will gravitate toward rarities like "Rampage." But it's not just about the games; enjoy a full menu of small-label beers while you check out the hipster crowd. ✉ *388 Union Ave., near Ainslie, Williamsburg* ☎ *718/302–6464* ⊕ *www.barcadenyc.com* Ⓜ *L to Lorimer St.*

Radegast Hall and Biergarten. The perfect alternative if you don't want to schlep all the way out to Queens for alfresco Slavic beers, Radegast Hall Biergarten serves Central European suds and hearty eats under a retractable roof. Schnitzel, goulash, and pretzels make for some authentic compliments to the beers here. ✉ *113 N. 3rd St., Williamsburg* ☎ *718/963–3973* ⊕ *radegasthall.com* Ⓜ *L to Bedford Ave.*

Brooklyn Brewery. Brooklyn was once known as America's brewing capital; at the turn of the 20th century Williamsburg alone was home to nearly 60 breweries. The originals are mostly gone, but this relative newcomer has been bringing back the hops since opening here in 1996. The Friday-evening happy hour means $3 beers—try the popular Brooklyn Lager, the Belgian-inspired Local 1, or one of the seasonal brews. Beer buffs can join a free guided tour on Saturday afternoons. ✉ *79 N. 11th St., between Berry St. and Wythe Ave., Williamsburg* ☎ *718/486–7422* ⊕ *www.brooklynbrewery.com* ☉ *Fri. 6–11 PM, Sat. and Sun. noon–6 PM* Ⓜ *L to Bedford Ave.; G to Nassau Ave.*

Pete's Candy Store. Off Williamsburg's beaten path, this bar has a retro feel, a friendly crowd, and cheerful bartenders. The back room, smaller than a subway car, frequently hosts intimate performances. Brainy hipsters come here for spelling bees and bingo, and on Wednesday nights infamous trivia contests. There's no actual candy here, so try a sandwich or craft beer instead. ✉ *709 Lorimer St., between Frost and Richardson Sts., Williamsburg* ☎ *718/302–3770* ⊕ *www.petescandystore.com* Ⓜ *L to Lorimer St.*

SHOPPING

Though the boutiques on Bedford Avenue are best for people-watching, you'll also find stores along Grand Street, and on many side streets, especially North 6th.

At the **Girdle Building** (✉ *218 Bedford Ave., Williamsburg*)—the closest thing Williamsburg has to a mall—pick up free newspapers and magazines that will help you get a read on the local scene. Attractions here include a small café, a new/used record store, achingly hip boutiques, and an art bookstore.

The small size of the **Bedford Cheese Shop** (✉ *229 Bedford Ave., at N. 4th St., Williamsburg* ☎ *718/599–7588*) belies the fact that this is one of the city's best cheese stores, packed with an encyclopedic assortment of artisan cheeses as well as small-producer cured meats, gourmet imported oils, chocolates, and other dry goods. Don't miss the quirky and occasionally salacious descriptions of the cheeses ("looks like dirty scrimshaw but tastes like a peat-covered goat teat").

One of the standout boutiques on Bedford, **Catbird** (⊠ *219 Bedford Ave., near N. 5th St., Williamsburg* ☎ *718/599–3457* ⊕ *www.catbirdnyc. com*), is a dollhouse-size shop whose shelves are filled with handmade jewelry, home accessories, and whimsical hats.

Brooklyn's thriving home-design scene is often credited to the opening of **Future Perfect** (⊠ *115 N. 6th St., at Berry St., Williamsburg* ☎ *718/599–6278* ⊕ *www.thefutureperfect.com*). Even if you're not planning on shipping home a Bone Chair made entirely of cow ribs, you'll have a great time browsing the playful and often ironic furnishings from better-known local Brooklyn designers and international exclusives. Future Perfect's sister store **A&G Merch** (⊠ *111 N. 6th St., Williamsburg* ☎ *718/388–1779* ⊕ *www.aandgmerch.com*) sells more affordable home accessories.

CARROLL GARDENS/COBBLE HILL/BOERUM HILL

On Atlantic Avenue's south side, the three adjacent neighborhoods of Carroll Gardens, Cobble Hill, and Boerum Hill form a quiet residential area of leafy streets lined with 19th-century town houses. The action swirls around Smith Street, a famed restaurant row augmented by fresh, fashionable boutiques, as well as Court Street's restaurants, bookstores, and old-fashioned bakeries. Nearby on Atlantic Avenue between Court and Clinton is a rapidly gentrifying Middle Eastern enclave, which includes the emporium **Sahadi's**, great for purchasing a veritable bazaar of olives, baklava, and other treats. Get to this neighborhood by taking the F or G train to Bergen Street-Carroll Street.

WHERE TO EAT

$$$ ✕ **Char No. 4.** With 300 plus whiskies to choose from, Char No. 4 is a
AMERICAN   connoisseur's dream. (The name refers to barrels in which the golden liquor is aged.) Complement your tipple with updated dishes from south of the Mason-Dixon line. Many of the appetizers involve bacon; don't miss the thick-cut bacon with peas and carrots, the BLT, or the cheese curds with pimento sauce. ⊠ *196 Smith St., Carroll Gardens* ☎ *718/643–2106* ⊕ *charno4.com* ⌕ *Reservations recommended* ⊟ *AE, MC, V* ⊘ *No lunch weekdays.*

$$$ ✕ **Saul.** Owner Saul Bolton's experience as a cook at famed Le Bernardin
AMERICAN   shows; the dynamic menu of seasonal specials features first-rate ingredients from the city's best purveyors. The food is so good that patrons only wish the portions were larger. ⊠ *140 Smith St., near Bergen, Carroll Gardens* ☎ *718/935–9844* ⊟ *AE, D, DC, MC, V* ⊘ *No lunch* Ⓜ *F, G to Bergen St.*

FORT GREENE

One of Brooklyn's most diverse neighborhoods, Fort Greene has long been a home to writers like Richard Wright, Marianne Moore, and John Steinbeck, and many musicians such as Betty Carter, Branford Marsalis, and even rapper Ol' Dirty Bastard. Architecture buffs will see many great examples of Eastlake and Italianate styles, especially in the facade of BAM, Brooklyn's performing arts jewel.

The Brooklyn Flea Market

Quirky, inclusive, and full of unclaimed treasure—that's Brooklyn in a nutshell, and it also aptly describes the Brooklyn Flea Market. This little market that could is now one of Brooklyn's most popular shopping attractions, luring locals and bargain hunters from afar with vintage finds, hip crafts, and crazy-delicious eats.

The Flea is a hybrid of traditional flea market, garage sale, and craft fair. It's a tumble of the expensive, the cheap, and the strange. Some vendors hawk high-end items like antique doors refashioned into tables, rescued fixtures from prewar houses, or mid-century lamps identical to those in *Mad Men*. The most "Brooklyn-y" component is the local artisans, and buying their one-of-a-kind handmade wares gives shoppers the altruistic feeling of supporting arts and crafts, whether that's silkscreened T-shirts of giant squid, tongue-and-cheek charm bracelets with little daggers, or hand-stitched stuffed elephants. You'll also find not a small number of oddly specialized booths. Exhibit A: the vendor who sells nothing beyond oil paintings of bicycles. Why not? Finally, there is plenty of bric-a-brac to sift through; great stuff that may not be practical (mink stoles, non-functional alarm clocks, *Star Wars* collectibles), but it makes for fun browsing.

When you've exhausted the shopping side of things, the Flea boasts some fantastic food options. You'll find Belgian waffles from Wafles and Dinges, funny franks from Asia Dogs, cheeses from Saxelby, organic ice cream from Blue Marble, even the popular McClure's pickles, all with plenty of coffee to get a second wind.

The set-up is slightly confusing, in that the Flea moves depending on the day of the week and the time of year. From March to November the market splits time between the parking lot of a local school on Saturdays and underneath the Brooklyn Bridge in Brooklyn Bridge Park on Sundays. During the colder months the Flea moves to an indoor location, also in DUMBO. See the Web site for more details. ⊠ *In spring and summer: Saturdays: Bishop Laughlin Memorial High School, 176 Lafayette Ave., between Clermont and Vanderbilt Ave., Fort Greene* ⊠ *Sundays: 22 Water St., DUMBO* ⊠ *In Winter: 76 Front St., DUMBO* ⊕ *brownstoner. com/brooklynflea* 🎫 *Free admission* ⊙ *Spring/summer: Sat. 10–5, Sun. 11–6; Winter: Sat. and Sun. 11–6.* Ⓜ *Saturdays: A, C to Lafayette Ave., G to Washington-Clinton Ave. Sundays: A, C to High St., F to York St.*

Today the city is attempting to build on the success of BAM by creating a cultural district around it. Here, you can take a modern dance class at the **Mark Morris Dance Center** (⊠ *3 Lafayette Ave.* ⊕ *www. markmorrisdancegroup.org*), see African diaspora performances at **651Arts** (⊠ *651 Fulton St.* ⊕ *www.651arts.org*), catch avant-garde theater at the **Irondale Center** (⊠ *85 S. Oxford St.* ⊕ *www.irondale.org*), or spend a weekend learning to blow glass at **UrbanGlass** (⊠ *647 Fulton St.* ⊕ *www.urbanglass.org*).

The Brooklyn Academy of Music. BAM is a comprehensive arts anchor for the borough, with diverse and cutting-edge offerings in opera, theater,

12

dance, music, film, and more shown in a 1908 neo-Italianate showpiece. Choreographer Karole Armitage, director Milos Forman, and composer Philip Glass have all recently presented work here. The movie theater shows both art-house and mainstream films.

BAM also holds performances at the nearby **Harvey Theater** (✉ *651 Fulton St.*), a 1904 vaudeville house whose renovation purposefully retained some of its crumbling beauty. ✉ *Peter Jay Sharp Bldg., 30 Lafayette Ave., between Ashland Pl. and St. Felix St., Fort Greene* ☎ *718/636–4100* ⊕ *www.bam.org* Ⓜ *G to Fulton St.; C to Lafayette Ave.; 2, 3, 4, 5, B, Q to Atlantic Ave.; D, M, N, R to Atlantic Ave.-Pacific St.*

WHERE TO EAT

$$ ✕ **BAMcafé.** Starting two hours before opera-house performances, enjoy
AMERICAN casual fare on the mezzanine level, often with live music. On Friday and Saturday when there is no opera-house performance, BAMcafé opens at 8 PM with a limited menu. ✉ *30 Lafayette Ave., at Ashland Pl., Fort Greene* ☎ *718/623–7811* ═ *AE, D, DC, MC, V* Ⓜ *D, M, N, R to Pacific St.; 2, 3, 4, 5, B, Q to Atlantic Ave.; C to Lafayette Ave.; G to Fulton St.*

$$$ ✕ **The General Greene.** One of the best examples of the hearty, stick-to-
AMERICAN your ribs fare that Brooklyn serves up these days, the General Greene serves big portions and big flavors. Dishes like pork ribs with yogurt sauce, lemon braised chicken, and even chorizo salad are favorites here, well paired with an impressive cocktail list. ✉ *226 DeKalb Ave., Fort Greene* ☎ *718/222–1510* ⊕ *thegeneralgreene.com* ⊗ *No reservations* ═ *AE, MC, V* Ⓜ *G to Clinton-Washington; C to Lafayette Ave.; 2, 3, 4, 5, to Nevins; B, M, Q, R to DeKalb Ave.*

$ ✕ **Smoke Joint.** Up the hill from BAM, find in-house-smoked "real New
BARBECUE York Barbecue," which translates to a mix of regional specialties like incredibly moist chicken, spicy dry-rubbed beef short ribs, collard greens, and meaty barbecued beans. Several kinds of sauces are served on the side, and the counter service couldn't be friendlier. ✉ *87 S. Elliot Pl., Fort Greene* ☎ *718/797–1011* ⊗ *Reservations not accepted* ═ *AE, D, MC, V* ⊘ *Closed Mon.* Ⓜ *G to Fulton St.; C to Lafayette Ave; 2, 3, 4, 5, B, Q to Atlantic Ave.; D, M, N, R to Pacific St.*

PROSPECT PARK/PROSPECT HEIGHTS/PARK SLOPE

Follow dog walkers and bicyclists to idyllic 526-acre **Prospect Park,** designed by the same landscapers as Central Park. Along with green lawns and shady trees, there are concerts, kids programs, and even a skating rink. Adjacent to the park are two of Brooklyn's main attractions: the **Brooklyn Botanic Garden,** a must-see during its springtime Cherry Blossom Festival, and the **Brooklyn Museum,** known for its Egyptian and feminist art collections.

The neighborhood that literally slopes down from the park, **Park Slope** is known affectionately as "Stroller Land." This family-friendly neighborhood is full of academics, writers, and late-blooming couples pushing Bugaboo strollers to its cafés and designer boutiques. One of Brooklyn's most comfortable places to live, Park Slope contains row after row of

Park Slope and Prospect Park

immaculate brownstones that date from its turn-of-the-20th-century heyday, when Park Slope had the nation's highest per-capita income. To see some of the neighborhood's most beautiful houses, walk between 7th Avenue and Prospect Park along any of the streets between Sterling Place and 4th Street.

★ **Brooklyn Botanic Garden.** One of the finest botanic gardens in the country, the 52 acres are a must-see, especially in spring and summer. A major attraction is the beguiling Japanese Hill-and-Pond Garden—complete with a 1-acre pond and blazing red *torii* gate, which signifies (accurately) that a shrine is nearby. Nearby, the Japanese cherry arbor turns into a breathtaking cloud of pink every spring, and the Cherry Blossom Festival is a hugely popular event.

Also be sure to wander through the Cranford Rose Garden (5,000 bushes, 1,200 varieties); the Fragrance Garden, designed especially for the blind; and the Shakespeare Garden, featuring more than 80 plants immortalized by the Bard. At the Steinhardt Conservatory, desert, tropical, temperate, and aquatic vegetation thrives. Don't miss the extraordinary C. V. Starr Bonsai Museum for close to 100 miniature Japanese specimens, some more than a century old. Near the conservatory are a café and a gift shop, with bulbs, plants, and gardening books as well as jewelry.

Entrances to the garden are on Eastern Parkway, next to the subway station; on Washington Avenue, behind the Brooklyn Museum; and on Flatbush Avenue at Empire Boulevard. Free garden tours meet at the front gate every weekend at 1 PM. ⊠ *900 Washington Ave., between Crown and Carroll Sts., Prospect Heights* ☎ *718/623–7200* ⊕ *www.bbg. org* ✎ *$8; free all day Tues. and Sat. before noon. Weekend combo ticket with Brooklyn Museum $16* ☉ *Mar.–late Oct.: grounds Tues.–Fri. 8–6, weekends 10–6; conservatory daily 10–5:30. Late Oct.–Mar.: grounds Tues.–Fri. 8–4:30, weekends 10–4:30; conservatory daily 10–4. Closed Mon. except holidays* Ⓜ *2, 3 to Eastern Pkwy.; B, Q to Prospect Park.*

★ **Brooklyn Museum.** The Brooklyn Museum has long stood in the shadow of Manhattan's Metropolitan. Though it has more than 1 million pieces in its permanent collection, from Rodin sculptures to Andean textiles and Assyrian wall reliefs, Brooklyn is still only the second-largest art museum in the United States—the Met is larger. But with a welcoming new design, more populist exhibitions, and neighborhood events, the city is finally starting to appreciate this hidden gem.

Along with changing exhibitions, highlights include Egyptian art, one of the best collections of its kind in the world; African and pre-Columbian art; and Native American art. Seek out the museum's works by Georgia O'Keeffe, Winslow Homer, John Singer Sargent, George Bellows, Thomas Eakins, and Milton Avery—all stunners. Also check out the Elizabeth A. Sackler Center for Feminist Art, which hosts traveling exhibits in addition to serving as the permanent home to Judy Chicago's installation *The Dinner Party* (1974–79). On the first Saturday of each month the museum throws an extremely popular free evening of art, music, dancing, film screenings, and readings, starting at 6 PM. ⊠ *200 Eastern Pkwy., at Washington Ave., Prospect Heights* ☎ *718/638–5000* ⊕ *www.brooklynmuseum.org* ✎ *$10 suggested donation. Weekend combo ticket with Brooklyn Botanic Garden $16* ☉ *Wed.–Fri. 10–5, weekends 11–6; 1st Sat. every month 11–11; call for program schedule* Ⓜ *2, 3 to Eastern Pkwy./Brooklyn Museum.*

Central Library. Across Grand Army Plaza from the park entrance is this sleek, modern temple of learning—the central location of the Brooklyn Public Library. The building resembles an open book, with the entrance at the book's spine; on the facade, gold-leaf figures celebrate art and science. Bright limestone walls and perfect proportions make this an impressive 20th-century New York building. Inside, more than 1.5 million books, public programs, and exhibitions in the lobby will keep you busy for at least a few hours. ⊠ *1 Grand Army Plaza, Prospect Heights* ☎ *718/230–2100* ⊕ *www.brooklynpubliclibrary.org* ☉ *Mon. and Fri. 9–6, Tues.–Thurs. 9–9, Sat. 10–6, Sun. closed* Ⓜ *2, 3 to Grand Army Plaza; Q to 7th Ave.*

☾ **Prospect Park.** Brooklyn residents are fiercely passionate about Prospect Park. Designed by Frederick Law Olmsted and Calvert Vaux, the park was completed in the late 1880s. Olmsted once said that he was prouder of it than any of his other works—including Manhattan's Central Park.

A good way to experience the park is to walk along its 3.5-mi circular drive and make detours off it as you wish. The drive is closed to cars at all times except weekday rush hours. Families with children should head straight for the eastern side, where most kids' attractions are clustered.

The park's north entrance is at **Grand Army Plaza**, where the Soldiers' and Sailors' Memorial Arch honors Civil War veterans. (Look familiar? It's patterned after the Arc de Triomphe in Paris.) Three heroic sculptural groupings adorn the arch: atop, a dynamic four-horse chariot; to either side, the victorious Union Army and Navy of the Civil War. The inner arch has bas-reliefs of presidents Abraham Lincoln and Ulysses S. Grant, sculpted by Thomas Eakins and William O'Donovan, respectively. To the northwest of the arch, Neptune and a passel of debauched Tritons leer over the edges of the **Bailey Fountain**. On Saturdays year-round a greenmarket at the plaza sells produce, flowers and plants, cheese, and baked goods to throngs of locals. Other days, you can find a few vendors selling snacks here and at the 9th Street entrance.

If you walk down the park's west drive from Grand Army Plaza, you'll first encounter **Litchfield Villa** (☎ *718/965–8951* 🎫 *Free* ☼ *Weekdays 9–5*), an Italianate mansion built in 1857 for a prominent railroad magnate. It has housed the park's headquarters since 1883; visitors are welcome to step inside and view the domed octagonal rotunda.

The **Prospect Park Band Shell** (☎ *718/965–8999 park hotline; 718/855–7882 Celebrate Brooklyn Festival* ⊕ *www.bricartsmedia.org*) is the home of the annual Celebrate Brooklyn Festival, which from mid-June through the last weekend in August sponsors free films and concerts that have included Afro-Caribbean jazz, David Byrne, and the Brooklyn Philharmonic.

A smaller cousin to Wollman Rink in Central Park, popular **Wollman Memorial Rink** offers skating in winter and pedal-boat rentals from spring through fall. ☎ *718/282–7789* 🎫 *$5, skate rental $6.50; pedal boats $16.33 per hr* ☼ *Rink: Thanksgiving–mid-Mar.; hrs vary, call for specifics. Pedal boats: May and June, Thurs.–Sun. noon–5; July–Labor Day, Thurs.–Sun. noon–6; Sept.–mid-Oct., weekends noon–5.*

Styled after Sansovino's 16th-century Library at St. Mark's in Venice, the **Prospect Park Audubon Center and Visitor Center at the Boathouse**, built in 1904, sits opposite the Lullwater Bridge, creating an idyllic spot for watching pedal boats and wildlife, or just taking a break at the café. Here, learn about nature through interactive exhibits, park tours, and educational programs especially for kids. On a nice day, take a ride on the electric boat to tour the Lullwater and Prospect Lake. You can also sign up for a bird-watching tour to see some of the 200 species spotted here. ✉ *Prospect Park* ☎ *718/287–3400* ⊕ *www.prospectpark. org/audubon* 🎫 *Audubon Center free; electric-boat tours $8* ☼ *Audubon Center: Apr.–Nov., Thurs.–Sun. noon–5; Dec.–Mar., weekends noon–4; call for program and tour times. Electric-boat tours: Apr.–Oct., Thurs.–Sun. noon–4:30; Sept.–mid-Oct., weekends noon–4:30, every 30 mins.*

12

Lefferts Historic House (☎ 718/789–2822 ☜ Free ☉ Apr.–Nov., Thurs.–Sun. noon–5; Dec.–Mar., school holidays noon–5) is a Dutch Colonial farmhouse built in 1783 and moved to Prospect Park in 1918. Rooms of the historic house-museum are furnished with antiques and reproductions from the 1820s, when the house was last redecorated. The museum hosts all kinds of activities for kids; call for information.

Climb aboard a giraffe or sit inside a dragon-pulled chariot at the immaculately restored **Prospect Park Carousel**, handcrafted in 1912 by master carver Charles Carmel. ☎ 718/282–7789 ☜ $1.50 per ride ☉ Apr.–June, Sept., and Oct., Thurs.–Sun. noon–5; July–Labor Day, Thurs.–Sun. noon–6.

Small and friendly, **Prospect Park Zoo** is perfect for those children who may be overwhelmed by the city's larger animal sanctuaries. Of the 400 inhabitants and 93 species, kids seem to be especially fond of the sea lions and the red pandas. An outdoor discovery trail has a simulated prairie-dog burrow, a duck pond, and kangaroos and wallabies in habitat. Be aware that there are no cafés, only vending machines. ✉ 450 Flatbush Ave., Prospect Heights ☎ 718/399–7339 ⊕ www.prospectparkzoo.com ☜ $7 ☉ Apr.–Oct., weekdays 10–5, weekends 10–5:30; Nov.–Mar., daily 10–4:30; last ticket ½ hr prior to closing Ⓜ 2, 3 to Eastern Pkwy.; B, Q to Prospect Park.

OFF THE BEATEN PATH

☺ **Brooklyn Children's Museum.** A mile east of Grand Army Plaza is the oldest children's museum in the country, now housed in a sparkling new Viñoly-designed "green" building. Here kids can become astronauts, run a bakery, create African-patterned fabric, and even become DJs, mixing the rhythms of the outdoors to make music. ✉ 145 Brooklyn Ave., Crown Heights ☎ 718/735–4400 ⊕ www.brooklynkids.org ☜ $7.50 ☉ Wed.–Fri. 11–5, weekends 10–5 Ⓜ C to Kingston-Throop Aves.; 3 to Kingston Ave.

WHERE TO EAT

$$
ITALIAN
★

✕ **al di là.** This northern Italian hot spot has been consistently packed since it first opened in 1988, and it's easy to understand why: affordable prices, a relaxed and charming environment, and simple yet soulfully comforting cuisine such as the red beet ravioli swimming in butter and poppy seeds. The no-reservations policy ensures that the place always has a buzz around it from waiting patrons. ✉ 248 5th Ave., at Carroll St., Park Slope ☎ 718/783–4565 ⌔ Reservations not accepted ▤ MC, V ☉ Closed Tues. No lunch Ⓜ F to 15th St.-Prospect Park; M, R to Union St.

$
PIZZA

✕ **Franny's.** Though many swear by Grimaldi's for the borough's best pie, this Park Slope pizza upstart has developed quite a following of its own. The crisp, thin-crust pizzas run the gamut, from a "naked" pie with olive oil and salt to their justly famous clam and garlic iteration. Many of the toppings are seasonal and locally sourced. ✉ 295 Flatbush Ave., Park Slope ☎ 718/230–0221 ⊕ frannysbrooklyn.com ⌔ No reservations ▤ MC, V ☉ No lunch weekdays Ⓜ B, Q to 7th Ave; 2, 3 to Bergen St.

¢ ✗ **Tom's Restaurant.** For friendly service and great diner fare, like fluffy
AMERICAN pumpkin-walnut pancakes served with homemade flavored butters,
head three blocks north of the Brooklyn Museum to this family-
owned, 70-year-old restaurant. On weekends lines are long, but your
wait is eased by free coffee and orange slices. ⊠ *782 Washington Ave.,
at Sterling Pl., Prospect Heights* ☎ *718/636–9738* ⌔ *Reservations not
accepted* ⊟ *No credit cards* ⊙ *Open 6 AM–4 PM. No dinner* Ⓜ *2, 3 to
Grand Army Plaza.*

NIGHTLIFE

Barbès. It's not *quite* like stepping into the funky Parisian neighborhood
of the same name, but this cozy bar does have French-accented bartenders, pressed-tin ceilings, and a red-tinted back room. Diverse events
there range from an energetic Slavic Soul Party to classical music concerts. ⊠ *376 9th St., at 6th Ave., Park Slope* ☎ *718/965–9177* ⊕ *www.
barbesbrooklyn.com* Ⓜ *F to 7th Ave.*

Southpaw. Folk, rock, and pop for refined tastes are on the bill at this
Park Slope hangout, recognized as one of South Brooklyn's most popular music venues. The sprawling space is packed with glam twenty-
somethings on any given night, but country music showcases and the
occasional kid-friendly family show on weekends keep everyone in the
neighborhood happy. ⊠ *125 5th Ave., between St. Johns Pl. and Sterling Pl., Park Slope* ☎ *718/230–0236* ⊕ *www.spsounds.com* Ⓜ *M, R
to Union St.*

Union Hall. You'll feel immediately comfortable at this large, airy hangout. Grab a beer up front in the classy library, or, if you're up for a
little sport, join friendly locals in a game of bocce ball. In the basement,
check out some rising indie rock stars on stage. ⊠ *702 Union St., at
6th Ave., Park Slope* ☎ *718/638–4400* ⊕ *www.unionhallny.com* Ⓜ *M,
R to Union St.*

SHOPPING

Seventh Avenue is Park Slope's main shopping street, with long-estab-
lished restaurants, bookstores, shops, cafés, bakeries, churches, and
real-estate agents (one favorite neighborhood pastime is window-shopping for new apartments). More fun, however, are the newer restaurants
and cute boutiques along 5th Avenue.

Start out with a snack from gourmet food store **Bierkraft** (⊠ *191 5th
Ave., near Union St., Park Slope* ☎ *718/230–7600*). In addition to
nearly 1,000 craft beers (available by the bottle), they also sell cheeses,
chocolates, olives, and other edible goodies.

Just one of the many excellent women's clothing stores dotting the area,
Bird (⊠ *316 5th Ave., between 2nd and 3rd Sts., Park Slope* ☎ *718/768–
4940*) is one of the oldest and best. In addition to their many well-
curated brands of women's clothing, like Mayle and 3.1 Phillip Lim,
Bird now stocks both men's apparel and baby clothes.

At **Brooklyn Superhero Supply Co.** (⊠ *372 5th Ave. at 7th St., Park Slope*
☎ *718/499–9884* ⊕ *www.superherosupplies.com*) young superheroes
can purchase capes, grappling hooks, secret identity kits, and more
from staff who never drop the game of pretend. Proceeds benefit the

free drop-in tutoring center (run by nonprofit organization 826NYC) located in a "secret lair" behind a swinging bookcase.

CONEY ISLAND AND BRIGHTON BEACH

12

Fodor's Choice
★
Experience the sounds, smells, and sights of a New York City summer: hot dogs and ice cream; suntan lotion; excited crowds; and weathered old men fishing.

Named Konijn Eiland (Rabbit Island) by the Dutch for its wild rabbit population, the Coney Island peninsula has a boardwalk, a 2.5-mi-long beach, amusement parks, and the **New York Aquarium.** Eating a Nathan's Famous hot dog (⊠ *1310 Surf Ave., Coney Island*) and strolling seaside has been a classic New York experience since 1916.

And then there are the freakish attractions at **Sideshows by the Seashore** and the **Coney Island Museum,** the heart-stopping plunge of the granddaddy of all roller coasters—the **Cyclone**—and the thwack of bats swung by the minor-league team the Cyclones at **Keyspan Park.** The area's banner day is the raucous Mermaid Parade, held in June. A fireworks display lights up the sky Friday nights from late June through Labor Day.

A pleasant stroll down the boardwalk is Brighton Beach, named after Britain's longstanding beach resort. In the early 1900s Brighton Beach was a resort in its own right, with seaside hotels that catered to rich Manhattan families visiting for the summer. Since the 1970s and '80s Brighton Beach has been known for its 100,000 Soviet émigrés.

To get to the heart of "Little Odessa" from Coney Island, walk about a mile east along the boardwalk to Brighton 1st Place, then head up to Brighton Beach Avenue. To get here from Manhattan directly, take the B or Q train to the Brighton Beach stop; the trip takes about an hour.

☺ **Cyclone.** One of the oldest roller coasters still operating, this world-famous, wood-and-steel colossus first roared around the tracks in 1927. Unfortunately, the adjacent, carnivalesque Astroland recently shut down, after pressure from developers. But fear not, thrill-seekers: the landmarked Cyclone will keep running, ensuring future generations of New Yorkers and visitors their most satisfying case of whiplash ever. ⊠ *1000 Surf Ave., at W. 10th St., Coney Island* ☎ *718/265-2100* �R *$5 per ride* ⊙ *Memorial Day–Labor Day, daily; call for seasonal hrs* Ⓜ *D, F, N, Q to Coney Island-Stillwell Ave.*

☺ **Deno's Wonder Wheel Park.** You get a new perspective atop the 150-foot-tall Wonder Wheel, built in 1920. Though it appears tame, its swinging cars will quicken your heart rate. Fortunately, Deno's lease runs until 2020, so Coney-lovers still have time for the Spook-a-rama, the Thunderbolt, and bumper cars. ⊠ *3059 Denos Vourderis Pl., at W. 12th St., Coney Island* ☎ *718/372-2592* ⊕ *www.wonderwheel.com* ⊠ *$6 per ride, 5 rides for $25* ⊙ *Memorial Day–Labor Day, daily 11–midnight; Apr., May, Sept., and Oct., weekends noon–9* Ⓜ *D, F, N, Q to Coney Island-Stillwell Ave.*

☺ **Keyspan Park.** Rekindle your Brooklyn baseball memories (or make some new ones) at a Brooklyn Cyclones game. When this Mets-owned single-A farm team moved to Brooklyn it brought professional baseball to the borough for the first time since 1957. Now the intimate, bright park is especially great for introducing kids to the game. The park often holds special promotions to get the little ones on the field. ⊠ *1904 Surf Ave., between 17th and 19th Sts., Coney Island* ☎ *718/449–8497* ⊕ *www.brooklyncyclones.com* 🎟 *$5–$8* ◷ *Games June–Sept.; call for schedule* Ⓜ *D, F, N, Q to Coney Island-Stillwell Ave.*

⟳ **New York Aquarium.** Home to more than 8,000 creatures of the ocean, New York City's only aquarium is also the nation's oldest. Tropical fish, sea horses, and jellyfish luxuriate in large tanks; otters, walruses, penguins, and seals lounge on a replicated Pacific coast; and a 90,000-gallon tank is home to several different types of sharks. ⊠ *W. 8th St. and Surf Ave.,Coney Island* ☎ *718/265–3474* ⊕ *www.nyaquarium.com* 🎟 *$17* ◷ *Early Apr.–Memorial Day and Labor Day–Oct., weekdays 10–5, weekends 10–5:30; Memorial Day–Labor Day, weekdays 10–6, weekends 10–7; Nov.–early Apr., daily 10–4:30; last ticket sold 45 mins before closing* Ⓜ *F, Q to W. 8th St.*

⟳ **Sideshows by the Seashore and the Coney Island Museum.** Step right up for a lively circus sideshow, complete with a fire-eater, sword swallower, snake charmer, and contortionist. Upstairs, the small museum has Coney Island memorabilia and a great deal of tourist information. ⊠ *1208 Surf Ave., at W. 12th St., Coney Island* ☎ *718/372–5159* ⊕ *www.coneyisland.com* 🎟 *Sideshow $7.50, museum 99¢* ◷ *Sideshows: Memorial Day–Labor Day, Wed.–Fri. 2–8, weekends 1–9; Apr., May, and Sept., weekends 1–8. Museum: weekends noon–5. Hrs vary, so call ahead.*

WHERE TO EAT

¢ **Nathan's Famous.** No visit to Coney Island would be complete without a hot dog from this stand that first opened in 1916. On the Fourth of July thousands come to see their world-famous hot dog eating contest; the record stands at 68 in 10 minutes. ⊠ *1310 Surf Ave., at Stillwell Ave., Coney Island* ☎ *718/946–2202* Ⓜ *D, F, N, Q to Coney Island Stillwell Ave.*

AMERICAN

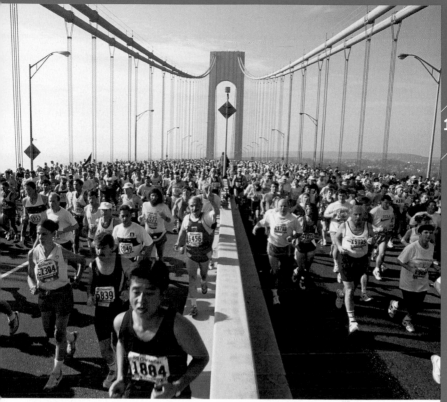

Queens, The Bronx, and Staten Island

WORD OF MOUTH

"[Combine] a visit to Arthur Avenue with a visit to the New York Botanical Garden which is located just north of the Belmont section. Take a MetroNorth train from Grand Central to the Botanical Garden stop. Walk across the street and enter the gardens. There are many acres of outdoor exhibits."

—ellenem

GETTING ORIENTED

MAKING THE MOST OF YOUR TIME

Queens is rich with superb museums. An afternoon in Long Island City and Astoria will enable you to take in the P.S. 1 Contemporary Art Center, the American Museum of the Moving Image, and the Noguchi Museum. After that, jump on the 7 train and have dinner in Jackson Heights or Flushing at one of the borough's excellent restaurants.

It is easy to spend a full day at either of the Bronx's treasures: the New York Botanical Garden or the Bronx Zoo. To visit both, start early and plan on a late lunch or early dinner in the Arthur Avenue area. The garden and the zoo are less crowded on weekdays during the school year.

Many tourists' only sight of Staten Island is during a round-trip ride on the ferry, but the borough also holds unexpected offerings in its small museums and historic villages. Set aside the better part of a day for Historic Richmond Town, and add on a couple hours for the Tibetan Museum.

GETTING HERE

Queens is served by many subway lines. To get to Astoria, take the N or W train. For Long Island City, take the E, V, or 7 train. To get to Jackson Heights, take the 7 subway train to the 74th Street-Broadway stop. You can also take the E, F, R, or V train to Roosevelt Avenue.

The Bronx is serviced by the 2, 4, 5, 6, B, and D subway trains. The attractions in the Bronx are spread out across the borough, so you'll need to take different lines to get where you want to go, and it's not necessarily convenient to make connections across town. The B, D, and 4 trains all go to Yankee Stadium, and the B and D continue uptown to take you to Arthur Avenue from the west. The 2 and 5 trains take you to the Bronx Zoo and to Arthur Avenue.

From the scenic and free Staten Island Ferry you can catch a local bus to attractions. Tell the driver where you're going, and ask about the return schedule.

13

FODOR'S CHOICE

Bronx Zoo

Citi Field

Historic Richmond Town

New York Botanical Garden

P.S. 1 Contemporary Art Center

Staten Island Ferry

Yankee Stadium

TOP EXPERIENCES

Traveling around the world through the restaurants of Queens

Standing in the shadow of the World's Fair Unisphere

Catching a Game at the new Yankee Stadium or Citi Field

BEST FOR KIDS

Bronx Zoo

The Museum of the Moving Image

Queens Zoo

NEARBY MUSEUMS

Jacques Marchais Museum of Tibetan Art

Museum of the Moving Image

New York Hall of Science

The Noguchi Museum

Queens Museum of Art

AREA SHOPS

Arthur Avenue Retail Market

Sightseeing
★★★
Nightlife
★★★
Dining
★★★★
Lodging
★
Shopping
★★★★

Many tourists miss out on seeing these three boroughs, and that's a shame. They contain some of the city's best restaurants, museums, and attractions. They're closer than you think, and certainly worth the trip.

Updated by
Alexander
Basek

Queens is a patchwork of diverse neighborhoods, each a small world with a distinct culture, all fascinating to explore. Thanks especially to the borough's strong immigrant population (almost 50%), you'll also find some of the city's most interesting cuisine here. Art lovers will definitely want to make the short trip for world-class museums such as P.S.1 Contemporary Art Center and the Noguchi Museum.

The **Bronx** is the city's most maligned and misunderstood borough. Its reputation as a gritty, down-and-out place is a little outdated, and more than a little incorrect. There's lots of beauty in the Bronx, including more parkland than any other borough, one of the world's finest botanical collections, and the largest metropolitan zoo in the country. Be aware that the borough covers a large area, and its attractions are spread out. However, on weekends from April through October the city operates the free Bronx Trolley, which departs from Manhattan in the morning, and offers hop on/hop off service to all major attractions. Whether you're relaxing at a ball game or scoping exotic species at the zoo, there's plenty of fun to be had here.

Staten Island is legally a part of New York City, but in many ways it's a world apart. The "Forgotten Borough," as some locals refer to it, is geographically more separate, less populous, politically more conservative, and ethnically more homogeneous than the rest of the city. Along with suburban sprawl, there are wonderful small museums, walkable woodlands, and a historic village replicating New York's rural past. And for a view of the skyline and the Statue of Liberty, nothing beats the 25-minute free ferry trip to Staten Island.

WHAT IT COSTS					
	¢	$	$$	$$$	$$$$
AT DINNER	under $10	$10–$17	$18–$24	$25–$35	over $35

Price per person for a median main course or equivalent combination of smaller dishes. Note: if a restaurant offers only prix-fixe (set-price) meals, it has been given the price category that reflects the full prix-fixe price.

13

QUEENS

L.I.C. AND ASTORIA

Just for the museums and restaurants alone, a short 15-minute trip on the 7 train from Grand Central or Times Square to **Long Island City** and **Astoria** is truly worth it. Long Island City (L.I.C. for short) is the outer-borough art capital, boasting the MoMA-affiliated **P.S. 1 Contemporary Art Center**, which presents experimental and formally innovative work; the **Noguchi Museum**, showcasing the work of Japanese-American sculptor Isamu Noguchi in a large, peaceful garden and galleries; and **Socrates Sculpture Park.**

Nearby Astoria, nicknamed Little Athens, was the center of Greek immigrant life in New York City for over 60 years. An increase in Greek affluence has meant that many have left the borough, but they still return for authentic restaurants, grocery stores, and churches. Here you can buy kalamata olives and salty sheep's milk feta from storeowners who can tell you where to go for the best spinach pie. Today substantial numbers of Asian, Eastern European, Irish, and Latino immigrants also live in Astoria. The heart of what remains of the Greek community is on Broadway, between 31st and Steinway streets. Thirtieth Avenue is another busy thoroughfare, with almost every kind of food store imaginable. Astoria is also home to the nation's only museum devoted to the art, technology, and history of film, TV, and digital media. The **American Museum of the Moving Image** has a slew of hands-on exhibits that allow visitors to edit, direct, and step into favorite movies and television shows.

TOP ATTRACTIONS

Museum of the Moving Image. Step inside the world of movie- and television-making at this museum full of Hollywood memorabilia. Exhibitions range from the history of the movie camera to the (literally) head-spinning special effects of *The Exorcist.* Try your hand at interactive stations that allow you to dub your voice into *Titanic,* create stop-action sequences, and more. Those wishing to improve their Space Invaders score should head to the darkened video arcade on the ground floor (games are moving images, too). Film buffs will love the film retrospectives, lectures, and other special programs. At press time, the Museum was still undergoing an extensive renovation and expansion, expected to be complete in the fall of 2010, when the temporary admission of $7 will be raised back to $10; call ahead to confirm access

Queens

MANHATTAN

STEINWAY

Socrates Sculpture Park

Isamu Noguchi Garden Museum

LONG ISLAND CITY

P.S.1 Contemporary Art Center

Sculpture Center

ASTORIA

SUNNYSIDE

Museum of the Moving Image

EAST ELMHURST

LaGuardia Airport

JACKSON HEIGHTS

Louis Armstrong House

ELMHURST

MASPETH

RIDGEWOOD

FLUSHING

Flushing Meadows-Corona Park

Queens Botanical Gardens

USTA Nat'l Tennis Center

Queens Museum of Art

Citi Field/ Shea Stadium

New York Hall of Science

Queens Zoo

REGO PARK

GLENDALE

FOREST HILLS

UTOPIA

JAMAICA

SOUTH JAMAICA

RICHMOND HILL

Northern Blvd.

Bayside Ave.

24th Ave.

73rd Ave.

164th St.

Main St.

Jamaica Ave.

Hillside Ave.

Central Pkwy.

108th St.

Myrtle Ave.

Queens Blvd.

Metropolitan Ave.

Woodhaven Blvd.

Grand Central Pkwy.

Ditmars Blvd.

Steinway St.

Northern Blvd.

31st St.

21st St.

35th Ave.

36th Ave.

25A

278

495

278

25

25

Brooklyn Queens Expwy.

Queens Midtown Tunnel

0 1 miles

0 3 km

QUEENS BY THE NUMBERS

Addresses in Queens can seem confusing at first. Not only are there 30th Street and 30th Avenue, there are also 30th Place and 30th Road, all next to each other. Then there are those hyphenated building numbers. But the system is actually much more logical than you might think. Sequentially numbered avenues run east-to-west, and sequentially numbered streets run north-to-south. If there are any smaller roads between avenues, they have the same number as the nearest avenue, and are called roads or drives. Similarly, smaller side roads between streets are called places or lanes. Thus, 30th Place is one block east of 30th Street. Most buildings have two pairs of numbers, separated by a hyphen. The first pair indicates the nearest cross street, while the second gives the location on the block. So 47-10 30th Place is 10 houses away from the corner of 47th Avenue and 30th Place. Logical, right? If this all still seems confusing to you, there's good news: locals are used to giving directions to visitors.

13

to certain galleries. ✉ *35th Ave. at 36th St., Astoria* ☎ *718/784–0077* ⊕ *www.movingimage.us* 🎟 *$10; free after 4 on Fri.* ☉ *Wed. and Thurs. 11–5, Fri. 11–8, weekends 11–6:30; screenings weekends and Fri. 7:30* Ⓜ *R, V to Steinway St.; N, W to 36th Ave.*

Noguchi Museum. In 1985 The Japanese-American sculptor Isamu Noguchi (1904–88) transformed this former photo-engraving plant into a place to display his modernist and earlier works. A peaceful central garden is surrounded by gallery buildings, providing room to show more than 250 pieces done in stone, metal, clay, and other materials. Temporary exhibits feature his collaborations with others, such as industrial designer Isamu Kenmochi. The museum is about a mile from subway stops; check the Web site for complete directions. On Sunday a shuttle bus leaves from the northwest corner of Park Avenue and 70th Street in Manhattan (in front of the Asia Society), hourly, beginning at 12:30; the round-trip costs $10. ✉ *9–01 33rd Rd., at Vernon Blvd., Long Island City* ☎ *718/204–7088* ⊕ *www.noguchi.org* 🎟 *$10; 1st Fri. of month, pay what you wish* ☉ *Wed.–Fri. 10–5, weekends 11–6* Ⓜ *N, W to Broadway.*

Fodor's Choice ★ **P.S. 1 Contemporary Art Center.** A pioneer in the "alternative-space" movement, P.S.1 rose from the ruins of an abandoned school in 1976 as a sort of community arts center for the future. Now a partner of MoMA, P.S.1 focuses on the work of currently active experimental and innovative artists. Long-term installations include work by Sol LeWitt and Pipilotti Rist. Every available corner of the enormous 100-room building is used; discover art not only in galleries but also on the rooftop, in the boiler room, and even in some bathrooms. Summer Saturdays from 3 to 9 PM outdoor dance parties attract a hip art-school crowd. ✉ *22–25 Jackson Ave., at 46th Ave., Long Island City* ☎ *718/784–2084* ⊕ *www.ps1.org* 🎟 *$5 suggested donation, free with MoMA entrance ticket* ☉ *Thurs.–Mon. noon–6* Ⓜ *7 to 45th Rd.–Courthouse Sq.; E, V to 23rd St.–Ely Ave.; G to 21st St.*

WORTH NOTING

SculptureCenter. Founded by artists in 1928 to exhibit innovative contemporary work, SculptureCenter now occupies a former trolley repair shop renovated by artist Maya Lin and architect David Hotson, not far from P.S.1. Their indoor and outdoor exhibitions spaces sometimes close between shows; call ahead before visiting. ⊠ *44–19 Purves St., at Jackson Ave., Long Island City* ☎ *718/361–1750* ⊕ *www.sculpture-center.org* ✑ *$5 suggested donation* ⊙ *Thurs.–Mon. 12–6* Ⓜ *7 to 45th Rd.--Courthouse Sq.; E, V to 23rd St.-Ely Ave.; G to Court Sq.*

⊛ **Socrates Sculpture Park.** In 1985 local artist Mark di Suvero and other residents rallied to transform what had been an abandoned landfill and illegal dump site into this 4.5-acre waterfront park devoted to public art. Today a superb view of the river and Manhattan frames changing exhibitions of contemporary sculptures and multimedia installations. Free public programs include art workshops and an annual outdoor film series (July and August, Wednesday evenings). ⊠ *32–01 Vernon Blvd., at Broadway, Long Island City* ☎ *718/956–1819* ⊕ *www.socratessculpturepark.org* ✑ *Free* ⊙ *Daily 10–sunset* Ⓜ *N, W to Broadway, then walk 8 blocks west or take Q104 bus along Broadway to Vernon Blvd.*

WHERE TO EAT

After you're done with the sights, why head back to Manhattan? End your day with dinner at one of Astoria's legendary Greek restaurants (on or near Broadway) or venture to the Middle Eastern restaurants farther out on Steinway Street.

$
EASTERN
EUROPEAN
✕ **Bohemian Beer Garden.** If your favorite outdoor activities include drinking beer and eating kielbasa, you'll love this place. The last survivor of the more than 800 beer gardens that once graced New York, this popular spot offers imported Czech beers and Central-European eats like pierogi and schnitzel. Get there early to avoid long lines. Just drinking? Bring cash, as credit cards are reserved for orders from the kitchen. Bad weather? Don't worry, indoor seating is available. ⊠ *29–19 24th Ave., between 29th and 31st Sts., Astoria* ☎ *718/274–4925* ▭ *MC, V* ⊙ *Closed Tues.* Ⓜ *N, W to Astoria Blvd.*

$
MIDDLE EASTERN
✕ **Kabab Café.** Middle-Eastern restaurants are a dime a dozen in NYC, but Egyptian-Mediterranean spots are a rarer find, attracting foodies like celebrity chef Anthony Bourdain. This charming yet eccentric 16-seat café, which excels at interesting home-style dishes, is a true hidden treasure. The menu changes nightly, but exceedingly tender lamb stuffed with pomegranate is always great. ⊠ *25–12 Steinway St., Astoria* ☎ *718/728–9858* ✑ *Reservations not accepted* ▭ *No credit cards* ⊙ *Closed Mon.* Ⓜ *N, W to Astoria-Ditmars Blvd.*

$
GREEK
✕ **Taverna Kyclades.** The current powerhouse of Hellenic eats in the neighborhood, Taverna Kyclades offers Greek classics at a higher level than you'd expect, given the simple decor and unassuming location. Fried calamari and grilled octopus make appearances at rock-bottom prices, despite their obvious quality, as do more out of the ordinary dishes like "caviar dip" and swordfish kebabs. Be prepared to wait for a table at peak times, as they don't take reservations. ⊠ *33–07 Ditmars Blvd., Astoria* ☎ *718/545–8666* ⊕ *tavernakyclades.com* ✑ *No reservations* ▭ *AE, MC, V* Ⓜ *N, W to Astoria-Ditmars Blvd.*

CLOSE UP

Filmmaking in Astoria

13

Hollywood may be the king of movi-emaking now, but in the early days of sound Queens was where it was at. In the 1920s such stars as Gloria Swanson, Rudolph Valentino, and Claudette Colbert all acted in one of the more than 100 films made at Astoria Studios. Built in 1919 by the film company that would become Paramount, "the Big House" was the largest and most important filmmaking studio in the country.

Though Astoria's ideal location provided easy access to Broadway and vaudeville stars, Hollywood's weather soon lured away most studios. Astoria was able to hold its own for a while longer, creating such films as the Marx Brothers classics *The Cocoanuts* and *Animal Crackers*. But in 1942 the studio was sold to the U.S. Army. It became the Signal

Corps Photographic Center, producing training films and documentaries, including Frank's Capra's classic seven-film series *Why We Fight*. The Army retained the studio until the early '70s, when it began to fall into disrepair and was transferred to the government.

In 1982 the city leased the studio to real-estate developer George S. Kaufman, in partnership with Alan King and Johnny Carson. Kaufman-Astoria Studios, with six stages, is a thriving operation once again, used for television series (*Sesame Street. Law & Order*) as well as movies (*The Wiz, Hair,* and *The Pink Panther*). Although the studio is not open to the public, movie buffs can hope to spot stars at the Studio Café, and learn more about the craft next door at the fantastic Museum of the Moving Image.

JACKSON HEIGHTS

Even in the diverse borough of Queens, Jackson Heights stands out for being a true polycultural neighborhood. In just a few blocks surrounding the three-way intersection of Roosevelt Avenue, 74th Street, and Broadway, you can find shops and restaurants catering to the area's strong Indian, Bangladeshi, Colombian, Mexican, and Ecuadorian communities. Built as a planned "garden community" in the 1920s, the area boasts many prewar apartments with elaborate block-long interior gardens as well as English-style homes. Celebs who grew up in the area include Lucy Liu and Gene Simmons. It's also the birthplace of the board game Scrabble.

WHERE TO EAT

$ ✕**Delhi Palace.** Jackson Heights is full of Indian restaurants, but Delhi
INDIAN Palace, specializing in north Indian cuisine, stands out from the competition. Fans cite their varied daily $10 buffet, friendly service, and fewer crowds than the popular Jackson Diner down the street. Try the thin and crispy potato-filled crepes called masala dosa, made to order. ⊠ *37–33 74th St., between Roosevelt and 37th Aves., Jackson Heights* 🖀 *718/507–0666* �‍ *AE, D, MC, V* Ⓜ *E, F, R, V to Jackson Hts.-Roosevelt Ave.; 7 to 74th St.-Broadway.*

$ ✕**Spicy Mina.** Since 2003, fans of Mina Azad's Bangladeshi food
ASIAN have eagerly followed her career. They mourned when her Sunnyside

The 7 Train: A Food Lover's Favorite Subway Line

Manhattan may be known for its fine four-star restaurants, but food lovers know that there's one train line to take to some of the best eats in the city. The 7 train snakes its way through the middle of Queens, and conveniently also through some of the best eating neighborhoods in New York. Because the tracks are elevated, it's easy to get a handle on your surroundings—and to know where to find the train once your explorations are through.

Irish expats have long settled in the adjoining neighborhoods of Woodside and Sunnyside (near the 61st Street stop), the site of many great Gaelic bars and a few restaurants. Get a proper Irish breakfast, including black and white pudding, at the casual **Stop Inn** (✉ 60–22 Roosevelt Ave., Woodside ☎ 718/779–0290). At **Donovan's** (✉ Roosevelt Ave. and 58th St., Woodside ☎ 718/429–9339) ask for extra napkins and get one of the best burgers in New York City, nicely charred and served with home-cut steak fries.

But the main reason foodies flock to Woodside is for the Thai restaurant **Sripraphai** (✉ 64–13 39th Ave., Woodside ☎ 718/899–9599), pronounced See-PRA-pie, widely considered the best Thai restaurant in New York. Don't miss the crispy watercress salad and the larb (ground pork with mint, lime juice and onions). It's closed Wednesdays.

At either the 74th Street or 82nd Street stop, diverse Jackson Heights not only offers outstanding Indian restaurants but also many other Southeast Asian spots and fantastic eats from all over Latin America. Named after a town in Puebla, Mexico, **Taqueria Coatzingo** (✉ 76–05

Roosevelt Ave., Jackson Heights ☎ 718/424–1977) has deeply flavorful mole poblano. Those in the know stick to daily handwritten specials like Pipian en Puerco Rojo—pork cooked in red pumpkin-seed sauce. **Chivito D'Oro III** (✉ 84–02 37th Ave., Jackson Heights ☎ 718/424–0600), a Uruguayan diner, serves up parades of grilled meats called parrilladas—easily enough for two. Since many Uraguayans are of Italian heritage, Chivito also serves delicate pastas.

The 7 train may save the best for last: at the end of the line is Flushing, home to the second-largest Chinatown in the United States. (First is San Francisco's.) Wide streets have few tourists and many interesting stores and restaurants, making the long trip worth it. The standout is **Spicy and Tasty** (✉ 39–07 Prince St., at 39th Ave., Flushing ☎ 718/359–1601), which lives up to its name with numbing Szechuan peppercorns and slicks of red chili oil. Tea-smoked duck has crispy skin and smoky, salty meat. Eggplant with garlic sauce tastes of ginger, tomatoes, and red chilies. Cool it all down with a Tsingtao beer.

A few tips: Bring cash, not many of these restaurants accept credit cards. Be prepared to encounter language difficulties, as English speakers are in the minority. In Manhattan, catch the 7 train at Times Square or Grand Central Terminal.

—Nina Callaway

restaurant closed, and cheered when she briefly popped up again, cooking in Manhattan. Now they trek to the border of Jackson Heights and Woodside to wait patiently through spotty service while she prepares elaborately spiced feasts from scratch, an anomaly in a sea of steam-table buffet restaurants. It's also BYOB. ✉ *64–23 Broadway, Woodside* ☎ *718/205–2340* ▭ *MC, V* Ⓜ *G, R, V to 65th St.*

> **DID YOU KNOW?**
>
> Flushing may seem like a strange name for a town, but it's an English adaptation of the original (and hard-to-pronounce) Dutch name, Vlissingen. The Dutch named it for a favorite port city in the Netherlands.

13

SHOPPING

At **Patel Brothers** (✉ *37–27 74th St., near 37th Ave.* ☎ *718/898–3445*) let your nose lead your way through the aisles of this Indian grocery store minichain, inhaling the heady scents of rich spices, rare Kesar mangoes, and other exotic produce. Then follow your curiosity through dozens of varieties of lentils and an entire aisle devoted to rice before stocking up on spicy fried snacks and cheap souvenirs for the folks back home.

For special keepsakes, head to **Sahil Sari Palace** (✉ *37–39 74th St., between Roosevelt and 37th Aves.* ☎ *718/426–9526*), filled with bolts of colorful silks and ready-to-wear sequined saris.

FLUSHING AND CORONA

Before it became a part of New York City, Queens was once many small independent townships. So it makes sense that the historic town of Flushing is today a microcosm of a larger city, including a bustling downtown area, fantastic restaurants, and bucolic suburbanlike streets nearby.

Next door, quiet Corona could easily be overlooked, but that would be a mistake. Here are two huge legacies: the music of Satchmo and the cooling simplicity of an Italian ice.

TOP ATTRACTIONS

Fodor's Choice
★

Citi Field. The Mets are justly proud of their brand-new stadium, designed to hark back to Ebbets Field (where the Dodgers played in Brooklyn) with a brick exterior and plenty of bells and whistles, from a batting cage and whiffle ball field to the original giant apple from Shea. The team christened it in 2009 with a terrible season, but thankfully, there are lots of other reasons to check it out even when the Mets are down on their luck. Chief among them: the Jackie Robinson Rotunda, a soaring multistory entrance and history exhibit dedicated to the Dodgers player who shattered baseball's color barrier. It's also a hit with foodies, who flock to the food court behind center field for Shake Shack burgers, surprisingly inexpensive beers like Czechvar and Leffe, and even lobster rolls and tacos. Though it seats fewer people than Shea by about 10,000, tickets are not hard to come by, especially later in the season. Still feeling nostalgic for the old Shea? Pay your respects at the plaque in the parking lot. ✉ *Roosevelt Ave. off Grand Central Pkwy.* ☎ *718/507–8499* ⊕ *www.mets.com* Ⓜ *7 to Mets/Willets Point.*

Where can I find . . . ?

DRINKS IN QUEENS	Dutch Kills 27–24 Jackson Ave. Swank cocktails at Queens prices.	Bohemian Beer Garden 29–19 24th Ave. Perfect on a summer night.
SNACKS IN THE BRONX	Zero Otto Nove 2357 Arthur Ave. Serious Neapolitan pizza without the hassle.	Mike's Deli 2344 Arthur Ave. Sandwiches as big as your head, friendly service, and a convenient location.
GOOD EATS IN STATEN ISLAND	Adobe Blues 63 Lafayette Ave. Southwestern food and more than 200 beers.	Café Botanica Snug Harbor Cultural Center, Cottage Row American classics, like fresh biscuits with whipped butter.

Flushing Meadows–Corona Park. Standing in the lush grass of this park, you'd never imagine that it was once a swamp and a dumping ground. But the gleaming Unisphere (an enormous 140-foot-high steel globe) might tip you off that this 1,255 acre-park was also the site of two World's Fairs.

Many New Yorkers head to a specific attraction, such as a Mets game or the science museum, not realizing the many discoveries to be made nearby. But savvy visitors can take advantage of "one-stop park shopping." Here are not only typical grassy knolls, barbecue pits, and sports fields, but also an art museum, a petting zoo, golf and minigolf, and even a model-plane field. It is too large to see everything in one day, so aim to hit a few primary spots. Though several destinations are clustered together on the northwest side of the park, be prepared for long peaceful walks in between. The flat grounds are ideal for family biking; rent bikes near the park entrance or Meadow Lake from March to October. ■**TIP**➔ Although the park is great in daytime, avoid visiting once it gets dark; there has been some crime in this area.

At the northwestern edge of the park, the **New York Hall of Science** (☎ 718/699–0005 ⊕ www.nyscience.org ⊠ $11; free Fri. 2–5 and Sun. 10–11 Sept.–June ☉ Sept.–June, Mon.–Thurs. 9:30–2, Fri. 9:30–5, weekends 10–6; July and Aug., weekdays 9:30–5, weekends 10–6) has more than 400 hands-on exhibitions that make science a playground for inquisitive minds of all ages. Climb aboard a replica of John Glenn's space capsule, throw a fastball and investigate its speed, or explore Charles and Ray Eames's classic Mathematica exhibition.

Behind the Hall of Science lies the intimate **Queens Zoo** (☎ 718/271–1500 ⊕ www.wcs.org ⊠ $7 ☉ Early Apr.–late Oct., weekdays 10–5, weekends 10–5:30; late Oct.–early Apr., daily 10–4:30; last ticket sold 30 mins before closing), whose small scale is especially well suited to easily tired young visitors. In only 11 acres you'll find North American animals such as bears, mountain lions, bald eagles, and pudu—the world's smallest deer. Buckminster Fuller's geodesic dome from the 1964 World's Fair is now the aviary. Across the street is a petting zoo.

Between the zoo and the Unisphere, you'll find the **Queens Museum of Art** (☎ 718/592–9700 ⊕ *www.queensmuseum.org* ✉ *$5 suggested donation* ☉ *Sept.–June, Wed.–Fri. 10–5, weekends noon–5; call for extended hrs in July and Aug.*). Don't miss the astonishing Panorama, a nearly 900,000-building model of NYC made for the 1964 World's Fair. Many unsuspecting park visitors looking for a bathroom instead find themselves spending hours checking out the intricate structures that replicate every block in the city. There are also rotating exhibitions of contemporary art and a permanent collection of Louis Comfort Tiffany stained glass. ⊠ *Between 111th St./Grand Central Pkwy and Van Wyck Expressway at 44th Ave., Flushing* Ⓜ *7 to 111th St. or Willets Point.*

USTA Billie Jean King National Tennis Center. Each August, 700,000 fans come here for the U.S. Open, which claims the title of highest-attended annual sporting event in the world. The rest of the year the 45 courts (33 outdoor and 12 indoor, all Deco Turf II) are open to the public for $20–$60 hourly. Make reservations up to two days in advance. ⊠ *Flushing Meadows–Corona Park* ☎ *718/760–6200* ⊕ *www.usta.com* Ⓜ *7 to Willets Point.*

WORTH NOTING

Louis Armstrong House Museum. For the last 28 years of his life the famed jazz musician lived in this modest three-story house in Corona with his wife Lucille. Take a guided 40-minute tour and note the difference between the rooms vividly decorated by Lucille in charming mid-century style and Louis's dark den, cluttered with phonographs and reel-to-reel tape recorders. Although photographs and family mementos throughout the house impart knowledge about Satchmo's life, it's in his den that you'll really understand his spirit. ⊠ *34–56 107th St., at 37th Ave., Corona* ☎ *718/478–8274* ⊕ *www.satchmo.net* ✉ *$8* ☉ *Tours hourly Tues.–Fri. 10–5, weekends noon–5* Ⓜ *7 to 103rd St.–Corona Plaza.*

NEED A BREAK? | If you're looking for authentic Queens experiences, there are few as true as eating an Italian ice from the **Lemon Ice King of Corona** (⊠ *52–02 108th St., at 52nd St., Corona* ☎ *718/699–5133*) while strolling by a nearby bocce court on a hot summer day. Though there aren't seats or friendly service, none of that will matter as soon as you taste one of the more than 30 flavors, homemade and fresh, from this 66-year-old institution.

THE BRONX

TOP ATTRACTIONS

Fodor'sChoice ★ Ⓒ **The Bronx Zoo.** When it opened its gates in 1899 the Bronx Zoo only had 843 animals. But today, with 265 acres and more than 4,000 animals (of more than 600 species), it's the largest metropolitan zoo in the United States. Get up close and personal with exotic creatures in outdoor settings that re-create natural habitats; you're often separated from them by no more than a moat or wall of glass. Don't miss the **Congo Gorilla Forest** (✉ *$3*) a 6.5-acre re-creation of a lush African rain forest

with two troops of lowland gorillas, as well as white-bearded DeB-
razza's monkeys, okapis, and red
river hogs. At **Tiger Mountain** an
open viewing shelter lets you get
incredibly close to Siberian tigers,
who frolic in a pool, lounge outside
(even in cold weather), and enjoy
daily "enrichment sessions" with
keepers. As the big cats are often
napping at midday, aim to visit in
the morning or evening. In the new

> ### ROSES AND SNUFF
>
> Much of the NY Botanical Gar-
> den's land was originally owned
> by tobacco manufacturers who
> grew extensive rose gardens to
> perfume their tobacco. You can
> still visit the 1840 Snuff Mill, the
> oldest extant tobacco factory in
> the country.

$62 million exhibit **Madagascar!**, the formality of the old Lion House
has been replaced with a verdant re-creation of one of the most threatened natural habitats in the world. Here you'll see adorable lemurs and
far-from-adorable hissing cockroaches.

Go on a minisafari via the **Wild Asia Monorail** ($4), open May–
October, weather permitting. As you wind your way through the forest, see Asian elephants, Indo-Chinese tigers, Indian rhinoceroses, gaur
(the world's largest cattle), Mongolian wild horses, and several deer
and antelope species. ■ TIP➔ Try to visit the most popular exhibits, such
as Congo Gorilla Forest, early to avoid lines later in the day. In winter the
outdoor exhibitions have fewer animals on view, but there are also fewer
crowds, and plenty of indoor exhibits to savor. From mid-November to January 1 the zoo is decorated with holiday lights and open until 9 PM. ⊠ *Bronx
River Pkwy. and Fordham Rd., Fordham* ☎ *718/367–1010* ⊕ *www.
bronxzoo.com* $15; *extra charge for some exhibits; free Wed., dona-
tion suggested; parking $12* ☯ *Apr.–Oct., weekdays 10–5, weekends
10–5:30; Nov.–Mar., daily 10–4:30; last ticket sold 30 mins before closing* Ⓜ *2, 5 to E. Tremont/West Farms, then walk 2 blocks up Boston Rd.
to zoo's Asia entrance; Bx11 express bus to Bronx River entrance.*

Fodor's Choice
★ **New York Botanical Garden.** Considered one of the leading botany centers
of the world, this 250-acre garden is one of the best reasons to make a
trip to the Bronx. Built around the dramatic gorge of the Bronx River,
the Garden offers lush indoor and outdoor gardens, acres of natural
forest, as well as classes, concerts, and special exhibits. Be astounded by
the captivating fragrance of the Peggy Rockefeller Rose Garden's 2,700
plants of more than 250 varieties; see intricate orchids that look like the
stuff of science fiction; relax in the quiet of the forest or the calm of the
Conservatory; or take a jaunt through the Everett Children's Adventure
Garden: a 12-acre, indoor-outdoor museum with a boulder maze, giant
animal topiaries, and a plant discovery center.

The Garden's roses bloom in June and September, but there's plenty
to see year-round. The Victorian-style **Enid A. Haupt Conservatory**
($20, *part of the Combination Ticket*) houses re-creations of misty
tropical rain forests and arid African and North American deserts as
well as exhibitions, such as the annual Holiday Train Show and the
Orchid Show. The **Combination Ticket** ($20) gives you access to the
Conservatory, Rock Garden, Native Plant Garden, Tram Tour, Everett
Children's Adventure Garden, and exhibits in the library.

The Jungle habitat at the Bronx Zoo will make you forget the surrounding urban jungle.

The most direct way to the Garden is via **Metro-North Railroad** (⊕ *www.mta.info/mnr*) from Grand Central Terminal (Harlem Local Line, Botanical Garden stop). Round-trip tickets are $10.50 to $14, depending on time of day. A cheaper alternative is to take the D or 4 train to Bedford Park Boulevard, then walk east. ⊠ *200th St. at Kazimiroff Blvd., Bedford Park* ☎ *718/817–8700* ⊕ *www.nybg.org* ☜ *Grounds only $6, free Sat. 10–noon and all day Wed.; All-Garden Pass $20; parking $12* ☽ *Tues.–Sun., 10 AM–6 PM.* Ⓜ *B, D, 4 to Bedford Park Blvd., then walk 8 blocks downhill to the garden; Metro-North to Botanical Garden.*

Fodor's Choice ★ **Yankee Stadium.** Fans are still mourning the original, legendary Yankee Stadium, which saw its last season in 2008. Though the team is still breaking it in, the new Yankee Stadium—right next to the House that Ruth Built—has gotten off to a good start, with the Yankees winning the World Series in its inaugural year. Tickets can be ridiculously expensive, but the experience is like watching baseball in Las Vegas's Bellagio hotel. Meaning, it's incredibly opulent and over-the-top: traditional white frieze adorning the stadium's top; inside, limestone and marble hallways are lined with photos of past Yankee greats; lower level seats have cushions, cup holders, and a boffo meatery, NYY Steak. Like the team, all the amenities don't come cheap. But the spirit of the original still remains. History buffs and hardcore fans should be sure to visit Monument Park, with plaques of past team members, by Center Field— it survived from the old stadium. Aside from the subway, you can also get here by Metro-North, to the Yankees-153rd St. Station. ⊠ *River*

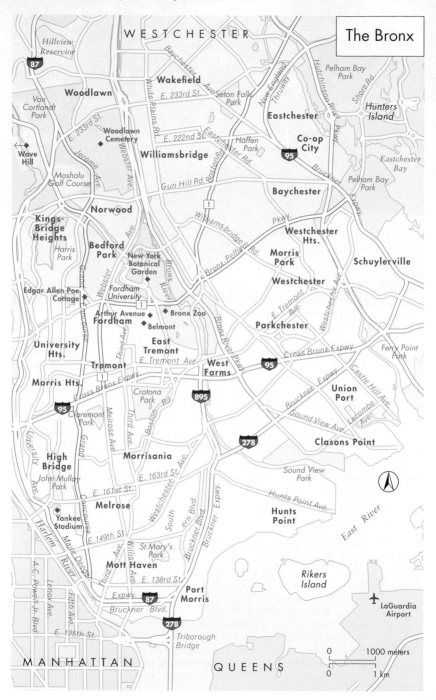

Ave. at 161st St., South Bronx ☎ *718/293–4300* ⊕ *www.yankees.com* Ⓜ *B (weekdays only), D, or 4 to 161st St.-Yankee Stadium.*

WORTH NOTING

Edgar Allan Poe Cottage. In hopes that the country air would help his sickly wife Virginia, the poet sought refuge at this tiny workman's cottage from 1846 until his death in 1849. The country air is gone, but visitors can see period furnishings, exhibits, and the spot where Poe wrote some of his most famous works. After Virginia's death in 1847 Poe sought solace in the church chimes at nearby St. John's College (now Fordham University); word has it that these haunting sounds inspired "The Bells." You may notice that the new visitor center has a winged roof and featherlike shingles; it was inspired by "The Raven." ⊠ *E. Kingsbridge Rd. at Grand Concourse, Kingsbridge Heights* ☎ *718/881–8900* ⊕ *www.bronxhistoricalsociety.org* ☞ *$5* ⊗ *Mon.–Fri. 9–5, Sat. 10–4, Sun. 1–5* Ⓜ *4, B, D to Kingsbridge Rd.*

13

OFF THE
BEATEN
PATH

Wave Hill. Drawn by stunning views of the Hudson River and New Jersey's dramatic cliffs, 19th-century Manhattan millionaires built summer homes in the Bronx suburb of Riverdale. One of the most magnificent, Wave Hill, is now a 28-acre public garden and cultural center that attracts green thumbs from all over the world. Along with exquisite gardens, grand beech and oak trees adorn wide lawns, an elegant pergola overlooks the majestic river view, and benches on curving pathways provide quiet respite. Wave Hill House (1843) and Glyndor House (1927) now house art exhibitions, Sunday concerts, and gardening workshops. Even England's Queen stayed here during a visit. It's worth the schlep. ⊠ *Independence Ave. at W. 249th St., Riverdale* ☎ *718/549–3200* ⊕ *www.wavehill.org* ☞ *$6; free Tues. and Sat. mornings* ⊗ *Mid-Apr.–mid-Oct., Tues.–Sun. 9–5:30; mid-Oct.–mid-Apr., Tues.–Sun. 9–4:30; closed Mon. except holidays. Free garden tours Sun. at 2:15* Ⓜ *1 to 231st St., then Bx7 or Bx10 bus to 252nd St. and Riverdale Ave. or free van service available hourly from station between 9:10* AM *and 3:10* PM*; Metro-North train: Hudson line to Riverdale then 15-min uphill walk.*

ARTHUR AVENUE (BELMONT)

Manhattan's Little Italy is sadly overrun with mediocre restaurants aimed at tourists, but Belmont, the Little Italy of the Bronx, is a real, thriving Italian-American community. Unless you have family in the area, the main reason to come here is for the food: eating it, buying it, looking at it fondly through windows. A secondary, but just as important, reason is chatting with shopkeepers so you can steal their recipes.

Nearly a century after pushcarts on Arthur Avenue catered to Italian-American workers constructing the zoo and Botanical Garden, the area teems with meat markets, bakeries, and cheese makers. There are long debates about which store or restaurant is the "best," but thanks to generations of Italian grandmothers, vendors here wouldn't dare offer anything less than superfresh, handmade foods.

Although the area is no longer solely Italian—many Latinos and Albanians share this neighborhood now—Italians dominate the food scene. Regulars mostly shop on Saturday afternoon; you'll find many stores shuttered on Sunday and after 6 PM. ⊠ *Arthur Ave. between Crescent Ave./E. 184th St. and E. 188th Sts., and 187th St. from Lorillard Pl. to Hughes Ave. Belmont* ⊕ *www.arthuravenue.com* Ⓜ *B, D, 4 to Fordham Rd., then Bx12 east; 2, 5 to Pelham Pkwy., then Bx12 west. On weekends and holidays Apr.–Oct., free Bronx Tour Trolley leaves from Fordham Plaza Metro-North and West Farms 2/5 stations.*

WHERE TO EAT

$ ✗ **Antonio's Trattoria.** Antonio's bills itself as "an Italian restaurant serv-
ITALIAN   ing simple food," but that's underselling it by far. Fantastic classic Italian fare is dished out here; do not miss the baked clams, the house-made ravioli, and the excellent pizzas. It's a bit off the main Arthur Avenue strip, but worth the trek. ⊠ *2370 Belmont Ave., Belmont* ☎ *718/733-6630* ⊕ *antoniostrattoria.com* ☉ *Closed Mon.* ⊟ *MC, V* Ⓜ *B, D to 182nd.*

$ ✗ **Zero Otto Nove.** Though insiders who can get a table swear by Rao's
ITALIAN   on 114th in Manhattan, Zero Otto Nove chugs along as one of the best Italian restaurants north of 96th street. The draw? Wood-oven fired pizza, perfectly chewy and larded with buffalo mozzarella. The San Matteo, which adds broccoli rabe to the mix, is just as addictive as the plain jane margherita. ⊠ *2357 Arthur Ave., Belmont* ☎ *718/220-1027* ⌢ *Reservations not accepted* ⊟ *MC, V* ☉ *Closed Mon.* Ⓜ *B, D to 182nd.*

SHOPPING

The covered **Arthur Avenue Retail Market** (⊠ *2344 Arthur Ave., at E. 187th St., Belmont* ☎ *718/367–5686* ⊕ *www.arthuravenue.com* Ⓜ *B, D, 4 to Fordham Rd., then 15-min walk or Bx12 east*), which houses more than a dozen vendors, was opened by Mayor Fiorello LaGuardia in an effort to get the pushcarts off the crowded streets. Inside, you'll find great sandwiches and pizza, barrels of olives, a butcher specializing in offal, and lots of fresh pastas. Cigars are rolled by hand right at the building's entrance, alongside Italian gifts and kitchenware. It's open Monday through Saturday 6–6.

Let an Italian nonna (grandmother) sell you homemade fresh pastas of every kind, shape, and flavor at **Borgatti's Ravioli & Egg Noodles** (⊠ *632 E. 187th St., between Belmont and Hughes Aves., Belmont* ☎ *718/367–3799*). It's closed all day Monday and Sunday afternoon, and frequently has shorter hours in summer.

Don't miss the porcine spectacle of **Calabria Pork Store** (⊠ *2338 Arthur Ave., between 186th St. and Crescent Ave., Belmont* ☎ *718/365–5145*), where a forest of house-aged salamis dangles thickly from the rafters. At **Calandra Cheese** (⊠ *2314 Arthur Ave., between 186th St. and Crescent Ave., Belmont* ☎ *718/365–7572*) bulbous spheres of freshly made cheese hang from the ceiling. Go for the cacciocavallo—a dry, salty mozzarella—or the clean-tasting ricotta.

The brick ovens at **Madonia Bros. Bakery** (⊠ *2348 Arthur Ave., at 187th St., Belmont* ☎ *718/295–5573*) have been turning out golden-brown

LIFE RING BUOY
WITH LINE

loaves since 1918, but the true stars are fresh, crispy cannoli, filled only when you order, with not-too-sweet ricotta cream.

At **Teitel Bros.** (✉ *2372 Arthur Ave., at E. 186th St., Belmont* ☎ *718/733–9400*), grab a number and stand elbow-to-elbow with locals buying pungent olives, hulking hunks of hard cheeses, pounds of dried beans, and gallons of olive oil.

STATEN ISLAND

Staten Island is full of surprises, from a premier collection of Tibetan art to a multifaceted historic village. To explore the borough, take the **Staten Island Ferry** from the southern tip of Manhattan. After you disembark, grab an S40 bus to the **Snug Harbor Cultural Center (about 10 minutes)** or take the S74 and combine visits to the **Tibetan Museum** and **Historic Richmond Town.**

TOP ATTRACTIONS

Fodor's Choice

★

☾

Historic Richmond Town. Think of Virginia's Colonial Williamsburg (the polar opposite of Brooklyn's scene-y Williamsburg), and you'll understand the appeal of Richmond Town. This 100-acre village, constructed from 1695 to the 19th century, was the site of Staten Island's original county seat. Fifteen of the site's 27 historic buildings are open to the public. Highlights include the Gothic Revival **Courthouse**, the one-room **General Store**, and the **Voorlezer's House**, one of the oldest buildings on the site. It served as a residence, a place of worship, and an elementary school. Also on-site is the **Staten Island Historical Society Museum,** built in 1848 as the second county clerk's and surrogate's office, which now houses Staten Island artifacts plus changing exhibitions about the island. Audio tours are free with admission.

You may see staff in period dress demonstrate Early American crafts and trades such as tinsmithing or basket making, though the general era meant to be re-created is 1820–1860. December brings a monthlong Christmas celebration. Take the S74–Richmond Road bus (30 minutes) or a car service (about $15) from the ferry terminal. ✉ *441 Clarke Ave., Richmondtown* ☎ *718/351–1611* ⊕ *www.historicrichmondtown.org* ▭ *$5* ☾ *July and Aug., Wed.–Fri. 11–5, weekends 1–5; Sept.–June, Wed.–Sun. 1–5* Ⓜ *S74 bus to St. Patrick's Pl.*

Jacques Marchais Museum of Tibetan Art. At the top of a hill sits this replica of a Tibetan monastery containing one of the largest collections of Tibetan and Himalayan sculpture, paintings, and artifacts outside Tibet. Meditate with visiting Buddhist monks, or just enjoy the peaceful views from the terraced garden. ✉ *338 Lighthouse Ave., Richmondtown* ☎ *718/987–3500* ⊕ *www.tibetanmuseum.org* ▭ *$5* ☾ *Wed.–Sun. 1–5* Ⓜ *S74 bus to Lighthouse Ave. and walk uphill 15 mins.*

Fodor's Choice

★

Staten Island Ferry. One of Staten Island's biggest attractions is free— the phenomenal view of Manhattan and the Statue of Liberty afforded by the 25-minute ferry ride across New York Harbor. From Whitehall Terminal at the southern tip of Manhattan, catch the ferry every half hour on weekdays and weekend afternoons. On weekend mornings until 11:30 AM, ferries run every hour on the half hour. From 11:30 AM

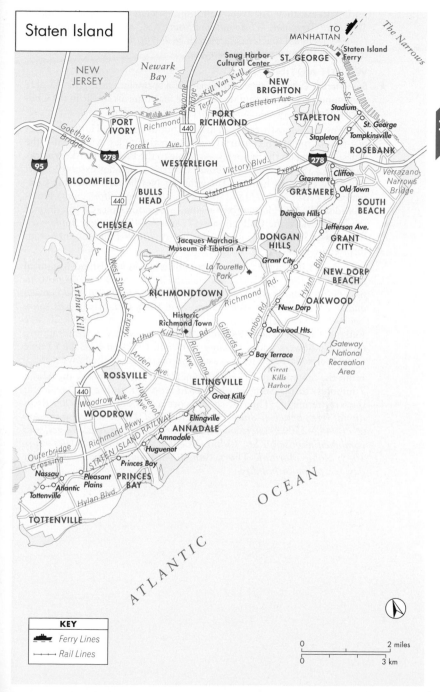

Staten Island

NEW JERSEY

Newark Bay

TO MANHATTAN

The Narrows

Snug Harbor Cultural Center

ST. GEORGE

Staten Island Ferry

NEW BRIGHTON

Kill Van Kull

Bayonne Bridge

Terr.

Castleton Ave.

Stadium

PORT RICHMOND

STAPLETON

St. George

Richmond Ave.

440

Stapleton

Tompkinsville

PORT IVORY

Forest Ave.

ROSEBANK

Goethals Bridge

278

WESTERLEIGH

Victory Blvd.

278

Verrazano Narrows Bridge

95

Staten Island Expwy.

Grasmere

Cliffon

440

BLOOMFIELD

BULLS HEAD

GRASMERE

Old Town

SOUTH BEACH

Dongan Hills

CHELSEA

Jefferson Ave.

Jacques Marchais Museum of Tibetan Art

DONGAN HILLS

GRANT CITY

West Shore Expwy.

La Tourette Park

Grant City

NEW DORP BEACH

Arthur Kill

RICHMONDTOWN

Richmond Rd.

Hylan Blvd.

OAKWOOD

Arthur Kill Rd.

Historic Richmond Town

Richmond Rd.

New Dorp

Giffords La.

Amboy Rd.

Oakwood Hts.

Arden Ave.

Richmond Ave.

Gateway National Recreation Area

Huguenot Ave.

ROSSVILLE

ELTINGVILLE

Bay Terrace

440

Woodrow Ave.

Great Kills

Great Kills Harbor

WOODROW

Eltingville

STATEN ISLAND RAILWAY

ANNADALE

Richmond Pkwy.

Annadale

Outerbridge Crossing

Huguenot

Nassau

Princes Bay

PRINCES BAY

Pleasant Plains

Atlantic

Hylan Blvd.

OCEAN

Tottenville

TOTTENVILLE

ATLANTIC

KEY

Ferry Lines

Rail Lines

0   2 miles

0   3 km

13

until 7:30 PM, they run every half hour. ⊹ *Runs between Manhattan's Whitehall Terminal, Whitehall and South Sts., and Staten Island's St. George Terminal* ⊕ *www.siferry.com* Ⓜ *4, 5 to Bowling Green; R, W to Whitehall St.; 1 to South Ferry.*

WORTH NOTING

★ **Snug Harbor Cultural Center.** Once part of a sprawling farm, this 83-acre community is now a popular spot to see maritime art, frolic in the **Children's Museum,** or take a stroll through lush gardens.

Made up of 26 mostly restored historic buildings, Snug Harbor's center is a row of mid-19th-century Greek Revival temples. Main Hall—the oldest building on the property—is home to the **Eleanor Proske Visitors Center** (🎫 *$3, including Newhouse Center*), which has exhibits on art and Snug Harbor's history. The adjacent **Newhouse Center for Contemporary Art** (🕾 *718/448–2500* 🎫 *$3, including visitor center*) shows multidisciplinary videos, mixed media, and performances. Next door at the **Noble Maritime Collection** (🕾 *718/447–6490* ⊕ *www.noblemaritime.org* 🎫 *$5*) an old seamens' dormitory is now a museum of ocean-inspired artwork.

Spread over the cultural center grounds is the **Staten Island Botanical Garden** (🕾 *718/273–8200* ⊕ *www.snug-harbor.org* 🎫 *Free; $5 for Chinese Garden and Secret Garden* ☉ *Daily dawn–dusk; Chinese Garden and Secret Garden Apr.–Sept., Tues.–Sun. 10–5; Oct.–Mar., Tues.–Sun. noon–4*), which includes an orchid collection, 9/11 memorial, 20-acre wetland, Chinese Scholar's Garden, and a sensory garden with fragrant, touchable flowers and a tinkling waterfall. Children love the Connie Gretz Secret Garden with its castle and maze among the flowers.

From the Staten Island Ferry terminal, take the S40 bus 2 mi (about 7 minutes) to the Snug Harbor Road stop. Or grab a car service at the ferry terminal. (The ride should cost you about $5.) ✉ *1000 Richmond Terr., between Snug Harbor Rd. and Tyson Ave., Livingston* 🕾 *718/448–2500* ⊕ *www.snug-harbor.org* 🎫 *$3; gardens and galleries combined admission $6; Cultural Center grounds free* ☉ *Tues.–Sun. 10–5; Noble Maritime Thurs.–Sun. 10–5; grounds dawn–dusk every day except major holidays.*

Museums

WORD OF MOUTH

"If you go to the Neue [Galerie] museum, definitely stop into Café Sabarsky for a fabulous dessert and Viennese coffee. The coffee here is some of the best I have ever tasted."

—Cries_Van_Notebook

MUSEUMS PLANNER

Underhyped

Frick Collection

Museum of the City
of New York

New York City Police Museum

The Paley Center for Media

Whitney Museum of Modern
Art

Best for Kids

Children's Museum of the Arts

Children's Museum of
Manhattan

Lower East Side Tenement
Museum

New York City Fire Museum

New York City Police Museum

Actually Free

Alexander Hamilton U.S. Custom House/National Museum
of the American Indian

Forbes Galleries

The Hispanic Society of
America

Museum of American
Illustration

Think Small

Manhattan could be called Museumpalooza—within just
one 30-block area (the main stage, aka Museum Mile, 5th
Avenue from 82nd Street to 105th Street)—there are nine
world-class institutions, and, within that general vicinity,
there are a dozen or so merely excellent ones. Trying to see
all of this wonderfulness in a week or two is, unfortunately,
impossible. Attempting to see all of even one or two of the
big museums is equally futile; your feet will go on strike
shortly before your brain shuts down with sensory overload.

So consider this your permission slip to think small. Pick
one—at most, two—of the bigger museums—the Metropolitan Museum of Art and/or the American Museum of Natural History are the obvious choices, though the Museum of
Modern Art is a definite contender—check out their Web
sites, and choose just two exhibit halls in your selected
museums to tour in depth. For a first visit to the Met, perhaps choose the Egyptian gallery and some of the period
rooms off the majorly renovated American Wing; in Natural History, the Dinosaur and Ocean Life halls. See them,
and then turn your attention to the city's smaller museums,
where there are hidden treasures; elsewhere, many of them
could be a city's cultural centerpiece.

Among our favorites are the Rubin Museum of Art on
West 17th Street, the first museum in the Western world
dedicated to the art of the Himalayas; the Museum of the
City of New York on 5th Avenue at 103rd Street, which
provides an outstanding overview of the city's origins;
the American Folk Art Museum on West 53rd Street; the
International Center of Photography on 6th Avenue and
43rd Street; and El Museo del Barrio at 104th Street and
5th Avenue, dedicated to Latino art and culture. (Bonus: all
our picks also have outstanding gift shops.) But choose the
museums that suit your interests however niche they may
be—there are institutions dedicated to water, toys, money,
film, television, transportation, assorted cultural heritages,
fashion, gardening, and many more.

Updated by
Jacqueline
Terrebonne

People visiting New York often confess to being over-whelmed by the honking traffic, the masses of people on the move, the 24/7 energy of the place. We've learned to tune that static out, but no matter how long you live here, you never cease to be amazed and somewhat besieged by the museums.

Artists have long since called New York home. For centuries they've drawn inspiration from the city's bustling mash-up of cultures. But the city's institutions do more than just display the works of its native sons and daughters; the plethora of museums offer the best the world has to offer at a depth and volume that is absolutely staggering.

There are so many wonderful things to explore in our incredible cultural institutions—and not a chance that a mere mortal can ever experience it all. The entire island is home to such a wealth of cultural treasure that it is both a blessing and—to those who despair of ever really doing it justice—a curse. You'll likely see more of the museums in your visit to Manhattan than the locals do in a few years of living here full time. But to see even a little bit, you'll need a plan.

This chapter is front-loaded with the shouldn't-miss museums: MoMA, the Guggenheim, and the Whitney are famous but often overlooked. The 800-pound gorillas, Natural History Museum and the Metropolitan Museum of Art are covered in depth in the following pages. Familiarizing yourself with their floor plans and permanent exhibits will help you make the most of your time.

Choose what museums you want to tour before you arrive. Then visit their Web sites to purchase tickets in advance when possible and peruse the information on special shows as well as daily events and tours. And if you have kids, make sure to check the family or educator's sections of the sites for interesting activities—scavenger hunts, puzzles, doodling, etc.—that can make a trip to the museum more fun for younger visitors. And, hey, they'll liven up those long marble halls for parents, too.

AMERICAN MUSEUM ᴼᶠ NATURAL HISTORY

Theodore Roosevelt
Memorial Hall

The largest natural history museum in the world is also one of the most impressive sights in New York. Four city blocks make up its 46 exhibition halls, which hold more than 30 million artifacts and wonders from the land, the sea, and outer space. With all those wonders, you won't be able to see everything on a single visit, but you can easily hit the highlights in half a day.

Before you begin, plan a route before setting out. Be sure to pick up a map when you pay your admission. The museum's four floors (and lower level) are mazelike.

To get the most from the museum's stunning riches, try to allow enough time to slow down and take advantage of the computer stations and the volunteer "Explainers," who are knowledgeable and able to point out their own favorite exhibits.

Getting into the museum can be time consuming. For the shortest lines, use the below-street-level entrance connected to the 81st Street subway station (look for the subway entrance to the left of the museum's steps). This entrance gives you quick access to bathrooms and the food court. The entrance on Central Park West, where the vast steps lead up into the impressive, barrel-ceilinged Theodore Roosevelt Rotunda, is the most impressive and memorable entrance at

the museum. Its central location makes a good starting place for exploring.

The Rose Center for Earth and Space, a must-visit, is attached to the museum. Enter from West 81st Street, where a path slopes down to the entrance, after which elevators and stairs descend to the ticket line on the lower level.

What to see? Check out the museum highlights on the following pages.

✉ Central Park West at W. 79th St., Upper West Side

Ⓜ Subway: B, C to 81st St.

☎ 212/769–5200

⊕ www.amnh.org

💲 $16 suggested donation, includes admission to Rose Center for Earth and Space

🕐 Daily 10–5:45. Rose Center until 8:45 on Fri.

Left, Spectrum of Life Wall

MUSEUM HIGHLIGHTS

Left, Tyrannosaurus rex
Above, Hadrosaurus

Dinosaurs and Mammals

An amazing assembly of dinosaur and mammal fossils covers the entire floor. The organization can be hard to grasp at first, so head to the **Wallace Orientation Center,** where a short film explains how each of the Fossil Halls lead into each other. You'll want to spend at least an hour here—the highlights include a *T. rex*, an *Apatosaurus* (formerly called a Brontosaurus), and the *Buettneria*, which resembles a modern-day crocodile.

The specimens are not in chronological order; they're put together based on their shared characteristics. Key branching-off points—a watertight egg, a grasping hand—are highlighted in the center of rooms and surrounded by related fossil groups. Check out the touch screens here; they make a complex topic more comprehensible.

Reptiles and Amphibians

Head for the Reptiles and Amphibians Hall to check out the Komodo dragon lizards and a 23-foot-long python skeleton. The weirdest display is the enlarged model of the Suriname toad *Pipa pipa*, whose young hatch from the female's back. The Primates Hall carries brief but interesting comparisons between apes, monkeys, and humans. Also on the third floor is the upper gallery of the famed Akeley Hall of African Mammals.

SPECIAL SHOWS AND NEW EXHIBITS

Special exhibits, the IMAX theater, and the Space Show cost extra. The timed tickets are available in advance at the museum's Web site and are sold same day at the door. Between October and May, don't miss the warm, plant-filled Butterfly Conservatory, where blue morphos, monarchs, and other butterflies flit and feed. Ten minutes is probably enough time to enjoy it.

THIRD FLOOR

Wallach
Orientation
Center

Café on 4

Vertebrate
Origins

Milstein Hall
of Advanced
Mammals

Saurischian
Dinosaurs

Astor Turret

Primitive
Mammals

Akeley Hall
of African
Mammals

Ornithischian
Dinosaurs

FOURTH FLOOR

Hayden Planetarium
Space Theater

Reptiles and
Amphibians

Rose Center for
Earth and Space

Ross Hall of
Meteorites

FIRST FLOOR

Guggenheim
Hall of Minerals

er Hall
luman
rigins

Morgan Memorial
Hall of Gems

Rose Center for
Earth and Space

Akeley
Hall of
African
Mammals

Big
Bang

Café on 1

Lefrak
IMSX
Theater

Heilbrunn Cosmic
Pathway

Milstein
Hall of
Ocean Life

Heilbrunn
Cosmic
Pathway

SECOND FLOOR

Hall of
Biodiversity

Gottesman Hall
of Planet Earth

Rose Center for
Earth and Space

Theodore Roosevelt
Memorial Hall

Akeley Hall of African Mammals

Opened in 1936, this hall is one of the most beloved parts of the museum. Its 28 dramatically lighted dioramas may seem merely kitschy at first glance, but take a little time to let their beauty and technical brilliance shine through.

The hall was the life's work of the explorer Carl Akeley, who came up with the idea for the hall, raised the funds for the expeditions, gathered specimens, and sketched landscape studies for what would become the stunning backgrounds. (The backgrounds themselves were painted by James Perry Wilson, whose works can be found throughout the museum.)

Akeley died a decade before the hall opened on an expedition in what's now Rwanda. His grave site is near the landscape portrayed in the gorilla diorama, completed after his death as a memorial to him and his work. The dioramas make irresistible photo ops. If you want to snap one yourself, it's best to turn off your flash to prevent reflections off the glass.

Hall of Human Origins

The Spitzer Hall of Human Origins is a comprehensive exhibit that allows visitors to draw their own conclusions about human evolution by presenting both the scientific methods and the material evidence that goes into evolutionary theory. Visitors gain insight into the techniques and thinking of scientists and anthropologists.

The exhibit then traces the evolution of our species over six million years of fossil record and spells out our ancestors' physical and intellectual advancements. Highlights include casts of our famous hairy relative "Lucy," who walked the plains of Africa over 1.8 million years ago.

Hall of Biodiversity

The small **Hall of Biodiversity** includes a shady replica of a Central African Republic rain forest. Within a few yards are 160 species of flora and fauna—and also evidence of the forest's destruction. Nearby, the **Spectrum of Life Wall** showcases 1,500 specimens and models, helping show just how weird life can get. The wall opens into the gaping Milstein Hall of Ocean Life, designed to give it an underwater glow and to show off the 94-foot model of a **blue whale** that's suspended from the ceiling. The hall focuses on the vast array of life in the ocean that covers our planet.

AMNH ON FILM

Does the inside of AMNH look familiar? It should. The museum is a popular location for movies filming in New York. Here are a few of its recent close ups:

Spider-Man2: Peter Parker (Toby Maguire) has yet another bad day wrestling with his secret identity while in the Rose Center.

Night at the Museum: Larry (Ben Stiller) is chased through the halls by a t. Rex and outsmarts a monkey in the Hall of African Mammals while working as a night security guard.

Blue Whale

The Squid & the Whale: Walt Berkman (Jesse Eisenberg) comes to a revelation that he is the squid and his father is the whale in front of the Hall of Ocean Life's famous diorama.

The Devil Wears Prada: Andrea (Anne Hathaway) wins over Miranda (Meryl Streep) by remembering the names of high society guests while attending a benefit here.

ROSE CENTER
FOR EARTH AND SPACE

The vast expanses of space and time involved in the creation of the universe can be hard to grasp even with the guiding hand of a museum, so visit the center when you're at your sharpest. The stunning glass building's centerpiece is the aluminum-clad Hayden Sphere, 87 feet in diameter. Enclosed within are the planetarium, called the Space Theater, and an audiovisual Big Bang presentation consisting of four minutes of narration by Maya Angelou, indistinct washes of color, and frightening bursts of sound. The rock-filled **Hall of Planet Earth** is particularly timely given the earthquakes and other natural disasters of recent years: one section uses a working earthquake monitor to help explain just what causes such seismic violence.

The Space Theater

At the Space Theater, the stage is the dome above you and the actors, heavenly projections. One of the world's largest virtual reality simulators, the theater uses surround sound and slight vibrations in the seats, to immerse you in scenes of planets, star clusters, and galaxies. The music of U2, Audioslave, and David Byrne among others inspire Sonic Vision, a digitally animated performance given every Friday and Saturday night.

TIME TO EAT?

Inside the Museum: The **main food court** on the lower level serves sandwiches for about $7.95; hamburgers cost $5.50. The animal- and planet-shaped cookies are draws for kids; adults should check out the barbecue station.

The small **Café on 4**, in a turret next to the fossil halls, sells pre-made sandwiches and salads, and yogurt and desserts, but nothing warm.

The über-white **Café on 1**, tucked away beside the Hall of Human Origins, sells warm sandwiches, soup, salads beer and wine at New York prices.

Outside the Museum: The nearest restaurants are expensive; to keep to a budget, head to a popular chain: **Uno Chicago Grill** (✉ Columbus Ave. and W. 81st St. ☎ 212/595–4700), where lunch specials run until 3 PM and kids' meals are $3.99 and up. For something special, try **Nice Matin** (Amsterdam Ave. and W. 79th St.), a French restaurant that specializes in food from the Nice region of France. They offer a brunch on the weekend from $7.50. Another option is a three course prix fixe dinner from 5:00–6:30 Monday–Friday that offers an array of selections from the menu for $32.50.

AMNH TALKS TO FODOR'S

Interview with Ellen V. Futter, President of the American Museum of Natural History, conducted by Michelle Delio.

If You Only Have an Hour: The American Museum of Natural History has the world's finest collection of dinosaur fossils, so a visit to the fourth-floor's Fossil Halls, where more than 600 specimens are on display, is a must. An extraordinarily high percentage of the specimens on view—85%—are real fossilized bones as opposed to casts. At most museums those percentages are reversed, so here visitors have the chance to see the real thing including T. rex, velociraptor, and triceratops.

What to Hit Next? The museum also is renowned for its habitat dioramas, which are considered among the finest examples in the world. Visits to the Akeley Hall of African Mammals, the Hall of North American Mammals, and the Sanford Hall of North American Birds provide an overview of the diorama arts—pioneered and advanced at the museum—while allowing visitors to come face-to-face with some glorious and beautiful animals depicted in their natural habitats—habitats which in many cases no longer exist in such pristine conditions.

Rose Center for Earth and Space

If You're Looking to Be Starstruck: Even if you don't have time to take in a space show in the Hayden Planetarium, the Rose Center for Earth and Space has lots of fascinating exhibits describing the vast range of sizes in the cosmos; the 13-billion-year history of the universe; the nature of galaxies, stars, and planets; and the dynamic features of our own unique planet Earth—all enclosed in a facility with spectacular award-winning architecture.

Hidden gems

The museum consists of 45 exhibition halls in 25 interconnected buildings so there are gems around every corner. Some lesser-known treasures include:

Star of India: The 563-carat Star of India, the largest and most famous star sapphire in the world, is displayed in the Morgan Memorial Hall of Gems.

WHERE'S PLUTO?

With all the controversy about what constitutes a planet, some visitors enjoy hunting for Pluto in the Cullman Hall of the Universe in the Rose Center for Earth and Space. We'll give you a hint: it's not with the other planets.

Black Smokers: These sulfide chimneys—collected during groundbreaking museum expeditions to the Pacific Ocean—are the only such specimens exhibited anywhere. Black smokers form around hot springs on the deep ocean floor and support a microbial community that does not live off sunlight but instead on the chemical energy of the Earth. Some of these microbes are considered the most ancient forms of life on Earth and may offer clues to the development of life here and the possibility of life elsewhere. See them in the Gottesman Hall of Planet Earth.

Spectrum of Life: The Hall of Biodiversity aims to showcase the glorious diversity of life on Earth resulting from 3.5 billion years of evolution. The impressive "Spectrum of Life" display is a 100-foot-long installation of more than 1,500 specimens and models—microorganisms and mammals, bacteria and beetles, fungi and fish. Use the computer workstations to learn more about the species depicted in each area.

Dodo: One of the museum's rarest treasures is the skeleton of a dodo bird, displayed along with other endangered or extinct species in the "Endangered Case" in the Hall of Biodiversity.

Small Dioramas: Tucked along the sides of the Hall of North American Mammals are two easy-to-miss corridors displaying a number of exquisitely rendered dioramas. In these jewel-box-like displays, some a mere 3 feet deep, you will see the smaller animals such as wolves galloping through a snowy night, a Canada lynx stalking a snowshoe hare, and a spotted skunk standing on its hands, preparing to spray a cacomistle, to name just a few of the evocative scenes.

Dinosaur Eggs: In 1993 museum scientists working in the Gobi Desert of Mongolia were the first to unearth fossilized embryos in dinosaur eggs, as well as the fossil of an adult oviraptor in a brooding posture over its nest. This discovery provided invaluable information about dinosaur gestation and revolutionized thinking about dinosaur behavior. Look for the display in the museum's Fossil Halls on the fourth floor.

Ross Terrace: In warmer months the Ross Terrace, with its fountains and cosmic theme, offers a wonderful outdoor spot for resting and reflecting, while providing a spectacular view of the Rose Center for Earth and Space.

Star of India

14

IN FOCUS AMERICAN MUSEUM OF NATURAL HISTORY

MOST INTERESTING OBJECT?

What's most interesting about the American Museum of Natural History is not any single object on exhibit, but the sheer range and scope of what you can experience here. Think of it is a field guide to the natural world, the universe, and the cultures of humanity—all under one roof. The experience of visiting the museum is ultimately about awakening a sense of discovery, wonder, awe, and stewardship of this Earth we call home.

THE METROPOLITAN MUSEUM OF ART

Mesmerizing carvings in the ancient Egyptian Temple of Dendur.

If the city held no other museum than the colossal Metropolitan Museum of Art, you could still occupy yourself for days roaming its labyrinthine corridors. Because the Metropolitan Museum has more than 2 million works of art representing 5,000 years of history, you're going to have to make tough choices. Looking at everything here could take a week.

Before you begin exploring the museum, check the museum's floor plan, available at all entrances, for location of the major wings and collections. Pick up the "Today's Events" flier at the desk where you buy your ticket. The museum offers gallery talks on a range of subjects; taking a tour with a staff curator can show you some of the collection's hidden secrets.

The posted adult admission, though only a suggestion, is one that's strongly encouraged. Whatever you choose to pay, admission includes all special exhibits and same-day entrance to the Cloisters (see page 231). The Met's audio guide costs an additional $7, and if you intend to stay more than an hour or so, it's worth it. The generally perceptive commentary covers museum highlights and directors' picks, with separate commentary tracks directed at kids.

If you want to avoid the crowds, visit weekday mornings. Also good are Friday and Saturday evenings, when live classical music plays from the Great Hall balcony. If the Great Hall (the main entrance) is mobbed, avoid the chaos by heading to the street-level entrance to the left of the main stairs, near 81st Street. Ticket lines and coat checks are much less ferocious here.

What to see? Check out the museum highlights on the following pages.

> ✉ 5th Ave. at 82nd St., Upper East Side
>
> Ⓜ Subway: 4, 5, 6 to 86th St.
>
> ☎ 212/535–7710
>
> 🌐 www.metmuseum.org
>
> 💵 $20 suggested donation
>
> 🕑 Tues.–Thurs. and Sun. 9:30–5:30, Fri. and Sat. 9:30–9

Left, Great Hall

MUSEUM HIGHLIGHTS

Egyptian Art

A major star is the **Temple of Dendur** (circa 15 BC), in a huge atrium to itself and with a moatlike pool of water to represent its original location near the Nile. The temple was commissioned by the Roman emperor Augustus to honor the goddess Isis and the sons of a Nubian chieftain. Look for the scratched-in graffiti from 19th-century Western explorers on the inside. Egypt gave the temple as a gift to the U.S. in 1965; it would have been submerged after the construction of the Aswan High Dam.

Temple of Dendur

The Egyptian collection as a whole covers 4,000 years of history, with papyrus pages from the Egyptian Book of the Dead, stone sarcophagi inscribed with hieroglyphics, and tombs. The galleries should be walked through counterclockwise from the Ancient Kingdom (2650–2150 BC), to the period under Roman rule (30 BC–400 AD). In the latter, keep an eye out for the enormous, bulbous **Sarcophagus of Horkhebil**, sculpted from basalt.

ART TO TAKE HOME

You don't have to pay admission to get to the mammoth gift shop on the first floor. One of the better souvenirs here is also one of the more reasonable: the Met's own **illustrated guide** to 858 of the best items in its collection ($19.95).

Greek and Roman Art

Today's tabloids have nothing on ancient Greece and Rome. They had it all—sex, cults, drugs, unrelenting violence, and, of course, stunning art. The recently redone Greek and Roman galleries encompass 6,000 works of art that reveal aspects of everyday life in these influential cultures.

The urnlike terracotta kraters were used by the Greeks for mixing wine and water at parties and other events. Given that, it's not surprising that most depict slightly racy scenes. Some of the most impressive can be found in the gallery covering 5th century BC.

Engelhard Court

On the mezzanine of the Roman galleries, the Etruscan bronze chariot from 650 BC depicts scenes from the life of Achilles. Notice how the simplistic Etruscan style in combination with the Greek influence evolved into the naturalistic Roman statues below.

The frescoes from a bedroom in the Villa of P. Fannius Synistor preserved by the explosion of Mt. Vesuvius in 79 AD give us a glimpse into the stylistic achievement of perspective in Roman painting.

Greek and Roman Galleries

SECOND FLOOR

MEZZANINES

FIRST FLOOR

5th Avenue

Visitors ponder European paintings on the 2nd floor.

American Wing

The **Henry R. Luce Center for the Study of American Art,** on a mezzanine between the first and second floors, is a storage room open to the public. Row after row of multilevel glass enclosures hold furniture, decorative objects, and paintings that couldn't otherwise be on display due to space constraints. There are enough works here to make up a small museum of their own—the **Pennsylvania Dutch chests** in row 25 are especially cool.

Also part of the collection is a group of five larger-than-life portraits by **John Singer Sargent.** One of them, *Madame X,* caused a scandal when it was first exhibited in Paris. The woman's pose, with one strap of her gown falling off her shoulder, seemed very suggestive to the onlookers of the time. Sargent later repainted the strap back up in its current, more proper position. Unfortunately these Sargent paintings are currently not on view, but check with information to see when they expect to put these pieces back on display.

TIME TO EAT?
INSIDE THE MUSEUM

The museum's restaurants are almost always full, and going to lunch at 2 PM doesn't mean there won't be a line. The **Petrie Café,** at the back of the 1st-floor European Sculpture Court, has waiter service, but aside from its wall of windows looking onto Central Park, it's very plain. Prices range from $12 for a sandwich to $21 for organic chicken salad. Tea, sweets, and savories are served from 2:30 PM to 4:30 PM during the week.

The **Great Hall Balcony Bar** is located on the second floor belcony overlooking the Great Hall. On Fridays and Saturdays, 4 PM TO 8:30 PM waiters serve appetizers and cocktails accompanied by live classical music.

The basement **cafeteria,** which has white tiles and a vaulted ceiling, has stations for pasta, main courses, antipasti, and sandwiches.

Tiffany

Arms and Armor

The **Equestrian Court**, where the knights are mounted on armored models of horses, is one of the most dramatic rooms in the museum. For a bird's-eye view, check it out again from the balconies in the Musical Instruments collection on the second floor.

European Sculpture and Decorative Arts

Among the many sculptures in the sun-filled Petrie Court, *Ugolino and His Sons* still stands out for the despairing poses of its subjects. Ugolino, a nobleman whose family's tragic story is told in Dante's *Inferno*, was punished for treason by being left to starve to death with his grandsons and sons in a locked tower. (It's not clear if putting such a sculpture so near the Petrie Court's café is some curator's idea of a joke or not.) By the way, the redbrick and granite wall on the court's north side is the museum's original entrance.

The newly renovated Wrightsman Galleries for French Decorative Arts on the first floor displays the opulence that caused Louis the XVI to lose his head. The blindingly golden Boiserie from the Hotel de Cabris, a remnant of French 18th century Neo-classical interiors, represents the finest collection of French decorative arts in the country.

Modern Art

The museum's most famous Picasso is probably his 1906 portrait *Gertrude Stein* in which the writer's face is stern and masklike. The portrait was bequeathed to the museum by Stein herself.

Of the Georgia O'Keeffes on view, 1931's *Red, White, and Blue* painting of a cow skull is a standout. The color, composition, and natural motif work together to create a work with religious as well as nationalist overtones.

European Paintings

On the second floor, the 13th- to 18th-century paintings are in one block, at the top of the Great Hall's stairs. To get to the 19th-century paintings and sculptures, walk through the the narrow corridor of Drawings, Prints, and Photographs. Both sections can be hard to navigate quickly, with a masterpiece around every corner.

Recently, the Met spent about $45 million to buy Duccio di Buoninsegna's *Madonna and Child,* painted circa 1300. The last remaining Duccio in private hands,

TIME TO EAT?
OUTSIDE THE MUSEUM

Because museum admission is good all day, you can always leave for lunch and come back later. The deli-style **City Market Café** (1100 Madison Ave., between. 82nd and 83rd Sts., 212/535–2070) with 10 small tables, serves pizzas, sandwiches, and make-your-own salad. At the fairly inexpensive sit-down eatery **Le Pain Quotidien** (1131 Madison Ave., at 84th St., 212/327–4900), the hungry dine at long communal tables for sandwiches (around $9), salads, and pastries high in both calories and quality. If you'd rather try for a typical New York diner, head for the **Amity Restaurant** (1134 Madison Ave, between 84th and 85th Sts.). A burger with fries costs under $10.

Equestrian Court (1930)

this painting, the size of a piece of typewriter paper, is unimpressive at first glance. The work, though rigid, represents a revolution in Byzantine art. The humanity reflected in the baby Jesus grabbing his mother's veil changed European painting.

The Triumph of Fame, a round, double-sided "commemorative birth tray" by Scheggia, shows a crowd of mounted knights saluting winged Fame, who holds both a cupid and a sword (they symbolize two timeless ways to get famous). The tray heralds the arrival of Lorenzo de' Medici (1449–92), who did indeed become a famed figure of the Italian Renaissance.

Vincent van Gogh,
Wheatfield with Cypresses

Rembrandt's masterful *Aristotle with a Bust of Homer* (1653) shows a philosopher contemplating worldly gains versus values through its play of light and use of symbols. Around Aristotle is a gold medal of Alexander the Great, one of the philosopher's students.

In the room dedicated to **Monet** you can get to all his greatest hits—poplar trees, haystacks, water lilies, and the Rouen Cathedral. The muted tones of Pissaro are followed by a room full of bright and garish colors announcing works by Gauguin, Matisse, and Van Gogh.

Asian Galleries

The serene **Astor Court,** which has its own skylight and pond of real-life koi (goldfish), is a model of a scholar's court garden in Soochow, China.

The Han dynasty (206 BC–220 AD) introduced the practice of sending the dead on to the afterlife with small objects to help them there. Keep an eye out for these **small clay figures,** which include farm animals (enclosed in barnyards) and dancing entertainers.

On display in a glass case in the center of an early-Chinese gallery is a complete set of 14 **bronze altar vessels.** Dating 1100 BC—800 AD, these green and slightly crusty pieces were used for worshipping ancestors.The Met displays some of its finest **Asian stoneware and porcelain** along the balcony overlooking the Great Hall.

The teak dome and minature balconies from a **Jain meeting hall** in western India were carved in the 16th century. Just about the entire surface is covered with musicians, animals, gods, and servants.

GREAT VIEWS

Looking for one of the best views in town? The Roof Garden (open May–October) exhibits contemporary sculptures, but most people take the elevator here to have a drink or snack while checking out Central Park and the skyline.

SOLOMON R. GUGGENHEIM MUSEUM

✉ *1071 5th Ave., between E. 88th and E. 89th Sts., Upper East Side*

☎ *212/423–3500*

⊕ *www.guggenheim.org*

🎫 *$18*

⊙ *Sun.–Wed. 9–5:45, Fri. and Sat. 9–8. Closed Thurs.*

Ⓜ *4, 5, 6 to 86th St.*

14

TIPS

■ Gallery talks provide richer understanding of the masterpieces in front of you. The museum offers tours at a terrific price: free!

■ Eat before trekking over to 5th Avenue; restaurants on Lexington offer more varied fare than the museum's cafeteria.

■ The museum is pay-what-you-wish on Saturday from 5:45 to 7:45. Lines can be long, so go early. The last tickets are handed out at 7:15.

Frank Lloyd Wright's landmark museum building is visited as much for its famous architecture as for its superlative art. Opened in 1959, shortly after Wright's death, the Guggenheim is acclaimed as one of the greatest buildings of the 20th century. After a three-year restoration project completed at the end of October 2008, the Guggenheim building is once again a glorious vision. Eleven coats of paint were removed, exterior cracks were fixed, and supporting structures were reinforced. Inside, under a 92-foot-high glass dome, a seemingly endless ramp spirals down past changing exhibits. The museum has strong holdings of Wassily Kandinsky, Paul Klee, Marc Chagall, Pablo Picasso, and Robert Mapplethorpe.

HIGHLIGHTS

Wright's design was criticized by some who believed that the distinctive building detracted from the art within, but the interior nautilus design allows artworks to be viewed from several different angles and distances. Be sure to notice not only what's in front of you but also what's across the spiral from you.

On permanent display, the museum's Thannhauser Collection is made up primarily of works by French impressionists and Postimpressionists van Gogh, Toulouse-Lautrec, Cézanne, and Matisse. Perhaps more than any other 20th-century painter, Wassily Kandinsky, one of the first "pure" abstract artists, has been closely linked to the museum's history. Beginning with the acquisition of his masterpiece *Composition 8* (1923) in 1930, the collection has grown to encompass more than 150 works.

MUSEUM OF MODERN ART (MOMA)

✉ *11 W. 53rd St., between 5th and 6th Aves., Midtown East*

☎ *212/708–9400*

⊕ *www.moma.org*

✉ *$20*

☉ *Sat.–Mon., Wed., and Thurs. 10:30–5:30, Fri. 10:30–8. Closed Tues.*

Ⓜ *E, V to 5th Ave./53rd St.; B, D, F, V to 47th–50th Sts. Rockefeller Center*

TIPS

■ Consider lining up for the free audio guide, especially if the scribbled and rather ambiguous nature of modern art occasionally confounds you.

■ Entrance between 4 and 8 pm on Friday is free, but come expecting to wait in line.

■ Check out the free Wi-Fi service within the museum to listen to audio tours as you wander through MoMA (log onto www.moma.org/wifi with your HTML browser-enabled device).

■ With so much art on display, it's hard to remember that the MoMA has three movie theaters. Film passes to the day's screenings are included with the price of admission.

■ Tickets to MoMA include free admission to its affiliated museum—the avant-garde P.S. 1 in Queens. Don't worry; you won't need to trek out to Queens on the same day. Save your ticket and you can go in for free any time within 30 days of your original purchase.

Novices and reluctant art enthusiasts are often awestruck by the masterpieces before them here, including Monet's *Water Lilies*, Picasso's *Les Demoiselles d'Avignon*, and van Gogh's *Starry Night*. In 2004, the museum's $425 million face-lift by Yoshio Taniguchi increased exhibition space by nearly 50%, including space to accommodate large-scale contemporary installations. Its current building gave the museum an opportunity for an increased focus on contemporary art, evident in the recent creation of a Media and Performance Art department. The museum continues to collect: most recently it obtained important works by Martin Kippenberger, David Wojnarowicz, Jasper Johns, Kara Walker, and Neo Rauch. One of the top research facilities in modern and contemporary art is housed inside the museum's eight-story "Education and Research" building.

HIGHLIGHTS

In addition to the artwork, one of the main draws of MoMA is the building itself. A maze of glass walkways permits art viewing from many angles.

The 110-foot atrium entrance (accessed from the museum's lobby on either 53rd or 54th Street) leads to the movie theaters and the main-floor restaurant, Modern, with Alsatian-inspired cuisine.

A favorite resting spot is the Abby Aldrich Rockefeller Sculpture Garden. Designed by Philip Johnson, it features Barnett Newman's *Broken Obelisk* (1962–69). The glass wall lets visitors look directly into the surrounding galleries from the garden.

Contemporary art (1970 to the present) from the museum's seven curatorial departments shares the second floor of the six-story building, and the sky-lighted top floor showcases an impressive lineup of changing exhibits.

WHITNEY MUSEUM OF AMERICAN ART

✉ *945 Madison Ave., at E. 75th St., Upper East Side*
☎ *800/WHITNEY*
⊕ *www.whitney.org*
🎟 *$15*
🕑 *Wed., Thurs., and weekends 11–6; Fri. 1–9*
Ⓜ *6 to 77th St.*

14

TIPS

■ After 6 pm on Friday the price of admission is pay-what-you-wish. On some of those nights the Whitney Live series presents new artists and reinterpretations of American classics. Be forewarned that this combination may result in long lines.

■ Sarabeth's at the Whitney serves a tasty selection of sandwiches, pastries, and soups.

With its bold collection of 20th- and 21st-centuy and contemporary American art, this museum presents an eclectic mix drawn from its permanent collection of more than 18,000 works in its permanent collection. The museum was originally a gallery in the studio of sculptor and collector Gertrude Vanderbilt Whitney, whose talent and taste were accompanied by the money of two wealthy families. In 1930, after the Met turned down Whitney's offer to donate her collection of 20th-century American art, she established an independent museum in Greenwich Village. Now uptown, the minimalist gray-granite building opened in 1966 and was designed by Marcel Breuer and Hamilton Smith.

HIGHLIGHTS

Start your visit on the fifth floor, where the eight sparse galleries house rotating exhibitions of postwar and contemporary works from the permanent collection by artists such as Jackson Pollock, Jim Dine, Jasper Johns, Mark Rothko, Chuck Close, Cindy Sherman, and Roy Lichtenstein.

Although the collection on display constantly changes, notable pieces often on view include Hopper's *Early Sunday Morning* (1930), Bellows's *Dempsey and Firpo* (1924), Alexander Calder's beloved *Circus,* and several of Georgia O'Keeffe's dazzling flower paintings.

The lower floors feature exhibitions of contemporary artists such as Kara Walker and Gordon Matta-Clark as well as retrospective exhibitions that focus on movements and themes in American art.

The often-controversial Whitney Biennial, which showcases the most important developments in American art over the previous two years, takes place in the spring of even-numbered years.

TOP MUSEUMS

American Folk Art Museum. Weather vanes, quilts, pottery, scrimshaw, sculpture, and paintings give an excellent overview of the freewheeling folk-art genre, but the exterior is a work of art as well: the eight-story building was designed in 2001 by husband-and-wife-team Tod Williams and Billie Tsein, and the facade, consisting of 63 hand-cast panels of alloyed bronze, reveals individual textures, sizes, and plays of light. You'll also find a large collection of contemporary self-taught artists of the 20th and 21st centuries, including the single larges collection of reclusive Chicago artist Henry Darger, known for his mythic, mural-sized painting. The museum's award-winning gift shop has an outstanding collection of handcrafted items. ⊠ *45 W. 53rd St., between 5th and 6th Aves., Midtown West* ☎ *212/265–1040* ⊕ *www.folkartmuseum. org* ▧ *$9; free Fri. 5:30 PM–7:30 PM* ☉ *Tues.–Thurs. and weekends 10:30–5:30, Fri. 10:30–7:30* Ⓜ *E, V to 5th Ave./53rd St.; B, D, E to 7th Ave.; B, D, F, V to 47th–50th Sts./Rockefeller Center.*

The Cloisters Museum and Gardens. Perched on a wooded hill in Fort Tryon Park, near Manhattan's northern tip, the Cloisters Museum and Gardens, which shelters the medieval collection of the Metropolitan Museum of Art, is a scenic destination on its own. Colonnaded walks connect authentic French and Spanish monastic cloisters, a French Romanesque chapel, a 12th-century chapter house, and a Romanesque apse. One room is devoted to the 15th- and 16th-century Unicorn Tapestries from around 1500—a must-see masterpiece of medieval mythology. The tomb effigies are another highlight. Two of the three enclosed gardens shelter more than 250 species of plants similar to those grown during the Middle Ages, including flowers, herbs, and medicinals; the third is an ornamental garden planted with both modern and medieval plants, providing color and fragrance from early spring until late fall. The Unicorn Garden blooms with flowers and plants depicted in the tapestries. Concerts of medieval music are held here regularly (concert tickets include same-day admission to the museum), and an outdoor café decorated with 15th-century carvings serves biscotti and espresso from May through October. ⊠ *99 Margaret Corbin Dr., Inwood* ☎ *212/923–3700* ⊕ *www.metmuseum.org* ▧ *$20 suggested donation* ☉ *Mar.–Oct., Tues.–Sun. 9:30–5:15; Nov.–Feb., Tues.–Sun. 9:30–4:45* Ⓜ *A to 190th St.*

Cooper-Hewitt National Design Museum. More than 2,000 years of international design are on display inside the 64-room mansion, formerly home to industrialist Andrew Carnegie. The 200,000-plus objects here include drawings, textiles, furniture, metalwork, ceramics, glass, and woodwork. Changing exhibitions are drawn from the permanent collection, highlighting everything from antique cutlery and Japanese sword fittings to robotics and animation. The museum's shows are invariably enlightening and often amusing. In summer some exhibits are displayed in the museum's lush garden. ⊠ *2 E. 91st St., at 5th Ave., Upper East Side* ☎ *212/849–8400* ⊕ *www.cooperhewitt.org* ▧ *$15* ☉ *Mon.–Fri. 10–5, Sat. 10–6, Sun. noon–6* Ⓜ *4, 5, 6 to 86th St.*

★ **Frick Collection.** Henry Clay Frick made his fortune amid the soot and smoke of Pittsburgh, where he was a coke (a coal fuel derivative) and steel baron. Decidedly removed from soot is this facility, once Frick's private New York residence. Édouard Manet's *The Bullfight* (1864) hangs in the East Gallery, which also exhibits the Chinard portrait bust (1809; bought in 2004). Two of the Frick's three Vermeers—*Officer and Laughing Girl* (circa 1658) and *Girl Interrupted at Her Music* (1660–61)—hang by the front staircase. Nearly 50 additional paintings, as well as sculpture, decorative arts, and furniture, are in the West and East galleries. Three Rembrandts, including *The Polish Rider* (circa 1655) and *Self-Portrait* (1658), as well as a third Vermeer, *Mistress and Maid* (circa 1665–70), hang in the former; paintings by El Greco, Goya, Millet, Greuze, and Hogarth in the latter. An audio guide, available in several languages, is included with admission, as are the year-round temporary exhibits. The tranquil indoor garden court is a great spot for a rest. Children under 10 are not admitted, 10–16 with adult only. ✉ *1 E. 70th St., at 5th Ave., Upper East Side* ☎ *212/288–0700* ⊕ *www.frick.org* ✍ *$18* ⊙ *Tues.–Sat. 10–6, Sun. 11–5* Ⓜ *6 to 68th St./ Hunter College.*

☾ ***Intrepid* Sea, Air & Space Museum.** The centerpiece of the newly renovated *Intrepid* Sea, Air & Space Museum complex is the 900-foot *Intrepid* aircraft carrier, making it Manhattan's only floating museum. The carrier's most trying moment of service, the day it was attacked in World War II by kamikaze pilots, is recounted in a multimedia presentation. Aircraft on deck include an A-12 Blackbird spy plane, a Concorde, helicopters, and thirty other aircraft. Docked alongside, and also part of the museum, is the *Growler,* a strategic-missile submarine. The interactive Exploreum contains 18 hands-on exhibits. Guests can experience a flight simulator, transmit messages in Morse code, and see what it was like to live aboard the massive carrier. ✉ *Hudson River, Pier 86, 12th Ave. at W. 46th St., Midtown West* ☎ *212/245–0072 or 877/957–7447* ⊕ *www.intrepidmuseum.org* ✍ *$22; free to active and retired U.S. military personnel and children under 3* ⊙ *Apr.–Sept., weekdays 10–5, weekends 10–6; Oct.–Mar., Tues.–Sun. 10–5; last admission 1 hr before closing* Ⓜ *A, C, E to 42nd St.; M42 bus to pier.*

★ **Museum of the City of New York.** Within a Colonial Revival building
☾ designed for the museum in the 1930s, the city's history and many quirks are revealed through engaging exhibits. Beginning in early 2010 and through 2012, the museum's permanent galleries will undergo a major renovation. The museum will still have a series of rotating exhibitions on subjects such as architecture, fashion, history, and politics. Don't miss *Timescapes*, a 25-minute media projection that innovatively illustrates New York's physical expansion and population changes. The museum hosts New York–centric lectures, films, and walking tours. ■**TIP→** When you're finished touring the museum, cross the street and stroll through the Vanderbilt Gates to enter the Conservatory Garden, one of Central Park's hidden gems. ✉ *1220 5th Ave., at E. 103rd St., Upper East Side* ☎ *212/534–1672* ⊕ *www.mcny.org* ✍ *$9 suggested donation* ⊙ *Tues.–Sun. 10–5* Ⓜ *6 to 103rd St.*

Major Museums

The Cloisters Museum and Gardens

Museum of the City of New York

Cooper-Hewitt

Guggenheim

Wards Island

Henry Hudson Pkwy.

Riverside Dr.

Broadway

Amsterdam Ave.

W. 96th St.

Central Park West

Central Park

E. 96th St.

5th Ave.

W. 86th St.

E. 86th St.

UPPER WEST SIDE

West End Ave.

Columbus Ave.

Metropolitan Museum of Art

UPPER EAST SIDE

Riverside Park

American Museum of Natural History

E. 79th St.

W. 72nd St.

Whitney Museum

E. 72nd St.

Frick Collection

Park Ave.

Roosevelt Island

FDR Dr.

E. 65th St.

Hudson River

Broadway

59th St.

57th St.

Queensboro Bridge

Museum of Modern Art (MoMA)

American Folk Art Museum

QUEENS

W. 50th St.

The Paley Center for Media

MIDTOWN

Intrepid Sea, Air, and Space Museum

W. 42nd St.

E. 42nd St.

Madison Ave.

Queens-Midtown Tunnel

Lincoln Tunnel

W. 34th St.

East River

11th Ave.

10th Ave.

9th Ave.

8th Ave.

7th Ave.

Broadway

5th Ave.

3rd Ave.

2nd Ave.

1st Ave.

W. 23rd St.

MURRAY HILL

CHELSEA

Ave. of the Americas

E. 23rd St.

GRAMERCY

Union Sq.

W. 14th St.

E. 14th St.

WEST VILLAGE

EAST VILLAGE

GREENWICH VILLAGE

Washington Sq.

Hudson River

West Side Hwy.

Houston St.

Williamsburg Bridge

NOLITA

Holland Tunnel

SOHO

Canal St.

W. Broadway

West St.

LITTLE ITALY

LOWER EAST SIDE

TRI-BECA

CHINATOWN

Manhattan Bridge

Chambers St.

Brooklyn Bridge

LOWER MANHATTAN

BROOKLYN

NEW JERSEY

Museum of Jewish Heritage

Museum of Jewish Heritage—A Living Memorial to the Holocaust. In a granite 85-foot hexagon at the southern end of Battery Park City, this museum pays tribute to the 6 million Jews who perished in the Holocaust. Architects Kevin Roche and John Dinkeloo built the museum in the shape of a Star of David, with three floors of exhibits demonstrating the dynamism of 20th-century Jewish culture. Visitors enter through a gallery that provides a context for the early-20th-century artifacts on the first floor: an elaborate screen hand-painted for the fall harvest festival of Sukkoth, wedding invitations, and tools used by Jewish tradesmen. Original documentary films play throughout the museum. The second floor details the rise of Nazism and anti-Semitism, and the ravages of the Holocaust. A gallery covers the doomed voyage of the SS *St. Louis,* a ship of German Jewish refugees that crossed the Atlantic twice in 1939 in search of a safe haven. Signs of hope are also on display, including a trumpet that Louis Bannet (the "Dutch Louis Armstrong") played for three years in the Auschwitz-Birkenau inmate orchestra. The third floor covers postwar Jewish life. The east wing contains a theater, memorial garden by artist Andy Goldsworthy, resource center, library, more galleries, classrooms, and a café. ⊠ *36 Battery Pl., Battery Park City, Lower Manhattan* ☎ *646/437 4200* ⊕ *www.mjhnyc.org* ⊠ *$12, free on Wed. from 4–10* ⊙ *Thurs. and Sun.–Tues. 10–5:45, Wed. 10–8, Fri. and eve of Jewish holidays 10–3* Ⓜ *4, 5 to Bowling Green.*

14

Fodor'sChoice ★ ☾ **The Paley Center for Media.** Three galleries of photographs and artifacts document the history of broadcasting in this 1989 limestone building by Philip Johnson and John Burgee. But the main draw here is the computerized catalog of more than 100,000 television and radio programs. If you want to see a performance of "Turkey Lurkey Time" from the 1969 Tony Awards, for example, type the name of the song, show, or performer into a computer terminal. You can then proceed to a semi-private screening area to watch your selection. People nearby might be watching classic comedies from the '50s, miniseries from the '70s, or news broadcasts from the '90s. Adding to the delight of screening TV shows from yesteryear is that the original commercials are still embedded in many of the programs; if ads are your thing you can also skip the programming altogether and watch different compilations of classic commercials. ⊠ *25 W. 52nd St., between 5th and 6th Aves., Midtown West* ☎ *212/621–6800* ⊕ *www.paleycenter.org* ⊠ *$10* ⊙ *Tues., Wed., and Fri.–Sun. noon–6; Thurs. noon–8* Ⓜ *E, V to 5th Ave./53rd St.; B, D, F, V to 47th–50th Sts./Rockefeller Center.*

MUSEUMS WORTH NOTING

☾ **Alexander Hamilton U.S. Custom House/National Museum of the American Indian.** The Beaux-Arts Alexander Hamilton U.S. Custom House (1907) is one of Lower Manhattan's finest buildings. Massive granite columns rise to a pediment topped by a double row of statues. Inside, the egg-shaped stairwell and rotunda embellished with shipping-theme murals (completed in the 1930s) are incredibly impressive. Changing presentations drawn from the National Museum of the American Indian in New York, a branch of the Smithsonian, are exhibited here with modern stylishness. The museum recently opened a new public gallery called "Infinity of Nations," which presents an encyclopedic survey of Native cultures from throughout the Americas, including 700 objects from ancient times to present day. The Diker Pavilion provides a venue for dance, music, and storytelling programs. Videos and films made by indigenous people from around the world are shown here regularly. ⊠ *1 Bowling Green, between State and Whitehall Sts., Lower Manhattan* ☎ *212/514–3700* ⊕ *www.americanindian.si.edu* ⊒ *Free* ⊙ *Mon.–Wed. and Fri.–Sun. 10–5, Thurs. 10–8* Ⓜ *4, 5 to Bowling Green.*

Asia Society and Museum. The Asian art collection of Mr. and Mrs. John D. Rockefeller III forms the core of the museum's holdings, which include South Asian stone and bronze sculptures; art from India, Nepal, Pakistan, and Afghanistan; bronze vessels, ceramics, sculpture, and paintings from China; Korean ceramics; and paintings, wooden sculptures, and ceramics from Japan. Founded in 1956, the society has a regular program of lectures, films, and performances, in addition to changing exhibitions of traditional and contemporary art. Trees grow in the Garden Court Café, which serves an eclectically Asian menu for lunch and dinner. ⊠ *725 Park Ave., at 70th St., Upper East Side* ☎ *212/288–6400* ⊕ *www.asiasociety.org* ⊒ *$10; free Fri. 6–9* ⊙ *Tues.– Sun. 11–6; open until 9 PM on Fri. from the day after Labor Day–July 3* Ⓜ *6 to 68th St./Hunter College.*

Chelsea Art Museum. In a former Christmas-ornament factory, this contemporary art museum was created to display a collection of postwar European art and to host traveling exhibitions from European museums. Exhibits examine relatively unexplored dimensions of 20th- and 21st-century art, as well as display the work of French abstract painter Jean Miotte. ⊠ *556 W. 22nd St., at 11th Ave., Chelsea* ☎ *212/255– 0719* ⊕ *www.chelseaartmuseum.org* ⊒ *$6* ⊙ *Tues., Wed., Fri., and Sat. noon–6, Thurs. noon–8* Ⓜ *C, E to 23rd St.*

☺ **Children's Museum of the Arts.** In this bi-level space a few blocks from Broadway, children ages 1 to 14 can amuse and educate themselves with various activities, including diving into a pool of colorful balls; playacting in costume; music making with real instruments; and art making, from computer art to old-fashioned painting, sculpting, and collage. ⊠ *182 Lafayette St., between Grand and Broome Sts., SoHo* ☎ *212/941–9198* ⊕ *www.cmany.org* ⊒ *$10* ⊙ *Wed. and Fri.–Sun. noon–5, Thurs. noon–6* Ⓜ *6 to Spring St.*

China Institute Gallery. A pair of stone lions guards the doorway of this pleasant redbrick town house. The institute's gallery is open for two exhibitions each year (September–November and March–June). Recent exhibitions include a collection of Chinese shadow puppets. The gallery is closed on holidays and between exhibits. ⊠ *125 E. 65th St., between Lexington and Park Aves., Upper East Side* ☎ *212/744–8181* ⊕ *www. chinainstitute.org* ⊒ *Gallery $5; free Tues. and Thurs. 6–8* ⊙ *Mon., Wed., Fri., and Sat. 10–5; Tues. and Thurs. 10–8* Ⓜ *6 to 68th St./Hunter College; F to 63rd St.-Lexington Ave.*

El Museo del Barrio. *El barrio* is Spanish for "the neighborhood" and the nickname for East Harlem, a largely Spanish-speaking Puerto Rican

Studio Museum in Harlem

Hispanic Society

El Museo del Barrio

Studio Museum in Harlem

Jewish Museum

National Academy

Neue Galerie New York

New-York Historical Society

Asia Society

China Institute Gallery

Museum of American Illustration

Museum of Arts & Design

Japan Society

International Center of Photography

Madame Tussaud's

Morgan Library

Museum of Sex

Chelsea Art Museum

Rubin Museum

Forbes Galleries

Grey Art Gallery

Museum of Comic & Cartoon Arts

Merchant's House

NYC Fire Museum

The New Museum

Lower East Side Tenement Museum

Children's Museum of the Arts

Museum of Chinese in the Americas (MoCA)

Museum of American Finance

NYC Police Museum

Skyscraper Museum

Alexander Hamilton U.S. Custom House

Randalls Island

Wards Island

UPPER WEST SIDE

Riverside Park

Central Park

UPPER EAST SIDE

Roosevelt Island

Queensboro Bridge

QUEENS

MIDTOWN

Queens-Midtown Tunnel

Lincoln Tunnel

MURRAY HILL

CHELSEA

GRAMERCY

Union Sq.

WEST VILLAGE

GREENWICH VILLAGE

Washington Sq.

EAST VILLAGE

Houston St.

NOLITA

Williamsburg Bridge

SOHO

LITTLE ITALY

LOWER EAST SIDE

TRI-BECA

CHINA-TOWN

Manhattan Bridge

Canal St.

Holland Tunnel

NEW JERSEY

Chambers St.

LOWER MANHATTAN

Brooklyn Bridge

BROOKLYN

Hudson River

East River

Henry Hudson Pkwy.

Riverside Dr.

West End Ave.

Amsterdam Ave.

Broadway

Columbus Ave.

Central Park West

Park Ave.

5 Ave.

Madison Ave.

FDR Dr.

W. 96th St.

W. 86th St.

W. 72nd St.

E. 96th St.

E. 86th St.

E. 79th St.

E. 72nd St.

E. 65th St.

59th St.

57th St.

W. 50th St.

W. 42nd St.

E. 42nd St.

W. 34th St.

11th Ave.

10th Ave.

9th Ave.

8th Ave.

7th Ave.

Ave. of the Americas

3rd Ave.

2nd Ave.

1st Ave.

W. 23rd St.

E. 23rd St.

W. 14th St.

E. 14th St.

West St.

W. Broadway

Broadway

Museums Worth Noting

and Dominican community. The museum, on the edge of this neighborhood, focuses on Latin American and Caribbean art. The more than 6,500-object permanent collection includes numerous pre-Columbian artifacts, sculpture, photography, film and video, and traditional art from all over Latin America. The collection of 360 *santos,* carved wooden folk-art figures from Puerto Rico, is a popular attraction. Thanks to a renovation in 2009, the museum now sports a glass facade and a redesigned courtyard. ⊠ *1230 5th Ave., between E. 104th and E. 105th Sts., Upper East Side* ☎ *212/831–7272* ⊕ *www.elmuseo.org* ⊠ *$6* ☉ *Wed.–Sun. 11–5* Ⓜ *6 to 103rd St.*

Forbes Galleries. Marvel at the idiosyncratic personal collection of the late publisher Malcolm Forbes, on view in the limestone Forbes Magazine Building. Those who like toys and flea-market finds (see the Trophies room) should definitely take a look at this small, personal museum. Military music is piped into the displays of toy warships and ocean liners. A tiny, dramatic diorama captures the adrenaline of the men on the gun deck of the HMS *Victory* during the Battle of Trafalgar. Of the 10,000 toy soldiers depicted in action, you'll see Aztecs resisting Cortez in 1521, Mussolini marching into Ethiopia in 1935, and a skirmish between "cowboys and Indians." ⊠ *62 5th Ave., at E. 12th St., Greenwich Village* ☎ *212/206–5548* ⊕ *www.forbesgalleries. com* ⊠ *Free* ☉ *Tues.–Sat. 10–4* Ⓜ *L, N, Q, R, W, 4, 5, 6 to 14th St./ Union Sq.*

Hispanic Society of America. This is the best collection of Spanish art outside the Prado in Madrid, with (primarily 15th- and 16th-century) paintings, sculptures, textiles, and decorative arts from Spain, Portugal, Italy, and South America. There are notable pieces by Goya, El Greco, and Velázquez. An entire room is filled with a collection of antique brass knockers. ⊠ *Audubon Terr., Broadway, between W. 155th and W. 156th Sts., entrance up steps to left, Harlem* ☎ *212/926–2234* ⊕ *www. hispanicsociety.org* ⊠ *Free* ☉ *Sept.–July, Tues.–Sat. 10–4:30, Sun. 1–4* Ⓜ *1 to 157th St.*

International Center of Photography *(ICP).* Founded in 1974 by photojournalist Cornell Capa (photographer Robert Capa's brother), this leading photography museum and school has a permanent collection focused on American and European documentary photography of the 1930s to the 1990s. Changing exhibits display work by famous and should-be-famous photographers and theme group shows on topics such as ecology, health, religion, science, war, and candid street shots. The gift shop offers amazing imagery on postcards, posters, and prints, and outstanding photography books. ⊠ *1133 6th Ave., at W. 43rd St., Midtown West* ☎ *212/857–0000* ⊕ *www.icp.org* ⊠ *$12* ☉ *Tues.–Thurs. and weekends 10–6, Fri. 10–8* Ⓜ *B, D, F, V to 42nd St.*

Japan Society. The stylish and serene lobby of the Japan Society has interior bamboo gardens linked by a second-floor waterfall. Works by well-known Japanese artists are exhibited in the second-floor gallery—past shows have included the first-ever retrospective of Yoko Ono's works and "Hiroshi Sugimoto: History of History." ⊠ *333 E. 47th St., between 1st and 2nd Aves., Midtown East* ☎ *212/832–1155* ⊕ *www.*

japansociety.org ⬚ *$10* ⊙ *Building weekdays 9:30–5:30. Gallery Tues.–Thurs. 11–6, Fri. 11–9, weekends 11–5* Ⓜ *6 to 51st St./Lexington Ave.; E, V to Lexington–3rd Aves./53rd St.*

Jewish Museum. Within a Gothic-style 1908 mansion, the museum draws on a large collection of art and ceremonial objects to explore Jewish identity and culture spanning over 4,000 years. The two-floor permanent exhibition "Culture and Continuity: The Jewish Journey" displays nearly 800 objects complemented by interactive media. The wide-ranging collection includes a 3rd-century Roman burial plaque, 20th-century sculpture by Elie Nadelman, and contemporary art from artists such as Marc Chagall and Man Ray. ⌧ *1109 5th Ave., at E. 92nd St., Upper East Side* ☎ *212/423–3200* ⊕ *www.jewishmuseum. org* ⬚ *$12; Sat. free all day* ⊙ *Sat.–Tues. 11–5:45, Thurs. 11–8, Fri. 11–4* Ⓜ *6 to 96th St.*

☾ **Lower East Side Tenement Museum.** Step back in time and into the partially restored 1863 tenement building at 97 Orchard Street, where you can squeeze through the preserved apartments of immigrants on one of four one-hour tours. This is America's first urban living-history museum dedicated to the life of immigrants—and one of the city's most underrated and overlooked. "Getting By" visits the homes of Natalie Gumpertz, a German-Jewish dressmaker (dating from 1878) and Adolph and Rosaria Baldizzi, Catholic immigrants from Sicily (1935). "Piecing it Together" visits the Levines' garment shop/apartment and the Rogarshevsky family from Eastern Europe (1918). The tour through the Confino family apartment is designed for children, who are greeted by a costumed interpreter playing Victoria Confino. Her family of Sephardic Jews came from Kastoria, Turkey, which is now part of Greece (1916). Another tour explores the life of the Moores, an Irish American family living in the building in 1869, and shows a re-created tenement rear yard. Building tours are limited to 15 people, so consider buying tickets in advance. A two-hour extended experience tour with chance for in-depth discussion is offered every day. Walking tours of the neighborhood are also held daily. The visitor information center and excellent gift shop displays a video with interviews of Lower East Side residents past and present. ⌧ *108 Orchard St., between Delancey and Broome Sts., Lower East Side* ☎ *212/982–8420* ⊕ *www.tenement.org* ⬚ *Tenement and walking tours $35; Confino apartment tour $20* ⊙ *Tours July–Aug. Fri.–Wed., 10–5, Thurs. 10–7:15; Sept.–June, daily, 11:15–5; check Web site for full details. Visitor center and gift shop daily 10–6* Ⓜ *B, D to Grand St.; F to Delancey St.; J, M, Z to Essex St.*

Madame Tussaud's New York. Sit in the Oval Office with President Obama, sing along with an American Idol, party in the V.I.P. room with the Jonas Brothers and Paris Hilton, or forecast tomorrow's weather with Al Roker. Much of the fun here comes from the photo opportunities—you're encouraged to pose with and touch the nearly 200 realistic replicas of the famous and infamous (disposable cameras are for sale). But there's more to do here than just pal around with the waxworks. Interactive options include a karaoke café, a celebrity walk down the red carpet, and a haunted town, the latter populated with both wax figures and real people. ⌧ *234 W. 42nd St., between 7th and 8th Aves.,*

14

Midtown West ☎ *212/512–9600* ⊕ *www.madame-tussauds.com* ✉ *$29* ⊙ *Weekdays 10–9, weekends 10–10* Ⓜ *1, 2, 3, 7, A, C, E, N, Q, R, W, S to 42nd St.*

Ⓒ **Merchant's House Museum.** Built in 1832, this redbrick house, combining Federal and Greek Revival styles, provides a glimpse into domestic life for the three decades before the Civil War. Retired merchant Seabury Tredwell and his descendants lived here from 1835 until 1933. The home became a museum in 1936 with the original furnishings and architectural features preserved; family memorabilia are also on display. Self-guided-tour are available without reservations. Kids under 12 get in free. ✉ *29 E. 4th St., between Bowery and Lafayette St., East Village* ☎ *212/777–1089* ⊕ *www.merchantshouse.org* ✉ *$8* ⊙ *Thurs.– Mon. noon–5* Ⓜ *6 to Astor Pl. or Bleecker St.; B, D, F, V to Broadway– Lafayette St.; R, W to 8th St.*

Morgan Library and Museum. The treasures inside this museum, gathered by John Pierpont Morgan (1837–1913), one of New York's wealthiest financiers, are exceptional: medieval and Renaissance illuminated manuscripts, old master drawings and prints, rare books, and autographed literary and musical manuscripts. Architect Renzo Piano's redesign of the museum was unveiled in April 2006. The original Renaissance-style building (1906) by Charles McKim of McKim, Mead & White has been preserved, but now there's twice the gallery space, an enlarged auditorium, a dining room, and a café. Crowning achievements produced on paper, from the Middle Ages to the 20th century, are on view here: letters penned by John Keats and Thomas Jefferson; a summary of the theory of relativity in Einstein's own elegant handwriting; three Gutenberg Bibles; drawings by Dürer, Leonardo da Vinci, Rubens, Blake, and Rembrandt; the only known manuscript fragment of Milton's *Paradise Lost;* Thoreau's journals; and original manuscripts and letters by Charlotte Brontë, Jane Austen, Thomas Pynchon, and many others.

The library shop is within an 1852 Italianate brownstone, once the home of Morgan's son, J. P. Morgan Jr. Outside on East 36th Street, the sphinx in the right-hand sculptured panel of the original library's facade was rumored to wear the face of architect Charles McKim. ✉ *225 Madison Ave., at 36th St., Murray Hill* ☎ *212/685–0008* ⊕ *www.themorgan. org* ✉ *$12* ⊙ *Tues.–Thurs. 10:30–5, Fri. 10:30–9, Sat. 10–6, Sun. 11–6* Ⓜ *B, D, F, N, Q, R, V, W to 34th St./Herald Sq.; 6 to 33rd St.*

Museum of American Finance. This Smithsonian Institution affiliate has made it big on Wall Street: in early 2008 it moved from a room in the Standard Oil Building on Broadway to the grandiose former banking hall of the Bank of New York. On view are artifacts of the financial market's history; interactive exhibits on the financial markets, banking, entrepreneurship, and Alexander Hamilton; and well-executed temporary exhibits. ✉ *48 Wall St., at William St., Lower Manhattan* ☎ *212/908–4110* ⊕ *www.financialhistory.org* ✉ *$2* ⊙ *Tues.–Sat. 10–4* Ⓜ *2, 3 to Wall St.*

Museum of American Illustration. Founded in 1901, the museum of the Society of Illustrators presents its annual "Oscars," a juried, international competition, from January to March. The best in children's book illustrations is featured October through November. In between are eclectic exhibitions on science fiction, fashion, political, and historical illustration. ✉ *128 E. 63rd St., between Lexington and Park Aves., Upper East Side* ☎ *212/838–2560* ⊕ *www.societyillustrators.org* ⊠ *Free* ⊘ *Tues. 10–8, Wed.–Fri. 10–5, Sat. noon–4* Ⓜ *F to 63rd St.; 4, 5, 6, N, R, W to 59th St./Lexington Ave.*

Museum of Arts and Design. In a whimsical building right next door to the Time-Warner center, the Museum of Art and Design celebrates joyful quirkiness and personal, sometimes even obsessive, artistic visions. The art is human-scale here, much of it neatly housed in display cases rather than on the walls, with a strong focus on contemporary jewelry, glass, ceramic, fiber, wood, and mixed-media works. Recent exhibits included "Slash: Paper Under the Knife," which showcased contemporary artworks entirely made from cut paper, and "Read My Pins," which displayed the brooch collection of former Secretary of State Madeline Albright. Thursday is a good time to drop by; the admission is pay-what-you-wish. ✉ *2 Columbus Circle, 59th St. at 8th Ave., Midtown* ☎ *212/299–7777* ⊕ *www.madmuseum.org* ⊠ *$15* ⊘ *Tues.–Sun. 11–6, Thurs. 11–9* Ⓜ *A, B, C, D, 1 to Columbus Circle/59th St.; N, Q, R, W to 57th St./7th Ave.; F to 57th St. /6th Ave.*

The Museum of Chinese in America (MOCA). Founded in 1980, this museum is dedicated to preserving and presenting the history of the Chinese people and their descendants in the United States., MOCA moved in early 2009 to its new home on Centre Street. The current 14,000-square-foot gallery space increased the size of the museum by more than five times. Designed by Maya Lin, architect of the Vietnam Veterans Memorial in Washington, D.C. MOCA features a permanent exhibit on Chinese-American history, "With a Single Step: Stories in the Making of America," which includes artworks, personal and domestic artifacts, historical documentation, and films. Chinese laundry tools, a traditional general store, and antique business signs are some of the unique objects on display. Rotating shows such as Here & Now, a contemporary art exhibit are on display in the second gallery. MOCA sponsors workshops, walking tours, lectures, and family events. ✉ *215 Centre St., between Grand and Howard Sts., Chinatown* ☎ *212/619–4785* ⊕ *www.moca-nyc.org* ⊠ *$7* ⊘ *Thurs. 11–9, Fri. 11–5, weekends 10–5, Mon. 11–5* Ⓜ *6, J, M, N, Q, R, W, Z to Canal St.*

Museum of Comic and Cartoon Art. Don't be put off by the uninspiring and small space, the Museum of Comic and Cartoon Art features smartly curated artist spotlights (such as Will Eisner, Todd McFarlane, and Kim Deitch) and genre exhibits. Recent shows included a retrospective of Saturday Morning Cartoons, which included a Smurf village along with the more predictable (but still swell) sketches, animation cells, videos, a horror-theme "Things That Go Bump" review, modern fairy tales, and a comprehensive look at the history and future of independent comics. New shows are mounted frequently, but MOCCA's Web site tends to list only coming-very-soon shows, so don't worry if nothing seems to be happening while you're planning your trip; check the site a week or so before you arrive in the city to see what's scheduled. And stay on the lookout for MOCCA's annual Art Festival, a comic and cartoon bonanza typically in June. ✉ *594 Broadway, Suite 401, between W. Houston and Broome Sts., SoHo* ☎ *212/254–3511* ⊕ *www.moccany. org* ⌨ *$5* ◔ *Tues.–Sat. noon–5 (Thurs. noon–6).* Ⓜ *B, D, F, G to Broadway/Layfayette St.; N, R to Prince St.*

Museum of Sex. Ponder the profound history and cultural significance of sex while staring at vintage pornographic photos, S&M paraphernalia, anti-masturbation devices from the 1800s, vintage condom tins, and silent movies. The subject matter is given serious curatorial treatment, though an alternative museum like this has to credit sex-product companies rather than foundations for sponsorship, and the gift shop preceding the galleries is full of fun sexual kitsch. On two floors, special exhibits and the permanent collection probe topics such as Japanese pornographic art from the 1700s or classic American pinup art. Evenings bring readings by cutting-edge authors and performance artists. No one under 18 is admitted. ✉ *233 5th Ave., entrance on 27th St., Flatiron District* ☎ *212/689–6337* ⊕ *www.museumofsex.com* ⌨ *$14.50* ◔ *Sun.–Fri. 11–6:30, Sat. 11–8* Ⓜ *R, W to 28th St.*

National Academy. Since its founding in 1825, the academy has required each member elected to its museum and School of Fine Arts (the oldest art school in New York) to donate a representative work of art. This criterion produced a strong collection of 19th- and 20th-century American art, as members have included Mary Cassatt, Samuel F. B. Morse, Winslow Homer, Frank Lloyd Wright, Jacob Lawrence, I. M. Pei, Robert Rauschenberg, Maya Lin, Frank Gehry, and Red Grooms. The collection's home is a 19th-century mansion donated in 1940 by sculptor and academy member Anna Hyatt Huntington. Huntington's bronze, *Diana of the Chase* (1922), is in the academy's foyer. ✉ *1083 5th Ave., between E. 89th and E. 90th Sts., Upper East Side* ☎ *212/369–4880* ⊕ *www.nationalacademy.org* ⌨ *$10* ◔ *Wed. and Thurs. noon–5, Fri.–Sun. 11–6* Ⓜ *4, 5, 6 to 86th St.*

Neue Galerie New York. Early-20th-century German and Austrian art and design are the focus here, with Gustav Klimt, Wassily Kandinsky, Paul Klee, Egon Schiele, Josef Hoffman, and other designers from the Wiener Werkstätte. The Neue Galerie was founded by the late art dealer Serge Sabarsky and cosmetics heir and art collector Ronald S. Lauder. The two-floor gallery, Viennese-style café, and design shop are in a 1914 wood- and marble-floored mansion designed by Carrère and Hastings, which was home to Mrs. Cornelius Vanderbilt III. An audio guide is included with admission. Note that children under 12 are not admitted, and teens 12–16 must be accompanied by an adult.

In an elegant, high-ceiling space below the Neue Galerie, **Café Sabarsky** serves Viennese coffee, cakes, strudels, and Sacher tortes (Monday and Wednesday 9–6, Thursday–Sunday 9–9). If you seek something more than a sugar fix, the savory menu includes trout crepes and Hungarian goulash. ✉ *1048 5th Ave., at E. 86th St., Upper East Side* ☎ *212/628–6200* ⊕ *www.neuegalerie.org* ⌨ *$15* ✄ *Children under 12 not admitted* ◔ *Thurs.–Mon. 11–6* Ⓜ *4, 5, 6 to 86th St.*

The New Museum. Focused on contemporary art, the New Museum moved to 235 Bowery in late 2007, marking the first time in its 30 years of existence that the institution has had its very own building. It's also the first building in downtown Manhattan constructed from the ground up with the purpose of being a museum. The seven-story, 60,000-square-foot structure—a glimmering metal mesh-clad assemblage of off-centered squares—was designed by avant-garde architects Kazuyo Sejima and Ryue Nishizawa. Previous exhibits include "Live Forever: Elizabeth Peyton," the painter's first survey in an American institution, and shows on computer hacking and life inside "the grid" of modern society. Be sure to run up to the seventh-floor "sky room" for a twirl around the panoramic balcony above Lower Manhattan. ⊠ *235 Bowery, at Prince St., Lower Manhattan* ☎ *212/219–1222* ⊕ *www. newmuseum.org* ✉ *$12* ⊗ *Wed., Sat., and Sun. noon–6, Thurs. and Fri. noon–9* Ⓜ *6 to Spring St.; F, V to 2nd Ave.*

14

�™ **New York City Fire Museum.** In the former headquarters of Engine 30, a handsome Beaux-Arts building dating from 1904, retired firefighters volunteer their time to answer visitors' questions. The collection of firefighting tools from the 18th century to the present includes hand-pulled and horse-drawn engines, pumps, and uniforms. A memorial exhibit with photos, paintings, children's artwork, and found objects relating to the September 11 attacks is also on view. On 9/11 the city's fire department lost 343 members at the World Trade Center. The museum is two subway stops (via the E train) north of the Ground Zero site. ⊠ *278 Spring St., near Varick St., SoHo* ☎ *212/691–1303* ⊕ *www. nycfiremuseum.org* ✉ *$5 suggested donation* ⊗ *Tues.–Sat. 10–5, Sun. 10–4* Ⓜ *C, E to Spring St.*

☃ **New York City Police Museum.** Why are police called cops? Why does a police badge have eight points? When was fingerprinting first used to solve a crime? Find the answers at this museum dedicated to New York's finest. The force's history from colonial times through the present is covered through permanent and rotating exhibits. A permanent exhibit, "9/11 Remembered," includes a video with interviews with those who were first responders to the attack. The Hall of Heroes honors police officers who have fallen in the line of duty. Special events include a vintage police-car show the first weekend in June, and the first Saturday in October, when kids get to meet police officers and events take place. ⊠ *100 Old Slip, near South St., Lower Manhattan* ☎ *212/480–3100* ⊕ *www.nycpolicemuseum.org* ✉ *$5 suggested donation* ⊗ *Mon.–Sat. 10–5* Ⓜ *2, 3 to Wall St.*

New-York Historical Society. Manhattan's oldest museum, founded in 1804, has one of the city's finest research libraries and a collection of 6 million pieces of art, literature, and memorabilia. Special exhibitions shed light on New York's—and America's—history, art, and architecture. Major exhibits have included Hudson River School landscapes and an examination of New York City's role in the slavery debate and the Civil War. Unlike other museums that keep much of their collections in storage, virtually all of the museum's huge and eclectic permanent collection—ranging from 19th-century cockroach traps to the armchair that George Washington sat in during his inaugural ceremony—are displayed in glass shelves in the museum's Henry Luce III Center for the Study of American Culture. It's a bit of a jumble, but you're bound to stumble across many wonderful things. ⊠ *2 W. 77th St., at Central Park W, Upper West Side* ☎ *212/873–3400* ⊕ *www.nyhistory.org* ⌑ *$12* ⊗ *Tues.–Thurs. and weekends 10–6, Fri. 10–8* Ⓜ *B, C to 81st St.*

Rubin Museum of Art. Opened in 2004, this sleek and serene museum is the largest in the western hemisphere dedicated to art of the Himalayas. It provides a great deal of the explanation for the colorful works, which are religious and rich with symbols. Six floors contain paintings on cloth, metal sculptures, and textiles dating from the 2nd century onward. Many of the works from areas such as Tibet, Nepal, southwest China, and India are all related to Buddhism, Hinduism, Bon, and other eastern religions. A pleasant café and gift shop are on the ground floor. ⊠ *150 W. 17th St., near 7th Ave., Chelsea* ☎ *212/620–5000* ⊕ *www. rmanyc.org* ⌑ *$10* ⊗ *Mon. and Thurs. 11–5, Wed. 11–7, Fri. 11–10, weekends 11–6* Ⓜ *1 to 18th St.*

Skyscraper Museum. This small museum will either delight or disappoint skyscraper fans. To evoke space, the stainless-steel floor and ceiling are polished to mirror quality, but the open room with column partitions does not include a comprehensive overview of the rise of the skyscraper. Focused exhibits change every few months; the newly expanded permanent display features highlights of New York and Chicago skyscraper history, including the daily photo journal a contractor kept during the Empire State Building's construction. Models of current or future buildings; short videos; and exhibits that reveal the influence of history, real estate, and individuals on architecture are regular features. ⊠ *39 Battery Pl., Battery Park City, Lower Manhattan* ☎ *212/968–1961* ⊕ *www. skyscraper.org* ⌑ *$5* ⊗ *Wed.–Sun. noon–6* Ⓜ *4, 5 to Bowling Green.*

Studio Museum in Harlem. Contemporary art by African-American, Caribbean, and African artists is the focus of this small museum with a light-filled sculpture garden. Its changing exhibits have included "Black Artists and Abstraction" and "Africa Comics." Three artists in residence present their works each year. ⊠ *144 W. 125th St., between Lenox Ave. and Adam Clayton Powell Jr. Blvd., Harlem* ☎ *212/864–4500* ⊕ *www.studiomuseum.org* ⌑ *$7 suggested donation* ⊗ *Wed.–Fri. and Sun. noon–6, Sat. 10–6* Ⓜ *2, 3 to 125th St.*

The Performing Arts

WORD OF MOUTH

"Seating is personal preference and does depend on the theater.
I like aisle seats best and will always opt for one if it's available.
For a musical, often first few rows of the mezzanine is better than
back of the orchestra but try to get as close to the center of the
theater as possible (not on extreme sides)."

—mclaurie

Updated by
Lynne Arany

"Where do you wait tables?" is the not-so-ironic question New York performers get when they say they're in the arts. But even more telling is that most of these toughened artists won't miss a beat when they respond with the restaurant's name. Fact is, if you're an aspiring performer here, you'd better be tough and competitive. There is a constant influx of artists from around the globe, and all these actors, singers, dancers, and musicians striving for their big break infuse the city with a crackling creative energy.

Just as tough are the audiences, many out-of-towners, many discerning local patrons, who help drive the arts scene as they thrive on keeping up with the latest—flocking to a concert hall to hear a world-class soprano deliver a flawless performance then crowding into a cramped café to support young writers floundering through their own prose.

New York has somewhere between 200 and 250 legitimate theaters (meaning those with theatrical performances, not movies or strip shows), and many more ad hoc venues—parks, churches, lofts, galleries, rooftops, even parking lots. The city is also a revolving door of special events: summer jazz, one-act-play marathons, film festivals, and music and dance celebrations from the classical to the avant-garde, to name just a few. It's this unrivaled wealth of culture and art that many New Yorkers cite as the reason why they're here, and the reason why many millions more say they're visiting here.

TICKETS 101

What do tickets sell for, anyway? Not counting the limited "premium seat" category (or discount deals), the top ticket price for Broadway musicals is now hovering at $130; the low end for musicals is in the $75 range. Nonmusical comedies and dramas start at about $60 and top out at about $120. Off-Broadway show tickets average $35–$80, while off-

off-Broadway shows can run as low as $10–$15. Tickets to an opera start at about $25 for nosebleed seats and can soar close to $400 for prime locations. Classical music concerts go for $25 to $100 or more, depending on the venue. Dance performances are usually in the $15 to $60 range, but expect seats for the ballet in choice spots to cost more.

Scoring tickets is fairly easy, especially if you have some flexibility. But if timing or cost is critical, the only way to ensure you'll get the seats you want is to make your purchase in advance—and that might be months ahead for a hit show. In general, tickets for Saturday evenings and for weekend matinees are the toughest to secure.

For opera, classical music, and dance performances, go to the box office or order tickets through the venue's Web site. For smaller performing-arts companies, and especially for off-Broadway shows, try **Ticket Central** (✉ *416 W. 42nd St., between 9th and 10th Aves., Midtown West* ☎ *212/279–4200* ⊕ *www.ticketcentral.com* ⊙ *Daily noon–8* PM Ⓜ *A, C, E to 42nd St.*); service charges are nominal here. **SmartTix** (☎ *212/868–4444* ⊕ *www.smarttix.com*) is relatively new, but a completely reliable resource for (usually) smaller performing-arts companies, including dance and music; their service charges are nominal as well. Inside the Times Square Information Center is the **Broadway Ticket Center** (✉ *1560 Broadway, between W. 46th and W. 47th Sts., Midtown West* ☎ *888/ BROADWAY* ⊕ *www.livebroadway.com* ⊙ *Ticket hours: Mon.–Sat. 9–7, Sun. 10–6* Ⓜ *1, 2, 3, 7, N, Q, R, W, S to 42nd St./Times Sq.; N, R, W to 49th St.*), where you can purchase full- and premium-price tickets for most Broadway (and some Off-Broadway) shows.

Sure bets for Broadway (and some other big-hall events) are the box office or either **Telecharge** (☎ *212/239–6200; 800/432–7250 outside NYC* ⊕ *www.telecharge.com*) or **Ticketmaster** (☎ *212/307–4100; 866/448–7849 automated service; 212/220–0500 premium tickets* ⊕ *www.ticketmaster.com*). Virtually all larger shows are listed with one service or the other, but never both; specifying "premium" will help you get elusive—and expensive (upwards of $200–$300)—seats. A broker or your hotel concierge should be able to procure last-minute tickets, but prices may even exceed "premium" rates. Be prepared to pay steep add-on fees (per ticket *and* per order) for all ticketing services.

■ **TIP→** Although most online ticket services provide seating maps to help you choose, the advantage of going to the box office is twofold: there are no add-on service fees, and a ticket seller can personally advise you about sight lines—and knee room—for the seat location you are considering. Broadway box offices do not usually have direct phone lines; their walk-in hours are generally 10 AM until curtain.

BROADWAY (AND OFF) AT A DISCOUNT

The cheapest—though chanciest—ticket opportunities are found at participating theater box offices on the day of the performance. These "Rush" tickets, usually about $25, may be distributed by lottery and are usually for front-row (possibly neck-craning) seats. Check the comprehensive planner on ⊕ *www.nytix.com* or go to the box office of the show you are interested in to discover whether they have such an offer and how to pursue it. Obstructed-view seats or those in the very rear balcony are sometimes available for advance purchase; the price point on these is usually in the $35–$40 range.

But for advanced discount purchases, the best seating is likely available by using a discount "code"—procure these 20%- to 50%-off codes online. (You will need to register on each Web site.) The excellent no-subscription-required ⊕ *www.broadwaybox.com* site is comprehensive and posts all discount codes currently available for Broadway shows. As with all discount codes offered through online subscriber services—**TheaterMania** (⊕ *www.theatermania.com*), **Playbill** (⊕ *www.playbill.com*), and **Best of Off Broadway** (⊕ *bestofoffbroadway.com*) among them—to avoid service charges, you must bring a printout of the offer to the box office, and make your purchase there.

For seats at 25%–50% off the usual price, go to one of the **TKTS booths** (⊠ *Duffy Sq. at W. 47th St. and Broadway, Midtown West* Ⓜ *1, 2, 3, 7, N, Q, R, S, W to 42nd St./Times Sq.; N, R, W to 49th St.; 1 to 50th St.* ⊠ *South St. Seaport at Front and John Sts., Lower Manhattan* Ⓜ *2, 3, 4, 5, A, C, E, J, M, Z to Fulton St./Broadway-Nassau* ⊠ *Downtown Brooklyn, at the Myrtle St. Promenade and Jay St., Brooklyn* Ⓜ *A, C, F to Jay St.-Borough Hall; M, R, 2, 3, 4, 5 to Court St.-Borough Hall* ⊕ *www.tdf.org*). Although they do tack on a $4 per ticket service charge, and not all shows are predictably available, the broad choices and ease of selection—and of course, the solid discount—make TKTS the go-to source for the flexible theatergoer. Check the electronic listings board near the ticket windows to mull over your options while you're on line. At the snazzily updated Duffy Square location (look for the bright red glass staircase), there is a separate *play only* window to further simplify—and speed—things. Duffy hours are Monday–Saturday 3–8 (for evening performances); for Wednesday and Saturday matinees 10–2; for Sunday matinees 11–3; Sunday evening shows, from 3 until a half hour before curtain. Seaport hours are Monday–Saturday 11–6, Sunday 11–4. Brooklyn hours are weekdays 11–6. With the exception of matinees at the Seaport and Brooklyn locations (they sell these for next-day performances only), all shows offered are for that same day. Credit cards, cash, or traveler's checks are accepted *at all locations.* ▪**TIP**➔ Planning ahead? Their Web site lists what was available at the booths in the previous week to give you an idea of what shows you'll find; and for all current shows it notes whether they are "frequently," "occasionally," "rarely," or "never" available at their booths.

THEATER

Broadway—not the Statue of Liberty or even the Empire State Building—is the city's number-one tourist attraction. Sure there's all that Technicolor neon, but it is the fabulous historic theaters—not to mention the popular productions within them—that draw most folks to the bedazzling showtime nexus at Times Square and 42nd Street. Yet to fully experience theater in New York you'll also want to consider the many offerings outside this area. From a splashy musical to an austere performance piece, from the Battery to the Bronx, New York has shows for every taste and budget—on just about any night (or day) of the week.

What's Playing Where

New York is rich with easily accessible and comprehensive listings resources in both print and online formats. The New York Times (⊕ www.nytimes. com) listings are concentrated in its Thursday, Friday, and Sunday papers, as well as online. The New Yorker (⊕ www.newyorker.com) is highly selective, but calls attention to performances with its succinct reviews. It hits the stands on Monday. In New York magazine (⊕ www.nymag.com), also on newsstands on Monday, see "The Week" section for hot-ticket events. Time Out New York's (⊕ time-outnewyork.com) short takes are comprehensive; read them online or pick up a copy of the weekly on Thursday.

The freebie tabloid the Village Voice (⊕ www.villagevoice.com) comes out on Wednesday; it has extensive listings—especially for theater, music, and dance—as well.

Online-only venues ⊕ www.nytheatre. com (especially for Broadway) and ⊕ www.nyconstage.org, ⊕ indiethe-ater.org, and ⊕ offoffonline.com (for Off- and Off-Off Broadway) provide synopses, schedules when theaters are dark, accessibility info, run times, seating charts, and links to ticket purchases. The best general source online for dance and smaller opera and classical music companies is ⊕ www.smarttix.com.

15

BROADWAY

Even if you're just a legend in your own mind, there's nothing quite like making your own grand entrance at a show on the Great White Way. As you find your way to your seat, the anticipation starts to rise; you sit, the houselights dim, and the orchestra strikes up the first notes of the overture, filling the theater with excitement. There is no other experience like it, and no visit to the city—at least your first or second visit—is really complete if you haven't seen a Broadway show (or three). So stow away your ticket stub, take one last glance at your Playbill, shut off your cellphone, and prepare to be transported.

Some of the 40 Broadway theaters are just as interesting for their history as for their current productions. The onetime Selwyn—the venerable home to the works of Coward, Kaufman, and Porter in their heyday—is now known as the **American Airlines Theatre** (⊠ 227 W. 42nd St., between 7th and 8th Aves., Midtown West ☎ 212/719–1300 ⊕ www. roundabouttheatre.org Ⓜ 1, 2, 3, 7, N, Q, R, W, S to 42nd St./Times Sq.; A, C, E to 42nd St./Port Authority). After incarnations as a burlesque hall and pornographic movie house, this splendidly restored 1918 Vene-tian-style playhouse is now home to the not-for-profit Roundabout Theatre Company, which is acclaimed for its revivals of classic musi-cals and plays, such as a Doug Hughes–directed production of A Man for All Seasons. The **Barrymore Theatre** (⊠ 243 W. 47th St., between Broadway and 8th Ave., Midtown West ☎ 212/239–6200 ⊕ www. shubertorganization.com Ⓜ 1, 2, 3, 7, N, Q, R, W, S to 42nd St./Times Sq.; C, E to 50th St.) was that rare Broadway house that stayed legit throughout the Depression and still honors its original namesake, Ethel Barrymore. The 1928 Elizabethan wonder greets theatergoers with two stone archways. Shows within have included David Rabe's original *Hurly Burly* in 1984 and the innovative revival of Sondheim's *Company* in 2006. Disney refurbished the elaborate 1903 Art Nouveau **New Amsterdam Theater** (⊠ *214 W. 42nd St., between 7th and 8th Aves., Midtown West* ☎ *212/282–2907* ⊕ *www.disneyonbroadway.com* Ⓜ *1, 2, 3, 7, N, Q, R, W, S to 42nd St./Times Sq.; A, C, E to 42nd St./Port Authority*), where Eddie Cantor, Will Rogers, Fanny Brice, and the Ziegfeld Follies once drew crowds. *The Lion King* ruled here for the first nine years of its run. Moorish Revival in style, the **St. James** (⊠ *246 W. 44th St., between Broadway and 8th Ave., Midtown West* ☎ *212/269–6300* Ⓜ *1, 2, 3, 7, N, Q, R, W, S to 42nd St./Times Sq.; A, C, E to 42nd St./ Port Authority*) went up in 1927, and has been running legit at least since the late 1930s. Home of Mel Brooks's juggernaut *The Producers* in its heyday, and where a Tony-laden revival of *Gypsy* held sway late in the first decade of the 21st century, the St. James is where Lauren Bacall was an usherette in the '40s, and where a little show called *Oklahoma!* premiered, with a rousing score and choreography to match, and changed the musical forever.

OFF-BROADWAY THEATERS

Off-Broadway houses—defined by seat count, not the theater's location—are where you can find showcases for emerging playwrights, unexpected stagings of classic plays, and perennial crowd-pleasers like *Stomp* and *Blue Man Group*. The venues themselves are found throughout the city—these shows indeed play in the Times Square area, but clusters of them mark a wide swath of Manhattan from Houston north to 14th Street; there are hot spots in the other boroughs as well.

At the cozy 178-seat theater belonging to the **Classic Stage Company** (⊠ *136 E. 13th St., between 3rd and 4th Aves., East Village* ☎ *212/677–4210* ⊕ *www.classicstage.org* Ⓜ *4, 5, 6, L, N, Q, R, W to Union Sq.*) you can see revivals—such as Chekhov's *Three Sisters* or Shakespeare's *The Tempest*—perhaps with a modern spin, and often with reigning theatrical stars.

The **New York Theater Workshop (NYTW)** (⊠ *79 E. 4th St., between Bowery and 2nd Ave., East Village* ☎ *212/460–5475* ⊕ *www.nytw.org* Ⓜ *F, V to 2nd Ave.; B, D, F, V to Broadway-Lafayette St.; 6 to Bleecker St.*) produces work by new and established playwrights. Tony Kushner's *Homebody Kabul* premiered at NYTW, and Jonathan Larson's *Rent* got its pre-Broadway start here. Hit the box office for Sunday night "Cheap-Tix"; those seats are $20—in cash, in advance only—as available.

Playwrights Horizons (⊠ *416 W. 42nd St., between 9th and 10th Aves., Midtown West* ☎ *212/564–1235; 212/279–4200 tickets* ⊕ *www. playwrightshorizons.org* Ⓜ *A, C, E to 42nd St./Port Authority*) is known for its support of new work by American playwrights. The first home for eventual Broadway hits such as *Grey Gardens* and Wendy Wasserstein's *The Heidi Chronicles*; this is where you will find the latest work from Craig Lucas and Doug Wright. **The Public Theater** (⊠ *425 Lafayette St., south of Astor Pl., East Village* ☎ *212/539–8500; 212/967–7555 tickets* ⊕ *www.publictheater.org* Ⓜ *6 to Astor Pl.; R, W to 8th St.*)

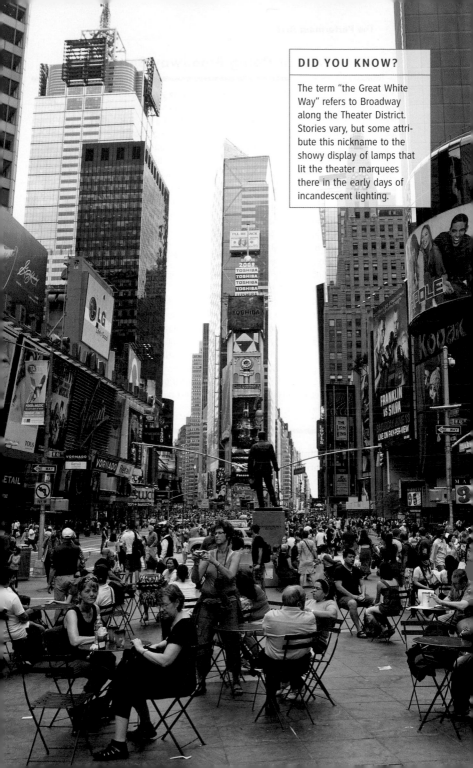

CLOSE UP | Three Tips for Doing Broadway Better

Whether you're handing over a hundred bucks for a top ticket or shoestringing it in a nosebleed seat, seeing one show or seven, you'll have better Broadway experiences to brag about if you take our advice.

Reserve ahead. The TKTS booth is great when you're up for what the fates make available, but for must-sees, we recommend booking early. While you're at it, don't forget to ask whether the regular cast is expected (an in-person stop at the box office is the most reliable way to score this information ahead, but don't hold them to it unless it's the day of performance. If there is a change then—and the replacement cast is not acceptable to you—you may get a refund). For musicals, live music will always add a special zing; confirm when ticketing to avoid surprises on the rare occasion when recorded music is used.

Know your seats. Front mezzanine is a great option; with seats that overhang the stage, they can be better (though not always less expensive) than many orchestra locations. Always book with a seating chart at hand (available online and at the box office); although even the priciest seats might be tight, it is always worth splurging for the best sight lines. Check accessibility, especially at older theaters with multiple flights of stairs and scarce elevators.

Know when to go. Surprisingly, Friday evening is a good option; Saturday night and weekday matinees are the most difficult. Do as the locals do and go on weeknights. Tuesday is especially promising, and typically an earlier curtain—7 or 7:30 instead of the usual 8 PM—helps ensure that you'll get a good night's sleep for your next day of touring.

---

presents fresh theater like the latest work of Suzan-Lori Parks, a 2008 Stephen Sondheim debut, and monologuist Mike Daisey's *If You See Something Say Something.* Many noted productions that began here (*Hair*, *A Chorus Line*) went on to Broadway. Go to the Public's box office one hour prior to curtain to secure one of their limited-availability (and cash only) $20 Rush Tix. In summer you won't want to miss their incomparable—and free—Shakespeare in the Park performances.

Signature Theatre Company (⊠ *Peter Norton Space, 555 W. 42nd St., between 10th and 11th Aves., Midtown West* ☎ *212/244–7529 info and tickets* ⊕ *www.signaturetheatre.org* Ⓜ *A, C, E to 42nd St./Port Authority*) devotes each season to works by a single playwright (August Wilson, Horton Foote, Sam Shepard, and Tony Kushner among them), or an entire tradition, such as the seminal works of the Negro Ensemble Company. All tickets are $20.

OFF-OFF BROADWAY AND PERFORMANCE ART

The following theaters are all small—even tiny—but host works that are often startling in their originality; expect their shows to stretch the boundaries of what's found on Broadway *and* off-Broadway.

HERE Arts Center (✉ *145 6th Ave., between Spring and Broome Sts., SoHo* ☎ *212/352–3101; 866/811–4111 tickets* ⊕ *www.here.org* Ⓜ *C, E to Spring St.*), the original home of Eve Ensler's 1997 Obie winner *The Vagina Monologues,* 2007's lauded *Removable Parts,* and all manner of genre-bending productions, also has an art gallery and café. **The Kitchen** (✉ *512 W. 19th St., between 10th and 11th Aves., Chelsea* ☎ *212/255–5793* ⊕ *www.thekitchen.org* Ⓜ *C, E to 23rd St.*) is *the* place for multimedia performance art, and has been a crucible for artists on the experimental edge—Charles Atlas, Kiki Smith, Elizabeth Streb—since 1971. Ellen Stewart, also known as La Mama, founded **La MaMa E.T.C.** (✉ *74A E. 4th St., between Bowery and 2nd Ave., East Village* ☎ *212/475–7710* ⊕ *www.lamama.org* Ⓜ *F, V to 2nd Ave.; B, D, F, V to Broadway-Lafayette St.; 6 to Bleecker St.*) in a tiny basement space in 1961. It's grown now, and her influential "Experimental Theater Club" continues to support new works that cross cultures and performance disciplines.

★ **Performance Space 122 (P.S. 122)** (✉ *150 1st Ave., at E. 9th St., East Village* ☎ *212/352–3101 tickets* ⊕ *www.ps122.org* Ⓜ *6 to Astor Pl.*) became a launching pad for now well-recognized talent like Karen Finley, Spalding Gray, Ann Magnuson, and Eric Bogosian back in the 1980s, and continues to offer a dazzling repertoire of performance from the fringe.

Fodor's Choice ★ **St. Ann's Warehouse** (✉ *38 Water St., between Main and Dock Sts., DUMBO, Brooklyn* ☎ *718/254–8779; 866/911–4111 tickets* ⊕ *stannswarehouse.org* Ⓜ *A, C to High St.; F to York St.*) has hosted everything from the National Theatre of Scotland's evisceration of war, *Black Watch,* to the strangely riveting Tiger Lillies, and is also a regular home for the Wooster Group's larger productions—such as their 2009 opera, *La Didone.*

A four-theater cultural complex, **Theater for the New City** (✉ *155 1st Ave., between E. 9th and E. 10th Sts., East Village* ☎ *212/254–1109* ⊕ *www.theaterforthenewcity.net* Ⓜ *6 to Astor Pl.*) puts on 30–40 new American plays each year, including works by Moises Kaufman and Mabou Mines.

THEATER FOR CHILDREN

★ ☺ **Just Kidding at Symphony Space** (✉ *2537 Broadway, at W. 95th St., Upper West Side* ☎ *212/864–5400* ⊕ *www.symphonyspace.org* Ⓜ *1, 2, 3 to 96th St.*) is a family series that has it all—musicals especially, but a nonstop parade of plays, sing-alongs, and puppets as well.

Fodor's Choice ★ ☺ In a magnificently restored century-old performance space, **The New Victory Theater** (✉ *209 W. 42nd St., between 7th and 8th Aves., Midtown West* ☎ *212/239–6200* ⊕ *www.newvictory.org* Ⓜ *1, 2, 3, 7, A, C, E, N, Q, R, W, S to 42nd St./Times Sq.*) presents supremely kid-pleasing plays, music, and dance performances, and even minicircuses. On weekends **The Paper Bag Players** (☎ *212/663–0390* ⊕ *www.thepaperbagplayers. org*), the country's oldest children's theater group, stage original—and exuberant—plays for youngsters under 10 at venues throughout the city. Finely detailed wooden marionettes and hand puppets are on the

15

bill at **Puppetworks** (✉ *338 6th Ave., at 4th St., Park Slope, Brooklyn* ☎ *718/965–3391 [reservations required]* ⊕ *www.puppetworks.org* Ⓜ *F to 7th Ave.*). Familiar childhood tales like *Little Red Riding Hood* and *Peter and the Wolf* come to life in this 75-seat neighborhood theater.

The **Swedish Cottage Marionette Theatre** (✉ *Swedish Cottage, West Dr., at W. 79th St., Central Park* ☎ *212/988–9093 [reservations required]* ⊕ *www.cityparksfoundation.org* or *www.centralparknyc.org* Ⓜ *B, C to 81st St.*) was originally part of Sweden's exhibit at the 1876 Centennial Exposition in Philadelphia (park designer Frederick Law Olmsted had it moved here the following year). The charming wooden 100-seat (and technically modern) playhouse presents classics like *Hansel and Gretel* and *Cinderella*.

MUSIC

"Gentlemen," conductor Serge Koussevitzky once told the assembled Boston Symphony Orchestra, "maybe it's good enough for Cleveland or Cincinnati, but it's not good enough for New York." In a nutshell he described New York's central position in the musical world. New York has the country's oldest symphony orchestra (the New York Philharmonic) as well as three renowned conservatories (the Juilliard School, the Manhattan School of Music, and Mannes College of Music). For more than a century, the best orchestras have made this a principal stop on their tours. The city is also a mecca for an astonishing variety of musicians playing everything from early music to minimalism, klezmer to Senegalese percussion. In summer the city comes fully alive with the best music it has to offer—performed outdoors from river to river and throughout the five boroughs—often for free.

CONCERT HALLS

The **Brooklyn Academy of Music (BAM)** (✉ *Howard Gilman Opera House, Peter Jay Sharp Bldg., 30 Lafayette Ave., between Ashland Pl. and St. Felix St., Fort Greene, Brooklyn* ☎ *718/636–4100* ⊕ *www.bam.org* Ⓜ *2, 3, 4, 5, B, Q to Atlantic Ave.*) is the performing home of the **Brooklyn Philharmonic** (☎ *718/488–5700* ⊕ *www.brooklynphilharmonic. org*), which, under the direction of Michael Christie, has some of the most adventurous symphonic programming to be found in the city. The impressive acoustics here perfectly complement this orchestra and the wide selection of nontraditional musical programming featured here throughout the year.

Fodor's Choice ★ ☾ **Carnegie Hall** (✉ *881 7th Ave., at W. 57th St., Midtown West* ☎ *212/247–7800* ⊕ *www.carnegiehall.org* Ⓜ *N, Q, R, W to 57th St.; B, D, E to 7th Ave.*) is one of the best venues—anywhere—to hear classical music. The world's top orchestras sound so good because of the incomparable acoustics of the fabulously steep Stern Auditorium. So do smaller ensembles and soloists such as sopranos Renée Fleming and Deborah Voight. A noted roster of Family Concerts is also part of Carnegie's programming. The subterranean **Zankel Hall**, with equally excellent acoustics, attracts performers such as the Kronos Quartet, Milton

Nascimento, and Ravi Shankar. Many young talents make their New York debuts in the **Weill Recital Hall.** ∎**TIP**➔ The Carnegie box office offers $10 Rush tickets on the day of performance, or you may buy partial-view seating in advance at 50% off the full ticket price.

★ **Lincoln Center for the Performing Arts** (✉ *W. 62nd to W. 66th Sts., Broad-*
☺ *way to Amsterdam Ave., Upper West Side* ☎*212/546–2656* ⊕*www. lincolncenter.org* Ⓜ *1 to 66th St./Lincoln Center*) is the city's musical nerve center, especially when it comes to classical music. Formal and U-shaped, the massive Avery Fisher Hall presents the world's great musicians and is home to the **New York Philharmonic** (☎*212/875–5656* ⊕*nyphil.org*), one of the finest symphony orchestras. Alan Gilbert conducts from late September to early June. Orchestra rehearsals at 9:45 AM are open to the public on selected weekday mornings (usually Wednesday or Thursday) for $16. A popular Young People's Concert series is offered on Saturday afternoons, four times throughout the season. The **Chamber Music Society of Lincoln Center** (☎*212/875–5788* ⊕*www.chambermusicsociety.org*) performs in Alice Tully Hall, which is considered to be as acoustically perfect as a concert hall can get. In August Lincoln Center's longest-running classical series, the **Mostly Mozart Festival** (☎*212/875–5399*), captures the crowds.

15

OTHER VENUES

In Brooklyn, **Bargemusic** (✉*Fulton Ferry Landing, at Old Fulton and Furman Sts., Brooklyn Heights* ☎*718/624–2083* ⊕*www.bargemusic. org* Ⓜ*A, C to High St.; 2, 3 to Clark St.*) keeps chamber music groups busy year-round on a re-outfitted harbor barge with a fabulous view of the Manhattan skyline. Anything you come to hear at the **Cathedral Church of St. John the Divine** (✉*1047 Amsterdam Ave., at W. 112th St., Upper West Side* ☎*212/316–7490* ⊕*www.stjohndivine.org* Ⓜ*1, B, C to 110th St./Cathedral Pkwy.*) will likely be an unforgettable experience, but the seasonal programming of the **Early Music New York** (☎*212/749–6600* ⊕*www.earlymusicny.org*) ensemble is essential.

In its Grace Rainey Rogers Auditorium (and occasionally in the Medieval Sculpture Hall and the Temple of Dendur) the **Metropolitan Museum of Art** (✉*1000 5th Ave., at E. 82nd St., Upper East Side* ☎*212/570–3949* ⊕*www.metmuseum.org* Ⓜ*4, 5, 6 to 86th St.*) offers a rich seasonal music program with concerts by leading classical and jazz musicians. Also part of the Met, and well worth the trip farther uptown, is **The Cloisters** (✉*Fort Tryon Park, Morningside Heights* ☎*212/650–2290* Ⓜ*A to 190th St.*), which has matinee performances of sacred and secular music from the Middle Ages. It all takes places within a 12th-century Spanish chapel. Well-known soloists and chamber music groups perform in **Kaufmann Concert Hall** (✉*Tisch Center for the Arts, 92nd St. Y, 1395 Lexington Ave., at E. 92nd St., Upper East Side* ☎*212/996–1100* ⊕*www.92y.org* Ⓜ*6 to 96th St.*).

★ Adventurous programming of jazz, classical, early and modern music, and dance continues at the **Miller Theatre** (✉*Columbia University, 2960 Broadway, at W. 116th St., Morningside Heights* ☎*212/854–1633; 212/854–7799 box office* ⊕*www.millertheatre.com* Ⓜ*1 to 116th St.*), which is now in the hands of 2009-appointed director Melissa Smey. A well-designed 688-seater, this is a hall that rewards serious listeners. **Symphony Space** (✉ *2537 Broadway, at W. 95th St., Upper West Side* ☎ *212/864–5400* ⊕ *www.symphonyspace.org* Ⓜ *1, 2, 3 to 96th St.*) presents an energetic roster of music (including its famed Wall to Wall composer programs), and is a regular host to **World Music Institute** (☎ *212/545–7536* ⊕ *www.worldmusicinstitute.org*) events.

☺ The **Tribeca Performing Arts Center** (✉ *199 Chambers St., at Greenwich St., TriBeCa* ☎ *212/220–1460* ⊕ *www.tribecapac.org* Ⓜ *1, 2, 3 to Chambers St.*) celebrates theater (with a clever children's series) and dance, but more so, jazz in all its forms; "Highlights in Jazz" and "Lost Jazz Shrines" are two of its special series. Count on the **Winter Garden** (✉ *World Financial Center, West St., between Vesey and Liberty Sts., Lower Manhattan* ☎ *212/945–2600* ⊕ *www.artsworldfinancialcenter. com* Ⓜ *E to World Trade Center; 1 to Rector St.*) for an inspired array of musical events from gospel to site-specific sonic installations . . . and a little dance as well—all free, and all befitting the spectacular setting.

OPERA

The greatest singers in the world clamor to test their mettle at the Metropolitan Opera, where they can work alongside internationally admired directors and designers. But there's plenty of talent to go around, and the city has no dearth of venues in which to appreciate masters of this grand art.

MAJOR COMPANIES

Fodor's Choice
★ The titan of American opera companies, the **Metropolitan Opera** (✉ *Lincoln, Center, Broadway/Columbus Ave., at W. 63rd.,Upper West Side* ☎ *212/362–6000* ⊕ *www.metopera.org* Ⓜ *1 to 66th St./Lincoln Center*), an institution since 1883, brings the world's leading singers to its vast stage at Lincoln Center from October to April. The company's music director and principal conductor, James Levine, ensures that the orchestra rivals the world's finest symphonies; with General Manager Peter Gelb at the helm, the Met is taking steps to embrace the 21st century. Ranging from the traditional to a growing consideration of the modern (*Doctor Atomic* in 2008, and new *Tosca* in 2009), all performances, including those sung in English are unobtrusively subtitled on small screens on the back of the seat in front of you. ■**TIP→** For programs Monday–Thursday, a limited number of same-day $20 rush orchestra-seat tickets are available at the Met box office two hours prior to curtain; seniors may buy them by phone or online beginning at noon. Standing-room tickets go on sale at 10 AM on the day of the performance (buy them online, by phone, or at the box office); they are $20 for the orchestra level and $15 for the family circle. Partial view seating (always discounted) is available on most levels, at all times; free "Open House" dress rehearsals are open to the general public.

Perhaps not as famous as its next-door neighbor, the **New York City Opera** (✉ *Lincoln Center, Broadway/Columbus Ave. at W. 63rd St.,*

Upper West Side ☎*212/870–5570; 212/721–6500 tickets* ⊕*www. nycopera.com* Ⓜ*1 to 66th St./Lincoln Center*) draws a crowd to its performances at the David H. Koch Theater. Founded in 1943, the company is known for its innovative and diverse repertory, and its soft spot for American composers. With the 2009 appointment of George Steel to General Manager and Artistic Director (George Manahan remains Music Director), you can expect to find a renewed commitment to fresh interpretations of the classics (*Madama Butterfly, Don Giovanni*), and the mounting of riskier and rarely seen productions (such as Hugo Weisgall's *Esther*). Placido Domingo and Beverly Sills began their careers at City Opera; generations of great voices follow in their footsteps. City Opera performs September to November and March to April. All performances of foreign-language operas have supertitles—line-by-line English translations—displayed above the stage. ■TIP➜ $25 orchestra-seating "Opera for All" Rush tickets, as available, go on sale for the entire week's performances at the box office beginning 10 AM Monday (they are also available online and by phone; refer to code: OFA1).

15

SMALLER COMPANIES

☙ **Dicapo Opera Theatre** (✉*184 E. 76th St., between Lexington and 3rd Aves. Upper East Side* ☎*212/288–9438; 212/868–4444 tickets* ⊕*www. dicapo.com* Ⓜ*6 to 77th St.*) may be in a church basement (albeit the resplendently French Provincial St. Jean Baptiste), but the 204-seater's boffo reputation—and its thoroughly modern facility—belie its humble-sounding setting. Productions range from Puccini to Tobias Picker's *Emmeline*. Their complementary children's programming, Opera for Kids, offers—at nominal seat prices—one-hour renditions of the classics on weekends.

The **New York Gilbert & Sullivan Players** (☎*212/769–1000* ⊕*www.nygasp. org*) stage lively productions of such G&S favorites as *The Pirates of Penzance* and *The Mikado,* plus rarities like Sullivan's last completed work, *The Rose of Persia*. Their New York performance season—usually throughout January—is spent primarily at City Center.

DANCE

Bodies in motion tend to stay in motion here in New York City. Ballet aficionados are spoiled with options at New York's landmark performing arts centers, and those in search of something less classical will find it in all corners of the city, including downtown venues that veer toward experimental fare.

BALLET

American Ballet Theatre (ABT) (☎*212/477–3030* ⊕*www.abt.org*) is renowned for its gorgeous renditions of the 19th-century classics (*Swan Lake, Giselle, La Bayardère*), as well as its modern repertoire, including works by such 20th-century masters as George Balanchine, Jerome Robbins, and Agnes de Mille. Since its founding in 1940, the company has nurtured a stellar array of dancers, including Mikhail Baryshnikov, Natalia Makarova, Rudolf Nureyev, Gelsey Kirkland, Cynthia Gregory, and 21st-century principals Gillian Murphy and Herman Cornejo. ABT has two New York seasons—eight weeks beginning in May at its home in the Metropolitan Opera House and a much shorter run in fall (usually a week or two in October) at another city venue.

☺ With more than 90 dancers, the **New York City Ballet** (☎ *212/870–5570* ⊕ *www.nycballet.com*) has an unmatched repertoire of 20th-century works. Its fall season, which runs from mid-November through December, includes the beloved annual production of George Balanchine's *The Nutcracker*. Its spring season runs from April through June; an eight-week Winter Repertory program runs in January and February. The company continues to stress the works themselves rather than individual performers, although that hasn't stopped principal dancers such as Jock Soto, Kyra Nichols, and Damian Woetzel (past), and Wendy Whelan and Benjamin Millepied (present) from earning the highest accolades. Along with New York City Opera, the company calls Lincoln Center's David H. Koch Theater home.

MODERN DANCE

The world's most innovative dance companies perform in New York throughout the year, especially in fall and spring, showcasing the works of such legendary and endlessly creative choreographers as Twyla Tharp, Lar Lubovitch, Bill T. Jones, Paul Taylor, Doug Varone, Trisha Brown, and Mark Morris, along with the influential repertory of Martha Graham and Merce Cunningham.

The 299-seat Jerome Robbins Theater opened in 2010 and with it, the first full season of the **Baryshnikov Arts Center (BAC)** (✉ *37 Arts, 450 W. 37 St., between 9th and 10th Aves., Garment District* ☎ *646/731–3200* ⊕ *www.bacnyc.org* Ⓜ *A, C, E, to 34th St./Penn Station*). Mikhail Baryshnikov's longtime vision has reached fruition in this modern facility for contemporary performance that is dedicated to movement, which can be as much about theater as it is about dance. The Elizabeth LeCompte-directed Wooster Group is in residence. Trisha Brown Dance Company had its 40th-anniversary program here, and a roster of boundary-breaking international choreographers (George Stamos, Donna Uchizono, and Emmanuèle Phuon), co-productions with the Kitchen and BAC Flicks are all part of the plan.

World-renowned dance troupes **Alvin Ailey American Dance Theater** (⊕ *www.alvinailey.org*) and **Paul Taylor Dance Company** (⊕ *www.ptdc. org*) present their primary New York seasons at **City Center** (✉ *131 W. 55th St., between 6th and 7th Aves., Midtown West* ☎ *212/581–1212* ⊕ *www. nycitycenter.org* Ⓜ *N, Q, R, W to 57th St./7th Ave.; F to 57th St./6th Ave.*). City Center's annual "Fall for Dance" festival is a must; all tickets are $10, the performances are world class and sell out very quickly.

★ **Dance Theater Workshop** (✉ *219 W. 19th St., between 7th and 8th Aves.,*
☺ *Chelsea* ☎ *212/924–0077* ⊕ *www.dtw.org* Ⓜ *1 to 18th St.; A, C, E, L to 14th St.-8th Ave.*) serves as a laboratory for new choreographers.

They are also known for their multimedia and kid-friendly "Family Matters" series.

Fodor'sChoice In a former Art Deco movie house in Chelsea, the 472-seat **Joyce The-**
★ **ater** (⊠ *175 8th Ave., at W. 19th St., Chelsea* ☎ *212/242–0800 tickets*
⊕ *www.joyce.org* Ⓜ *A, C, E to 14th St.; L to 8th Ave.*) has superb
sight lines and presents a full spectrum of contemporary dance. **Garth**
Fagan Dance (⊕ *garthfagandance.org*), **Ballet Hispanico** (⊕ *www.*
ballethispanico.org), and taut and athletic **Parsons Dance** (⊕ *www.*
parsonsdance.org) are regulars on the Joyce's always rewarding lineup.
Their **Joyce SoHo** location (⊠ *155 Mercer St., between Houston and*
Prince Sts., SoHo ☎ *212/352–3101 tickets* ⊕ *www.joyce.org* Ⓜ *R, W*
to Prince St.; B, D, F, V to Broadway/Lafayette St.) showcases more
experimental work.

PERFORMING ARTS CENTERS

Fodor'sChoice America's oldest performing arts center, the **Brooklyn Academy of Music**
★ **(BAM)** (⊠ *Peter Jay Sharp Bldg., 30 Lafayette Ave., between Ashland*
Pl. and St. Felix St., Fort Greene, Brooklyn ☎ *718/636–4100* ⊕ *www.*
bam.org Ⓜ *2, 3, 4, 5, B, Q to Atlantic Ave.*), presented its first show
in 1861. Today BAM has a much-deserved reputation for grand-scale
stagings of contemporary dance, music, opera, and theatrical productions, and its film programming. The main performance spaces are
the 2,100-seat **Howard Gilman Opera House,** a restored Renaissance
Revival palace built in 1908, and the 874-seat **Harvey Theater,** an
updated 1904 theater a block away at 651 Fulton Street. Every fall
BAM's multimedia Next Wave Festival fills the house with a global
audience. Year-round you can catch other live performances (including the **Brooklyn Philharmonic** (⊕ *www.brooklynphilharmonic.org*), a
movie at the **BAM Rose Cinemas,** or hit the industrial-glam **BAMcafé**
(☎ *718/623–4139 reservations*), which becomes a cabaret venue on
Friday and Saturday nights.

Carnegie Hall (⊠ *881 7th Ave., at W. 57th St., Midtown West* ☎ *212/247–*
7800 ⊕ *www.carnegiehall.org* Ⓜ *N, Q, R, W to 57th St.; B, D, E to*
7th Ave.) is, of course, one of the world's most famous concert halls.
Virtually every important musician of the 20th century performed in
this century-old Italian Renaissance–style building, often at the peak of
his or her creative powers. Tchaikovsky conducted the opening-night
concert on May 5, 1891, Leonard Bernstein had his debut here, and
Vladimir Horowitz made his historic return to the concert stage here.
Performances are given in the grand 2,804-seat **Isaac Stern Auditorium,**
the 268-seat **Weill Recital Hall,** and the modern and stylish 644-seat
Judy and Arthur Zankel Hall on the lower level. Although the emphasis
is on classical music, Carnegie Hall also hosts jazz, pop, cabaret, and
folk music concerts.

★ **City Center** (⊠ *131 W. 55th St., between 6th and 7th Aves., Midtown*
West ☎ *212/581–1212 CityTix* ⊕ *www.nycitycenter.org* Ⓜ *N, Q, R, W*
to 57th St./7th Ave.; F to 57th St./6th Ave.) has a neo-Moorish look (it
was built in 1923 for the Ancient and Accepted Order of the Mystic

Shrine). Pause as you enter to admire the beautifully ornate tile work that plasters the lobby. The 2,750-seat main stage is perfectly suited for its role as a showplace for world-class dance troupes and special theatrical events. The popular Encores! musicals-in-concert series are staged here, as are—on the smaller **City Center Stages I** and **II**—a number of productions and programs of the Manhattan Theatre Club.

Lincoln Center for the Performing Arts (✉ *W. 62nd to W. 66th Sts., Broadway to Amsterdam Ave., Upper West Side* ☎ *212/875–5456 Customer Service 9* AM*–9* PM *daily; 212/721–6500 CenterCharge; 212/875–5375 for accessibility information;* ⊕ *www.lincolncenter.org* Ⓜ *1 to 66th St./ Lincoln Center*) is a 16-acre complex. Just in time for its 50th anniversary—which coincided with the 2009–2010 season—the wraps came off most of the construction geared to improving and enhancing this stately facility. Among the cultural lights comprising Lincoln Center's main campus are the **Metropolitan Opera House** (☎ *212/362–6000*), which also presents American Ballet Theatre; the **David H. Koch Theater** (formerly the New York State Theater) (☎ *212/870–5570*), home to New York City Opera and New York City Ballet; **Avery Fisher Hall** (☎ *212/875–5030*), where the New York Philharmonic performs; **Alice Tully Hall** (☎ *212/671–4050*), home to the Chamber Music Society of Lincoln Center; the **Vivian Beaumont and Mitzi E. Newhouse** theaters (☎ *212/362–7600*); the **New York Public Library for the Performing Arts** (☎ *212/870–1630*); and the Film Society of Lincoln Center's **Walter Reade Theater** (☎ *212/875–5600*), which will remain open throughout a planned expansion into the **Elinor Bunin-Monroe Film Center**. The predominantly travertine-clad buildings were designed by multiple architects, all of whom applied a classical aesthetic to their cleanly modern structures. Avery Fisher, designed by Max Abramovitz, broke ground first. Opened in 1962, it was then known as Philharmonic Hall. The 2,738-seater's original acoustics were greatly improved with a 1976 renovation by Philip Johnson and John Burgee. Philip Johnson also designed the State (now Koch) Theater, which opened in 1964; a spruced-up interior is part of the Center's 50th-anniversary refurb. In 1965 came Eero Saarinen's finely scaled theaters for plays and musicals, the 1,047-seat Beaumont and the 334-seat Newhouse. The 3,800-seat Met, with its Austrian-crystal chandeliers and Marc Chagall paintings, premiered in 1966. Alice Tully Hall, designed by Pietro Belluschi for a music and film audience of 1,100, followed in 1969; when it reopened for the spring 2009 season, concertgoers were greeted by improved acoustics and an aesthetic transformation by Diller Scofidio + Renfro (in collaboration with FX Fowle Architects).

An outpost a few blocks south of the main campus was dedicated to **Jazz at Lincoln Center** (✉ *Time Warner Center, Broadway at W. 60th St., Columbus Circle* ☎ *212/258–9800* ⊕ *www.jalc.org* Ⓜ *1, A, B, C, D to 59th St./Columbus Circle*) in 2004. Stages in Rafael Viñoly's crisply modern **Frederick P. Rose Hall** feature the 1,100-seat **Rose Theater** (where a worthy Jazz for Young People series joins the buoyant adult programming a few times each year). Also here is the **Allen Room,** an elegant and intimate 310–460 seater, and the even more intimate 140-seat Dizzy's Club Coca-Cola. Back on the main campus, seasonal

15

festivals—music, theater, dance, film, and more—abound, and often take place in the grand plaza surrounding the famous fountain, refurbished now as well, and in adjacent Damrosch Park.

■**TIP→** Day-of-show tickets for most Lincoln Center venues may now be purchased in person at the David Rubenstein Atrium on Broadway between W. 62nd and W. 63rd Sts; there is a limit of two tickets per customer. Although the box office there is closed on Mondays, they will sell any available tickets for Monday performances on Sunday. Box office hours: Tuesday–Saturday noon–7:45; Sunday noon–5:45.

Radio City Music Hall (✉ *1260 6th Ave., between W. 50th and W. 51st Sts., Midtown West* ☎ *212/247–4777* ⊕ *www.radiocity.com* Ⓜ *B, D, F to 47th–50th/Rockefeller Center*) is the famed home of the scissor-kicking Rockettes and the Radio City Christmas Spectacular, but this stunning Art Deco showplace also packs its some 6,000 seats for musical events and the occasional film, set perhaps, to a live orchestra.

FILM

On any given week New York City theaters screen all the major new releases, classics renowned and obscure, foreign films, small independent flicks, hard-to-find documentaries, and experimental video. The theaters themselves run the gamut from sleek multiplexes with large screens and stadium seating to shoe-box-size screening rooms with room for fewer than a hundred people.

GETTING TICKETS

New Yorkers have such a ravenous appetite for celluloid that even barely publicized independent projects can expect a full house, as can revivals of obscure movies and foreign film. Sold-out shows are common, so it's a good idea to purchase tickets in advance. Tickets to most theaters in New York are $12 or $12.50. Although there are no bargain matinees in Manhattan, discounts for senior citizens and children are usually available. For quick access to showtimes and locations, try the ticket services listed below or the *New York Times* (⊕ *www.nytimes. com*). For print listings, Friday's *New York Times* has comprehensive listings by neighborhood. *Time Out New York* (⊕ *www.timeoutny.com*) splits out "Art-house & Indie Cinema" listings, which can be very helpful when you're not sure what you want to see.

Oddly enough, no one phone or online ticket service handles advance ticket purchase for all of the city's screens. Although the occasional indie house allows purchases directly through its own Web site, for chains and most independents you'll need to contact one of the following to charge tickets ahead. There's usually a service fee of $1 to $2 for phone or online orders. **Fandango** (☎ *800/326–3264 [FANDANGO]* ⊕ *www. fandango.com*) handles AMC Loews, City Cinemas, and Regal theaters. **Moviefone** (☎ *212/777–3456 [777–FILM]* ⊕ *www.moviefone.com*) covers the remaining chains, including Landmark and Clearview.

If you prefer to get your tickets the old-fashioned way, a good rule of thumb is to hit the box office three hours ahead of showtime; this is especially true for evening performances and most new releases. If you're seeing a blockbuster, you'll need even more lead time. Save last-minute arrivals for smaller films, or something that has been out awhile; in those cases you may still have to hunt for the few remaining seats.

FIRST-RUN MOVIES

Wherever you are in New York City, you usually don't have to walk far to find a theater showing recent releases; nationwide chains and cookie-cutter multiplexes abound. But noting that "first-run" in New York is as much about independent ventures, documentaries, and foreign films as it is about commercial blockbusters, we list below the one-of-a-kind venues that make moviegoing a unique New York City experience.

Foreign, independent, and, some mainstream films are screened at the **Angelika Film Center** (☒ *18 W. Houston St., at Mercer St., Greenwich Village* ☎ *212/995–2000* ⊕ *www.angelikafilmcenter.com* Ⓜ *B, D, F, V to Broadway-Lafayette St.; 6 to Bleecker St.*). Despite its (six) tunnel-like theaters, and the occasionally audible subway rumble below, it's usually packed; get a snack at their café while you wait for your movie to be called. **Cinema Village** (☒ *22 E. 12th St., between University Pl. and 5th Ave., Greenwich Village* ☎ *212/924–3363* ⊕ *www.cinemavillage.com* Ⓜ *4, 5, 6, L, N, Q, R, W to 14th St./Union Sq.*) has three tiny screening rooms (with surprisingly good sight lines) that show a smart selection of hard-to-find first-run domestic and foreign films.

Adjacent to the Plaza Hotel sits the **Paris** (☒ *4 W. 58th St., between 5th and 6th Aves., Midtown West* ☎ *212/688–3800* Ⓜ *N, R, W to 5th Ave./59th St.; F to 57th St.*)—a rare stately remnant of the single-screen era. Opened in 1948, it retains its wide screen (and its balcony) and is a fine showcase for new movies, often foreign and with a limited release.

Movie lovers adore the **Quad Cinema** (☒ *34 W. 13th St., between 5th and 6th Aves., Greenwich Village* ☎ *212/255–8800* ⊕ *www.quadcinema.com* Ⓜ *1, 2, 3, F, V to 14th St.; L to 6th Ave.*), probably because the four tiny theaters feel so much like a private screening room. First-run art and foreign films are the fare here. Within a sleekly renovated space—remnants of its life as a vaudeville theater are all but gone—the **Sunshine Cinema** (☒ *143 E. Houston St., between 1st and 2nd Aves., Lower East Side* ☎ *212/330–8182* ⊕ *www.landmarktheatres.com* Ⓜ *F, V to 2nd Ave.*) has five decent-size screens showing a mix of art-house and smaller-release mainstream films.

The **Village East Cinema** (☒ *181–189 2nd Ave., at E. 12th St., East Village* ☎ *212/529–6799* ⊕ *www.villageeastcinema.com* Ⓜ *6 to Astor Pl.; L to 1st Ave.*), with programming akin to that of its sister Angelika, is housed in a former Yiddish theater that was restored and converted to a six-screen multiplex. Catch a film that's screening in the original theater space upstairs (you can call ahead to find out); its Moorish Revival-style decor, domed ceiling, and grand chandelier are best appreciated from the balcony.

★ Its vintage is late 1960s, but the **Ziegfeld** (☒ *141 W. 54th St., between 6th and 7th Aves., Midtown West* ☎ *212/307–1862* Ⓜ *F to 57th St./6th*

15

Ave.; N, Q, R, W to 57th St./7th Ave.) is as close as you'll come to a movie-palace experience in New York today. Wide screen, chandeliers and crimson decor, good sight lines, and solid sound system make the Ziegfeld a special place to view anything it serves up; grand-opening red-carpet galas often take place here as well.

SERIES AND REVIVALS

Although many of the screens listed here also show first-run releases, old favorites and rarities are the heart of their programming. These gems—which include every genre from noir to the most au courant experimental work—frequently screen at museums, cultural societies, and other public spaces, such as the **French Institute** (☎ *212/355– 6100* ⊕ *www.fiaf.org*), **Scandinavia House** (☎ *212/879–9779* ⊕ *www. scandinaviahouse.org*), **Instituto Cervantes** (☎ *212/308–7720* ⊕ *www. cervantes.org*), and even branches of the **New York Public Library** (⊕ *www.nypl.org*).

Dedicated to preserving and exhibiting independent and avant-garde film, **Anthology Film Archives** (⊠ *32 2nd Ave., at E. 2nd St., East Village* ☎ *212/505–5181* ⊕ *www.anthologyfilmarchives.org* Ⓜ *F, V to 2nd Ave.*) comprises a film repository and two gem-like screening rooms in a renovated redbrick courthouse. This is a good place for hard-to-find films and videos. The Essential Cinema series delves into the works of filmmakers like Stan Brakhage, Robert Bresson, and more. The four-screen **BAM Rose Cinemas** (⊠ *Brooklyn Academy of Music, Peter Jay Sharp Bldg., 30 Lafayette Ave., between Ashland Pl. and St. Felix St., Fort Greene, Brooklyn* ☎ *718/636–4100* ⊕ *www.bam.org* Ⓜ *2, 3, 4, 5, B, Q to Atlantic Ave.*) includes BAMcinématek, an eclectic repertory series (from "Freaky Cats" to "Hungarians in Hollywood"), as well as the latest from Sundance plus first-run foreign-language and popular independent films.

Fodor'sChoice ★ In addition to premiering new releases, **Film Forum** (⊠ *209 W. Houston St., between 6th Ave. and Varick St., Greenwich Village* ☎ *212/727– 8110* ⊕ *www.filmforum.org* Ⓜ *1 to Houston St.*), a very special non-profit theater with three small screening rooms, hosts movies by directors from Hitchcock to Bertolucci; genre series with themes from pre-Code to samurai; and newly restored prints of classic works. The small café serves tasty cakes and fresh-popped popcorn.

The **Museum of Modern Art (MoMA)** (⊠ *11 W. 53rd St., between 5th and 6th Aves., Midtown West* ☎ *212/708–9400* ⊕ *www.moma.org* Ⓜ *E, V to 5th Ave./53rd St.; B, D, F, V to 47th–50th Sts./Rockefeller Center*) has some of the most engaging international repertory you'll find anywhere; it's shown in the state-of-the-art Roy and Niuta Titus theaters 1 and 2. Movie tickets are available at the museum for same-day screenings (a limited number are released up to one week in advance for an extra fee); they're free if you have purchased museum admission.

🅒 The **Museum of the Moving Image** (⊠ *35th Ave. at 36th St., Astoria* ☎ *718/784–0077* ⊕ *www.movingimage.us* Ⓜ *R, V to Steinway St.; N, W to 36th Ave.*) presents special film programming in two new screening rooms added in 2010. The museum's facelift brings with it in-person appearances by moviemaker luminaries along with the retrospectives and themed repertory they featured previously, like a Robert Altman series, or the splashy tribute "Glorious Technicolor!" It's also a great choice for kids: besides the hands-on "Behind the Screen" museum display, the draw is Tut's Fever Movie Palace—the fab Red Grooms and Lysiane Luong–designed installation that screens classic shorts daily.

The film programs at **92YTribeca** (⊠ *200 Hudson St., at Canal St., TriBeCa* ☎ *212/601–1000* ⊕ *www.92y.org/92yTribeca* Ⓜ *1, E to Canal St.*) emphasize participation, with directors often on hand, and a Q&A afterwards is the norm. View a fresh and eclectic take on series concepts, with the likes of the Found Footage Festival, a late-night sing-along series, Camp Nostalgia, and Desi Diaspora films to the latest by documentarians Chris Hegedus and D.A. Pennebaker.

Ⓒ **SonyWonder Technology Lab** (⊠ *550 Madison Ave., between E. 55th and E. 56th Sts., Midtown East* ☎ *212/833–7858 tickets* ⊕ *www.sonywondertechlab.com* Ⓜ *E, V to 5th Ave.–53rd St.*), the kid-oriented hands-on extravaganza of high-tech how-to for moviemaking and more, shows free films of the Dora the Explorer and Sesame Street genre. Children under 18 must be accompanied by an adult. You may reserve tickets by phone up to a week ahead.

Ⓒ "Thalia Film Sundays" are the thing at **Symphony Space** (☎ *212/864–5400* ⊕ *www.symphonyspace.org*), a former art-house. A mix of rarely-available foreign features and documentaries for adult viewers on Sunday evenings is complemented on Saturday mornings by zany children's programming—like the animated Gustafer Yellowgold Show and a "Winter Wondershorts" series.

★ The comfy 268-seat auditorium of the **Walter Reade Theater** (⊠ *Lincoln Center, 165 W. 65th St., between Broadway and Amsterdam Ave., Upper West Side* ☎ *212/875–5600* ⊕ *www.filmlinc.com* Ⓜ *1 to 66th St./Lincoln Center*) has what may be the best sight lines in town. It presents series devoted to "the best in world cinema" that run the gamut from silents (with occasional live organ accompaniment) and documentaries to retrospectives and recent releases, often on the same theme or from the same country. And here's where to come on certain Saturdays to catch The Met: Live in HD screenings.

FESTIVALS, INDOORS AND OUT

New York's preeminent film event is the annual **New York Film Festival**; sponsored by the Film Society of Lincoln Center (☎ *212/875–5050* ⊕ *www.filmlinc.com*), it runs annually from late September into October. Screenings—which feature many U.S. premieres—are announced more than a month in advance and sell out rapidly. Venues are usually Lincoln Center's Alice Tully Hall and Walter Reade Theater. Each January the Film Society joins forces with The Jewish Museum to produce the **New York Jewish Film Festival,** then in March it joins with MoMA to present **New Directors/New Films.**

Ⓒ While it sponsors year-round kids programming around town, the centerpiece of the superbly curated **New York International Children's Film**

15

Festival (NYICFF) (☎ *212/349–0330* ⊕ *www.gkids.com*) takes place in a two-week window (most years in late February–early March), when it screens some 100 new films and videos for ages 3–18. The festival shows are very popular—it's a rare opportunity to see them on a big screen—and they sell out early.

Fodor's Choice ★ An immediately embraced 2002 addition to the New York film-o-philic scene, the **Tribeca Film Festival** (⊕ *www.tribecafilmfestival.org*) takes place in mostly downtown venues for about two weeks starting in late April, and features mainstream premieres along with indie treasures. The **Tribeca Family Film Festival** (⊕ *www.tribecafilmfestival. org*) crowds gravitate to its back-to-back street fair and movie day for ages six and up.

Summer in New York sees a bonanza of alfresco film. Even better, it's usually free (but arrive early to secure a space; screenings begin at dusk). You'll want to check out lovely **Bryant Park** (✉ *42nd St., between 5th and 6th Aves., Midtown West* ☎ *212/512–5700* ⊕ *www.bryantpark.org* Ⓜ *B, D, F, V to 42nd St./Bryant Park; 7 to 5th Ave.*) for its Monday night festival, June–August.

�馨 **Hudson River Park** runs its "RiverFlicks" series in July and August. Movies for "grown-ups" screen on Wednesday evenings on Pier 54 (*at W. 13th St., Greenwich Village* ⊕ *www.hudsonriverpark.org* Ⓜ *A, C, E to 14th St.; L to 8th Ave.*); RiverFlicks for kids are shown on Pier 46, on Fridays.

READINGS AND LECTURES

Literary figures great and small share their work at dozens of readings held each week in the city.

Time Out New York magazine (⊕ *timeoutnewyork.com)* is your source for the best roundup of poetry and spoken-word events. Admission to most of these events is usually under $15, and often free—although certain luminaries might command as much as $25 or $35.

SERIES AND SPECIAL EVENTS

The **Center for Architecture** (✉ *536 LaGuardia Pl., between W. 3rd and Bleecker Sts., Greenwich Village* ☎ *212/683–0023* ⊕ *www.aiany.org* Ⓜ *A, B, C, D, E, F, V to W. 4th St./Washington Sq.*), a glass-faced gallery, hosts lively discussions (which may be accompanied by films or other visuals) on topics like radical architecture in Mexico City or visionary American architects of the 1930s. WNYC Radio invites the public into their intimate (125 seats) and brand new (2009) technologically forward-thinking digs, **The Jerome L. Greene Performance Space (The Greene Space)** (✉ *44 Charlton St., at Varick St. Tribeca* ☎ *646/829–4400* ⊕ *www.thegreenespace.org* Ⓜ *C, E to Spring St.; 1 to Houston St. or Canal St.*). Live shows—music, audio theater, interviews—match their renowned, and equally forward-thinking, on-air programming. The **Lesbian, Gay, Bisexual & Transgender Community Center** (✉ *208 W. 13th St., between 6th and 7th Aves., West Village* ☎ *212/620–7310* ⊕ *www.*

gaycenter.org Ⓜ *1, 2, 3, F, V to 14th St.; L to 6th Ave.*) sponsors "Second Tuesdays" and "Center Voices," both series of engaging and topical talks (and occasional films or musical events), with themes ranging from out lawyers to Elaine Stritch. In the historic Villard Houses, the nonprofit **Municipal Art Society** (✉ *Urban Center, 457 Madison Ave., at E. 51st St., Midtown East* ☎ *212/935–3960* ⊕ *www.mas.org* Ⓜ *6 to 51st St.; E, V to 5th Ave./53rd St.*) is dedicated to preserving New York's architectural treasures. It presents a free lecture series at noon on Thursday, with well-known authors addressing topics from subway ornamentation to houses of worship; their walking tours are also good. At **The New School** (✉ *66 W. 12th St., between 5th and 6th Aves., Greenwich Village* ☎ *212/229–5488* ⊕ *www.newschool.edu/events* Ⓜ *1, 2, 3, F, V to 14th St.*) topical panels predominate; expect incisive and thought-provoking results, whether the subject is economics or design. The **New York Public Library** (✉ *Celeste Bartos Forum, W. 42nd St. at 5th Ave., Midtown West* ☎ *212/868–4444* ⊕ *www.nypl.org/live* Ⓜ *B, D, F, V to 42nd St.*) presents "LIVE from the NYPL," a rich program of lectures and reading events at the famous main library and its branches elsewhere in the city. The venerable **New York Studio School** (✉ *8 W. 8th St., between 5th and 6th Aves., Greenwich Village* ☎ *212/673–6466* ⊕ *www.nyss.org* Ⓜ *A, B, C, D, E, F to W. 4th St./Washington Sq.*) hosts two—usually free—evening lecture series on contemporary issues in art. Hear from both emerging and established artists, and from some of the biggest names in art history and criticism. Authors, poets, and playwrights, as well as political pundits, industry leaders, and media bigwigs, take the stage at the **92nd Street Y** (✉ *1395 Lexington Ave., at E. 92nd St., Upper East Side* ☎ *212/415–5500* ⊕ *www.92y.org* Ⓜ *6 to 96th St.*). The intent at **92YTribeca** (✉ *200 Hudson St., at Canal St., Tribeca* ☎ *212/601–1000* ⊕ *www.92y.org* Ⓜ *1, E to Canal St.*) is to appeal to a twenty- to thirty-ish set, but just about anyone should find something to their liking in their extensive daytime and evening lineups. Try talks on American Media & the Green Movement to JewBu: Exploring Jewish Dharma, and themes from the arts, food, and technology. **Symphony Space** (✉ *2537 Broadway, at W. 95th St., Upper West Side* ☎ *212/864–5400* ⊕ *www.symphonyspace.org* Ⓜ *1, 2, 3 to 96th St.*) hosts a celebrated roster of literary events, including Bloomsday and the famed "Selected Shorts" series of stories read by prominent actors and broadcast live on National Public Radio.

★ Insight into the creative process is what the superb **Works & Process** (✉ *Guggenheim Museum, 1071 5th Ave., at E. 89th St., Upper East Side* ☎ *212/423–3587* ⊕ *www.worksandprocess.org* Ⓜ *4, 5, 6 to 86th St.*) program is all about. Often drawing on dance and theater works-in-progress, live performances are complemented with illuminating discussions with their (always top-notch) choreographers, playwrights, and directors.

15

FICTION AND POETRY READINGS

Fodor's Choice ★ "Poetry Czar" Bob Holman's **Bowery Poetry Club** (✉ *308 Bowery, at Bleecker St., Lower East Side* ☎ *212/614–0505* ⊕ *www.bowerypoetry. com* Ⓜ *B, D, F, V to Broadway–Lafayette St.; 6 to Bleecker St.*) serves up coffee and comestibles along with its ingenious poetry events. Expect every permutation of the spoken word—and art and music, too.

★ The **Cornelia Street Café** (✉ *29 Cornelia St., between W. 4th and Bleecker Sts., Greenwich Village* ☎ *212/989–9319* ⊕ *www.corneliastreetcafe. com* Ⓜ *A, B, C, D, E, F, V to W. 4th St./Washington Sq.*) is a good bet for original poetry—the Pink Pony West open-mike series takes place here—and fiction readings, live jazz, and a good meal as well.

The **Nuyorican Poets Café** (✉ *236 E. 3rd St., between Aves. B and C, East Village* ☎ *212/505–8183* ⊕ *www.nuyorican.org* Ⓜ *F, V to 2nd Ave.*) schedules daily readings, open-mike events, and screenplay readings, and hosts the granddaddy of the current spoken word scene, the "Friday Night Poetry Slam."

Having settled into its new home hard by the Hudson in 2009, **Poets House** (✉ *10 River Terr., at Murray St., Battery Park City* ☎ *212/431–7920* ⊕ *www.poetshouse.org* Ⓜ *E to Fulton St.; 1, 2, 3 to Chambers St.*) finally has a setting that rises to its theme: it is an open resource for all ages, one that offers a huge library and readings and events that exalt the art of poetry.

The Poetry Project (✉ *At St. Mark's Church in-the-Bowery, 131 E. 10th St., at 2nd Ave., East Village* ☎ *212/674–0910* ⊕ *poetryproject.org* Ⓜ *6 to Astor Pl.*) had its start in 1966, and has been a source of sustenance for poets (and their audiences) ever since. This is where Allen Ginsberg, Amiri Baraka, and Sam Shepard first found their voices, and where you're likely to find folks of the same caliber today.

☾ The famed **Strand Bookstore** (✉ *828 Broadway, at E. 12th St., East Village* ☎ *212/473–1452* ⊕ *www.strandbooks.com* Ⓜ *L, N, Q, R, W, 4, 5, 6 to 14th St./Union Sq.*) hosts the occasional nonfiction panel and special Family Hour events, but its primary fare is current fiction readings with authors like Marisha Pessl, Colson Whitehead, Calvin Trillin, and Mark Kurlansky.

Nightlife

WORD OF MOUTH

"The Iridium is an intimate and funky room where we spent a delightful evening on a recent visit to New York. The late, great Les Paul played there on Monday nights until shortly before his death."

— happytrailstoyou

Updated by
Gary Lippman

"Everybody's working for the weekend"? Maybe in New Jersey. But the natives here in "Fun City," as it used to be called, seldom wait for the weekend to party. In fact, many zealous New Yorkers prefer to do it during the week. (Thursday's particularly popular. Friday and Saturday can be less of a local crowd.)

The nightlife scene still resides largely downtown—in dives in the East Village and Lower East Side, classic jazz joints in the West Village, and the Meatpacking District's and Chelsea's see-and-be-seen clubs. Still, Midtown, especially around Hell's Kitchen, has developed quite the vibrant scene, too, and plenty of preppy hangouts dot the Upper East and Upper West sides. (*For venues in Brooklyn, see Chapter 12.*)

Keep in mind that *when* you go is just as important as *where* you go. A spot only sizzles when it's hopping—a club that is packed at 11 might empty out by midnight, and a bar that raged last night may be completely empty tonight. These days, night prowlers are more loyal to floating parties, DJs, and club promoters than to any specific addresses.

For those of you trying to give NYC its "Fun City" rep back, *Paper* magazine has a good list of the roving parties. You can check their online nightlife guide, *PM* (NYC), via their Web site ⊕ *www.papermag. com*. Another streetwise mag, *The L Magazine* (⊕ *www.thelmagazine. com*), lists what's happening day by day at many of the city's lounges and clubs, as well as dance and comedy performances. The *Village Voice,* a free weekly newspaper, probably has more club ads than any other rag in the world. Also check out the *New York Press,* which has pages and pages of nightlife listings. The *New York Times* has listings of cabaret and jazz shows, most comprehensively in their Friday and Sunday Arts section. Bear in mind that a venue's life span is often measured in months, not years. Phone ahead to make sure your target hasn't closed or turned into a polka hall (although, you never know—that could be fun, too).

CLUBS AND ENTERTAINMENT

CLASSIC NEW YORK

If we're talking about quintessential old-school Manhattan, these social landmarks are all distinguished by an unbeatable location, a unique style, a rich history, or a combination of the three.

Fodor's Choice ★ **Campbell Apartment.** Commuting professionals pack into this Grand Central Terminal bar on their way to catch trains home during the evening rush, but don't let the crush of humanity scare you away—you can have a deeply romantic time here in one of Manhattan's more beautiful rooms. The restored space dates to the 1920s, when it was the private office of an executive named John W. Campbell, and as the exquisite decor suggests, old Campy knew how to live. Try out the good life as you knock back a well-built cocktail from an overstuffed chair. Just try to avoid that evening rush. ☒ *15 Vanderbilt Ave. entrance, Grand Central Station, Midtown East* ☎ *212/953–0409* ⊕ *www.hospitalityholdings. com* Ⓜ *4, 5, 6, 7, S to 42nd St./Grand Central.*

Fodor's Choice ★ **The Carlyle.** The hotel's discreetly sophisticated Café Carlyle hosts such top cabaret and jazz performers as Christine Ebersole, John Pizzarelli, and Steve Tyrell. Stop by on a Monday night and take in Woody Allen, who swings on the clarinet with the Eddy Davis New Orleans Jazz Band. The less fancy-schmancy (though still pricey) **Bemelmans Bar,** with a mural by the author of the *Madeline* books, features a rotating cast of pianist-singers. ☒ *35 E. 76th St., between Madison and Park Aves., Upper East Side* ☎ *212/744–1600* ⊕ *www.thecarlyle.com* Ⓜ *6 to 77th St.*

Four Seasons. Maybe it's true that, as some wag once said, "History is made at night." But New York City (and American) history are made at lunchtime, too, here in Philip Johnson's landmark temple of modern design. Come nightfall, watch for politicos and media moguls in the Grill Room, or enjoy the 300-plus selections in the new Garden Room. ☒ *99 E. 52nd St., between Park and Lexington Aves., Midtown East* ☎ *212/754–9494* ⊕ *www.fourseasonsrestaurant.com* Ⓜ *E, V to Lexington Ave./53rd St.; 6 to 51st St.*

King Cole Bar. A justly beloved Maxfield Parrish mural of "Old King Cole" himself, as well as his psychedelic court, adds to the already considerable elegance at this romantic and essential Midtown meeting place. Try a Bloody Mary—this is where drink was introduced to Americans. ☒ *St. Regis Hotel, 2 E. 55th St., between 5th and Madison Aves., Midtown East* ☎ *212/753–4500* ☎ *www.starwoodhotels.com* Ⓜ *E, V to 5th Ave./53rd St.*

Oak Room. One of the great classic cabaret venues, the Algonquin's Oak Room is formal (jackets are mandatory; ties are the norm) and decorated sumptuously. You might find the hopelessly romantic singer Andrea Marcovicci, among other top-notch performers, crooning here. ☒ *Algonquin Hotel, 59 W. 44th St., between 5th and 6th Aves., Midtown West* ☎ *212/840–6800* Ⓜ *B, D, F, V to 42nd St.; 7 to 5th Ave.*

16

★ **'21' Club**. A row of lawn jockeys welcomes you to this former speakeasy, celebrated for having pulled in famous writers and movie stars through most of the past century. Privilege and whimsy are mixed together here: the well-dressed can enjoy well-prepared American cuisine in the well-appointed Bar Room as well as enjoy well-made drinks next to a roaring fire in the cozy front lounge. ⊠ *21 W. 52nd St., between 5th and 6th Aves., Midtown West* ☎ *212/582–7200* ⊕ *www.21club.com* Ⓜ *B, D, F, V to 47–50th Sts./Rockefeller Center.*

DANCE CLUBS AND DJ VENUES

The listings here aren't the absolutely "hottest" nightclubs in New York at the moment. Why? Because those velvet ropes are near-impossible to penetrate. But don't let that keep you in your hotel; unless you're a glamour snob, the accessible clubs listed below are more fun for less money.

Apt. Music is the priority at this polished (and hard to spot) bi-level club, which features a cozy chill lounge-restaurant at street level as well as, down in a tiny, luminous wood-paneled basement, some of the world's top DJs. Oh, and Sunday nights are especially cracking here. ⊠ *419 W. 13th St., between 9th Ave. and Washington St., Meatpacking District* ☎ *212/414–4245* ☎ *www.aptnyc.com* ☎ *212/414–4245* Ⓜ *A, C, E to 14th St.; L to 8th Ave.*

Canal Room. Polished wood floors, potted palms, and stylish chairs give this intimate club—known for its Artist You Should Know series—an air of glamour. Musicians perform here several times a month, but they also come just to enjoy themselves. The owners' record-business connections, a spectacular sound system, celeb sightings, and DJs with reputations as big as their turntables (size does matter) keep the crowds moving, even if they are a touch "Bridge and Tunnel" lately. ⊠ *285 West Broadway, at Canal St., TriBeCa* ☎ *212/941–8100* ⊕ *www.canalroom. com* Ⓜ *A, C, E to Canal St.*

Cielo. Relatively mature dance club–goers (if the word "mature" can ever be applied to such a crowd) gravitate to this small but sturdy Meatpacking District "musichead" mecca to toss back cocktails, dig the quality sound system, groove to top-flight DJs spinning soulful Latin beats and techno, boogie on the sunken dance floor, and smoke in the no-frills garden outside. On Monday nights are the award-winning "Deep Space" parties, where resident DJ François K. (as well as guest spinmeisters like Dmitri from Paris) rev up the faithful with everything from dubstep to Stravinsky. ⊠ *18 Little W. 12th St., between 9th Ave. and Washington St., Meatpacking District* ☎ *212/645–5700* ⊕ *www. cieloclub.com* Ⓜ *A, C, E to 14th St.; L to 8th Ave.*

Fodor's Choice **Kiss And Fly**. One of New York's most discerning nightlife experts, the ★ dance-music artist Sir Ivan, swears by Kiss And Fly, and it's obvious why: this modest-size dance club has sensational music (pumped as loud as can be, of course), a beautiful interior design (dig all the butterfly motifs), and creative lighting that actually lets you see who you're dancing/speaking/kissing/sipping with. It's pricey, tough to get into, and a bit snooty, but now that you've been duly warned, have a ball.

✉ *409 W. 13th St., between 9th Ave. and Washington St., Meatpacking District* ☎ *212/255–1933* ⊕ *www.kissandflyclub.com* Ⓜ *A, C, E to 14th St.; L to 8th Ave.*

Pacha. Maybe you've been to the exclusive Pacha clubs in Buenos Aires, Ibiza, and London. Congratulations. But the jewel in the crown of the Pacha empire may well be here. Assuming you pass muster to enter, you'll find four stories' worth of high-tech fittings (blinding lights, go-go girls, humungous sound), plus celeb DJs, celeb customers, even celeb bathroom attendants! (OK, maybe not that last part.) ✉ *618 W. 46st St., between 11th and 12th Aves., Midtown West* ☎ *212/209–7500* ⊕ *www.pachanyc.com* Ⓜ *C, E to 50th St.*

Fodor's Choice
★ **Santos Party House.** "Now *this* is what I call a dance club," says the legendary DJ (and legendary record producer) Arthur Baker about this glorious new downtown dance club, where the velvet ropes part for everyone, and "creativity" rather than "superficiality" (or "Grease") is the word. Co-owned by the rocker Andrew W.K., the bi-level Santos ain't fancy, but that's the point, and the customers are as eclectic (everybody from punks to Upper East Siders) as the DJs (including Mr. Baker, who flies in regularly from London). Hence the musical vibe (underground dance, mostly) is simply kaleidoscopic. ✉ *100 Lafayette St., between White and Walker Sts., TriBeCa* ☎ *212/584–5892* ⊕ *www. santospartyhouse.com* Ⓜ *J, M, Z, N, Q, R, W, 6 to Canal St.*

16

JAZZ CLUBS

Birdland. This place gets its name from bebop saxophone great Charlie "Yardbird" (or just "Bird") Parker, so expect serious musicians such as John Pizzarelli, the Dave Holland Sextet, and Chico O'Farrill's Afro-Cuban Jazz Orchestra (on Sunday nights). The dining room serves moderately priced American fare with a Cajun accent. If you sit at the bar your cover charge includes a drink. ✉ *315 W. 44th St., between 8th and 9th Aves., Midtown West* ☎ *212/581–3080* ⊕ *www.birdlandjazz.com* Ⓜ *A, C, E to 42nd St./Port Authority.*

Fodor's Choice
★ **Blue Note.** Considered by many (not least its current owners) to be "the jazz capital of the world," the Blue Note was once the stomping ground for such legends as Dizzy Gillespie, and still hosts a varied repertoire from Chris Botti to the Count Basie Orchestra to Boz Scaggs. Expect a steep cover charge except for late shows on weekends, when the music might less jazzy and more funky. ✉ *131 W. 3rd St., near 6th Ave., Greenwich Village* ☎ *212/475–8592* ⊕ *www.bluenotejazz.com* Ⓜ *A, B, C, D, E, F, V to W. 4th St.*

Garage Restaurant & Café. Good news for you budget-minded jazzers: there's no cover *and* no minimum at this Village hot spot, where two jazz groups jam seven nights a week and a fireplace sets the mood upstairs. ✉ *99 7th Ave. S, between Bleecker and Christopher Sts., Greenwich Village* ☎ *212/645–0600* ⊕ *www.garagerest.com* Ⓜ *1 to Christopher St./Sheridan Sq.*

Iridium. This cozy, top-drawer club is a sure bet for big-name talent like the David Murray Black Saint Quartet and Michael Wolff. The sight

Continued on page 298

NEW YORK NIGHTS

New York is the city that never sleeps—and when you come to visit, you might not, either. It doesn't matter if you're a disco queen, a lounge lizard, a class act, or a prisoner of rock n' roll; the nightlife options here will give you your fix. So pop some No-Doz, drink that third cup of coffee, do whatever it takes for you to rev up. You can catch up on sleep when you're dead . . . or in Cleveland.

A NIGHT OF JAZZ
GREENWICH VILLAGE

It's no surprise that the Village, a legendary haunt for Beat poets, avant-garde performance artists, and countercultural politicos, is also a hotbed of jazz. This neighborhood's vibe is all about experimentation and free expression . . . so put on your dark glasses and your artfully distressed leather jacket, grab your Gauloises (for the sidewalk, anyhow), and get ready to groove.

Making advance reservations may not entirely jibe with jazz's spontaneous sensibility, but it's necessary if you want to get into some of the Village's best-known venues. Booking weeks ahead for a table at the **Blue Note** will only ensure that you have a memorable night; you'll be able to see jazz greats like Herbie Hancock,

McCoy Tyner, Cassandra Wilson, Eddie Palmer, Nellie McKay, and Chris Botti right up close from one of the cramped 40-or-so tables. This is also a great place to have dinner; the Note serves up some bodacious barbecue, especially at Sunday brunch.

Another spot that's worth pre-booking for is the nearby "Carnegie Hall of Cool," the **Village Vanguard**. John Coltrane and Sonny Rollins used to jam here regularly, and modern-day jazz giants like Wynton Marsalis make rare appearances. When the headline act's not huge, though, you can sometimes wander in at 8 (when the doors open) and still snag a seat.

OUTSIDE THE BOX

Although the Village has the highest concentration of jazz clubs in the city, a few fabulous venues that are worth the cab fare uptown. **Smoke**, way up near Columbia University, is a true jazz-lover's haven. The 16-piece "Smoke Big Band" blasts your brainpan off on Thursdays. A less arduous trip to Midtown will bring you to **Iridium**, where late guitar great Les Paul once played on Monday nights. A bit farther south near Times Square is the famous 60-year-old **Birdland**, named for the late great Charlie Parker; the cover charge here includes a drink.

With smaller, less famous Village venues, you can extemporize a bit; these places are almost always packed with jazzers, but you can show up without a reservation (often without paying a cover charge) and still catch some top-quality music. The **Garage Restaurant & Café** is one such spot; you can have a steak dinner in front of the giant fireplace while listening to great local trios and quartets (or, on Monday, big-band swing). The **Knickerbocker Bar & Grill** is another place where you can satisfy both your gastronomic and musical appetites; on Friday and Saturday nights live ensembles play while diners dig in to St. Louis ribs or slow baked salmon.

Arthur's Tavern is another no-cover venue, with a coolly grotty dark-wood (or, more accurately, dark wood–veneer) ambience; you can chill out in the piano bar or catch a jazz trio from one of the

dining room tables. **Sweet Rhythm**, also a great choice, is even greater if you're a starving student; on Monday nights, a jazz ensemble from the nearby New School University's music program takes the stage, and anyone with student ID gets in free.

For addresses and phone numbers of these venues, see the main Nightlife listings in this chapter.

A NIGHT OF CLUBBING
THE MEATPACKING DISTRICT AND CHELSEA

Ever since Studio 54 hung its first mirrored ball and ignited a citywide disco inferno, New York has been a playground for the young late-night club set. The '70s may be over; the multilevel megaclubs of the '80s and pulsing raves of the '90s are now largely in the past. But if DJ-spun grooves and packed dance floors are what you love, there's still plenty of New York spots where you can party like it's 1999 (or 1989, or 1979).

It's best to start your long evening with some sustenance, so your first stop—no earlier than 9 PM—should be one of the Meatpacking District's super-hip eateries. **Spice Market** and **Pastis** serve excellent food (Southeast Asian and French bistro, respectively), and will also ease you into the clubland vibe; they both have killer cocktails, a see-and-be-seen crowd, and sometimes even lines of people waiting to get inside (hence advance reservations are highly recommended).

Once you've lingered until a more respectable hour (midnight so), meander over to one of the neighborhood's more civilized clubs. **APT's** basement room, where funk and soul are in heavy rotation, has just a narrow slice of dance floor between the bar and a seating area; it's a safe place to do some preliminary

OUTSIDE THE BOX

Although the Meatpacking and Chelsea neighborhoods are Clubland Central, a couple of New York's best clubs are a bit off the beaten path and worth seeking out.

If you've had your fill of velvet-rope snootiness, direct your dancing feet to the Santos Party House, where a democratic entry policy rules. What it lacks in frills, Santos more than makes up for in fun.

HOW TO GET IN

Unless you're a model, movie star, or recording artist, there's no surefire way to make sure you'll get past the velvet ropes at top New York clubs. But there are some things you can do to increase your chances.

■ **Arranging for bottle service** is an expensive proposition, but it's one of the only ways to reserve a table for you and your friends inside a club. Bottle service means you agree to purchase an entire bottle (or several) of, say, vodka or champagne, which is then used to serve your group. You won't be paying liquor-store prices, though; a bottle of Grey Goose with mixers can easily set you back a couple hundred dollars.

■ **Surrounding yourself with good-looking, sexily dressed females** is always a good bet when you're trying to catch the doorman's eye. Club owners and managers want to keep their venues packed with eye candy—so if you're a girl, pour yourself into tight jeans, stiletto heels, and some sort of dressy top, and grab your friends. If you're a guy, do your best to cobble together an entourage, and steer clear of sports jerseys, baseball hats, sneakers.

■ **Showing up early** may make you feel like a loser—nothing's more dismal than a cavernous, empty dance floor—but it's easier to get in when the door staff is simply trying to get bodies inside.

■ **Cash** has been known to part even the most stubborn velvet ropes like the Red Sea. So if you're not famous, good-looking, or rich enough for bottle service, you can always try slipping the doorman a $20 (just do it discreetly, and don't consider it a guarantee).

head-bobbing. **Cielo,** where deep-house DJs reign, is another relatively chill and intimate place to dance. A glorious new Meatpacking marvel is **Kiss and Fly,** where plenty of groovy dancing gets done along with all the kissing and flying. An incandescent interior based on a butterfly motif is eye-popping, but the crowd and how they move grabs the most attention.

When the wee hours arrive, it's time to get serious; New York's biggest and wildest clubs only really come alive around 1 AM. Many of these are in Chelsea, the next neighborhood over and just a short cab ride away from the Meatpacking District. **Marquee** (289 10th Ave., 646/473–0202) is similarly fabulous, but with with a high quotient of beautiful people. It, like the other ultra-glamorous dance clubs in town (Oak, the Gates, Avenue, M2), can be a tough door to get past.

No matter where your night of clubbing takes you, have at least $150 on you. Many places don't take plastic, and if they do, you'll only exasperate the people behind you if you whip it out. Most clubs charge a cover ranging from $5 to $25, depending on the night and venue. Have another $40–$50 socked away for round-trip cab fare: it's a relatively small price to pay for the convenience and the designated driver.

16

IN FOCUS NEW YORK NIGHTS

For addresses and phone numbers of these venues, see the main Nightlife listings in this chapter.

A NIGHT OF ELEGANCE
MIDTOWN, THE UPPER EAST AND UPPER WEST SIDES

I like the city air
I like to drink of it
The more I know New York
The more I think of it

It hardly matters that these Cole Porter lyrics (from "I Happen to Like New York") are decades old. The nighttime Manhattan that Porter knew—of moonlit walks in Central Park, swanky piano bars, chandeliered dining rooms, and dancing cheek to cheek—is still alive and kicking. Some of the city's classiest nightspots have been around since Porter himself was a regular, and some are more newly minted—but all of them share a sense of old-world, uniquely New York style.

If you prefer a clubbier, less formal but still elegant meal, try the **'21' Club,** where you can enjoy one of the city's best, and most expensive, hamburgers ($30) in front of a roaring fire. (Jackets are required for men at dinnertime.)

For post-dinner drinks, head east to the gorgeously wood-paneled **Campbell Apartment**—a small warren of rooms inside Grand Central that was once the private residence of a New York tycoon.

Cocktails with Fitzgerald-esque names will literally help get you in the spirit. Or, head north to the posh Carlyle Hotel, where you can slip into one of the leather banquettes and listen to live piano music at **Bemelmans Bar.** The Carlyle is also home to the famed **Café Carlyle,** where big-name entertainers like Judy Collins dazzle in an intimate setting (you'll need to buy tickets well in advance for these shows). Another nearby spot for live music (except in the summertime, when it's closed) is **Feinstein's** at the Regency Hotel (540 Park Ave., 212/759–4100).

CLASSIC CHAMPAGNE COCKTAILS

If sipping bubbly while gazing at the New York skyline sounds like the epitome of class, you're in luck; many of the elegant nightspots listed here serve up signature Champagne cocktails. Here are a few you can try:

The Flapper's Delight, at the Campbell Apartment: Champagne with papaya juice and amaretto

The ChamPino, at Bemelmans Bar: A concoction made with Champagne, Campari, and sweet vermouth

The Kir Royale, once served at the now-closed, Rainbow Room: An oldie but goodie, made with Champagne and crème de cassis

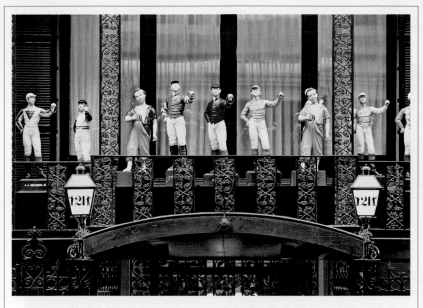

A cheeky row of lawn jockeys mark the entrance to the '21' Club

Featured performers here have included Florence Henderson.

Another sort of elegance is the urban intellectual sort, and this too can be found. At the venerable **Lexington Bar and Books,** the shelves are filled with those pre-Kindle curios, otherwise known as books, giving it a clubby feel. Even if these book-lined walls don't draw you in, the waitresses in pearl, the cozy furnishings, and the elite cocktails, cognacs, and malts will.

As mentioned, some of the swankiest bars and cocktail lounges are located in Manhattan's fabled hotels, the grand dames of lodging, such as the St. Regis, home to the tiny but essential **King Cole Bar** where artist Maxfield Parrish's bar-long mural looks as luminous as ever. The Plaza, the Pierre, and the Sherry-Netherland, also offer supremely elegant nightcap settings.

BACK IN THE DAY

The '21' Club, founded during Prohibition, began its life as a speakeasy. The club was raided several times, but it never closed, largely because of the ingenious preventive measures set up by its owners, Jack Kreindler and Charlie Berns. One of these was a mechanical system of pulleys that, when activated, immediately swept all the alcohol bottles off the bar shelves and down a chute, away from the prying eyes of police.

A glorious newcomer to this group is the dark-wood paneled **Lobby Lounge** of the Mandarin Oriental hotel. The Lounge's views are flat-out sensational and their signature cocktails, like the Blood and Seoul (made of vodka, lemon juice, tomato juice, and spicy Korean kimchee), are good enough to become a conversation piece.

For addresses and phone numbers of these venues, see the main Nightlife listings in this chapter.

A NIGHT OF ROCK N' ROLL
THE LOWER EAST SIDE

The Ramones, Patti Smith, the New York Dolls, the Velvet Underground, Television, Blondie . . . easily half the bands that are today considered American punk rock legends cut their teeth in the gritty grottoes of the Lower East Side. Now that the neighborhood's undergone a revival—it's become home base for a new generation of jaded, creative young things—new live-music venues have been popping up around the old dives like weeds in a junkyard. Some of these are full-blown performance spaces, others just bars with a guitarist, an amp, and a drummer crammed into a corner; but the good news is, if you don't like the band playing in one place, you'll have to walk only a block or two to get to the next one. And hey—now that smoking's been banned, you can actually see what's happening on stage.

The venerable **Bowery Ballroom**, a staple of the downtown music scene, is the perfect place to start your a rock n' roll pilgrimage. You'll need advance tickets to see the bands that play here, especially ultra-hip headliners like Arctic Monkeys, Dr. Dog, and the Yeah Yeah Yeahs. But the relatively small size of the auditorium, the great acoustics, and the beer-sloshing enthusiasm of the crowd make it worth the Ticketmaster prices. On your way out, you may find yourself passing 315 Bowery, the address of the legendary and now defunct **CBGB**. A battle-scarred, stinking pit even in its 1970s heyday—when bands like Suicides, Talking Heads, and Blondie launched their careers here—the club finally closed its doors in October of 2006 and is now a rock-themed clothing store.

The nearby intersection of Ludlow and Stanton streets is a mecca of sorts; small but rocking clubs seem to radiate in every direction for several blocks. This is the part of the LES that can get as crowded as a suburban mall late at night; between around 11 and 3 or 4 AM., the sidewalks are awash in young hipsters smoking Luckies and parading their thrift-store best. (If you want to blend in here, think scruffy retro-chic; no logos, no Manolos, no bling.) A favorite of this crowd is **Pianos,** once a piano shop (the new owners didn't bother to change the sign) and now an intimate performance space for acoustic and rock bands. **Arlene's Grocery,** just a block away, has been pulling in alternative music acts for more than a decade; The Strokes played here before anyone else had heard of them. If you need to channel your own inner Julian Casablancas, come on Monday night and join in the super-popular Rock n' Roll Karaoke party.

Heading less than a block east on Stanton will bring you to the deceptively un-rocklike **Cake Shop,** which looks like a record store crossed with a bakery. It is—at least on the first floor—but downstairs is a whole other story. Here, up-and-coming punk and garage bands play for a crowd of too-cool twenty-somethings (who also like to tank up on Fridays with the two-for-one happy hour, 5–8). Following Ludlow up to Houston, though, will take you right to **Mercury Lounge,** whose back room is famous for hosting big names before they were big. The White Stripes played here in their early days—the late, great Jeff Buckley would try out new material here; more recent performers, like Cold War Kids and Voxtrot are already starting to hit the mainstream.

16

IN FOCUS NEW YORK NIGHTS

For addresses and phone numbers of these venues, see the main Nightlife listings in this chapter.

Drinks with a Panoramic Punch

In New York you can take in the sights without leaving your bar stool. The **River Café** (✉ *1 Water St., near Old Fulton St., DUMBO, Brooklyn* ☎ *718/522–5200*), under the Brooklyn Bridge, has unobstructed views of the city skyline. (⇨ *See chapter 12.*) From the 23rd floor of the Peninsula Hotel you can nearly touch the sky at the **Salon de Ning** (✉ *700 5th Ave., at W. 55th St., Midtown West* ☎ *212/956–2888*). Still hungry for high altitude without low-attitude? Try the East River-side **Top of the Tower** (✉ *Beekman Tower Hotel, 3 Mitchell Pl., near 1st Ave. at E. 49th St., Midtown East* ☎ *212/980–4796* ⊕ *www.thebeekmanhotel.com* Ⓜ *6 to 51st St./Lexington Ave.; E, V to Lexington*

Ave./53rd St.). Or hit the Gansvoort Hotel's Meatpacking District-centric **Plunge** ✉ *18 9th Ave., at W. 13th St., Meatpacking District* ☎ *212/660–6766* ⊕ *www.hotelgansevoort.com* Ⓜ *A, C, E to 14th St.; L to 8th Ave.*). The only sight more beautiful than the skyline is its reflection in the East River at the **Water Club** (✉ *500 E. 30th St., at FDR Dr. and East River, Midtown East* ☎ *212/683–3333*). And the southwest side of Central Park never looks as lovely as when you behold it from the bar at the top of the Time-Warner building's Mandarin Oriental Hotel (✉ *80 Columbus Circle, Upper West Side* ☎ *212/806–8800*), which is one of the classiest havens in town even without that gorgeous view.

lines are good, and the sound system was designed with the help of Les Paul, the inventor of the solid-body electric guitar, who used to play here every Monday night. The rest of the week sees a mix of artists like Chuck Mangione and the Eddie Daniels Band. ✉ *1650 Broadway, at W. 51st St., Midtown West* ☎ *212/582–2121* ⊕ *www.iridiumjazzclub.com* Ⓜ *1 to 50th St.; N, R, W to 49th St.*

☺ **Jazz Standard.** The Standard's sizable underground room draws the top names in the business. As a part of Danny Meyer's Southern-food restaurant Blue Smoke, it's one of the few spots where you can get dry-rubbed ribs to go with your bebop. Bring the kids for the Jazz Standard Youth Orchestra concerts every Sunday afternoon. ✉ *116 E. 27th St., between Park and Lexington Aves., Murray Hill* ☎ *212/576–2232* ⊕ *www.jazzstandard.net* Ⓜ *6 to 28th St.*

Knickerbocker Bar and Grill. Jazz acts are on the menu on Friday and Saturday nights at this old-fashioned steak house, a longtime staple of the city's more intimate music scene. ✉ *33 University Pl., at E. 9th St., Greenwich Village* ☎ *212/228–8490* ⊕ *www.knickerbockerbarandgrill.com* Ⓜ *R, W to 8th St.*

Lenox Lounge. This impeccably detailed Art Deco lounge opened in the 1930s, and currently hosts jazz ensembles, blues acts, and jam sessions in the Zebra Room. The restaurant in back serves great food to go with the soulful music. ✉ *288 Lenox Ave., between W. 124th and W. 125th Sts., Harlem* ☎ *212/427–0253* ⊕ *www.lenoxlounge.com* Ⓜ *2, 3 to 125th St.*

Smoke. If you can't wait until sunset to get your riffs on, head uptown to this lounge near Columbia University, where the music starts as early as

6 PM. Performers include some of the top names in the business, including turban-wearing organist Dr. Lonnie Smith and the drummer Jimmy Cobb (who laid down the beat on Miles Davis's seminal album *Kind of Blue*). ✉ *2751 Broadway, between W. 105th and W. 106th Sts., Upper West Side* ☎ *212/864–6662* ⊕ *www.smokejazz.com* Ⓜ *1 to 103rd St.*

Fodor's Choice ★ **Village Vanguard.** This prototypical jazz club, tucked into a cellar in Greenwich Village since the 1940s, has been the haunt of legends like Thelonious Monk and Barbra Streisand (who recently came back for a one-night-only gig). Today you can hear jams from the jazz-star likes of Bill Charlap and Ravi Coltrane, and on Monday nights, the sizable resident "Vanguard Jazz Orchestra" blows its collective heart out. ✉ *178 7th Ave. S, between W. 11th and Perry Sts., Greenwich Village* ☎ *212/255–4037* ⊕ *www.villagevanguard.com* Ⓜ *1, 2, 3 to 14th St.*

ROCK CLUBS

Arlene's Grocery. On Monday nights crowds pack into this converted convenience store for Rock and Roll Karaoke, where they live out their rock-star dreams by singing favorite punk anthems onstage with a live band. The other six nights of the week are for local bands, and accordingly hit-or-miss. ✉ *95 Stanton St., between Ludlow and Orchard Sts., Lower East Side* ☎ *212/995–1652* ⊕ *www.arlenesgrocery.net* Ⓜ *F, V to 2nd Ave.*

Fodor's Choice ★ **Bowery Ballroom.** This theater with Art Deco accents is probably the city's top midsize concert venue. Packing in the crowds here is a rite of passage for musicians on the cusp of stardom, including the Gossip, Manic Street Preachers, and the exuberant Go! Team. Grab one of the tables on the balcony (if you can), stand (and thus get sandwiched) on the main floor, or retreat to comfortable bar in the basement, which really fills up after each show. ✉ *6 Delancey St., between the Bowery and Chrystie St., Lower East Side* ☎ *212/533–2111* ⊕ *www.boweryballroom.com* Ⓜ *J, M, Z to Bowery St.*

Fodor's Choice ★ **The Fillmore New York @ Irving Plaza.** This two-story venue, now affiliated with San Francisco's legendary club of the same name, is known for its solid rock performances, both indie (DJ Shadow and Sleater-Kinney) and more mainstream (Lenny Kravitz, Blues Traveller)—even if they can get a little pricey. Red walls and chandeliers add a Gothic touch. And if the main floor gets too cramped, seek sanctuary in the form of the chill upstairs bar. ✉ *17 Irving Pl., at E. 15th St., Gramercy* ☎ *212/777–6800* ⊕ *www.irvingplaza.com* Ⓜ *4, 5, 6, L, N, Q, R, W to 14th St./Union Sq.*

★ **(Le) Poisson Rouge.** Underneath the site of the late, lamented Village Gate jazz emporium is this cutting-edge jewel of a place, whose name means "The Red Fish" and whose parentheses around "Le" remain a sacred mystery. Blending just the right mix of posh notes (the lush decor, the fine dining) and brave music programming (jazz, classical, electronic, cabaret, rock, folk—even with the splendiferous Ralph's World, children's music), the Poisson is quite simply an essential NYC fixture. ✉ *9158 Bleecker St., at Thompson St., West Village* ☎ *212/796–0741* ⊕ *www.lepoissonrouge.com* Ⓜ *A, B, C, D, E, F, V to W. 4th St.*

16

Lit Lounge. With a rock roster that's included musical forces as diverse as Devendra Banhart and the Hold Steady, Lit is a wonderfully grungy East Village classic. The raucous arty crowd hits not only shows but its charming art gallery "Fuse," and its theme parties, which cater to fans of specific bands (the White Stripes, Devo, and the Buzzcocks, to name just three). ⊠ *93 2nd Ave., Grand Central Station, East Village* ☎ *212/777–7987* ⊕ *www.litloungenyc.com* Ⓜ *F, V to Lower East Side/2nd Ave., 6 to Astor Pl.*

Mercury Lounge. You'll have to squeeze past all the sardine-packed hipsters in the front bar to reach the stage, but it's worth it. Not only does this top-quality venue, a "little sister to the Bowery Bar," specialize in cool bands on the indie scene (Holly Golightly, Echo and the Bunnymen, and the Apostle of Hustle, anyone?), but it was where the late great Jeff Buckley used to stop by to do spontaneous solo shows. ⊠ *217 E. Houston St., at Ave. A, Lower East Side* ☎ *212/260–4700* ⊕ *www. mercuryloungenyc.com* Ⓜ *F, V to 2nd Ave.*

WORLD MUSIC VENUES

Fodor'sChoice
★
S.O.B.'s. The initials stand for "Sounds Of Brazil" (no, not what you— and everybody else—might think), and this is *the* place for reggae, African, and Latin music, with some jazz gigs like Marcus Miller sprinkled in. The late, great Cuban sensation Cachao used to hold court here, as does calypso's Mighty Sparrow when he's up north. Don't miss the monthly Southeast Asian party "Basement Bhangra," the Haitian dance parties, or the bossa nova brunches. Dinner is served as well. ⊠ *204 Varick St., at W. Houston St., SoHo* ☎ *212/243–4940* ⊕ *www.sobs. com* Ⓜ *1 to Houston St.*

ACOUSTIC AND BLUES VENUES

B.B. King Blues Club & Grill. This lavish Times Square club is vast and shiny and host to a range of musicians from the Harlem Gospel Choir to George Clinton and the P-Funk All-Stars. It's also where surviving rock legends like Little Richard, Chuck Berry, and, yes, the still-relentlessly touring owner play as well. (If you happen to meet Mr. King here, give our regards to "Lucille," his guitar.) ⊠ *237 W. 42nd St., between 7th and 8th Aves., Midtown West* ☎ *212/997–4144* ⊕ *www.bbkingblues. com* Ⓜ *1, 2, 3, 7, A, C, E, N, Q, R, W, S to 42nd St./Port Authority.*

Fodor'sChoice
★
Living Room. Terre Roche, Connie Acher, and other ace singer-song-writers—some solo, some with their bands—are found at this unpretentiously delightful club. Craving a more intimate experience? Head upstairs to Googie's Lounge, their humbler acoustic space with just a piano. (Or else sashay next door to **Cakeshop,** which has music and boozin' in a shabby-chic setting.) ⊠ *154 Ludlow St., between Stanton and Rivington Sts., Lower East Side* ☎ *212/533–7235* ⊕ *www. livingroomny.com* Ⓜ *F, V to 2nd Ave.*

COMEDY CLUBS

Caroline's on Broadway. This high-gloss club presents established names as well as comedians on the edge of stardom. Janeane Garofalo, David Alan Grier, Colin Quinn, and Gilbert Gottfried have headlined. ⊠ *1626 Broadway, between W. 49th and W. 50th Sts., Midtown West* ☎ *212/757–4100* ⊕ *www.carolines.com* Ⓜ *N, R, W to 49th St.; 1 to 50th St.*

Chicago City Limits. This crew touts itself as performing in the longest-running improv show in the city. The shows, heavy on audience participation, take place Wednesday through Saturday and seldom fail to whip visitors into what the comics might call a "phun phrenzy." ⊠ *318 W. 53rd St., between 8th and 9th Aves., Midtown West* ☎ *212/888–5233* ⊕ *www.chicagocitylimits.com* Ⓜ *C, E to 50th St.*

Fodor's Choice
★ **Comix.** With big-name comics in its main room and up-and-comers in the smaller "Ochi's Lounge," Comix brings comedy to the Meatpacking District (whose pretensions can be pretty comical in themselves). Another plus: it looks a whole lot better than most local lairs of laughter. ⊠ *1353 W. 14th St., between 8th and 9th Ave., Meatpacking District* ☎ *212/524-2500* ⊕ *www.comixny.com* Ⓜ *A, C, E to 14th St.*

Fodor's Choice
★ **Upright Citizens Brigade Theatre.** Raucous sketch comedy, audience-initiated improv, and classic stand-up take turns onstage here at the city's absolute capital for alternative comedy. There are even classes available; the Upright Citizens bill their program as the world's largest improv school, where you can catch indie comic darlings like *SNL*'s Amy Poehler or *Human Giant*'s Rob Huebel. ⊠ *307 W. 26th St., between 8th and 9th Aves., Chelsea* ☎ *212/366–9176* ⊕ *www.uprightcitizens.org* Ⓜ *C, E to 23rd St.*

CABARET AND PERFORMANCE SPACES

In addition to the Carlyle and the Oak Room (⇨ *Classic New York*), here are some of the best venues.

The Duplex. No matter who's performing, the largely gay audience hoots and hollers in support of the often kitschy performers at this music-scene staple on busy Sheridan Square since 1951. Singers and comedians hold court in the cabaret theater, while those itching to take a shot at open-mike head downstairs to the lively piano bar. ⊠ *61 Christopher St., at 7th Ave. S, Greenwich Village* ☎ *212/255–5438* ⊕ *www.theduplex.com* Ⓜ *1 to Christopher St.*

Feinstein's at the Regency. That the world-touring Michael Feinstein performs a residency here only once a year (usually in winter) and still gets the venue named after him speaks volumes about the charismatic cabaret star. This tastefully appointed space in Loew's Regency Hotel presents Broadway babe and *30 Rock* regular Jane Krakowski and other top names in the business—plus, when we're lucky, Tony Danza. ⊠ *540 Park Ave., at E. 61st St., Upper East Side* ☎ *212/339–4095* ⊕ *www.feinsteinsattheregency.com* Ⓜ *4, 5, 6, N, R, W to 59th St.–Lexington Ave.*

16

Fodor's Choice   **Joe's Pub**. Wood paneling, red-velvet walls, and comfy sofas make a
   ★   lush setting for top-notch performers and the A-list celebrities who
love them, or pretend to. Named for the Public Theater's near-mythic
impresario Joe Papp, and located inside the Public, Joe's doesn't have
a bad seat—but if you want to occupy one, buy tickets beforehand
and/or arrive at least half an hour early for the Italian-inspired dinner
menu. ⊠ *425 Lafayette St., between E. 4th St. and Astor Pl., East Village* ☎ *212/539–8770* ⊕ *www.joespub.com* Ⓜ *6 to Astor Pl.*

BARS

LOWER MANHATTAN, SOHO, AND TRIBECA

B-flat. The decor is red-on-red here, and the Asian-style cocktails are particularly groovy. (Literally. One, with yuzu juice and vodka, is dubbed
"the Groovy.") Get some fine Japanese food-treats to keep yourself
upright, and check out the upstairs area with amazing wall- and ceiling-murals of the Tokyo Bar. ⊠ *277 Church St., between Franklin and White Sts., TriBeCa* ☎ *212/219–2970* ⊕ *www.bflat.info* Ⓜ *1 to Franklin St.*

Fodor's Choice   **Brandy Library**. Alas, the only book in this exquisite, wood-panelled
   ★   room is the leather-bound menu listing hundreds of brandies and single-
malt Scotches. The bottles are on gorgeous backlighted "bookshelves,"
though, and you can learn what makes each of them special by chatting
with the spirit sommelier—or by attending Saturday's 5–8 PM free-of-
charge single-malt tastings. ⊠ *25 N. Moore St., between Varick and Hudson Sts., TriBeCa* ☎ *212/226–5545* ⊕ *www.brandylibrary.com* Ⓜ *1 to Franklin St.*

Ear Inn. Since the early 1800s this sturdy old New York classic (at one
time also a bordello) has been packing in, and amiably spooking, customers. According to legend, the place is haunted by a randy ghost,
so beware—that hand you feel in your lap might not be your lover's.
That hardly scares away patrons. In fact, it may be a selling point, as
the staff encourages you to report all sightings. (No doubt "sightings"
increase after a few drinks.) ⊠ *7326 Spring St., between Greenwich and Washington Sts., SoHo* ☎ *212/226–9060* ⊕ *www.earinn.com* Ⓜ *1 to Houston St., C, E to Spring St.*

M1-5. For the more bohemian of TriBeCa pubgoers, this lipstick-red,
high-ceilinged spot is a vast playground (as in pool and darts). A reggae jukebox helps keep it real, as do discounts for local artists on the
diverse cocktail menu. Extra points, too, for the bar's name, which cites
TriBeCa's warehouse zoning law. ⊠ *52 Walker St., between Broadway and Church St., TriBeCa* ☎ *212/965–1701* ⊕ *www.m1-5.com* Ⓜ *J, M, Z, N, Q, R, W, 6 to Canal St.*

   ★   **MercBar**. A well-turned-out local crowd and Europeans-in-the-know
come to this dark, otherwise nondescript, yet forever popular bar for the
wonderful martinis. Its street number is barely visible, so look for the
French doors, which stay open in summer. ⊠ *151 Mercer St., between Prince and W. Houston Sts., SoHo* ☎ *212/966–2727* ⊕ *www.mercbar.com* Ⓜ *R, W to Prince St.*

Pegu Club. Modeled after an officers' club in what's now Myanmar, the Pegu manages to feel expansive and calm even when packed. The well dressed and flirtatious come here partly for the exotically lovely surroundings, but primarily for the cocktails, which are innovative, prepared with superlative ingredients, and predictably pricey. ⊠ *77 W. Houston St. (2nd fl.) , between West Broadway and Wooster St., SoHo* ☎ *212/473–7348* ⊕ *www.peguclub.com* Ⓜ *B, D, F, V to Broadway-Lafayette St.; 6 to Bleecker St.*

Fodor's Choice
★
Pravda. Cocktails rule at this Eastern European–style bar. Choose from more than 70 brands of vodka, including house infusions, or opt for a house martini. The speakeasy-like space, with an atmospheric vaulted ceiling and charmingly tiny upstairs bar, is illuminated with candles. It has the friendliest hosts this side of Moscow, too. Table reservations are usually needed for the Russian-inspired fare, especially on weekends. ⊠ *281 Lafayette St., between Prince and E. Houston Sts., SoHo* ☎ *212/226–4944* ⊕ *www.pravdany.com* Ⓜ *B, D, F, V to Broadway-Lafayette St.; 6 to Bleecker St.*

Smith and Mills. Attractive scenesters frolic giddily at this tiny gem of a ginmill, where mixologists who resemble Daniel Day-Lewis dispense elixirs (and caviar) from a bar hung with pots and pans. There are cozy table-nooks for couples, and an elevator-toilet (yes, you read that correctly) for anyone who feels "nature's call" while heeding "the call of the wild." ⊠ *71 N. Moore St., between Hudson and Greenwich Sts., TriBeCa* ☎ *212/219–8568* ⊕ *www.cafenyc.com* Ⓜ *1 to Franklin St.*

Thom Bar. This lounge inside the 60 Thompson boutique hotel is the perfect place to perch on a banquette, ogle the attractive crowd (locals as well as out of-towners) and splurge on a "Thom Martini." Pick a weeknight if you want your drink to be a more relaxed one—the weekends get predictably full. ⊠ *60 Thompson St., between Spring and Broome Sts., SoHo* ☎ *212/219–3200* ⊕ *www.60thompson.com* Ⓜ *C, E to Spring St.*

CHELSEA, THE MEATPACKING DISTRICT, AND GREENWICH VILLAGE

Fodor's Choice
★
Cornelia Street Café. Share a bottle of merlot at a street-side table on a quaint West Village lane. Downstairs you can catch live jazz or a poetry reading, or take in the superb monthly "Entertaining Science" evenings hosted by the Nobel laureate chemist Roald Hoffmann. ⊠ *29 Cornelia St., between W. 4th and Bleecker Sts., Greenwich Village* ☎ *212/989–9319* ⊕ *www.corneliastreetcafe.com* Ⓜ *A, B, C, D, E, F, V to W. 4th St./Washington Sq.*

The Dove. On a colorful block that evokes the Greenwich Village of yore—cigar store, vegetarian cafés, a bootleg music shop, and not one but two stores specializing in chess—is this wonderful bar whose elegant atmosphere (red-velvet wallpaper, white-wood paneling) is belied by the revelry of the very sexy young customers. ⊠ *228 Thompson St., between W. 3rd and Bleecker Sts., West Village* ☎ *212/254–1435* ⊕ *www.thedoveparlour.com* Ⓜ *E to Spring St.*

Half King. Writer Sebastian Junger (*The Perfect Storm*) is one of the owners of this would-be literary mecca. We say "would-be" because

16

the ambience can be more pub-like than writerly—but that's fine, since the King draws such a friendly crowd (media types, mostly). We like it best for its Monday night readings, gallery exhibits, and Irish-American menu. ⊠ *505 W. 23rd St., between 10th and 11th Aves., Chelsea* ☎ *212/462–4300* ⊕ *www.thehalfking.com* Ⓜ *C, E to 23rd St.*

Hogs & Heifers. This raucous place is all about the saucy barkeeps using megaphones to berate male customers and bait the females to get up on the bar and dance (and add their bras to the collection on the wall). Celebrities of the *Us Weekly* variety still drop in from time to time to get their names in the gossip columns. ⊠ *859 Washington St., at W. 13th St., Meatpacking District* ☎ *212/929–0655* ⊕ *www.hogsandheifers.com* Ⓜ *A, C, E to 14th St.; L to 8th Ave.*

Hudson Bar and Books. Along with its sister branches—Beekman Bar and Books on Beekman Place and Lexington Bar and Books on, yep, Lexington—the Hudson reflects a literary bent on its cocktails with names like "the Dewey Decimal," "the Cervantes Spritzer," and "Alphabet Absinthe" (topped off with floating letter-shaped sugar cubes). Despite that, it's hardly a hushed library where well-read butlers serve you; no—the atmosphere here is more about book decor than serious literature. (It's usually too dim to read or to write anyway.) Still, it is seriously gorgeous in a clubby way with wood-paneling and leather banquettes. And the cigars and swell cocktail menu stimulate all kinds of conversation, literary or otherwise. ⊠ *636 Hudson St., at Horatio St., West Village* ☎ *212/229–2642* ⊕ *www.barandbooks.cz* Ⓜ *A, C, E to 14th St., L to 8th Ave.*

Fodor's Choice
★ **Little Branch.** The owners of the secretive, hard-to-access lounge Milk & Honey have created this open-to-everyone cousin, the site of NY's legendary '80s Milk Bar, with the same simple yet quality cocktails. The dim lighting and snug booths make it the ideal spot for you to hide from creditors or share a romantic first kiss in equal measure. ⊠ *20 7th Ave., at Leroy St., Greenwich Village* ☎ *212/929–4360* Ⓜ *1 to Houston St.*

New York City Motorcycle Federation. Q: What's better than a hip shop that sells the finest in motorcycle fashion and accoutrements? A: When said shop turns into a rockin' café–bar at night. It's all about multitasking at this modest-size but wonderful new nightspot, which lets you ogle artfully designed leathers, crash helmets, and chrome gadgets while you're ogling some of the West Village's sexiest young denizens. Of course, you don't have to be a Hell's Angel to feel at home here—the vibe is more Ducati than Harley—and you can enjoy the place by day as well as night, because they start serving beer and wine (as well as other refreshments, but no hard liquor) from the morning on. But don't scorn as "square" all those non-boozing shoppers and browsers—they're probably already high on metaphorical bike fumes. ⊠ *257 6th Ave., between Downing and Houston Sts., West Village* ☎ *212/255–1234* ⊕ *www. motorcyclefederation.com* Ⓜ *1 to Sheridan Square-Christopher St.*

Fodor's Choice
★ **Plunge.** Simply stated, the Gansvoort Hotel's slick rooftop bar would worth visiting even without its mouthwatering views. The adjectives "sleek" and "glossy" could easily be illustrated by Plunge, where the lighting is soft, the furnishings are cool and comfy (at least to a degree),

the music isn't too loud, servers of both genders are sexy, and the ample space—indoor as well as outdoor—make it practically iconic. ✉ *18 9th Ave., at W. 13th St., Meatpacking District* ☏ *212/660–6766* ⊕ *www. hotelgansevoort.com* Ⓜ *A, C, E to 14th St.; L to 8th Ave.*

675 Bar. How can you not love a spot where the bouncer greets you with a grin instead of a scowl, board games abound, a giant black-lacquered horse stands guard next to the pool table, the drinks get amply poured, and each small room along the subterranean stone corridor is decorated in a different creative way? As an ideal spot for both dates (plenty of dark corners) and raucous merriment (bright big central space), the 675 scores highest for having less attitude than the rest of this supremely haughty nightlife neighborhood. ✉ *675 Hudson St., between Hudson St. and 9th Ave. (enter on 13th St.), Meatpacking District* ☏ *212/699–2410* ⊕ *www.675bar.com* Ⓜ *A,C, E to 14th St., L to 8th Ave.*

Spice Market. The posh come here to gorge on Asian street fare served with upscale twists and the equally exotic cocktails. Ginger margaritas, anyone? Or kumquat *mojito*? (When in season). And if you're looking for tranquillity, the multilevel open space has slowly rotating fans, intricately carved woodwork, and flowing curtains that create a palpable aura of calm. ✉ *403 W. 13th St., at 9th Ave., Meatpacking District* ☏ *212/675–2322* ✉ *spicemarketnewyork.com* Ⓜ *A, C, E to 14th St.; L to 8th Ave.*

The Standard Hotel Beer Garden, Grill, and Living Room. Practically the official bar of the High Line park, the Standard is a lush diversion. Initially, media stories swirled around the riotous behavior of hotel guests here who displayed themselves to High Line visitors leaving their shades wide open during salacious activities. But the real story is in the sprawling and already riotous beer-garden, grill bar, and very cool indoor "Living Room" lounge. As for the chic hotspot on the roof, unofficially called "The Boom Boom Room," it's currently the hardest "door" in town ("hardest," that is, to get through), but given the quality of the accessible fun down below, we'll forgive their snobbery. ✉ *848 Washington St., at W. 13th St., Meatpacking District* ☏ *212/645–4646* ⊕ *www.standardhotels.com* Ⓜ *A, C, E, L to 8th Ave.-14th St.*

Fodor's Choice
★ **Tillman's**. Nothing in Chelsea is quite like this glorious "Old Harlem" lounge, resplendent as it is with fireplace, banquettes, good eats, even better cocktails, inventive decor, jazz and blues sounds on the soundtrack, and tastefully uniformed servers complete with a cigarette girl. ✉ *165 W. 26th St., between 6th and 7th Ave., Chelsea* ☏ *212/627–8320* ⊕ *www.tillmansnyc.com* Ⓜ *F, V, 1 to 28th St.*

Vol de Nuit. Tucked away from the street, the "Belgian Beer Bar" (as everybody calls it) features a European-style, enclosed outdoor courtyard and a cozy interior, all red light and shadows. NYU grad-student types come for the mammoth selection of beers on tap as well as for the fries, which are served with a Belgian flair, in a paper cone with an array of sauces on the side. ✉ *148 W. 4th St., at 6th Ave., Greenwich Village* ☏ *212/982–3388* ⊕ *www.voldenuitbar.com* Ⓜ *A, B, C, D, E, F, V to W. 4th St./Washington Sq.*

Fodor's Choice
★

White Horse Tavern. According to New York legend, Dylan Thomas drank himself to death in this historic and quintessential West Village tavern founded in 1880. The Horse remains perpetually popular with literary types, but thankfully it's lacking more death-by-alcohol-poisoning cases of late. When the weather's nice, try to snag a seat at one of the sidewalk tables for prime—and, given the neighborhood, we do mean prime—people-watching. ⊠ *567 Hudson St., at W. 11th St., Greenwich Village* ☎ *212/989–3956* Ⓜ *1 to Christopher St./Sheridan Sq.*

LOWER EAST SIDE AND EAST VILLAGE THROUGH EAST 20S

Fodor's Choice
★

Back Room. The Prohibition-era atmospheric touches here include tin ceilings, chandeliers, velvet wallpaper, mirrored bars, amply sized fireplace, and "hidden" outdoor entrance (which you'll find easily enough, though the back-alley walk to the second, indoor entrance puts you in the speakeasy spirit). The music consists of rock CDs rather than a live spinmeister, and the drinks come in old-fashioned teacups or wrapped in paper bags. These, and other prize quirks, attract a slightly older clientele than many of its rowdy "boho" (aka bohemian) neighbors do. ⊠ *102 Norfolk St., between Delancey St. and Rivington St., Lower East Side* Ⓜ *F to Delancey St.; J, M, Z to Essex St.*

B Bar. Long lines of people peer through Venetian blinds at the stylish downtown crowd within this long-running but still fairly trendy bar-and-grill. It's a far cry from this spot's former gas-station days, so dress your best if you want a seat in the vast covered outdoor space, one of New York's finest to drink in. ⊠ *40 E. 4th St., at the Bowery, East Village* ☎ *212/475–2220* ⊕ *www.bbarandgrill.com* Ⓜ *6 to Astor Pl.*

Beauty Bar. Grab a seat in a barber chair or under a dryer at this made-over hair salon where, during happy hour, the manicurist will do your nails for a fee that includes a drink. (How's that for multitasking!) The DJ spins everything from Britpop to rock—a great soundtrack for primping. ⊠ *231 E. 14th St., between 2nd and 3rd Aves., East Village* ☎ *212/539–1389* ⊕ *www.beautybar.com* Ⓜ *4, 5, 6, L, N, Q, R, W to 14th St./Union Sq.*

Fodor's Choice
★

The Bourgeois Pig. What do you get when you serve all kinds of different fondue concoctions as well as all kinds of inventively delicious cocktails in a velvety yet chilled-out French bordello setting that's smack dab in the middle of the East Village? This keeper of a lounge, that's what. ⊠ *111 E. 7th St., between 1st Ave. and Ave. A, East Village* ☎ *212/475–2246* ⊕ *www.thebourgeoispigny.com* Ⓜ *F, V to Lower East Side/2nd Ave., 6 to Astor Pl.*

★

The Bowery Hotel Lobby Bar and Patio. Combining Old World hunting-lodge elegance with the height of comfort, the spanking new Bowery sets a standard for what all hotel lobbies should feature: sofas you can get lost in, a grand fireplace, a beautiful garden, an unusually friendly staff, and enough good vibes to compensate for the loss of CBGB down the block. ⊠ *333 The Bowery , between 2nd and 3rd Aves. East Village* ☎ *212/505–9100* ⊕ *www.theboweryhotel.com* Ⓜ *F, V to Lower East Side/2nd Ave., 6 to Astor Pl.*

Death and Company. It's all about "speakeasy chic" at this sister lounge to the equally imaginative and classy nearby bars Mayahuel and Bourgeois Pig. A hilarious wall mural toward the rear sets the tone for the tongue-and-cheek Satanic vibe here, but in the end, it's all about the outlandishly delicious cocktails. ⊠ *4 E. 6th St., between 1st Ave. and Ave. A, East Village* ☏ *212/388–0882* ⊕ *www.deathandcompany.com* Ⓜ *F, V to Lower East Side/2nd Ave., 6 to Astor Pl.*

Good World Bar & Grill. On an isolated street in Chinatown is this glass-fronted bar full of artists, writers, their subjects, and the attractive customers who distract said artists from their muse. Expect a catwalk-worthy (and sometimes, it seems, catwalk-veteran) staff; expect superb music; and expect—believe it or not—tasty Nordic specialties like gravlax, herring, and Swedish meatballs. ⊠ *3 Orchard St., between Canal and Division Sts., Lower East Side* ☏ *212/925–9975* ⊕ *www. goodworldbar.com* Ⓜ *F to East Broadway.*

Lucky Cheng's. Although gastronomes deride its subpar Asian fare, Lucky Cheng's is famous for its mostly stunning drag queens who cavort and kick up their heels with the tourists as well as the bachelorettes singing karaoke in the lounge downstairs. ⊠ *24 1st Ave., between E. 1st and E. 2nd Sts., East Village* ☏ *212/473–0516* ⊕ *www.planetluckychengs. com* Ⓜ *F, V to 2nd Ave.*

Fodor's Choice ★ **Mayahuel.** This is the newest kid on the downtown, designer-bar block, and what a kid: all manner of Aztec spirits (raspberry tea–infused tequilas! pineapple-infused mescal!) make for the fiendishly rococo cocktails here, courtesy of master mixologist Philip Ward. Equally good are tapas such as popcorn with lime, cheese, and chili. The bi-level setting conjures a sort of demonic south-of-the border bordello. As for the name, it derives from an Aztec legend (the fun menu fills you in). ⊠ *304 E. 6th St.,between 1st and 2nd Ave., East Village* ☏ *212/253–5888* ⊕ *www. mayahuel.com* Ⓜ *F, V to Lower East Side/2nd Ave., 6 to Astor Pl., R, W to 8th St.-Broadway.*

McSorley's Old Ale House. One of New York's oldest saloons (it claims to have opened in 1854) and immortalized by *New Yorker* writer Joseph Mitchell, McSorley's is a must-visit for beer lovers, even if only two kinds of brew are served: "McSorley's Light" and "McSorley's Dark." It's also essential for blarney lovers, and much friendlier to women than it used to be before the '80s. (The motto here once was "Good ale, raw onions, and no ladies.") Go early to avoid the down-the-block lines on Friday and Saturday night. ⊠ *15 E. 7th St., between 2nd and 3rd Aves., East Village* ☏ *212/473–9148* ⊕ *www.mcsorleysnewyork. com* Ⓜ *6 to Astor Pl.*

Old Town Bar & Restaurant. The proudly unpretentious bi-level Old Town is redolent of old New York, and why not—it's been around since 1892. Tavern-style grub, mahogany everywhere, and atmosphere, atmosphere, atmosphere make this a fun stop on any pub crawl. ⊠ *45 E. 18th St., between Broadway and Park Ave. S, Gramercy* ☏ *212/529–6732* ⊕ *www. oldtownbar.com* Ⓜ *4, 5, 6, L, N, Q, R, W to 14th St./Union Sq.*

16

Fodor's Choice
★ **Otto's Shrunken Head.** Who says NYC doesn't appeal to all tastes? Should you get a sudden urge to visit a tiki bar while in the East Village—and who doesn't sometimes?—the ultrapopular Otto's is your ticket. You'll find more than just a bamboo bar here: namely fish lamps, a tattooed, punk rock crowd, cute little banquettes, drinking mugs in the form of shrunken heads, beef jerky for sale, rock bands wailing in the backroom, and DJs prone to spinning anything from '50s rock to that great sole chestnut of black surf music, "Soul Gidget." ⊠ *538 E. 14th St., between Aves. A and B, East Village* ☎ *212/228–2240* ⊕ *www. ottosshrunkenhead.com* Ⓜ *L to 1st Ave.*

PDT. Those who crave their cocktails with a little cloak-and-dagger will flip over PDT (which stands for "Please Don't Tell"). Housed below the unassuming hot-dog joint "Crif Dogs," this pseudo-speakeasy can only be reached through a phone booth on the main floor. Patrons with phoned-in reservations are escorted through the phone booth's false back into the building's underbelly, which is decorated with warm wooden beams and tongue-in-cheek taxidermy. ⊠ *113 St. Marks Pl., between 1st Ave. and Ave. A, East Village* ☎ *212/614–0386* ⊕ *www. pdtnyc.com* Ⓜ *6 to Astor Pl.*

Fodor's Choice
★ **Pete's Tavern.** Allegedly the place where that great transplanted New Yorker O. Henry wrote his sweet tale *The Gift of the Magi* (in the booth up front), Pete's has charm to spare even today, when it's crowded with locals enjoying a beer or a (fantastic) burger. ⊠ *129 E. 18th St., at Irving Pl., Gramercy* ☎ *212/473–7676* ⊕ *www.petestavern.com* Ⓜ *4, 5, 6, L, N, Q, R, W to 14th St./Union Sq.*

★ **The Pink Pony.** Maintaining a defiantly boho feel on trendy Ludlow Street, this shabby-chic bar-café draws young writers, filmmakers, and designers who come to escape the cacophony from nearby music venues and make conversation over bottles of cheap wine and cup after cup (after cup) of coffee. ⊠ *176 Ludlow St., between E. Houston and Stanton Sts., Lower East Side* ☎ *212/253–1922* Ⓜ *www.pinkponynyc. com* Ⓜ *F, V to 2nd Ave.*

Fodor's Choice
★ **Spitzer's Corner.** No, you won't rub shoulders with disgraced ex-governor Eliot Spitzer here. Instead, you'll find a well-turned-out and attractive crowd making the scene at this equally attractive bar-restaurant with forty types of beer, delicious munchies, floor-to-ceiling windows that pop open in fine weather, and wooden walls supposedly taken from pickle barrels. (Fortunately, the air is free of any scents from the barrel's former contents.) ⊠ *101 Rivington St., at Ludlow St., Lower East Side* ☎ *212/228–0027* ⊕ *www.spitzerscorner.com* Ⓜ *F to Delancey St., J, M, Z to Essex St.*

Sweet and Vicious. The name of this unpretentious butterfly-logo'ed lounge doesn't signify the looks (sweet) and attitude (vicious) of certain downtown pretty things that frequent the bars on this LES stretch. That crowd haunts many of the fine bars on this eastern stretch of Spring Street (e.g., Bar Marche, Room 18, Bread, and the down-home Spring Tavern). So what makes this bar in particular so sweet? A sizable back garden. ⊠ *5 Spring St., between the Bowery and Elizabeth St., Lower East Side* ☎ *212/224–7915* Ⓜ *6 to Spring St., J, M to Bowery.*

Fodor's Choice
★

Temple Bar. Unmarked and famous for its classic cocktails and romantic atmosphere, the Temple is prime first-date territory, especially once you drift past the sleekly wonderful bar to the back, where, swathed in almost complete darkness, you can lounge on a comfy banquette, order an Old-Fashioned, and do what people on first dates do. ✉ *332 Lafayette St., between Bleecker and E. Houston Sts., East Village* ☎ *212/925–4242* ⊕ *www.templebarnyc.com* Ⓜ *B, D, F, V to Broadway–Lafayette St.; 6 to Bleecker St.*

White Star. Master mixologist Sasha Petraske won kudos for his innovative cocktails at Milk and Honey, but the hassles associated with that bar (reservations, membership, etc.) mean that White Star, its elegantly less-is-more sister bar, is a better choice. Named for the Moroccan lamps that hang above the bar (and front door), the Star features nattily dressed barkeeps, a scintillating drinks menu, and a tiny sunken back room that is one of NYC's best sites for a double date. ✉ *21 Essex St., between Canal and Hester Sts., Lower East Side* ☎ *212/995–5464* ⊕ *www.nycgo.com* Ⓜ *F to East Broadway.*

MIDTOWN AND THE THEATER DISTRICT

Algonquin Hotel. Playing up its history as the home of the Algonquin Roundtable, that famed literary clique that included sharp-tongued Dorothy Parker, this veritable institution would still draw a crowd even if it just opened thanks to its clubby, oak-panel lobby and comfortable sofas. ✉ *59 W. 44th St., between 5th and 6th Aves., Midtown West* ☎ *212/840–6800* ⊕ *www.algonquinhotel.com* Ⓜ *B, D, F, V to 42nd St.*

The Cabin Club at the Pine Tree Lodge Bar. Who says that the zaniest places are all below 14th Street? This insane theme bar offers serious competition. Think "summer camp on psychedelics"—we're talking mounted wildlife, rafts, and other outdoorsy-kitsch decor. Don't overlook the very spacious backyard or the racy raccoon picture in the comfy sideroom—you'll never view those critters the same way again. ✉ *326 E. 35th St., between 1st and 2nd Aves., Midtown East* ☎ *212/481–5490* Ⓜ *6 to 34th St.*

Cellar Bar. Underneath the Bryant Park Hotel—and a tiled, arched ceiling—is one of the more spectacular spaces in Midtown. As a DJ with a taste for classic R&B spins the night away, a fashion-industry crowd gets up to dance—and spills its collective drink. ✉ *40 W. 40th St., between 5th and 6th Aves., Midtown West* ☎ *212/642–2260* ⊕ *www.bryantparkhotel.com* Ⓜ *B, D, F, V to 42nd St.; 7 to 5th Ave.*

Fodor's Choice
★

Galway Hooker. The name actually refers to a kind of Irish fishing boat (but then, you knew that already, right?). It's sought out as one of Midtown's most authentic, and best, Irish pubs. Even on a block with a high number of fine drinking establishments (check out **The Ginger Man** and **Under The Volcano**), the Hooker stands out thanks to its gorgeous circular bar, intriguing orange lighting, spirited after-work crowd, and bartenders, some of which might just actually hail from the Emerald Isle. Snag one of their business cards, too—on the back are words of wisdom from the best Irish writers. ✉ *7 E. 36th St., between 5th and Madison*

16

Aves., Midtown East ☎ *212/725–2353* ⊕ *www.galwayhookernyc.com* Ⓜ *6 to 34th St.*

Hudson Bar. Not quite as popular as it once was, though its rotating DJs can still hold their own, the Hudson Hotel's signature bar features a hand-painted ceiling as well as lights shining up from the glass floor. ⊠ *356 W. 58th St., between 8th and 9th Aves., Midtown West* ☎ *212/554–6303* ⊕ *www.hudsonhotel.com* Ⓜ *1, A, B, C, D to 59th St.*

Fodor's Choice ★ **Joe Allen.** Everybody's en route either to or from a show at this "old reliable" on the boisterous Restaurant Row, celebrated in the musical version of *All About Eve*. Chances are you'll even spot a Broadway star at the bar or in the dining room. Still, our favorite thing about Joe's is not the fun show crowd but the hilarious "flop wall," adorned with posters from musicals that bombed, sometimes spectacularly. (Check out the hilarious ones for *Paradox Lust, Got To Go Disco*, and *Dude*, which was the unfortunate sequel to *Hair*.) For added mirth, head outside and then upstairs for the quiet jewel **Bar Central.** ⊠ *326 W. 46th St., between 8th and 9th Aves., Midtown West* ☎ *212/581–6464* ⊕ *www. joeallenrestaurant.com* Ⓜ *A, C, E to 42nd St.*

★ **P.J. Clarke's.** Mirrors and polished wood and other old-time flair adorn New York's most famous Irish bar, a redbrick brawler of a joint. Steeped in Hollywood lore—Steve McQueen was once a regular, and scenes from the 1945 movie *Lost Weekend* were shot here—Clarke's draws in the after-work crowd that appreciates drinking beer and eating exceptionally juicy burgers around a sense of history. ⊠ *915 3rd Ave., at E. 55th St., Midtown East* ☎ *212/317–1616* ⊕ *www.pjclarkes.com* Ⓜ *4, 5, 6, N, R, W to 59th St–Lexington Ave.*

Russian Vodka Room. Forget **Russian Samovar** across the block—here's where the serious vodka drinking goes down, along with (almost) everything that goes along with serious vodka drinking. The Vodka Room features a glowing, sophistocated front room with nightly piano player (and the superlative Dmitri Kolesnik Jazz Trio on Mondays, free of charge), a more sumptuous back room, a generous "Attitude Adjustment Hour" (that's Russki for "Happy Hour"), and more exotically infused vodkas (horseradish! ginger! pepper!) than you can shake a babushka at. For those who crave variety, a vodka tasting menu is available, as are culinary standards like borscht. ⊠ *265 W. 52nd St., between Broadway and 8th Aves., Midtown West* ☎ *212/307–5835* ⊕ *www.russianvodkaroom.com* Ⓜ *C, E, 1 to 50th St.*

Salon de Ning. Take a break from 5th Avenue shopping at this glass-lined penthouse bar on the 23rd floor of the über-ritzy Peninsula Hotel. Drinks are pricey, of course, but what isn't in this neighborhood? Plus, the views are inarguably worth it, especially from the rooftop terraces. ⊠ *Peninsula Hotel, 700 5th Ave., at W. 55th St., Midtown West* ☎ *212/956–2888* Ⓜ *E, V to 5th Ave./53rd St.*

Top of the Tower. There are lounges at higher altitudes, but this one on the 26th floor wins wide acclaim for its atmosphere of subdued elegance and East Side location, within spitting distance of the United Nations. (But no spitting on the diplomats, please—it's not diplomatic.) There's live piano music Wednesday–Sunday nights. ⊠ *Beekman Tower Hotel,*

3 Mitchell Pl., near 1st Ave. at E. 49th St., Midtown East ☎ *212/980–4796* ⊕ *www.thebeekmanhotel.com* Ⓜ *6 to 51st St./Lexington Ave.; E, V to Lexington Ave./53rd St.*

★ **The Volstead**. Named for "the Volstead Act" which instituted Prohibition back in the '20s, this new subterranean bastion of cool is simply indispensable. In a gorgeous though tasteful setting that features just the right mix of mirrors, chandeliers, polished wood, and velvet wallpaper, a friendly staff and an ace barkeep serve up specialties like "Jalapeno Margaritas" and "Strawberry Caiproskas." ⊠ *125 E. 54th St., between Park and Lexington Aves., Midtown East* ☎ *212/583–0411* ⊕ *www. thevolstead.com* Ⓜ *E, V to 53rd St.*

Water Club. You're not sailing on the East River, but you might feel as if you are once you step onto the alluring outdoor deck here. This is a special-occasion place—particularly if you've already sampled all the landlocked ones in town. A fireplace warms the downstairs bar, and there's piano music every night except Sunday. ⊠ *500 E. 30th St., at FDR Dr., Midtown East* ☎ *212/683–3333* ⊕ *www.thewaterclub.com* Ⓜ *6 to 28th St.*

UPPER EAST SIDE

American Trash. You might tell from the name that this isn't exactly your granddad's UES drinking establishment. Bicycle tires, golf clubs, and other castoffs cover the walls and ceiling, ensuring that the 20-year-old Trash, a sanctum of sleaze, merits its descriptive name. Eight plasma TVs, three video games, a defiantly rock-and-roll jukebox, and a pool table keep the neighborhood crowd (as well as stray bikers who hate them) busy. Some nights local bands play classic rock. ⊠ *1471 1st Ave., between E. 76th and E. 77th Sts., Upper East Side* ☎ *212/988–9008* ⊕ *www.americantrashnyc.com* Ⓜ *6 to 77th St.*

Fodor's Choice **Auction House**. This Victorian lounge brings a touch of downtown chic
★ to the sometimes suburban-feeling Upper East Side with its candle-lighted tables, high tin ceilings, and velvet couches. Rap and hip-hop fans should look elsewhere (the only tunes coming out of this joint are alternative and rock), and baseball caps and sneakers are strictly forbidden here, as are—at the other end of the spectrum—fur coats. ⊠ *300 E. 89th St., between 1st and 2nd Aves., Upper East Side* ☎ *212/427–4458* Ⓜ *4, 5, 6 to 86th St.*

★ **Opia**. The motto for this upscale-yet-unpretentious bar-restaurant—"If you like us, tell your friends, and if you don't, tell your enemies!"—isn't necessary, given its manifold charms: a drop-dead gorgeous design, plenty of space for canoodling and cavorting, a romantic balcony (though 57th Street isn't exactly a scenic beach), plus no cover or minimum for the live jazz on Monday nights. Opia is ideal for couples in full-on infatuation or spouses hoping to remember the wine-and-roses days before the kids. ⊠ *130 E. 57th St., between Lexington and 3rd Aves., Upper East Side* ☎ *212/688–3939* ⊕ *www.opiarestaurant.com* Ⓜ *N, R, 6, to 59th St.*

16

UPPER WEST SIDE

Ding Dong Lounge. "Gabba gabba hey," kids—the CBGB's punk ethos is most alive and well not downtown but way up near Columbia University, at this out-and-out rock'n'roll bar. All manner of music posters (along with punk chanteuse Patti Smith's actual birth certificate) adorn the walls; the bathrooms are wallpapered entirely with do-it-yourself concert flyers. An exuberant young student crowd swills the many beers on tap, and candles at every table do little to dispel the near-total darkness. Just wear night-vision goggles—and maybe a crash helmet, given how often the DJs really shake up the joint. ⊠ *929 Columbus Ave., between W. 105th and W. 106th Sts., Upper West Side* ☎ *212/663–2600* Ⓜ *www.dingdonglounge.com* Ⓜ *B, C to 103rd St.*

The Empire Hotel Rooftop Bar. The only thing better than hanging out in Lincoln Center on a lovely night is hanging out a dozen stories above Lincoln Center. Thanks to the radically refurbished Empire Hotel's sprawling new rooftop bar, you can enjoy that pleasure even on nights that are less than lovely. We're talking thousands of square feet here, most of it outdoor and heated, with three terraces' worth of elegant furnishings, lighting, cabanas, and chaise longues. We're talking an attractive crowd, the single friendliest hostess in New York City, plus fabulous Friday night parties overseen by the great promoter Adam Sands. And we're talking cameras, because you'll want to bring yours and snap the great vistas and for the towering red-neon "EMPIRE HOTEL" right above your head. ⊠ *244 W. 65th St., between Broadway and Columbus Ave., Upper West Side* ☎ *212/956–3313* Ⓜ *1 to 66th St./Lincoln Center.*

Shark Bar. The fantastic bar at this soul-food (and soul-music) restaurant fills with eye candy every night. As if that's not enough to bite you, rapper LL Cool J ("Ladies Love Cool James" to his mother) has been known to mingle among the usual young black executives, music-industry bigwigs, and professional athletes. ⊠ *307 Amsterdam Ave., between W. 74th and W. 75th Sts., Upper West Side* ☎ *212/874–8500* Ⓜ *1, 2, 3 to 72nd St.*

GAY AND LESBIAN

New York is San Francisco's only real competition as the gayest city in these United States of ours. (Miami? Atlanta? Not even *close*.) For the latest listings of nightlife options, check out gay publications such as *Next* (⊕ *www.nextmagazine.net*), *MetroSource* (⊕ *www.metrosource. com*), and *Paper* (⊕ *www.papermag.com*). *GO Magazine* (⊕ *www. gomag.com*) is a good source for lesbian happenings.

DANCE CLUBS AND PARTIES

Fodor's Choice
★

Beige. Gay men in fashion and advertising predominate at this long-running Tuesday get-together at the B-Bar. An occasional celebrity or two keeps it lively, and with the right weather, the garden doubles or even triples the populace. Dress up, or look so freaking hot that you don't have to. ⊠ *B Bar, 40 E. 4th St., at the Bowery, East Village* ☎ *212/475–2220* Ⓜ *6 to Astor Pl.*

Big Apple Ranch. Taking Brokeback Mountain style to the dance floor, the Ranch lets you unleash your inner "cowboy dancer" every Saturday night, with half-hour two-step lessons at 8 PM, line dancing at 8:30 PM, and then a down-home country-and-western dance party. Make sure the DJ plays some Hank Williams, just to keep things honest (and remember these immortal words from Hank: "I don't need nobody standing by me in a barfight 'cept for my mama with a broken bottle in her hand") ⊠ *Dance Manhattan, 39 W. 19th St., 5th fl., between 5th and 6th Aves., Chelsea* ☎ *212/358–5752* ⊕ *www.bigappleranch.com* Ⓜ *F, R, V, W to 23rd St., 1 to 18th St.*

Fodor's Choice
★ **Splash Bar New York.** At this large, perennially crowded Chelsea bar-club, beefy go-go boys vie for attention with equally buff bartenders who, for some reason (can't the management afford uniforms?) don't have on much more than underwear. The daily happy hour, with campy music videos on three huge screens, is a hit. Our only caveat: late-night covers can be high. ⊠ *50 W. 17th St., between 5th and 6th Aves., Chelsea* ☎ *212/691–0073* ⊕ *www.splashbar.com* Ⓜ *6 to Astor Pl.*

LOUNGES

Evolve. Rising from the ashes of a popular gay club on the same site, this glossy, raucous Chelsea-style bar/club gets the Upper East Side rocking, with its sexy-yet-genial staff and its theme nights like "Pop-off Thursday," "Bulge Friday," and "Disco Balls Sunday." ⊠ *234 E. 58th St., between 2nd and 3rd Aves., Midtown East* ☎ *212/355–3395* ⊕ *www.evolvenyc.com* Ⓜ *4, 5, 6, N, R, W to 59th St./Lexington Ave.*

Posh. Lest you think that Hell's Kitchen has no fine gay lounges, Posh has walls covered in fine canvasses by local artists, trophies over the bar, ample room for kibitzing and dancing, plenty of neon decor, and hours that are "4 PM to 4 AM GUARANTEED." Who says nothing is certain anymore in these confusing times? ⊠ *405 W. 51st St., at 9th Ave., Midtown West* ☎ *212/957–2222* ⊕ *www.poshbarnyc.com* Ⓜ *C, E to 50th St.*

Urge. A bi-level bastion of East Village boy action, Urge has two levels of muscley hipsters, go-go boys, drag acts on Sundays, Bingo Mondays, and a contest on Wednesdays whose name we can't print here. Best of all, it's located cheek by jowl with several other fun East Village gay bars like the new **DTOX**. ⊠ *33 2nd Ave. at 2nd St., East Village* ☎ *212/645–8613* ⊕ *www.theurgenyc.com* Ⓜ *F, V to Lower East Side/2nd Ave.*

NEIGHBORHOOD BARS

The Cubby Hole. Early in the evening the crowd is mixed at this neighborhood institution, where the DJs, the unpretentious decor, and the inexpensive margaritas are popular. Later on, the women take charge—and how. ⊠ *281 W. 12th St., at W. 4th St., Greenwich Village* ☎ *212/243–9041* ⊕ *www.cubbyholebar.com* Ⓜ *A, C, E to 14th St.; L to 8th Ave.*

16

Gym Sports Bar. At New York's first gay sports bar, the plentiful flat-screen TVs and cheap Budweisers draw athletic enthusiasts of every stripe, from athlete to armchair. Nobly enough, the bar sponsors—and frequently hosts parties for—a number of local gay sports teams. The only problem: Couldn't they have thought up a more savory name for the place? ⊠ *167 8th Ave., at W. 18th St., Chelsea* ☎ *212/337–2439* ⊕ *www.gymsportsbar.com* Ⓜ *A, C, E to 14th St.; L to 8th Ave.*

FodorsChoice   **Henrietta Hudson**. The nightly parties at this laid-back West Village HQ
★   for the Sapphic set attract young professional women, out-of-towners, and longtime regulars. Because the DJ and the pool table quickly create a crowd, though, stake your claim to a spot early, especially on—yup, you guessed it—weekends. ⊠ *438 Hudson St., at Morton St., Greenwich Village* ☎ *212/924–3347* ⊕ *www.henriettahudson.com* Ⓜ *1 to Christopher St./Sheridan Sq.*

PIANO BARS

FodorsChoice   **Brandy's Piano Bar**. A singing waitstaff warms up the mixed crowd at
★   this delightful and intimate Upper East Side lounge, getting everyone in the mood to belt out their favorite tunes. In fact, the Brandy's scene is so cheerful that some patrons have used this as a musical Prozac keeping depression at bay. ⊠ *235 E. 84th St., between 2nd and 3rd Aves., Upper East Side* ☎ *212/744–4949* ⊕ *www.brandysnyc.com* Ⓜ *4, 5, 6 to 86th St.*

The Townhouse. The elegant yin to the rowdy yang of **Evolve**, which is just across the block at East 58th Street. Distinguished mature men from the Upper East Side meet younger would-be versions of themselves at this "gentlemen's club," which looks like the home of a blueblood with superb taste. As always the attire is "uptown casual," if not fancier. ⊠ *236 E. 58th St., between 2nd and 3rd Aves., Midtown East* ☎ *212/754–4649* ⊕ *www.townhouseny.com* Ⓜ *4, 5, 6, N, R, W to 59th St.–Lexington Ave.*

Shopping

WORD OF MOUTH

"If you go to Century 21 go first thing in the morning when the doors open, and they open early. Don't miss the shoes which I think are the best part of Century 21. The store starts to fill up around 10–11ish and then it just gets overwhelming."

—williamscb13

Updated by
Nicole Crane

New York shopping is a nonstop eye-opener, from the pristine couture houses flanking Madison Avenue to quirkier shops downtown. No matter which threshold you cross, shopping here promises to be an event. For every bursting department store there's an echoing, minimalist boutique; for every familiar national brand there's a secret local favorite. The foremost American and international companies stake their flagships here; meanwhile, small neighborhood shops guarantee unexpected pleasures. National chains often make their New York branches something special, with unique sales environments and exclusive merchandise.

Even for most New Yorkers, window shopping is unavoidable. Residents can't help passing tempting displays while running to the office or dashing out for coffee. The must-hit shopping neighborhoods concentrate their temptations, sometimes with boutiques in nearly every address on a block, so you can easily spend a couple of hours just browsing.

Special neighborhood profiles throughout this chapter will point you to the best areas and give you expert navigating tips. The individual reviews in this chapter are organized by type of merchandise, in alphabetical order by category. Many specialty stores have several branches in the city; in these cases we have listed the locations in the busier shopping neighborhoods. Happy hunting!

ANTIQUES AND VINTAGE FURNITURE

Antiquing is a fine art in Manhattan. Goods include everything from rarefied museum-quality pieces to wacky and affordable bric-a-brac. Premier shopping areas are on Madison Avenue north of 57th Street, and East 60th Street between 2nd and 3rd avenues, where more than

20 shops, dealing in everything from 18th-century French furniture to Art Deco lighting fixtures, cluster on one block. Around West 11th and 12th streets between University Place and Broadway a tantalizing array can be seen in the windows of about two dozen dealers, many of whom have TO THE TRADE signs on their doors; a card from your architect or decorator, however, may get you inside.

AMERICAN AND ENGLISH

Florian Papp. The shine of gilt—on ormolu clocks, chaise longues, and marble-top tables—lures casual customers in, but this store has an unassailed reputation among knowledgeable collectors. ✉ *962 Madison Ave., between E. 75th and E. 76th Sts., Upper East Side* ☎ *212/288–6770* Ⓜ *6 to 77th St.*

Kentshire Galleries. Pristine furniture is displayed in room settings here (the downtown location spans seven floors), with an emphasis on formal English pieces from the 18th and 19th centuries, particularly the Georgian and Regency periods. The collection of period and estate jewelry at the Upper East Side outlet is a showstopper, from Edwardian pearl earrings to Art Deco diamond brooches. ✉ *37 E. 12th St., between University Pl. and Broadway, Greenwich Village* ☎ *212/673–6644* Ⓜ *4, 5, 6, L, N, Q, R, W to 14th St./Union Sq.* ✉ *700 Madison Ave., between E. 62nd and E. 63rd Sts., Upper East Side* ☎ *212/421–1100* Ⓜ *6 to 68th St./Hunter College.*

Leigh Keno American Antiques. Twins Leigh and Leslie Keno set an auction record in the American antiques field by paying $2.75 million for a hairy paw–foot Philadelphia wing chair. They have a good eye and an interesting inventory; gaze up at a tall case clock or down at the delicate legs of a tea table. It's best to make an appointment. ✉ *127 E. 69th St., between Park and Lexington Aves., Upper East Side* ☎ *212/734–2381* Ⓜ *6 to 68th St./Hunter College.*

Newel Art Galleries. Near the East Side's interior-design district, this huge collection spans from the Renaissance through the 20th century. The non-furniture finds, from figureheads to bell jars, make for prime conversation pieces. ✉ *425 E. 53rd St., between 1st Ave. and Sutton Pl., Midtown East* ☎ *212/758–1970* Ⓜ *6 to 51st St./Lexington Ave.; E, V to Lexington–3rd Aves./53rd St.*

ASIAN

Chinese Porcelain Company. Though the name of this prestigious shop indicates one of its specialties, its stock covers more ground, ranging from lacquerware to Khmer sculpture to 18th-century French furniture. ✉ *475 Park Ave., at E. 58th St., Midtown East* ☎ *212/838–7744* Ⓜ *N, R, W to 5th Ave.*

Flying Cranes Antiques. Here you can find a well-regarded collection of rare, museum-quality pieces from the Meiji period, the time known as Japan's Golden Age. Items include ceramics, cloisonné, metalwork, carvings, ikebana baskets, and samurai swords and fittings. ✉ *Manhattan Art and Antiques Center, 1050 2nd Ave., between E. 55th and E. 56th Sts., Midtown East* ☎ *212/223–4600* Ⓜ *N, R, W, 4, 5, 6 to 59th St./Lexington Ave.*

Jacques Carcanagues, Inc. Carrying goods from Japan to India, this SoHo gallery offers an eclectic array of objects, from pillboxes to 18th-century Burmese Buddhas. ✉ *21 Greene St., between Grand and Canal Sts., SoHo* ☎ *212/925–8110* Ⓜ *4, 5, 6, R, W to Canal St.*

EUROPEAN

Newel Art Galleries and Florian Papp, covered under American and English antiques, and the Chinese Porcelain Company, listed under Asian antiques, also carry European pieces.

L'Antiquaire & The Connoisseur, Inc. Proprietor Helen Fioratti has written a guide to French antiques, but she's equally knowledgeable about her Italian and Spanish furniture and decorative objects from the 15th through the 18th century, as well as about the medieval arts. ✉ *36 E. 73rd St., between Madison and Park Aves., Upper East Side* ☎ *212/517–9176* Ⓜ *6 to 77th St.*

Leo Kaplan Ltd. The impeccable items here include Art Nouveau glass and pottery, porcelain from 18th-century England, antique and modern paperweights, and Russian artwork. ✉ *114 E. 57th St., between Park and Lexington Aves., Upper East Side* ☎ *212/355–7212* Ⓜ *N, R, W, 4, 5, 6 to 59th St./Lexington Ave.*

Les Pierre Antiques. Pierre Deux popularized French Provincial through reproductions; come here for a strong selection of the real thing, from etchings to sconces to armoires. Inside one of the period birdcages flutters a pet dove. ✉ *369 Bleecker St., at Charles St., Greenwich Village* ☎ *212/243–7740* Ⓜ *1 to Christopher St./Sheridan Sq.*

20TH-CENTURY FURNITURE AND MEMORABILIA

Las Venus. Step into this kitsch palace and you may feel as though a time machine has zapped you back to the '50s, '60s, or groovy '70s—depending on which vintage pieces are in stock. Look for bubble lamps, lots of brocade, and Knoll knockoffs; a second location around the corner catches the overflow. ✉ *163 Ludlow St., between E. Houston and Stanton Sts., Lower East Side* ☎ *212/982–0608* Ⓜ *F, V to 2nd Ave.*

Lost City Arts. In addition to mod furniture, like pod and Eames chairs, and industrial memorabilia, such as neon gas-station clocks, Lost City can help you relive the Machine Age with an in-house, retromodern line of furniture. ✉ *18 Cooper Sq., at E. 5th St., East Village* ☎ *212/375–0500* Ⓜ *6 to Astor Pl.*

17

BEAUTY

FRAGRANCE

★ **Aedes De Venustas.** Swathed in red velvet, this jewel-box-size store stocks a well-edited selection of hard-to-find skin-care lines like Annick Goutal and Duchess Marden; fragrance from Creed, Costes, and Heeley; and pricey candles from Diptyque and Mariage Freres. Their signature giftwrap is as beautiful as what's inside the box. ✉ *9 Christopher St., between 6th and 7th Aves., Greenwich Village* ☎ *212/206–8674* Ⓜ *1 to Christopher St./Sheridan Sq.*

SOHO

Somehow, everything looks a bit more beautiful here. Maybe it's because of the way sunlight filters down the cast-iron facades, glinting off the shop windows. Maybe it's because the uneven cobblestone streets prompt you to slow down, giving you time to notice details.

Jaded locals call this neighborhood a touristy outdoor mall. True, you'll see plenty of familiar company names, and several common, less expensive chains, like Banana Republic and Sephora, have made land grabs on Broadway. There's also a certain amount of luxury one-upmanship, as stores like Prada, Chanel, and Louis Vuitton have planted themselves here for downtown cred. But you can still hit a few clothing and housewares boutiques you won't find elsewhere in this country. The hottest shopping area runs west from Broadway over to 6th Avenue, between West Houston and Grand streets. Don't overlook a couple of streets east of Broadway: Crosby and Lafayette each have a handful of intriguing shops. —by Jennifer Paull

BEST TIME TO GO

Wednesday through Friday afternoons, when all the stores are open and the people-watching is prime, but the streets aren't hideously crowded. On weekends, Broadway and Prince Street can feel like a cattle drive.

BEST SOUVENIR FOR YOUR IN-LAWS

If they're caffeine fiends, consider the house-blend coffees and teas at **Dean & Deluca** (✉ *560 Broadway, at Prince St.*), which you can pair with sophisticated snacks in a D&D tote or metal lunch box.

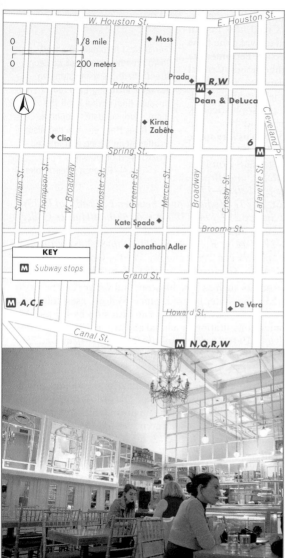

17

BEST FOR

WHAT TO WEAR

Prada: the high-concept, Rem Koolhaas–designed store steals the spotlight from the clothes.

Kirna Zabête: uncommon, sought-after women's clothing in a cheerful, unpretentious space.

Kate Spade: the mother lode for clever handbags, plus retro-ish shoes and a few baubles.

HOUSEWARES

Moss: exquisite, innovative design for everything from wineglasses to bathtubs.

Clio: low-key vibe but high-scoring selection of unique tableware.

Jonathan Adler: a loving spin on mid-century mod (and kitsch) in ceramics and furniture.

De Vera: eclectic selection of antiques and new objets d'art, from Murano glass to Japanese lacquer.

REFUELING

For something on the fly, drop by **Balthazar Bakery** (✉ *80 Spring St., between Broadway and Crosby St.* ☎ *212/965–1785*) for a scone, cannele, or sticky bun with a potent cup of coffee. If you'd rather have a seat, make your way to the tearoom hidden in the back of Marie Belle for a cup of their excellent hot chocolate.

★ **Bond No. 9.** Created by the same fragrance team as Creed, this line of scents is intended to evoke the New York City experience. Perfumes are named after neighborhoods: Central Park, a men's fragrance, is woodsy and "green"; the feminine Park Avenue is regal and sophisticated, with hints of iris and rose. The Bond Street shop, with its airy space and wood-panel Tea Library, is a lovely place to linger. ✉ *9 Bond St., between Lafayette St. and Broadway, East Village* ☎ *212/228–1732*

> **WORD OF MOUTH**
>
> "For SoHo, I recommend a walk down Broadway south of Houston Street. There are many stores in this area, including the Prada Museum (that's what I call the shop), Bloomingdale's, Sephora, Pearl River Mart, etc. You can also wander along Spring and Prince toward West Broadway."
> —Proenza_Preschooler

Ⓜ *6 to Bleecker St.* ✉ *897 Madison Ave., between E. 72nd and E. 73rd Sts., Upper East Side* ☎ *212/794–4480* Ⓜ *6 to 68th St/Hunter College* ✉ *680 Madison Ave., between E. 61st and E. 62nd Sts., Upper East Side* ☎ *212/838–2780* Ⓜ *N, R, W, 4, 5, 6 to 59th St./Lexington Ave.* ✉ *399 Bleecker St., between Perry and W. 11 Sts., Greenwich Village* ☎ *212/633–1641* Ⓜ *1 to Christopher St.; A, C, E to 14th St.*

Jo Malone. Unisex scents such as lime blossom and vetiver can be worn alone or, in the Malone style, layered. Since Malone uses colognes, not perfumes, it's not overpowering. You can also stop by for a quick fragrance-combining consultation or a hand and arm massage from one of the store's stylists. ✉ *946 Madison Ave., between E. 74th and E. 75th Sts., Upper East Side* ☎ *212/472–0074* Ⓜ *6 to 77th St.*

MAKEUP AND SKIN CARE

Fresh. It sounds good enough to eat: a brown-sugar skin-care line, pomegranate hair conditioner, pear-cassis cologne. The 3rd Avenue location offers decadent skin and body treatments—many of which are free with the purchase of product—in a back spa room. ✉ *57 Spring St., between Lafayette and Mulberry Sts., SoHo* ☎ *212/925–0099* Ⓜ *6 to Spring St.* ✉ *1367 3rd Ave., at E. 78th St., Upper East Side* ☎ *212/585–3400* Ⓜ *6 to 77th St.* ✉ *159 Columbus Ave., between W. 67th and W. 68th Sts., Upper West Side* ☎ *212/787–3505* Ⓜ *1 to 66th St.* ✉ *388 Bleecker St., between Perry and W. 11th Sts., Greenwich Village* ☎ *917/408–1850* Ⓜ *1, 2, 3 to 14th St.* ✉ *872 Broadway, at 18th St., Flatiron District* ☎ *212/477–1100* Ⓜ *N, R to 23rd St.*

Fodor'sChoice
★ **Kiehl's Since 1851.** At this favored haunt of top models and stylists, white-smocked assistants can help you choose between the lotions and potions, all of which are packaged in deceptively simple-looking bottles and jars. Some of the products, such as the pineapple-papaya facial scrub, Silk Groom hair-styling aid, and the superrich Creme de Corps, have attained near-cult status among beautyphiles. ■TIP→ Kiehl's is also known for being generous with samples, so be sure to ask for your own bag of take-home testers. ✉ *109 3rd Ave., at E. 13th St., East Village* ☎ *212/677–3171* Ⓜ *4, 5, 6, L, N, Q, R, W to 14th St./Union Sq.* ✉ *154 Columbus Ave., at W. 67th St., Upper West Side* ☎ *212/799–3438* Ⓜ *1 to 66th St./Lincoln Center.*

Studio Beauty Mix @ Korres. Greece's oldest homeopathic pharmacy rolls out its line of herb- and flower-based skin treatments. Best sellers like wild-rose moisturizer and thyme-honey cream line the modular shelves of the gallerylike store. ⊠ *110 Wooster St., between Prince and Spring Sts., SoHo* ☎ *212/219–0683* Ⓜ *N, R to Prince St.*

★ **Santa Maria Novella.** A heavy, iron-barred door leads to a hushed, scented inner sanctum of products from this medieval Florentine pharmacy. Many of the colognes, creams, and soaps are intriguingly archaic, such as the iris toothpaste and the Vinegar of the Seven Thieves (a variant on smelling salts). Everything is packaged in bottles and jars with antique-style apothecary labels. ⊠ *285 Lafayette St., between E. Houston and Prince Sts., SoHo* ☎ *212/925–0001* Ⓜ *N, R to Prince St.*

BOOKS

CHILDREN'S BOOKS

Books of Wonder. The friendly, knowledgeable staff can help select gifts for all reading levels from the extensive, beautiful selection of children's books. Oziana is a specialty. An outpost of the Cupcake Café gives little browsers a second wind. ⊠ *18 W. 18th St., between 5th and 6th Aves., Chelsea* ☎ *212/989–3270* Ⓜ *F, V to 14th St.*

Scholastic Store. An 11-foot orange dinosaur—with a cushioned tail doubling as a reading sofa—and a life-size Magic School Bus welcome kids to this truly fun emporium. With games, toys, DVDs, computers, arts and crafts workshops, and above all, books, this downtown spot is so family-friendly it has a separate entrance just for strollers (at 130 Mercer Street). ⊠ *557 Broadway, at Prince St., SoHo* ☎ *212/343–6166* Ⓜ *R, W to Prince St.*

GENERAL INTEREST

Barnes & Noble. Without argument, this is the biggest bookstore presence in the city. ⊠ *1972 Broadway, at W. 66th St., Upper West Side* ☎ *212/595–6859* Ⓜ *1 to 66th St./Lincoln Center* ⊠ *33 E. 17th St., at Union Sq., Flatiron District* ☎ *212/253–0810* Ⓜ *4, 5, 6, N, Q, R, W to 14th St./Union Sq.*

bookbook. Published diaries, letters, biographies, and autobiographies fill this neighborly store. There's also a thoughtful assortment of general nonfiction, fiction, guidebooks, and children's books. But the real focus here is the carefully selected sale tables that spill out onto the sidewalk—they have deals on everything from Graham Greene to Chuck Palahniuk. ⊠ *266 Bleecker St., between 6th and 7th Aves., Greenwich Village* ☎ *212/807–8655* Ⓜ *1 to Christopher St./Sheridan Sq.*

Borders. The smart, cheery flagship Columbus Circle branch of this second-biggest bookstore chain in the city is worth a browse. ⊠ *461 Park Ave., at E. 57th St., Midtown East* ☎ *212/980–6785* Ⓜ *N, R, W, 4, 5, 6 to 59th St./Lexington Ave.* ⊠ *10 Columbus Circle, at 59th St., Upper West Side* ☎ *212/823–9775* Ⓜ *1, A, B, C, D to Columbus Circle.*

17

The Complete Traveller Antiquarian Bookstore. Founded in the '80s by two former travel writers, this store specializes in rare and antique voyage-related books, and promises the country's largest selection of out-of-print Baedeker travel guides. They stock surprisingly affordable vintage maps, unusual tomes with

WORD OF MOUTH

"We are blessed with the original McNally [Jackson] book stores. I would have to say these are the best, most fun bookstores I have ever been in."   —ita

New York City themes, and a full spectrum of books—from history and geography to poetry and fiction—that emphasize travel. ⊠ *199 Madison Ave., at 35th St., Murray Hill* ☎ *212/685–9007* Ⓜ *6 to 33rd St.*

★ **Crawford Doyle Booksellers.** You're as likely to see an old edition of Wodehouse as a best seller in the window of this shop. You'll find a quality selection of fiction, nonfiction, and biographies, plus some rare books on the balcony. Salespeople offer their opinions *and* ask for yours. ⊠ *1082 Madison Ave., between E. 81st and E. 82nd Sts., Upper East Side* ☎ *212/288–6300* Ⓜ *4, 5, 6 to 86th St.*

Idlewild. Named for the pre-1960s JFK Airport, this travel-inspired bookstore groups its goods by destination. It has much more than guidebooks, though; novels, histories, cookbooks, and children's books share each segment, giving you a fascinating look at any given locale. If those chairs look familiar, you may have spent a layover in one of them, once upon a time in the American Airlines terminal. ⊠ *12 W. 19th St., 2nd fl., at 5th Ave., West Village* ☎ *212/414–8888* Ⓜ *4, 5, 6, L, Q, R, W to 14th St./Union Sq.*

★ **McNally Jackson.** McNally makes a happy counterpart to the nearby Housing Works bookstore (at 126 Crosby Street); both places have that welcoming vibe. Check the tables up front for hot-off-the-press novels, nonfiction, and manifestos. Upstairs you'll find fiction arranged by the authors' region of origin, a great way to learn more about, say, Asian or South American writing. The staff are by and large literary themselves, so ask for recommendations if you're browsing. Literature extends beyond the packed shelves here—just grab a coffee from what owner Sarah McNally calls the "booksiest bookstore café" to see for yourself—even the light fixtures are made from books. ⊠ *52 Prince St., between Lafayette and Mulberry Sts., SoHo* ☎ *212/274–1160* Ⓜ *R, W to Prince St.*

Partners & Crime. Signed first editions, helpful staff, a rental library, and whodunits galore—new and out-of-print—make this a must-browse for fans. Revered mystery writers give readings here. ⊠ *44 Greenwich Ave., between 6th and 7th Aves., Greenwich Village* ☎ *212/243–0440* Ⓜ *F, V, 1, 2, 3 to 14th St.*

★ **St. Mark's Bookshop.** Downtown residents, NYU students, and intellectuals in general love this store, spending hours poking through popular and oddball fiction and nonfiction. You'll find a truly eclectic, attitudinal collection of books here, not unlike the salespeople. On the main floor, books on critical theory are right up front, across from new fiction titles—this is perhaps the only place where you can find Jacques Derrida facing off against T. C. Boyle. Cultural and art books are up

CLOSE UP

Deals and Steals

Even a temporary New Yorker loves a bargain. Scoring a good deal is a rite of passage for everyone, economic bracket be darned. The city offers everything from low-cost department stores like Century 21 to hawkers of pseudo Rolex watches and Kate Spade bags stationed at street corners and in Canal Street stalls. And then there are the sample sales.

If a seasonal sale makes New Yorkers' eyes gleam, a sample sale throws shoppers into a frenzy. With so many designer flagships and corporate headquarters in town, merchandise fallout periodically leads to tremendous deals. Although, technically, the phrase "sample sale" refers to stock that's a sample design, show model, leftover, or is already discounted, the term is now also used for sales of current-season goods. Location adds a bit of an illicit thrill to the event: sales are held in hotels, warehouses, offices, or loft spaces, where items both incredible and unfortunate jam a motley assortment of racks,

tables, and bins. Generally, there is a makeshift communal dressing room, but mirrors are scarce, so veteran sample-sale shoppers come prepared for wriggling in the aisles; some wear skirts, tights, and tank tops for modest quick-changes. Two rules of thumb: grab first and inspect later, and call in advance to find out what methods of payment are accepted. One of the ultimate experiences is the Barneys Warehouse Sale, held in February and August in Chelsea. Other luscious sales range from the Vera Wang bridal-gown sale (early winter) to TSE cashmere (spring and late fall).

How to find out about these events? The level of publicity and regularity of sales vary. The print and online versions of *New York* magazine are always worth checking for sample sale tip-offs, as are regular bulletins on Racked (⊕ *racked.com*) and Daily Candy (⊕ *www.dailycandy.com*). If you're interested in specific designers, call their shops and inquire—you may get lucky.

17

---

front as well; literature and literary journals fill the back of the store. ■**TIP→** It's open daily until midnight. ⊠ *31 3rd Ave., between 8th and 9th Sts., East Village* ☎ *212/260–7853* Ⓜ *6 to Astor Pl.*

Shakespeare & Co. Booksellers. The stock here represents what's happening in just about every field of publishing today: students can grab a last-minute Gertrude Stein for class, then rummage through the homages to cult pop-culture figures. Late hours at the Broadway location (until 11 PM on weekdays; 9 PM on weekends) are a plus. ⊠ *939 Lexington Ave., between E. 68th and E. 69th Sts., Upper East Side* ☎ *212/570–0201* Ⓜ *6 to 68th St./Hunter College* ⊠ *137 E. 23rd St., at Lexington Ave., Gramercy* ☎ *212/505–2021* Ⓜ *6 to 23rd St.* ⊠ *716 Broadway, at Washington Pl., Greenwich Village* ☎ *212/529–1330* Ⓜ *R, W to 8th St.*

Fodor's Choice ★ **The Strand.** This downtown hangout proudly claims to have "18 miles of books." Craning your neck among the tall-as-trees stacks will likely net you something from the mix of new and old. Take an elevator ride to the third floor for rare book selections. ⊠ *828 Broadway, at E. 12th St., East Village* ☎ *212/473–1452* Ⓜ *L, N, Q, R, W, 4, 5, 6 to 14th St./Union Sq.*

★ **Three Lives & Co.** Three Lives has one of the city's best book selections. The display tables and counters highlight the latest literary fiction and serious nonfiction, classics, quirky gift books, and gorgeously illustrated tomes. The staff members' literary knowledge is formidable, and they can help you find most any book—even if it's not carried in the store. ⊠ *154 W. 10th St., at Waverly Pl., Greenwich Village* ☎ *212/741–2069* Ⓜ *1 to Christopher St./Sheridan Sq.*

MUSIC AND THEATER

Colony Music. Siphoning energy from Times Square, this place keeps its neon blinking until 1 AM Monday through Saturday, and midnight on Sunday. Inspired by the Broadway musical or concert you've just seen? Snap up the sheet music, CD, or karaoke set here. ⊠ *1619 Broadway, at W. 49th St., Midtown West* ☎ *212/265–2050* Ⓜ *R, W to 49th St.*

Drama Book Shop. If you're looking for a script, be it a lesser-known Russian translation or a Broadway hit, chances are you can find it here. The range of books spans film, music, dance, TV, and biographies. ⊠ *250 W. 40th St., between 7th and 8th Aves., Midtown West* ☎ *212/944–0595* Ⓜ *A, C, E to 42nd St./Port Authority.*

RARE AND USED BOOKS

Crawford Doyle Booksellers, Complete Traveller, and the Strand, covered under General Interest, also carry rare and used titles.

Argosy Bookstore. This sedate landmark, established in 1925, keeps a scholarly stock of books and autographs. It's also a great place to look for low-price maps and prints. ⊠ *116 E. 59th St., between Park and Lexington Aves., Midtown East* ☎ *212/753–4455* Ⓜ *N, R, W, 4, 5, 6 to 59th St./Lexington Ave.*

Skyline Books. An endearingly scruffy, small, old-school space makes this the Woody Allen of used-book stores. Come here for out-of-print books in all categories, a large Beat Generation selection, literary first editions, and books on photography and art. ⊠ *13 W. 18th St., between 5th and 6th Aves., Chelsea* ☎ *212/759–5463* Ⓜ *4, 5, 6, N, Q, R, W to 14th St./Union Sq.*

Westsider Rare & Used Books. This wonderfully crammed space is a lifesaver on the otherwise sparse Upper West Side. Squeeze in among the stacks of art books and fiction; clamber up the steep stairway and you'll find all sorts of rare books. ⊠ *2246 Broadway, between W. 80th and W. 81st Sts., Upper West Side* ☎ *212/362–0706* Ⓜ *1 to 79th St.*

CAMERAS AND ELECTRONICS

Apple Store. After Apple's first store, in a former SoHo post office, hooked the e-mail generation, the brand took things a step further. The 5th Avenue location, topped by a giant translucent cube, is open 24 hours a day, every day, to satisfy those wee-hours computer cravings. ■**TIP→** In-store events include hour-long tutorials; from getting to know your iPhone to navigating new Mac software, they run the gamut. At all stores you'll have to elbow through a crowd, but they're the best places to check out the latest equipment, software, demos, and troubleshooting

Genius Bars. ✉ *103 Prince St., at Greene St., SoHo* ☎ *212/226–3126* Ⓜ *R, W to Prince St.* ✉ *767 5th Ave., between E. 58th and E. 59th Sts., Midtown East* ☎ *212/336–1440* Ⓜ *R, W to 60th St.* ✉ *401 W. 14th St., at 9th Ave., Meatpacking District* ☎ *212/444–3400* Ⓜ *A, C, E to 14th St.* ✉ *1981 Broadway, at 67th St., Upper West Side* ☎ *212/209–3400* Ⓜ *1 to 66th St./Lincoln Center.*

Fodor's Choice
★
B&H Photo Video and Pro Audio. As baskets of purchases trundle along on tracks overhead, you can plunge into the excellent selection of imaging, audio, video, and lighting equipment. The staff is generous with advice, and will happily compare merchandise. Low prices, good customer service, and a liberal returns policy make this a favorite with pros and amateurs alike. ■TIP→ Be sure to leave a few extra minutes for the checkout procedure; also, keep in mind that the store is closed Saturday. ✉ *420 9th Ave., between W. 33rd and W. 34th Sts., Midtown West* ☎ *212/444–5000* Ⓜ *A, C, E, 1, 2, 3 to 34th St./Penn Station.*

J&R Music World. Just south of City Hall, J&R has emerged as the city's most competitively priced one-stop electronics outlet, with an enormous selection of video equipment, computers, stereos, and cameras. The staff is hands-on and super knowledgeable; many of them are A/V wizards who've worked here since the early 1990s. Home office supplies are at No. 1, computers at No. 15, small appliances at No. 27. ✉ *23 Park Row, between Beekman and Ann Sts., Lower Manhattan* ☎ *212/238–9000* Ⓜ *4, 5, 6 to Brooklyn Bridge/City Hall.*

SONY Style. This equipment and music store comes in a glossy package, with imaginative window displays and a downstairs demonstration area for the integrated systems. You'll find all the latest stereo and entertainment systems, digital cameras, and MP3 players on the shelves. ✉ *550 Madison Ave., at E. 55th St., Midtown East* ☎ *212/833–8800* Ⓜ *E, V, 6 to 51st St./Lexington Ave.*

CHILDREN'S CLOTHING

PLAY CLOTHES

Oilily. Stylized flowers, stripes, and animal shapes splash across these brightly colored play and school clothes from the trippy Dutch brand. Note that the store only stocks the boys' line in sizes up to 12 months. ✉ *465 West Broadway, between Prince and Houston Sts., SoHo* ☎ *212/871–0201* Ⓜ *6 to Spring St.*

Petit Bateau. Fine cotton is spun into comfortable underwear, play clothes, and pajamas; T-shirts come in dozens of colors and to every specification, with V-necks, round necks, snap-fronts, and more. ✉ *1094 Madison Ave., at E. 82nd St., Upper East Side* ☎ *212/988–8884* Ⓜ *4, 5, 6 to 86th St.*

17

NOLITA

The Nabokovian nickname, shorthand for "North of Little Italy," covers a neighborhood that has taken the commercial baton from SoHo and run with it.

Like SoHo, NoLita has gone from a locals-only, understated area to a crowded weekend magnet, as much about people-watching as it is about shopping. Still, unlike those of its SoHo neighbor, these stores remain largely one-of-a-kind. Running along the parallel north–south spines of Elizabeth, Mott, and Mulberry streets, between East Houston and Kenmare streets, NoLita's boutiques tend to be small and, as real estate dictates, somewhat pricey. —J.P.

BEST TIME TO GO

Wednesday through Friday afternoons if you're keen to shop without too many distractions, weekends for more people to scope out. Shops stay open latest (usually until 8 PM) Thursday through Saturday.

BEST SOUVENIR FOR YOUR BABYSITTER

Beautifully packaged, petal-topped candles exclusive to **Red Flower** (✉ *13 Prince St., at Elizabeth St.* ☎ *212/966–5301*) in dreamy scents like jasmine and Japanese peony. Or perhaps some calming chamomile or lavender bath products from the ancient Italian perfumer-pharmacist **Santa Maria Novella**.

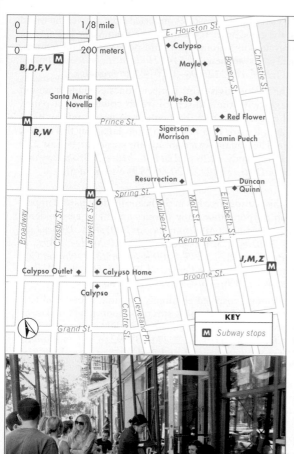

REFUELING

Hit the takeout window of **Café Gitane** (✉ *242 Mott St., at Prince St.* ☎ *212/334–9552*) for the best espresso; it comes with a little square of dark chocolate for an extra boost. Or, if you don't mind getting your fingers messy, stop by **Café Habana to Go** (✉ *17 Prince St., at Elizabeth St.* ☎ *212/625–2002*) for an addictively salty, cheese-topped ear of grilled corn.

BEST FOR

TOO-COOL-FOR-SCHOOL CLOTHES
Mayle: ladylike looks with two dashes of retro flair and a pinch of eccentricity.

Duncan Quinn: whether customized or off the rack, these button-downs and suits are perfectly cut.

Resurrection: mint-condition vintage Pucci and Courrèges make this a stylist's gold mine.

Calypso: almost half-a-dozen boutiques in Nolita alone for softly exotic clothes and housewares.

FOXY SHOES
Sigerson Morrison: this strappy-sandal success has the biggest footprint in the 'hood.

... AND OTHER ACCESSORIES
Jamin Puech: run-away-bohemian-heiress handbags dripping with embroidery and fringe.

Me&Ro: Indian-inspired gold and silver jewelry, from shoulder-duster earrings to tiny lotus-petal pendants.

17

Shoofly. Children's shoes and accessories imported from all over the world are the name of the game here. You can choose from Mary Janes, wing tips, and motorcycle boots along with pom-pom hats, plaid fedoras, brightly patterned socks, and jewelry. ⊠ *42 Hudson St., between Thomas and Duane Sts., TriBeCa* ☎ *212/406–3270* Ⓜ *1 to Franklin St.*

★ **Space Kiddets**. The funky (Elvis-print rompers, onesies made from old concert tees) mixes with the old-school (retro cowboy-print pants, brightly colored clogs, New York borough-pride gear) and the high-end (Lilli Gaufrette, Kenzo, Boo Foo Woo from Japan) at this casual, trendsetting store. The original space around the corner, at 46 East 21st Street, now stocks toys only. ⊠ *26 E. 22nd St., between Broadway and Park Ave., Flatiron District* ☎ *212/420–9878* Ⓜ *6 to 23rd St.*

PRECIOUS

Bonpoint. The sophistication here lies in the beautiful designs and impeccable workmanship—pony-hair baby booties and hand-embroidered jumpers and blouses. ⊠ *1269 Madison Ave., at E. 91st St., Upper East Side* ☎ *212/722–7720* Ⓜ *4, 5, 6 to 86th St.* ⊠ *810 Madison Ave., at 68th St., Upper East Side* ☎ *212/879–0900* Ⓜ *6 to 68th St./Hunter College* ⊠ *392 Bleecker St., between Perry and W. 11th Sts., West Village* ☎ *212/647–1700* Ⓜ *1 to Christopher St./Sheridan Sq.*

Bu and the Duck. Vintage-inspired children's clothing, shoes, and toys distinguish this shop. The Italian-made spectator boots might make you wish your own feet were tiny again. ⊠ *106 Franklin St., between West Broadway and Church St., TriBeCa* ☎ *212/431–9226* Ⓜ *1 to Franklin St.* ⊠ *316 E. 81st St., between 1st and 2nd Aves., Upper East Side* ☎ *212/794–0721* Ⓜ *6 to 77th St.*

Flora and Henri. The padded twill coats, slate-blue pleated skirts, and pin-dot cotton dresses here are cute but not overly so. They'll stand up to wear and tear; witness the sturdy Italian-made shoes. ⊠ *1023 Lexington Ave., between E. 73rd and E. 74th Sts., Upper East Side* ☎ *212/249–1695* Ⓜ *6 to 77th St.*

Infinity. Mothers gossip near the dressing rooms as their daughters try on slinky Les Tout Petits dresses, Miss Sixty Jeans, and cheeky tees with slogans like "chicks ahoy." The aggressively trendy and the rather sweet meet in a welter of preteen accessories. ⊠ *1116 Madison Ave., at E. 83rd St., Upper East Side* ☎ *212/517–4232* Ⓜ *4, 5, 6 to 86th St.*

Les Petits Chapelais. Designed and made in France, these kids' clothes are adorable but also practical. Corduroy outfits have details like embroidered flowers and contrasting cuffs; soft fleecy jackets are reversible, and sweaters have easy-zip-up fronts and hoodies. ⊠ *86 Thompson St., between Spring and Prince Sts., SoHo* ☎ *212/625–1023* Ⓜ *C, E to Spring St.*

Lilliput. At both locations, which face each other across the street, kids can up their coolness quotient with Paul Smith sweaters, sequined party dresses, and denim wear by Diesel. The difference is that the shop at No. 265 carries it all up to size 8, whereas the original shop goes up to teens. ⊠ *240 Lafayette St., between Prince and Spring Sts., SoHo* ☎ *212/965–9201* Ⓜ *R, W to Prince St.* ⊠ *265 Lafayette St., between Prince and Spring Sts., SoHo* ☎ *212/965–9567* Ⓜ *6 to Spring St.*

CHOCOLATE

Chocolate Bar. Along with this shop's signature and retro chocolate bars (the latter include such flavors as caramel apple and coconut cream pie) is an array of filled chocolate bonbons. At the café counter you can get a steaming cup of cocoa. The bar is open until 10 PM nightly. ✉ *19 8th Ave., between Jane and West 12th Sts., West Village* ☎ *212/366–1541* Ⓜ *A, C, E, to 14th St.*

François Chocolate Bar. On the fourth floor of the ultraglam jewelry store Mauboussin, you'll find this sweet reminder of François Payard's shuttered Upper East Side patisserie. Here, exposed brick and "*chocolat*"-painted walls are home to a comforting assortment of signature Payard pastries, and playful additions like pound cakes and parfaits, or "verrines," boasting layers like raspberry balsamic compote and Earl Grey mousse. Macaroons—think White Chocolate and Sesame ganache—go for only $2 a pop. ✉ *714 Madison Avenue, between E. 63rd and E. 64th Sts., Upper East Side* ☎ *212/759–1600* Ⓜ *F to Lexington Ave./63rd St.*

★ **Jacques Torres Chocolate Haven.** Visit the café and shop here and you'll literally be surrounded by chocolate. The glass-walled downtown space is in the heart of Torres's chocolate factory, so you can watch the goodies being made while you sip a richly spiced cocoa. Uptown you'll find an intimate European-style store and café with leather armchairs you can sink into. ■**TIP➔** Signature taste: the "wicked" chocolate, laced with cinnamon and chili pepper. ✉ *350 Hudson St., at King St., SoHo* ☎ *212/414–2462* Ⓜ *1 to Houston St.* ✉ *285 Amsterdam Ave., between 74th and 75th Sts., Upper West Side* ☎ *212/787–3256* Ⓜ *1, 2, 3 to 72nd St.*

Kee's Chocolates. Walking into this small store, you might get a whiff of warm chocolate or spy a few smeared spatulas in the back, attesting to the candy's homemade origin. Yet what's in the case looks preternaturally perfect: dark chocolates filled with *yuzu* (a Japanese citrus), covered with freshly crushed pistachios, or flavored with lemon and basil. ✉ *80 Thompson St., between Spring and Broome Sts., SoHo* ☎ *212/334–3284* Ⓜ *A, C to Spring St.*

★ **La Maison du Chocolat.** Stop in at this chocolatier's small tea salon to dive into a cup of thick, heavenly hot chocolate. The Paris-based outfit sells handmade truffles, chocolates, and pastries that could lull you into a chocolate stupor. ✉ *1018 Madison Ave., between E. 78th and 79th Sts., Upper East Side* ☎ *212/744–7117* Ⓜ *6 to 77th St.* ✉ *30 Rockefeller Center, between 5th and 6th Aves., Midtown West* ☎ *212/265–9404* Ⓜ *B, D, F, V to 47th–50th St./Rockefeller Center* ✉ *63 Wall St., between Pearl and Hanover Sts., Financial District* ☎ *212/952–1123* Ⓜ *2, 3 to Wall St.*

Li-Lac Chocolates. They've been feeding the Village's sweet tooth since 1923. You can buy dark-chocolate-dipped marzipan acorns here by the pound, as well as such specialty items as chocolate-molded Statues of Liberty. ✉ *40 8th Ave., at Jane St., Greenwich Village* ☎ *212/924–2280* Ⓜ *A, C, E to 14th St.*

17

Cool Spots for Souvenirs

What to get from the city that has everything? Major tourist attractions keep their gift shops well stocked with all the standard souvenirs, and dozens of gift shops dot the Times Square area. If you're looking for grungier souvenirs of downtown (T-shirts with salty messages, tattoos), troll St. Marks Place between 2nd and 3rd avenues in the East Village. *But for more unique mementos of the city, see this chapter's neighborhood spotlights for ideas and try the sources below.*

City Store. Discover all kinds of books and pamphlets that explain New York City's government, from pocket maps, NYPD T-shirts, and wallets printed with subway routes to manhole-cover floormats and salt and pepper shakers shaped like squad cars. The store shuts at 4:30 on weekdays and is closed weekends. ⊠ *1 Centre St., at Chambers St., Lower Manhattan* ☎ *212/669–8246* Ⓜ *4, 5, 6 to City Hall/Brooklyn Bridge.*

Eleni's. Take a bite out of the Big Apple—in cookie form—with these perfectly decorated treats. The "New York, New York" tin includes sugar cookies that mimic local icons like yellow cabs and the Statue of Liberty. ⊠ *Chelsea Market, 75 9th Ave., between W. 15th and W. 16th Sts., Chelsea* ☎ *212/255–6804* Ⓜ *A, C, E to 14th St., L to 8th Ave.*

H&H Bagels. Looking for a taste of the city? Although a slice of pizza may not travel so well, bagels are another story. H&H can pack its bagels to withstand any plane ride—and in true New York spirit, the store is open 24 hours a day. ⊠ *2239 Broadway, at W. 80th St., Upper West Side* ☎ *212/595–8003* Ⓜ *1 to 79th St.*

New York City Transit Museum Gift Shop. In the symbolic heart of New York City's transit system, all the store's merchandise is somehow linked to the MTA, from straphanger ties to umbrellas decorated with subway-line logos. ⊠ *Grand Central Terminal, Vanderbilt Pl. and E. 42nd St., Midtown East* ☎ *212/878–0106* Ⓜ *4, 5, 6, 7 to 42nd St./Grand Central Terminal.*

★ **MarieBelle.** The handmade chocolates here are nothing less than works of art. Square truffles and bonbons—which come in such flavors as Earl Grey tea, cappuccino, passion fruit, and saffron—are painted with edible dyes (cocoa butter dyed with natural coloring) so each resembles a miniature painting. Tins of aromatic tea leaves and Aztec hot chocolate are also available. ⊠ *484 Broome St., between West Broadway and Wooster St., SoHo* ☎ *212/925–6999* Ⓜ *R, W to Prince St.* ⊠ *762 Madison Ave., between 65th and 66th Sts., Upper East Side* ☎ *212/249–4588* Ⓜ *6 to 68th St./Hunter College.*

Max Brenner: Chocolate by the Bald Man. This isn't the place to make a fuss about cocoa percentages or impeccable handcrafted bonbons; instead, this Aussie arrival is all about a Wonka-ish sense of entertainment. The cafés encourage the messy enjoyment of gooey creations like chocolate fondues. Take-away treats include pralines and whipped chocolate truffles rolled in powdered sugar and cocoa. ⊠ *841 Broadway, between*

E. 13th and E. 14th Sts., East Village ☎ *212/388–0030* Ⓜ *L, N, Q, R, W, 4, 5, 6 to 14th St./Union Sq.*

Fodor's Choice **Vosges Haut Chocolat.** This chandeliered salon takes chocolate couture
★ to a new level. Many of the creations are internationally themed: the Budapest bonbons combine dark chocolate and Hungarian paprika, the Black Pearls contain wasabi, but the most unexpected treat might be the chocolate bacon bars. ✉ *132 Spring St., between Greene and Wooster Sts., SoHo* ☎ *212/625–2929* Ⓜ *R, W to Prince St.* ✉ *1100 Madison Ave., at 83rd St., Upper East Side* ☎ *212/717–2929* Ⓜ *4, 5, 6 to 86th St.*

CLOTHING: DISCOUNT

Besides the following standby, don't overlook the discount department stores, especially Century 21.

Loehmann's. Label searchers can turn up $40 Polo/Ralph Lauren chinos and Donna Karan and Yves Saint Laurent suits in the men's department here on a regular basis. Head up to the "back room" on the top floor for the best women's designers, but you may need to make a repeat visit or two before emerging victorious. ✉ *101 7th Ave., at W. 16th St., Chelsea* ☎ *212/352–0856* Ⓜ *1, 2, 3 to 14th St.* ✉ *2101 Broadway, at W. 73rd and 74th Sts., Upper West Side* ☎ *212/882–9990* Ⓜ *1, 2, 3 to 72nd St.*

17

CLOTHING: JUST FOR MEN

Duncan Quinn. Shooting for nothing less than sartorial splendor, this designer provides everything from chalk-stripe suits to cuff links in a shop not much bigger than its silk pocket squares. Only a few of each style of shirt are made, so the odds are slim that you will see someone else in your blue, violet, or orange button-down with contrast-color under cuffs. Bespoke customers can choose from thousands of fabrics. ✉ *8 Spring St., between Elizabeth and Bowery Sts., NoLita* ☎ *212/226–7030* Ⓜ *6 to Spring St.*

Dunhill. Corporate brass come here for finely tailored clothing, both ready- and custom-made, and smoking accessories; the walk-in humidor stores top-quality tobacco and cigars. ✉ *545 Madison Ave., at E. 55th St., Midtown East* ☎ *212/753–9292* Ⓜ *F to 57th St.*

John Varvatos. Over the past few years Varvatos has amplified his rock and roll ties, with rock-star photos in his stores and ad campaigns starring Franz Ferdinand and ZZ Top. He may have overstepped himself, though, by taking over the CBGB club space to use as another boutique for hawking expensive, soft-shouldered suits, cotton crewnecks, and jeans in leather, velvet, or denim. ✉ *122 Spring St., at Greene St., SoHo* ☎ *212/965–0700* Ⓜ *6 to Spring St.* ✉ *315 Bowery, between E. 1st and E. 2nd Sts., East Village* ☎ *212/358–0315* Ⓜ *F, V to Lower East Side/2nd Ave.*

Nom de Guerre. Brave the narrow staircase at this basement-level hipster hideaway to find racks filled mainly with the house men's line, plus a selection of items by A.P.C., Comme de Garçons, and others. There's an Army-Navyish vibe, with camo-green dressing-room curtains and a concrete floor, but the staff is militant only about style and fit. ⊠ *640 Broadway, at Bleecker St., Greenwich Village* ☎ *212/253–2891* Ⓜ *F, V to Broadway-Lafayette.*

★ **Sean.** These snug shops carry low-key, well-priced, and comfortable apparel from France—wool and cotton painter's coats, very-narrow-wale corduroy pants, and a respectable collection of suits and dress shirts. ⊠ *199 Prince St., between Sullivan and MacDougal Sts., SoHo* ☎ *212/598–5980* Ⓜ *R, W to Prince St.* ⊠ *224 Columbus Ave., between W. 70th and W. 71st Sts., Upper West Side* ☎ *212/769–1489* Ⓜ *B, C to 72nd St.*

Tom Ford. After making his name sexing up the Gucci women's lines, Ford lasers in on the XY set for his next major retail effort. The suits are relatively traditional (and impeccably made), but the shirts are more interesting, as they come in literally hundreds of colors. Glide up the ebony staircase for the made-to-measure services, which will customize anything from suits to pajamas. ⊠ *845 Madison Ave., at E. 70th St., Upper East Side* ☎ *212/359–0300* Ⓜ *6 to 68th St./Hunter College.*

Vilebrequin. Allow St-Tropez to influence your swimsuit; these striped, floral, and solid-color French-made trunks come in sunny hues. Water-proof pocket inserts keep your essentials safe from beachcombers. Many styles come in boys' sizes, too. ⊠ *1070 Madison Ave., at E. 81st St., Upper East Side* ☎ *212/650–0353* Ⓜ *6 to 77th St.* ⊠ *436 West Broadway, between Prince and Spring Sts., SoHo* ☎ *212/431–0673* Ⓜ *R, W to Prince St.*

CLOTHING: MEN'S AND WOMEN'S

CASUAL AND COOL

Agnès b. With this quintessentially French line, women can look like Parisian schoolgirls—in snap-front tops, slender pants, sweet floral prints—or like a chic *maman* in tailored dark suits and leather jackets. For men, the designer's love for the movies makes it easy to come out looking a little Godard around the edges: turtleneck sweaters, lean black suits, and black-leather porkpie hats demand the sangfroid of Belmondo. The Upper East Side store is women's only. ⊠ *13 E. 16th St., between 5th Ave. and Union Sq. W, Flatiron District* ☎ *212/741–2585* Ⓜ *N, Q, R, W, 4, 5, 6 to 14th St./Union Sq.* ⊠ *1063 Madison Ave., between E. 80th and E. 81st Sts., Upper East Side* ☎ *212/570–9333* Ⓜ *6 to 77th St.*

A.P.C. This hip French boutique proves to be deceptively simple. Watch your step on the uneven wooden floorboards while choosing narrow gabardine and corduroy suits or dark denim jeans and jackets, some with a hint of military. ⊠ *131 Mercer St., between Prince and Spring Sts., SoHo* ☎ *212/966–9685* Ⓜ *6 to Spring St.; R, W to Prince St.*

Christopher Fischer Featherweight cashmere sweaters, wraps, and throws in every hue from Easter-egg pastels to rich jewel tones have made Fischer the darling of Hamptonites. His shop also carries leather accessories and such home wares as throw pillows and wooden bowls from South Africa. ⊠ *80 Wooster St., between Spring and Broome Sts., SoHo* ☏ *212/965–9009* Ⓜ *R, W to Prince St.* ⊠ *1225 Madison Ave., between 88th and 89th Sts., Upper East Side* ☏ *212/831–8880* Ⓜ *4, 5, 6 to 86th St.*

Destination. The model pigs guarding this store fit right in with the Meatpacking District. Inside are clothes and accessories that telegraph "south of 14th Street": hard-to-find, roomy Jacques le Corre bags, skull jewelry, and cult sunglasses. ⊠ *32–36 Little W. 12th St., between Greenwich and Washington Sts., Meatpacking District* ☏ *212/727–2031* Ⓜ *1 to Christopher St./Sheridan Sq.*

DKNY. Cocktail-party ensembles, chunky-knit sweaters, and knock-around denim vie for notice; the "pure" line is reserved for all-natural fibers. A scattering of vintage pieces, such as leather bomber jackets and 1930s jewelry, ensures that you can have something no one else has. Scout out the nonwearables, too; the candles and home accessories are unfailingly cool. Then you can belly up to the juice bar or listen to a featured CD. ⊠ *655 Madison Ave., at E. 60th St., Upper East Side* ☏ *212/223–3569* Ⓜ *N, R, W, 4, 5, 6 to 59th St./Lexington Ave.* ⊠ *420 West Broadway, between Prince and Spring Sts., SoHo* ☏ *646/613–1100* Ⓜ *C, E to Spring St.*

Tommy Hilfiger. With their patriotic red, white, and blue logos, bright colors, and casual, outdoorsy look, these clothes have a recognizably American style. The Fifth Avenue store takes a more upscale tack, with tailored suits for men, smart sweater sets and pencil skirts for women, and broadcloth shirts for both; the Soho location also carries children's clothing, Bleecker Street has an eclectic mix of sportswear and hand-picked vintage pieces, and Broadway stocks men's and women's denim. ⊠ *681 5th Ave., at 54th St., Midtown East* ☏ *212/223–1824* Ⓜ *E, V to 53rd St.* ⊠ *372 West Broadway, at Broome St., SoHo* ☏ *917/237–0983* Ⓜ *R, W to Prince St.* ⊠ *375 Bleecker St., between Charles and Perry Sts., West Village* ☏ *646/638–4812* Ⓜ *1 to Christopher St./Sheridan Sq.* ⊠ *500 Broadway, between Spring and Broome Sts., Greenwich Village* ☏ *212/334–0042* Ⓜ *6 to Spring St.*

Ìrma. This unprepossessing nook with its squeaky plank floors is actually home to some of the most hard-to-find designers in the city. Besides carrying a good selection of Vivienne Westwood, the store stockpiles whisper-light cashmere by Kristesen du Nord, ready-to-wear from Canadian brand Ports 1961, and Belstaff motorcycle boots and jackets. ⊠ *378 Bleecker St., between Charles and Perry Sts., Greenwich Village* ☏ *212/206–7475* Ⓜ *A, C, E, F, V to W. 4th St./Washington Sq.*

J. Crew. The preppy-chic brand has opened some special storefronts in New York, in addition to the many standard branches around town. A selection of menswear has taken over an old-time TriBeCa tavern, keeping the original wood bar and adding vintage photos and a fitting room that doubles as an art gallery—another menswear location recently

17

popped up in SoHo. Some of the best finds are accessories: Borsalino hats and Selima Optique sunglasses (both in exclusive designs), vintage tie bars, money clips, and books. Uptown, there's a posh, one-off Women's Collection shop, where whitewashed walls set off color-coded rows of calfskin jackets, cashmere sweaters, and snakeskin handbags, and a children's store carrying the brand's irresistible crewcuts line. Specialty stores also carry some staples like denim and corduroy. ⊠ *235 West Broadway, at White St., TriBeCa* ☎ *212/226–5476* Ⓜ *1 to Franklin St.* ⊠ *484 Broadway, at Broome St., Soho* ☎ *212/343–1227* Ⓜ *N, Q, R, W to Canal St.* ⊠ *1035 Madison Ave., at 79th St., Upper East Side* ☎ *212/249–3869* Ⓜ *6 to 77th St./Lexington Ave.* ⊠ *Crewcuts, 1190 Madison Ave., at 87th St., Upper East Side* ☎ *212/348–9803* Ⓜ *4, 5, 6 to 86th St./Lexington Ave.*

Paul Frank. The flat visage of Julius the monkey, the original Paul Frank character, plasters vinyl wallets, flannel PJs, skateboards, and, of course, T-shirts. Also look for tees evoking such formative elements of '80s youth as corn dogs and break dancing. A selection of monkey-free accessories, including perfect weekender bags, is more stylish than sassy. ⊠ *195 Mulberry St., at Kenmare St., NoLita* ☎ *212/965–5079* Ⓜ *6 to Spring St.*

R by 45rpm. Japanese interpretations of Western styles, from peacoats to bandannas, are marked by their attention to detail. Look for hand-stressed denim. ⊠ *169 Mercer St., between W. Houston and Prince Sts., SoHo* ☎ *917/237–0045* Ⓜ *R, W to Prince St.*

Reiss. These casual-but-tailored clothes have sleek details and a relatively gentle price. Women's blouses and skirts have delicate pleats; jersey dresses are delicately draped. Men's mohair trousers are complemented by shrunken blazers, military-inspired peacoats, and trim leather jackets. ⊠ *387 West Broadway, between Spring and Broome Sts., SoHo* ☎ *212/925–5707* Ⓜ *R, W to Prince St.* ⊠ *309–313 Bleecker St., between 7th Ave. and Grove St., Greenwich Village* ☎ *212/488–2411* Ⓜ *1 to Christopher St./Sheridan Sq.* ⊠ *197–199 Columbus Ave., 76 W. 69th St., Upper West Side* ☎ *212/799–5560* Ⓜ *1 to 66th St.*

Fodor's Choice
★
UNIQLO. Past the 30-foot wall of seasonal staples near the entrance of this Japanese retail giant, a tri-level space bursts with affordable, well-tailored basics. Cashmere crew- and V-necks (most under $100), slim-fit denims, and casual coats share space with edgier tees designed by Japanese graphic artists. Most of the clothing has been tweaked or made specifically for the American market. ∎**TIP→** Weekday mornings are the best time to avoid long lines for the dressing rooms. ⊠ *546 Broadway, between Prince and Spring Sts., SoHo* ☎ *917/237–8800* Ⓜ *R, W to Prince St.*

HIGH DESIGN

Burberry. The signature check is hardly square these days, as bikinis, leather pants, and messenger-style bags join the traditional gabardine trench coats. The flagship store on East 57th Street is the mother lode; the SoHo branch has an abbreviated assortment. ⊠ *9 E. 57th St., between 5th and Madison Aves., Midtown East* ☎ *212/407–7100*

Ⓜ N, R, W to 5th Ave./59th St. ⊠ 131 Spring St., between Greene and Wooster Sts., SoHo ☎ 212/925–9300 Ⓜ R, W to Prince St.

Calvin Klein. Though the namesake designer has bowed out, the label keeps channeling his particular style. This stark flagship store emphasizes the luxe end of the clothing line. Men's suits tend to be soft around the edges; women's evening gowns are often a fluid pouring of silk. There are also shoes, accessories, housewares, and makeup. ⊠ 654 Madison Ave., at E. 60th St., Upper East Side ☎ 212/292–9000 Ⓜ N, R, W, 4, 5, 6 to 59th St./Lexington Ave.

Christian Dior. The New York outpost of one of France's most venerable fashion houses makes its home in the dazzlingly modern LVMH tower. The designs bring elements of everything from raceways to skate punks to haute couture. If you're not in the market for an investment gown, peruse the glam accessories, like the latest status bag. The Dior menswear boutique is next door; the rocking cigarette-thin suits are often pilfered by women. ⊠ 21 E. 57th St., at Madison Ave., Midtown East ☎ 212/931–2950 Ⓜ E, V to 5th Ave./53rd St. ⊠ Men's store, 17 E. 57th St., between 5th and Madison Aves., Midtown East ☎ 212/421–6009 Ⓜ E, V to 5th Ave./53rd St.

Comme des Garçons. The designs in this stark, white, swoopy space consistently push the fashion envelope with brash patterns, unlikely juxtapositions (tulle and neoprene), and cuts that are meant to be thought-provoking, not flattering. Architecture students come just for the interior design. ⊠ 520 W. 22nd St., between 10th and 11th Aves., Chelsea ☎ 212/604–9200 Ⓜ C, E to 23rd St.

Costume National. Although entering this chrome-lined shop may seem intimidating (all those hard, shiny surfaces), the sexy, slim-cut leather coats and sheer black shirts for both men and women are chic and beautifully made. ⊠ 160 Mercer St., between Prince and W. Houston Sts., SoHo ☎ 212/431–1530 Ⓜ C, E to Spring St.

Dolce & Gabbana. It's easy to feel like an Italian movie star amid these extravagant (in every sense) clothes. Pinstripes are a favorite; for women, they could be paired with something sheer, furred, or leopard-print, and for men they elongate the sharp suits. ⊠ 825 Madison Ave., between E. 68th and E. 69th Sts., Upper East Side ☎ 212/249–4100 Ⓜ 6 to 68th St./Hunter College.

Emporio Armani. At this middle child of the Armani trio, the clothes are dressy without quite being formal, and are frequently offered in cream, muted blues, and ever-cool shades of soot. ⊠ 410 West Broadway, at Spring St., SoHo ☎ 646/613–8099 Ⓜ C, E to Spring St.

Etro. Trademark paisleys sprawl over richly covered suits, dresses, and lustrous pillows at this Italian designer's boutique, while juicy colors and rich detailing and embroidery keep things modern. ⊠ 720 Madison Ave., between E. 63rd and E. 64th Sts., Upper East Side ☎ 212/317–9096 Ⓜ 6 to 68th St./Hunter College.

Gianni Versace. Filling a five-story flagship store, the sometimes outrageous designs and colors of Versace clothes might not be to everyone's

17

FIFTH AVENUE AND 57TH STREET

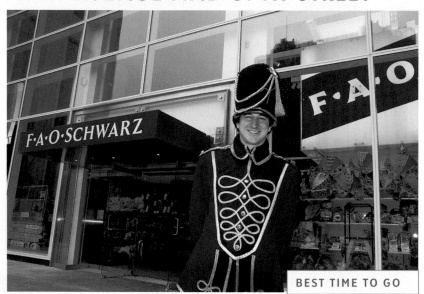

Fifth Avenue from Rockefeller Center to Central Park South pogos between landmark department stores, glossy international designer boutiques, and casual national chains. What they all have in common: massive flagship spaces.

The intersection of 5th Avenue with 57th Street distills this mix of old and new, exclusive and accessible. From these corners you'll see blue-chip New York classics (jeweler Tiffany & Co., the Bergdorf Goodman department stores), luxury giants (Gucci and the glass box of Louis Vuitton), a high-tech wonderland (another glass box for Apple), and show-off digs for informal brands (Nike-Town, Abercrombie & Fitch). Capping this shopping stretch at East 58th Street is the colossal, exceptional toy store FAO Schwarz. If you're keen to shop the high end or to see the impressive flagships, it's worth coming to this neighborhood—but if large-scale doesn't do it for you, you're better off heading downtown. —J.P.

BEST TIME TO GO

Wednesday through Friday if you're trying to avoid crowds. Weekends before the winter holidays get extremely hectic and can spark "sidewalk rage" in even the most patient shopper—try to come earlier in the week, especially if you want to see the fantastic department-store window displays.

BEST SOUVENIR FOR KIDS

An incredibly lifelike stuffed animal from **FAO Schwarz**. They've got exclusive Steiff "purebred" dogs, for instance, that come with authenticity certificates from the American Kennel Club.

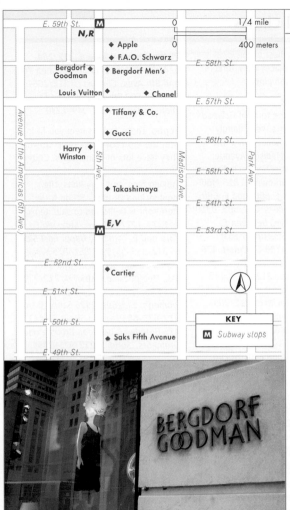

REFUELING

Soothe frazzled nerves with a stop at **Fika** (✉ *41 W. 58th St., between 5th and 6th Aves.* ☎ *212/832–0022*), a calm, friendly Swedish café. Settle in for a gravlax salad, a bracing cup of coffee, and an airy-yet-buttery *drömmar* cookie. If you'd rather stay in the energetic current of 5th Avenue, nab a table, or a seat with a fold-down tray, at the time-warped **Prime Burger** (✉ *5 E. 51st St., between 5th and Madison Aves.* ☎ *212/759–4729*). You'll find all the diner standbys; if you order a burger, you'll have to specify all the toppings you'd like with it.

BEST FOR

DEPARTMENT STORES
Saks Fifth Avenue: fashion and nothing but.

Bergdorf Goodman:
these partner stores (one for women, the other for men; guess which has the housewares) are both genteelly tasteful.

Takashimaya New York:
a cool and collected Japanese emporium with a gorgeous florist on the top floor.

FLAGSHIP STORES
Louis Vuitton: every permutation of the signature handbags and leather goods, plus the jet-set clothing line upstairs.

Chanel: all the hallmarks, from little black dresses to double-C jewelry.

Apple: all sorts of chip-driven devices, 24 hours a day.

Gucci: check out classic designs and goodies exclusive to this store.

SERIOUS JEWELRY
Tiffany & Co.: hum "Moon River," check out the dazzling gems and pearls, then head upstairs for all sorts of silver ornaments.

Cartier: both classic and slinky new designs glitter in a turn-of-the-20th-century mansion.

Harry Winston: the ultimate for diamonds (just ask Marilyn Monroe).

17

Cool Local Chains

Following are the best of the local chain stores, the places New Yorkers head to in a fashion pinch.

Calypso. An island-vacation vibe swept the city in the form of Calypso's colorful silk women's wear, dangly jewelry, and boho housewares. The flagship's now on Madison Avenue; several themed branches, including an outlet, cluster downtown. ✉ *815 Madison Ave., between E. 68th and E. 69th Sts., Upper East Side* ☎ *212/585-0310* ✉ *935 Madison Ave., between E. 74th and E. 75th Sts., Upper East Side* ☎ *212/585-4100* ✉ *Outlet, 426 Broome St., between Lafayette and Crosby Sts., SoHo* ☎ *212/274-0449* ✉ *280 Mott St., between E. Houston and Prince Sts., NoLita* ☎ *212/965-0990* ✉ *407 Broome St., between Lafayette and Centre Sts., NoLita* ☎ *212/941-9700* ✉ *Home, 199 Lafayette St., at Broome St., NoLita* ☎ *212/925-6200* ✉ *654 Hudson St., at Gansevoort St., Meatpacking District* ☎ *646/638-3000* ✉ *191 Lafayette St., at Broome St., NoLita* ☎ *212/941-6512* ✉ *137 West Broadway, between Thomas and Duane Sts., TriBeCa* ☎ *212/608-2222.*

Ricky's. The loud and fun drugstores—there are over two-dozen in the city—attract an eclectic, mostly young crowd who come just as often for the crazy-color wigs or fishnet stockings as they do for the body glitter and Neutrogena soap. Every fall the stores turn into Halloween central, with a huge assortment of feather boas, masks, and spray-on hair color. ✉ *590 Broadway, at Prince St., SoHo* ☎ *212/226-5552* ✉ *7 E. 14th St., Union Sq.* ☎ *212/691-7930* ✉ *466 6th Ave., at W. 12th St., Greenwich Village* ☎ *212/924-3401* ✉ *44 E. 8th St., between Broadway and University Pl., Greenwich Village* ☎ *212/254-5247* ✉ *267 W. 23rd St., between 7th and 8th Aves., Chelsea* ☎ *212/206-0234* ✉ *509 5th Ave., at 42nd St., Midtown East* ☎ *212/949-7230.*

Scoop. These clothes help you fit in with the too-cool-to-dress-up crowd. They have lots of jeans (Levi's, Citizens of Humanity), slinky tops, vintage-looking tees, and cozy knits. The Meatpacking District's Scoop It Up storefront is dedicated to sale items. ✉ *1273-1277 3rd Ave., between E. 73rd and E. 74th Sts., Upper East Side* ☎ *212/535-5577* ✉ *861-875 Washington St., between 13th and 14th Sts., Meatpacking District* ☎ *212/929-1244 men's shop; 212/691-1905 women's; 212/691-1926 Scoop It Up; 212/633-6535 Scoop Street* ✉ *473-475 Broadway, between Broome and Grand Sts., SoHo* ☎ *212/925-3539.*

Searle. Mostly strung along the East Side, these stores have a devoted following for their coats, and there are plenty of other designer items to layer, from cowl-neck sweaters to fitted tees. ✉ *1051 3rd Ave., at E. 62nd St., Upper East Side* ☎ *212/838-5990* ✉ *635 Madison Ave., between E. 59th and E. 60th Sts., Midtown East* ☎ *212/753-9021* ✉ *1296 3rd Ave., between E. 74th and E. 75th Sts., Upper East Side* ☎ *212/717-5200* ✉ *1124 Madison Ave., at E. 84th St., Upper East Side* ☎ *212/988-7318.*

taste (or budget), but they're never boring. ⊠ *647 5th Ave., near E. 51st St., Midtown East* ☎ *212/317–0224* Ⓜ *E, V to 5th Ave./53rd St.*

★ **Gucci.** The 5th Avenue flagship store sets a new standard for giantism—it spans 46,000 square feet with floor-to-ceiling glass windows. This three-floor incarnation has a special "heritage" department, plus goods exclusive to the store. With a female designer in place, the clothing is less aggressively sexy than it was in the Tom Ford era. Skintight pants might be paired with a luxe leather jacket; silk tops leave a little more to the imagination. The accessories, like wraparound shades or snakeskin shoes, many with signature horsebit detailing, continue to spark consumer frenzies. ⊠ *725 5th Ave., at 56th St., Midtown East* ☎ *212/826–2600* Ⓜ *N, R, W to 5th Ave./59th St.* ⊠ *840 Madison Ave., between E. 69th and E. 70th Sts., Upper East Side* ☎ *212/717–2619* Ⓜ *6 to 68th St./Hunter College.*

Hermès. Sweep up and down the curving stairway in this contemporary flagship while on the prowl for the classic, distinctively patterned silk scarves and neckties, the coveted Kelly and Birkin handbags, or the beautifully simple separates. True to its roots, Hermès still stocks saddles and other equestrian items. ⊠ *691 Madison Ave., at E. 62nd St., Upper East Side* ☎ *212/751–3181* Ⓜ *N, R, W, 4, 5, 6 to 59th St./Lexington Ave.*

Issey Miyake. Pleats of a Fortuny-like tightness are the Miyake signature—but instead of Fortuny's silks, these clothes are in polyester or ultra-high-tech textiles, often forming sculptural shapes. **Pleats Please** carries a line with simpler silhouettes, from tunics to long dresses. ⊠ *802 Madison Ave., between 67th and 68th Sts., Upper East Side* ☎ *212/439–7822* Ⓜ *6 to 68th St./Hunter College* ⊠ *119 Hudson St., at N. Moore St., TriBeCa* ☎ *212/226–0100* Ⓜ *1 to Franklin St.* ⊠ *Pleats Please, 128 Wooster St., at Prince St., SoHo* ☎ *212/226–3600* Ⓜ *R, W to Prince St.*

Jeffrey. The Meatpacking District really arrived when this Atlanta-based mini-Barneys opened its doors. You can find an incredible array of designer shoes—Valentino, Lanvin, and red-soled Christian Louboutin are some of the best sellers—plus überlabels like Marni and Gucci. ⊠ *449 W. 14th St., between 9th and 10th Aves., Meatpacking District* ☎ *212/206–1272* Ⓜ *A, C, E, L to 14th St./8th Ave.*

Fodor's Choice ★ **Marc Jacobs.** The West Village is getting steadily infiltrated with boutiques carrying the more casual lines of the Jacobs juggernaut. The saturation zone teems with tongue-in-cheek tees, downplayed duds in plaids and stripes, and the eternally popular shoes and bags. In SoHo a former garage is filled with ladylike designs made with luxurious fabrics: silk, cashmere, wool bouclé, and tweeds ranging from the demure to the flamboyant. The details, though—oversize buttons, circular patch pockets, and military-style grommet belts—add a sartorial wink. ⊠ *163 Mercer St., between W. Houston and Prince Sts., SoHo* ☎ *212/343–1490* Ⓜ *R, W to Prince St.* ⊠ *Accessories boutique: 385 Bleecker St., at Perry St., Greenwich Village* ☎ *212/924–6126* Ⓜ *1 to Christopher St./Sheridan Sq.* ⊠ *Men's Accessories:298 W. 4th St., at Bank St., West Village* ☎ *212/929–0304* Ⓜ *1 to Christopher St./Sheridan Sq.* ⊠ *Men's:*

17

301 W. 4th St., at Bank St., West Village ☏ *212/929–0304* Ⓜ *1 to Christopher St./Sheridan Sq.* ✉ *Little Marc: 382 Bleecker St., between Perry and Charles Sts., West Village* ☏ *212/206–6644* Ⓜ *1 to Christopher St./Sheridan Sq.* ✉ *403–405 Bleecker St., at W. 11th St., Greenwich Village* ☏ *212/924–0026* Ⓜ *1 to Christopher St./Sheridan Sq.*

★ **Polo/Ralph Lauren.** One of New York's most distinctive shopping experiences, Lauren's flagship store graces the turn-of-the-20th-century Rhinelander mansion. Clothes range from summer-in-the-Hamptons madras to exquisite silk gowns and Purple Label men's suits. **Polo Sport** carries casual clothes and sports gear, from puffy anoraks to wickaway tanks. The Village branches of **Ralph Lauren,** on the other hand, are small, tightly packed boutiques. They pull together sequin-slicked skirts, sturdy cable knits and tweeds, western and denim, and the odd bit of vintage. ✉ *867 Madison Ave., at E. 72nd St., Upper East Side* ☏ *212/606–2100* Ⓜ *6 to 68th St./Hunter College* ✉ *Polo Sport, 1055 Madison Ave., at 80th St., Upper East Side* ☏ *212/434–8000* Ⓜ *6 to 68th St./Hunter College* ✉ *379 West Broadway, between Spring and Broome Sts., SoHo* ☏ *212/625–1660* Ⓜ *C, E to Spring St.* ✉ *380–381 Bleecker St., at Perry St., Greenwich Village* ☏ *212/645–5513* Ⓜ *1 to Christopher St./Sheridan Sq.*

Fodor's Choice ★ **Prada.** The design shop's gossamer silks, slick black suits, and luxe shoes and leather goods are among the all-time great Italian fashion coups. The uptown stores pulse with pale green walls (remember this if you start questioning your skin tone). The 57th Street branch carries just the shoes, bags, and other accessories. The SoHo location, an ultramodern space designed by Rem Koolhaas, incorporates so many technological innovations that it was written up in *Popular Science.* The dressing-room gadgets alone include liquid crystal displays, changeable lighting, and scanners that link you to the store's database. ✉ *724 5th Ave., between W. 56th and W. 57th Sts., Midtown West* ☏ *212/664–0010* Ⓜ *Q, W to 5th Ave./60th St.* ✉ *45 E. 57th St., between Madison and Park Aves., Midtown East* ☏ *212/308–2332* Ⓜ *E, V to 5th Ave./53rd St.* ✉ *841 Madison Ave., at E. 70th St., Upper East Side* ☏ *212/327–4200* Ⓜ *6 to 68th St./Hunter College* ✉ *575 Broadway, at Prince St., SoHo* ☏ *212/334–8888* Ⓜ *R, W to Prince St.*

Roberto Cavalli. Rock-star style (at rock-star prices) delivers denim decked with fur, feathers, prints, and even shredded silk overlays. ✉ *711 Madison Ave., at E. 63rd St., Upper East Side* ☏ *212/755–7722* Ⓜ *N, R, W to 5th Ave./59th St.*

Valentino. The mix here is at once audacious and beautifully cut; the fur or feather trimmings, low necklines, and opulent fabrics are about as close as you can get to celluloid glamour. No one does a better red. ✉ *747 Madison Ave., at E. 65th St., Upper East Side* ☏ *212/772–6969* Ⓜ *6 to 68th St./Hunter College.*

Yohji Yamamoto. Although almost entirely black and white, these clothes aren't as severe as they seem. Whimsical details, like giant polka dots, shirts with drawstring hems, and slouchy, rolled trouser cuffs, add a dash of levity. ✉ *103 Grand St., at Mercer St., SoHo* ☏ *212/966–9066*

Ⓜ J, M, N, Q, R, W, Z, 6 to Canal St. ✉ 1 Gansevoort St., at W. 13th St., Meatpacking District ☎ 212/966–3615 Ⓜ A, C, E to 14th St.

Yves Saint Laurent Rive Gauche. Tom Ford's successor, Stephano Pilati, is lightening up the fabled French house; think seduction instead of sexpot, with ruffles, wide belts, and safari-style jackets. ✉ 855 Madison Ave., between E. 70th and E. 71st Sts., Upper East Side ☎ 212/988–3821 Ⓜ 6 to 68th St./Hunter College ✉ 3 E. 57th St., between 5th and Madison Aves., Midtown East ☎ 212/980–2970 Ⓜ N, R, W to 5th Ave./59th St.

TAILORED

Barbour. The company's waxed jackets are built to withstand raw British weather. The tweeds, moleskin pants, lamb's-wool sweaters, and tattersall shirts invariably call up images of country rambles. Trusty hunting dog is not included. ✉ 1047 Madison Ave., at E. 80th St., Upper East Side ☎ 212/570–2600 Ⓜ 6 to 77th St.

Brooks Brothers. The clothes at this classic American haberdasher are, as ever, traditional, comfortable, and fairly priced. Summer seersucker, navy blue blazers, and the peerless oxford shirts have been staples for generations. The women's selection has variations thereof. The Bleecker Street Black Fleece storefront sells the brand's more upscale Thom Browne-designed line. ■ TIP→ At the Madison Avenue store you can step into a computer scanner to get precisely measured for a custom shirt or suit; appointments are recommended. ✉ 346 Madison Ave., at E. 44th St., Midtown East ☎ 212/682–8800 Ⓜ 4, 5, 6, 7, S to 42nd St./Grand Central ✉ 1270 Avenue of the Americas, between 50th and 51st Sts., Midtown West ☎ 212/247–9374 Ⓜ B, D, F, to 47th–50th Sts./Rockefeller Center ✉ 1934 Broadway, at 65th St., Upper West Side ☎ 212/362–2374 Ⓜ 1 to 66th St./Lincoln Center ✉ Black Fleece, 351 Bleecker St., at W. 10th St., Midtown East ☎ 212/929–2763 Ⓜ 1 to Christopher St./Sheridan Sq. ✉ 1 Church St., at Liberty St., Lower Manhattan ☎ 212/267–2400 Ⓜ R, W to Cortlandt St.

Paul Smith. Victorian mahogany cases complement the dandyish British styles they hold. Embroidered vests, brightly striped socks, scarves, and shirts, and tongue-in-cheek cuff links leaven the classic, double-backvent suits for men. Women head for the tailored suits and separates, classic outerwear, and plush knits. Plus, you'll find furniture and a selection of photography books, cordial glasses, and other such oddments that beg for a cultured bachelor pad. ✉ 142 Greene St., between Prince and W. Houston Sts., SoHo ☎ 646/613–3060 Ⓜ R, W to Prince St. ✉ 108 5th Ave., at E. 16th St., Flatiron District ☎ 212/627–9770 Ⓜ F, V to 14th St.

Seize sur Vingt. In bringing a contemporary sensibility to custom tailoring, this store realized an ideal fusion. Brighten a suit or cotton moleskin flat-front pants with a checked or striped shirt; all can be made to order. Women are also the beneficiaries of the store's crisp button-downs and single-pleat trousers. ✉ 78 Greene St., between Spring and Broome Sts., SoHo ☎ 212/625–1620 Ⓜ R, W to Prince St.

17

Street Vendors

If you're looking for original or repro-duced artwork, the two areas to visit for street vendors are the stretch of 5th Avenue in front of the Metropoli-tan Museum of Art (roughly between 81st and 82nd streets) and the SoHo area of West Broadway, between Houston and Broome streets. In both areas you'll find dozens of artists sell-ing original paintings, drawings, and photographs (some lovely, some lurid), as well as photo reproductions of famous New York scenes (the Chrysler building, South Street Seaport). Prices can start as low as $10.

The east–west streets in SoHo are an excellent place to look for handmade crafts: Spring and Prince streets, especially, are jammed with tables full of beaded jewelry, tooled leather belts, and homemade hats and purses. These streets are also great places to find deals on art books; several vendors have titles featuring the work of artists from Diego Rivera to Annie Leibovitz, all for about 20% less than you'd pay at a chain. It's best to know which books you want ahead of time, though; street vendors wrap theirs in clear plastic, and can get testy if you unwrap them but don't wind up buying.

Faux-designer handbags, sunglasses, wallets, and watches are some of the most popular street buys in town—but crackdowns on knockoffs have made them harder to find. The hub used to be Canal Street, roughly between Greene and Lafayette streets, but many vendors there have swept their booths clean of fake Vuitton, Prada, Gucci, and Fendi merchandise. You might have better luck finding a Faux-lex near Herald Square or Madison Square Garden; and good old-fashioned fake handbags are still sold by isolated vendors around such shopping areas as Rockefeller Center and Lexington Avenue near Bloom-ingdale's. The one thing Canal Street is still good for, though, is cheap lug-gage: for $30–$40 (be sure to haggle), you can walk away with a giant roll-ing suitcase to lug home all your loot.

WITH AN EDGE

A Bathing Ape. Known simply as BAPE to devotees, this exclusive label has a cult following in its native Tokyo. At first it may be hard to see what the fuss is about. A small selection of camouflage gear and lim-ited-edition T-shirts is placed throughout the minimalist space; the real scene-stealers are the flashy retro-style sneakers in neon colors. ⊠ *91 Greene St., between Prince and Spring Sts., SoHo* ☎ *212/925–0222* Ⓜ *R, W to Prince St.*

DDC Lab. The superhip street-wear offerings include bomber jackets and pleated skirts in the brand's signature paper-thin, washable Lycra-leather. The overdyed denim comes in black and navy, along with some supersaturated seasonal hues. ⊠ *427 W. 14th St., at Washington St., Meatpacking District* ☎ *212/414–5801* Ⓜ *A, C, E to 14th St.*

Patricia Field. If you loved Carrie Bradshaw's wild outfits on *Sex and the City*, this is the place for you. As well as designing costumes for the show, Field has been a longtime purveyor of flamboyant club-kid gear. Her East Village emporium is chockablock with teeny kilts, lamé, marabou, pleather, and vinyl, as well as wigs in every color and stiletto heels in some very large sizes. ✉ *302 Bowery, between Bleecker and E. Houston Sts., East Village* ☎ *212/966–4066* Ⓜ *6 to Bleecker St.*

Seven New York. Björk-worthy levels of experimental fashion are achieved at this boutique; check out the designs of such cutting-edge designers as Cosmic Wonder, Preen, Henrik Vibskov, and Gareth Pugh. ✉ *110 Mercer St., between Prince and Spring Sts., SoHo* ☎ *646/654–0156* Ⓜ *N, R to Prince St.*

Trash and Vaudeville. Goths, punks, and other nightcrawlers have favored this standby for years. You might hear the Ramones on the sound system while you browse through bondage-inspired pants and skirts covered in straps, buckles, and other hardware. You'll also find striped stovepipe pants, vinyl corsets, and crinolines painted with flames. ✉ *4 St. Marks Pl., between 2nd and 3rd Aves., East Village* ☎ *212/982–3590* Ⓜ *6 to Astor Pl.*

CLOTHING: VINTAGE AND RESALE

Allan & Suzi. The proprietors, whom you'll no doubt find behind the counter, are the godparents of fashion collecting. Their wacky shop preserves 1980s shoulder pads and 1940s gowns for posterity (or sale). ✉ *416 Amsterdam Ave., between W. 79th and W. 80th Sts., Upper West Side* ☎ *212/724–7445* Ⓜ *1 to 79th St.*

Cheap Jack's. Jack's two-floor space may be 12,000 square feet, but it's still jammed with interesting, not-too-expensive duds. There's almost everything you could wish for: track suits, bomber jackets, early 1980s madras shirts, old prom dresses, and fur-trimmed wool ladies' suits with the eau-de-mothball stamp of authenticity. ✉ *303 5th Ave., at 31st St., Midtown West* ☎ *212/777–9564* Ⓜ *N, Q, R, W to 34th St./Herald Sq.*

Fisch for the Hip. These resale racks are evenly split between men's and women's clothes, with a well-edited selection throughout. You may find last season's Catherine Malandrino chiffon dress with its tags intact, or a Zegna jacket for under $300. Look for multiple discounts on such wardrobe warhorses as little black dresses. ✉ *153 W. 18th St., between 6th and 7th Aves., Chelsea* ☎ *212/633–9053* Ⓜ *F, V, 1, 2, 3 to 14th St.*

Frock. Models and stylists frequent this tiny shop for vintage women's wear from the 1960s, '70s, and '80s. The store carries pieces from such new-wave, mid-'80s designers as Thierry Mugler, Stephen Sprouse, and Claude Montana, not to mention leather, snakeskin, and lizard clutch purses from Chanel, Carlos Falchi, and Charles Jourdan. ✉ *170 Elizabeth St., between Spring and Kenmare Sts., Nolita* ☎ *212/594–5380* Ⓜ *B, D, F, V to Broadway/Lafayette St.*

INA. Although you may spot something vintage, like a 1960s Yves Saint Laurent velvet bolero, most clothing at these small boutiques harks back only a few seasons, and in some cases, the item has never been worn. The 19 Prince Street and flagship Bleecker Street locations rack up menswear; the other stores carry women's resale. The Spring Street location has a consistently good spread of womens' shoes, but also consistently surly

17

service. ✉ *101 Thompson St., between Prince and Spring Sts., SoHo* ☎ *212/941–4757* Ⓜ *6 to Spring St.* ✉ *21 Prince St., between Elizabeth and Mott Sts., NoLita* ☎ *212/334–9048* Ⓜ *6 to Spring St.* ✉ *19 Prince St., between Elizabeth and Mott Sts., NoLita* ☎ *212/334–2210* Ⓜ *6 to Spring St.* ✉ *15 Bleecker St., at Elizabeth St., NoLita* ☎ *212/228–8511* Ⓜ *6 to Bleecker St.* ✉ *208 E. 73rd St., between 2nd and 3rd Aves., Upper East Side* ☎ *212/249–0014* Ⓜ *6 to 77th St.*

New York Vintage. No patience to search through flea markets? Ransack the racks of women's wear in this narrow Chelsea space, where the prime picks have been winnowed for you. The 1930s chiffon blouses, '50s circle skirts, and '60s cocktail dresses are well kept; there's a good selection of handbags and pumps, too. ✉ *117 W. 25th St., between 6th and 7th Aves., Chelsea* ☎ *212/647–1107* Ⓜ *1 to 28th St.*

★ **Resurrection.** With original Chanels, Puccis, and foxy boots, this store is a retro-chic gold mine. Prices, however, are decidedly 21st century. Designers like Marc Jacobs and Anna Sui have sought inspiration among the racks, and the store returns the love by presenting occasional in-store designer exhibits, often with pieces from an honoree's personal collection. ✉ *217 Mott St., between Prince and Spring Sts., NoLita* ☎ *212/625–1374* Ⓜ *6 to Spring St.*

Screaming Mimi's. Vintage 1950s through '80s clothes and retro-wear includes everything from djellabas to soccer shirts to prom dresses. You can also find a selection of huge tinted sunglasses, in case you feel like channeling Yoko Ono or one of the Olsen twins. Don't forget to check out the balcony full of vintage designer duds. ✉ *382 Lafayette St., between 4th and Great Jones Sts., East Village* ☎ *212/677–6464* Ⓜ *B, D, F, V to Broadway–Lafayette St.*

What Goes Around Comes Around. Thanks to the staff's sharp eyes, the denim and leather racks here are a reliable choice. You can also find such hip-again items as rabbit-fur jackets, designer dresses, and some terrific one-of-a-kind vintage rock-concert T-shirts. If the idea of forking over $100 for an Alice Cooper number pains you, just remember: unlike the copies everyone else is wearing, you'll be sporting the real deal. ✉ *351 West Broadway, between Grand and Broome Sts., SoHo* ☎ *212/343–9303* Ⓜ *J, M, N, Q, R, W, Z, 6 to Canal St.*

CLOTHING: WOMEN ONLY

CASUAL AND COOL

Comptoir des Cotonniers. The "cotton counter" angles for multigenerational shopping, lining up stylish, comfortable basics for babies, twentysomethings, ladies of a certain age, and everyone in between. There's a subtle Parisian vibe to the understated tunics, dresses, and separates; colors tend to be earthy. The brand's first U.S. branch has a nature-friendly minimalist look, with pale wood floors and lots of natural light. ✉ *155 Spring St., at West Broadway, SoHo* ☎ *212/274–0830* Ⓜ *C, E to Spring St.*

Foley & Corinna. Images of flowers and butterflies waft along the walls, while the racks divulge both vintage finds, like embroidered leather jackets, and Foley's own line of new clothes. Many looks are lingerie-inspired, with flounces and lace. ⌧ *114 Stanton St., between Ludlow and Essex Sts., Lower East Side* ☎ *212/529–2338* Ⓜ *F to 2nd Ave. or Delancey St.*

Intermix. This boutique is stocked with a healthy mid- to high-range lineup of established and emerging designers—think Chloé, Stella McCartney, and Elizabeth and James. You'll find everything from denim to silk frocks, plus a just-enough layout of shoes and accessories. ⌧ *210 Columbus Ave., between W. 69th and W. 70th Sts., Upper West Side* ☎ *212/769–9116* Ⓜ *1, 2, 3 to 72nd St.* ⌧ *1003 Madison Ave., between E. 77th and E. 78th Sts., Upper East Side* ☎ *212/249–7858* Ⓜ *6 to 77th St.* ⌧ *125 5th Ave., between 19th and 20th Sts., Flatiron* ☎ *212/533–9720* Ⓜ *R, W to 23rd St.* ⌧ *98 Prince St., SoHo* ☎ *212/966–5303* Ⓜ *R, W to Prince St.* ⌧ *365 Bleecker St., at Charles St., Greenwich Village* ☎ *212/929–7180* Ⓜ *1 to Christopher St./Sheridan Sq.*

TG-170. Silk Alice Ritter blouses, peacoats, and a terrific assortment of one-of-a-kind Swiss Freitag messenger bags (made from colorful reused trucking tarps) can be found at this downtown store. ⌧ *170 Ludlow St., between E. Houston and Stanton Sts., Lower East Side* ☎ *212/995–8660* Ⓜ *F, J, M, Z to Delancey St./Essex St.*

Topshop. A household name in the United Kingdom, this cheap-chic chain burnished its image with designs by supermodel Kate Moss, then finally crossed the pond to open its first stateside boutique here. Mirrored walls reflect racks and racks of quick-to-be-snatched pieces—items here really do go fast. The styles are trendy but not painfully so—and prices are fair, with dresses and jeans around $90. Male stylistas will rejoice—Topman has moved into the ground level. ⌧ *480 Broadway, at Broome St., SoHo* ☎ *212/966–9555* Ⓜ *6 to Spring St.; R, W to Prince St.*

CHIC (BUT NOT CHEAP)

Anna Sui. The violet-and-black salon, hung with Beardsley prints and alterna-rock posters, is the ideal setting for Sui's bohemian, flapper- and rocker-influenced designs and colorful beauty products. ⌧ *113 Greene St., between Prince and Spring Sts., SoHo* ☎ *212/941–8406* Ⓜ *R, W to Prince St.*

Castor & Pollux. The store's interior signals a finely tuned balance of high taste (vintage Bergdorf Goodman display cases) and quirkiness (grass-cloth wall coverings and small horse sculptures). Hard-to-find brands like the Risto Bimbiloski are mixed with better-known names like Acne and Kimberly Ovitz. There's also an eye-catching in-house line of jewelry and clutches. ⌧ *238 W. 10th St., at Hudson St., West Village* ☎ *212/645–6572* Ⓜ *1 to Christopher St./Sheridan Sq.*

Charles Nolan. Formerly an exclusive designer for Saks, Nolan offers impeccable craftsmanship: colorful quilted jackets have decorative stitching; body-skimming skirts are beautifully cut; and silken trousers have a creamy drape. Don't overlook the front-of-store gift selection including chunky glass candlesticks and cashmere scrunch scarves. ⌧ *30 Gansevoort St., at Hudson St., Meatpacking District* ☎ *212/924–4888* Ⓜ *A, C, E to 14th St.*

17

MADISON AVENUE

If you're craving a couture fix, cab it straight to Madison Avenue between East 57th and East 79th streets. Here the greatest Italian, French, and American fashion houses form a platinum-card corridor for ladies who lunch. (If you're going to be pointedly overlooked by a salesperson, odds are it will happen here.)

Most occupy large, glass-facade spaces but there are some exceptions, from intimate boutiques in old brownstones to the imposing turn-of-the-20th-century mansion now home to Ralph Lauren. Barneys, a full-fledged if very select department store, fits right in with the avenue's recherché roll call. But Madison isn't just a fashion funnel. A couple of marvelous booksellers and several outstanding antiques dealers and art galleries share this address as well. —J.P.

BEST TIME TO GO

Saturday is the busiest day and thus better for people-watching. Perhaps because of the European influence, the pace is calmer here, especially on weekdays. Avoid coming on a Sunday, since several stores close, especially in summer when they figure their main clientele is out in the Hamptons.

BEST SOUVENIR FOR AN EX-MANHATTANITE

Take a whiff of the Manhattan-inspired perfumes like Chelsea Flowers and Park Avenue at **Bond No. 9.** Can't decide? Snap up the sampler box with travel-size spray scents wrapped like bonbons.

BEST FOR

INTERNATIONAL MEGA-DESIGNERS

Barneys: dozens of the most cutting-edge names.

Polo/Ralph Lauren: haute-WASP style in a Rhinelander mansion.

Hermès: those divine silk scarves and handbags are waiting....

Giorgio Armani: a sleek setting for perfectly cut suits and dramatic evening wear.

Yves Saint Laurent Rive Gauche: Left Bank chic, *fabuleux* accessories.

Vera Wang: Big Occasion gowns, bridal and beyond.

FANCY CHILDREN'S CLOTHES

Bonpoint: precious European designs with hand-embroidering, velvet ribbons, you get the picture.

Petit Bateau: all superfine, hypoallergenic, colorful cotton, all the time.

REFUELING

Join the Upper East Side yummy mummies and their trilingual children at the local branch of **Le Pain Quotidien** (✉ *1131 Madison Ave., between E. 84th and E. 85th Sts.* ☎ *212/327–4900*) for a fruit tart, vegetarian soup, or steaming bowl of cocoa. If you're willing to pull yourself away from Madison Avenue, the front room of American-style bakeshop **Two Little Red Hens** (✉ *1652 2nd Ave., between E. 85th and E. 86th Sts.* ☎ *212/452–0476*) has a handful of small tables where you can order a latticed pie or a lemon curd-filled, lemon-cream-cheese-frosted cupcake.

CLOSE UP

Department Store Discounts

At a few major department stores visitors from out of town can ring up a special discount as a shopping incentive. If you show identification to prove you live outside New York State, you're eligible for a markdown. Score one for the tourist team!

Bloomingdale's: go to the visitor center on the balcony level between the ground and second floors. With your out-of-town ID you'll get a card for an 11% discount on all purchases

bought that day. You can apply for this card on any given visit.

Lord & Taylor: hit the ground-floor information desk to pick up a coupon for 15% off that day's purchases.

Macy's: stop by the visitor center on the balcony level between the ground and second floors for an out-of-state 10% discount voucher. The coupon is valid for five days for U.S. visitors and one month for international visitors.

Ludivine. If it's being worn in Paris, it's being sold here, from the vibrant string bikinis of Naelie to the draped tunics and nonchalant bags by Vanessa Bruno. Notify denim tosses off a Gallic-rocker look. Most of the lines are French-designed and -made, though a few like-minded Italians have slipped in. ⊠ *172 W. 4th St., between Jones and Cornelia Sts., Greenwich Village* 🕾 *646/336–6576* Ⓜ *1 to Christopher St./Sheridan Sq.* ⊠ *1216 Lexington Ave., between 82nd and 83rd Sts., Upper East Side* 🕾 *212/249–4053* Ⓜ *4, 5, 6 to 86th St.*

Lyell. Browse the racks for enticing vintage—and vintage-inspired—finds like draped silk dresses that would do well for dancing to Benny Goodman. ⊠ *173 Elizabeth St., between Spring and Kenmare Sts., NoLita* 🕾 *212/966–8484* Ⓜ *6 to Spring St.*

★ **Malia Mills.** Fit fanatics have met their match here. Bikini tops and bottoms are sold separately: halters, bandeaus, and triangle tops, plus boy-cut, side-tie, and low-ride bottoms. There are a few one-pieces, too. If you've got a warm-weather honeymoon coming up, you may want the bikini with "Just Married" across your bum. ⊠ *199 Mulberry St., between Spring and Kenmare Sts., NoLita* 🕾 *212/625–2311* Ⓜ *6 to Spring St.* ⊠ *1031 Lexington Ave., at E. 74th St., Upper East Side* 🕾 *212/517–7485* Ⓜ *6 to 77th St.* ⊠ *220 Columbus Ave., at 70th St., Upper West Side* 🕾 *212/874–7200* Ⓜ *B, C to 72nd St.*

Marina Rinaldi. These plus-size tailored suits, hip-slung belts, and sweeping coats know just how to flatter. ⊠ *800 Madison Ave., between E. 67th and E. 68th Sts., Upper East Side* 🕾 *212/734–4333* Ⓜ *6 to 68th St./Hunter College.*

Marni. Weaving among the suspended garments in Marni's first U.S. store, you may fall prey to a hemp-cloth duster jacket, brightly striped cotton trousers, or a coyly creased floral blouse. ⊠ *161 Mercer St., between W. Houston and Prince Sts., SoHo* 🕾 *212/343–3912* Ⓜ *R, W to Prince St.*

Max Mara. Think subtle colors and plush fabrics—straight skirts in cashmere or heathered wool, tuxedo-style evening jackets, and several choices of wool and cashmere camel overcoats. The SoHo location just carries the Sportmax collection. ✉ *813 Madison Ave., at E. 68th St., Upper East Side* ☎ *212/879–6100* Ⓜ *6 to 68th St./Hunter College* ✉ *450 West Broadway, between W. Houston and Prince Sts., SoHo* ☎ *212/674–1817* Ⓜ *C, E to Spring St.*

Michael Kors. In his deft reworkings of American classics, *Project Runway* judge Kors gives sportswear the luxury treatment, as with cream-color cashmere pullovers. An industrial element is creeping in, too, with chunky gold-chain detailing on buttery leather bags and jewelry. At the Soho location you'll also find clothing and accessories from the designer's little sister lines, KORS Michael Kors and MICHAEL Michael Kors. ✉ *974 Madison Ave., at E. 76th St., Upper East Side* ☎ *212/452–4685* Ⓜ *6 to 77th St.* ✉ *101 Prince St., between Mercer and Green Sts., SoHo* ☎ *212/965–0401* Ⓜ *N, R, W to Prince St.*

Miu Miu. Prada front woman Miuccia Prada established a secondary line (bearing her childhood nickname, Miu Miu) to showcase her more experimental ideas. Look for Prada-esque styles in more daring colors and cuts, such as high-waisted skirts with scalloped edges, Peter Pan–collar dresses in trippy patterns, and patent-leather pumps. ✉ *100 Prince St., between Mercer and Greene Sts., SoHo* ☎ *212/334–5156* Ⓜ *R, W to Prince St.* ✉ *11 E. 57th St., between Madison and 5th Aves., Upper East Side* ☎ *212/641–2980* Ⓜ *N, R, W to 59th St.*

Tory Burch. Bright-orange lacquer zings through this space, which, in a reversal of the usual flow, brings uptown downtown. Orange joins navy, flamingo pink, and mossy green on espadrilles, printed cotton blouses, and signature side-split tunics, available in bold prints or with embellished necklines. ✉ *257 Elizabeth St., between E. Houston and Prince Sts., NoLita* ☎ *212/334–3000* Ⓜ *R, W to Prince St.* ✉ *38–40 Little West 12th St., at Washington St., Meatpacking District* ☎ *212/929–0125* Ⓜ *A, C, F, L to 14th St./8th Ave.*

FLIRTY

BCBG/Max Azria. If flirtation's your sport, you'll find your sportswear here: fluttering skirts, beaded camisoles, chiffon dresses, and leather pants fill the racks. ✉ *120 Wooster St., between Prince and Spring Sts., SoHo* ☎ *212/625–2723* Ⓜ *R, W to Prince St.* ✉ *770 Madison Ave., at E. 66th St., Upper East Side* ☎ *212/717–4225* Ⓜ *6 to 68th St./Hunter College.*

Betsey Johnson. The SoHo store departs from the traditional (if such a word can be applied) hot-pink interior; instead its walls are white-washed with painted roses, and there's a bordello-red lounge area in back. Besides the quirkily printed dresses, available in all stores, there's the edgy Archives line. This is not the place for natural fibers—it's ruled by rayon, stretch, and the occasional faux fur. ✉ *138 Wooster St., between Prince and W. Houston Sts., SoHo* ☎ *212/995–5048* Ⓜ *R, W to Prince St.* ✉ *251 E. 60th St., between 2nd and 3rd Aves., Upper East Side* ☎ *212/319–7699* Ⓜ *N, R, W, 4, 5, 6 to 59th St./Lexington Ave.* ✉ *248 Columbus Ave., between W. 71st and W. 72nd Sts., Upper West Side* ☎ *212/362–3364* Ⓜ *1, 2, 3 to 72nd St.* ✉ *1060 Madison Ave.,*

17

between E. 80th and E. 81st Sts., Upper East Side ☎ *212/734–1257* Ⓜ *6 to 77th St.*

Catherine Malandrino. Designs here evoke the flapper era: frothy chiffon dresses with embroidered Empire waists, beaded necklines, and tiny matching fur stoles let you pretend you're Daisy Buchanan. ✉ *468 Broome St., at Greene St., SoHo* ☎ *212/925–6765* Ⓜ *6 to Spring St.* ✉ *652 Hudson St., at W. 13th St., Meatpacking District* ☎ *212/929– 8710* Ⓜ *A, C, E to 14th St.*

Cynthia Rowley. As one half of the *Swell* team, you can expect this designer to be a party-outfit pro. She delivers with such flirty picks as bow-top pumps, swingy, swirly halter dresses with heart-shaped appliqués, and handbags with small inset mirrors, ideal for checking your lipstick. The *Swell* books are on hand, too, natch. ✉ *376 Bleecker St., between Charles and Perry Sts., Greenwich Village* ☎ *212/242–3803* Ⓜ *1 to Christopher St./Sheridan Sq.*

Diane von Furstenberg. Flit through the perennial wrap dresses or tops with a deep-V neckline, some with ruffles along the edge to accentuate the plunge. The space has just a hint of disco, with flecks of mirrors spangling the ceiling. ✉ *874 Washington St., at 14th St., Meatpacking District* ☎ *646/486–4800* Ⓜ *A, C, E to 14th St.*

Morgane Le Fay. The clothes here used to have a sort of billowy, Stevie Nicks quality, but though they're still Renaissance-inspired, the designs are more streamlined. Silk organza gowns have Empire waists and crinkly skirts; fitted velvet jackets have covered buttons. ✉ *980 Madison Ave., between E. 75th and E. 76th Sts., Upper East Side* ☎ *212/879–9700* Ⓜ *6 to 68th St./Hunter College* ✉ *67 Wooster St., between Broome and Spring Sts., SoHo* ☎ *212/219–7672* Ⓜ *C, E to Spring St.*

Nanette Lepore. "Girly" may well be the description that comes to mind as you browse through this cheerful shop; skirts are pleated and adorned with bows, jackets are enhanced by embroidery and floral appliqués, fur shrugs have tiny sleeves. ✉ *958 Madison Ave., between E. 75th and E. 76th Sts., Upper East Side* ☎ *212/452–3056* Ⓜ *6 to 77th St.* ✉ *423 Broome St., between Lafayette and Crosby Sts., NoLita* ☎ *212/219–8265* Ⓜ *6 to Spring St.*

Rebecca Taylor. Subdued hues of taupe, cream, and rose frame the racks of lace-overlay dresses and silk-piped trousers. Appliqués and embroideries add fillips of craftiness. ✉ *260 Mott St., between Prince and W. Houston Sts., NoLita* ☎ *212/966–0406* Ⓜ *6 to Spring St.*

★ **Tracy Reese.** Unabashedly girly garb is Reese's specialty, as she plays with lush fabrics (silk chiffon is a favorite), quirky color combos, and notice-me embellishments like rhinestones and ruffles. The cuts flatter all sorts of figures, often emphasizing the waist. This flagship carries both the ladylike Tracy Reese line and the funkier, lower-price Plenty label. ✉ *641 Hudson St., between Horatio and Gansevoort Sts., Meatpacking District* ☎ *212/807–0505* Ⓜ *A, C, E to 14th St.*

Vivienne Tam. Tam is known for her playful "China chic" take on familiar Asian images. Cold-weather creations in jewel-color silk are embroidered;

the warm-weather clothes are floaty and romantic. ✉ *40 Mercer St., at Grand St., SoHo* ☎ *212/966–2398* Ⓜ *R, W to Prince St.*

HAUTE DESIGN

Alexander McQueen. No matter how flouncy the late McQueen's ensembles became, they retained idiosyncratic, unsettling elements. Delicate, floaty dresses might be printed with eagles; fitted pantsuits could be juxtaposed with stiff leather corsets or Victorian lace. ✉ *417 W. 14th St., between 9th and 10th Aves., Meatpacking District* ☎ *212/645–1797* Ⓜ *A, C, E to 14th St.*

Balenciaga. Nicolas Ghesquière, a current *amour fou* in the fashion world, took a page from the neighboring galleries for the first U.S. store. His clothing's not always the most wearable, but it's always stimulating. You might luck onto a reissue from the (Cristobal) Balenciaga archives, made up in modern fabrics. The stash of more accessible handbags and shoes is worth a browse. ✉ *542 W. 22nd St., between 10th and 11th Aves., Chelsea* ☎ *212/206–0872* Ⓜ *C, E to 23rd St.*

Carolina Herrera. This couture deserves a truly outstanding occasion; the beading and sequin work are stunning. Expect anything from demure, shimmering bands of decoration to knockout swaths of beaded lace. ✉ *954 Madison Ave., at E. 75th St., Upper East Side* ☎ *212/249–6552* Ⓜ *6 to 77th St.*

Chanel. The Midtown flagship has often been compared to a Chanel suit—slim, elegant, and timeless. Inside wait the famed suits themselves, along with other pillars of Chanel style: chic little black dresses and evening gowns, chain handled bags, and yards of pearls. Downtown's branch concentrates on more contemporary forays, including ski gear, while Madison's boutique is dedicated to shoes, handbags, and other accessories. The jewelry outpost gleams with showstopper pieces based on Chanel's own jewels, as well as stars and comets sparkling with diamonds and gold worked into a quilted design. ✉ *139 Spring St., at Wooster St., SoHo* ☎ *212/334–0055* Ⓜ *C, E to Spring St.* ✉ *15 E. 57th St., between 5th and Madison Aves., Midtown East* ☎ *212/355–5050* Ⓜ *N, R, W to 5th Ave./59th St.* ✉ *737 Madison Ave., at E. 64th St., Upper East Side* ☎ *212/535–5505* Ⓜ *6 to 68th St./Hunter College* ✉ *Chanel Fine Jewelry, 733 Madison Ave., at E. 64th St., Upper East Side* ☎ *212/535–5828* Ⓜ *6 to 68th St./Hunter College.*

★ **Kirna Zabête.** A heavy-hitting lineup of prestigious designers—Balenciaga, Alexander Wang, Lanvin, Proenza Schouler—is managed with an exceptionally cheerful flair. Step downstairs for dog apparel, French Bull home accessories, and hip infant gear from Kit and Lili. ✉ *96 Greene St., between Spring and Prince Sts., SoHo* ☎ *212/941–9656* Ⓜ *R, W to Prince St.*

O.M.O. Norma Kamali. A fashion fixture from the 1980s has a newly modern, though still '80s-influenced, line. Her luminously white store carries bold black-and-white-patterned bathing suits, slinky separates in velvet and jersey, and poofy "sleeping-bag coats." You can also choose from a selection of skin-care products, olive oils, and fragrances. ✉ *11 W. 56th St., between 5th and 6th Aves., Midtown West* ☎ *212/957–9797* Ⓜ *E, V to 5th Ave./53rd St.*

17

Oscar de la Renta. The ladylike yet lighthearted runway designs of this upper-crust favorite got their first U.S. store here. Skirts swing, ruffles billow, embroidery brightens up tweed, and even a tennis dress looks like something you could go dancing in. ⊠ *772 Madison Ave., at E. 66th St., Upper East Side* ☎ *212/288–5810* Ⓜ *6 to 68th St./Hunter College.*

Philosophy di Alberta Ferretti. The designer's eye for delicate detailing is evident in the perforated hemlines, embroidered stitching, and sprinkling of beads across gauzy fabrics or soft knits. ⊠ *452 West Broadway, between W. Houston and Prince Sts., SoHo* ☎ *212/460–5500* Ⓜ *F, V to Broadway–Lafayette St.*

★ **Stella McCartney.** A devout vegetarian setting up shop in the Meatpacking District may seem odd, but it's further proof that chic trumps many other considerations. You could put together an outfit of head-to-toe satin or chiffon, but it's more in keeping to mix it with shredded denim or a pair of knee-high Ultrasuede cowboy boots (since leather is verboten, shoes and accessories come in satin, canvas, and synthetics). The dressing rooms are so beautiful you might just want to move in. ⊠ *429 W. 14th St., between 9th and 10th Aves., Meatpacking District* ☎ *212/255–1556* Ⓜ *A, C, E to 14th St.*

Vera Wang. Though practically synonymous with made-to-order, modern-princess bridal gowns, Wang's also a star at evening wear. Her gowns manage to pull off vintage-inspired shapes (mermaid sheaths, portrait necklines) and lots of satin, beading, and embroidery while still looking elegantly streamlined. Periodic prêt-à-porter sales offer the dresses for a (relative) song. A second store in SoHo, at 158 Mercer Street has also recently opened; it stocks the ready-to-wear lines. ⊠ *991 Madison Ave., at E. 77th St., Upper East Side* ☎ *212/628–3400* Ⓜ *6 to 77th St.* ⊠ *158 Mercer St., between Prince and W. Houston Sts., SoHo* ☎ *212/382–2184* Ⓜ *N, R, W to Prince St.*

DEPARTMENT STORES

Most department stores keep regular hours on weekdays and are open late (until 8 or 9) at least one night a week. Many have personal shoppers who can walk you through the store at no charge, as well as concierges who will answer all manner of questions. Some have restaurants or cafés that offer decent meals and pick-me-up snacks.

Fodor'sChoice
★
Barneys New York. Barneys continues to provide fashion-conscious and big-budget shoppers with irresistible, must-have items at its uptown flagship store. The extensive menswear selection has a handful of edgier designers, though made-to-measure is always available. The women's department showcases posh designers of all stripes, from the subdued lines of Armani and Jil Sander to the irrepressible Alaïa and Zac Posen. The shoe selection trots out Prada boots and strappy Blahniks; the cosmetics department will keep you in Kiehl's, Sue Devitt, and Gendarme; jewelry runs from the whimsical (Mark Davis) to the classic (Ileana Makri). Expanded versions of the less expensive **Co-op** department occupy the old Barneys' warehouse space on West 18th Street and a niche on Wooster Street. ⊠ *660 Madison Ave., between E. 60th and E. 61st*

Sts., Upper East Side ☎ *212/826–8900* Ⓜ *N, R, W, 4, 5, 6 to 59th St./Lexington Ave.* ✉ *Barneys Co-op, 236 W. 18th St., between 7th and 8th Aves., Chelsea* ☎ *212/593–7800* Ⓜ *A, C, E to 14th St.* ✉ *116 Wooster St., between Prince and Spring Sts., SoHo* ☎ *212/965–9964* Ⓜ *R, W to Prince St.*

Bergdorf Goodman. Good taste reigns in an elegant and understated setting, but remember that elegant doesn't necessarily mean sedate.

Bergdorf's carries some brilliant lines, such as Marchesa, Narciso Rodriguez, and Carmen Marc Valvo. In the basement Level of Beauty, find a seat in the manicure–pedicure lounge (no appointments) for a bit of impromptu pampering. The home department has rooms full of magnificent linens, tableware, and gifts. Across the street is another entire store devoted to menswear: made-to-measure shirts, custom suits, designer lines by the likes of Ralph Lauren and Gucci, and scads of accessories, from hip flasks to silk scarves. ✉ *754 5th Ave., between W. 57th and W. 58th Sts., Midtown West* ✉ *Men's store, 745 5th Ave., at 58th St., Midtown East* ☎ *212/753–7300* Ⓜ *N, R, W to 5th Ave./59th St.*

Bloomingdale's. Only a few stores in New York occupy an entire city block; the uptown branch of this New York institution is one of them. The main floor is a crazy, glittery maze of mirrored cosmetic counters and perfume-spraying salespeople. Once you get past this dizzying scene, you can find good buys on designer clothes, bedding, and housewares. The downtown location is smaller, and has a well-edited, higher-end selection of merchandise, so you can focus your search for that Michael Kors handbag or pricey pair of stilettos. ✉ *1000 3rd Ave., main entrance at E. 59th St. and Lexington Ave., Midtown East* ☎ *212/705–2000* Ⓜ *N, R, W, 4, 5, 6 to 59th St./Lexington Ave.* ✉ *504 Broadway, between Spring and Broome Sts., SoHo* ☎ *212/729–5900* Ⓜ *R, W to Prince St.*

Fodor's Choice
★
Century 21. For many New Yorkers this downtown fixture—right across the street from the former World Trade Center site—remains the mother lode of discount shopping. Four floors are crammed with everything from Gucci sunglasses and half-price cashmere sweaters to Ralph Lauren towels, though you'll have to weed through racks of less fabulous stuff to find that gem. The best bets in the men's department are shoes and the designer briefs; the full floor of designer women's wear can yield some dazzling finds, such as a Calvin Klein leather trench coat for less than $600 or a sweeping crinoline skirt from Jean Paul Gaultier. ■**TIP**➔ Since lines for the communal dressing rooms can be prohibitively long, you might want to wear a bodysuit under your clothes for quick, between-the-racks try-ons. ✉ *22 Cortlandt St., between Broadway and Church St., Lower Manhattan* ☎ *212/227–9092* Ⓜ *R, W to Cortlandt St.*

17

THE MEATPACKING DISTRICT

For nearly a century, this industrial western edge of downtown Manhattan was defined by slaughterhouses and meatpacking plants, blood-splattered cobblestoned streets, and men lugging carcasses into warehouses way before dawn.

But in the late 1990s the area between West 14th Street, Gansevoort Street, Hudson Street, and 11th Avenue speedily transformed into another kind of meat market. Many of the old warehouses now house ultrachic shops, nightclubs, and restaurants packed with angular fashionistas. Jeffrey, a pint-size department store, was an early arrival, followed by edgy but established designers like Stella McCartney and a few lofty furniture stores. Despite the influx of a few chains—albeit stylish ones like Scoop—eclectic boutiques keep popping up. The one thing it's hard to find here is a bargain. —J.P.

BEST TIME TO GO

Wednesday through Friday afternoons. Most stores are open daily, but a few are closed Monday and Tuesday. On weekends some stores stay open until 7 or 8 PM, overlapping with the overeager nightlife crowd.

BEST SOUVENIR FOR YOUR GIRLFRIEND (OR BOHO AUNT)

Necklaces strung with candy-color vintage glass beads from **Auto** (✉ *803 and 805 Washington St., at Horatio St.* ☎ *212/229-2292*), a boutique focusing on New York–based jewelry designers.

BEST FOR

FABULOUS FROCKS
Jeffrey: culls the coolest outfits from high-end labels.

Alexander McQueen: impeccably tailored, take-no-prisoners style.

Catherine Malandrino: romantic chiffon and swingy layers, at more-reasonable prices.

DENIM
Earnest Sewn (✉ *821 Washington St.* ☎ *212/242–3414*) : customize the cut, buttons, and pockets of your cult jeans.

DDC Lab: high-tech yet earthy, with vegetable indigo dyes, hand-scratching, and sometimes a dash of Lycra.

KILLER ACCESSORIES
Ten Thousand Things: unusual stones in delicate, handwrought settings.

La Perla: the most minxy outpost for this brand's lace lingerie.

Christian Louboutin: vampy heels with telltale crimson soles.

17

REFUELING

Hit the buzzing bistro **Pastis** (✉ *9 9th Ave., at Little W. 12th St.* ☎ *212/929–4844*) for a croque monsieur, a bracing coffee, or a cocktail with the namesake hooch. For a quicker stop, follow the smell of grilled meat to **Pop Burger** (✉ *58–60 9th Ave., between 14th and 15th Sts.* ☎ *212/414–8686*). The mini burgers are tempting, but locals swear by the sides: crispy fries and thick-as-cement milkshakes.

Henri Bendel. Behind the graceful Lalique windows you'll discover a mecca of niche boutiques stocking mostly beauty and accessories. Bendel's dedication to the unusual begins in the ground-floor cosmetics area and percolates through the floors of women's lingerie and add-ons like jewelry, scarves, and sunglasses. Designers such as Alice + Olivia, Michael Kors, Matthew Williamson, and Milly have room to breathe here. Bendel's in-house lines, which include the signature cashmeres and brown-and-white dopp kits, are displayed throughout. This isn't a fully comprehensive store, though; for instance, there is no true shoe department. ⊠ *712 5th Ave., between W. 55th and W. 56th Sts., Midtown West* ☎ *212/247–1100* Ⓜ *E, V to 5th Ave./53rd St.*

Lord & Taylor. Comfortably conservative and never overwhelming, Lord & Taylor is a stronghold of classic American designer clothes. Instead of unpronounceable labels, you can find Ellen Tracy, Jones New York, and a lot of casual wear. The store tends to attract an older, decidedly untrendy crowd. It also has a large selection of reasonably priced full-length gowns. ⊠ *424 5th Ave., between W. 38th and W. 39th Sts., Midtown West* ☎ *212/391–3344* Ⓜ *B, D, F, N, Q, R, V, W to 34th St./Herald Sq.*

Macy's. Macy's headquarters store claims to be the largest retail store in America; expect to lose your bearings at least once. Fashion-wise, there's a concentration on the mainstream rather than on the luxe. One strong suit is denim, with everything from Hilfiger and Calvin Klein to Earl Jeans and Paper Denim & Cloth. There's also a reliably good selection of American designs from Ralph Lauren, DKNY, and Sean John. For cooking gear and housewares, the Cellar nearly outdoes Zabar's. ⊠ *Herald Sq., 151 W. 34th St., between 6th and 7th Aves., Midtown West* ☎ *212/695–4400* Ⓜ *B, D, F, N, Q, R, V, W to 34th St./Herald Sq.*

★   **Pearl River Mart**. If you want to redecorate your entire apartment with a Chinese theme for less than $1,000, this is the place to do it. Every Asian-style furnishing, houseware, and trinket can be found here, from bamboo rice steamers and ceramic tea sets to paper lanterns and grinning wooden Buddha statues. On the main floor, under a ceiling festooned with dragon kites and rice-paper parasols, you can buy kimono-style robes, pajamas, and embroidered satin slippers for the whole family. There's also a dry-goods section, where you can load up on packages of ginger candy, jasmine tea, and cellophane noodles. ⊠ *477 Broadway, between Broome and Grand Sts., SoHo* ☎ *212/431–4770* Ⓜ *N, R, Q, W to Canal St.*

Saks Fifth Avenue. A fashion- and beauty-only department store, Saks sells an astonishing array of clothing. The choice of American and European designers is impressive without being esoteric—the women's selection includes Gucci, Narciso Rodriguez, and Marc Jacobs, plus devastating ball gowns galore. The footwear collections are gratifyingly broad, from Ferragamo to Juicy. In the men's department, sportswear stars such as John Varvatos counterbalance formal wear and current trends. The ground-floor beauty department stocks everything from the classic (Sisley, Lancôme, La Prairie) to the fun and edgy (Nars,

M.A.C.). ⊠ *611 5th Ave., between E. 49th and E. 50th Sts., Midtown East* ☎ *212/753–4000* Ⓜ *E, V to 5th Ave./53rd St.*

Takashimaya New York. This pristine branch of Japan's largest department store carries stylish accessories and fine household items, all of which reflect a combination of Eastern and Western designs. There's also a lovely basement-level tearoom, top-floor floral section, and an expanded children's department store anchored by a merry-go-round and a high-design playhouse. ⊠ *693 5th Ave., between E. 54th and E. 55th Sts., Midtown East* ☎ *212/350–0100* Ⓜ *E, V to 5th Ave./53rd St.*

HOME DECOR

Fodor'sChoice **ABC Carpet & Home.** ABC seems to cover most of the furnishings alpha-
★ bet; over several floors it encompasses everything from rustic furniture to 19th-century repros, refinished Chinese chests, and Vitra chairs, not to mention that loose category "country French." The ground floor teems with a treasure-attic's worth of accessories. Two restaurants offer places to refuel. Rugs and carpets are unrolled across the street at 881 Broadway. ⊠ *888 Broadway, at E. 19th St., Flatiron District* ☎ *212/473–3000* Ⓜ *L, N, Q, R, W, 4, 5, 6 to 14th St./Union Sq.*

Armani Casa. In keeping with the Armani aesthetic, the minimalist furniture and home wares have a subdued color scheme (gold, grays, black, and a crimson accent here and there). You might find lacquered ebony-stain boxes, square-cut porcelain bowls and plates, or silky linens and pillows. ⊠ *97 Greene St., between Prince and Spring Sts., SoHo* ☎ *212/334–1271* Ⓜ *R, W to Prince St.*

Clio. Take a shortcut to find the accessories you've seen in the shelter mags. This boutique sets its table with delicate Czech glass vases, bone china with raised dots, and colorful handblown glass bottles. ⊠ *92 Thompson St., between Prince and Spring Sts., SoHo* ☎ *212/966–8991* Ⓜ *C, E to Spring St.*

★ **The Conran Shop.** The small glass pavilion beneath the 59th Street Bridge caps this British stylemonger's vast underground showroom of kitchen and garden implements, fabrics, furniture, and glassware. Even the shower curtains are cool. ⊠ *407 E. 59th St., at 1st Ave., Midtown East* ☎ *212/755–9079* Ⓜ *N, R, W, 4, 5, 6 to 59th St./Lexington Ave.*

★ **de Vera.** The objets d'art here all seem to have stories behind them. Many are antique and hint of colonial travels: Indian carvings, Japanese lacquer boxes, 19th-century British earrings. Others exemplify modern forms of traditional workmanship, such as the Murano glass vases or incredibly lifelike glass insects. ⊠ *1 Crosby St., at Howard St., SoHo* ☎ *212/625–0838* Ⓜ *N, Q, R, W, 6 to Canal St.*

Design Within Reach. "An interesting plainness is the most difficult and precious thing to achieve" reads one of the quotes discreetly placed on the walls here. You can get a lot closer to Mies van der Rohe's ideal with these tasteful mid-20th-century pieces, such as Noguchi's paper column lamps and Eero Saarinen's womb ottoman, plus contemporary furnishings in the same spirit, such as Jesús Gasca's beech "globus" chair. ⊠ *408 W. 14th St., at 9th Ave., Meatpacking District*

17

☎ 212/242–9449 Ⓜ A, C, E to 14th St. ✉ 142 Wooster St., between Prince and W. Houston Sts., SoHo ☎ 212/471–0280 Ⓜ F, V to Broadway-Lafayette ✉ 110 Greene St., between Prince and Spring Sts., SoHo ☎ 212/475–0001 Ⓜ F, V to Broadway–Lafayette ✉ 27 E. 62nd St., between Park and Madison Aves., Upper East Side ☎ 212/888–4539 Ⓜ N, R, W, 4, 5, 6 to 59th St./ Lexington Ave. ✉ 124 Hudson St.,

between Beach and N. Moore Sts., TriBeCa ☎ 212/219–2217 Ⓜ 1 to Franklin St. ✉ 341 Columbus Ave., at W. 76th St., Upper West Side ☎ 212/799–5900 Ⓜ 1, 2, 3 to 72nd St. ✉ 903 Broadway, at 20th St., Flatrion ☎ 212/477–1155 Ⓜ N, R, W to 23rd St.

Fishs Eddy. The dishes, china, and glassware for resale come from all walks of crockery life, from corporate dining rooms to failed restaurants. New wares often look retro, such as a service with a ticker-tape border. They also stock lots of oddball pieces, such as finger bowls. ✉ 889 Broadway, at E. 19th St., Flatiron District ☎ 212/420–9020 Ⓜ L, N, Q, R, W, 4, 5, 6 to 14th St./Union Sq.

Jonathan Adler. Adler gets mid-20th-century-modern—and modernist— styles to lighten up with his striped, striated, or curvy handmade pottery (ranging from a $30 vase to a chunky $400 lamp) as well as the hand-loomed wool pillow covers, rugs, and throws with blunt graphics (stripes, crosses, circles). ✉ 47 Greene St., between Broome and Grand Sts., SoHo ☎ 212/941–8950 Ⓜ N, Q, R, W, 6 to Canal St. ✉ 37 Greenwich Ave., at Charles St., Greenwich Village ☎ 212/488–2803 Ⓜ 1 to Christopher St./Sheridan Sq. ✉ 304 Columbus Ave., at 74th St., Upper West Side ☎ 212/787–0017 Ⓜ 1, 2, 3 to 72nd St. ✉ 1097 Madison Ave., at 83rd St., Upper East Side ☎ 212/772–2410 Ⓜ 4, 5, 6 to 86th St.

Kiosk. Is it a gallery or a boutique? Duck under the neon arrow sign, head up the stairway, and you'll come upon this novelty shop–cum–art installation. The owners travel the globe in search of locally unique, interestingly designed or packaged items, then sell their gleanings at this outpost. A new destination is highlighted every few months. You might find wooden rattles from Vermont, beeswax crayons from Finland, or lavender from Provence. ✉ 95 Spring St., 2nd fl., at Broadway, SoHo ☎ 212/226–8601 Ⓜ R, W to Prince St.

Fodor'sChoice
★

Moss. International designers put a fantastic spin on even the most utilitarian objects, which are carefully brought together by Murray Moss at his store–cum–design museum. The latest innovations from Jasper Morrison, Ted Muehling, and Philippe Starck are interspersed with classic Baccarat and Lobmeyr crystal and limited-edition studio works from Dutch designers Studio Job and Maarten Baas. The neighboring Moss Gallery spotlights work that's even more arty. ✉ 150 Greene St., between W. Houston and Prince Sts., SoHo ☎ 212/204–7100 Ⓜ R, W to Prince St.

★ **Muji.** If you're into simple, chic, cheap style, Muji will be your trifecta. The name of this Japanese import translates to "no brand" and indeed, you won't find a logo plastered on the housewares or clothes. Instead, their hallmark is streamlined, often monochrome design. The whole range of goods, from milky porcelain teapots to wooden toys, is invariably user-friendly. At the Midtown branch you can glimpse the lobby of the *New York Times.* ✉ *455 Broadway, at Grand St., SoHo* ☎ *212/334–2002* Ⓜ *N, Q, R, W to Canal St.* ✉ *16 W. 19th St., between 5th and 6th Aves., Chelsea* ☎ *212/414–9024* Ⓜ *1 to 18th St; R to 22nd St.* ✉ *620 8th Ave., at W. 40th St., Midtown West* ☎ *212/382–2300* Ⓜ *A, C, E to 42nd St./Port Authority.*

Mxyplyzyk. Hard to pronounce (*mixy plit sick*) and hard to resist, this is a trove of impulse buys—creative riffs on household standbys such as dishes (made from colorful drinking straws), handbags (fashioned to look like boccie balls), and toothbrush holders (shaped like giant teeth). ✉ *125 Greenwich Ave., at W. 13th St., Greenwich Village* ☎ *212/989–4300* Ⓜ *A, C, E, L to 14th St./8th Ave.*

★ **Olatz.** The wife and muse of painter Julian, Olatz Schnabel modeled her linen shop on a historic Havana pharmacy after the couple visited Cuba. The black-and white checkerboard floors and mint-green walls breathe a sort of lazy, faded elegance, a spot-on backdrop to her collection of luxurious sheets, blankets, and pajama sets, all of which have sky-high thread counts and are bordered with bold stripes or intricate damask embroidery. ✉ *43 Clarkson St., between Hudson and Greenwich Sts., Greenwich Village* ☎ *212/255–8627* Ⓜ *1 to Houston St.*

17

Pylones. Even the most utilitarian items get a goofy, colorful makeover from this French company. Toasters and thermoses are coated in stripes or flowers, hairbrushes have pictures of frogs or ladybugs on their backs, and whisks are reimagined as squid. ■**TIP→** There are plenty of fun gifts for less than $20, such as old-fashioned robot toys and candy-color boxes. ✉ *69 Spring St., between Crosby and Lafayette Sts., SoHo* ☎ *212/431–3244* Ⓜ *6 to Spring St.*

William-Wayne & Co. Silver julep cups, Viennese playing cards, butler's trays, candelabras made from coral, and other whimsical decorative items all vie for your attention at this shop. ✉ *40 University Pl., at E. 9th St., Greenwich Village* ☎ *212/533–4711* Ⓜ *6 to Astor Pl.* ✉ *846 Lexington Ave., at E. 64th St., Upper East Side* ☎ *212/737–8934* Ⓜ *6 to 68th St./Hunter College* ✉ *850 Lexington Ave., at E. 64th St., Upper East Side* ☎ *212/288–9243* Ⓜ *6 to 68th St./Hunter College.*

JEWELRY

FOR EVERY DAY

Alexis Bittar. Bittar began selling his first jewelry line, made from Depression-era glass, on a corner in SoHo. Now the Brooklyn-born designer has multiple Manhattan stores showcasing his hand-sculpted and hand-painted treasures. He makes clean-lined, big-statement jewelry from vermeil, colored Lucite, pearls, and vintage glass. The stores mirror this aesthetic with a mix of old and new, like antiqued white Victorian-era lion's claw tables and Plexiglass walls. ⊠ *465 Broome St., between Mercer and Greene Sts., SoHo* ☎ *212/625–8340* Ⓜ *R, W to Prince St.* ⊠ *353 Bleecker St., between Charles and Christopher Sts., West Village* ☎ *212/727–1093* Ⓜ *1 to Christopher St./Sheridan Sq.*

Beads of Paradise. Browse a rich selection of African trade-bead necklaces, earrings, and rare artifacts. You can also choose from troves of semi-precious and natural beads to create your own designs. ⊠ *16 E. 17th St., between 5th Ave. and Broadway, Flatiron District* ☎ *212/620– 0642* Ⓜ *4, 5, 6, N, Q, R, W to 14th St./Union Sq.*

Dinosaur Designs. Translucent and colorful, this antipodean work uses an untraditional medium: resin. Some resins look like semiprecious stone, such as onyx or jade; the rest delve into stronger colors like aqua or crimson. Cruise the stacks of chunky bangles and cuffs or rows of rings; prices start at $50. There's some striking tableware, too. ⊠ *250 Mott St., between Prince and E. Houston Sts., NoLita* ☎ *212/680–3523* Ⓜ *R, W to Prince St.*

★ **Fragments**. This spot glitters with pieces by nimble new jewelry designers, many of them local. Most use semiprecious stones—you could try on turquoise-bead shoulder-duster earrings, an oversize opal ring, or a tourmaline pendant—but a few bust out the sapphires and rubies. ⊠ *116 Prince St., between Greene and Wooster Sts., SoHo* ☎ *212/334– 9588* Ⓜ *R, W to Prince St.*

Me&Ro. Eastern styling has gained these designers a cult following. The Indian-inspired, hand-finished gold bangles and earrings covered with tiny dangling rubies, sapphires, or brown diamonds may look bohemian, but most of the prices target the trust-fund set. Sterling Silver starts at $150. ⊠ *241 Elizabeth St., between Prince and E. Houston Sts., NoLita* ☎ *917/237–9215* Ⓜ *R, W to Prince St.*

Robert Lee Morris. Gold and silver take on bold, sculptural shapes here: cuff bracelets are chunky but fluidly curved, and necklaces and earrings have dangling hammered disks for a "wind chime" effect. Some pieces incorporate diamonds; others have semiprecious stones like turquoise or citrine. ⊠ *400 West Broadway, between Broome and Spring Sts., SoHo* ☎ *212/431–9405* Ⓜ *C, E to Spring St.*

Stuart Moore. Many of the Teutonic designs are minimalist, almost industrial-seeming: diamonds are set in brushed platinum, and some rings and cuff links have a geometric, architectural aesthetic. Pieces here tend to be modest in scale. ⊠ *411 West Broadway, at Spring St., SoHo* ☎ *212/941–1023* Ⓜ *A, C, E to Spring St.*

Fodor'sChoice **Ten Thousand Things**. You might find yourself wishing for 10,000 things ★ from the showcases in this gallerylike space. Designs run from thin gold and silver chains to bold resin pieces. Many shapes are abstract reflections of natural forms, like buttercups or seedpods. Unusual stones beckon from the glass cases, such as the pendants of purple rubies or labradorites. ⊠ *423 W. 14th St., between 9th and 10th Aves., Meatpacking District* ☎ *212/352–1333* Ⓜ *A, C, E to 14th St.*

Versani. Silver teams up with all kinds of materials here: leather, denim, and snakeskin, as well as semiprecious stones. There's a good selection of silver rings and pendants under $50. ✉ *152 Mercer St., between Prince and W. Houston Sts., SoHo* ☎ *212/941–7770* Ⓜ *R, W to Prince St.* ✉ *227 Mulberry St., between Prince and Spring Sts., NoLita* ☎ *212/431–4944* Ⓜ *6 to Spring St.*

MONEY'S NO OBJECT

A La Vieille Russie. Stop here to behold bibelots by Fabergé and others, enameled or encrusted with jewels. ✉ *781 5th Ave., at E. 59th St., Midtown East* ☎ *212/752–1727* Ⓜ *N, R, W to 5th Ave./59th St.*

Asprey. Its net spreads to cater to all kinds of luxury tastes, from leather goods and rare books to polo equipment and cashmere sweaters. Asprey's claim to fame, though, is jewelry; its own eponymous diamond cut has A-shaped facets. ✉ *853 Madison Ave., between 70th and 71st Sts., Upper East Side* ☎ *212/688–1811* Ⓜ *6 to 68th St./Hunter College.*

Bulgari. This Italian company is certainly not shy about its name, which encircles gems, watch faces, and an ever-growing accessories line. There are beautiful, weighty rings, pieces mixing gold with stainless steel or porcelain, the brand's signature cabochon multi-colored sapphires, and the latest Serpenti collection of coiled jewels and watches meant to resemble gold snakes flecked with diamonds. ✉ *730 5th Ave., at W. 57th St., Midtown West* ☎ *212/315–9000* Ⓜ *N, R, W to 5th Ave.*

Fred Leighton. If you're in the market for vintage diamonds, this is the place, whether your taste is for tiaras, Art Deco settings, or sparklers once worn by a Vanderbilt. ✉ *773 Madison Ave., at E. 66th St., Upper East Side* ☎ *212/288–1872* Ⓜ *6 to 68th St./Hunter College.*

H. Stern. Sleek designs pose in an equally modern 5th Avenue setting; smooth cabochon-cut stones, most from South America, glow in pale wooden display cases. The designers make notable use of semiprecious stones such as citrine, tourmaline, and topaz. ✉ *645 5th Ave., between E. 51st and E. 52nd Sts., Midtown East* ☎ *212/688–0300* Ⓜ *E, V to 5th Ave./53rd St.*

Ivanka Trump. Compared to the style of Trump *père*, this small jewelry boutique is quite discreet. All things being relative, though, The Donald's daughter would like to see you dripping with her diamonds. Drop earrings, briolette tassels, and lots of icy rings are shown in an unstuffy yet glam salon. ✉ *685 Madison Ave., between E. 61st and E. 62nd Sts., Midtown East* ☎ *212/756–9912* Ⓜ *N, R, W, 4, 5, 6 to 59th St./Lexington Ave.*

Mikimoto. The Japanese originator of the cultured pearl, Mikimoto presents a glowing display of high-luster pearls. Besides the creamy strands from their own pearl farms, check out the dazzlingly colored South Sea pearls, dramatic black-lip and silver-lip varieties, and rare conch pearls. ✉ *730 5th Ave., between W. 56th and W. 57th Sts., Midtown West* ☎ *212/457–4600* Ⓜ *F to 57th St.*

NEW YORK CLASSICS

Cartier. Pierre Cartier allegedly won the 5th Avenue mansion location by trading two strands of perfectly matched natural pearls with Mrs. Morton Plant. The jewelry is still incredibly persuasive, from such

17

LOWER EAST SIDE

Once home to multitudes of Jewish immigrants from Russia and Eastern Europe, the Lower East Side has traditionally been New Yorkers' bargain beat. The center of it all is Orchard Street, where vendors still holler, "Lady, have I got a deal for you!"

Here tiny, no-nonsense clothing stores and scrappy stalls hang on to the past, while funky local designers gradually claim more turf. A few cool vintage clothing and furniture spots bridge the two camps. Ludlow Street, one block east of Orchard, has become the main drag for twentysomethings with attitude, its boutiques wedged in between bars and low-key restaurants. Anything too polished is looked on with suspicion—and that goes for you, too. For the full scope of this area, prowl from Allen to Essex streets, south of East Houston Street down to Broome Street. A tip: wear closed shoes to stay clear of broken glass and other crud on the sidewalks. —J.P.

BEST TIME TO GO

Come on a Sunday afternoon, when Orchard Street between East Houston and Delancey streets becomes a vehicle-free pedestrian zone. On Saturday the old-school stores close for the Jewish Sabbath.

BEST SOUVENIR FOR YOUR FAVE KITCHEN AIDE

Raid the **Lower East Side Tenement Museum** gift shop (⊠ *108 Orchard St., between Delancey and Broome Sts.* ☎ *212/982–8420*) for a cheery reproduction 1950 Empire State souvenir kitchen towel and some retro fridge magnets with skyscrapers trumpeting "New York the Wonder City."

17

BEST FOR

VINTAGE
Edith Machinist: big names from the 1970s and '80s, whopping shoulder pads, and often hefty price tags.

Las Venus: Danish modern furniture, princess phones, boomerang ashtrays in punchy colors.

CLOTHES WITH BITE
TG-170: rock-chick wardrobe staples like superdark, tight jeans and tough Freitag bags.

Foley & Corinna: mixes vintage-y new clothes with the truly vintage.

OLD-WORLD FOOD
Russ & Daughters (⊠ 179 E. Houston St. at 1st Ave.): smoked salmon, pickled herring, and babka, oh my.

The Pickle Guys (⊠ 49 Essex St. ☎ 212/656–9739) : move beyond the half-sours to the zingy full-sour and horseradish pickle spears.

REFUELING

Get your calcium with a stop at **il laboratorio del gelato** (⊠ 95 Orchard St., between Delancey and Broome Sts. ☎ 212/343–9922) for creamy scoops in unusual flavors like nutmeg, ricotta, or ginger. Cake with your gelato? Zip to **Sugar Sweet Sunshine** (⊠ 126 Rivington St., between Essex and Norfolk Sts. ☎ 212/995–1960), a homey little bakery where you can nibble on a cupcake with chocolate-almond frosting or a slice of red velvet cake.

CLOSE UP

Holiday Markets

Between Thanksgiving and Christmas, holiday markets—rows of wooden stalls, many with red-and-white-stripe awnings—spring up around town. The gifts and goods vary from year to year, but there are some perennial offerings: colorful handmade knitwear and jewelry; sweet-smelling soaps, candles, and lotions with hand-lettered labels; glittery Christmas ornaments of every stripe; and New York–theme gift items (a group called Gritty City offers T-shirts, coin purses, and undies printed with pictures of taxicabs and manhole covers).

Though the holiday market in **Grand Central Terminal's Vanderbilt Hall** is indoors, most vendors set up outside. There's one every year at **Columbus Circle,** near the southwest entrance to Central Park, and another at **Bryant Park,** behind the New York City Public Library. The largest and most popular, however, is at the south end of **Union Square,** where you can go from the greenmarket to the stalls like the downtowners who meet in the afternoon or after work to look for unique or last-minute gifts.

established favorites as the interlocking rings to the more recent additions such as the handcufflike Menotte bracelets. ⊠ *653 5th Ave., at E. 52nd St., Midtown East* ☎ *212/753–0111* Ⓜ *E, V to 5th Ave./53rd St.* ⊠ *828 Madison Ave., at E. 69th St., Upper East Side* ☎ *212/472–6400* Ⓜ *6 to 68th St./Hunter College.*

Harry Winston. Ice-clear diamonds of impeccable quality sparkle in Harry Winston's inner sanctum. They're set in everything from emerald-cut solitaire rings to wreath necklaces resembling strings of flowers. No wonder the jeweler was immortalized in the song "Diamonds Are a Girl's Best Friend." ⊠ *718 5th Ave., at W. 56th St., Midtown West* ☎ *212/245–2000* Ⓜ *F to 57th St.*

Fodor's Choice ★ **Tiffany & Co.** The display windows can be soigné, funny, or just plain breathtaking. Alongside the $80,000 platinum-and-diamond bracelets, a lot here is affordable on a whim (check out the sterling silver floor)—and everything comes wrapped in that unmistakable Tiffany blue. ⊠ *727 5th Ave., at E. 57th St., Midtown East* ☎ *212/755–8000* Ⓜ *N, R, W to 5th Ave./59th St.* ⊠ *37 Wall St., between Broad and William Sts., Lower Manhattan* ☎ *212/514–8015* Ⓜ *2, 3 to Wall St.*

LINGERIE

Agent Provocateur. The bustiest mannequins in Manhattan vamp in the front window of this British underpinnings phenom. Showpieces include boned corsets, lace sets with contrast-color trim, bottoms tied with satin ribbons, and a few fetish-type leather ensembles. A great selection of stockings is complemented by the garter belts to secure them. ⊠ *133 Mercer St., between Prince and Spring Sts., SoHo* ☎ *212/965–0229* Ⓜ *R, W to Prince St.*

★ **Bra Smyth.** Chic and sweetly sexy French and Canadian underthings in soft cottons and silks line the shelves of this Uptown staple. In addition to the selection of bridal-ready white bustiers and custom-fit swimsuits (made, cleverly, in bra-cup sizes), the store is best known for its knowledgeable staff, many of whom can offer tips on proper fit and size you up on sight. Cup sizes run from AA to H. ✉ *905 Madison Ave., at 73rd St., Upper East Side* ☎ *212/772–9400* Ⓜ *6 to 68th St./Hunter College* ✉ *2177 Broadway, at 77th St., Upper West Side* ☎ *212/721–5111* Ⓜ *1 to 79th St.*

La Perla. From the Leavers lace, soutache, and embroidery to unadorned tulle, these underthings are so gorgeous they've inspired a trilogy of books. Look for the sets of sheer underwear embroidered with the days of the week in Italian—a grown-up alternative to Bloomie's classic bloomers. ✉ *803 Madison Ave., between E. 67th and E. 68th Sts., Upper East Side* ☎ *212/570–0050* Ⓜ *6 to 68th St./Hunter College* ✉ *93 Greene St., between Prince and Spring Sts., SoHo* ☎ *212/219–0999* Ⓜ *R, W to Prince St.* ✉ *425 W. 14th St., between 9th and 10th Aves., Meatpacking District* ☎ *212/242–6662* Ⓜ *A, C, E to 14th St.*

La Petite Coquette. Among the signed photos on the walls is one of ultimate authority—from Frederique, longtime Victoria's Secret model. The store's own line of silk slips, camisoles, and other underpinnings comes in a range of colors, and as befits the name, they have special petite cuts. ✉ *51 University Pl., between E. 9th and E. 10th Sts., Greenwich Village* ☎ *212/473–2478* Ⓜ *R, W to 8th St.*

Mixona. The minx-at-heart will have a field day among the lace and mesh bras of Andres Sarda and the flirty, lower-cut bras by Aubade. Some lines trace back to such major design houses as Blumarine and Dolce & Gabbana. There's also a house line of silk sleepwear and a small selection of indie label ready-to-wear clothing. ■TIP➔ There are usually good finds on the sales racks in back. ✉ *262 Mott St., between Prince and E. Houston Sts., NoLita* ☎ *646/613–0100* Ⓜ *R, W to Prince St.*

LUGGAGE, LEATHER GOODS AND HANDBAGS

Altman Luggage. Great bargains—a Samsonite Pullman for a little more than $100—are the thing at this discount store, which also stocks tough Timberland and Swiss Army backpacks. ✉ *135 Orchard St., between Delancey and Rivington Sts., Lower East Side* ☎ *212/254–7275* Ⓜ *F, J, M, Z to Delancey St./Essex St.*

Anya Hindmarch. Although some of these divine British handbags in calf, satin, or velvet are ready for a very proper occasion, others cut loose like the Be a Bag collection—you can have a bag printed with any personal photo. ✉ *29 E. 60th St., between Madison and Park Aves., Upper East Side* ☎ *212/750–3974* Ⓜ *N, R, W to 5th Ave./59th St.* ✉ *115 Greene St., between Prince and Spring Sts., SoHo* ☎ *212/343–8147* Ⓜ *R, W to Prince St.*

Bottega Veneta. The signature crosshatch weave graces leather handbags, slouchy satchels, and shoes; the especially satisfying brown shades extend from fawn to deep chocolate. ✉ *697 5th Ave., between E. 54th*

17

and E. 55th Sts., Midtown East ☎ *212/371–5511* Ⓜ *N, R, W, 4, 5, 6 to 59th St./Lexington Ave.*

Crouch & Fitzgerald. Since 1839 this store has offered an unimpeachable selection of hard- and soft-sided luggage, as well as a huge number of attaché cases. ✉ *400 Madison Ave., at E. 48th St., Midtown East* ☎ *212/755–5888* Ⓜ *B, D, F, V to 47th–50th St./Rockefeller Center.*

Fendi. Once known for its furs, Fendi is now synonymous with decadent handbags. The purses are beaded, embroidered, and fantastically embellished within an inch of their lives, resulting in prices that skyrocket over $1,000. Fancy leathers, furs, and other accessories are also available. ✉ *677 5th Ave., between E. 53rd and E. 54th Sts., Midtown East* ☎ *212/759–4646* Ⓜ *E, F to 5th Ave./53rd St.*

★ **Flight 001**. Frequent flyers can one-stop-shop at this travel-theme store. Carry-on bags, passport holders, and personal-size down pillows share shelf space with mini–alarm clocks, satin sleep masks, and even paper soap. ✉ *96 Greenwich Ave., between W. 12th and Jane Sts., Greenwich Village* ☎ *212/989–0001* Ⓜ *A, C, E to 14th St.*

Furla. Shoulder bags, oblong clutches, and roomy totes can be quite proper or attention-getting, from a cocoa-brown, croc-embossed zipper-top to a patent leather, cherry-red purse. ✉ *598 Madison Ave., at E. 57th St., Midtown East* ☎ *212/980–3208* Ⓜ *N, R, 4, 5, 6 to 59th St.* ✉ *727 Madison Ave., between E. 63rd and E. 64th Sts., Upper East Side* ☎ *212/755–8986* Ⓜ *N, R, W, 4, 5, 6 to 59th St./Lexington Ave.*

Henry Beguelin. The aroma of leather pervades this boutique on the ground floor of the Hotel Gansevoort, and it's no wonder: everything here, even the floor, is made from it. Many of the pieces have an ethnic-bohemian look, with fringe and beading on jackets and swingy skirts. ✉ *18 9th Ave., at W. 13th St., Meatpacking District* ☎ *212/647–8415* Ⓜ *A, C, E to 14th St.*

High Way. Some of these breezy, colorful handbags come trimmed with grosgrain ribbon or with a coin-purse-like snapping closure. Others open like minigarment bags to disclose a wealth of inner pockets. ✉ *238 Mott St., between Prince and Spring Sts., NoLita* ☎ *212/966–4388* Ⓜ *6 to Bleecker St.*

Jamin Puech. Wanderlust is evident in many of these bags; the colors, embroideries, fringes, and fabrics may suggest Morocco and Polynesia, and the bags can cost as much as an off-season plane ticket to the Continent. ✉ *14 Prince St., at Elizabeth St., NoLita* ☎ *212/431–5200* Ⓜ *R, W to Prince St.*

Fodor's Choice ★ **Kate Spade**. These eminently desirable (and oft-copied) handbags in lush-color leather, tweed, and canvas have a classic but kicky retro style. Totes and shoulder bags are lined in fun fabrics; wicker baskets for summer are jazzed up with bright leather accents or shaped like birdhouses. The Broome Street shop also carries shoes, hats, scarves, linens, sunglasses, and baby and travel accessories. Around the corner you'll find **Jack Spade** filled with bags, dopp kits, and other men's accessories in a nostalgic setting (a second location is on Bleecker Street). ✉ *454 Broome St., between Mercer and Greene Sts., SoHo* ☎ *212/274–1991*

Ⓜ *C, E to Spring St.* ✉ *Jack Spade, 56 Greene St., between Broome and Spring Sts., SoHo* ☎ *212/625–1820* Ⓜ *C, E to Prince St.* ✉ *Jack Spade, 401 Bleecker St., at 11th St., Flatiron District* ☎ *212/675–4085* Ⓜ *1, 2, 3 to 14th St.* ✉ *135 5th Ave., at 20th St., Flatiron District* ☎ *212/358–0420* Ⓜ *N, R, W to 23rd St.*

Leiber. A door handle twinkling with Swarovski crystals signals the entrance to the Kingdom of Sparkle. Instantly recognizable handbags are completely frosted in crystals, from simple, colorful rectangles to minaudières shaped like animals or flowers. Crystals also spangle the heels of satin pumps and the bows of oversize (to cut the glare?) sunglasses. ✉ *680 Madison Ave., at E. 61st St., Upper East Side* ☎ *212/223–2999* Ⓜ *4, 5, 6 to E. 59th St.*

Longchamp. Its Le Pliage nylon bags have become an Upper East Side staple, and can be spotted everywhere in the Hamptons. The store carries the entire line of luggage, wallets, and totes in a rainbow of colors. ✉ *713 Madison Ave., between E. 63rd and E. 64th Sts., Upper East Side* ☎ *212/223–1500* Ⓜ *N, R, W, 4, 5, 6 to 59th St./Lexington Ave.* ✉ *132 Spring St., at Elizabeth St., SoHo* ☎ *212/343–7444* Ⓜ *N, R, W to Prince St.*

Fodor'sChoice
★
Louis Vuitton. In the mammoth 57th Street store vintage examples of Vuitton's famous monogrammed trunks float above the fray on the ground floor, where shoppers angle for the latest accessories. Joining the initials are the Damier check pattern and colorful striated leathers, plus devastatingly chic clothes and shoes designed by Marc Jacobs. ✉ *1 E. 57th St., at 5th Ave., Midtown East* ☎ *212/758–8877* Ⓜ *E, V to 5th Ave./53rd St.* ✉ *116 Greene St., between Prince and Spring Sts., SoHo* ☎ *212/274–9090* Ⓜ *R, W to Prince St.*

17

Lulu Guinness. Hit this black-and-white striped salon for such whimsically retro accessories as handbags (some lip-shaped) adorned with appliqué, beads, and bows; polka-dot scarves; and umbrellas patterned with poodles. ✉ *394 Bleecker St., between W. 11th and Perry Sts., Greenwich Village* ☎ *212/367–2120* Ⓜ *1 to Christopher St./Sheridan Sq.*

Fodor'sChoice
★
Belle by Sigerson Morrison. Ready to seduce your shoulder as well as your feet, this outpost stocks Sigerson Morrison's Belle line of shoes and the core brand's stylish, but practical, bags, the latter in calfskin, pigskin, suede, and the occasional fabric, and often equipped with zippered exterior pockets for cell phones and other things you need close at hand. ✉ *242 Mott St., between Prince and E. Houston Sts., NoLita* ☎ *212/941–5404* Ⓜ *R, W to Prince St.*

Token Store. You know you want one, so visit the source of the Manhattan Portage messenger-bag fad. Although they're a dime a dozen around these parts, these sturdy nylon and canvas numbers cost real money—$20 to $100—and will impress the folks back home. The store also carries Manhattan Portage's newer, more-high-end line of leather carryalls, totes, and travel bags for those who grew up carting the messenger style, but now need something a bit more professional. ✉ *258 Elizabeth St., between E. Houston and Prince Sts., NoLita* ☎ *212/226–9655* Ⓜ *R, W to Prince St.*

MUSEUM STORES

Cooper-Hewitt, National Design Museum. Prowl the shelves here for intriguing urban oddments and ornaments, like sculptural tableware, rare design books, rose corsages made from bulletproof material, and ceramic versions of New York deli coffee cups. ⊠ *2 E. 91st St., at 5th Ave., Upper East Side* ☎ *212/849–8355* Ⓜ *4, 5, 6 to 86th St.*

Metropolitan Museum of Art Shop. Of the three locations, the store in the museum has a phenomenal book selection, as well as posters, art videos, and computer programs. Reproductions of jewelry, statuettes, and other *objets* fill the gleaming cases in every branch. ⊠ *1000 5th Ave., at E. 82nd St., Upper East Side* ☎ *212/570–3894* Ⓜ *4, 5, 6 to 86th St.* ⊠ *15 W. 49th St., between 5th and 6th Aves., Rockefeller Center, Midtown West* ☎ *212/332–1360* Ⓜ *B, D, F, V to 47th–50th Sts./Rockefeller Center.*

Museum of Arts and Design. In this museum's new home, the gift shop stocks beautiful handmade tableware, unusual jewelry, and other adornments, often tied in to ongoing exhibits. ⊠ *2 Columbus Circle, at 8th Ave., Midtown West* ☎ *212/299–7777* Ⓜ *1, A, B, C, D to 59th St./Columbus Circle.*

★ **Museum of Modern Art Design and Book Store.** The redesigned MoMA expanded its in-house shop with a huge selection of art posters and more than 2,000 titles on painting, sculpture, film, and photography. **Across the street is the MoMA Design Store, where you can find Charles and Ray Eames furniture reproductions, vases designed by Alvar Aalto, and lots of clever trinkets.** The SoHo branch combines most of the virtues of the first two, although its book selection is smaller. ⊠ *11 W. 53rd St., between 5th and 6th Aves., Midtown West* ☎ *212/708–9700* Ⓜ *E, V to 5th Ave./53rd St.* ⊠ *MoMA Design Store, 44 W. 53rd St., between 5th and 6th Aves., Midtown West* ☎ *212/767–1050* Ⓜ *E, V to 5th Ave./53rd St.* ⊠ *81 Spring St., between Broadway and Crosby St., SoHo* ☎ *212/613–1367* Ⓜ *6 to Spring St.*

Museum of the City of New York. Satisfy your curiosity about New York City's past, present, or future with the terrific selection of books, cards, toys, and photography posters. ⊠ *1220 5th Ave., at E. 103rd St., Upper East Side* ☎ *212/534–1672* Ⓜ *6 to 103rd St.*

Neue Galerie. Like the museum, this bookshop focuses on German, Austrian, and Central European art. The solid selection includes catalogs, literature, and decorative items, including lovely wrapping papers. ⊠ *1048 5th Ave., between E. 85th and E. 86th Sts., Upper East Side* ☎ *212/628–6200* Ⓜ *4, 5, 6 to 86th St.*

MUSIC AND VIDEO

The city's best record stores provide browsers with a window to New York's cooler subcultures. The East Village is especially good for dance tracks and used music.

Bleecker Bob's Golden Oldies Record Shop. One of the oldest independent record stores in town, this pleasingly shabby-looking shop with its old-fashioned neon sign sells punk, jazz, metal, and reggae, plus good old rock on vinyl, until the wee hours. ⊠ *118 W. 3rd St., at MacDougal St., Greenwich Village* ☎ *212/475–9677* Ⓜ *A, C, E, F, V to W. 4th St./Washington Sq.*

Jazz Record Center. Long-lost Ellingtons and other rare pressings come to light here; the jazz-record specialist also stocks collectibles, DVDs, videos, posters, CDs, and LPs. ⊠ *236 W. 26th St., between 7th and 8th Aves., 8th fl., Chelsea* ☎ *212/675–4480* Ⓜ *1 to 28th St.*

Fodor's Choice ★ **Other Music.** The antidote to music megastores, this niche spot carries hard-to-find genres on CD and vinyl, from Japanese electronica and Krautrock to acid folk and Americana. ■**TIP**➔ There's also a great selection of used CDs, including seminal punk classics from the Clash and the Stooges. ⊠ *15 E. 4th St., between Lafayette St. and Broadway, East Village* ☎ *212/477–8150* Ⓜ *6 to Astor Pl.*

PAPER, GREETING CARDS, AND STATIONERY

Industries Stationery. The date books, calendars, and paper goods here are all clean-lined and bold. Journals might have wooden or bright yellow leather covers, and note cards are patterned in Marimekko-ish designs. ⊠ *91 Crosby St., between Prince and Spring Sts., SoHo* ☎ *212/334–4447* Ⓜ *N, R to Prince St.*

17

Fodor's Choice ★ **Kate's Paperie.** Avid correspondents and gift givers adore Kate's, which rustles with fabulous wrapping papers, ribbons, blank books, writing implements of all kinds, and more. ⊠ *72 Spring St., between Crosby and Lafayette Sts., SoHo* ☎ *212/941–9816* Ⓜ *6 to Spring St.* ⊠ *8 W. 13th St., between 5th and 6th Aves., Greenwich Village* ☎ *212/633–0570* Ⓜ *F, V to 14th St.* ⊠ *1282 3rd Ave., between E. 73rd and E. 74th Sts., Upper East Side* ☎ *212/396–3670* Ⓜ *6 to 77th St.* ⊠ *140 W. 57th St., between 6th and 7th Aves., Midtown West* ☎ *212/459–0700* Ⓜ *F to 57th St.*

Smythson of Bond Street. Stationery fit for a queen—literally—check out the royal warrant from England's HRH. But keepsakes here are far from stuffy: make notes on your purchases, deepest thoughts, or conquests in softbound leather diaries with appropriate gilded titles, such as Happiness is Shopping and Dreams and Thoughts. They also carry an array of elegant formal stationery, address books, and buttery leather travel accessories. ⊠ *4 W. 57th St., between 5th and 6th Aves., Midtown West* ☎ *212/265–4573* Ⓜ *F to 57th St.*

PERFORMING ARTS MEMORABILIA

Drama Book Shop. The comprehensive stock here includes scripts, scores, and librettos. ⊠ *250 W. 40th St., between 7th and 8th Aves., Midtown West* ☎ *212/944–0595* Ⓜ *A, C, E to 42nd St./Port Authority.*

WEST VILLAGE

It's easy to feel like a local, not a tourist, while shopping in the West Village. Unlike 5th Avenue or SoHo, the pace is slower, the streets relatively quiet, and the scale small. This is the place to come for unusual finds rather than global-brand goods (well, if you don't count Marc Jacobs).

Bleecker Street is a particularly good place to indulge all sorts of shopping appetites. Foodies love the blocks between 6th and 7th avenues for the specialty purveyors like Murray's Cheese (254 Bleecker St.). Fashion foragers prowl the stretch between West 10th Street and 8th Avenue, while avid readers lose themselves in the book-book bookshop. Hudson Street and Greenwich Avenue are also prime boutique-browsing territory. Christopher Street, true to its connection with the lesbian and gay community, has a handful of rainbow-flag stops. High rents mean there are fewer student-oriented shops around NYU than you might expect.

BEST TIME TO GO

Tuesday through Friday afternoons for a focused shopping stint, Saturday afternoon if you get a buzz from people-watching or the competitive aspect of busier boutiques. (Keep in mind that most stores here are small, so even a half-dozen fellow browers can make a shop feel crowded.) On Sunday the area's a bit bogged down by brunchers, and stores have shorter hours.

BEST SOUVENIR FOR A SWEET TOOTH

At the intersection of 8th Ave. and Jane St., **Li-Lac Chocolates** sells butter-crunch, almond bark, and assorted chocolate truffles.

BEST FOR

NONCHALANT-CHIC CLOTHES

Marc Jacobs: the casual (but not cheap) line with seemingly unstoppable downtown street cred.

Castor & Pollux: feminine pieces that feel simultaneously vintage and modern.

Irma: the place to pair cult jeans, motorcycle boots, and a revealing top.

Ludivine: a direct feed to the Parisian femme's fashion scene.

Cynthia Rowley: party-friendly outfits for when a girl needs a halter top or a filmy dress.

HOME DECOR

Mxyplyzyk: household necessities and accessories get a jolt of saucy humor.

Olatz: divine bedding and pajamas in a Havana-inspired setting.

Albertine General: antique and antique-inspired curiosities like martini glasses, silver spoons, and vintage postcards.

17

REFUELING

Skip Magnolia Bakery; there's always a line, and besides, there's a vast number of other great places for a pick-me-up in this neighborhood. The house-made sweets at **Amy's Bread** (⊠ *250 Bleecker St., at Leroy St.* ☎ *212/675–7802*), like the layer-cake slices and "kitchen sink" cookies, are both homey and delicious. Try an Irish soda roll or a sandwich on raisin-and-fennel bread. A few doors away at **Cones** (⊠ *272 Bleecker St., between Morton and Jones Sts.* ☎ *212/414–1795*), you can lap up a rich ginger or banana ice cream.

Movie Star News. As you flip through images from blockbusters, cult faves, and memorable bombs, it's hard to doubt their claim that they have the world's largest variety of movie photos and posters. Behind the counter are signed photos of many of the stars seen on the posters. ■TIP➔ A poster of a New York film such as *Manhattan, The Royal Tenenbaums, or Taxi Driver* makes for a good souvenir for less than $20. ☒ *134 W. 18th St., between 6th and 7th Aves., Chelsea* ☎ *212/620–8160* Ⓜ *1, 2, 3 to 14th St.*

One Shubert Alley. Souvenir posters, tees, and other knickknacks memorializing past and present Broadway hits reign at this Theater District shop. ☒ *1 Shubert Alley, between W. 44th and W. 45th Sts., Midtown West* ☎ *212/944–4133* Ⓜ *N, Q, R, S, W, 1, 2, 3 to 42nd St./Times Sq.*

Triton Gallery. Theatrical posters large and small are available, and the selection is democratic, with everything from Marlene Dietrich's *Blue Angel* to recent Broadway shows represented. ☒ *630 9th Ave., between W. 44th and W. 45th Sts., Suite. 808, Midtown West* ☎ *212/765–2472* Ⓜ *A, E to 42nd St./Port Authority.*

SHOES

MEN'S AND WOMEN'S SHOES

Bally. A few curveballs, like olive-green or slate-blue wing tips, liven up the mainly conservative selection. Carry-ons and clothing, such as deerskin or lamb jackets, join the shoe leather. ☒ *628 Madison Ave., at E. 59th St., Midtown East* ☎ *212/751–9082* Ⓜ *N, R, W, 4, 5, 6 to 59th St./Lexington Ave.*

Camper. These Euro-fave walking shoes, with their sturdy leather uppers and nubby rubber soles, have also proved popular on the cobblestone streets of SoHo. Comfort is a priority; all the slip-ons and lace-ups here have generously rounded toes and a springy feel. ☒ *125 Prince St., at Wooster St., SoHo* ☎ *212/358–1841* Ⓜ *R, W to Prince St.*

Cole-Haan. No longer wedded to staid moccasin styles, Cole-Haan has of late broken into stylish territory. Shoes for both sexes now come in exotic skins like python and crocodile; for warm weather, check out the orange suede thongs for men and metallic stiletto sandals for women. The handbag line is much more playful, too. ☒ *620 5th Ave., at Rockefeller Center, Midtown West* ☎ *212/765–9747* Ⓜ *E, V to 5th Ave./53rd St.* ☒ *667 Madison Ave., at E. 61st St., Upper East Side* ☎ *212/421–8440* Ⓜ *N, R, W, 4, 5, 6 to 59th St./Lexington Ave.* ☒ *10 Columbus Circle, at W. 59th St., Midtown West* ☎ *212/823–9420* Ⓜ *1, A, B, C, D to Columbus Circle.*

J.M. Weston. Specially treated calfskin for the soles and handcrafted construction have made these a French favorite; they could also double the price of your outfit. Blue suede sneakers stand out among the shining leather oxfords and moccasins. ☒ *812 Madison Ave., at E. 68th St., Upper East Side* ☎ *212/535–2100* Ⓜ *6 to 68th St./Hunter College.*

John Fluevog Shoes. The inventor of the Angelic sole (protects against water, acid, "and Satan"), Fluevog, designs chunky, funky shoes and boots. ✉ *250 Mulberry St., at Prince St., NoLita* ☎ *212/431–4484* Ⓜ *R, W to Prince St.*

Salvatore Ferragamo. Elegance typifies these designs, from black-tie patent to weekender ankle boots. The company reworks some of their women's styles from previous decades, like the girlish Audrey (as in Hepburn) ballet flat, released seasonally for limited runs. ✉ *655 5th Ave., at E. 52nd St., Midtown East* ☎ *212/759–3822* Ⓜ *E, V to 53rd St.*

Fodor's Choice ★ **Sigerson Morrison.** The details—just-right T-straps, small buckles, metallic leathers—make the women's shoes irresistible. Prices rise well above $300, so the sales are big events. ✉ *28 Prince St., between Mott and Elizabeth Sts., NoLita* ☎ *212/219–3893* Ⓜ *F, V to Broadway-Lafayette St.* ✉ *19 East 71st St., between 5th and Madison Aves., Upper East Side* ☎ *212/734–2100* Ⓜ *6 to 77th St.*

Stuart Weitzman. The broad range of styles, from wing tips to strappy sandals, is enhanced by an even wider range of sizes and widths. ✉ *625 Madison Ave., between E. 58th and E. 59th Sts., Midtown East* ☎ *212/750–2555* Ⓜ *N, R, W, 4, 5, 6 to 59th St./Lexington Ave.* ✉ *10 Columbus Circle, at W. 59th St., Midtown West* ☎ *212/823–9560* Ⓜ *1, A, B, C, D to Columbus Circle.*

Tod's. Diego Della Valle's coveted driving moccasins, casual loafers, and boots in colorful leather, suede, and pony skin are right at home on Madison Avenue. Though most of the women's selection is made up of low-heeled or flat styles, an increasing number of high heels are bent on driving sales, rather than cars. Men's choices stay low to the track with rubber-sole loafers, sneakers, and oxfords. ✉ *650 Madison Ave., near E. 60th St., Upper East Side* ☎ *212/644–5945* Ⓜ *N, R, W to 5th Ave./59th St.*

MEN'S SHOES

Billy Martin's. Quality hand-tooled and custom-made boots for the urban cowboy are carried here. To complete the look, you can add a suede shirt or a turquoise-and-silver belt. ✉ *1034 3rd Ave., between 61st and 62nd Sts., Upper East Side* ☎ *212/861–3100* Ⓜ *N, R, 4, 5, 6 to 59th St.*

Church's English Shoes. The high quality of these shoes is indisputable; you could choose something highly polished for an embassy dinner, a loafer or a crepe-sole suede ankle boot for a weekend, or even a black-and-white spectator style worthy of Fred Astaire. ✉ *689 Madison Ave., at E. 62nd St., Upper East Side* ☎ *212/758–5200* Ⓜ *N, R, 4, 5, 6 to 59th St.*

John Lobb. These British shoes often use waxed leather, the better to contend with London levels of dampness. Ankle boots with padded collars or zips join the traditional oxfords and derbies; some shoes have elegantly tapered toes. ✉ *680 Madison Ave., between E. 61st and E. 62nd Sts., Upper East Side* ☎ *212/888–9797* Ⓜ *N, R, 4, 5, 6 to 59th St.*

17

WOMEN'S SHOES

Christian Louboutin. Lipstick-red soles are the signature of Louboutin's delicately sexy couture slippers and stilettos, and his latest, larger downtown store has carpeting to match. The pointy-toe creations come trimmed with brocade, tassels, buttons, or satin ribbons. ⊠ *965 Madison Ave., between E. 75th and E. 76th Sts., Upper East Side* ☎ *212/396–1884* Ⓜ *6 to 77th St.* ⊠ *59 Horatio St., between Hudson and Greenwich Sts., Meatpacking District* ☎ *212/255–1910* Ⓜ *A, C, E to 14th St.*

Iris. As the Italian shoe manufacturers for splashy brands like Galliano, Viktor & Rolf, Marc Jacobs, and Chloé, Iris's sole U.S. store is able to carry every style from those lines, including pieces not previously available on our shores. ⊠ *827 Washington St., at Little W. 12th St., Meatpacking District* ☎ *212/645–0950* Ⓜ *A, C, E, L to 14th St.*

Jimmy Choo. Pointy toes, low vamps, narrow heels, ankle-wrapping straps—these British-made shoes are undeniably vampy, and sometimes more comfortable than they look. ⊠ *716 Madison Ave., between E. 63rd and E. 64th Sts., Upper East Side* ☎ *212/759–7078* Ⓜ *6 to 68th St./Hunter College* ⊠ *645 5th Ave., at E. 51st St., Midtown East* ☎ *212/593–0800* Ⓜ *B, D, F, V to 47th–50th Sts./Rockefeller Center.*

Manolo Blahnik. These are, notoriously, some of the most expensive shoes money can buy. They're also devastatingly sexy, with pointed toes, low-cut vamps, and spindly heels. Mercifully, the summer stock includes flat (but still exquisite) sandals; look for gladiator styles with ankle laces, or thongs embellished with sparkly beads. Pray for a sale. ⊠ *31 W. 54th St., between 5th and 6th Aves., Midtown West* ☎ *212/582–3007* Ⓜ *E, V to 5th Ave./53rd St.*

Robert Clergerie. Not without its sense of fun, this place is often best in summer, when the sandal selection includes curvaceous soles and beaded starfish shapes. ⊠ *19 E. 62nd St., between 5th and Madison Aves., Upper East Side* ☎ *212/207–8600* Ⓜ *R, W to 5th Ave.*

TOYS AND GAMES

Most of these stores are geared to children, but a few shops that cater to grown-up toy-lovers are mixed in. *In addition to the stores listed below, see Pylones in Home Decor.*

American Girl Place. No toy pink convertibles here; instead, the namesake dolls are historically themed, from Felicity of colonial Virginia to Kit of Depression-era Cincinnati. Each character has her own affiliated books, furniture, clothes, and accessories. There's a doll hairdressing station, a café, and even a theater showing a musical based on the dolls' stories. ⊠ *609 5th Ave., at E. 49th St., Midtown East* ☎ *212/371–2220* Ⓜ *B, D, F, V to 47th–50th Sts./Rockefeller Center.*

Dinosaur Hill. These toys leave the run-of-the-mill far behind, with mini-bongo drums, craft kits, jack-in-the-boxes, and a throng of marionettes and hand puppets, from mermaids to farmers to demons. ⊠ *306 E. 9th St., between 1st and 2nd Aves., East Village* ☎ *212/473–5850* Ⓜ *R, W to 8th St.; 6 to Astor Pl.*

Fodor's Choice **FAO Schwarz Fifth Avenue.** A New York classic that's better than ever, this
★ children's paradise more than lives up to the hype. The ground floor
is a zoo of extraordinary stuffed animals, from cuddly $20 teddies to
towering, life-size elephants and giraffes (with larger-than-life prices to
match). FAO Schweetz stocks M&Ms in every color of the rainbow;
upstairs, you can dance on the giant musical floor keyboard, browse
through Barbies wearing Armani and Juicy Couture, and design your
own muppet puppet. ⊠ *767 5th Ave., at E. 58th St., Midtown East*
☎ *212/644–9400* Ⓜ *4, 5, 6 to E. 59th St.*

Kidrobot. Even if you've never heard of Urban Vinyl Toys, which, in
quainter times, were simply referred to as "action figures," you can
get a kick out of this shop, where adult and kid collectors flock to
stock up on the latest toys from Asian designers. This is a far cry from
Mattel—the artist-driven figures are more likely to represent smoking
cupcakes. ⊠ *118 Prince St., between Greene and Wooster Sts., SoHo*
☎ *212/966–6688* Ⓜ *N, R to Prince St.*

Kidding Around. This unpretentious shop is piled high with old-fashioned
wooden toys, Playmobil and Corolle dolls, and a fun selection of hand
puppets. The costume racks are rich with dress-up potential. ⊠ *60 W.
15th St., between 5th and 6th Aves., Flatiron District* ☎ *212/645–6337*
Ⓜ *L, N, Q, R, W, 4, 5, 6 to 14th St./Union Sq.*

Toys "R" Us. The Times Square megastore is so big that a three-story
Ferris wheel revolves inside. With all the movie tie-in merchandise,
video games, yo-yos, stuffed animals, and what seems to be the entire
Mattel oeuvre, this store has a lock on sheer volume. ⊠ *1514 Broadway, at W. 44th St., Midtown West* ☎ *646/366–8800* Ⓜ *1, N, Q, R, W
to 42nd St./Times Sq.*

WINE

Acker Merrall & Condit. Known for its selection of red burgundies, this
store has knowledgeable, helpful personnel. ⊠ *160 W. 72nd St., between
Amsterdam and Columbus Aves., Upper West Side* ☎ *212/787–1700*
Ⓜ *1, 2, 3 to 72nd St.*

Astor Wines & Spirits. This is a key spot for everything from well-priced
champagne to Poire Williams to Riesling, in a beautiful location with
a wine library and an organic wines area. ■**TIP**➜ A selection of house
favorites is discounted 15% every Tuesday. ⊠ *399 Lafayette St., at E. 4th
St., East Village* ☎ *212/674–7500* Ⓜ *6 to Astor Pl.*

Best Cellars. In a novel move, the stock here is organized by the wine's
characteristics (sweet, fruity) rather than by region. Even better, the
prices are amazingly low—between $10 and $14 a bottle. ⊠ *1291
Lexington Ave., between E. 86th and E. 87th Sts., Upper East Side*
☎ *212/426–4200* Ⓜ *4, 5, 6 to 86th St.*

★ **Bottlerocket.** Bright and approachable, this shop puts a new spin on wine
shopping. Vintages are organized by quirky factors like their compatibil-
ity with local take-out menus and who they'd best suit as gifts (ranging
from "Someone You Barely Know" to "The Boss"). A reference library,

kids' play nook, and doggie area make the space extra welcoming. ⊠ *5 W. 19th St., between 5th and 6th Aves., Chelsea* ☎ *212/929–2323* Ⓜ *N, R, Q, 4, 5, 6 to 14th St.*

Union Square Wine & Spirits. Tastings are easy at this well-stocked store, thanks to Enomatic machines. These card-operated contraptions let you sample dozens of wines. ⊠ *140 4th Ave., at 13th St., East Village* ☎ *212/675–8100* Ⓜ *L, N, Q, R, W, 4, 5, 6 to 14th St./Union Sq.*

Where to Eat

WORD OF MOUTH

"There are some GREAT prix fixe lunches in midtown at wonderful restaurants. Maybe not 'hip' but very food worthy. Nougatine, the bar area of Jean Georges in the Trump International hotel, has a $28 lunch. Asiate in the Mandarin Oriental has a $24 lunch Mon–Fri. Le Bernardin known as the finest seafood/French in the city and does a $69 lunch."

—mclaurie

Updated
by Adeena
Sussman

Ready to take a bite out of New York? Hope you've come hungry. In a city where creativity is expressed in many ways, the food scene takes center stage, with literally thousands of ways to get an authentic taste of what Gotham is all about. Whether they're lining up at street stands, gobbling down legendary deli and diner grub, or chasing a coveted reservation at the latest celebrity-chef venue, New Yorkers are a demanding, yet appreciative audience.

Every neighborhood offers temptations high, low, and in-between, meaning there's truly something for every taste, whim, and price point. No matter how you approach dining out here, you can't go wrong. Planning a day of shopping among the glittering boutique flagships along Fifth and Madison? Stop into one of the Upper East Side's storied restaurants for a repast among the ladies-who-lunch. Clubbing in the Meatpacking District? Tuck into a meal at eateries as trendy as their patrons. Craving authentic ethnic? From food trucks to hidden joints, there are almost more choices than there are appetites. Recent years have also seen entire food categories, from ramen noodles to mac 'n cheese, riffed upon and turned into fetishistic obsessions.

Amid newfound economic realities, there's been a revived appreciation for value, meaning you can tap into wallet-friendly choices at every end of the spectrum. At many restaurants you'll also notice an almost religious reverence for seasonal cuisine. And don't forget—New York is still home to more celebrity chefs than any other city. Your chances of running into your favorite cookbook author, Food Network celeb, or paparazzi-friendly chef are higher, adding even more star wattage to a restaurant scene with an already through-the-roof glamour quotient. Ready, set, eat. Rest assured, this city will do its part to satisfy your appetite.

HARLEM
BBQ and
soul food
reign supreme

UPPER EAST SIDE
pricey
neighborhood
joints

UPPER WEST SIDE
casual &
family-friendly

MIDTOWN WEST
mostly overpriced;
some great
steakhouses

MIDTOWN EAST
expense-account
dining

W. 86th St.
E. 86th St.
E. 65th St.
E. 59th St.
E. 57th St.
W. 57th St.
50th St.
W. 42nd St.
E. 42nd St.
W. 34th St.

Hudson River

West End Ave.
Amsterdam Ave.
Columbus Ave.
Central Park West
Riverside Dr.
Henry Hudson Pkwy.
Broadway

5th Ave.
Madison Ave.
Park Ave.
Lexington Ave.
1st Ave.
FDR Dr.

Queensboro Bridge
Roosevelt Island

QUEENS

Lincoln Tunnel

Queens-Midtown Tunnel

TUDOR CITY

11th Ave.
10th Ave.
9th Ave.
8th Ave.
7th Ave.
Ave. of the Americas
5th Ave.
Broadway
Madison Ave.
Park Ave.
3rd Ave.
2nd Ave.
1st Ave.

CHELSEA
reliable, casual
spots

MURRAY HILL
a.k.a Curry Hill,
great Indian
restaurants

KIPS BAY

FLATIRON DISTRICT
stylish, upscale
eateries

GRAMERCY
E. 23rd St.

STUYVESANT TOWN

East River

UNION SQUARE
foodie haven

W. 14th St.
E. 14th St.

Avenue B
Avenue C

MEATPACKING DISTRICT
flashy
hotspots

GREENWICH VILLAGE
shabby-chic
restaurants and
hip gastropubs

EAST VILLAGE
cheap eats, great
ethnic food

West Side Hwy.

E. Houston St.

Williamsburg Bridge

NOLITA
hipster
hangouts

LOWER EAST SIDE
edgy, DIY
resto-bars

Delancey St.

SOHO
pricey bistros
and glamorous
lounges

W. Houston St.

LITTLE ITALY
red-sauce
factories

Holland Tunnel

Canal St.

TRIBECA
swanky lounges,
sophisticated
dining

CHINATOWN
dim-sum palaces,
noodle shops,
Asian bakeries

Manhattan Bridge

West Broadway
West St.
W. Broadway

Chambers St.

CITY HALL

Brooklyn Bridge

Hudson R.

LOWER MANHATTAN
upscale haunts

BROOKLYN

WHERE TO EAT PLANNER

Eating Out Strategy

Where should we eat? With thousands of Manhattan eateries competing for your attention, it may seem like a daunting question. But fret not—our expert writers and editors have done most of the legwork. The 160-plus selections here represent the best this city has to offer—from hot dogs to haute cuisine. Search "Best Bets" for top recommendations by price, cuisine, and experience. Sample local flavor in the neighborhood features. Or find a review quickly in the alphabetical listings. Dive in, and enjoy! For restaurants in the Outer Boroughs, see the Brooklyn chapter, and the Queens, Bronx, and Staten Island chapter.

Children

Though it's unusual to see children in the dining rooms of Manhattan's most elite restaurants, dining with youngsters in New York does not have to mean culinary exile. Many of the restaurants reviewed in this chapter are excellent choices for families, and are marked with a ☺ symbol.

Reservations

It's still a good idea to plan ahead. Some renowned restaurants are booked weeks or even months in advance. If that's the case, you can get lucky at the last minute if you're flexible—and friendly. Most restaurants keep a few tables open for walk-ins and VIPs. Show up for dinner early (5:30 PM) or late (after 10 PM), and politely inquire about any last-minute vacancies or cancellations. Occasionally, an eatery may take your credit-card number and ask you to call the day before your scheduled meal to reconfirm: don't forget or you could lose out, or possibly be charged for your oversight.

What to Wear

When in the nation's style capital, do as the natives do: dress up to eat out. Whatever your style, dial it up a notch. Have some fun while you're at it. Pull out the clothes you've been saving for a special occasion and get glamorous. Unfair as it is, the way you look can influence how you're treated—and where you're seated. Generally speaking, jeans and a button-down shirt will suffice at most table-service restaurants in the $ to $$ range. Moving up from there, some pricier restaurants require jackets, and some insist on ties. In reviews, we note dress only when a jacket or jacket and tie is required. If you have doubts, call the restaurant and ask.

Tipping and Taxes

In most restaurants, tip the waiter 15%–20%. (To figure out a 20% tip quickly, just move the decimal point one place to the left on your total and double that amount.) Bills for parties of six or more sometimes include the tip already. Tip at least $1 per drink at the bar, and $1 for each coat checked. Never tip the maître d' unless you're out to impress your guests or expect to pay another visit soon.

Smoking

Smoking is prohibited in all enclosed public spaces in New York City, including restaurants and bars.

Hours

New Yorkers seem ready to eat at any hour. Many restaurants stay open between lunch and dinner, some offer late-night seating, and still others serve around-the-clock. Restaurants that serve breakfast often do so until noon or later. Restaurants in the East Village, the Lower East Side, SoHo, TriBeCa, and Greenwich Village are likely to remain open late, while Midtown spots and those in the Theater and Financial districts and uptown generally close earlier. Unless otherwise noted, the restaurants listed in this guide are open daily for lunch and dinner.

Prices

If you're watching your budget, be sure to ask the price of daily specials recited by the waiter. The charge for specials at some restaurants is noticeably out of line with the other prices on the menu. Beware of the $10 bottle of water; ask for tap water instead. And always review your bill.

If you eat early or late, you may be able to take advantage of a prix-fixe deal not offered at peak hours. Most upscale restaurants offer great lunch deals, with special menus at cut-rate prices designed to give customers a true taste of the place.

Credit cards are widely accepted, but many restaurants (particularly smaller ones downtown) accept only cash. If you plan to use a credit card, it's a good idea to confirm that it is acceptable when making reservations or before sitting down to eat.

Some restaurants are marked with a price range ($$–$$$, for example). This indicates one of two things: either the average cost straddles two categories, or if you order strategically, you can get out for less than most diners spend.

WHAT IT COSTS AT DINNER

	¢	$	$$	$$$	$$$$
RESTAURANTS	under $10	$10–$17	$18–$24	$25–$35	over $35

Price per person for a median main course or equivalent combination of smaller dishes. Note: if a restaurant offers only prix-fixe (set-price) meals, it has been given the price category that reflects the full prix-fixe price.

In This Chapter

Using the Maps

Throughout the chapter, you'll see mapping symbols and coordinates (⊕ 3:F2) after property names or reviews. To locate the property on a map, turn to the New York City Dining and Lodging Atlas at the end of this chapter. The first number after the ⊕ symbol indicates the map number. Following that is the property's coordinate on the map grid.

18

Double Check

The nature of the restaurant industry means that places open and close in a New York minute. It's always a good idea to phone ahead and make sure your restaurant is still turning over tables.

BEST BETS FOR NEW YORK CITY DINING

With thousands of restaurants to choose from, how will you decide where to eat? Fodor's writers and editors have selected their favorite restaurants by price, cuisine, and experience in the Best Bets lists below. In the first column, Fodor's Choice properties represent the "best of the best" in every price category. You can also search by neighborhood for excellent eats—just peruse the following pages. Or find specific details about a restaurant in the full reviews, listed later in the chapter.

FODOR'S CHOICE ★

A Voce, $$$, p. 422
Adour Alain Ducasse, $$$$, p. 438
Aldea, $$$, p. 422
Baoguette, $, p. 410
Bar Boulud, $$, p. 447
Burger Joint, ¢, p. 433
Candle 79, $$, p. 443
Daniel, $$$$, p. 443
DBGB Kitchen & Bar, $$, p. 410
Eleven Madison Park, $$$$, p. 424
Emporio, $$, p. 407
Fatty Crab, $, p. 420
Hundred Acres, $$, p. 407
Kampuchea, $, p. 413
Katz's Delicatessen, $, p. 413
L'Atelier de Joël Robuchon, $$$$, p. 440
Marea, $$$$, p. 450
Momofuku Ko, $$$$, p. 411

Nha Trang, ¢, p. 402
Per Se, $$$$, p. 450
Shake Shack, ¢, p. 426, 451
Tía Pol, $$, p. 431

Best by Price

¢

Burger Joint, p. 433
Financier Patisserie, p. 403
Gray's Papaya, p. 444
Nha Trang, p. 402
Shake Shack, p. 426, 451
Veniero's Pasticceria, p. 412

$

Back Forty, p. 410
Baoguette, p. 410
Bubby's, p. 404
City Bakery, p. 423
Fatty Crab, p. 449
Kampuchea, p. 413
Katz's Delicatessen, p. 413

Mexicana Mama, p. 421
Momofuku Noodle Bar, p. 412

$$

Arturo's, p. 415
Balthazar, p. 406
Bar Boulud, p. 447
Candle 79, p. 443
Emporio, p. 407
Hill Country, p. 425
'inoteca, p. 413
Tía Pol, p. 431

$$$

A Voce, p. 422
Babbo, p. 415
Bagatelle, p. 417
BLT Steak, p. 438
Craft, p. 429
Del Posto, p. 418
Minetta Tavern, p. 421
The Modern (Bar Room), p. 435
Scarpetta, p. 418

The Standard Grill, p. 419

$$$$

Adour Alain Ducasse, p. 438
Eleven Madison Park, p. 424
Jean Georges, p. 449
L'Atelier de Joël Robuchon, p. 440
Le Bernardin, p. 434
Marea, p. 450
Per Se, p. 450

Best by Cuisine

AMERICAN

Back Forty, p. 410
Gramercy Tavern, p. 425
Hundred Acres, p. 407
Park Avenue, p. 446
Per Se, p. 450

BARBECUE

Blue Smoke, p. 394
Dinosaur Bar-B-Que, p. 447
Hill Country, p. 425
R.U.B. BBQ, p. 430
Wildwood Barbecue, p. 427

CHINESE

Chinatown Brasserie, p. 410
Grand Sichuan International, p. 444
Great New York Noodletown, p. 402
Joe's Shanghai, p. 402
Shun Lee Palace, p. 442

FRENCH

Adour Alain Ducasse, p. 438

Bar Boulud, p. 447

Daniel, p. 443

Jean Georges, p. 449

Le Bernardin, p. 434

The Modern and Bar Room, p. 435

INDIAN

Tabla, p. 426

Tamarind, p. 427

ITALIAN

Alloro, p. 442

Babbo, p. 415

Convivio, p. 439

Emporio, p. 407

'ino, p. 421

'inoteca, p. 413

Lupa, p. 416

Marea, p. 450

Scarpetta, p. 418

JAPANESE

Kuruma Zushi, p. 439

Matsugen, p. 405

Sushi of Gari, p. 447

Sushi Yasuda, p. 442

MEDITERRANEAN

Aldea, p. 422

August, p. 419

Il Buco, p. 411

Picholine, p. 450

MEXICAN

Maya, p. 446

Mexicana Mama, p. 421

Toloache, p. 437

NEW AMERICAN

Blue Ribbon Brasserie, p. 407

Craft, p. 429

Eleven Madison Park, p. 424

Hundred Acres, p. 407

The Standard Grill, p. 419

PIZZA

Arturo's, p. 415

Esca, p. 434

Keste, p. 393

Lombardi's, p. 409

Marea, p. 450

Mary's Fish Camp, p. 417

BLT Fish, p. 423

SPANISH

Boqueria, p. 423

Tía Pol, p. 431

STEAK HOUSE

BLT Prime, p. 427

BLT Steak, p. 438

Porter House, p. 451

Sparks Steakhouse, p. 442

VIETNAMESE

Baoguette, p. 410

Nha Trang, p. 402

Best by Experience

BRUNCH

Aquavit, p. 438

Balthazar, p. 406

Bubby's, p. 404

Hundred Acres, p. 407

Sarabeth's, p. 445

BUSINESS DINING

BLT Steak, p. 438

DB Bistro Moderne, p. 433

Four Seasons, p. 439

Gotham Bar & Grill, p. 416

Jean Georges, p. 449

The Modern, p. 435

CELEB-SPOTTING

Balthazar, p. 406

Café Boulud, p. 442

DBGB Kitchen & Bar, p. 410

Four Seasons, p. 439

Minetta Tavern, p. 421

Nobu, p. 405

The Standard Grill, p. 419

CHILD-FRIENDLY

Bubby's, p. 404

Carmine's, p. 433

City Bakery, p. 423

Fatty Crab Upper West Side, p. 420

Joe's Shanghai, p. 402

Lombardi's, p. 409

Odeon, p. 406

Serafina, p. 445

Veniero's Pasticceria, p. 412

GOOD FOR GROUPS

Buddakan, p. 430

Carmine's, p. 433

Churrascaria Plataforma, p. 433

Emporio, p. 407

Hundred Acres, p. 407

Nobu, p. 405

Vento, p. 419

GREAT VIEW

Asiate, p. 447

Marea, p. 450

Michael Jordan's The Steakhouse NYC, p. 440

Per Se, p. 450

Porter House, p. 451

LATE-NIGHT DINING

Balthazar, p. 406

Blue Ribbon Brasserie, p. 407

DBGB Kitchen & Bar, p. 410

Emporio, p. 407

Fatty Crab, p. 420

Pastis, p. 418

Minetta Tavern, p. 421

The Standard Grill, p. 419

WINE LIST

Babbo, p. 415

Corton, p. 404

Del Posto, p. 418

'inoteca, p. 413

Marea, p. 450

The Modern and Bar Room, p. 435

'21' Club, p. 437

18

LOWER MANHATTAN

BELOW CANAL STREET, INCLUDING CHINATOWN AND TRIBECA

Post-9/11 development and attractive pricing have meant thousands of new residents in Lower Manhattan, fueling an up-and-coming—yet still slow-moving—neighborhood scene.

The most visible changes? Restaurants in and around the Financial District no longer adhere to banker's hours, and formal dining rooms have been outnumbered by casual cafés and wine bars. On the pedestrian-only Stone Street, throngs of young professionals gather for after-work drinks and dinner at nearby bistros, oyster bars, and steak houses.

To the north, Chinatown beckons adventurous diners with restaurants representing numerous regional cuisines of China, including Cantonese-, Szechuan-, Hunan-, Fujian-, Shanghai-, and Hong Kong–style cooking. Malaysian and Vietnamese restaurants also have taken root here, and the neighborhood continues to grow rapidly, encroaching into what was Little Italy.

To the west, TriBeCa still holds an air of exclusivity, though glamorous dining rooms in converted warehouses have now been joined by more casual spots with later hours.

TRIBECA BRUNCH

Locals descend on **Bubby's** (✉ 120 Hudson St., at N. Moore St. ☎ 212/219–0666 ✛ 2:C5) for Southern-accented comfort fare like buttermilk biscuits or house-made pork sausages. But save room for dessert: the restaurant started in 1990 as a pie company, and the whiskey apple pie with pecan crumble is a crowd favorite. If you're looking for a more elegant atmosphere, try **Capsouto Frères** (✉ 451 Washington St., near Watts St. ☎ 212/966–4900 ✛ 2:C5), a landmark French bistro that makes the city's best sweet and savory soufflés. We love the praline soufflé with hazelnut crème anglaise, and the three-cheese savory soufflé.

CHINATOWN CHOWDOWN

With more than 200 restaurants in just under 2 square mi, deciding where to dine may take longer than the actual meal. Here are our favorite places to enjoy Chinatown's diverse bounty.

Cantonese: For Hong Kong–style dim sum, head to **Ping's Seafood** (✉ 22 Mott St., near Worth St. ☎ 212/602–9988 ✛ 2:F6) or **HSF** (✉ 46 Bowery, near Canal St. ☎ 212/374–1319 ✛ 2:F5). Both spots are crowded, but offer addictive fare like turnip cakes, steamed pork buns, and fried sesame-seed balls.

One of the best deals in Chinatown is at **Dumpling House** (✉ 118 Eldridge St., near Broome St. ☎ 212/625–8008 ✛ 2:G4), where sizzling pork-and-chive dumplings are four for a buck.

Malaysian: There's something for everyone at **New Malaysia** (✉ 48 Bowery, near Canal St. ☎ 212/964–0284 ✛ 2:G5) like roti canai and delicious red-bean and coconut-milk drinks.

Shanghainese: The city's best soup dumplings—doughy pouches filled with ground pork and meaty broth—are ripe for the slurping at **Joe's Shanghai** (✉ 9 Pell St., near Bowery ☎ 212/233–8888 ✛ 2:F5).

Szechuan: Foodies go ga-ga for the twice-cooked pork in bean sauce and scallion pancakes at **Grand Sichuan** (✉ 125 Canal St., at Chrystie St. ☎ 212/625–9212 ✛ 2:G5). At the **Peking Duck House** (✉ 28 Mott St., near Mosco St. ☎ 212/227–1810 ✛ 2:F5), don't miss the stunning signature dish. Crispy-skinned Peking duck comes with pancakes, scallions, cucumbers, and hoisin sauce.

FINANCIAL DISTRICT'S RESTO ROW

Nestled alongside skyscrapers and the towering New York Stock Exchange, Stone Street is a two-block restaurant oasis that feels more like a village than the center of the financial universe. After the market closes, Wall Streeters head to **Ulysses'** (✉ 95 Pearl St., near Hanover Sq. ☎ 212/482–0400 ✛ 1:E4), a popular pub with 19 beers on tap and over 50 bottled beers.

Clerks might stop in for a broccoli rabe–and–sausage pie (they don't do slices) at **Adrienne's Pizza Bar** (✉ 54 Stone St., near Hanover Sq. ☎ 212/248–3838 ✛ 1:E4), while high-rolling brokers continue down the block to **Harry's Steak** (✉ 1 Hanover Sq., at Stone St., 212/785–9200 ✛ 1:E4) for a dry-aged porterhouse and a reserve-collection cabernet from a 2,800-strong cellar. Those with a sweet tooth end up at **Financier Patisserie** (✉ 62 Stone St., between Mill La. and Hanover Sq. ☎ 212/344–5600 ✛ 1:E4).

AND FOR DESSERT ...

Bouley Bakery (✉ 120 West Broadway, near Duane St. ☎ 212/964–2525 ✛ 2:D6). Renowned chef David Bouley's bustling TriBeCa bakery is both a downtown dessert haven and the entryway to Bouley's three-floor bakery/café, market, and upstairs dining complex. But you won't need to go farther than the first floor to satisfy your sweet tooth. The breads and pastries here represent many classic French favorites, including poppy-seed and fig loaves, brioche, croissants, and pains au chocolat. If you're looking for something more decadent, try the eclairs, meringues, Napoleons, fruit tarts, or one of Bouley's artisanal cakes. The colorful macaroons will make your mouth water with flavors like passion fruit filled with milk chocolate, raspberry with dark chocolate filling, and pistachio. One very special macaroon is called the Ispahna. It's filled with a buttercream, rosewater, raspberry, and lychee mixture.

18

SOHO, NOLITA, AND LITTLE ITALY

In this high-rent neighborhood dining options are somewhat limited, resulting in crowded restaurants with steep prices. But snacking is a great strategy for experiencing the local flavor without buyer's remorse.

Longtime New Yorkers lament that SoHo has evolved from a red-hot art district into a big-brand outdoor mall. Shoppers engulf the neighborhood on weekends like angry bees, turning Lafayette Street into a buzzing hive of commerce. As a result, popular spots can be tough to get into during prime times.

In NoLita, the trendy next-door neighborhood of indie boutiques and restaurants, the spirit of old SoHo prevails. Modest eateries are squeezed between boutiques featuring products from up-and-coming designers.

If you want authentic Italian food, don't head south to Little Italy: most of the pasta factories along the main strip of Mulberry Street have developed reputations as tourist traps. As with SoHo, it's a better bet to snack your way through this area.

FRESH-BAKED

Follow the beguiling scent of fresh-baked bread to **Balthazar Bakery** (⊠ 80 Spring St., near Crosby St. ☎ 212/965–1785 ✛ 2:E4), where you'll find baguettes, boules, batards, brioche, and several other different breads. The bakery—an extension of Keith McNally's well-loved Balthazar restaurant— boasts an extensive menu of panini, sandwiches, quiches, and homemade soups, plus newly added fresh breakfast egg dishes. The pastry chefs also turn out custom-made pastries, cakes, and cookies. Try the berry noisette tart or coconut cake, or keep it simple with a few of Balthazar Bakery's buttery lemon, or chocolate madeleines.

SOHO SIPS AND SNACKS

3 QUICK BITES

Relax and refuel at one of these neighborhood haunts.

Cuban sandwich at Café Habana (✉ 17 Prince St., at Elizabeth St. ☎ 212/625–2002 ✛ 2:F3): This popular pan-Latin dive also boasts excellent Mexican-style grilled corn and café con leche. The Cuban sandwich features roasted pork, ham, Swiss cheese, pickles, and chipotle mayo.

Tacos at La Esquina (✉ 106 Kenmare St. ☎ 646/613–7100 ✛ 2:F4): Order tasty pulled chicken or char-grilled steak tacos and tortas to go from the counter-service taqueria, or squeeze into the small café around the corner for a bigger sit-down meal.

Emporio (✉ 231 Mott St., near Prince St. ☎ 212/358–1707 ✛ 2:F3): Visit this cozy Italian restaurant at happy hour, weekdays 5 PM to 7 PM, when cocktails and wine come with free snacks. The daily selection may include olives, ricotta frittata, cheeses, pizzas, and cubed Italian ham.

ELEVATE YOUR COCKTAIL CONSCIOUSNESS

The American cocktail renaissance is underway at **Pegu Club** (✉ 77 W. Houston St., near West Broadway ☎ 212/473–7348 ✛ 2:D3), where renowned mixologist Audrey Saunders developed impeccable modern cocktail recipes steeped in pre-Prohibition tradition.

Inspired by a 19th-century British officer's club in Burma, the intimate second-floor lounge has a colonial aura, outfitted with palm trees, dark woods, and low-slung brown velvet couches.

But libations command the starring role, with fresh-squeezed juices and house infusions in every cocktail. Watching the barkeeps ply their trade making drinks like an Earl Grey martini with tea-infused gin, or the Jamaican Firefly features fresh ginger beer with rum and lime, makes the bar a prime perch.

"You have to look at well-crafted cocktails as fine cuisine with elements of sweet, sour, bitter, and spicy," Saunders says. "With well-crafted cocktails, you have parallel complexities, not just fruit and booze. You need spices and herbs and other ingredients to add complexity."

AND FOR DESSERT . . .

MarieBelle (✉ 484 Broome St., between Wooster St. and West Broadway ☎ 212/925–6999 ✛ 2:D4). Slip into MarieBelle to experience chocolate nirvana in a Parisian-style café setting. At the front of the shop you'll find an assortment of artisanal chocolates filled with velvety ganache. But real chocoholics head to the Cacao Bar at the back of the store for MarieBelle's überrich hot chocolate, crafted from ground cacao beans instead of cocoa powder, then mixed with boiling water (European style) or steamed milk (American style). For an unusual treat, try the spicy hot chocolate—it has a real kick to it. Tea lovers will be delighted by MarieBelle's diverse hand-blended selection. Not to worry if you're visiting during the late spring or summer, skip the hot chocolate and cool off with MarieBelle's Aztec iced chocolate—the warm-weather version of her decadent cacao elixir—or the house-made chocolate gelato.

18

EAST VILLAGE AND LOWER EAST SIDE

With luxury condos on Avenue C, the East Village—once Manhattan's edgiest enclave—has become yet another high-rent neighborhood. Nearby, the Lower East Side, home to generations of immigrant newcomers, is undergoing a similar transformation.

Both neighborhoods still offer some of the best meal deals in the city, and the influx of flush new residents has steadily raised the bar on quality eats. Dirt-cheap legends like **Katz's,** the all-night Jewish deli, coexist these days with high-end destinations featuring tasting menus and hard-to-score tables. There's something for every budget and craving, from yakitori parlors to mid-priced trattorias. St. Mark's Place is the center of New York's downtown Little Tokyo, while 6th Street is its Indian row. On the Lower East Side, meanwhile, cute little bistros have been inching into new gentrified stretches south of Delancey Street. And the neighborhoods have even given birth to their own homegrown star chefs, wildly creative renegades with cultish followings like **Momofuku**'s David Chang and **wd~50**'s Wylie Dufresne.

TOP BUDGET EATS

Be careful with the incendiary hot sauce at **Mamoun's Falafel** (⊠ 22 St. Marks Pl., between 2nd and 3rd Aves. ☎ 212/674–8685 ✛ 3:G5), where tahini-topped pitas are packed with fresh, green-on-the-inside falafel balls. Gluttony reigns at **Crif Dogs** (⊠ 113 St. Mark's Pl., at. Ave. A ☎ 212/614–2728 ✛ 3:H5); indulge in a bacon-wrapped, deep fried hot dog and chili-cheese tater tots. Next door, **Tuck Shop** (⊠ 115 St. Mark's Pl., between Ave. A and Ave. B ☎ 212/979–5200 ✛ 3:H5) offers Australian street food. Try a spicy beef meat pie followed by a dense, sweet vanilla slice (vanilla custard surrounded by puff pastry and topped with icing).

RAMEN REVOLUTION

A Japanese ramen noodle revolution has stormed the East Village, starting with **Momofuku Noodle Bar** (⊠ 171 1st Ave., between 10th and 11th Sts. ☎ 212/777–7773 ✛ 3:H5), David Chang's flagship restaurant. Chang's ramen features fatty slabs of Berkshire pork belly and shredded pork shoulder in savory broth topped with fresh vegetables and a slow-poached egg. At **Ippudo** (⊠ 65 4th Ave., between 9th and 10th Sts. ☎ 212/388–0088 ✛ 3:G5), the first American branch of the Japanese chain, draws crowds that wait up to two hours for noodles in a thick miso brew and a slick of spicy oil. Japanese expats flock to **Rai Rai Ken** (⊠ 214 E. 10th St., between 1st and 2nd Aves. ☎ 212/477–7030 ✛ 3:H5) for ramen sunk into one of three signature broths. **Minca** (⊠ 536 E. 5th St., between Aves. A and B ☎ 212/505–8001 ✛ 2:G2) has received the least fanfare, but its ramen may very well be the best. Start your meal with light, pan-fried whole shrimp gyoza and then dive into the Shoyu (soy sauce) pork ramen.

LATE-NIGHT EATS

From dirt-cheap to stylish, the city's best late-night eats can be found right here. Grab a gargantuan slice at table-less **Artichoke Pizza** (⊠ 328 E. 14th St., between 1st and 2nd Aves. ☎ 212/228–2004 ✛ 3:H4), where lines snake until 5 AM for the artichoke-spinach slice, which tastes like cheesy dip on crackers. For authentic Ukrainian cuisine, 24-hour diner gem **Veselka** (⊠ 144 2nd Ave. at 9th St. ☎ 212/228–9682 ✛ 3:H5) offers a solid burger and even better potato pierogies. Grab a chewy chocolate chip–M&M cookie for dessert. The swanky tapas restaurant & lounge **Stanton Social** (⊠ 99 Stanton St., between Orchard and Ludlow Sts. ☎ 212/995–0099 ✛ 2:G3) offers shareable Kobe beef sliders, French onion soup dumplings, and fresh doughnut holes until 2 AM nightly (3 on weekends).

AND FOR DESSERT...

The standing-only, workbench-like tables at **Momofuku Milk Bar** (⊠ 207 2nd Ave., at 13th St., ☎ 212/254–3500 ✛ 3:H4) provide clear views of pastry chef Christina Tosi tinkering with her constantly evolving menu of creations such as curiously flavored soft-serve ice cream (cereal-milk, lemon verbena) and Candy Bar Pie, a Proustian bomb of caramel, peanut-butter nougat, and pretzels atop a chocolate-cookie crust. If taking a seat is preferred, scoot into the cozy couches and chairs at **Sugar Sweet Sunshine** (⊠ 126 Rivington St., between Essex and Norfolk Sts. ☎ 212/995–1960 ✛ 2:G3), the brainchild of two former Magnolia Bakery employees. Sugar Sweet's cupcakes are far superior; try the chocolate-almond "Gooey Gooey," or the cream cheese frosting–topped pumpkin flavor. The real star showstopper? Swoon-inducing banana pudding incorporating slices of ripe fruit and crumbled Nilla wafers suspended in decadent vanilla pudding.

18

GREENWICH VILLAGE
WITH WEST VILLAGE AND MEATPACKING DISTRICT

Dining styles collide on the West Side, with quaint, chef-driven eateries in Greenwich Village facing off against the Meatpacking District's massive, celebrity-fueled hot spots.

Francophiles and fashonistas flock to Pastis, a brasserie in the Meatpacking District, for its stylish scene and standout seared tuna incise.

Greenwich Village's bohemian days may have faded with the Beatnik era, but the romantic allure of its tiny bistros, bars, and cafés remains. Around New York University, shabby-chic eateries and takeout joints line the streets and are patronized by a student clientele. Avoid heavily trafficked thoroughfares like Bleecker Street (unless you're tapping into the new artisan pizza craze), as most of the Village's culinary gems lie tucked away on side streets and alleyways, especially west of 7th Avenue, in the West Village. The vibe here is low-key and friendly, with patrons squeezed together at tiny tables in matchbox-size eateries.

For a glitzier scene, head to the Meatpacking District, which has transformed in recent years from a gritty commercial warehouse area to the celebrity-chef–driven epicenter of the city's dining scene. The vibe is flashy, favored by actors, models, and their suitors.

DOSA TO GO

Snap up a savory snack from Thiru Kumar's cart perched at West 4th and Sullivan streets. Also known as the **Dosa Man** (✛ 2:D2) of Washington Square Park, Kumar serves traditional South Indian fare like *masala dosa* (crepes stuffed with potato and onion), *idlis* (steamed lentil flour cakes), and *samosas* (savory potato-stuffed dumplings), all served with spicy vegetable soup and coconut chutney for about $5.

THE MEATPACKING DISTRICT 2 WAYS

	SAVE	SPLURGE
Creative Asian tapas	Chef Zak Pelaccio's affordable cantina **Fatty Crab** (✉ 643 Hudson St., betw. Gansevoort and Horatio Sts. ☎ 212/352–3590 ⊹ 3:C5) doubles as a late-night chef hangout. Stop in for chili-spiced crab and hard-to-find Japanese beers.	It may no longer be brand-new, but scene-seekers frequent **Spice Market** (✉ 403 W. 13th St., at 9th Ave. ☎ 212/675–2322 ⊹ 3:B4), chef Jean-Georges Vongerichten's sprawling hot spot, for treats like Ginger Margaritas and spicy black-pepper shrimp.
Molto Italian flavor	Meet up with friends at **Vento** (✉ 675 Hudson St., at 14th St. ☎ 212/699–2400 ⊹ 3:B4), where affordable small plates and wood-fired pizzas are served in a lively atmosphere.	Mario Batali's fine-dining flagship, **Del Posto** (✉ 85 10th Ave., betw. 15th and 16th Sts. ☎ 212/497–8090 ⊹ 3:A4), features luxe touches like live piano, stools for ladies' purses, and $49 risotto for two.

AND FOR DESSERT . . .

Sweet Revenge (✉ 62 Carmine St., between Bedford St. and 7th Ave. ☎ 212/242–2240, ⊕ www.sweetrevengenyc. com ⊹ 2:C2).

Everyone loves beer, wine, and cupcakes, but only Sweet Revenge brings them all together in a cozy neighborhood spot. Vibrantly flavored and delicately rich, the cupcakes are the real draw. Nut-studded peanut butter–buttercream tops a moist, crumbly peanut-butter cake housing a chocolate ganache center you'll want to measure out in every bite. Pair it with the suggested Argentinean red or German Hefeweizen or combine any of the other 15 wines and beers with a special cupcake of the day, such as the "Very Strawberry," with fresh strawberries baked into vanilla cake topped with strawberry cream-cheese frosting. There are also sandwiches and savory cakes, but indulgence is a dish best served sweet. $10 gets you a glass of sangria or wine and a cupcake from 4 to 8 PM Monday through Friday.

PIZZA THREE WAYS IN THE WEST VILLAGE

SLICE

Flavor reigns at **Bleecker Street Pizza** (✉ 69 7th Ave. S, at Bleecker St. ☎ 212/924–4466 ⊹ 2:B2), where the thin-crusted "Nonna Maria" is topped with garlicky marinara, grated mozzarella, fresh mozzarella, and freshly grated parmigano reggiano. You may not find a seat inside tiny **Joe's Pizza** (✉ 7 Carmine St. at 6th Ave. ☎ 212/366–1182 ⊹ 2:C2), but you will get one of the best versions of a purists' New York slice.

CLASSIC COAL OVEN

Founded in 1957, **Arturo's** (✉ 106 W. Houston St. at Thompson St. ☎ 212/677–3820 ⊹ 2:D3) is a double throwback: it's a jazz bar and friendly neighborhood coal-oven pizza restaurant where crackly-crusted pies are a guarantee. If you can brave the organized chaos and the usual wait, a gooey meatball pie awaits.

AUTHENTIC NEAPOLITAN

At the back of the long, narrow **Keste Pizza & Vino** (✉ 271 Bleecker Street, between 6th and 7th Aves. ☎ 212/243–1500 ⊹ 2:C2) sits a beautiful, tiled wood-fired oven that cooks Manhattan's most authentic Neapolitan pies at 1,000 degrees. Blistered and chewy around the edges, each pie gives way to a softer center pooled with San Marzano tomato sauce and imported buffalo mozzarella.

18

UNION SQUARE

WITH GRAMERCY, MURRAY HILL, AND FLATIRON DISTRICT

The blocks around Union Square and its open-air greenmarket are filled with upscale foodie havens featuring market-driven menus. But fancy seasonal fare isn't all the area offers: Curry Hill and Koreatown are just blocks away.

Some of the city's most popular restaurants, including **Craft** and **Union Square Cafe,** are located in the area northwest of Union Square, called the Flatiron District. The neighborhood is also a hot shopping destination, with plenty of refueling spots like City Bakery, a gourmet deli and sweets spot that's a standby for many New Yorkers. Heading up from Union Square, Park Avenue South and streets nearby are packed with crowd-pleasers like Blue Smoke, Dos Caminos, and Les Halles.

Lexington Avenue between 27th and 29th streets is known as Curry Hill (it borders Murray Hill) for its wall-to-wall Indian restaurants, spice shops, and takeout joints. The area near Koreatown, on West 32nd Street, between 5th and 6th avenues, may look deserted, as eateries often lack visible signage—it's best to go with a specific spot in mind than to try your luck window-shopping.

BURGER BLISS

This area is prime burger turf. The **Stand** (⊠ 24 E. 12th St., near University Pl. ☎ 212/488–5900 ✛ 3:F4) offers upscale fast fare in a sleek setting. We recommend the bacon-and-egg cheeseburger, topped with cheddar and hard-boiled egg mayo. For an Old New York feel, try the classic burgers at the **Old Town Bar** (⊠ 45 E. 18th St., near Park Ave. S ☎ 212/529–6732 ✛ 3:F3), where they've been serving 'em up for over 100 years. Or, if the weather is nice, head up to Madison Square Park, where burger lovers are always queued up at **Shake Shack** (⊠ 23rd St. near Madison Ave. ☎ 212/889–6600 ✛ 3:F2). Leave room for frozen custard.

TASTE OF THE CITY: ZACH BROOKS, FOOD BLOGGER FOR MIDTOWN LUNCH

Three years ago, Zach Brooks was a corporate nine-to-fiver looking for cheap lunchtime eats near his Midtown office. What began as a blog blossomed into a full-time career. Brooks now chronicles the dozens of "mobile restaurants" and other cheap eats in Midtown Manhattan. Here we get the inside scoop on the evolution of the food-cart scene.

Q: What is your criterion for a place to make it on site?

A: Midtown lunch is all about value, authenticity, and everything has to be under $10.

Q: Why has street food become such a force in the New York culinary scene?

A: It's definitely the Web and the bloggers, but it's also a word-of-mouth cultural thing.... But at the end of the day, nothing gets you like a line. You walk by and the smells are intoxicating, it pulls you in.

Q: What do you say to people who suggest that eating street food isn't safe?

A: Don't be scared. In many ways, it's the safest kind of food. You are basically looking in the kitchen, at the person who is preparing your food. None of the actual carts are operating without permits and licenses.

Q: How do you feel about the gourmet street carts?

A: The quality only gets better, and the cream always rises the top. As long as the food is good and cheap, I'm all for it. Anyone who is selling good food on the street for cheaper than you can get in a restaurant? I love it.

ZACH'S STREET CART BEST BETS

Halal Cart. SW corner, 53rd St./6th Ave.: Renowned platter of chicken or gyro meat, rice, hot sauce, and yogurt-based white sauce. **Biryani Cart.** SW Corner, 46th St./6th Ave.: Killer chicken Biryani and chicken tikka masala. **Kwikmeal Cart** (⊕ www.53rdand6th.com). NW corner 45th St./6th Ave.: Fragrant chicken and lamb over rice. **Trini Paki Boys** 43rd St./6th Ave.: Pakistani-style seasoned chicken, but with a Trinidadian pepper sauce. **Schnitzel & Things** (⊕ www.schnitzelandthings.com) 50th St./6th Ave. (location varies): Three types of breaded schnitzel and lots of great sauces. **Treats Truck** (⊕ www.treatstruck.com) 45th St./6th Ave. (location varies): Amazing peanut-butter-sandwich cookies, cinnamon-laced Mexican brownies.

AND FOR DESSERT...

Max Brenner: Chocolate by the Bald Man (✉ 841 Broadway, near 13th St. ☎ 212/388-0030 ⊹ 3:F4).
Sure, it's an international chain, but if you're looking for a major chocolate fix, you can count on this place to provide your poison. Max Brenner: Chocolate by the Bald Man is a Willy Wonka–esque chocolate emporium filled with college kids, families, and tourists—chocolate lovers, one and all. The extensive chocoholic menu boasts flavored chocolate beverages in custom-made sipping "hug mugs," chocolate fondues, cookies, cakes, brownies, and ice creams, even chocolate pizzas. If the Max Brenner scene isn't for you, check out the more sophisticated **City Bakery** (✉ 3 W. 18th St., between 5th and 6th Aves. ☎ 212/366-1414 ⊹ 3:E3) a few blocks to the north and west, where you can sip gourmet cocoa as thick as mud and nosh on crème brulée tartlettes with chocolate crusts or bag some addictively salty pretzel croissants to go.

18

MIDTOWN WEST AND CHELSEA

STEAK WITH STYLE

Big is the buzz in Times Square and neighboring hoods, where neon-lighted billboards, towering skyscrapers, and Broadway theaters play starring roles. But watch out for restaurant rip-offs in this urban-theme-park environment.

It's true that tourist traps abound on the Great White Way, but fortunately you needn't head far from Times Square to score a stellar meal. Just move away from the bright lights and unrelenting foot traffic that clogs the area. On calmer side streets and in adjoining Hell's Kitchen there are excellent dining options for budget travelers and expense-account diners alike. Some of the best steak houses and Italian restaurants are located here, and many eateries offer budget pretheater dinners and prix-fixe lunch menus to draw in new business.

But if the constant hustle and bustle unsettles your stomach, head south to Chelsea, a calmer neighborhood filled with art galleries and casual eateries. Chelsea may not be a white-hot dining destination, but you can eat well if you know where to go.

The design at **Quality Meats** (⊠ 57 W. 58th St., near 6th Ave. ☎ 212/371–7777 ✛ 4:D1), pictured above, is inspired by classic New York City butcher shops in its use of warm wood, stainless steel, and white marble. Sit at the bar to peruse the extensive menu of wines and single-malt Scotches. Then retire to the dining room for sophisticated riffs on steak-house classics like beef Wellington. Steak aficionados should know that Midtown has quality meats on every block. Here are more sure bets: **Ben Benson's** (⊠ 123 W. 52nd St., near 6th Ave. ☎ 212/581–8888 ✛ 4:D2) and **Uncle Jack's** (⊠ 440 9th Ave., at 35th St. ☎ 212/244–0005 ✛ 4:B6).

DINING IN TIMES SQUARE

There are plenty of chain eateries here that charge a pre-mium for a substandard, rushed meal. But we've narrowed the field, selecting the best spots for a range of experiences and prices—from fun family dining to pretheater favorites.

For family-style fun, you can't miss the retro, 1950s-style **Ellen's Stardust Diner** (✉ 1650 Broadway, at 51st St. ☎ 212/956–5151 ✛ 4:C3), complete with a singing waitstaff. Enjoy all-American classics such as meat loaf and chicken potpie while your waiters and waitresses serenade you with Broadway tunes.

Unlike the mostly kitschy theme restaurants that occupy Times Square, the sleek **Blue Fin** (✉ 1567 Broadway, near 47th St. ☎ 212/918–1400 ✛ 4:C3) seafood restaurant is a refreshing departure. Watch the crowds go by from the corner glass bar or head upstairs.

Toloache (✉ 251 W. 50th St., between Broadway and 8th Ave. ☎ 212/581–1818 ✛ 4:B3), a festive Mexican cantina, is a top foodie destination for its fresh ceviches, guacamoles, and standout dishes like the Negra Modelo–braised brisket taco or the quesadilla with black truffle and *huitlacoche* (corn fungus).

A mixed crowd of tourists, theatergoers, and thespians fre-quents **Joe Allen Restaurant** (✉ 326 W. 46th St., between 8th and 9th Aves. ☎ 212/581–6464 ✛ 4:B3), a pretheater favorite. This casual yet classy restaurant serves reliable American cuisine. Don't fret about missing the show—the Broadway-knowledgeable staff will make sure you get to the theater in time for the opening number.

Plates of fresh antipasti are displayed right as you walk into **Bond 45** (✉ 154 W. 45th St., between 6th and 7th Aves. ☎ 212/869–4545 ✛ 4:C4). This Italian eatery, with a dark-wood bar and leather-backed booths, serves a variety of piz-zas, pastas, and steaks. With a separate pretheater menu, this Theater District hot spot is an ideal option for dining and then dashing to your show of choice.

AND FOR DESSERT ...

Kyotofu
(✉ 705 9th Ave., near 48th St. ☎ 212/974–6012 ✛ 4:A3).
Even if you're not crazy about tofu, the soy-based delights at this Japanese dessert bar will make you reconsider the merits of the soybean. Kyotofu's signature sweet tofu with Kuromitsu black sugar syrup is so creamy and delicious you think it's a traditional panna cotta. The strawberry shortcake with strawberry sake sorbet and the warm miso chocolate cake with chocolate soybean ganache and green-tea cream are two more totally compelling favorites. Kyotofu's menu is full of intriguing options, so your best bet, on your first visit, is to go for the Kaiseki prix-fixe, a three-course tasting menu that enables you to try six different mini-desserts. Their menu changes seasonally, and it also includes savory brunch, lunch, and din-ner options as well as an extensive sake and shochu cocktail list.

18

MIDTOWN EAST/UPPER EAST SIDE

Power brokers like to seal their deals over lunch on the East Side, so that means more than a few suits and ties at the restaurants during the day.

At night Midtown's streets are relatively quiet, but the restaurants are filled with expense-account diners celebrating their successes. Some of the most formal dining rooms and most expensive meals in town can be found here, at restaurants like the landmark **Four Seasons** and **L'Atelier de Joël Robuchon** or the **Modern**.

Farther uptown, the Upper East Side is jam-packed with pricey neighborhood eateries that cater to the area's well-heeled residents. Long viewed as an enclave of the privileged, these neighborhoods have plenty of elegant restaurants that serve the society "ladies who lunch" and bankers looking forward to a steak and single-malt Scotch at the end of the day. However, visitors to Museum Mile and 5th Avenue shopping areas need not be put off. Whether you're looking to celebrate a special occasion or just want to grab a quick bite, you're sure to find something here for almost any budget.

URBAN PICNIC

For a uniquely New York experience, take a picnic lunch to one of the outdoor plazas that line Park Avenue from 51st to 53rd streets and seat yourself alongside scores of local office workers. (For architecture buffs, the Mies van der Rohe-designed Seagram Building is at 375 Park Avenue, at 52nd Street). First, pick up your wares at the **Market at Grand Central Terminal** (Main Concourse, East), a trusted resource for gourmet goods on-the-go. Your menu could include fresh-baked bread from **Corrado Bread & Pastry**; olives or prosciutto from **Ceriello Fine Foods**; and fresh mozzarella from **Murray's Cheese**.

MUSEUM MUNCHING

	SAVE	SPLURGE
Museum of Modern Art	The **La Bonne Soupe** (✉ 48 W. 55th St., betw. 5th and 6th Aves. ☎ 212/586–7650 ✛ 4:E2) special includes a bowl of soup with bread, salad, a glass of wine, and dessert for $17.25.	The **Modern's Bar Room** (✉ 9 W. 53rd St., near 5th Ave. ☎ 212/333–1220 ✛ 4:D2) offers Alsatian-inspired fare—don't miss the sinful tarte flambé, charred flat bread topped with bacon, onion, and creme fraîche.
Neue Galerie	**Pintaile's** (✉ 26 E. 91st St., at Madison Ave. ☎ 212/722–1967 ✛ 6:F5) pizza offers delicious slices with a thin whole-wheat crust and gourmet toppings like roasted eggplant, wild mushrooms, and chorizo.	**Café Sabarsky** (✉ 1048 5th Ave., near 86th St. ☎ 212/288–0665 ✛ 6:E6) entices museumgoers with hearty sandwiches and entrées like sausage and goulash. Rich pastries complete the caloric spree.
Metropolitan Museum of Art	Grab a bite at Belgian chain **Le Pain Quotidien** (✉ 1131 Madison Ave, betw. 84th and 85th Sts. ☎ 212/327–4900 ✛ 5:F1), which offers an array of light fare, like cheese boards and gourmet salads.	**E.A.T.** (✉ 1064 Madison Ave., betw. 80th and 81st Sts. ☎ 212/772–0022 ✛ 5:F2), Eli Zabar's upscale American diner, may have high prices, but devotees return for excellent soups, sandwiches, and salads.

FORAGING IN CENTRAL PARK

There are plenty of pushcarts offering hot dogs and sodas, but if you're looking to soak up Central Park's magical ambience in an elegant setting, head for the **Central Park Boathouse Restaurant** (✉ E. 72nd St. at Park Dr. N ☎ 212/517–2233 ✛ 5:E3), which overlooks the gondola lake. There you can relax on the outdoor deck with a glass of wine and a cheese plate, or go for a more formal meal inside the restaurant. In warmer months the restaurant can get crowded: go for a late lunch or early-evening cocktail.

AND FOR DESSERT . . .

Little Pie Company (✉ 107 E. 42nd St., Grand Central Terminal's Lower Dining Concourse ☎ 212/983–3538 ✛ 4:F4). The Grand Central Dining Concourse is not your typical food court—it contains outposts for some of the city's most popular edibles, including a pie-lover favorite: the Little Pie Company. The flakey crusts here are baked from scratch with fresh, all-natural ingredients. And they don't skimp on the fillings either, like fresh fruit, chocolate, or custard. Little Pie Company favorites include the Sour Cream Apple Walnut Pie, which is topped with a brown sugar, cinnamon, and walnut streusel, the Three Berry Pie (strawberry, blueberry, and raspberry), the Key Lime Pie (yep, made with real key lime juice), and the decadent triple chocolate Mississippi Mud Pie. You'll also find seasonal pies, such as a 100% pure pumpkin pie and their Southern Pecan pie with Texas pecans.

18

UPPER WEST SIDE/HARLEM

Anchoring the dining experience in this section of town are the high-end restaurants at the Time Warner Center, which some call a "fine-dining food court." Head farther uptown for cheaper eats, but also a burgeoning gourmet dining scene.

Dining room at Per Se in the Time Warner building.

With Lincoln Center theatergoers, hungry shoppers, and visitors to Central Park nearby, chefs are finally waking up to the captive built-in audience of tourists and locals alike. The main avenues are indeed lined with restaurants, but until recently many of them have been mediocre. Now the better-known destination-dining spots beyond the Time Warner Center—among them **Jean Georges, Picholine, Telepan, and Dovetail**—have been joined by newcomers like **Salumeria Rossi, Fatty Crab** and **Ed's Chowder,** all second or third restaurants from well-known chefs. Brunch is still a good bet, too. The flaky scones and fluffy omelets at **Sarabeth's,** not to mention blintzes and bagels at **Barney Greengrass,** are worth seeking out. For more adventurous eating, head up to Harlem for the city's best Southern cooking.

BRUNCH FAVES

If you haven't yet sorted out the city's obsession for smoked fish on a bagel, now's your chance to find out. **Barney Greengrass** (✉ 541 Amsterdam Ave., near 86th St. ☎ 212/724–4707 ✛ 6:B6) is the Upper West Side's best-loved brunch institution. Try succulent sable, luxuriant nova, egg and onion scramble, and the famed sturgeon. Caveats: reservations are not accepted, and the bill can hit $30-plus per person.

WHAT'S HOT IN HARLEM?

Visitors in decades past may remember Harlem as an area scarred by crime and poverty. But times have changed: the Harlem of today is a vibrant community with excellent restaurants of all stripes. Those unfamiliar with the area may consider catching a cab late in the evening. But don't be scared off: Harlem's ethnic eats are worth the trip.

Here are our top picks for savoring the multicultural flavor of the neighborhood:

Miss Mamie's Spoonbread Too (✉ 366 W. 110th St., near Manhattan Ave. ☎ 212/865–6744 ✚ 6:B2) is a much-loved Southern spot that's known for its friendly staff as well as its fried chicken, grits, and corn bread. Local politicians are sometimes seen rubbing elbows with the Columbia University students who gather here.

Native (✉ 161 Lenox Ave., at 118th St. ☎ 212/665–2525 ✚ 6:C1) is a mildly Caribbean restaurant serving flavorful rice bowls and entrées that span a broad range of cuisines. Boasting a curry chicken, smoked salmon linguine, and Moroccan fried chicken with collard greens and mashed potatoes this eatery manages to be all over the map and still find its way.

Sylvia's (✉ 328 Lenox Ave., near 127th St. ☎ 212/996–0660 ✚ 6:D1): This Harlem mainstay has been serving soul-food favorites like smothered chicken, barbecue ribs, collard greens, and mashed potatoes to a dedicated crowd of locals, tourists, and college students since 1962. The food is so popular that owner Sylvia Woods bottled her signature sauces and spices for the masses, available for purchase at the restaurant and online.

AND FOR DESSERT . . .

Levain Bakery (✉ 167 W. 74th St., near Amsterdam Ave. ☎ 212/874–6080 ✚ 5:B3). A big cookie for the big city. Completely unpretentious and utterly delicious, Levain's cookies are rich and hefty. In fact, they clock in at 6 ounces each! Choose from the chocolate-chip walnut, dark chocolate chocolate chip, dark chocolate peanut-butter chip, or oatmeal raisin. Batches are baked fresh daily, and they taste best when they're warm and melty right out of the oven, so it's definitely worth seeking out this small basement bakery for a cookie craving. Levain's also bakes artisanal breads, including banana chocolate chip and pumpkin ginger spice, sour cream coffee cake, chocolate-chip and cinnamon brioche, sourdough rolls stuffed with Valrhona chocolate, blueberry muffins, a variety of scones, and bomboloncini—their unique jelly doughnuts.

18

RESTAURANT REVIEWS

Listed Alphabetically within Neighborhoods

LOWER MANHATTAN

CHINATOWN

¢ ✕**Great New York Noodletown.** Although the soups and noodles are
CHINESE unbeatable at this no-frills restaurant, what you should order are the
window decorations—the hanging lacquered ducks and roasted pork,
which are listed on a simple board hung on the wall and superb served
with pungent garlic-and-ginger sauce on the side. Seasonal specialties
like duck with flowering chives and salt-baked soft-shell crabs are excellent. So is the *congee*, or rice porridge, available with any number of
garnishes. Solo diners may end up at a communal table. ⊠ *28 Bowery,
at Bayard St., Chinatown* ☎ *212/349–0923* ⊟ *No credit cards* Ⓜ *6, J,
M, Z to Canal St.; B, D to Grand St.* ✛ *2:F5.*

$ ✕**Jing Fong.** Come to this dim sum palace for a jolting taste of Hong
CHINESE Kong. On weekend mornings people pour into the escalator to Jing
Fong's carnivalesque third-floor dining room. Servers push carts of
steamed dumplings, barbecue pork buns, and shrimp balls. For adventurous eaters, there's chicken feet, tripe, and snails. Arrive early for the
best selection, and save room for mango pudding. ⊠ *20 Elizabeth St.,
2nd fl., between Bayard and Canal Sts., Chinatown* ☎ *212/964–5256*
⊟ *AE, MC, V* Ⓜ *6, J, M, N, Q, R, W, Z to Canal St.* ✛ *2:F5.*

$ ✕**Joe's Shanghai.** Joe opened his first Shanghai restaurant in Queens in
CHINESE 1995, but buoyed by the accolades accorded his steamed soup dumplings—filled with a rich, fragrant broth and ground pork or pork-crab-
meat mixture—he saw fit to open in Manhattan's Chinatown. There's
always a wait, but the line moves fast. Try the crisp turnip shortcakes
to start, homemade Shanghai noodles, and rich pork meatballs braised
in brown sauce. Other, more familiar Chinese dishes are also excellent.
Another Joe's Shanghai is located at 24 W. 56th Street, between 5th and
6th Avenues. ⊠ *9 Pell St., between the Bowery and Mott St., Chinatown*
☎ *212/233–8888* ⊕ *www.joeshanghairestaurants.com* ⌕ *Reservations
accepted at midtown location; also credit cards at Midtown location*
⊟ *No credit cards* Ⓜ *6, J, M, N, Q, R, W, Z to Canal St.* ✛ *2:F5.*

¢ ✕**Nha Trang.** You can get a great meal for under $10 at this low-atmo-
VIETNAMESE sphere Vietnamese restaurant in Chinatown. Start with crispy spring
Fodor's Choice rolls, sweet-and-sour seafood soup, or shrimp grilled on sugarcane.
★ For a follow-up, don't miss the thin pork chops, which are marinated
in a sweet vinegary sauce and grilled until charred. Another favorite
is deep-fried squid on shredded lettuce with a tangy dipping sauce. If
the line is long, which it usually is, even with a second location around
the corner at 148 Centre Street, you may be asked to sit at a table with
strangers. ⊠ *87 Baxter St., between Bayard and Canal Sts., Chinatown*
☎ *212/233–5948* ⊟ *No credit cards* Ⓜ *6, J, M, N, Q, R, W, Z to Canal
St.* ✛ *2:F5.*

$$ ✕**Peking Duck House.** This Chinatown institution is the place to go in
CHINESE New York for authentic Peking duck. Although the restaurant offers a
full Chinese menu, everyone—and we mean everyone—orders the duck.

Begin, as most tables do, with an order of Shanghai soup dumplings, then move onto the bird. It's carved up table-side with plenty of fanfare—crisp burnished skin separated from moist flesh. Roll up the duck, with hoisin and scallions, in tender steamed pancakes. ✉ *28 Mott St., at Mosco St., Chinatown* ☎ *212/227–1810* ⊕ *www.pekingduckhousenyc. com* ▭ *AE, MC, V* Ⓜ *6, J, M, N, Q, R, W, Z to Canal St.* ✛ *2:F5.*

$$ ✕**Ping's Seafood.** Although the original location in Queens still has the
CHINESE most elaborate menu with the most extensive selection of live seafood,
ⓒ the Manhattan location is more accessible both geographically and gastronomically. Helpful menus have pictures of most of the specialties. Among them are Dungeness crab in black bean sauce, crisp fried tofu, silken braised *e-fu* noodles, and crisp Peking duck. Pricier than some other Chinatown haunts, Ping's is thought by many to be a notch above in setting and service. ✉ *22 Mott St., near Pell St., Chinatown* ☎ *212/602–9988* ⚏ *Reservations essential* ▭ *AE, MC, V* Ⓜ *6, J, M, N, Q, R, W, Z to Canal St.* ✛ *2:F6.*

FINANCIAL DISTRICT

¢ ✕**Financier Patisserie.** On the cobblestone pedestrian street that has
CAFÉ become the Financial District's restaurant row, this quaint patisserie serves up excellent pastries and delicious savory foods, like truffle mushroom bisque and a panini pressed with prosciutto, fig jam, mascarpone, and arugula. After lunch, relax with a cappuccino and a *financier,* an almond tea cake, or an elegant French pastry. In warm weather, perch at an outdoor table and watch Manhattanites buzz by. Another location is nearby at 35 Cedar St., between Pearl and William Streets. ✉ *62 Stone St., between Mill La. and Hanover Sq., Lower Manhattan* ☎ *212/344–5600* ⊕ *www.financierpastries.com* ⚏ *Reservations not accepted* ▭ *AE, DC, MC, V* ☾ *Closed Sun. No dinner* Ⓜ *2, 3 to Wall St.; 4, 5 to Bowling Green* ✛ *1:E4.*

$$ ✕**Harry's Steak and Harry's Café.** Its noise-dampening acoustics and maze
STEAKHOUSE of underground nooks combine to make Harry's Steak—the fine-dining half of the resurrected Harry's of Hanover—the city's most intimate steak house. Request the grotto for a stealthy rendezvous, or the long dozen-seater for a raucous night out with the boys. Begin with savory baked clams buried in smoked bacon and bread crumbs or the lively tomato trio, starring thick beefsteak slices topped with bacon and blue cheese, mozzarella and basil, and shaved onion with ranch dressing. The star attraction—prime aged porterhouse for two—is nicely encrusted with sea salt and a good match for buttery mashed potatoes infused with sweet roasted shallots and thick steak sauce spooned from Mason jars. ✉ *1 Hanover Sq., between Stone and Pearl Sts., Financial District* ☎ *212/785–9200* ⊕ *www.harrysnyc.com* ⚏ *Reservations essential for Harry's Steak* ▭ *AE, D, MC, V* ☾ *Closed Sun.* Ⓜ *4, 5 to Bowling Green; 2, 3 to Wall St.* ✛ *1:E4.*

$$ ✕**P. J. Clarke's.** This East Side institution has been dispensing burgers
AMERICAN and beer for more than a century. Despite a physical upgrade under new owners in 2002, the original P. J. Clarke's (there's now another offshoot way downtown) maintains the beveled-glass and scuffed-wood look of an old-time saloon. Many of the bartenders and patrons are as much of a fixture as the decor. More civilized at lunchtime, weekday

18

evenings the bar area heaves with an after-work mob. Pull up a stool if you can for superlative bar food, like clams casino and the signature burger smothered in creamy béarnaise. A few other P. J. Clarke locations have sprouted up at 915 3rd Avenue (at 55th Street), 44 West 63rd St., near Columbus Avenue, and 205 East 55th Street, off 2nd Avenue. ✉ *250 Vesey St., at World Financial Center, Financial District* ☎ *212/285–1500* ▭ *AE, DC, MC, V* Ⓜ *A, C, E, 1, 2, 3, 9 to Chambers St.* ✛ *1:B3.*

$$$$ ✕ **SHO Shaun Hergatt.** This new restaurant in the Setai Hotel befits the
NEW AMERICAN riches of nearby Wall Street. Though it launched at the height of the recession, the decor screams all-out extravagance in every way. After passing through a dramatic corridor composed of glass-encased wine bottles, you enter a sprawling series of rooms adorned with framed silver rings, striated wood walls, and luxurious Asian-inspired fabrics. Australian chef Shaun Hergatt, visible in the open kitchen, brings a light touch to the luxurious cuisine in dishes like peekytoe crab with galangal gelee and sea urchin, and an ingot of three-day short rib over a rich parsnip puree that looks—and tastes—like a savory candy bar. The $69 three-course prix-fixe is a reasonable antidote to an expensive à la carte menu. ✉ *40 Broad St., at Exchange Pl., Lower Manhattan* ☎ *212/809–3993* ⊕ *wwwshoshaunhergatt.com* ⌕ *Reservations essential* ▭ *AE, MC, V* Ⓜ *R, W to Rector St., 2, 3, 4, 5 to Wall St., J, M, Z to Broad Street,* ✛ *1:D4.*

TRIBECA

$ ✕ **Bubby's.** Crowds clamoring for coffee and freshly squeezed juice line
AMERICAN up for brunch at this TriBeCa mainstay, but the restaurant serves fine
☺ lunches and dinners as well. The dining room is homey and comfortable, with big windows; in summer, neighbors sit at tables outside with their dogs. For brunch you can order almost anything, including homemade granola, sour-cream pancakes with bananas and strawberries, and *huevos rancheros* with guacamole and grits. Eclectic comfort food—mac 'n cheese, fried chicken—make up the lunch and dinner menus. ✉ *120 Hudson St., at N. Moore St., TriBeCa* ☎ *212/219–0666* ⊕ *www. bubbys.com* ▭ *D, DC, MC, V* Ⓜ *1 to Franklin St.* ✛ *1:C1.*

$$$$ ✕ **Corton.** Über-restaurateur Drew Neiporent has transformed the for-
FRENCH mer Montrachet space into a spare, elegant dining room. It's the perfect stage for young whiz-kid chef Paul Liebrandt's understated, mildly experimental cuisine. The walls are decorated with subtle white trompe-l'oeil designs of cherry blossoms and birds, but the real adornment is on the plate, where Liebrandt transports diners with dishes like his "from the garden" composition: an assemblage of nearly 20 vegetable components that redefines what produce can do. Heirloom eggs are presented at the table in a basket, then spirited back to the kitchen for a slow poach before being served with a rich yellow cauliflower puree and Serrano gelee. Desserts include chocolate tart with grapefruit and hazelnut. The well-curated wine list includes a cost-conscious selection of "country French" bottles. ✉ *239 W. Broadway, between Walker and White Sts., TriBeCa* ☎ *212/219–2777* ⊕ *www.cortonnyc.com* ⌕ *Reservations essential* ▭ *AE, D, DC, MC, V* ☾ *Closed Sun. No lunch* Ⓜ *1 to Franklin St., A, C, E to Canal St.* ✛ *2:D5.*

$$$
AMERICAN
✗**The Harrison.** Jimmy Bradley's formula for the perfect neighborhood eatery, which he mastered at the Red Cat in Chelsea, works like a charm in TriBeCa. The warm, woody room serves as a relaxed backdrop for the seasonal American food from chef Amanda Freitag, like English-cut lamb loin with baby carrots and fennel, and malt-vinegar mayo. Desserts, including an ice cream–brownie sandwich with Sazerac caramel, are at once accessible and sophisticated. ✉ *355 Greenwich St., at Harrison St., TriBeCa* ☎ *212/274–9310* ⊕ *www.theharrison.com* ⚓ *Reservations essential* 🖃 *AE, D, DC, MC, V* ☾ *No lunch* Ⓜ *1 to Franklin St.* ✛ *2:C6.*

$
AMERICAN
✗**Kitchenette.** This small, comfy restaurant lives up to its name with tables so close together you're likely to make new friends. The dining room feels like a breakfast nook, and the food tastes like your mom made it—provided she's a great cook. There are no frills, just solid cooking, friendly service, and a long line at peak times. For brunch don't miss the blackberry-cherry pancakes or the baked vanilla brûlée French toast. Lemon-Parmesan chicken with seasonal vegetables is a heavenly dinner. ✉ *156 Chambers St., near Greenwich St., TriBeCa* ☎ *212/267–6740* ⊕ *www.kitchenetterestaurant.com* 🖃 *AE, MC, V* Ⓜ *1, 2, 3, A, C to Chambers St.* ✛ *1:C2.*

$$–$$$
ITALIAN
✗**Locanda Verdi.** The second time's the charm for Robert DeNiro, who along with his partners closed Ago, their first attempt at a restaurant in the clubby Greenwich Hotel. Chef Andrew Carmellini, an acolyte of Daniel Boulud, made a smart move from A Voce to cook here, and he's clearly in his element. The space is warm and welcoming, with accents of brick and wood and large windows that open to the street, weather permitting. The menu is full of aspirational comfort food that hits the mark, especially the *cicchetti* (small plates) such as blue crab crostino with jalapeños and a mound of sheep's-milk ricotta scattered with sea salt and herbs. Five draft beers, along with more than a dozen wines by the glass, make an already hopping bar scene even more of a draw. ✉ *379 Greenwich St., at N. Moore St., TriBeCa* ☎ *212/925–3797* ⊕ *www.locandaverdenyc.com* ⚓ *Reservations essential* 🖃 *AE, MC, V* Ⓜ *1 to Franklin St.* ✛ *1:B1.*

18

$$
JAPANESE
✗**Matsugen.** Matsugen is Jean-Georges Vongerichten's latest Manhattan venture, offering authentic Japanese cuisine. The contemporary design includes long communal dining tables and a fish tank filled with unusual crustaceans. Classic Japanese dishes are offered, such as sushi, sashimi, Wagyu beef, and shabu-shabu (where diners try their own hand at cooking lobster and pork loin in a pot of boiling water at their table). The real stars here, however, are the more than a dozen takes on soba noodles, which are made from buckwheat flour—served hot, chilled, and with additions such as tofu, duck, yams, and prawns. The extensive sake menu makes for a nice accompaniment to the meal. If you're not in the mood to sit in the main dining room, the large bar area in the front of the restaurant has comfortable chairs and is ideal for lingering. ✉ *241 Church St., at Leonard St., TriBeCa* ☎ *212/925–0202* ⊕ *www. jean-georges.com* 🖃 *D, DC, MC, V* Ⓜ *1 to Franklin St.* ✛ *2:D5.*

$$$
JAPANESE
✗**Nobu.** At this huge, bustling TriBeCa dining room (or its sister location uptown), you may just spot a celeb or two. New York's most

famous Japanese restaurant has gained a lot of competition in recent years, but this is still the destination for the innovative Japanese cuisine Nobu Matsuhisa made famous (even if the chef himself is rarely in attendance these days). Dishes like fresh yellowtail sashimi with jalapeño, rock shrimp tempura, or miso-marinated Chilean sea bass continue to draw huge crowds. Put yourself in the hands of the chef by ordering the tasting menu, the *omakase*, specify how much you want to spend, and let the kitchen do the rest. Can't get reservations? Try your luck at the first-come, first-served **Nobu Next Door at 105 Hudson St.**, with a similar menu plus a sushi bar. ⊠ *105 Hudson St., at Franklin St., TriBeCa* ☎ *212/219–0500* ⊕ *www.myriadrestaurantgroup.com* ⌲ *Reservations essential* ▣ *AE, D, DC, MC, V* ⊙ *No lunch weekends* Ⓜ *1 to Franklin St.* ✛ *1:B1.*

$$$
BISTRO
Ⓒ

✗ **Odeon.** New Yorkers change hangouts faster than they can press speed-dial, but this spot has managed to maintain its quality and flair for more than 25 years. The neo-Art Deco room is still packed nightly with revelers. Now children are also welcome. The pleasant service and well-chosen wine list are always in style. The bistro-menu highlights include *frisée aux lardons* with poached farm egg, grilled NY strip steak, and slow-cooked cod with baby leeks and fennel confit. ⊠ *145 West Broadway, between Duane and Thomas Sts., TriBeCa* ☎ *212/233–0507* ⊕ *www.theodeonrestaurant.com* ▣ *AE, D, DC, MC, V* Ⓜ *1, 2, 3, A, C to Chambers St.* ✛ *2:D6.*

SOHO WITH NOLITA AND LITTLE ITALY

SOHO

$$$
SEAFOOD

✗ **Aquagrill.** Owned by a husband-and-wife team, Aquagrill is a popular SoHo standard. The lively neighborhood eatery makes its own pastries and baked goods—including the bread for its challah French toast with cinnamon apples and pecan butter. Fans rave about the lunchtime $21.50 prix-fixe Shucker Special—a half-dozen oysters with homemade soup or chowder and a salad. Dinner specialties include roasted Dungeness crab cake napoleon with sun-dried tomato oil, and falafel-crusted salmon. Try the knockout chocolate tasting plate, with handmade chocolates, warm chocolate cake, white chocolate mousse, and milk-chocolate ice cream. ⊠ *210 Spring St., at 6th Ave., SoHo* ☎ *212/274–0505* ⊕ *www.aquagrill.com* ⌲ *Reservations essential* ▣ *AE, D, DC, MC, V* Ⓜ *C, E to Spring St.* ✛ *2:D4.*

$$
BRASSERIE

✗ **Balthazar.** Even with long waits and excruciating noise levels, most out-of-towners agree that it's worth making reservations to experience restaurateur Keith McNally's flagship, a painstakingly accurate reproduction of a Parisian brasserie. Like the decor, entrées re-create French classics: Gruyère-topped onion soup; steak-frites; and icy tiers of crab, oysters, and other pristine shellfish. Brunch is still one of the toughest tables in town. The best strategy is to go at off-hours, or on weekdays for breakfast, to miss the crush of hungry New Yorkers. ⊠ *80 Spring St., between Broadway and Crosby St., SoHo* ☎ *212/965–1414* ⊕ *www.balthazarny.com* ⌲ *Reservations essential* ▣ *AE, MC, V* Ⓜ *6 to Spring St.; N, R, W to Prince St.; B, D, F, V to Broadway–Lafayette* ✛ *2:E4.*

$$ ✕ **Blue Ribbon Brasserie.** After 18 years, Blue Ribbon remains *the* late-night foodie hangout. Join the genial hubbub for midnight noshing, namely the beef marrow with oxtail marmalade and the renowned raw-bar platters. Trustafarians, literary types, chefs, designers—a good-looking gang—fill this dark box of a room until 4 AM. The menu appears standard at first blush, but it's not. Try the duck club sandwich, or the Wor matzah ball soup, a heady brew filled with the sacrilegious combo of seafood and traditional Jewish dumplings. ✉ *97 Sullivan St., between Prince and Spring Sts., SoHo* ☎ *212/274–0404* ⊕ *www.blueribbonrestaurants.com* ⌚ *Reservations not accepted* ▭ *AE, D, DC, MC, V* ⊘ *No lunch* Ⓜ *C, E to Spring St.; R, W to Prince St.* ✛ *2:D3.*

NEW AMERICAN

$$ ✕ **Blue Ribbon Sushi.** Sushi, like pizza, attracts plenty of opinionated fanatics. Stick to the excellent raw fish and specials here if you're a purist. Others might want to try one of the experimental rolls: the Blue Ribbon—lobster, shiso, and black caviar—is popular. The dark, intimate nooks, minimalist design, and servers with downtown attitude attract a stylish crowd that doesn't mind waiting for a table or for chilled sake served in traditional wooden boxes. ✉ *119 Sullivan St., between Prince and Spring Sts., SoHo* ☎ *212/343–0404* ⊕ *www.blueribbonrestaurants.com* ⌚ *Reservations not accepted* ▭ *AE, D, DC, MC, V* Ⓜ *C, E to Spring St.; R, W to Prince St.* ✛ *2:D3.*

JAPANESE

$$ ✕ **Emporio.** In a neighborhood whose long, boutique-lined blocks can sometimes feel deserted after dark, Emporio is a chic, welcoming hangout with warmth to spare. The brick-lined front room is a gathering spot for happy hour at the bar, featuring an appetizing selection of free small bites like frittata, white-bean salad, and ham-and-spinach *tramezzini* (finger sandwiches). The centerpiece of the large, skylit back room—great for small and large parties alike—is a wood-fired oven which turns out crisp, thin-crusted pizzas topped with staples like prosciutto, buffalo mozzarella, and arugula. Service is solicitous but not speedy, allowing time to linger into the late hours over a bottle of wine from a copious selection. Try house-made pastas like chewy garganelli with pork sausage and house-made ragu, entrées like whole roasted branzino with grilled lemon, then finish with piping-hot dessert calzone filled with ricotta, Nutella, and hazelnuts, or a delicate panna cotta with poached plums. ✉ *231 Mott St.,between Prince and Spring Sts. NoLita* ☎ *212/966–1234* ⊕ *www.auroraristorante.com/emporio* ▭ *AE, D, DC, MC, V* Ⓜ *B, D, F, V, A, C, E to W. 4th St., 6 to Bleecker St.* ✛ *2:F3.*

ITALIAN
Fodor's Choice
★

$$ ✕ **Hundred Acres.** The owners of Cookshop and Five Points have set up new digs on MacDougal Street. Their latest restaurant, Hundred Acres, has a rustic, country feel and offers simple yet sophisticated cooking à la Marc Meyer and Cookshop chef Joel Hough. Don't count on a big menu: the daily choices are limited to seven main dishes and one special entrée. The steamed littleneck clams appetizer served with garlic-oregano butter, pickled corn, cilantro, and garlic toasts is particularly delicious. For the mains, try the Montauk bluefish with spinach, chickpeas, and fiery harissa or the Hampshire pork shank with polenta and rhubarb chutney. The classic burger made from pasture-raised beef, topped with Vermont cheddar and served with fries and Vidalia onion mayonnaise, should not be missed. ✉ *38 MacDougal St.,*

NEW AMERICAN
Fodor's Choice
★

18

between Houston and Prince Sts., Soho ☎ *212/475–7500* ⊕ *hundreda-cresnyc.com* ▭ *AE, DC, MC, V* Ⓜ *1 to Houston; C, E to Spring St., N, R, W to Prince St.* ✛ *2:D3.*

$ ✗ **La Esquina.** Anchoring a downtown corner under a bright neon sign,
MEXICAN   La Esquina looks nothing more than a fast-food taqueria. But beyond the top-notch, dirt-cheap tacos sold to-go until 5 in the morning lurks an entire restaurant complex. Just around the corner you'll find a modestly priced sit-down café featuring those same tacos along with more ambitious fare like fine chiles rellenos (stuffed peppers) and *carne asada* (grilled meat). Meanwhile, the real hipster draw remains completely hidden from sight. La Esquina's basement brasserie, like a Mexican speakeasy, is accessible by reservation only, through an unmarked door just inside the ground-floor taqueria. Once inside, you'll discover a buzzy subterranean scene along with potent margaritas and robust upscale fare. Though prices downstairs are high, portions are huge. ⊠ *106 Kenmare St., between Cleveland Pl. and Lafayette St., SoHo* ☎ *646/613–7100* ▭ *AE, MC, V* Ⓜ *6 to Spring St.* ✛ *2:F4.*

$$$ ✗ **Lure.** Outfitted like the interior of a sleek luxury liner, Lure offers oce-
SEAFOOD   anic fare prepared in multiple culinary styles. From the sushi bar, feast on Lure House Rolls, shrimp tempura rolls crowned with spicy tuna and Japanese tartar sauce. From the kitchen, order creative dishes like steamed branzino with oyster mushrooms, scallions, and ponzu sauce, or Manila clams over pancetta-studded linguine. For an all-American treat, you can't go wrong with a classic lobster roll on brioche. ⊠ *142 Mercer St., at Prince St., SoHo* ☎ *212/431–7676* ⊕ *www.lurefishbar. com* ▭ *AE, MC, V* ⊘ *No lunch weekends* Ⓜ *6 to Bleecker St.; B, D, F, V to Broadway-Lafayette St.; N, R, W to Prince St.* ✛ *2:E3.*

$ ✗ **MarieBelle.** Practically invisible from the front of the chocolate empo-
CAFÉ   rium, the back entry to the Cacao Bar opens into a sweet, high-ceiling,
☺   12-table hot-chocolate shop. Most people order the Aztec, European-style (that's 60% Colombian chocolate mixed with hot water—no cocoa powder here!). The first sip is startlingly rich but not too dense. American-style, made with milk, is sweeter. Preface it with a salad or sandwich from the dainty lunch menu, or request one of the expensive but ravishing flavored chocolates sold out front, like passion fruit, or *dulce de leche.* Another location at 762 Madison Avenue, off 65th Street, gives Upper East Siders their sweet treats. ⊠ *484 Broome St., between West Broadway and Wooster St., SoHo* ☎ *212/925–6999* ⊕ *www.mariebelle.com* ⚆ *Reservations not accepted* ▭ *AE, D, MC, V* ⊘ *No dinner* Ⓜ *6 to Spring St.; A, C, E to Canal St.* ✛ *2:D4.*

$$$ ✗ **Savoy.** Chef-owner Peter Hoffman's two-story restaurant has the
AMERICAN   coziness of a country inn, with blazing fireplaces upstairs and downstairs, soft wood accents, and windows looking onto the cobblestone street. Hoffman is one of the city's strongest proponents of using local, seasonal ingredients, which shows in disarmingly simple dishes like a confit of pork shoulder with delicata squash, apple, and chorizo, and salt-crusted baked duck with mashed turnips, poached plums and carrots. The wine list emphasizes small producers, and the recession-friendly lunch special offers three small plates for $16. ⊠ *70 Prince St., at Crosby St., SoHo* ☎ *212/219–8570* ⊕ *www.savoynyc.com* ▭ *AE,*

MC, V ⊗ No lunch Sun. Ⓜ *R, W to Prince St.; 6 to Spring St.; F, V to Broadway–Lafayette St.* ✛ *2:E3.*

NOLITA

$$$ ✕ **Peasant.** The crowd at this rustic restaurant is stylishly urban. Inspired
ITALIAN by the proverbial "peasant" cuisine where meals were prepared in the
kitchen hearth, chef-owner Frank DeCarlo cooks all of his wonderful
food in a bank of wood- or charcoal-burning ovens, from which the
heady aroma of garlic perfumes the room. Don't fill up on the crusty
bread and fresh ricotta, though, or you'll miss out on other flavorful
Italian fare like sizzling sardines that arrive in terra-cotta pots, or rotis-
serie lamb that's redolent of fresh herbs. ✉ *194 Elizabeth St., between
Spring and Prince Sts., NoLita* ☎ *212/965–9511* ⊕ *www.peasantnyc.
com* ⚲ *Reservations essential* ⊟ *AE, MC, V ⊗ Closed Mon. No lunch*
Ⓜ *6 to Spring St.; R, W to Prince St.* ✛ *2:F3.*

$$ ✕ **Public.** Public's space is complex and sophisticated, with soaring ceil-
ECLECTIC ings and whitewashed brick walls, skylights, fireplaces, three dining
areas, a vast bar, and even the occasional elegant bookcase. The menu
flaunts its nonconformity, and brunch at Public is a local favorite, with
exotic dishes like coconut pancakes topped with fresh ricotta, mango,
and lime syrup, and a juicy venison burger. Australian barramundi
fish, served with vanilla-celeriac puree and braised garlic greens, dem-
onstrates a light, yet adventurous, touch. Standout desserts include
a chocolate mousse with tahini ice cream and sesame candy. ✉ *210
Elizabeth St., between Prince and Spring Sts., NoLita* ☎ *212/343–7011*
⊕ *www.public-nyc.com* ⊟ *AE, D, MC, V ⊗ No lunch weekdays* Ⓜ *6 to
Spring St.; N, R to Prince St.; J, M to Bowery* ✛ *2:F3.*

LITTLE ITALY

$ ✕ **Lombardi's.** Brick walls, red-and-white checkered tablecloths, and the
PIZZA aroma of thin-crust pies emerging from the coal oven set the mood for
☯ some of the best pizza in Manhattan. Lombardi's has served pizza since
1905 (though not in the same location), and business has not died down
a bit. The mozzarella is always fresh, resulting in an almost grease-
less slice, and the toppings, such as meatballs, pancetta, or imported
anchovies, are also top quality. Lombardi's is perhaps best known for
its toothsome clam pizza, which features freshly shucked clams, garlic
oil, pecorino-Romano cheese, and parsley. ✉ *32 Spring St., at Mott St.,
Little Italy* ☎ *212/941–7994* ⊕ *www.firstpizza.com* ⊟ *No credit cards*
Ⓜ *6 to Spring St.; B, D, F, V to Broadway–Lafayette St.* ✛ *2:F4.*

18

EAST VILLAGE AND LOWER EAST SIDE

EAST VILLAGE

$$$ ✕ **Apiary.** Set on a busy strip of the East Village, Apiary is a chic refuge
NEW AMERICAN for a mature dinner in a young neighborhood. The restaurant is partly
owned by furniture design company Ligne Roset, and the contemporary
space holds sleek furnishings by the brand. The à la carte menu, cour-
tesy of talented Veritas alumnus Scott Bryan, isn't huge, but is devoted
to seasonal—and whenever possible— local food. Expect dishes like
crispy sweetbreads with romesco sauce and chanterelle risotto with

peas, lemon, and herbs. A cost-conscious $35 prix-fixe menu, offered Monday through Thursday, offers many menu standouts at a fraction of the price. The extensive wine list features many domestic picks, but also takes drinkers on an international oenological tour. Monday is no-corkage night. ⊠ *60 3rd Ave., at 11th St., East Village* ☎ *212/254–0888* ⊕ *www.apiarynyc.com* ☐ *AE, D, DC, MC, V* ☺ *No lunch weekdays* Ⓜ *6 to Astor Pl.; R, W to 8th St.; L to 3rd Ave.* ✛ *3:G5.*

$ ✕ **Back Forty.** Pioneering chef Peter Hoffman, a longtime leader in pro-
AMERICAN moting local, sustainable food, attracts a devoted crowd at this casual restaurant that feels like a neighborhood joint. Despite Hoffman's pedigree, Back Forty displays plenty of humility. Prices on the short, rustic, greenmarket menu are low, and the homey decor features a pastoral mural behind the bar and rusty farm tools on the walls. Begin with bar snacks like chicken-liver mousse on toast washed down with a fine house cocktail like the rum and Concord Collins. The simple family-style dinner selections include a perfect grilled trout; a moist, shareable pan-roasted chicken; and a wide array of seasonal sides including the cauliflower gratin and roasted brussels sprouts with maple-cider vinegar and lemon-thyme butter. A hearty and popular brunch is now served Saturdays. ⊠ *190 Ave. B, at 12th St., East Village* ☎ *212/388–1990* ⊕ *www.backfortynyc.com* ☐ *AE, MC, V* ☺ *No lunch Mon.–Sat.* Ⓜ *L to 1st Ave.* ✛ *3:H4.*

$ ✕ **Baoguette.** Vietnamese *Banh Mi* have taken New York by storm in
VIETNAMESE the past couple of years, and Baoguette, a chainlet from restaurateur
Fodor's Choice Michael Hunh, is a great place to try these spicy, multilayered baguette
★ sandwiches. This is the flagship decorated with raffia walls and large photos of Vietnamese street scenes, and though there a few tables, the majority of customers get take-out sandwiches. Try the namesake sandwich, layered with savory pâté, flavorful pulled pork, and aromatic herbs, or the addictive Sloppy Bao, a sweet and savory sloppy joe with curried beef, mango, and lemongrass. ⊠ *37 St. Marks Pl., between 2nd and 3rd Aves., East Village* ☎ *212/380–1487* ⊕ *www.baoguettecafe. com* ⚛ *Reservations not accepted* ☐ *No credit cards* Ⓜ *R, W to 8th St./ NYU; 6 to Astor Pl./4th Ave.* ✛ *2:F1.*

$$ ✕ **Chinatown Brasserie.** This large, bi-level 175-seat dining room is thrill-
CHINESE ingly vibrant, featuring dark cherry banquettes and 8 stunning crimson pagoda silk lanterns suspended from two central columns. Chicken and pine nuts are wrapped in Bibb lettuce. Crispy Peking duck is roasted in a special barbecuing oven, then sliced and presented on a long platter with the crackling skin still attached to the succulent flesh. Fresh Mandarin pancakes, julienned scallions, and sweet, pungent hoisin sauce are on hand. Dark-chocolate fortune cookies contain salient quotes from Albert Einstein and Ronald Reagan. ⊠ *380 Lafayette St., at Great Jones St., East Village* ☎ *212/533–7000* ⊕ *www.chinatownbrasserie. com* ☐ *AE, MC, V* Ⓜ *6 to Bleecker St.; B, D, F, V to Broadway and Lafayette St.* ✛ *2:E2.*

$$ ✕ **DBGB Kitchen & Bar.** The latest addition to Daniel Boulud's New
GASTROPUB York City restaurant fleet, DBGB forgoes the white tablecloths, formal
Fodor's Choice service, and steep prices found at the famed chef's fancier digs, and
★ instead pays homage to the grittier, younger feel of its Lower East Side

location. (The name is a wink to CBGB.) Lined with shelves of pots, plates, and pans (not to mention copperware donated by renowned chefs from around the world), the dining room gives way to a partially open kitchen where you can catch the chefs preparing Boulud's take on French and German-inspired pub fare. The menu features 13 different varieties of sausages (the *tunisienne*, a spicy lamb and mint merguez is a particular standout), decadently sinful burgers (the aptly-named "piggy" burger, a juicy beef patty topped with a generous portion of Daisy Mae pulled pork, jalapeño mayonnaise, and mustard vinegar slaw in a cheddar-cornbread bun—not for the weak-willed), and classic entrées like steak-frites, and lemon and rosemary roasted chicken. The $22 three-course, lunch prix-fixe is quite a steal. ⊠ *299 Bowery, between Houston and 1st St., Lower East Side* ☎ *212/933–5300* ⊕ *www.danielnyc.com* ⚒ *Reservations essential* ☰ *AE, D, DC, MC, V* ⊘ *No lunch Mon.* ⊹ *2:F2.*

$$ ✗ **Gnocco.** Owners Pierluigi Palazzo and Gianluca Giavonetti named the
ITALIAN place not after gnocchi but after a regional specialty—deep-fried dough bites served alongside capicolla, salami, and aged prosciutto. Head to the roomy canopied garden out back for savory salads, an endlessly rotating selection of house-made pasta specials, pizza topped with mozzarella, truffles, and mushrooms, and hearty entrées like pork tenderloin in a balsamic emulsion with flakes of grana padano cheese. ⊠ *337 E. 10th St., between Aves. A and B, East Village* ☎ *212/677–1913* ⊕ *www. gnocco.com* ☰ *AE* Ⓜ *L. to 1st Ave.; 6 to Astor Pl.* ⊹ *3:H5.*

$$$ ✗ **Il Buco.** The unabashed clutter of vintage kitchen gadgets and tableware
MEDITERRANEAN harks back to Il Buco's past as an antiques store. Each table, two of which are communal, is unique—the effect is a festive, almost romantic country-house atmosphere. The restaurant features meats and produce from local farms for the daily entrées and Mediterranean tapaslike appetizers. Call ahead to book the intimate wine cellar for dinner. ⊠ *47 Bond St., between Bowery and Lafayette St., East Village* ☎ *212/533–1932* ⊕ *www.ilbuco.com* ☰ *AE, MC, V* ⊘ *No lunch Sun. and Mon.* Ⓜ *6 to Bleecker St.; B, D, F, V to Broadway-Lafayette St.* ⊹ *2:F2.*

$$$$ ✗ **Jewel Bako.** In a minefield of cheap, often inferior sushi houses gleams
JAPANESE tiny Jewel Bako. One of the best sushi restaurants in the East Village, the futuristic bamboo tunnel of a dining room is gorgeous, but try to nab a place at the sushi bar and put yourself in the hands of sushi master Yoshi Kousaka. His five-course *omakase*, or chef's menu, starts at $95. (A less-expensive sushi or sashimi *omakase* is $50.) You'll be served only what's freshest and best. ⊠ *239 E. 5th St., between 2nd and 3rd Aves., East Village* ☎ *212/979–1012* ⚒ *Reservations essential* ☰ *AE, MC, V* ⊘ *Closed Sun. No lunch* Ⓜ *6 to Astor Pl.* ⊹ *3:G6.*

$$$$ ✗ **Momofuku Ko.** A seasonal tasting menu full of clever combinations and
ASIAN esoteric ingredients explains the deafening buzz for James Beard Award–
Fodor's Choice winning chef David Chang's latest venture. Ko's small, intimate space
★ is sparsely furnished with a counter of blond wood and only a dozen stools. Diners get to see Ko's chefs in action as they prepare all manner of inventive dishes, including a signature preparation of frozen foie gras torchon grated over lychee fruits and white wine gelee. Reservations can only be made online, no more than seven days ahead, and are extremely

18

difficult to get. Log on at 10 AM (credit-card number needed just to get in the system), when new reservations are available, and keep hitting reload. ✉ *163 1st Ave., at E. 10th St., East Village* ☎ *212/228–0031 or 212/475–7899* ⊕ *www.momofuku.com* ☜ *Reservations essential* ▤ *AE, MC, V* ☽ *No lunch* Ⓜ *L to 1st Ave.; 6 to Astor Pl.* ✛ *3:H5.*

$
ASIAN
✕ **Momofuku Noodle Bar.** Chef-owner David Chang has created a shrine to ramen with this stylish 70-seat restaurant. His riff on the Japanese classic features *haute* ingredients like Berkshire pork, free-range chicken, and organic produce. His modern take on pork buns with cucumber and scallions is phenomenal—worth the trip alone. Go early or late—the tiny restaurant is packed during regular mealtimes. New this year: a phenomenal fried-chicken meal, featuring triple-fried and Old Bay varieties, with a variety of accoutrements (available by special reservations only on their Web site momofuku.com). ✉ *171 1st Ave., between E. 10th and E. 11 Sts., East Village* ☎ *212/777–7773* ⊕ *www. momofuku.com/noodle* ☜ *Reservations not accepted* ▤ *AE, MC, V* Ⓜ *L to 1st Ave.* ✛ *3:H5.*

$$
ASIAN
✕ **Momofuku Ssäm Bar.** New York foodies have been salivating over chef David Chang's Asian-influenced fare since he opened his first restaurant, a Japanese noodle shop, in 2004. Momofuku Ssäm Bar, the wunderkind's much larger follow-up, is packed nightly with downtown diners cut from the same cloth as the pierced and tattooed waitstaff and cooks. The no-reservation policy means you'll likely have to wait for a chance to perch at the communal food bar and nibble on Chang's truly original small-plate cuisine. Dishes from the seasonally changing menu arrive like tapas for sharing. Although the chef works mostly with Asian flavors, his food is impossible to pigeonhole. Chang's not-to-be-missed riff on a classic Chinese pork bun helped build his cult following. On their Web site, momofuku.com, you can special-order a festive Bo Ssäm dinner featuring a slow-roasted pork shoulder, oysters, Asian greens, and a variety of sauces—all piled into crispy lettuce leaves. ✉ *207 2nd Ave., at 13th St., East Village* ☎ *212/254–3500* ⊕ *www. momofuku.com/ssam* ☜ *Reservations not accepted* ▤ *AE, MC, V* Ⓜ *L to 1st Ave.* ✛ *3:H4.*

$$
NEW AMERICAN
✕ **Prune.** There's just something very right-on about the food at Prune, a cozy treasure of a restaurant serving eclectic, well-executed American food from cult chef Gabrielle Hamilton. The choices change with the season, but you might find braised rabbit legs in vinegar sauce, whole grilled fish with fennel oil and chunky sea salt, or roasted marrow bones with parsley salad and toast points. There's usually a wait, and the quarters are very cramped, so don't expect to feel comfortable lingering at your rickety wooden table. Desserts, like ricotta ice cream with salted caramel croutons, are irresistible, and on weekends lines form early for the restaurant's deservedly popular brunch. ✉ *54 E. 1st St., between 1st and 2nd Aves., East Village* ☎ *212/677–6221* ⊕ *www. prunerestaurant.com* ☜ *Reservations essential* ▤ *AE, MC, V* Ⓜ *F, V to 2nd Ave.* ✛ *2:F2.*

¢
CAFÉ
☺
✕ **Veniero's Pasticceria.** More than a century old, this bustling bakery-café sells every kind of Italian *dolce* (sweet), from cherry-topped cookies to creamy cannoli and flaky *sfogliatelle*. A wine license means you can top

off an evening with a bottle of red. ✉ *342 E. 11th St., near 1st Ave., East Village* ☎ *212/674–7070* ⊕ *www.venierospastry.com* ⌕ *Reservations not accepted* 🖃*AE, D, DC, MC, V* Ⓜ *6 to Astor Pl.; L to 1st Ave.* ✛ *3:H5.*

LOWER EAST SIDE

$$
ITALIAN
✕ **'inoteca.** The Italian terms on the menu may be a little daunting, but the food is not. An Italian small-plates concept with an excellent by-the-glass wine list, this rustic eatery is perpetually packed. (Reservations are accepted for parties of 6 or more.) Come for cheese and charcuterie plates, the famous truffled egg toast, and delicious panini sandwiches filled with cured meat, runny cheeses, and hot peppers. Menu staples include fresh salads and creative entrées like lentils, fennel, celery root, capers, and saffron, and roast lamb cannelloni with white beans, spinach, and pecorino with house-made sausage. ✉ *98 Rivington St., at Ludlow St., Lower East Side* ☎ *212/614–0473* ⊕ *www.inotecanyc.com* 🖃*AE, MC, V* Ⓜ *F, J, M, Z to Delancey St.* ✛ *2:G3.*

$
CAMBODIAN
Fodor's Choice
★
✕ **Kampuchea Restaurant.** Cambodian-born Ratha Chau is the driving force at this sophisticated Southeast Asian street-food spot. With exposed-brick walls, elevated bar-style seating, and a well-planned wine list, it's the most stylish noodle bar we've ever encountered. Kampuchea's menu changes often, according to both the bounty of the season and chef-owner Chau's culinary desires. Diners are encouraged to dabble different sections of the menu, moving from the small plates onto the sandwiches and crepes, and then to the big-bowl noodle soups and stews. Dishes like grilled corn lathered in coconut mayo, coconut flakes, and chili powder rotate with the seasons. Spicy house-cured pickles or the melt-in-your mouth crispy pork belly go down easily with a fresh watermelon juice or a lychee fizz. Next, go for the savory pork crepe scattered with peanuts or the shiitake mushroom crepe with soybeans and butternut squash. For sandwiches, the sweet pulled oxtail with spicy tamarind is a fantastic combo. Finally, the Phnom Penh Katiev noodle soup with ground pork, duck confit, chicken, and tiger shrimp and the bountiful Spicy Noodle Soup with jasmine rice, chicken, and tiger shrimp are both delicious, and each one is definitely big enough to share. Just remember, with all those chilies, Kampuchea's dishes are often spicy, so let your server know if you need to take a walk on the "mild" side, or just cool off with a refreshing glass of Riesling while reveling in the knowledge that you found one of New York's best hidden eats. ✉ *78 Rivington St., at Allen St., Lower East Side* ☎ *212/529–3901* ⊕ *www.kampucheanyc.com* 🖃 *D, DC, MC, V* Ⓜ *F to Delancey St.; J, M, Z to Essex St.* ✛ *2:G3.*

$
DELI
Fodor's Choice
★
✕ **Katz's Delicatessen.** Everything and nothing has changed at Katz's since it first opened in 1888, when the neighborhood was dominated by Jewish immigrants. The rows of Formica tables, the long self-service counter, and such signs as "Send a salami to your boy in the army" are all completely authentic. What's different are the area's demographics, but all types still flock here for succulent hand-carved corned beef and pastrami sandwiches, soul-warming soups, juicy hot dogs, and crisp half-sour pickles. ✉*205 E. Houston St., at Ludlow St., Lower East*

18

Side ☎ *212/254–2246* ⊕ *www.katzdeli.com* ▭ *AE, MC, V* Ⓜ *F, V to 2nd Ave.* ✛ *2:G2.*

$$$ ✕**Rayuela.** The young and sexy frequent this vibrant Lower East Side
LATIN restaurant to sample Latin cuisine courtesy of Máximo Tejada, the chef
who built his reputation cooking at New York City's popular Pipa and
Lucy Latin Kitchen. This bi-level eatery and bar has a dining area, a
ceviche bar, and—growing in the center of the restaurant—an olive
tree. The menu features small plates with more than a dozen ceviches
and tapas, including the must-have lobster with Uruguayan caviar. If
you'd like a predinner drink, arrive early to grab a stool at the bar
and enjoy a standout cocktail, like the pisco made with sour lime juice
and foamy egg white. ⊠ *165 Allen St., between Rivington and Stanton
Sts., Lower East Side* ☎ *212/253–8840* ⊕ *www.rayuelanyc.com* ▭ *AE,
D, DC, MC, V* ⊘ *No lunch* Ⓜ *F, V to 2nd Ave.; J, M, Z to Essex and
Delancey Sts.* ✛ *2:G3.*

$ ✕**Schiller's Liquor Bar.** It's the kind of hip Lower East Side hangout where
BISTRO you'd be equally comfortable as a celebrity or a parent with a stroller.
ⓒ The folks at Schiller's work hard to make it feel as if it's decades old.
Vintage mirrored panels, forever-in-style subway tiles, a tin ceiling, and
a checkered floor lend a Parisian feel. Cuban sandwiches and steak-
frites reveal a steady hand in the kitchen. At lunch, dollar doughnuts
and baguettes with sweet or savory fillings are standouts. At dinner a
standard bistro menu fills out the list. ⊠ *131 Rivington St., at Norfolk
St., Lower East Side* ☎ *212/260–4555* ⊕ *www.schillersny.com* ▭ *AE,
MC, V* Ⓜ *F to Delancey St.; J, M, Z to Essex St.* ✛ *2:G3.*

$$ ✕**The Stanton Social.** A perennial neighborhood favorite, this is the place
ITALIAN to come for an expansive menu of tapas-style dining from talented chef
Chris Santos, plus a perfectly calibrated cocktail menu. Come before
seven if you want to be able to hear your fellow diners speak, but the
people-watching and shared dishes are good at any hour. Try the gooey,
Gruyère-topped onion soup dumplings, juicy Kobe beef sliders, and
wasabi-crusted salmon. Downstairs feels like a more traditional dining
room, while the second level features a buzzy bar. The late-night lounge
area, decorated with cherry-blossom wallpaper and red leather uphol-
stery, turns into a quasi-nightclub the later it gets. The Stanton Social
is also great option for brunch—the spicy lobster Benedict is a must.
⊠ *99 Stanton St., between Ludlow and Orchard Sts., Lower East Side*
☎ *212/995–0099* ⊕ *www.thestantonsocial.com* ⬠ *Reservations essential* ▭ *AE, MC, V* ⊘ *No lunch* Ⓜ *F, V to 2nd Ave.* ✛ *2:G3.*

$$$ ✕**wd~50.** Chef Wylie Dufresne—the mad genius and early progenitor
NEW AMERICAN of the molecular gastronomy trend—mixes colors, flavors, and textures
with a masterful hand here. His staff encourages people to feel at ease
trying things like hanger steak tartare with smoked almonds, bananas
and hibiscus scallops with pine-needle udon, and grapefruit dashi. Des-
serts follow suit: licorice custard with sake sorbet and pears, anyone?
⊠ *50 Clinton St., between Rivington and Stanton Sts., Lower East Side*
☎ *212/477–2900* ⊕ *www.wd-50.com* ▭ *AE, D, DC, MC, V* ⊘ *No lunch
Sat.–Tues.* Ⓜ *F to Delancey St.; J, M, Z to Essex St.* ✛ *2:H3.*

GREENWICH VILLAGE WITH MEATPACKING DISTRICT AND WEST VILLAGE

GREENWICH VILLAGE

$$
PIZZA
☺ ✗**Arturo's**. Few guidebooks list this classic New York pizzeria, but the jam-packed room and pleasantly smoky scent foreshadow a satisfying meal. There's a full menu of Italian classics, but don't be fooled: pizza is the main event. The thin-crust beauties are cooked in a coal oven, emerging sizzling with simple toppings like pepperoni, sausage, and eggplant. Monday to Thursday you can call ahead to reserve a table; weekends, be prepared to wait and salivate. ⊠ *106 W. Houston St., near Thompson St., Greenwich Village* ☎ *212/677–3820* ▭ *AE, DC, MC, V* ☾ *No lunch* Ⓜ *1 to Houston St.; B, D, F, V to Broadway-Lafayette St.* ✣ *2:D3.*

$$$
ITALIAN ✗**Babbo**. After one bite of the ethereal homemade pasta or tender barbecued squab with roast beet farrotto, you'll understand why it's so hard to get reservations at Mario Batali's casually elegant restaurant. The complex and satisfying menu hits numerous high points, such as "mint love letters," ravioli filled with pureed peas, ricotta, and fresh mint, finished with spicy lamb sausage ragout; and rabbit with brussels sprouts, house-made pancetta, and carrot vinaigrette. Babbo is the perfect spot for a raucous celebratory dinner with flowing wine and festive banter. But be forewarned: if anyone in your party is hard of hearing, or bothered by loud rock music, choose someplace more sedate. ⊠ *110 Waverly Pl., between MacDougal St. and 6th Ave., Greenwich Village* ☎ *212/777–0303* ⊕ *www.babbonyc.com* ✍ *Reservations essential* ▭ *AE, MC, V* ☾ *No lunch* Ⓜ *A, B, C, D, F, F, V to W. 4th St.* ✣ *2:C1.*

$$$
NEW AMERICAN ✗**Blue Hill**. This tasteful, sophisticated chocolate-brown den of a restaurant—formerly a speakeasy—on a quiet, quaint side street maintains an impeccable reputation for excellence and consistency under the leadership of Dan Barber. The Obamas even stopped by here for dinner, shutting down the street for one of their "date nights." Part of the "slow food," sustainable agriculture movement, Blue Hill mostly uses ingredients grown or raised within 200 miles, including the Four Season Farm at Stone Barns Center for Food and Agriculture, Barber's second culinary project in nearby Westchester County. The chefs produce precisely cooked and elegantly constructed food such as wild striped bass with potato and clam chowder and house-cured *guanciale* (pork jowl). ⊠ *75 Washington Pl., between Washington Sq. W and 6th Ave., Greenwich Village* ☎ *212/539–1776* ⊕ *www.bluehillnyc.com* ✍ *Reservations essential* ▭ *AE, D, DC, MC, V* ☾ *No lunch* Ⓜ *A, B, C, D, E, F, V to W. 4th St.* ✣ *2:C1.*

$$
BISTRO ✗**Blue Ribbon Bakery**. When the owners renovated this space, they uncovered a 100-year-old wood-burning oven. They relined it with volcanic brick and let it dictate the destiny of their restaurant. The bakery/restaurant has an eclectic menu featuring substantial sandwiches on homemade bread (from the oven, of course), small plates, a legendary bread pudding, and entrées that span the globe, from hummus to grilled catfish with chorizo, bacon-studded collards, and sweet potatoes. The basement dining room is dark and intimate; upstairs is a Parisian-style

18

café. ✉ *35 Downing St., at Bedford St., Greenwich Village* ☎ *212/337–0404* ⊕ *www.blueribbonrestaurants.com* ▭ *AE, D, DC, MC, V* Ⓜ *1 to Houston St.; A, B, C, D, E, F, V to W. 4th St.* ✛ *2:C2.*

\$\$\$ ✕ **Centro Vinoteca**. Though *Top Chef* contestant and Eleven Madison
ITALIAN Park alum Leah Cohen left the kitchen, this bi-level Italian spot decked
out in gleaming white tiles and a wall of windows looking out onto 7th
Avenue remains popular. A recently revamped menu focuses on Italian
classics with flair, like a bitter green salad of local mutsu apples, endive,
radicchio, frisee, walnuts, and Gorgonzola dressing, and a grilled piz-
zette with mozzarella, fennel sausage, and arugula. Several dishes use
local supplier DiPalo's cheeses, including a ricotta cavatelli with a red
wine–braised short rib sauce. Main courses lean toward the substantial,
like a grilled Angus rib eye with balsamic braised cipollini mushrooms.
And in true Italian form, the kitchen stays open till midnight. ✉ *74 7th
Ave. S, at Barrow St., Greenwich Village* ☎ *212/367–7470* ⊕ *www.
centrovinoteca.com* ▭ *AE, MC, V* Ⓜ *1 to Christopher St./Sheridan Sq.;
A, B, C, D, E, F, V to W. 4th St.-Washington Sq.* ✛ *2:B2.*

\$\$ ✕ **Five Points**. This cheerful restaurant is a refreshing oasis, with a rush-
AMERICAN ing stream of water running through a hollowed-out log for the entire
length of the dining room. Chef-owner Marc Meyer's menus are seasonal and market-driven. Expect plump chilled oysters, exemplary
Caesar salad, and splendid house-made pasta, followed by the likes
of pan-seared day-boat halibut with cucumber gazpacho and chopped
tomato salsa; and grilled baby lamb chops with rosemary potatoes,
mint-yogurt sauce, and black-olive-stuffed tomato. Weekend brunch
is one of the very best in the city, and prices are quite friendly. New
to the menu: lunch, meaning Five Points is open all day long. ✉ *31
Great Jones St., between Lafayette St. and Bowery, Greenwich Village* ☎ *212/253–5700* ⊕ *www.fivepointsrestaurant.com* ⌂ *Reservations
essential* ▭ *AE, MC, V* Ⓜ *6 to Bleecker St.; B, D, F, V to Broadway-
Lafayette St.* ✛ *3:G6.*

\$\$\$\$ ✕ **Gotham Bar & Grill**. A culinary landmark, Gotham Bar & Grill is
AMERICAN every bit as thrilling as it was when it opened in 1984. Celebrated chef
Alfred Portale, who made the blueprint for "architectural food," that
is, towers of stacked ingredients, builds on a foundation of simple, clean
flavors. People come for Portale's transcendent preparations: no rack
of lamb is tenderer, no seafood salad sweeter.—at a price. There's also a
fantastic three-course \$31 prix-fixe lunch from noon to 2:30 weekdays.
✉ *12 E. 12th St., between 5th Ave. and University Pl., Greenwich Village* ☎ *212/620–4020* ⊕ *www.gothambarandgrill.com* ▭ *AE, D, DC,
MC, V* ☾ *No lunch weekends* Ⓜ *L, N, Q, R, W, 4, 5, 6 to 14th St./
Union Sq.* ✛ *3:E4.*

\$\$ ✕ **Lupa**. Even the most hard-to-please connoisseurs have a soft spot
ITALIAN for Lupa, Mario Batali and Joseph Bastianich's "downscale" Roman
trattoria. Rough-hewn wood, great Italian wines, and simple preparations with top-quality ingredients define the restaurant. People come
repeatedly for dishes such as ricotta gnocchi with sweet-sausage ragout,
house-made salumi, and sardines with fennel and cracked wheat. The
front of the restaurant is seated on a first-come, first-served basis;

reservations are taken for the back. ✉ *170 Thompson St., between Bleecker and W. Houston Sts., Greenwich Village* ☎ *212/982–5089* ⊕ *www.luparestaurant.com* ▤ *AE, MC, V* Ⓜ *A, B, C, D, E, F, V to W. 4th St.* ✛ *2:D3.*

$$
SEAFOOD
✗ **Mary's Fish Camp.** The neighborhood's second New England fish house (the result of a split between Pearl Oyster Bar's partners) proves you can't have too much of a good thing. There's usually a wait here for the excellent fried oysters, chowders, and, of course, the sweet lobster roll with crisp fries. That lobster roll is a citywide favorite—get here early or it may be sold out. ✉ *64 Charles St., at W. 4th St., Greenwich Village* ☎ *646/486–2185* 🖎 *Reservations not accepted* ▤ *AE, MC, V* ◷ *Closed Sun.* Ⓜ *1 to Christopher St./Sheridan Sq.* ✛ *2:B1.*

¢
MIDDLE EASTERN
✗ **Moustache.** There's typically a crowd waiting outside for one of the copper-topped tables at this appealing Middle Eastern neighborhood restaurant. The focal point is the perfect pita that accompanies tasty salads like lemony chickpea and spinach, and hearty lentil and bulgur. Also delicious is *lahambajin,* spicy ground lamb on a crispy flat crust. For entrées, try the leg of lamb or merguez sausage sandwiches. Service is slow but friendly. ✉ *90 Bedford St., between Barrow and Grove Sts., Greenwich Village* ☎ *212/229–2220* 🖎 *Reservations not accepted* ▤ *No credit cards* Ⓜ *1 to Christopher St./Sheridan Sq.* ✛ *2:B2.*

$$
BRASSERIE
✗ **Paris Commune.** Wraparound floor-to-ceiling windows, dark cherry banquettes, and papered-and-clothed tables characterize this old favorite's new space, along with a certain self-assurance. Begin exploring the classic bistro menu with dishes like the salad of beets, Stilton, apples, and nuts, followed by a marinated free-range chicken served with crispy frites. Desserts, like banana beignets with passion fruit soup an lavender honey, make for a creative finish. ✉ *99 Bank St., at Greenwich St., Greenwich Village* ☎ *212/929–0509* ⊕ *www.pariscommune.net* ▤ *AE, MC, V* Ⓜ *1 to Christopher St./Sheridan Sq.; A, C, E to 14th St.; L to 8th Ave.* ✛ *2:A1.*

$$$
AUSTRIAN
✗ **Wallsé.** Kurt Gutenbrunner's modern Austrian menu at this neighborhood restaurant with a quasi–Wiener Werkstätte look is soulful and satisfying, with a strong emphasis on Austrian tradition and urban New York attitude. It's hard to argue with such dishes as Wiener schnitzel with potato-cucumber salad and lingonberries or venison goulash with spaetzle and brussels sprouts. Desserts do Vienna proud: apple-walnut strudel is served with apple sorbet. ✉ *344 W. 11th St., at Washington St., Greenwich Village* ☎ *212/352–2300* ⊕ *www.wallse.com* 🖎 *Reservations essential* ▤ *AE, DC, MC, V* ◷ *No lunch weekdays* Ⓜ *1 to Christopher St./Sheridan Sq.; A, C, E to 14th St.; L to 8th Ave.* ✛ *3:B6.*

MEATPACKING DISTRICT

$$$
FRENCH
✗ **Bagatelle.** Situate yourself at a table in Bagatelle's elegant and spacious white dining room, sip on a cocktail like La Poire Royale (pear vodka, pear brandy, pear purée, Cointreau, and champagne), and watch the Meatpacking District's beautiful people strut by and coo at the bar. Executive chef Nicolas Cantrel's menu of Provençal bistro classics includes some appealing appetizers: buttery elbow pasta with veal juice, ham, and Swiss cheese. Entrées, such as filet mignon accompanied by frites and béarnaise sauce, are substantial but quotidien. Definitely leave

18

room for dessert, especially "le Paris Brest"—choux pastry, praline cream, and almonds. The wine list includes many French varietals; only a few are offered by the glass. ⊠ *409 W. 13th St., between 9th Ave. and Washington St., Meatpacking District* ☎ *212/675–2400* ▱ *AE, D, MC, V* ⊘ *No lunch weekdays* Ⓜ *A, C, E to 14th St.; L to 8th Ave.* ✛ *3:B4.*

$$$ ✗ **Del Posto.** Mario Batali's high-profile stab at four-star immortality
ITALIAN   helped kick off the big-box restaurant boom in the Meatpacking District. Much more formal than his still hugely popular Babbo, the restaurant initially struck many as too grown-up for a big kid like Batali. The dining room—with its sweeping staircase, formal decor, and live tinkling from a baby grand—has the feel of an opulent hotel lobby. But Del Posto prevailed and is now regarded as one of the most consistently dazzling special-occasion spots in a neighborhood overrun with overpriced eateries. A partnership with TV chef Lidia Bastianich, the restaurant offers pitch-perfect risotto made fresh to order for two persons or more (and served in the oversize pan), big shareable roast hunks of meat (veal chops), as well as ethereal pastas. For a little taste of the experience, come for a cocktail and sample the bargain bar menu. ⊠ *85 10th Ave., between 15th and 16th Sts., Meatpacking District* ☎ *212/497–8090* ⊕ *www.delposto.com* ▱ *AE, MC, V* ⊘ *No lunch Tues.–Sat.* Ⓜ *A, C, E to 14th St.; L to 8th Ave.* ✛ *3:A4.*

$$$ ✗ **Pastis.** A trendy spin-off of Balthazar in SoHo, Pastis looks like it was
BRASSERIE   shipped in, tile by nicotine-stained tile, from Pigalle. At night throngs of whippet-thin cell-phone-slinging boys and girls gather at the bar up front to sip martinis and be seen. French favorites are front and center, including toothsome steak-frites with béarnaise, mussels steamed in Pernod, and tasty apple tartlet with phyllo crust. ⊠ *9 9th Ave., at Little W. 12th St., Meatpacking District* ☎ *212/929–4844* ⊕ *www.pastisny. com* ⌕ *Reservations essential* ▱ *AE, MC, V* Ⓜ *A, C, E to 14th St.; L to 8th Ave.* ✛ *3:B4.*

$$$ ✗ **Scarpetta.** Chef Scott Conant left L'Impero and Alto, to open Scar-
ITALIAN   petta, a critical darling since day one, located adjacent to the glitz of the Meatpacking District. Walk past the bar into the polished dining room, where orange belts loop around mirrors and a retractable roof ushers in natural light. For a rousing start, try the creamy, rich polenta and mushrooms before enjoying one of the house-made pastas, like the al dente tagliatelle laced with strands of tender lamb ragout or his signature capretto (baby goat). Save room for dessert: the Amadei chocolate cake with burnt-caramel gelato brings à la mode to a whole new level. ⊠ *355 W. 14th St., at 9th Ave., Meatpacking District* ☎ *212/691–0555* ⊕ *www.scarpettanyc.com* ▱ *AE, D, DC, MC, V* ⊘ *No lunch* Ⓜ *A, C, E to 14th St.; L to 8th Ave.* ✛ *3:B4.*

$$$ ✗ **Spice Market.** This playground for New York's elite is set in a cav-
ASIAN   ernous space amid embroidered curtains and artifacts from Burma, India, and Malaysia. Chef Jean-Georges Vongerichten's playful takes on Southeast Asian street food will keep you asking the waiters for information: what exactly was in that? Sometimes the playfulness works, sometimes it doesn't, but don't miss the steamed lobster with garlic, ginger, and dried chili, or the squid salad with papaya and cashews. ⊠ *403 W. 13th St., at 9th Ave., Meatpacking District* ☎ *212/675–2322*

⊕ *www.jean-georges.com* ⌕ *Reservations essential* ▭ *AE, D, DC, MC, V* Ⓜ *A, C, E to 14th St.; L to 8th Ave.* ✛ *3:B4.*

$$$ ✕ **The Standard Grill.** Hotelier Andre Balasz has created an instant scene
AMERICAN for celebs, fashion-industry insiders, and aspiration common folk, all
who cluster at this buzzy restaurant inside his new Standard Hotel.
In warm weather the spacious outdoor seating area is a great place to
watch the new High Line park and sample $10 cocktails like a straw-
berry Pimm's cup or ginger cocktail in a copper mug. The indoor bar
is low-lit and sexy, with a raw bar and charcuterie station that works
on overdrive to put out plates of oysters and Italian cured meats for
the two dining rooms—the more casual one in front, with wainscoted
walls and views of Washington Street, and the larger room in the back,
with a floor whimsically comprised of thousands of glittering copper
pennies under Lucite. Chef Dan Silverman's food is comfort-luxe, with
dishes like roast chicken for two in a cast-iron skillet and delicious moist
trout with a currant and pine-nut relish. For dessert, there's a nearly
obscene chocolate mousse that comes with four silicone spatulas in
lieu of spoons. A late-night menu is offered until 4 AM. ▭ *846 Wash-
ington St., between Little W. 12th and 13th Sts., Meatpacking District*
☎ *212/645-4100* ⊕ *www.thestandardgrill.com* Ⓜ *A, C, E to 14th St./
Broadway, L to 14th St./8th Ave.* ✛ *3:4A.*

$ ✕ **Vento.** The pan-Italian menu here features small plates as well as
ITALIAN pizzas and full-size entrées at friendly prices. You can make a meal of
small tastes, from a full array of sliced Italian meats to chilled artichokes
with pecorino cheese, or opt for full portions of dishes like extra-virgin-
olive-oil-poached salmon with pink grapefruit and arugula salad, or
slow-roasted veal breast in a morel mushroom sauce. For dessert, chewy
zeppole are dusted with cinnamon sugar. ▭ *675 Hudson St., at W. 14th
St., Meatpacking District* ☎ *212/699–2400* ⊕ *www.brguestrestaurants.
com* ▭ *AE, MC, V* Ⓜ *A, C, E to 14th St.; L to 8th Ave.* ✛ *3:B4.*

WEST VILLAGE

$$ ✕ **August.** Rustic simplicity is the unifying theme at this bustling West
MEDITERRANEAN Village eatery helmed by Terrence Gallivan (The Modern and Gordon
Ramsay's in the London Hotel). A wood-burning oven in the dining
room turns out regional European dishes like tarte flambé; an Alsatian
flat bread topped with onion, bacon, and crème fraîche; and Sicilian
orata, a meaty white fish grilled whole and doused with citrus, olive oil,
and fresh herbs. Wood-planed floors and an arched cork ceiling envelop
the busy 40-seat dining room. For a quieter meal, ask for a table in the
glass-enclosed 15-seat atrium in back. ▭ *359 Bleecker St., at Charles
St., West Village* ☎ *212/929–8727* ⊕ *www.augustny.com* ⌕ *Reservations essential* ▭ *AE, MC, V* Ⓜ *1 to Christopher St./Sheridan Sq.; A,
B, C, D, E, F, V to W. 4th St.* ✛ *3:C6.*

$$$ ✕ **Bar Blanc Bistro.** With high-contrast white-leather banquettes and dark
AMERICAN wood accents, this recently redesigned eatery showcases the market-
driven cuisine of Sebastiaan Zijp, who previously worked at some of
the city's top restaurants. More of a chill neighborhood spot than a
destination restaurant, the atmosphere is buzzy around cocktail hour
with a clientele of well-heeled locals. Zijp has created a collection of
compelling dishes, including starters like house-made country terrine,

18

braised pork cheek salad, and seared scallops with curried carrots. Main courses are upscale but homey, like lacquered salmon with roasted local vegetables and slow roasted chicken with polenta. ⊠ *142 W. 10th St., West Village* ☎ *212/255–2330* ⊕ *www.barblanc.com* ▭ *MC, V* ⊙ *No lunch* Ⓜ *A, C, E, B, D, F, V to W. 4th St.* ✛ *3:D5.*

$$$
NEW AMERICAN

✕ **Commerce.** This former speakeasy harks back to days gone by with its Diego Rivera–style murals, vintage sconces, and restored subway tiles. The young crowd comes not only for the decor, but to taste Chef Harold Moore's seasonal cuisine. Appetizers range from truffle-flecked asparagus and morels with poached egg to yuzu-marinated hamachi ceviche. The entrées are just as vibrant: bright, sweet peas offset pristine halibut, and the shareable roast chicken, presented table-side, is served with foie-gras bread stuffing. There's also a new tavern menu offered on Saturdays, starring dishes like 20-herb salad with Manchego cheese and braised beef short rib sandwich. The smart, nimble waitstaff constantly replenishes your bread basket with warm baguettes and brioche, and steers you toward the dainty pineapple cheesecake with cilantro sorbet for a sweet ending. For a quieter meal, choose one of the booths near the bar. ⊠ *50 Commerce St., West Village* ☎ *212/524–2301* ⊕ *www. commercerestaurant.com* ▭ *AE, MC, V* ⊙ *No lunch* Ⓜ *1 to Christopher St./Sheridan Sq.; A, B, C, D, E, F, V to W. 4th St.* ✛ *2:B2.*

$$
ITALIAN

✕ **dell'anima.** Lines snake out the door of this neighborhood favorite. Check out the open kitchen, where the stylish crowd converges to watch chefs prepare authentic Italian dishes like simple arugula salad or a bowl of agnolotti pasta with squash, sage, and almonds. The lamb shank with polenta is the ultimate cold-weather comfort food, especially when paired with one of the restaurant's 400 wines. If you can't get a table, head to the 10-seat bar and drown your sorrows in a glass of limoncello. Stop in for complimentary *apertivo* snacks between 4 and 6 PM on weekends. ⊠ *38 8th Ave., at Jane St., West Village* ☎ *212/366–6633* ⊕ *www.dellanima.com* ▭ *AE, MC, V* ⊙ *No lunch weekends* Ⓜ *A, C, E to 14th St.; L to 8th Ave.* ✛ *3:C5.*

$$
KOREAN

✕ **Do Hwa.** If anyone in New York is responsible for making Korean food cool and user-friendly, it is the mother-daughter team behind this perennially popular restaurant and its East Village sister, Dok Suni's. Jenny Kwak and her mother, Myung Ja, serve home cooking in the form of *kalbi jim* (braised short ribs), *bibimbop* (a spicy, mix-it-yourself vegetable-and-rice dish), and other favorites that may not be as pungent as they are in Little Korea, but satisfying nevertheless. ⊠ *55 Carmine St., between Bedford St. and 7th Ave., West Village* ☎ *212/414–1224* ⊕ *www.dohwanyc.com* ▭ *AE, D, MC, V* ⊙ *No lunch weekends* Ⓜ *1 to Houston St.; A, B, C, D, E, F, V to W. 4th St.* ✛ *2:C2.*

$
MALAYSIAN
Fodor's Choice
★

✕ **Fatty Crab.** This rustic Malaysian cantina showcases the exciting cuisine of chef Zak Pelaccio, who spent years cooking at famous French restaurants before escaping to Southeast Asia for a year, where he fell in love with the flavors of the region. Start with the addictive pickled watermelon and crispy pork salad, an improbable combination that's both refreshing and decadent. The Berkshire pork tea sandwiches are another juicy winner. The can't-miss signature dish is chili crab—cracked Dungeness crab in a pool of rich, spicy chili sauce, served with bread for dipping. It's messy for sure, but worth rolling up your sleeves for. Friday and Saturday the kitchen is open until 2 AM. ✉ *643 Hudson St., between Gansevoort and Horatio Sts., West Village* ☎ *212/352–3590* ⊕ *www.fattycrab.com* ☜ *Reservations not accepted for parties of 6 or fewer* ⊟ *AE, D, MC, V* Ⓜ *A, C, E to 14th St.; L to 8th Ave.* ✛ *3:C5.*

$ ✕ **'ino.** 'Ino's the kind of place you want in every neighborhood, but the
ITALIAN West Village is the lucky winner here. Every inch of space is economized in this cozy, brick-lined eatery, where the chefs turn out an astonishing variety of fresh bruschetta, tramezzini (soft-bread sandwiches), and panini—not to mention soups and salad—from a tiny, well-organized kitchen. Grab a newspaper from the ledge and sit at one of the bar seats to sample a great selection of Italian wines by the glass. Everything's delicious, but the truffled egg toast, available for brunch or anytime with an oozing yolk and gooey fontina cheese, is the menu's star attraction. ✉ *21 Bedford St., between Downing and W. Houston Sts., Greenwich Village* ☎ *212/989–5769* ⊕ *www.cafeino.com* ☜ *Reservations not accepted* ⊟ *AE, MC, V* Ⓜ *A, B C, D, E, F, V to W. 4th St.; 1 to Varick St.* ✛ *2:C2.*

$$ ✕ **The Little Owl.** This tiny neighborhood joint, with seating for 28 peo-
NEW AMERICAN ple, is exceptionally eager to please. The menu is congruently small, which actually makes it easier to decide what you want. And what you want are the pork-veal-beef-pecorino-cheese meatball "sliders" or miniburgers. The unusually juicy pork loin chop, served with Parmesan butter beans and wild dandelion greens, is gigantic, and hugely satisfying. Raspberry-filled beignets, served with a ramekin of warm Nutella, are otherworldly. ✉ *90 Bedford St., at Grove St., West Village* ☎ *212/741–4695* ⊕ *www.thelittleowlnyc.com* ☜ *Reservations essential* ⊟ *AE, MC, V* Ⓜ *1 to Christopher St./Sheridan Sq.; A, B, C, D, E, F, V to W. 4th St.* ✛ *3:D6.*

$ ✕ **Mexicana Mama.** This quaint, colorful—and very popular—space
MEXICAN serves vividly flavored fare. The kitchen is serious enough to create four different salsas daily, including a rotating "special salsa" that incorporates an authentic Mexican chile. Several dishes come with your choice of salsa and filling. The tomato-habanero salsa is simply unforgettable; cream tames the habaneros, but only slightly. Three chili-roasted pork tacos are also filled with piquant Chihuahua cheese and black beans, and served over Mexican rice and avocado cubes. Quesadillas are made with fresh corn tortillas (for a change!), filled with that melted Chihuahua cheese and your choice of chicken, barbacoa beef, chicken mole, or a daily special vegetable filling. For dessert, look no further than the eggy flan in flavors like caramel or cinnamon. ✉ *525 Hudson St., near Charles St., West Village* ☎ *212/924–4119* ⊟ *No credit cards* Ⓜ *1 to Christopher St./Sheridan Sq.; A, B, C, D, E, F, V to W. 4th St.* ◷ *Closed Mon.* ✛ *3:C6.*

$$$ ✕ **Minetta Tavern.** By converting a moribund 80-year-old Italian restau-
NEW AMERICAN rant into a cozy hot spot, restaurateur Keith McNally created another hit. Try early and often to score reservations and sample creations like buttery trout *meuniere;* bone marrow on toast; expertly aged steaks; and the celebrated Black Label burger, a pile of meat lashed with clarified butter and topped with caramelized onions and—for the brave—an

18

added layer of cheese. The bar room, with its original details intact, is great for people-watching. A table in the back, with its original mural depicting West Village life and wall-to-wall photos of famous and infamous customers from eras gone by—makes sweet-talking the reservationist worth your while. ⊠ *113 MacDougal St., between Bleecker and West 3rd Sts., West Village* ☎ *212/475–3850* ⊕ *www.minettatavernny. com* ⚲ *Reservations essential* ⊟ *AE, D, DC, MC, V* Ⓜ *A, B, C, D, E, F, V to W. 4th St.* ✛ *2:C2.*

$$$ ✕**Perry St.** Pay no mind to the cars whizzing by on the nearby West
NEW AMERICAN Side Highway; inside, the clean lines of this austere dining room with its gauze-swaddled wraparound windows and straight-backed cream banquettes get you to focus on the main event on your plate. Food from owner Jean-Georges Vongerichten's son Cedric, recently named executive chef. Black-pepper crab dumplings are plated with delicate snow peas. Fried chicken is served with mushroom spaetzle and ginger vinaigrette, and a retro char-grilled cheeseburger is lavished with Russian dressing and crispy onions. Vongerichten's restaurants can be pricey, but give the man credit for offering prix-fixe specials at lunch and dinner: $26 and $38, respectively. ⊠ *176 Perry St., at West St., West Village* ☎ *212/352–1900* ⊕ *www.jean-georges.com* ⊟ *AE, D, MC, V* Ⓜ *1 to Christopher St./Sheridan Sq.* ✛ *2:A2.*

UNION SQUARE WITH FLATIRON DISTRICT, GRAMERCY PARK, AND MURRAY HILL

FLATIRON DISTRICT

$$$ ✕**Aldea.** Bouley alumnus George Mendes has opened a restaurant that
MEDITERANNEAN uses his Portuguese heritage as inspiration and takes it to new heights.
Fodor's Choice Although there are no bad seats in the sleekly appointed bilevel space
★ decorated with touches of wood, glass, and blue accents, watching Mendes work in his spotless tiled kitchen from one of the seats at the chef's counter in the back is undeniably exciting. *Petiscos* (small bites) like cubes of crisp pork belly with apple cider and caramelized endive and an earthy pork and duck terrine with sweet muscat gelee reveal sophisticated cooking techniques and flavors presented in highly addictive packages. A delicate matsutake mushroom broth floated with a slow-poached egg is edged with a subtle brace of pine. On the $75 five-course chef's tasting menu, the sea urchin on a crispy toast flat is a standout, as is the duck confit with chorizo and shatteringly crunchy duck-skin cracklings. ⊠ *31 W. 17th St., between 5th and 6th Aves., Flatiron District* ☎ *212/675–7223* ⊕ *www.aldearestaurant.com* ⚲ *Reservations essential* ⊟ *AE, MC, V* ☉ *Closed Sun. No lunch Sat.* Ⓜ *N, R, Q, W, 4, 5, 6 to 14th St./Union Square; F, V to 14th St. and 6th Ave.* ✛ *3:3E.*

$$$ ✕**A Voce.** Executive chef Missy Robbins has a passion for Italian cuisine,
ITALIAN and it shows. The American-born Robbins honed her Italian chops in
Fodor's Choice northern Italy at the highly acclaimed Agli Amici restaurant in Friuli.
★ For five years prior to joining A Voce, she was the executive chef at Chicago's Spiaggia. Her menu is inspired and represents regional dishes from all over Italy, including melt-in-your-mouth Swiss chard and Cresenza cheese–stuffed cassoncini pockets with prosciutto from Puglia,

and spaghetti alla chitarra from Abruzzo. The pasta is prepared fresh every day, and Robbins's fish and meat dishes are exceptional. The *agnello in due modi* entrée is especially well prepared, with tender lamb chops and a flavorful vegetable soffrito. For dessert, try the Tuscan bomboloni doughnuts with dark-chocolate dipping sauce. The attentive staff also help to make the dining experience here a real pleasure. A Voce's atmosphere is warm, and the 90-seat dining room has a retro Italian feel to it—walnut floors, pale green leather-top tables, and Eames chairs. There's also additional seating on the patio when weather permits. ☒ *41 Madison Ave., between 25th and 26th Sts., Flatiron District* ☎ *212/545–8555* ⊕ *www.avocerestaurant.com* ▭ *AE, MC, V* Ⓜ *N, R to 23rd St.* ✛ *3:F2.*

$$$
SEAFOOD ✕**BLT Fish.** Two stories above the less formal Fish Shack, BLT Fish is an elegantly appointed dining room set under a spectacular skylight. "BLT" stands for Bistro Laurent Tourondel, and he proves once again, as at BLT Steak uptown, that he embellishes his dishes more successfully than nearly anyone. Tourondel's signature roasted Alaskan black cod is simply marinated overnight, then roasted. The piping-hot result is among the best seafood dishes in town. Whole fish is sold by the pound, with most fish averaging 1–3 pounds each. At about $32 per pound, that can really add up. ☒ *21 W. 17th St., between 5th and 6th Aves., Flatiron District* ☎ *212/691–8888* ⊕ *www.bltfish.com* ⟆ *Reservations essential* ▭ *AE, D, DC, MC, V* ☉ *Closed Sun. No lunch* Ⓜ *4, 5, 6, L, N, Q, R, W to Union Sq./14th St.; F, V, L to 6th Ave./14th St.* ✛ *3:E3.*

$$
SPANISH ✕**Boqueria.** This warm, buzzy restaurant features comfortable wheat color leather banquettes and, if you want to make friends, a communal table running down the center of the dining room. Chef Seamus Mullen spent two years tromping around Spanish kitchens, and he came to New York armed with dozens of ideas for classic tapas and even better midsize dishes and entrées. Fried quail eggs and chorizo on roasted bread are even better than they sound. Salt cod, suckling pig, and mushroom croquettes are perched on dabs of flavored aioli. *Garbanzos al Pinotxo* is a luscious mix of chickpeas, morcilla, a steamed hen's egg, and toasted pine nuts. Traditional churros come with a thick hot chocolate for dipping. ☒ *53 W. 19th St., between 5th and 6th Aves., Flatiron District* ☎ *212/255–4160* ⊕ *www.boquerianyc.com* ⟆ *Reservations not accepted for parties of 6 or fewer* ▭ *AE, D, MC, V* Ⓜ *6, F, R, V, W to 23rd St.* ✛ *3:E3.*

$
CAFÉ
☾ ✕**City Bakery.** This self-service bakery-restaurant has the urban aesthetic to match its name. Chef-owner Maury Rubin's baked goods—giant cookies, addictively flaky, salty-sweet pretzel croissants, elegant caramel tarts—are unfailingly rich. A major draw is the salad bar that may seem overpriced, but the large selection of impeccably fresh food, including whole sides of baked salmon, roasted vegetables, soups, and several Asian-accented dishes, delivers bang for the buck. Much of the produce comes from the nearby farmers' market. In winter the bakery hosts a hot-chocolate festival; in summer it's lemonade time. Weekend brunch includes limited table-side service, and a new happy-hour menu features craft beers, local wines, and a menu with items capped at $10. ☒ *3 W. 18th St., between 5th and 6th Aves., Flatiron District* ☎ *212/366–1414*

18

⊕ *www.thecitybakery.com* ✍ *Reservations not accepted* ▭ *AE, MC, V* ⊙ *No dinner* Ⓜ *L, N, Q, R, W, 4, 5, 6 to 14th St./Union Sq.; F, V to 14th St.* ✛ *3:E3.*

$$ ╳ **Craftbar.** The casual sibling to Tom Colicchio's Craft is a spacious
NEW AMERICAN and inviting bargain. The menu features assertive seasonal cooking similar to what you can find at the upscale flagship just around the corner. The small-plates category on the menu elevates tiny nibbles like sausage-stuffed fried sage leaves or addictive fluffy salt cod croquettes to temptations that make you forget the main course entirely. The rest of the menu is eclectic enough to satisfy, from broccoli rabe and fennel sausage to braised fork-tender short ribs with Anson Mills grits, a fried egg, and shisito peppers. ✉ *900 Broadway, between 19th and 20th Sts., Flatiron District* ☎ *212/461–4300* ⊕ *www.craftrestaurant.com/craftbar. html* ✍ *Reservations essential* ▭ *AE, D, DC, MC, V* Ⓜ *L, N, Q, R, W, 4, 5, 6 to 14th St./Union Sq.* ✛ *3:F3.*

$$ ╳ **Dos Caminos.** Stephen Hanson, the visionary behind a dozen New
MEXICAN York restaurants, has created a hit with the Dos Caminos brand. Start
ↂ with guacamole, served in a granite mortar called a *molcajete,* and peruse the selection of 150 tequilas. Beef tacos studded with chilies, and slow-roasted pork ribs in chipotle barbecue sauce are solid choices. On weekend nights at both locations, the noise level can get out of control. ✉ *373 Park Ave. S, between E. 26th and E. 27th Sts., Flatiron District* ☎ *212/294–1000* ⊕ *www.brguestrestaurants.com* ✍ *Reservations essential* ▭ *AE, DC, MC, V* Ⓜ *6 to 28th St.* ✛ *3:F2.*

¢ ╳ **Eisenberg's Sandwich Shop.** Since 1929 this narrow coffee shop with
CAFÉ its timeworn counter and cramped tables has provided the city with some of the best tuna-, chicken-, and egg-salad sandwiches. On chilly days Eisenberg's classic matzoh-ball soup also really hits the spot. The lively and friendly staff use the cryptic language of soda jerks, in which "whiskey down" means rye toast and "Adam and Eve on a raft" means two eggs on toast. Considering the mayhem in the place, it's a pleasant surprise that you always get your meal, quickly and precisely as ordered. ✉ *174 5th Ave., between E. 22nd and E. 23rd Sts., Flatiron District* ☎ *212/675–5096* ⊕ *www.eisenbergsnyc.com* ✍ *Reservations not accepted* ▭ *AE, D, MC, V* ⊙ *No dinner* Ⓜ *R, W, 6 to 23rd St.* ✛ *3:E2.*

$$$$ ╳ **Eleven Madison Park.** Under Swiss-born chef Daniel Humm, who was
NEW AMERICAN lured from San Francisco's Campton Place by restaurateur Danny Meyer,
Fodor'sChoice this Art Nouveau jewel overlooking Madison Park has become one of
★ the city's most consistently exciting places to dine. Humm announces his lofty intentions with dishes like foie gras with golden raisin brioche and African kili pepper, butter-poached Scottish langoustines with carrot-orange nage, and Jamison Farm herb-roasted lamb with tomato confit and Niçoise olives. Don't forget your breakfast cake—a gift from the chef—as you walk out the door. ✉ *11 Madison Ave., at 24th St., Flatiron District* ☎ *212/889–0905* ⊕ *www.elevenmadisonpark.com* ✍ *Reservations essential* ▭ *AE, D, DC, MC, V* ⊙ *Closed Sun. No lunch weekends* Ⓜ *N, R, W, 6 to 23rd St.* ✛ *3:E2.*

$$$$
AMERICAN

✕ **Gramercy Tavern.** Danny Meyer's intensely popular restaurant tops many a New Yorker's favorite restaurant list, and chef Michael Anthony has settled in comfortably in the kitchen of one of New York's classic settings. In front, the first-come, first-served tavern presents a lighter menu—including a value-packed three-course prix-fixe—along with great craft beers and cocktails scrawled on a board at the bar. The more formal dining

room has a prix-fixe American menu; three courses at dinner is $86. Choose from seasonal dishes such as marinated sea scallops with pickled peppers and fresh grapes, and rack of lamb with salsify, hazelnuts, and exotic mushrooms. Meyer's restaurants—he owns several well-regarded eateries in the city—are renowned for their food and hospitality, and Gramercy Tavern sets the standard. ⊠ *42 E. 20th St., between Broadway and Park Ave. S, Flatiron District* ☎ *212/477–0777* ⊕ *www. gramercytavern.com* ⌖ *Reservations essential for main dining room; reservations not accepted for the Tavern* ⊟ *AE, D, DC, MC, V* Ⓜ *6, R, W to 23rd St.* ✛ *3:F3.*

$$
BARBECUE

✕ **Hill Country.** This enormous barbecue joint is perfect for big groups and carnivorous appetites. The menu was devised by 'cue queen Elizabeth Karmel, and the current pitmaster has a championship knack for real Texas barbecue. The beef-centric menu features meaty ribs and exceptionally succulent slow-smoked brisket (check your diet at the door and go for the moist, fatty option). Plump pork sausages, in regular and jalapeño cheese versions, are flown in direct from Kreuz Market in Lockhart, Texas. The market-style setup can mean long lines for meat, sold by the pound, or ribs at cutter-manned stations. Bring your tray downstairs for a fine bourbon selection and nightly live music. ⊠ *30 W. 26th St., between Broadway and 6th Ave., Flatiron District* ☎ *212/255–4544* ⊕ *www.hillcountryny.com* ⊟ *AE, MC, V* Ⓜ *N, R, W to 28th St.; 6 to 28th St.; F, V to 23rd St.* ✛ *3:E2.*

$
MIDDLE EASTERN

✕ **Ilili.** Famed Washington, D.C., restaurateur and chef Philippe Massoud brings his culinary talents to New York City with this bi-level, 400-seat eatery that showcases cuisine from his native Lebanon. The menu includes standard Middle Eastern fare, but also unexpected dishes like bone marrow with sour-cherry tabbouleh and black cod with fragrant rice and tahini. Waiters never fail to refresh the basket of hot, fluffy, house-baked pita bread. A glass of Lebanese or French wine is a nice accompaniment to the cuisine. Late-night entertainment includes belly dancing. ⊠ *236 5th Ave., between 27th and 28th Sts., Flatiron District* ☎ *212/683–2929* ⊕ *www.ililinyc.com* ⊟ *AE, D, DC, MC, V* ⊙ *No lunch weekends* Ⓜ *N, R, W to 28th St.* ✛ *3:E2.*

$$$$
STEAKHOUSE

✕ **Primehouse New York.** This sleek steak house comes from the reliable group that operates Dos Caminos, Vento, and several other perpetually mobbed New York restaurants. Here you'll find classic presentations

18

like Caesar salad and steak tartare prepared table-side, and respectable dry-aged prime cuts, ranging from hanger steak ($21) to porterhouse for two ($96). For something lighter, try skate sautéed in lemon–brown-butter sauce, or the Berkshire pork chop with fig glaze and apple compote. The mod space has a cream-and-black motif that recalls the Jetsons' futuristic 1960s feel, interspersed with geometric M. C. Escher–like patterns. ⊠ *381 Park Ave. S, at 27th St., Flatiron District* ☎ *212/824–2600* ⊕ *www.brguestrestaurants.com/restaurants/ primehouse_new_york* ☰ *AE, MC, V* Ⓜ *6, R, W to 28th St.* ⊹ *3:F2.*

$$　✕ **SD26.** The charming father-daughter restaurant team of Tony and
ITALIAN　Marisa May closed uptown's San Domenico to open this more casual, yet still impressive, Italian spot. The cavernous main dining room, decorated with a constellation of pinpoint lights and ringed with more intimate tables and banquettes, speaks to a fresher, more modern approach than its predecessor. The food—pappardelle with wild boar ragu, smoked lobster with porcini mushrooms and orange segments— is a refreshing mix of classic and forward-thinking. Expect a personal greeting from either father or daughter before your meal comes to an end. ⊠ *19 E. 26th St., between 5th and Madison Aves., Flatiron District* ☎ *212/265–5959* ⊕ *www.sd26ny.com* ⌸ *Reservations essential* ☰ *AE, MC, V, DC* Ⓜ *R, W to 23rd St. and 5th Ave.* ⊹ *3:2E.*

¢　✕ **Shake Shack.** Though the newer, uptown location of Danny Meyer's
BURGER　patties 'n shakes joint is bigger by far, this is where it all began. Here in
Fodor's Choice　Madison Square Park there's no indoor seating—just snaking outdoor
★　lines. Tip: check the "Shack Cam" from their Web site to gauge your wait. If it's raining, you may be in luck— inclement weather can mean shorter lines. Fresh steer burgers are ground daily, and a single will run you from $3.75 to $4.75, depending on what you want on it. For a burger on-the-go, they're decidedly tasty. For a few more bucks you can also order doubles and stacks or a vegetarian 'Shroom Burger—a super-rich melty Muenster and cheddar cheese–stuffed, fried portobello, topped with lettuce, tomato, and Shack sauce. The Shake Shack also offers beef and bird (chicken) hot dogs, french fries and fries drizzled with Shack-made cheddar and American cheese sauce, and a variety of delicious frozen custard desserts, and—of course—shakes! ⊠ *Madison Square Park near Madison Ave. and E. 23rd St., Flatiron District* ☎ *212/889–6600* ⊕ *www.shakeshack.com* ☰ *AE, D, MC, V* Ⓜ *N, R, W, 6 to 23rd St.* ⊹ *3:F2.*

$$$$　✕ **Tabla.** In concert with restaurant guru Danny Meyer, chef Floyd Car-
INDIAN　doz creates exciting cuisine based on the tastes of his native India, filtered through his European training. Indian ingredients garnish familiar fish and meats like striped bass, chicken, and lamb. In a recent change, the downstairs area is no longer a separate, more casual Bread Bar. But fans of the cheesy kulcha bread and spicy cauliflower can take heart; many of Bread Bar's greatest hits are now on the Tabla menu. There's also a $25 prix-fixe deal every day for lunch. ⊠ *11 Madison Ave., at E. 25th St., Flatiron District* ☎ *212/889–0667* ⊕ *www.tablany.com* ⌸ *Reservations essential* ☰ *AE, D, DC, MC, V* ⊘ *No lunch Sun.* Ⓜ *R, W, 6 to 23rd St.* ⊹ *3:F2.*

$$ ✗ **Tamarind**. Many consider Tamarind Manhattan's best Indian restau-
INDIAN rant. Forsaking the usual brass, beads, sitar, and darkness, you'll find
a lustrous skylighted dining room awash in soothing neutral colors
and awaft with tantalizing fragrances. Your welcoming hosts, owner
Avtar Walia and his nephew, general manager Gary, practically reinvent
charm. The busy kitchen offers multiregional dishes, some familiar (tan-
doori chicken, a searing lamb vindaloo), some unique (succulent veni-
son chops in a vigorously spiced cranberry sauce, she-crab soup with
saffron, nutmeg, and ginger juice). The more intriguing a dish sounds,
the better it turns out to be. Next door is a quaint teahouse–café–take-
out shop. ⊠ *41–43 E. 22nd St., between Broadway and Park Ave. S,
Flatiron District* ☎ *212/674–7400* ⊕ *www.tamarinde22.com* ⚑ *Reser-
vations essential* ▭ *AE, DC, MC, V* Ⓜ *N, R, 6 to 23rd St.* ✛ *3:F2.*

$$ ✗ **Wildwood Barbecue**. Prolific restaurateur Steve Hanson's latest venture
BARBECUE has been smokin' since day one, appeasing rabid barbecue aficionados.
Pit master (and former Queens cop) "Big Lou" Elrose deserves credit for
excellent ribs: succulent lamb and saucy baby back. Dine at the bar or at
adjacent high tables, where the animated scene is fueled by whiskey and
potent mint juleps. Families should settle in the dining room for fiery
fried jalapeño slices called "bottle caps," shareable platters of apricot-
glazed chicken and pulled pork, and towering carrot and chocolate
layer cakes. A crafty combination of reclaimed wood, distressed garage
doors, recycled paper, blackboards, and bell jars has made a trendy
Manhattan block feel kitschy and comfortable. ⊠ *225 Park Ave. S, at
18th St., Flatiron District* ☎ *212/533–2500* ⊕ *www.brguestrestaurants.
com/restaurants/wildwood_bbq* ▭ *AE, D, DC, MC, V* Ⓜ *4, 5, 6, L, N,
Q, R, W to 14th St./Union Sq.* ✛ *3:F3.*

GRAMERCY PARK

$$$$ ✗ **BLT Prime**. A masculine, vivacious space is the showcase for Laurent
STEAKHOUSE Tourondel's third "BLT" restaurant featuring Franco-American cuisine.
Menu specials are scrawled on a blackboard. Everything is served à la
carte, and prices are high, but so is the quality of every dish. Tourondel
has brought his signature steaming-hot Gruyère popovers downtown
from BLT Steak. They're light and buttery with an addictive texture.
Although there are poultry, veal, and lamb dishes on the menu, from
lemon-rosemary chicken to a lamb T-bone, steaks are the main event.
The dry-aged USDA prime steaks are broiled at 1,700, some spread
lightly with herb butter and offered with a choice of sauce (the béarnaise is perfection). ⊠ *111 E. 22nd St., between Lexington and Park
Aves., Gramercy Park* ☎ *212/995–8500* ⊕ *www.bltprime.com* ⚑ *Reservations essential* ▭ *AE, DC, MC, V* ☻ *No lunch* Ⓜ *6, R, W to 23rd
St.* ✛ *3:F3.*

$$ ✗ **Casa Mono**. Andy Nusser put in his time cooking Italian under Mario
SPANISH Batali at Babbo before an obsession with Spain landed him his own
acclaimed Iberian niche. The perennially cramped and crowded Casa
Mono sends its overflow to Bar Jamon, the annex wine-and-ham bar
next door. Pick at plates of *jamon serrano* while awaiting the call
for a prime seat at the counter overlooking the chef's open kitchen.
Though everything is delectably shareable, of particular note are all
things seared *à la plancha* (on the hot top), including blistered peppers

and garlic-kissed mushrooms. Like his renowned mentor, Nusser has a weakness for the most neglected cuts of meat. Check your food fears at the door and order up the blood sausage, cockscombs, and tripe. ⊠ *52 Irving Pl., at E. 17th St., Gramercy Park* ☎ *212/253–2773* ⊕ *www. casamononyc.com* ⊟ *AE, DC, MC, V* Ⓜ *4, 5, 6, L, N, Q, R, W to Union Sq.* ✛ *3:G3.*

$$$
AMERICAN

✕**Irving Mill.** This seasonal American hot spot has become a neighborhood favorite. The large dining room has a homey feel, with beige accents and traditional wood walls, and the waitstaff is eager to please with warm, unobtrusive service. Their menu isn't huge, but the choices incorporate the freshest produce and meat. Winter selections include celery-root chowder and baby beet salad as starters, and braised rabbit and roasted arctic char as mains. If you can't snag a reservation in the main dining room, try the Front Tap Room, which accepts walk-ins. ⊠ *116 E/ 16th St., between Union Square E and Irving Pl., Gramercy Park* ☎ *212/254–1600* ⊕ *www.irvingmill.com* ⊟ *AE, D, DC, MC, V* Ⓜ *4, 5, 6, L, N, Q, R, W to 14th St./Union Sq.* ✛ *3:F4.*

MURRAY HILL

$$
BRASSERIE

✕**Artisanal.** This spacious brasserie is a beloved shrine to cheese, the passion of chef-owner Terrance Brennan. Though service can be spotty, gastronomes and business lunchers still flock here for the more than 150 cheeses—available for on-site sampling or retail sale—then stay to enjoy their selections with one of 120 wines by the glass. Hot *fromage*-imbued fare also is satisfying, with preparations like addictive gougères, onion soup gratiné, and several types of fondue. For curd-adverse customers, steak-frites or selections from the raw bar should satisfy. ⊠ *2 Park Ave., at E. 32nd St., Murray Hill* ☎ *212/725–8585* ⊕ *www.artisanalbistro. com* ⌟ *Reservations essential* ⊟ *AE, D, DC, MC, V* Ⓜ *6 to 33rd St.* ✛ *3:F1.*

$
KOREAN

✕**Gahm Mi Oak.** The deconstructed industrial design, inexpensive 24-hour menu, and late-night hours attract a young and stylish crowd here. Every item on the limited menu goes well with *soju*, a Korean spirit, or beer. There are even photos on the menu to help bleary-eyed revelers order. Korean-style fried mung-bean pancakes with scallions, onions, carrots, and ground pork make for addictive stomach-lining fare. The kimchi is renowned, as is the *sul long tang*, a milky ox-bone soup with thin slices of beef, rice, and noodles that is reputed to be an effective hangover cure. ⊠ *43 W. 32nd St., between 5th Ave. and Broadway, Murray Hill* ☎ *212/695–4113* ⌟ *Reservations not accepted* ⊟ *AE, D, DC, MC, V* Ⓜ *B, D, F, N, Q, R, V, W to 34th St./Herald Sq.* ✛ *3:E1.*

$$
BRASSERIE
☼

✕**Les Halles.** This local hangout, owned by Philippe Lajaunie since 1990 and benefiting from the celebrity of former executive chef and writer Anthony Bourdain, is boisterous and unpretentious—just like a true French brasserie. A good bet is steak-frites—with fries regarded by some as the best in New York. Other prime choices include crispy duck-leg confit with frisée salad, blood sausage with caramelized apples, and steak tartare, prepared table-side. Another Les Halles is in Lower Manhattan at 15 John Street. ⊠ *411 Park Ave. S, between E. 28th*

and E. 29th Sts., Murray Hill ☎ *212/679–4111* ⊕ *www.leshalles.net*
🍴 *Reservations essential* 🖃 *AE, DC, MC, V* Ⓜ *6 to 28th St.* ✛ *3:F1*

$ ✕ **Turkish Kitchen.** This striking multilevel room with crimson walls,
TURKISH chairs with red-skirted slipcovers, and colorful kilims is Manhattan's
busiest and best Turkish restaurant. For appetizers, choose from the
likes of velvety char-grilled eggplant or tender octopus salad, creamy
hummus, or poached beef dumplings. The luscious stuffed cabbage
is downright irresistible. The restaurant also hosts one of the most
alluring Sunday brunch buffets in town, featuring 90 items, Turkish
and American—all house-made, including a dozen breads. ✉ *386 3rd
Ave., between E. 27th and E. 28th Sts., Murray Hill* ☎ *212/679–6633*
⊕ *www.turkishkitchen.com* 🖃 *AE, D, DC, MC, V* ☽ *No lunch Sat.* Ⓜ *6
to 28th St.* ✛ *3:G2.*

UNION SQUARE

$$$ ✕ **Craft.** Dining here is like a luscious choose-your-own-adventure game.
NEW AMERICAN Every delectable dish comes à la carte, including sides for your roasted
guinea hen or braised monkfish. Craft is *Top Chef* head judge Tom
Colicchio's flagship in a mini-empire of excellent restaurants around the
country, including the upscale Craftbar and Craftsteak brands, as well
as grab-and-go sandwich bars called 'wichcraft. Just about everything
here is exceptionally prepared with little fuss, from simple yet intrigu-
ing starters (grilled French sardines) and sides (the justly famous variety
of roasted mushrooms, including oysters, trumpets, chanterelles, and
hen-of-the-woods) to desserts (warm chocolate tart with buttermilk
ice cream, cinnamon custard, and cashews). The serene dining room
features burnished dark wood, custom tables, a curved leather wall,
and a succession of dangling radiant bulbs. ✉ *43 E. 19th St., between
Broadway and Park Ave. S, Union Square* ☎ *212/780–0880* ⊕ *www.
craftrestaurant.com* 🍴 *Reservations essential* 🖃 *AE, D, DC, MC, V*
☽ *No lunch* Ⓜ *L, N, Q, R, W, 4, 5, 6 to 14th St./Union Sq.* ✛ *3:F3.*

¢ ✕ **Republic.** When Republic first opened it was one of very few places
ASIAN to get an Asian-style noodle bowl with a stylish edge. Many have fol-
lowed in its footsteps—and some are better—but for window shoppers,
greenmarketers, and anyone else in the Union Square area, this place
gets the job done. The look is like a cross between a downtown art gal-
lery and a Japanese school cafeteria, and the young waitstaff dressed in
black T-shirts and jeans hold remote-control ordering devices to accel-
erate the already speedy service. Sit at the long, bluestone bar or at the
picnic-style tables and order appetizers such as smoky grilled eggplant
and luscious fried wontons. Entrées are all based on noodles or rice.
Spicy coconut chicken soup and Vietnamese-style barbecued pork are
particularly delicious. ✉ *37 Union Sq. W, between E. 16th and E. 17th
Sts., Union Square* ☎ *212/627–7172* ⊕ *www.thinknoodles.com* 🍴 *Res-
ervations not accepted* 🖃 *AE, DC, MC, V* Ⓜ *L, N, Q, R, W, 4, 5, 6 to
14th St./Union Sq.* ✛ *3:F4.*

$$$ ✕ **Tocqueville.** Hidden just steps from busy Union Square, Tocqueville
NEW AMERICAN is a refined dining oasis that's a secret even to many New York food-
ies. Guests enter through an austere reception area that gives no indi-
cation of the luxury appointments inside. Past heavy curtains and a
six-seat bar, the dining area is an intimate, modern room lined with

18

warm gold- and sand-toned fabrics. Chef-owner Marco Moreira's signature starter is the unctuous sea urchin and angel-hair carbonara. Main courses are steeped in French tradition, but with international flavors, like pan-roasted turbot with mushroom fondue and kohlrabi and sea-bean confit, and lemon verbena–scented tofu with lily-bulb puree. The three-course $24 prix-fixe lunch is a steal. ⊠ *1 E. 15th St., between 5th Ave. and Union Sq. W, Union Square* ☎ *212/647–1515* ⊕ *www.tocquevillerestaurant.com* ⟁ *Reservations essential* ⊟ *AE, MC, V* Ⓜ *L, N, Q, R, W, 4, 5, 6 to 14th St./Union Sq.* ✛ *3:F4.*

$$$ ✕ **Union Square Cafe.** When he opened Union Square Cafe in 1985,
AMERICAN   Danny Meyer changed the American restaurant landscape. The combination of upscale food and unpretentious but focused service sparked a revolution. Today chef Carmen Quagliata still draws devotees with his crowd-pleasing menu. Wood paneling and white walls are hung with splashy modern paintings; in addition to the three dining areas, there's a long bar ideal for solo diners. The cuisine is American with a thick Italian accent: for example, the grilled, marinated filet mignon of tuna can land on the same table as creamy polenta with mascarpone. ⊠ *21 E. 16th St., between 5th Ave. and Union Sq. W, Union Square* ☎ *212/243–4020* ⊕ *www.unionsquarecafe.com* ⟁ *Reservations essential* ⊟ *AE, D, DC, MC, V* Ⓜ *L, N, Q, R, W, 4, 5, 6 to 14th St./Union Sq.* ✛ *3:F4.*

MIDTOWN WEST AND CHELSEA

CHELSEA

$$$ ✕ **Buddakan.** Few—if any—restaurants in Manhattan can rival the
ASIAN   16,000-square-foot Buddakan in terms of sheer magnitude and buoyant theatricality. And in a neighborhood whose eateries often get by on sizzle alone, the food here has real substance as well. Restaurateur Steven Starr created a New York edition of his Philadelphia original. Here the upstairs bar is a great end-of-day meet-up spot for pert cocktails and appetizers, while the vast downstairs is like a dining hall in a medieval castle, complete with a communal table spanning the room. Highly pedigreed chef Lon Symensma has cooked at Spice Market in New York City. His ethereal tuna spring rolls are narrow flutes of ruby tuna tartare in a crisp contrapuntal fried shell, and edamame dumplings reveal a creamy light green center. Crisp-tender sizzling short ribs are served with tender wide noodles and highly comforting results, and there are dozens of other tempting dishes large and small. Considering the droves of patrons, service is surprisingly attentive. ⊠ *75 9th Ave., between 15th and 16th Sts., Chelsea* ☎ *212/989–6699* ⊕ *www. buddakannyc.com* ⟁ *Reservations essential* ⊟ *AE, D, MC, V* ◐ *No lunch* Ⓜ *A, C, E to 14th St.; L to 8th Ave.* ✛ *3:B4.*

$ ✕ **R.U.B. BBQ.** Among the American barbecue capitals, Kansas City's
BARBECUE   smoked fare stands out as perhaps the most versatile, characterized by dry rubs with sauces strictly on the side. Executive chef Paul Kirk is from Kansas City, and is a legend on the growing New York City barbecue competition circuit. This is not a restaurant for the timid of appetite. Platters are so bountiful that even the side dishes come in overwhelming quantities. The shameless menu promises everything from

beef, pork, ham, pastrami, and turkey to chicken, sausage, and, of course ribs. Burned ends—delicious charred-crisp, rich edges of beef brisket—are legendary, and they sell out every night. For dessert, don't miss the batter-fried Oreos. In fact, many items on the menu sell out by 8 PM, so it's wise to arrive fairly early. ⊠ *208 W. 23rd St., between 7th and 8th Aves., Chelsea* ☎ *212/524–4300* ⊕ *www.rubbbq.net* ⌁ *Reservations not accepted* ⊟ *AE, D, MC, V* Ⓜ *1, C, E, F, V to 23rd St.* ✛ *3:D2.*

$$ × **Tía Pol.** This tiny, dark, out-of-the way, but highly popular tapas bar

SPANISH
Fodor's Choice is usually packed, but there are good reasons for that: it's one of the
★ best in town with a welcoming vibe, a dozen reasonably priced Spanish wines by the glass, and charm to spare. The tables and stools are small (and high), but the flavors are enormous. One of the most original tapas has become a signature here: bittersweet chocolate smeared on a baguette disc and topped with salty Spanish chorizo. *Patatas bravas,* (rough-cut potatoes deep-fried and served with a dollop of spicy aioli) are so addictive you won't want to share them. The pork loin, piquillo pepper, and mild tetilla cheese sandwich is scrumptious, and so is the Galician octopus terrine. In fact, everything on the menu is transporting and delicious. ⊠ *205 10th Ave., between 22nd and 23rd Sts., Chelsea* ☎ *212/675–8805* ⊕ *www.tiapol.com* ⌁ *Reservations essential for groups of 6–8* ⊟ *AE, MC, V* ☟ *No lunch Mon.* Ⓜ *C, E to 23rd St.* ✛ *3:A2.*

18

MIDTOWN WEST

$$$$ × **Aureole.** An island of fine dining in the heart of bustling Times Square,

NEW AMERICAN Aureole is the second act of a New York classic from Charlie Palmer and his handpicked executive chef, Christopher Lee. From the street, a curved second-story corridor hosting the restaurant's storied wine collection beckons. A welcoming front bar room serves a more casual, yet refined, menu with dishes like a cheddar-bacon burger dolloped with pickled ramp mayonnaise. The dining room, with its abundance of flowers, is the place to hobnob with expense-account diners and pre-theater revelers alike. For dinner, starters like the sea-scallop "sandwich" topped with foie gras and passion fruit coulis is a treat, and the $115 "parallel tasting" offers the menu's greatest hits, with an optional wine pairing. ⊠ *135 W. 42nd St., between Broadway and 6th Ave, Midtown West* ☎ *212/319–1660* ⊕ *www.charlie palmer.com/properties/ aureoleny.com* ⌁ *Reservations essential* ⊟ *AE, D, DC, MC, V* Ⓜ *B, D, F, V to 42nd St./Bryant Park; 1, 2, 3, 9, N, R, Q, W to 42nd St./Times Square* ✛ *4:D4.*

$$$ × **Bar Americain.** Celeb chef Bobby Flay's largest Manhattan restaurant

BRASSERIE is the soaring Bar Americain. The 200-seat two-story space looks like a dining room on a luxury liner. (Complete with a gift shop: you can purchase his many cookbooks in the front.) This is not food for the faint-of-heart: Flay piles on the butter, cream, and endless varieties of bacon. Southern-inflected brasserie fare includes gold corn Johnny-cakes with barbecued pulled pork and cranberry butter, smoked chicken with hatch-green chili spoon bread and black-pepper vinegar sauce, and roasted duck breast surrounded by dirty wild rice with bourbon-soaked pecans. Slightly naughtier are the éclairs piped with whiskey-infused pastry cream and burnished with a burnt-sugar glaze.

Brunch, featuring dishes like biscuits and cream gravy with sausage and scrambled eggs, is delicious. ⊠ *152 W. 52nd St., between 6th and 7th Aves., Midtown West* ☎ *212/265–9700* ⊕ *www.baramericain.com/* ♨ *Reservations essential* ▤ *AE, D, MC, V* Ⓜ *B, D, E to 7th Ave.; 1, C, E to 50th St.; N, R, W to 49th St.* ✛ *4:C2.*

$$$ ✕ **Becco.** An ingenious concept makes Becco a prime Restaurant Row
ITALIAN choice for time-constrained theatergoers. There are two pricing scenarios: one includes an all-you-can-eat selection of antipasti and three pastas served hot out of pans that waiters circulate around the dining room; the other adds a generous entrée to the mix. The pasta selection changes daily, but often includes gnocchi, fresh ravioli, and fettuccine in a cream sauce. The entrées include braised veal shank, grilled double-cut pork chop, and rack of lamb, among other selections. ⊠ *355 W. 46th St., between 8th and 9th Aves., Midtown West* ☎ *212/397–7597* ⊕ *www.becco-nyc.com* ♨ *Reservations essential* ▤ *AE, D, DC, MC, V* Ⓜ *A, C, E to 42nd St.* ✛ *4:B3.*

$$$$ ✕ **Ben Benson's Steakhouse.** Among the most venerable steak houses
STEAKHOUSE around, Ben Benson's feels like a clubby hunting lodge. The gracefully choreographed, intensely focused staff will bring you only the finest dry-aged prime meats and only the freshest seafood, all classically prepared, teeming with familiar and beloved flavors. The trimmings are ravishing, too: comforting creamed spinach, sizzling onion rings, and decadent hash browns are essential. Power lunches were practically invented here; just being in the place makes you feel important. ⊠ *123 W. 52nd St., between 6th and 7th Aves., Midtown West* ☎ *212/581–8888* ⊕ *www. benbensons.com* ♨ *Reservations essential* ▤ *AE, D, DC, MC, V* ⊗ *No lunch weekends* Ⓜ *B, D, E to 7th Ave.; 1 to 50th St.; N, R, W to 49th St.* ✛ *4:D2.*

$$$ ✕ **Brasserie Ruhlmann.** In a plush 120-seat dining room with just enough
BRASSERIE Art Deco touches to harmonize with its Rockefeller Center setting, the sublime French bistro cookery, courtesy of Laurent Tourondel, is on display. There is a decorous countenance to the room, but the staff is so friendly that the place could never be stuffy. Seventeen excellent wines are available by the glass, as well as ten half-bottles. A pristine raw bar, featuring a selection of pedigreed oysters, is a great way to begin, or opt for a blue crab salad over mache with a honey-lime vinaigrette. If it's on the menu, order braised rabbit nestled in mustard cream on a bed of fresh pappardelle, sprinkled with pitted cherries. Desserts like Floating

Island—delicately baked meringue floating on a pond of crème anglaise—are embellished by a tangled flurry of spun sugar. ⊠ *45 Rockefeller Plaza, 50th St. between 5th and 6th Aves., Midtown West* ☎ *212/974–2020* ⊕ *www.brasserieruhlmann.com* ⚑ *Reservations essential* ⊟ *AE, MC, V* Ⓜ *B, D, F, V to 47th–50th Sts./Rockefeller Center* ✛ *4:D3.*

¢ ✕ **Burger Joint**. What's a college burger bar, done up in particleboard and
BURGER rec-room decor straight out of a *Happy Days* episode, doing hidden
Fodor's Choice inside of a five-star Midtown hotel? This tongue-in-cheek lunch spot,
★ hidden behind a heavy red velvet curtain in the Parker Meridien hotel, does such boisterous midweek business that lines often snake through the lobby. Stepping behind the curtain, you can find baseball cap–wearing grease-spattered cooks dispensing paper-wrapped cheeseburgers and crisp thin fries. Forget Kobe beef or foie gras—these burgers are straightforward, cheap, and delicious. ⊠ *118 W. 57th St., between 6th and 7th Aves., Midtown West* ☎ *212/245–5000* ⊕ *www.parkermeridien.com* ⊟ *No credit cards* Ⓜ *F, N, Q, R, W to 57th St.* ✛ *4:D1.*

$$ ✕ **Carmine's**. Savvy New Yorkers line up early for the affordable fam-
ITALIAN ily-style meals at this large, busy Midtown eatery. Family photos line
ⓒ the walls, and there's a convivial feeling amid all the Times Square hubbub. Don't be fooled: Carmine's may be huge, but it fills up with families carbo-loading for a day of sightseeing or a night of theater on Broadway. There are no reservations taken for parties of fewer than six people after 7 PM, but those who wait are rewarded with mountains of such popular, toothsome viands as fried calamari, linguine with white clam sauce, chicken parmigiana, and veal saltimbocca. ⊠ *200 W. 44th St., between Broadway and 8th Ave., Midtown West* ☎ *212/221–3800* ⊕ *www.carminesnyc.com* ⊟ *AE, D, DC, MC, V* Ⓜ *A, C, E, N, Q, R, W, S, 1, 2, 3, 7 to 42nd St./Times Sq.* ✛ *4:C4*

$$$$ ✕ **Churrascaria Plataforma**. This sprawling, boisterous shrine to meat,
BRAZILIAN with its all-you-can-eat prix-fixe menu, is best experienced with a group of ravenous friends. A *caipirinha,* featuring cacacha sugarcane liquor, sugar, and lime, will kick things off nicely. Follow up with a trip to the salad bar piled with vegetables, meats, and cheeses. But restrain yourself—there's a parade of all manner of grilled meats and poultry, from pork ribs to chicken hearts, delivered to the table on long skewers until you beg for mercy. ⊠ *316 W. 49th St., between 8th and 9th Aves., Midtown West* ☎ *212/245–0505* ⊕ *www.churrascariaplataforma.com* ⚑ *Reservations essential* ⊟ *AE, D, DC, MC, V* Ⓜ *C, E to 50th St.* ✛ *4:B3.*

$$$ ✕ **DB Bistro Moderne**. Daniel Boulud's "casual bistro" (it's neither, actu-
FRENCH ally) consists of two elegantly appointed dining rooms. The menu features classic dishes like Nantucket Bay scallops or hanger steak exquisitely prepared. Ever the trendsetter, Boulud's $32 db hamburger, available at lunch and dinner, and stuffed with braised short ribs, foie gras, and black truffles, is the patty credited with kick-starting the whole gourmet burger trend. Yes, it's worth every penny. ⊠ *55 W. 44th St., between 5th and 6th Aves., Midtown West* ☎ *212/391–2400* ⊕ *www. danielnyc.com/dbbistro.html* ⚑ *Reservations essential* ⊟ *AE, DC, MC, V* ☾ *No lunch Sun.* Ⓜ *B, D, F, V to 42nd St./Bryant Park; 7 to 5th Ave./ Bryant Park* ✛ *4:D4.*

18

$$$
SEAFOOD

✗ **Esca.** Italian for "bait," this restaurant, courtesy of partners Mario Batali, Joe Bastianich, and longtime chef David Pasternack, lures diners in with delectable raw preparations called *crudo*—such as tilefish with orange and Sardinian oil or pink snapper with a sprinkle of crunchy red clay salt—and hooks them with such entrées as whole, salt-crusted *branzino*, sea bass for two, or *bucatini* pasta with spicy baby octopus. The menu changes daily. Batali's partner, Joe Bastianich, is in charge of the wine cellar, so expect an adventurous list of Italian bottles. ✉ *402 W. 43rd St., at 9th Ave., Midtown West* ☎ *212/564–7272* ⊕ *www.esca-nyc.com* ⌔ *Reservations essential* ▭ *AE, DC, MC, V* ☯ *No lunch Sun.* Ⓜ *A, C, E to 42nd St.* ✛ *4:A4.*

$$
AMERICAN

✗ **Five Napkin Burger.** This perennially packed Hell's Kitchen burger/brasserie has been a magnet for burger lovers since day one. Bottles of Maker's Mark line the sleek, alluringly lit the bar in the back, a collection of antique butcher's scales hangs on a tile wall near the kitchen, and meat hooks dangle from the ceiling between the light fixtures. Though there are many menu distractions—deep-fried pickles, warm artichoke dip, and an iceberg-wedge salad among them—the main attractions are the juicy burgers, like the original 10-oz chuck with a tangle of onions, Gruyère cheese, and rosemary aioli. There's a patty variety for everyone, including a ground lamb *kofta* and an onion ring–topped ahi tuna burger. For dessert, have an über-thick black-and-white malted milkshake. ✉ *630 9th Ave., between 44th and 45th Sts., Hell's Kitchen* ☎ *212/757–2277* ⊕ *www.fivenapkinburger.com* ⌔ *Reservations accepted, walk-ins welcome* ▭ *AE, D, MC, V* Ⓜ *A, C, E to 42nd St./8th Ave.* ✛ *4:B4.*

$$–$$$$
FRENCH

✗ **Gordon Ramsay at The London and Maze.** With more than a dozen restaurants around the world—and an ever-busy TV schedule—you're not likely to find British chef Gordon Ramsay at his eponymous Midtown restaurant. What you will find, however, are Ramsay's trembling acolytes producing flawless facsimiles of his classically muted haute cuisine. The flagship fine-dining restaurant is an exorbitant time commitment, with menus that start at $110 for three courses and stretch to $150 for seven. It is hidden behind opaque glass doors just beyond the comparatively casual, and much more reasonably priced, Maze. The lower-key annex, in a silver-gray dining room, specializes in elegant small-plate cuisine (often very small). Although dinner is a mix-and-match affair, the $35 prix-fixe three-course lunch is one of the top bargains in Midtown. ✉ *151 W. 54th St., between 6th and 7th Aves., Midtown West* ☎ *212/468–8888* ⊕ *www.thelondonnyc.com/gordon_ramsay.com* ▭ *AE, D, DC, MC, V* ☯ *No lunch. No dinner Sun. and Mon.* Ⓜ *B, D, E to 7th Ave.; N, Q, R, W to 57th St.* ✛ *4:D2.*

$$$$
FRENCH

✗ **Le Bernardin.** Owner Maguy LeCoze presides over the teak-panel dining room at this trendsetting French seafood restaurant, and chef-partner Eric Ripert works magic with anything that swims—preferring at times not to cook it at all. Deceptively simple dishes such as poached lobster in rich coconut-ginger soup or crispy spiced black bass in a Peking duck bouillon are typical of his style. It is widely agreed that there's no beating Le Bernardin for thrilling cuisine, seafood or otherwise, coupled with some of the finest desserts in town and a wine list as deep as the Atlantic. ✉ *155 W. 51st St., between 6th and 7th Aves., Midtown West* ☎ *212/554–1515* ⊕ *www.le-bernardin.com* ✍ *Reservations essential, Jacket required* ▭ *AE, DC, MC, V* ⊙ *Closed Sun. No lunch Sat.* Ⓜ *1 to 50th St.; R, W to 49th St.; B, D, F, V to 47th–50th Sts./Rockefeller Center.* ✛ *4:C2.*

$$ **✕ Lugo Caffé.** The area around Madison Square Garden is a restaurant
ITALIAN wasteland with the rare sparkling exception of Lugo Caffé, founded by
an Italian menswear line. Locals rejoiced at the introduction of this spacious Italian "brasserie" offering comfort food with a *Dolce Vita* twist all day long. Stop by for an espresso and *cornetto* pastry in the morning. Later, a single menu presents lunch, *aperitivo*, and dinner options, which include grazing portions of salumi, cheeses, and vegetable dishes like eggplant caponata, Tuscan bean salad, and grilled zucchini with pine nuts. Fuller meals of Neapolitan-style pizzas, house-made pastas, and grilled meats and fish also are commendable. ✉ *1 Penn Plaza (33rd St. and 8th Ave.), Garment District* ☎ *212/760–2700* ⊕ *www.lugocaffe. com* ▭ *AE, MC, V* Ⓜ *A, C, E to 34th St.; 1, 2, 3 to 34th St.* ✛ *4:C6.*

$$ **✕ Marseille.** With great food and a convenient location near several
MEDITERRANEAN Broadway theaters, Marseille is perpetually packed. Executive chef
and partner Andy d'Amico's Mediterranean creations are continually impressive. His bouillabaisse, the signature dish of the region for which the restaurant is named, is a mélange of mussels, shrimp, rouget, and bass swimming in a fragrant fish broth, topped with a garlicky crouton and served with rouille on the side. Leave room for the spongy beignets with chocolate and raspberry dipping sauces. ✉ *630 9th Ave., at W. 44th St., Midtown West* ☎ *212/333–2323* ⊕ *www.marseillenyc. com* ✍ *Reservations essential* ▭ *AE, MC, V* Ⓜ *A, C, E to 42nd St./Port Authority Bus Terminal* ✛ *4:B4.*

$ **✕ Meskerem.** The tasty Ethiopian delicacies offered in this Hell's Kitchen
ETHIOPIAN storefront include *kitfo*, spiced ground steak, which you can order raw,
rare, or well done, and *yebeg alecha,* tender pieces of lamb marinated in Ethiopian butter flavored with curry, rosemary, and an herb called *kosart,* and then sautéed with fresh ginger and more curry. The vegetarian combination, served on injera, a fermented and slightly porous flat bread used as a utensil to sop up the food, is a great deal. ✉ *468 W. 47th St., near 10th Ave., Midtown West* ☎ *212/664–0520* ▭ *AE, D, DC, MC, V* Ⓜ *C, E to 50th St.* ✛ *4:A3.*

$$$–$$$$ **✕ The Modern and Bar Room.** Both spots competing for the title of the
FRENCH country's best museum restaurant sit side by side on the ground floor of
the New York MoMA. The Modern, run by restaurateur Danny Meyer, is two restaurants in one. Both offer the dazzling food of Alsatian chef Gabriel Kreuther. The formal dining room features a view of the museum's sculpture garden and an ambitious, pricey, prix-fixe menu. The far more accessible and popular Bar Room lies just beyond a partition. Here you can find a dizzying collection of shareable plates, like the refreshing arctic char tartare and oysters with leeks and caviar. Two or three make a fine if extravagant afternoon snack—double that number and you have a full meal. ✉ *9 W. 53rd St., between 5th and 6th Aves., Midtown West* ☎ *212/333–1220* ⊕ *www.themodernnyc.com* ▭ *AE, D, DC, MC, V* ⊙ *Closed Sun.* Ⓜ *E, V to 5th Ave./53rd St.* ✛ *4:D2.*

18

$$$$
SEAFOOD

✕ **Oceana.** Entering the newly revamped Oceana is like walking into the dressy stateroom of a modern luxury ocean liner. Floor-to-ceiling windows look out both north and west, the cocktail bar offers cutting-edge concoctions like a fusion of bourbon, Italian bitters, elderflower, and cardamom. The arrestingly designed raw bar backed with Mediterranean-hued ceramics offers stunningly fresh choices. You would expect gorgeous oysters at a restaurant called Oceana, and you get them: they're so full-flavored that they transcend their chilliness. Chef Ben Pollinger has all the skill and confidence necessary to serve some of the most vivid and delicious seafood in town. A "contemporary appetizer" section features items like marinated cucumber with cucumber, apple, and toasted spices. Grilled whole fish like halibut, swordfish, and crispy wild striped bass are served with perfect sauces such as tomatillo salsa and Moroccan-style Hollandaise. Thai-style red snapper comes with tender silk squash, crisp jicama, and a kaffir-saffron broth. ⊠ *1221 6th Ave., at W. 49th St., Midtown West* ☎ *212/759–5941* ⊕ *www.livanosrestaurantgroup.com* ☁ *Reservations essential* ⊟ *AE, DC, MC, V* Ⓜ *E, V to 53rd St./5th Ave.* ✢ *4:D3.*

$$$
AUSTRIAN/
GERMAN

✕ **Seäsonal Restaurant and Weinbar.** Partners and executive chefs Wolfgang Ban and Eduard Frauender have brought something *neu* to Midtown: a swanky Austrian-German restaurant and Weinbar. With its sculptural ceiling lighting, elliptical bar, and contemporary Austrian and German art, Seäsonal feels more "downtown" than you'd expect from such central Midtown digs. The decor is modern European, with white walls, wood floors, and leather cubby seating. The cuisine is sophisticated and contemporary, yet still steeped in regional traditions. The chefs are committed to using fresh, seasonal ingredients, and whenever possible, locally sourced products. Appetizers like the foie-gras terrine and the cheese ravioli with smoked chanterelle mushrooms will delight you with their contrasting lightness and intensity of flavor. Main dishes, such as the pumpkin seed-crusted black sea bass with butternut squash and black truffles, and the classic Wiener schnitzel served with a crescent potato-cucumber salad, will pleasure your palate with simple but striking flavor combinations. Seäsonal's Weinbar features a distinctive selection of wines from emerging Austrian and German winemakers— definitely the right place for your Riesling fix. ⊠ *132 W. 58th St., Midtown West* ☎ *212/957–5550* ⊕ *www.seasonalnyc.com* ⊟ *AE, DC, MC, V* Ⓜ *F to 57th St./6th Ave.* ✢ *4:D1.*

$$
ITALIAN

✕ **Sosa Borella.** This is one of the Theater District's top spots for reliable food at a reasonable cost. This bi-level, casual Italian eatery is an inviting and friendly space where diners choose from a wide range of options. The lunch menu features staples like warm sandwiches and entrée-size salads, while the dinner menu is slightly gussied up with meat, fish, and pasta dishes (the rich agnolotti with lamb Bolognese sauce, topped with a wedge of grilled pecorino cheese is a must-try). The freshly baked bread served at the beginning of the meal with pesto dipping sauce is a nice touch as you wait for your meal. The service, at times, can be slow, so leave yourself plenty of time before the show. ⊠ *832 8th Ave., between 50th and 51st Sts., Midtown West* ☎ *212/262–8282* ⊕ *www. sosaborella.com* ⊟ *AE, MC, V* Ⓜ *C, E, 1 to 50th St.* ✢ *4:B3.*

$$ ✕**Toloache**. Make a quick detour off
MEXICAN heavily trafficked Broadway into this pleasantly bustling Mexican cantina that's one of the best dining options around Times Square. The bi-level eatery has a festive, celebratory vibe, with several seating options (bar, balcony, main dining room, and ceviche bar), oversize bronze chandeliers, and gold and terra-cotta tones throughout. Foodies flock here for three types of guacamole (traditional, fruited, and spicy), a trio of well-executed ceviches, and dishes like the Mexico City–style tacos with Negra Modelo–braised brisket, quesadillas studded with black truffle and *huitlacoche* (a corn fungus). There's an extensive tequila selection—upwards of 100 brands. Adventurous palates will be drawn to tacos featuring chili-studded dried grasshoppers, lobes of seared foie gras, and caramelized veal sweetbreads. ✉ *251 W. 50th St., near 8th Ave., Midtown West* ☎ *212/581–1818* ⊕ *www. toloachenyc.com* ▭ *AE, D, MC, V* Ⓜ *1, C, E to 50th St.; N, R, W to 49th St.* ✛ *4:B3.*

$$$$ ✕**'21' Club**. Tradition's the thing at this town-house landmark, a former
AMERICAN speakeasy that opened in 1929. Toys donated by famous patrons—e.g., John McEnroe's tennis racket or Howard Hughes's model plane—hang from the ceiling. Down below, Chef John Greeley tries to satisfy everyone with standards like the famous '21' burger and Dover sole with brown butter, and more modern dishes, such as smoked Berkshire pork belly with butter beans and Tuscan kale, but the food is almost secondary to the restaurant's storied past. Fellas, a jacket is required, but thanks to a more relaxed dress code you can leave your tie at home. ✉ *21 W. 52nd St., between 5th and 6th Aves., Midtown West* ☎ *212/582–7200* ⊕ *www.21club.com* ⚞ *Jacket required* ▭ *AE, D, DC, MC, V* ☾ *Closed Sun. No lunch Sat.* Ⓜ *E, V to 53rd St./5th Ave.; B, D, F, V to 47th–50th Sts./Rockefeller Center.* ✛ *4:D2.*

$$$$ ✕**Uncle Jack's Steakhouse**. Surpassing even its celebrated flagship restau-
STEAKHOUSE rant in Bayside, Queens, Uncle Jack's soars directly into the pantheon of the best steak houses in Manhattan. As in most great steak houses, you can feel the testosterone throbbing all through the place. The space is vast and gorgeously appointed, and service is swift and focused. USDA Prime steaks are dry-aged for 21 days. Australian lobster tails are so enormous they have to be served carved, yet the flesh is meltingly tender. ✉ *440 9th Ave., between W. 34th and W. 35th Sts., Midtown West* ☎ *212/244–0005* ⊕ *www.unclejacks.com* ⚞ *Reservations essential* ▭ *AE, MC, V* ☾ *No lunch weekends* Ⓜ *A, C, E to 34th St./Penn Station* ✛ *4:B6.*

$$ ✕**Virgil's Real BBQ**. Neon, wood, and Formica set the scene at this
BARBECUE massive roadhouse in the Theater District. Start with stuffed jalape-
☻ ños or—especially—unbelievably succulent barbecued chicken wings.

18

Then, what the hell: go for the "Pig Out"—a rack of pork ribs, Texas hot links, pulled pork, rack of lamb, chicken, and, of course, more. It's that kind of place. There are also five domestic microbrews on tap and a good list of top beers from around the world. The place is absolutely mobbed pre-theater, so if that's when you're going, arrive by 6 PM or you'll miss your curtain. ⊠ *152 W. 44th St., between 6th Ave. and Broadway, Midtown West* ☎ *212/921–9494* ⊕ *www.virgilsbbq. com* ♠ *Reservations essential* ⊟ *AE, MC, V* Ⓜ *N, Q, R, W, S, 1, 2, 3, 7 to 42nd St./Times Sq.* ⊕ *4:C4.*

MIDTOWN EAST AND UPPER EAST SIDE

MIDTOWN EAST

$$$$
MODERN FRENCH
Fodor's Choice
★

✕ **Adour Alain Ducasse.** Master chef Alain Ducasse adds to his growing empire with the upscale and elegant Adour, located in the equally sophisticated St. Regis Hotel. Celebratory couples of all ages gravitate to the Left and Right Bank rooms, while a mix of tourists, shoppers, and businessmen settle on plush burgundy chairs and banquettes in the regal but relaxed main dining room. Beautifully baked baguettes and fragrant olive and sourdough rolls are flown in, parbaked, from Paris, and finished downstairs. Deep pockets splurge on artfully arranged dishes, such as sweetbreads meunière-stye with an unctuous poached egg "purse," and butter-poached Maine lobster with trumpet mushrooms and Champagne sauce. Sommeliers help decipher an international wine list (displayed on interactive computer screens at the bar) with bottles that range from $35 to $19,000. ⊠ *2 E. 55th St., near 5th Ave., Midtown East* ☎ *212/710–2277* ⊕ *www.adour-stregis.com* ♠ *Reservations essential* ⊟ *AE, D, DC, MC, V* ☉ *No lunch* Ⓜ *E, V to 5th Ave./53rd St.; F to 57th St.* ⊕ *4:E2.*

$$$$
SCANDINAVIAN

✕ **Aquavit and Aquavit Café.** Celebrity chef Marcus Samuelsson may not be in the kitchen every night, but you'd never know it from the impeccable cuisine and service at this fine-dining restaurant and upscale café. The elegant atmosphere features warm woods and modern decor from a Scandinavian design team. In the café, try a two-course dinner of daily "Swedish home cooking" specials, or order à la carte to try the herring sampler, with boldly flavored selections like curry and apple, and vodka-lime. Hot-smoked arctic char served with langoustines and chanterelles, is a standout. The main dining room is prix-fixe only, with a three-course dinner for $78 or a chef's tasting at $105. ⊠ *65 E. 55th St., between Madison and Park Aves., Midtown East* ☎ *212/307–7311* ⊕ *www.aquavit.org* ♠ *Reservations essential* ⊟ *AE, DC, MC, V* ☉ *No lunch Sat., except in café* Ⓜ *E, V to 5th Ave./53rd St.* ⊕ *4:F2.*

$$$
STEAKHOUSE

✕ **BLT Steak.** Chef Laurent Tourondel raises the bar for steak houses in this classy space decked out in beige and suede with resin-topped black tables. As soon as you're settled, puffy Gruyère popovers arrive still steaming. The no-muss, no-fuss menu is nonetheless large, and so are the portions of supple crab cakes with celery-infused mayonnaise and luscious ruby tuna tartare with avocado, ramped up with soy-lime dressing. A veal chop crusted with rosemary and Parmesan lends new depth to the meat. At lunch, the quintessential BLT includes Kobe beef, foie gras, bacon, and tomato on a split ciabatta bun, with a cute plastic pig toothpick indicating desired doneness. Sides and desserts, like a killer peanut butter–chocolate mousse with banana ice cream, are all superior. ✉ *106 E. 57th St., between Lexington and Park Aves., Midtown East* ☎ *212/752–7470* ⊕ *www.bltsteak.com* ⌧ *Reservations essential* ▱ *AE, DC, MC, V* ☉ *Closed Sun. No lunch Sat.* Ⓜ *4, 5, 6, N, R, W to 59th St./Lexington Ave.* ✚ *4:F1.*

$$ ✕ **Convivio.** Formerly L'Impero, this renamed restaurant in charming
ITALIAN Tudor City has earned a devoted following under the helm of well-respected chef Michael White. The orange-and-white room has 110 seats, all filled with locals, tourists, and diplomats who come for the chic ambience, polished service, and even better food. Tasty *sfizi*, or nibbles—such as sweet and sour baby eggplant and saffron risotto *arancini*—foreshadow White's legendary house-made pastas, like braised rabbit–filled ravioli with escarole and wild mushrooms or fusilli with pork shoulder ragu and a fondue of caciocavallo cheese. Eclectic and flavorsome entrées, like crispy Long Island duck breast with Swiss chard and butternut squash, round out the menu, which is meant to be enjoyed as a $59 prix-fixe. The spot has several outdoor tables for alfresco dining and a spacious bar area for drinking from the all-Italian beer list, or from the 550-bottle wine list with many Sicilian selections. ✉ *45 Tudor City Pl., between 42nd and 43rd Sts., Midtown East* ☎ *212/599–5045* ⊕ *www.convivionyc.com* ▱ *AE, D, DC, MC, V* ☉ *Closed Sun. No lunch weekends* Ⓜ *4, 5, 6, 7, S to Grand Central* ✚ *4:H4.*

$$$$ ✕ **Four Seasons.** The landmark Seagram Building houses one of Amer-
AMERICAN ica's most famous restaurants, truly an only-in-New York experience. Owners Alex Von Bider and Julian Niccolini supervise the seating chart like hawks, placing power players in finance, entertainment, and New York society in prime positions for maximum visibility. The stark Grill Room, birthplace of the power lunch, has one of the best bars in New York. Illuminated trees and a gurgling Carrara marble pool characterize the more romantic Pool Room. The menu changes seasonally; there's a $65 prix-fixe pre-theater dinner—a delicious indulgence. After the death of longtime chef Christian Albin, Italian chef Fabio Trabocchi has taken the reigns. You can't go wrong with classic dishes like Dover sole, filet mignon, or crispy duck, but the restaurant moves with the times, so expect roving seasonal specials featuring luxe ingredients and preparations. Finish with pear William, Grand Marnier, or a chocolate soufflé. ✉ *99 E. 52nd St., between Park and Lexington Aves., Midtown East* ☎ *212/754–9494* ⊕ *www.fourseasonsrestaurant.com* ⌧ *Reservations essential. Jacket required* ▱ *AE, D, DC, MC, V* ☉ *Closed Sun. No lunch Sat.* Ⓜ *E, V to Lexington Ave./53rd St.; 6 to 51st St.* ✚ *4:F2.*

$$$$ ✕ **Kuruma Zushi.** Only a small sign in Japanese indicates the location
JAPANESE of this extraordinary restaurant that serves only sushi and sashimi. Bypass the tables, sit at the sushi bar, and put yourself in the hands of Toshishiro Uezu, the chef-owner. Among the selections are hard-to-find fish that Uezu imports directly from Japan. The most attentive, pampering service staff in the city completes the wildly expensive experience. The showstopping chef's *omakase* will cost you $250, but it's a multicourse feast you'll never forget. ✉ *7 E. 47th St., 2nd fl., between 5th and Madison Aves., Midtown East* ☎ *212/317–2802* ⌧ *Reservations*

18

essential $=$ *AE, MC, V* ✆ *Closed Sun.* Ⓜ *4, 5, 6, 7 to 42nd St./Grand Central* ✛ *4:E3.*

$$$$ ✕ **L'Atelier de Joël Robuchon.** The New York branch of Joël Robuchon's
FRENCH superluxurious tapas bar, inside the Four Seasons Hotel, features essen-
Fodor'sChoice tially the same food (with a more natural-hue decor) as the Paris origi-
★ nal. And that, it turns out, is a very good thing. The perfectionist chef
has installed a longtime protégé to uphold the standards that can make
a Robuchon meal a life-changing experience. Skip the regular-size appetizers and entrées. Instead, secure a seat at the pear-wood counter and
cobble together your own small-plate feast. But be warned; with heady
ingredients like Scottish langoustines (tempura fried), Osetra caviar
atop crabmeat and coral gelee, and foie gras (paired with caramelized eel), Robuchon's little bites come at a steep price. ✉ *57 E. 57th
St., between Madison and Park Aves., Midtown East* ☎ *212/350–6658*
⊕ *www.fourseasons.com/newyorkfs/dining.html* ✍ *Reservations essential* $=$ *AE, MC, V* ✆ *No lunch* Ⓜ *4, 5, 6 to 59th St.* ✛ *4:F1.*

$$$$ ✕ **Le Cirque.** Impresario-owner Sirio Maccioni still presides over a din-
FRENCH ing room filled nightly with a who's who of political, business, and
society circles—regulars who've table-hopped from Le Cirque's first
incarnation to its latest, in a glass-enclosed aerie on the ground floor
of the Bloomberg headquarters. Billowing silk, tall gauzy shades, and
porcelain monkeys in a display-case pillar create a playful big-top effect.
The menu strikes a balance between the creative and classic. Dover sole,
filleted table-side, gives way to more avant-garde preparations like a
duo of seared foie gras and sushi-grade tuna. Desserts, too, have a split
personality, with the menu divided into the "classic" and "new." The
foot-tall napoleon that seems to arrive at every second table is an old
favorite, but newer creations like the rich, peanut-butter "candy bar"
also satisfy high-society sweet tooths. Though jackets are still required
in the dining room, things are more relaxed in the casual wine lounge.
✉ *151 E. 58th St., at Lexington Ave., Midtown East* ☎ *212/644–0202*
⊕ *www.lecirque.com* ✍ *Reservations essential* $=$ *AE, D, DC, MC, V*
✆ *Closed Sun. No lunch Sat.* Ⓜ *4, 5, 6, N, R, W to Lexington Ave./59th
St.* ✛ *4:F1.*

$$$ ✕ **Michael Jordan's The Steakhouse NYC.** Don't be dissuaded by the fact that
STEAKHOUSE this place is technically part of a chain: there's nowhere remotely like it.
The handsomely appointed space in Grand Central Terminal, hung with
gracious filigree chandeliers, overlooks one of the most famous interiors
in America. Start with the stack of soft, toasted bread soldiers in a pool
of hot Gorgonzola fondue. Pristine oysters make a great prelude for a
prime dry-aged rib eye or a 2½-pound lobster, grilled, steamed, sautéed,
or broiled. Sides, like creamy mac 'n cheese and a crispy rosemary hash-
brown cake, are equally tempting. ✉ *Grand Central Terminal, West
Balcony, 23 Vanderbilt Ave., between E. 43rd and E. 44th Sts., Mid-
town East* ☎ *212/655–2300* ⊕ *www.theglaziergroup.com/restaurants/
michaeljordan* ✍ *Reservations essential* $=$ *AE, D, DC, MC, V* Ⓜ *4, 5,
6, 7 to 42nd St./Grand Central* ✛ *4:F4.*

$$ ✕ **Mint.** With a delightful dining room splashed with bright colors and
INDIAN flattering lighting, and executive chef and owner Gary Sikka's brightly
seasoned dishes, this newcomer has joined the ranks of the best Indian

restaurants in town. The large menu includes rarely encountered specialties from Goa and Sikkim. Freshly grilled moist ground lamb kebabs deliver a slow burn to the palate. Chili heat punctuates other spices in the lamb vindaloo, resulting in a well-rounded array of savory flavors. Finish with carrot pudding with saffron and coconut flakes. ⊠ *150 E. 50th St., between Lexington and 3rd Aves., Midtown East* ☎ *212/644–8888* ═ *AE, D, DC, MC, V* Ⓜ *6, E, V to 51st St./ Lexington Ave.* ✛ *4:G3.*

> ### WORD OF MOUTH
>
> "My wife and I love to go to the Grand Central Oyster Bar and have a dozen oysters, bottle of champagne, chowder and split a fish entree and then head to the Campbell Apartment for cocktails. Great way to spend an evening."
>
> —ksucat

$$$
SEAFOOD

✗ **Oyster Bar.** Nestled deep in the belly of Grand Central Station, the Oyster Bar has been a worthy seafood destination for over nine decades. Sit at the counter for the fried oyster po'boy, or slurp an assortment of bracingly fresh oysters before having a steaming bowl of clam chowder washed down with an ice-cold brew. Or experience the forgotten pleasure of fresh, unadorned seafood such as lobster with drawn butter or grilled herring in season. Avoid anything that sounds too complicated, like cream-smothered seafood pan roasts. ⊠ *Grand Central Station, dining concourse, E. 42nd St. at Vanderbilt Ave., Midtown East* ☎ *212/490–6650* ⊕ *www.oysterbarny.com* ⌕ *Reservations essential* ═ *AE, D, MC, V* ⊗ *Closed Sun.* Ⓜ *4, 5, 6, 7, S to 42nd St./Grand Central* ✛ *4:F4.*

$$$
STEAKHOUSE

✗ **Palm.** They may have added tablecloths, but it would take more than that to hide the brusque, no-nonsense nature of this West Side branch of the legendary steak house. The steak is always impeccable, and the Nova Scotia lobsters are so big—4 pounds and up—there may not be room at the table for such classic side dishes as rich creamed spinach, served family-style for two or more. The "half-and-half" side combination of cottage-fried potatoes and fried onions is particularly addictive. There may be other locations, but due to its perch near the theater district and Midtown businesses, this is the one with the most action. ⊠ *837 2nd Ave., between 44th and 45th Sts., Midtown East* ☎ *212/687–2953* ⊕ *www.thepalm.com* ⌕ *Reservations essential* ═ *AE, D, DC, MC, V* ⊗ *Closed Sun. No lunch Sat.* Ⓜ *4, 5, 6, 7, S to Grand Central* ✛ *4:G4*

$
AMERICAN

✗ **Second Avenue Deli.** It may no longer be on Second Avenue, but the new incarnation of the East Village institution—one block over and about a mile uptown—is still delivering on its longtime tradition of overstuffed "three-decker" sandwiches filled with house-cured pastrami, matzo-ball soup, and other Old World specialties. Hot open sandwiches, like juicy beef brisket served with gravy and french fries, may be a heart-attack on a plate, but, hey, you only love once. Even better, you can now get Old World specialties like kasha varnishkes, carrot tzimmes, and potato kugel 24 hours a day. ⊠ *162 E. 33rd St., between Lexington and 3rd Aves., Midtown East* ☎ *212/689–9000* ⊕ *www.2ndavenuedeli.com* ═ *AE, MC, V* Ⓜ *6 to 33rd St./Lexington Ave.* ✛ *4:G6.*

18

$$$ ✗ **Shun Lee Palace.** If you want inexpensive Cantonese food without
CHINESE pretensions, head to Chinatown; but if you prefer to be pampered and
don't mind spending a lot of money, this is the place. The cuisine is
absolutely classic Chinese. Beijing panfried dumplings make a good
starter, and rack of lamb Szechuan style, grilled with scallions and gar-
lic, is a popular entrée. Beijing duck is sure to please. ⊠ *155 E. 55th
St., between Lexington and 3rd Aves., Midtown East* ☎ *212/371–8844*
⊕ *www.shunleepalace.lanteck.net/index2.htm* ✍ *Reservations essen-
tial* ⊟ *AE, DC, MC, V* Ⓜ *N, R, W, 4, 5, 6 to 59th St./Lexington Ave.*
✛ *4:G2.*

$$$$ ✗ **Sparks Steakhouse.** Magnums of wines that cost more than most peo-
STEAKHOUSE ple earn in a week festoon the large dining rooms of this classic New
York steak house. Although seafood is given more than fair play on the
menu, Sparks is really about dry-aged steak. The extra-thick lamb and
veal chops are also noteworthy. Classic sides of hash browns, creamed
spinach, sautéed mushrooms, and grilled onions are all you need to
complete the experience. ⊠ *210 E. 46th St., between 2nd and 3rd Aves.,
Midtown East* ☎ *212/687–4855* ⊕ *www.sparkssteakhouse.com* ✍ *Res-
ervations essential* ⊟ *AE, D, DC, MC, V* ☉ *Closed Sun. No lunch Sat.*
Ⓜ *4, 5, 6, 7, S to 42nd St./Grand Central* ✛ *4:G3.*

$$ ✗ **Sushi Yasuda.** The sleek bamboo-lined space in which chef Naomichi
JAPANESE Yasuda works his aquatic sorcery is as elegant as his food. Whether he's
using fish flown in daily from Japan or the creamiest sea urchin, Yasuda
makes sushi so fresh and delicate it melts in your mouth. A number of
special appetizers change daily (crispy fried eel backbone is a surprising treat), and a fine selection of sake and beer complements the lovely
food. Try to sit at the bar, which the chef hand-crafted himself out of
imported Japanese materials. ⊠ *204 E. 43rd St., between 2nd and 3rd
Aves., Midtown East* ☎ *212/972–1001* ⊕ *www.sushiyasuda.com* ⊟ *AE,
D, MC, V* ☉ *Closed Sun. No lunch Sat.* Ⓜ *4, 5, 6, 7 to 42nd St./Grand
Central* ✛ *4:G4.*

UPPER EAST SIDE

$$$ ✗ **Alloro.** Italian chef Salvatore Corea and his wife Gina, a native New
ITALIAN Yorker, are living their dream of opening an old-fashioned family-run
restaurant here on the Upper East Side just a block away from the
apartment they share with their two young daughters. It's not Corea's
first New York restaurant endeavor—he's opened three other success-
ful venues in the city (Cacio e Pepe, Spiga, and Bocca), but Alloro is
his first venture with his wife, and judging by the friendly vibe and the
delicious dishes coming out of Corea's *cucina,* it's off to a great start.
Chef Corea's creative take on traditional, regional Italian cuisines leads
the way for delicious dishes, like *paccheri,* a wide tube-shaped pasta,
with a white ragout of quail, porcini mushrooms, black truffles, and
fresh blueberries. Both the filet mignon with the potato pie and wild
mushrooms and the duck breast served with polenta cake are fantastic.
⊠ *307 E. 77th St., near 2nd Ave., Upper East Side* ☎ *212/535–2866*
⊕ *www.alloronyc.com* ⊟ *AE, MC, V* Ⓜ *6 to 77th St.* ✛ *5:H2.*

$$$$ ✗ **Café Boulud.** Manhattan's who's who in business, politics, and the art
FRENCH world come to hobnob at this café-in-name-only. The food and service
are top-notch at Daniel Boulud's conservative (but not stuffy) restaurant

in the Surrey Hotel, which recently underwent a sumptuous renovation. The menu, overseen by Boulud protégé Gavin Kaysen, is divided into four parts: under La Tradition you can find classic French dishes such as roasted duck breast "Montmorency" with cherry chutney, green Swiss chard, and baby turnips; Le Potager tempts with lemon ricotta ravioli; La Saison follows the rhythms of the season; and Le Voyage reinterprets cuisines of the world. ⊠ *20 E. 76th St., between 5th and Madison Aves., Upper East Side* ☎ *212/772–2600* ⊕ *www.danielnyc. com/cafeboulud* ⌖ *Reservations essential* ▭ *AE, DC, MC, V* Ⓜ *6 to 77th St.* ✣ *5:F3.*

$$ ✗ **Café d'Alsace.** Unusually comfortable burgundy banquettes, huge
BRASSERIE antiqued mirrors, and low lighting that makes everyone look fabulous characterize this Alsatian gem. Start with a house cocktail—say, L'Alsacien, in which the aperitif Belle de Brillet meets cognac, pear, and fresh lemon in a happy union. Standouts include the *tarte flambé*, a *fromage-blanc*–topped flat bread scattered with tawny caramelized onions and hunks of bacon. The *choucroute garnie* entrée comes in a cast-iron kettle that keeps it piping hot for the entire meal. Sausages, smoked pork breast, and pork belly are so carefully braised that everything comes out in perfect harmony. Delicious bread pudding is studded with strawberries. ⊠ *1695 2nd Ave., at E. 88th St., Upper East Side* ☎ *212/722–5133* ⊕ *www.cafedalsace.com* ▭ *AE, MC, V* Ⓜ *4, 5, 6 to 86th St.* ✣ *6:G6.*

$$ ✗ **Candle 79.** The Upper East Side may seem like an unlikely place for
VEGETARIAN gourmet vegan fare, but the people behind Candle 79 have lit upon a
Fodor's Choice formula that would work in any neighborhood. The elegant, bilevel
★ space, done up in warm, autumnal tones with touches of wood and rich fabric, is far from the health-food stereotype. Try for a second-floor table overlooking the street, and refresh yourself with a house-made elixir made with fresh grated ginger, agave nectar, and lime that will forever convert you from the canned alternative. Appetizers like rice balls with tempeh bacon may sound like hippie throwbacks, but they taste more like well-executed trattoria fare. Signature dishes include the seitan piccata, which replaces the usual protein with a vegetarian substitute and is so well made and well seasoned that you would never miss the meat. Salads, soups, desserts, and entrées are all stunningly fresh and made with local, organic, seasonal produce. There's also an impressive list of organic wines and sakes. ⊠ *154 E. 79th St., at Lexington Ave.* ☎ *212/537–7179* ⊕ *www.candle79.com* ⌖ *Reservations essential* ▭ *AE, MC, V* Ⓜ *6 to 77th St./Lexington Ave.* ✣ *5:G2.*

$$$$ ✗ **Daniel.** Celebrity-chef Daniel Boulud has created one of the most
FRENCH elegant dining experiences in Manhattan today, in an expansive space
Fodor's Choice that recently underwent a multimillion-dollar renovation. The prix-
★ fixe–only menu (there are à la carte selections in the elegant lounge and bar) is predominantly French, with such modern classics as turbot on Himalayan salt with an ale-and-gingerbread sauce; and a duo of dry-aged Angus black beef featuring meltingly tender red wine–braised short ribs and seared rib eye with black trumpet mushrooms and Gorgonzola cream. Equally impressive are the serious artwork, professional service, the extensive wine list, and masterful cocktails by Xavier, one of the

18

CLOSE UP

Local Chains Worth Checking Out

The following are some great local chain restaurants, the places New Yorkers head to when hunger strikes, but standard for good food still run high.

$ ✕ **Grand Sichuan International**. This regional Chinese chainlet may be low on ambience, but it serves delicious Szechuan specialties like fiery *dan dan* noodles or crab soup dumplings. ⊠ *19–23 St. Marks Pl., near 3rd Ave., East Village* ☎ *212/529–4800* ⊟ *AE, MC, V* Ⓜ *6 to Astor Pl.* ✛ *2:F1* ⊠ *229 9th Ave., at W. 24th St., Chelsea* ☎ *212/620–5200* ⊟ *AE, D, MC, V* Ⓜ *C, E to 23rd St.* ✛ *3:B2* ⊠ *15 7th Ave. S, between Leroy and Carmine Sts., East Village* ☎ *212/645–0222* ⊟ *AE, MC, V* Ⓜ *1 to Houston St.; A, B, C, D, E, F, V to W. 4th St.* ✛ *2:C3.*

¢ ✕ **Gray's Papaya**. It's a stand-up, takeout dive. And, yes, limos do sometimes stop here for the legendary hot dogs. More often than not, though, it's neighbors or commuters who know how good the slim, traditional, juicy all-beef dogs are. ⊠ *402 6th Ave., at W. 8th St., Greenwich Village* ☎ *212/260–3532* ⌂ *Reservations not accepted* ⊟ *No credit cards* Ⓜ *A, B, C, D, E, F, V to W. 4th St.* ✛ *3:D5* ⊠ *539 8th Ave., at 37th St., Midtown West* ☎ *212/904–1588* ⌂ *Reservations not accepted* ⊟ *No credit cards* Ⓜ *A, C, E to 34th St./Penn Station* ✛ *4:B5* ⊠ *2090 Broadway, at 72nd St., Upper West Side* ☎ *212/799–0243* ⌂ *Reservations not accepted* ⊟ *No credit cards* Ⓜ *1, 2, 3 to 72nd St.* ✛ *5:B4.*

$ ✕ **Le Pain Quotidien**. This international Belgian chain brings its homeland ingredients with it, treating New Yorkers to crusty organic breads, jams, chocolate, and other specialty products. You can grab a snack to go or stay and eat breakfast, lunch, or dinner at communal or private tables with waiter service. Come for a steaming latte and croissant in the morning or a tartine (open-faced sandwich) at noon. ⊠ *252 E. 77th St., near 2nd Ave., Upper East Side* ☎ *212/249–8600* Ⓜ *6 to 77th St.* ✛ *5:G2* ⊠ *38 E. 19th St., between Broadway and Park Ave. S, Flatiron District* ☎ *212/673–7900* Ⓜ *R, W, 6 to 23rd St.* ✛ *3:F3* ⊠ *124 7th Ave., between W. 17th and 18th Sts., Chelsea* ☎ *212/255–2777* Ⓜ *1 to 18th St.* ✛ *3:D3* ⊠ *1270 1st Ave., at 68th St., Upper East Side* ☎ *212/988–5001* Ⓜ *6 to 68th St.* ✛ *5:H4* ⊠ *100 Grand St., at Mercer St., SoHo* ☎ *212/625–9009* ⊕ *www.lepainquotidien.com* ⌂ *Reservations not accepted* ⊟ *AE, DC, MC, V* Ⓜ *N, Q, R, W to Canal St.* ✛ *2:E4* ⊠ *60 W. 65th St., near Columbus Ave., Upper West Side* ☎ *212/721–4001* Ⓜ *1 to 66th St.* ✛ *5:C5* ⊠ *922 7th Ave., at 58th St., Midtown* ☎ *212/757–0775* Ⓜ *N, Q, R, W to 57th St.* ✛ *4:C1* ⊠ *1271 Avenue of the Americas at 50th St. Midtown West* ☎ *646/462–4165* Ⓜ *B, D, F, V to 47–50th Sts./Rockefeller Center* ✛ *3:F3* ⊠ *50 W. 72nd St., near Central Park W, Upper West Side* ☎ *212/712–9700* Ⓜ *B, C to 72nd St.* ✛ *5:C4* ⊠ *10 5th Ave., at 8th St., Greenwich Village* ☎ *212/253–2324* Ⓜ *R, W to 8th St.* ✛ *2:D1* ⊠ *833 Lexington Ave., near 64th St., Upper East Side* ☎ *212/755–5810* Ⓜ *F to 63rd St.* ✛ *5:G5* ⊠ *801 Broadway, between E. 11th and E. 12th Sts., East Village* ☎ *212/677–5277* Ⓜ *4, 5, 6, L, N, Q, R, W to 14th St./Union Sq.* ✛ *3:F4.*

¢ ✗ **Ollie's Noodle Shop**. This local chain offers Chinese fare in a no-frills setting. Fans rave about the Cantonese-style barbecued meats (duck, pork, chicken), steamed dumplings and buns, and Mandarin noodle soups. The locations in the Theater District and near Lincoln Center are great for arts patrons in search of a quick budget meal. It's a feast that—with beer or cocktails—comes in under $20 a person. ✉ *1991 Broadway, at W. 68th St., Upper West Side* ☎ *212/595-8181* 🪑 *Reservations not accepted* ⊟ *AE, MC, V* Ⓜ *1 to 66th St./Lincoln Center* ✛ *5:D4* ✉ *2957 Broadway, at W. 116th St., Upper West Side* ☎ *212/932-3300* Ⓜ *1 to 116th St./Columbia Univ.* ✛ *6:A1* ✉ *200B W. 44th St., near Broadway, Midtown* ☎ *212/921-5988* Ⓜ *1, 2, 3, 7, N, Q, R, W, S to Times Sq./42nd St.* ✛ *4:C4.*

$$ ✗ **Sarabeth's**. Lining up for brunch here is as much an Upper West Side tradition as taking a sunny Sunday afternoon stroll in nearby Riverside Park. Locals love the bric-a-brac-filled restaurant for sweet morning-time dishes like lemon ricotta pancakes, as well as for the comforting dinners. The afternoon tea includes buttery scones with Sarabeth's signature jams, savory nibbles, and outstanding baked goods. Dinner entrées include chicken potpie and truffle mac 'n cheese. ✉ *423 Amsterdam Ave., at W. 80th St., Upper West Side* ☎ *212/496-6280* ⊕ *www.sarabeth.com* ⊟ *AE, D, DC, MC, V* Ⓜ *1 to 79th St.* ✛ *5:B2* ✉ *1295 Madison Ave., at 92nd St., Upper East Side* ☎ *212/410-7335* ⊕ *www.sarabeth.com* ⊟ *AE, DC, MC, V* Ⓜ *6 to 96th St.* ✛ *6:F5* ✉ *40 Central Park S, near 6th Ave., Midtown West* ☎ *212/826-5959* ⊕ *www.sarabeth.com* ⊟ *AE, D, DC,* *MC, V* Ⓜ *N, R, W to 5th Ave./59th St.* ✛ *5:E6* ✉ *Whitney Museum of American Art, 945 Madison Ave., at 75th St., Upper East Side* ☎ *212/570-3670* ◷ *Closed Mon.* ⊕ *www.sarabeth.com* ⊟ *AE, D, DC, MC, V* Ⓜ *6 to 77th St.* ✛ *5:F3* ✉ *Chelsea Market, 75 9th Ave., Chelsea* ☎ *212/989-2424* ⊕ *www.sarabeth.com* ⊟ *AE, MC, V* Ⓜ *A, C, E to 14th St.; L to 8th Ave.* ✛ *3:B4* ✉ *Lord & Taylor, 424 Fifth Ave., Midtown East* ☎ *212/828-5060* ⊕ *www.sarabeth.com* ⊟ *AE, MC, V* Ⓜ *B, D, F, V, 7 to 42nd St./Bryant Park* ✛ *4:E5.*

$$ ✗ **Serafina**. Each location of Serafina features different design details—Mediterranean-hue friezes or an outdoor terrace, for instance. Looks aside, the real draw here is some authentic Neopolitan pizza—they even filter the water for the pizza dough to make it more closely resemble the water in Naples. Beyond the designer pizzas are antipasti, salads, and pastas. ✉ *210 W. 55th St., at Broadway, Midtown West* ☎ *212/315-1700* Ⓜ *N, Q, R, W to 57th St./7th Ave.* ✛ *4:C2* ✉ *29 E. 61st St., between Madison and Park Aves., Upper East Side* ☎ *212/702-9898* Ⓜ *N, R, W, 4, 5, 6 to 59th St./Lexington Ave.* ✛ *5:F6* ✉ *1022 Madison Ave., at E. 79th St., Upper East Side* ☎ *212/734-2676* ⊕ *www.serafinarestaurant.com* ⊟ *AE, DC, MC, V* Ⓜ *6 to 77th St.* ✛ *5:F2* ✉ *38 E. 58th St., near Madison Ave., Upper East Side* ☎ *212/832-8888* Ⓜ *N, R, W to 5th Ave.* ✛ *5:F6* ✉ *224 W. 49th St., between 7th and 8th Aves., Midtown West* ☎ *212/247-1000* Ⓜ *C, E, to 50th St.* ✛ *4:C3.*

city's most respected mixologists. Don't forget the decadent desserts and overflowing cheese trolley. A three-course vegetarian menu is also available. ✉ *60 E. 65th St., between Madison and Park Aves., Upper East Side* ☎ *212/288–0033* ⊕ *www.danielnyc.com/daniel* ⌚ *Reservations essential. Jacket required* ▭ *AE, DC, MC, V* ☽ *Closed Sun. No lunch* Ⓜ *6 to 68th St./Hunter College* ✛ *5:F5.*

$$$ ✗ **Maya.** The upscale-hacienda appearance of this justifiably popular
MEXICAN   restaurant showcases some of the best Mexican food in the city, courtesy of pioneering Mexican chef Richard Sandoval. Begin with a fresh mango mojito, then tuck into delicious roasted corn soup with huitlacoche dumplings, stuffed poblano peppers, and smoky filet mignon taco with jalapeño escabeche. Finish with caramelized goat's-milk crepes and cinnamon ice cream and you'll leave wearing a big grin. ✉ *1191 1st Ave., between E. 64th and E. 65th Sts., Upper East Side* ☎ *212/585–1818* ⊕ *www.modernmexican.com/mayany* ⌚ *Reservations essential* ▭ *AE, D, DC, MC, V* ☽ *No lunch* Ⓜ *6 to 68th St./Hunter College* ✛ *5:H5.*

$$$ ✗ **Park Avenue Summer/Autumn/Winter/Spring.** New York's most self-con-
AMERICAN   sciously seasonal restaurant swaps out much more than its menu as temperatures change. Four times a year the restaurant—the formerly staid Park Avenue Café—shuts its doors for a head-to-toe makeover, switching, for instance, from a summery blond-wood beach-house motif to dark-wood-and-copper fall-foliage tones. Chef Craig Koketsu's seasonal food lives up to the striking surroundings. Summer brings a bounty of fresh-shucked corn, with a big, juicy veal chop and heirloom tomatoes. Come autumn the kitchen turns its focus to mushrooms, truffles (on a flaky halibut fillet accompanied by a brioche-crusted poached egg), and game (local quail, big venison chops scattered with pomegranate and pumpkin seeds). Desserts, by award-winning pastry chef Richard Leach, include hard-to-resist elegant creations like sweet-corn ice cream with rhubarb, warm caramel, and popcorn. ✉ *100 E. 63rd St., at Park Ave., Upper East Side* ☎ *212/644–1900* ⊕ *www.parkavenyc.com* ⌚ *Reservations essential* ▭ *AE, D, DC, MC, V* Ⓜ *F to Lexington Ave./63rd St.; 4, 5, 6 to 59th Sts.; N, R, W to 5th Ave./59th St.* ✛ *5:F6.*

$$$ ✗ **Sfoglia.** Veiled from the street by linen curtains, this tiny Manhattan
ITALIAN   offshoot of its Nantucket namesake does a fine impression of a shabby-chic Tuscan farmhouse. The fastidious decor includes big wooden communal tables, plush pillows, vintage posters of Italian food, and Murano glass chandeliers. The food, too, has an air of photo-styled casual perfection. A complimentary bowl of plump glistening olives comes artfully tossed with lemon and herbs. A too-quickly devoured basket of crusty bread arrives fresh from the oven sprinkled with sea salt. The oft-changing menu might include sweet-potato gnocchi with braised oxtail, apples, and leeks or pan-roasted orata redolent with the scent of saffron. The baked-to-order *torta del giorno*—a seasonal buttery fruit tart—is a showstopping finale that feeds a crowd. But good luck getting a table—for a spot so out-of-the-way, Sfoglia is one of the toughest reservations in town. ✉ *1402 Lexington Ave., at 92nd St., Upper East Side* ☎ *212/831–1402* ⊕ *www.sfogliarestaurant.com* ⌚ *Reservations essential* ▭ *AE, MC, V* ☽ *No lunch Sun, and Mon.* Ⓜ *4, 5, 6 to 86th St.* ✛ *6:G5.*

$$ ✕ **Sushi of Gari.** Options at this popular sushi restaurant range from the
JAPANESE ordinary (California roll) to such exotic options as tuna with creamy
tofu sauce, miso-marinated cod, or Japanese yellowtail with jalapeño.
Japanese noodles (udon or soba) and meat dishes such as teriyaki and
negimaki (scallions rolled in thinly sliced beef) are well prepared. Res-
ervations are recommended. Another location at 370 Columbus Avenue
gives Upper West Siders their udon fix. ✉ *402 E. 78th St., at 1st Ave.,
Upper East Side* ☎ *212/517–5340* ⊕ *www.sushiofgari.com* ⊟ *AE, MC,
V* ⊙ *No lunch* Ⓜ *6 to 77th St.* ⊹ *5:H2.*

UPPER WEST SIDE AND HARLEM

HARLEM

$ ✕ **Dinosaur Bar-B-Que.** New York's reputation for inferior barbecue
BARBECUE improved instantly when John Stage opened the third outpost of his
Syracuse-based joint in 2004, installing it in a riverside meatpacking
warehouse in Harlem. Here the city's friendliest waitstaff serves piled-
high plates of pulled pork, ribs, chicken, brisket, and knockout wings;
a well-stocked bar corrals the Columbia students. ✉ *646 W. 131st St.,
at 12th Ave., Harlem* ☎ *212/694–1777* ⊕ *www.dinosaurbarbque.com*
⊟ *AE, D, DC, MC, V* Ⓜ *1 to 125th St.* ⊹ *6:A2.*

UPPER WEST SIDE

$$$$ ✕ **Asiate.** The unparalleled view is reason enough to visit Asiate's pris-
ASIAN tine dining room, perched on the 35th floor of the Time Warner Center
in the Mandarin Oriental Hotel. Artfully positioned tables and mini-
malist decor help direct eyes to the windows, which peer over Central
Park. At night crystalline lights reflect in the glass, creating a magical
effect. Young chef Brandon Kida creates contemporary dishes with an
Asian influence. One of his signature dishes is soba noodles with Osetra
caviar and wasabi cream; another standout is Wagyu beef tenderloin
with smoked potato puree and braised short rib. Professional, atten-
tive service helps foster an atmosphere of dreamlike luxury. The res-
taurant offers prix-fixe menus only, and an illustrious wine collection
housing 1,300 bottles. ✉ *Time Warner Center, 80 Columbus Circle,
35th fl., at W. 60th St., Upper West Side* ☎ *212/805–8881* ⊕ *www.
mandarinoriental.com/newyork/dining/asiate* ⊟ *AE, D, DC, MC, V*
Ⓜ *A, B, C, D, 1 to 59th St./Columbus Circle* ⊹ *5:C6.*

$$ ✕ **Bar Boulud.** Acclaimed French chef Daniel Boulud, known for upscale
FRENCH New York City eateries Daniel and Café Boulud, shows diners his more
Fodor's Choice casual side with this lively contemporary bistro and wine bar. The long
★ narrow space accommodates 100 people and has a 14-seat round table
for special wine-themed tastings. An additional level has three rooms for
larger parties. The menu emphasizes charcuterie, including terrines and
pâtés designed by Parisian charcutier Gilles Verot, who relocated just to
work with Boulud, as well as traditional French bistro dishes like steak
frites and *poulet rôti à l'ail* (roast chicken with garlic mashed potatoes).
The 500-bottle wine list is heavy on wines from Burgundy and the
Rhône Valley. Wallet watchers won't feel left out: a pre-theater three-
course menu starts at $42, and weekend brunch has two hearty courses
plus coffee and dessert for $42. ✉ *1900 Broadway, between 63rd and*

18

64th Sts., Upper West Side ☎ *212/595–0303* ⊕ *www.barboulud.com* ⊟ *AE, DC, MC, V* Ⓜ *1 to 66th St./Lincoln Center; 1, A, C, B, D to 59th St./Columbus Circle* ✛ *5:B5.*

$ ✕ **Barney Greengrass.** At this New York Jewish landmark brusque wait-
DELI   ers send out stellar smoked salmon, sturgeon, and whitefish to a happy crowd packed to the gills at small Formica tables. Split a fish plat-ter with bagels, cream cheese, and other fixings, or get your velvety nova scrambled with eggs and buttery caramelized onions. If you're still hungry, go for a plate of cheese blintzes or the to-die-for chopped liver. Beware: the weekend brunch wait can exceed an hour. ⊠ *541 Amsterdam Ave., between W. 86th and W. 87th Sts., Upper West Side* ☎ *212/724–4707* ⊕ *www.barneygreengrass.com* ⌂ *Reservations not accepted* ⊟ *No credit cards* ⊘ *Closed Mon. No dinner* Ⓜ *1, B, C to 86th St.* ✛ *6:B6.*

$ ✕ **Big Nick's.** This cramped, 24-hour neighborhood diner is decorated
DINER   with photographs of the celebrities who've visited, but the primary draw is the burgers, which are huge and juicy. The endless menu lists every conceivable burger topping, from avocado and bacon to Greek tzatziki sauce. The classic Bistro Burger has mushrooms, Swiss, and fried onions on toasted challah bread. ⊠ *2175 Broadway, between W. 76th and W. 77th Sts., Upper West Side* ☎ *212/362–9238* ⊕ *www.bignicksnyc.com* ⊟ *MC, V* Ⓜ *1 to 79th St.; 1, 2, 3 to 72nd St.* ✛ *5:A3.*

$ ✕ **Bouchon Bakery.** Never mind that you're in the middle of a shopping
CAFÉ   mall under a Samsung sign, soups and sandwiches don't get much more luxurious than this. Acclaimed chef Thomas Keller's low-key lunch spot (one floor down from his extravagant flagship, Per Se) draws long lines for good reason. Share a mason jar of salmon rillettes—an unctuous spread of cooked and smoked salmon folded around crème fraîche and butter—then move onto one of the fork-and-knife open-faced tartines, like the tuna niçoise. When a sandwich has this much pedigree, $13 is actually a bargain. Grab dessert to go, a fresh macaroon or éclair, from the nearby bakery window. ⊠ *10 Columbus Circle, 3rd fl., at 60th St., Upper West Side* ☎ *212/823–9366* ⊕ *www.bouchonbakery.com* ⊟ *AE, MC, V* Ⓜ *1, A, B, C, D to 59th St./Columbus Circle* ✛ *5:C6.*

$$ ✕ **Café Luxembourg.** The old soul of the Lincoln Center neighborhood
BRASSERIE   seems to inhabit the tiled and mirrored walls of this lively, cramped restaurant, where West End Avenue regulars are greeted with kisses, and musicians and audience members pack the room after a concert. The menu (served until 11 PM Sunday through Tuesday and until mid-night from Wednesday through Saturday) includes dishes like steak tartare and lobster roll alongside dishes with a more contemporary spin like pan-seared sea scallops with roasted fennel and carrots. ⊠ *200 W. 70th St., between Amsterdam and West End Aves., Upper West Side* ☎ *212/873–7411* ⊕ *www.cafeluxembourg.com* ⌂ *Reservations essen-tial* ⊟ *AE, DC, MC, V* Ⓜ *1, 2, 3, B, C to 72nd St.* ✛ *5:A4.*

$$ ✕ **Carmine's.** Set on a nondescript block of Broadway, this branch of
ITALIAN   the Italian family-style mainstay is a favorite for families celebrating
☺   special occasions, pre-prom groups of teens, and plain old folks who come for the tried-and-true menu items like fried calamari, linguine with white clam sauce, chicken parmigiana, and veal saltimbocca all

served in mountainous portions. Family photos line the walls, there's a groaning antipasti table filled with savory meats, cheese, and salads, and there's a convivial feeling amid the organized chaos. On weekends, only parties of 6 or more can make dinner reservations. ✉ *2450 Broadway, between 90th and 91st Sts., Upper West Side* ☎ *212/362–2200* ⊕ *www.carminesnyc.com* ☰ *AE, D, DC, MC, V* Ⓜ *1,2,3, to 96th St./Broadway* ✢ *6:5A.*

$$$ ✗ **Dovetail.** Inside Dovetail, chef-owner John Fraser's subdued town

AMERICAN house and restaurant, cream-color walls, and maple panels create a warm, soothing atmosphere, and a recent expansion allows for more dining-room space and a larger bar area. The menu, which changes daily, features refined but hearty dishes. Seek solace from winter temperatures with the earthy gnocchi topped with veal short-rib ragout and foie gras butter. Tender lamb is heightened by exotic Indian spices, yogurt, and winter tabbouleh. The savory feast continues with pastry chef Vera Tong's salty but sweet bacon bread-and-butter pudding. ✉ *103 W. 77th St., at Columbus Ave., Upper West Side* ☎ *212/362–3800* ⊕ *www.dovetailnyc.com* ☰ *AE, DC, MC, V* ☺ *No lunch Mon.–Sat.* Ⓜ *1 to 79th St.; B, C to 81st St./Museum of Natural History* ✢ *5:B3.*

$ ✗ **Fatty Crab.** The uptown branch of Zac Pelaccio's downtown Malaysian

MALAYSIAN street-food joint has two major advantages over its downtown sibling: more seats and a reservations line. Other than that, the menu mimics the Hudson Street locale's laundry list of crowd-pleasing favorites like coconut-rich short rib Rendang and soft buns filled with Berhskire pork, cilantro, and savory sauce. Perhaps in deference to the stroller-toting population in the neighborhood, baby-sized onesies bearing the restaurant's logo are hung out for sale. ✉ *2170 Broadway between 76th and 77th Sts., Upper West Side* ☎ *212/496–2722* ⊕ *www.fattycrab.com* ☰ *AE, D, MC, V* Ⓜ *1 to 79th St./Broadway* ✢ *5:A3.*

$$$$ ✗ **Jean Georges.** This culinary temple focuses wholly on *chef celebre*

FRENCH Jean-Georges Vongerichten's spectacular creations. Some approach the limits of the taste universe, like foie-gras brûlée with spiced fig jam and ice-wine verjus. Others are models of simplicity, like slow-cooked cod with warm vegetable vinaigrette. Exceedingly personalized service and a well-selected wine list contribute to an unforgettable meal. For Jean Georges on a budget, try the prix-fixe lunch in the front room, Nougatine. ✉ *1 Central Park W, at W. 59th St., Upper West Side* ☎ *212/299–3900* ⊕ *www.jean-georges.com* ⌁ *Reservations essential. Jacket required* ☰ *AE, DC, MC, V* ☺ *Closed Sun.* Ⓜ *A, B, C, D, 1 to 59th St./Columbus Circle* ✢ *5:C6.*

$ ✗ **Kefi.** Michael Psilakis's homage to his grandmother's Greek cook-

GREEK ing has moved to an expansive space a few blocks northof the now-closed original location. Among the mezes, the meatballs with roasted garlic, olives, and tomato is a standout; the flavorful roast chicken, potatoes, red peppers, garlic, and thyme makes for a winning entrée; and the béchamel-rich Kefi mac 'n cheese is irresistible. Reasonable prices—appetizers are no more than $9.95, and main courses max out at $16.95—make it easy to stick around for a piece of traditional walnut cake with walnut ice cream. ✉ *505 Columbus Ave., between 84th and 85th Sts., Upper West Side* ☎ *212/873–0200* ☰ *AE, DC, MC, V* ☺ *No lunch Mon.* Ⓜ *1 to 86th St.; B,C to 86th St.* ✢ *5:B1.*

18

$$$$
ITALIAN
Fodor's Choice
★

✕ **Marea.** Carefully sourced, meticulously prepared fish and seafood take center-stage at this glossy, well-pedigreed restaurant. Large picture windows in the dining room offer expansive views of Central Park South, and silver-dipped shells on pedestals decorate the dining room. No expense is spared in importing the very best of the ocean's bounty, beginning with an entire menu of raw *crudo* dishes—think scallops with orange, wild fennel, and arugula—that is rapidly becoming the restaurant's signature, and can be enjoyed in the main dining room or an 8-seat bar at the end of the front room's shimmering onyx wall. You'd be remiss, though, if you skipped the pastas that made chef Michael White famous at the East Side's Convivio. They're served here in lusty iterations like rich fusilli with octopus and bone marrow and spaghetti with sea urchin. Whole fish like roasted turbot and and salt-baked snapper are equally showstopping. Service is flawless, and even the dishware-scalloped china embossed with the restaurant's name, tiny shell-shaped espresso cups—is special. ⊠ *240 Central Park S, between Broadway and 7th Ave., Midtown West* ☎ *212/582–5100* ⊕ *www. marea-nyc.com* ⟝ *Reservations essential* ⊟ *AE, MC, V* Ⓜ *A, B, C, D, 1, 9 to Columbus Circle* ✛ *4:B1.*

$$$$
AMERICAN
Fodor's Choice
★

✕ **Per Se.** The New York interpretation of what many consider America's finest restaurant, Napa Valley's French Laundry, Per Se is chef Thomas Keller's Broadway stage. Keller equally embraces French technique, a religious fervor for seasonality, and a witty playfulness that speaks to his confidence in the kitchen. The large dining room is understated and elegant, with touches of wood, towering florals, and—the best design touch of all—sweeping windows with views of Central Park. Keller's dishes are now world renowned, such as his tiny cones of tuna tartare topped with crème fraiche, and "oysters and pearls," delicate tiny mollusks suspended in a creamy custard with tapioca. Dessert service is a multicourse celebration of all things sweet, including a choice of 27 house-made chocolates, a rejoinder of truffles and, of course, treats to take home. Waiters, who can, and may, recite the provenance of the tiniest turnip, are also some of the nicest, most disarming servers in town. There's also a new à la carte "salon" menu available in the front bar room, but let's face it: if you manage to snag a reservation, there's nothing else to do but submit to the $275 prix-fixe. For reservations, call exactly two months in advance of your hoped-for dining date and keep your fingers crossed. ⊠ *Time Warner Center, 10 Columbus Circle, 4th fl., at W. 60th St., Upper West Side* ☎ *212/823–9335* ⊕ *www.perseny.com* ⟝ *Reservations essential. Jacket required* ⊟ *AE, MC, V* ☽ *No lunch Mon.–Thurs.* Ⓜ *A, B, C, D, 1 to 59th St./Columbus Circle* ✛ *5:C6.*

$$$$
MEDITERRANEAN

✕ **Picholine.** Having undergone a spiffy renovation in recent years, Terrence Brennan's classic French restaurant, done up in tones of eggplant and lavender, still has a dignified atmosphere, but it's now caught up with the times. His kitchen maintains a strong emphasis on contemporary Mediterranean cuisine and relies conspicuously on artisanal farmers and food producers. The menu is divided into four relatively small sections: Preludes, Pastas, Day Boats, and the Land, and you are invited to construct your own tasting by selecting three or four sections. The kitchen's spin on chicken Kiev is particularly brilliant: an heirloom chicken breast is pressed into a fat juicy tube and rolled in crushed cornflakes before it is deep-fried. Slice into the soft cylinder and it spills its luscious "liquid foie gras" filling. Don't miss the famous cheese course, which Brennan practically invented here. There's also a more limited three-course prix-fixe for $58, one of the best deals in the neighborhood. ⊠ *35 W. 64th St., between Broadway and Central Park W, Upper West Side* ☎ *212/724–8585* ⊕ *www.picholinenyc.com* ⌂ *Reservations essential* ⊟ *AE, DC, MC, V* ☉ *No lunch. Closed Sun.* Ⓜ *1 to 66th St./ Lincoln Center* ⊹ *5:C5.*

$$$$ ✕**Porter House**. With clubby interiors by Jeffrey Beers and an adjoin-
STEAKHOUSE ing lounge area, Porter House marks the splashy return to the scene of former Windows on the World chef Michael Lomonaco. Filling the meat-and-potatoes slot in the Time Warner Center's upscale "Restaurant Collection," the masculine throwback highlights American wines and pedigreed super-size meat. The neighborhood, long underserved on the steak-house front, has quickly warmed to Lomonaco's simple, solid American fare. Begin with his smoky clams casino or rich tarragon-kissed oyster pan roast. Steaks are huge and expertly seasoned, and come with the usual battery of à la carte sides—creamed spinach, roasted mushrooms, and mashed potatoes. ⊠ *10 Columbus Circle, 4th fl., at 60th St., Upper West Side* ☎ *212/823–9500* ⊕ *www. porterhousenewyork.com* ⊟ *AE, MC, V* Ⓜ *1, A, B, C, D to 59th St./ Columbus Circle* ⊹ *5:C6.*

$ ✕**Salumeria Rosi**. Just up the block from Gray's Papaya sits this compact
ITALIAN temple to a whole different subset of cured meats. Chef Cesare Casella has created a showcase for dozens of varieties of prosciutto, coppa, mortadella, and more, carved from a professional slicer for consumption on the spot or as indulgent takeout from the immaculate glass-walled display case. There's also a more ambitious menu of small plates, including a salad of arugula and lemon with Parmesan, and balsamic-glazed sweet and sour onions. If you're lucky, you may catch a glimpse of the avuncular chef with his signature rosemary sprig peeking from his breast pocket. ⊠ *283 Amsterdam Ave., between 73rd and 74th Sts., Upper West Side* ☎ *212/877–4700* ⊕ *www.salumeriarosi.com* ⊟ *AE, D, MC, V* Ⓜ *1 to 79th St./Broadway* ⊹ *5:B3.*

¢ ✕**Shake Shack**. Local restaurant legend Danny Meyer has gone a little
BURGER low-brow with his fast-ish food venture, Shake Shack—and New York-
Fodor's Choice ers are loving it. The Upper West Side Shack is an eat-in joint located
★ just across Columbus Avenue from the American Museum of Natural History. While the lines may be long at lunchtime, the grub is good and well priced. Fresh steer burgers are ground daily, and a single will run you from $3.75 to $4.75, depending on what you want on it. For a few more bucks you can also order doubles and stacks or a vegetarian 'Shroom Burger—a melty Muenster and cheddar cheese–stuffed portobello. The Shake Shack also offers beef and bird (chicken) hot dogs, french fries, and fries drizzled with Shack-made cheddar and American cheese sauce, and a variety of delicious frozen custard desserts and—of course—thick shakes! ⊠ *366 Columbus Ave., at W. 77th St., Upper*

18

West Side ☎ *646/747–8770* ⊕ *www.shakeshacknyc.com* ⊟ *AE, D, MC, V* Ⓜ *B, C to 81st St.* ✛ *5:B2.*

$$$
AMERICAN

✕ **Telepan.** Chef/owner Bill Telepan is a regular at the neighborhood greenmarket, and it shows in his seasonal, produce-driven menu, which is divided into three courses: appetizers of salads, light fish dishes, and soups; middle courses of eggs, pasta, or vegetables; and main courses of meat and fish. A trio of tiny *amuses-bouches* such as wild mushroom cappuccino, arrive to tease your palate, and the servers are refreshingly well-versed on the wine list. The menu features house-made brook trout, served on celery-root blini with green-apple sour cream is a well-deserved favorite, as is anything on the menu which contains eggs, like the "open-egg" ravioli with wild mushrooms and parmigiano broth. For dessert, a crunchy peanut-butter and milk-chocolate gianduja duo with peanut-brittle ice cream is sublime. ✉ *72 W. 69th St., between Columbus Ave. and Central Park W, Upper West Side* ☎ *212/580–4300* ⊕ *www.telepan-ny.com* ⊟ *AE, D, DC, MC, V* ⊘ *No lunch Mon.–Tues.* Ⓜ *1 to 66th St./Lincoln Center; 1, 2, 3 to 72nd St.; B, C to 72nd St.* ✛ *5:B4.*

New York City Dining and Lodging Atlas

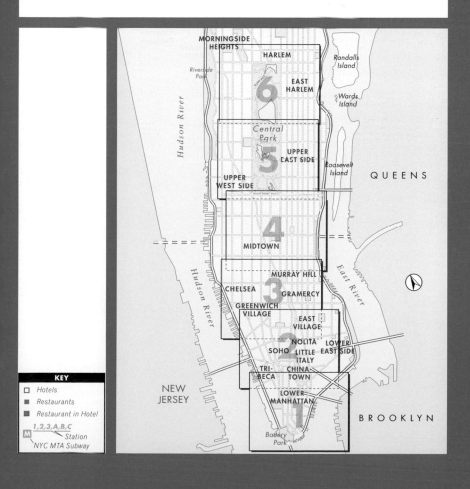

KEY

☐ Hotels
■ Restaurants
■ Restaurant in Hotel

Ⓜ 1,2,3,A,B,C Station
NYC MTA Subway

Map 2

- Chinatown
- East Village
- Greenwich Village
- Little Italy
- Lower E. Side
- NoLita
- SoHo
- Tribeca
- West Village

GREENWICH VILLAGE

W. 12th St.
W. 10th St.
W. 9th St.
Abingdon Square
Le Pain Quotidien
W. 8th St.
Bank St.
W. 11th St.
Perry St.
W. 4th St.
Charles St.
Waverly Pl.
Greenwich Ave.
Gay St.

Paris Commune
Mary's Fish Camp
Washington Square Hotel

Hudson St.
W. 10th St.
Christopher St.
Sheridan Square
West Washington Pl.
Blue Hill
Babbo
Waverly Pl.
Washington Square Park
University Pl.

Keste Pizza & Vino
Centro Vinoteca
Grove St.
Jones St.
Cornelia St.
A, B, C, E, F, V
West 4th St.
Dosa Man
La Guardia Pl.

Perry St.
Greenwich St.
Moustache
Commerce
Bedford St.
Bleeker Street Pizza
Bleeker St.
Minetta Tavern
W. 3rd St.

Washington St.
Father Demo Square
Bleecker St.

Do Hwa
Leroy St.
Carmine St.
Blue Ribbon Bakery
Lupa
Arturo's

Barrow St.
Grand Sichuan International
Sweet Revenge
'ino
Sullivan St.
W. Houston St.
Dos Caminos
Pegu Club

Morton St.
James J. Walker Park
Downing St.
MacDougal St.
Ave. of the Americas
Hundred Acres

Leroy St.
Hudson St.
SOHO

Clarkson St.
60 Thompson

W. Houston St.
King St.
Varick St.
Blue Ribbon Sushi
Blue Ribbon Brasserie
Thompson St.
West Broadway
Wooster St.
Greene St.

Charlton St.
Vandam St.
C, E
Aquagrill

Spring St.
Dominick St.
MarieBelle

Hudson River Park

Greenwich St.
Broome St.
Holland Tunnel Entrance
(Sixth Ave.)

Canal St.
Grand St.
SoHo Grand

Holland Tunnel
A, C, E
Canal St.

Watts St.
Capsouto Fréres
Holland Tunnel Entrance/Exit
Varick St.
Lispenard St.

Desbrosses St.
Sixth Ave.
Tribeca Grand
Church St.

Vestry St.
Hudson St.
Corton

Laight St.
Beach St.
Matsugen

Hubert St.
N. Moore St.
Bubby's
West Broadway
Leonard St.

Hudson River
Nobu
Franklin St.
Worth St.

West Side Highway
Greenwich Hotel
TRIBECA

The Harrison
Odeon
Thomas St.
Duane Street Hotel

9A
Harrison St.
Jay St.
Bouley Bakery

Duane St.
Independence Plaza
Reade St.
1, 2, 3
A, C

Chambers St.

0   1,000 ft
0   300 m

A   B   C   D

Where to Stay

WORD OF MOUTH

"Has anyone stayed at [the Library Hotel]? We're just looking for some feedback."

—mark

"You will love it! So quaint, cozy. They have a great library room where they serve breakfast and snacks throughout the day."

—XXX

Updated by
Alexander
Basek

It's a buyer's market for hotels here in New York. But does that mean that New York is cheap? Not exactly. Deals are plentiful—if you're not set on specific properties. With occupancy down across the city, hotels are slashing rates—especially if you're willing to wait until the last minute. That said, if you want to stay in a specific place and the rate seems reasonable, book it—it's just as likely to go up, especially during peak seasons (spring and fall).

And how to choose? Well, the first thing to consider is location (check out our "Where Should I Stay?" chart on the following page). Many New York City visitors insist on staying in the hectic Midtown area, but other neighborhoods are often just as convenient. Less-touristy areas, such as Gramercy, the Lower East Side, the Upper West Side—even Brooklyn—offer a far more realistic sense of New York life.

Also consider timing: the least expensive months to book rooms in the city are January and February. If you're flexible on dates, ask the reservationist if there's a cheaper time to stay during your preferred traveling month—that way you can avoid peak dates, like Fashion Week and the New York marathon. And be sure to ask about possible weekend packages that could include a third night free. (The Financial District in particular can be a discount gold mine on the weekend.)

Another source of bargains? Chain hotels. Many have moved into the city, offering reasonable room rates. In addition to favorites like the Sheraton, Hilton, and Hyatt brands, there are Best Westerns, Days Inns, and Comfort Inns. These rates aren't as low as you'll find outside Manhattan, but they're certainly getting closer.

WHERE SHOULD I STAY?

	NEIGHBORHOOD VIBE	PROS	CONS
Lower Manhattan (below Canal St., with TriBeCa and the Financial District)	Mostly skyscraper hotels in an area that buzzes with activity during weekday hours, but can be eerily quiet at night.	Low crime area; easy subway access to uptown sights; great walking paths along the waterfront and in Battery Park.	Construction and congestion near World Trade Center site; limited choice of restaurants and shopping.
SoHo, NoLita, and Little Italy	Swanky, high-end hotels with hip restaurants and lounges patronized by New Yorkers and travelers alike.	Scores of upscale clothing boutiques and art galleries nearby; safe area for meandering walks; easy subway access.	Not budget-friendly; streets are crowded on weekends; few major monuments nearby.
Greenwich Village (with West Village and Meatpacking District)	More hotels are opening, in one of the city's trendiest restaurant and nightlife areas.	Easy subway access to anywhere in town; great shopping, dining, and drinking venues.	Winding streets can be tough to navigate; most hotels are on the pricey side.
Union Square (with Gramercy, Murray Hill, and Flatiron)	A residential area where you'll get a feel for what it's really like to live in the city.	Patches of calm respite from the hustle-and-bustle of downtown and Midtown; low crime area.	Limited subway access; Gramercy or Murray Hill area may be too quiet for some.
East Village and Lower East Side	The epicenter of edgy New York, great for travelers looking to party.	Great low-cost options for young adults. Excellent chef-owned restaurants and independent boutiques nearby.	One of the least subway-accessible Manhattan neighborhoods; expect late-night noise.
Midtown East and Upper East Side	Business travelers flock to Midtown for its central location and its power dining restaurants	Easy regional rail and subway access; near tourist attractions like Central Park and several museums.	Most hotels here are expensive; the streets are quiet after 9 PM; few budget dining options.
Midtown West and Chelsea	Mostly big-name hotel chains and luxury business suites in the area around Times Square, where out-of-towners tend to congregate.	Near Broadway theaters; easy access to regional trains and most subway lines; budget options are available in chain hotels and indies alike.	Streets are often packed with pedestrians; restaurants are chain-owned and often overpriced; area around Port Authority can feel gritty.
Upper West Side	High-priced hotels in a residential neighborhood near Central Park, Lincoln Center, and several museums.	Low crime area; tree-lined streets; great delis and laid-back neighborhood eateries.	The 1 train can be dreadfully slow; most hotels are on the pricey side.

19

NEW YORK CITY LODGING PLANNER

Strategy

With hundreds of Manhattan hotels, making a choice may seem like a daunting question. But fret not—our expert writers and editors have done most of the legwork. The 120-plus selections here represent the best this city has to offer—from the best budget motels to the sleekest designer hotels. Scan "Best Bets" on the following pages for top recommendations by price and experience. Or find a review quickly in the listings— search by neighborhood, then alphabetically. Happy hunting!

Need a Reservation?

Hotel reservations are an absolute necessity when planning your trip to New York— although rooms are easier to come by these days. Competition for clients also means properties must undergo frequent improvements, especially during July and August, so when booking, ask about any renovations, lest you get a room within earshot of construction. In this ever-changing city travelers can find themselves temporarily, and most inconveniently, without commonplace amenities such as room service or spa access if their hotel is upgrading.

Services

Unless otherwise noted in the individual descriptions, all the hotels listed have private baths, central heating, air-conditioning, and private phones. Almost all hotels have data ports and phones with voice mail, as well as valet service. Many now have wireless Internet (Wi-Fi) available, although it's not always free. Most large hotels have video or high-speed checkout capability, and many can arrange babysitting. Pools are a rarity, but most properties have gyms or health clubs, and sometimes full-scale spas; hotels without facilities usually have arrangements for guests at nearby gyms, sometimes for a fee.

Parking

Bringing a car to Manhattan can significantly add to your expenses. Many properties in all price ranges do have parking facilities, but they are often at independent garages that charge as much as $20 or more per day, and valet parking can cost up to $60 a day. The city's exorbitant 18.375% parking tax can turn any car you drive into the Big Apple into a lemon.

Family Travel

New York has gone to great lengths to attract family vacationers, and hotels have followed the family-friendly trend. Some properties provide such diversions as Web TV and in-room video games; others have suites with kitchenettes and fold-out sofa beds. Most full-service Manhattan hotels provide rollaway beds, babysitting, and stroller rental, but be sure to make arrangements when booking the room, not when you arrive.

Does Size Matter?

If room size is important to you, ask the reservationist how many square feet a room has, not just if it's big. A hotel room in New York is considered quite large if it's 500 square feet. Very large rooms, such as those at the Four Seasons, are 600 square feet. To stay anywhere larger you'll have to get a multi-room suite. Small rooms are a tight 150 to 200 square feet, or sometimes even less. Very small rooms are less than 100 square feet; you'll find these at inns and lodges, and they're sold as a single for only one person. There are studio apartments in the city that are 250 square feet and include a kitchen; 1,000 square feet is considered a huge abode in this very compact and crowded urban playland.

Prices

There's no denying that New York City hotels are expensive, but rates run the full range. For high-end hotels like the Mandarin Oriental at Central Park, prices start at $895 a night for a standard room in high season, which runs from September through December. At the low end of the spending spectrum, a bunk at the Jane starts at $99 for a single. But don't be put off by the prices printed here—many hotels slash their rates significantly for promotions and Web-only deals.

The price ratings we've printed are based on standard double rooms at high season, excluding holidays. Although we list all the facilities that are available at a property, we don't specify what is included and what costs extra. Those policies are subject to change without notice, so it's always best to ask what's included when you make your reservation.

WHAT IT COSTS

	¢	$	$$	$$$	$$$$
FOR TWO PEOPLE	under $150	$150–$299	$300–$449	$450–$600	over $600

Prices are for a standard double room, excluding 14.75% city and state taxes.

In This Chapter

Using the Maps

Throughout the chapter, you'll see mapping symbols and coordinates (✛ 3:F2) after property names or reviews. To locate the property on a map, turn to the New York City Dining and Lodging Atlas at the end of the Where to Eat chapter. The first number after the ✛ symbol indicates the map number. Following that is the property's coordinate on the map grid.

19

BEST BETS FOR NEW YORK CITY LODGING

Fodor's offers a selective listing of quality lodging experiences in every price range, from the city's best budget motel to its most sophisticated luxury hotel. Here we've compiled our top recommendations by price and experience. The very best properties—in other words, those that provide a particularly remarkable experience in their price range—are designated in the listings with the Fodor's Choice logo.

Fodor's Choice ★

Ace Hotel, $, p. 483
Crosby Street Hotel, $$$, p. 477
Inn at Irving Place, $$, p. 485
Inn on 23rd, $, p. 492
Library Hotel, $$, p. 510
Mandarin Oriental, $$$$, p. 499
The Peninsula, $$$$, p. 512
Plaza Hotel, $$$$, p. 501
Ritz-Carlton New York, Central Park, $$$$, p. 503
The St. Regis, $$$$, p. 513
The Standard, $, p. 483
Thompson LES, $$, p. 481

Best By Price

¢

Carlton Arms, p. 488
La Quinta Inn, p. 498
Pod Hotel, p. 512

$

Ace Hotel, p. 483
Herald Square Hotel, p. 488
Hotel Beacon, p. 518
Hotel 41, p. 496
Hotel Metro, p. 497
Inn on 23rd, p. 492
The President, p. 501
Room Mate Grace, p. 503
The Standard, p. 483
W Hotel New York, p. 514

$$

Casablanca Hotel, p. 494
Holiday Inn SoHo, p. 478
Inn at Irving Place, p. 485
Library Hotel, p. 510
The Mansfield, p. 500
Maritime Hotel, p. 492
Thompson LES, p. 481

$$$

Gramercy Park Hotel, p. 483
The Mercer, p. 478
The Michelangelo, p. 500

$$$$

The Carlyle, p. 515
Mandarin Oriental, p. 499
The Peninsula, p. 512
Ritz-Carlton New York, Central Park, p. 503
The St. Regis, p. 513

Best By Experience

BEST AFTERNOON TEA

The Carlyle, p. 515
Four Seasons, p. 510
Inn at Irving Place, p. 485
The London NYC, p. 499
Plaza Hotel, p. 501
The St. Regis, p. 513

BEST BEDS

Four Seasons, p. 510
Ink48, p. 497
Inn at Irving Place, p. 485
The Mansfield, p. 500
Ritz-Carltons, p. 476, 503

BEST FOR BUSINESS

Bryant Park Hotel, p. 493
The Peninsula, p. 512
Ritz-Carlton, Battery Park, p. 476
The St. Regis, p. 513
Trump International Hotel and Towers, p. 520

BEST CELEBRITY RETREAT

Ace Hotel, p. 483
The Lowell, p. 517
Mandarin Oriental, p. 499
The Mercer, p. 478
The Standard, p. 483

BEST CONCIERGE

Four Seasons, p. 510

Le Parker Meridien, p. 498

The London NYC, p. 499

Mandarin Oriental, p. 499

Ritz-Carlton Battery Park, p. 476

BEST GYM

Le Parker Meridien, p. 498

The London NYC, p. 499

Trump International Hotel and Towers, p. 520

BEST HIPSTER HOTELS

Ace Hotel, p. 483

Bowery Hotel, p. 480

Gramercy Park Hotel, p. 483

The Standard, p. 483

Thompson LES, p. 481

BEST FOR HISTORY BUFFS

The Carlyle, p. 515

Inn at Irving Place, p. 485

The Plaza Hotel, p. 501

The St. Regis, p. 513

The Waldorf=Astoria, p. 514

BEST HOTEL BAR

Bemelmans Bar at the Carlyle, p. 515

Breslin Bar at the Ace Hotel, p. 483

King Cole Bar at St. Regis, p. 513

Lobby Bar at the Bowery Hotel, p. 480

Rose Bar at the Gramercy Park Hotel, p. 483

Oak Bar at the Plaza Hotel, p. 501

BEST HOTEL RESTAURANT

Asiate at Mandarin Oriental, p. 499

Gordon Ramsay and Maze at the London NYC, p. 499

Jean Georges at Trump International Hotel and Towers, p. 520

L'Atelier de Joël Robuchon at Four Seasons, p. 510

Standard Grill at the The Standard, p. 483

BEST FOR KIDS

Affinia 50, p. 508

Embassy Suites New York, p. 475

Le Parker Meridien, p. 498

BEST LOBBY

Ace Hotel, p. 483

Four Seasons, p. 510

Gramercy Park Hotel, p. 483

Mandarin Oriental, p. 499

The Peninsula, p. 512

The St. Regis, p. 513

BEST NEIGHBORHOOD EXPERIENCE

The Carlyle, p. 515

The Franklin, p. 516

Inn at Irving Place, p. 485

The Standard, p. 483

BEST NEW HOTELS

Ace Hotel, p. 483

The London NYC, p. 499

On the Ave, p. 520

The President, p. 501

The Standard, p. 483

Thompson LES, p. 481

BEST FOR PETS

The Carlyle, p. 515

Loews Regency, p. 511

Ritz-Carlton Battery Park, p. 476

Ritz-Carlton New York, Central Park, p. 503

70 Park Avenue, p. 490

BEST POOL

Hotel Gansevoort, p. 482

Mandarin Oriental, p. 499

Millennium UN Plaza, p. 511

The Peninsula, p. 512

Thompson LES, p. 481

Trump International Hotel and Towers, p. 520

BEST-KEPT SECRET

The Franklin, p. 516

Inn at Irving Place, p. 485

Inn on 23rd, p. 492

The Lowell, p. 517

The President, p. 501

BEST SERVICE

The Carlyle, p. 515

Four Seasons, p. 510

The Peninsula, p. 512

The Plaza Hotel, p. 501

Ritz-Carlton Battery Park, p. 476

SoHo Grand, p. 479

BEST TOILETRIES

Gramercy Park Hotel, p. 483

Hotel Gansevoort, p. 482

The Peninsula, p. 512

The St. Regis, p. 513

SoHo Grand, p. 479

Tribeca Grand, p. 477

BEST VIEWS

The Carlyle, p. 515

Cooper Square Hotel, p. 479

Ritz Carlton New York, Central Park, p. 503

The Standard, p. 483

Trump International Hotel and Towers, p. 520

MOST ROMANTIC

Inn at Irving Place, p. 485

Library Hotel, p. 510

Ritz-Carlton Battery Park, p. 476

The Standard, p. 483

19

BROOKLYN

$ 🏨 **New York Marriott at the Brooklyn Bridge.** What Manhattan hotel has room for an Olympic-length lap pool, a 1,100-car garage, and even a dedicated kosher kitchen? Just like many New Yorkers before you, you'll find that one virtue of staying in Brooklyn is all the extra space. Rooms are classic Marriott—large, comfortable, plain guest rooms enhanced by niceties such as high ceilings, massaging showerheads, and rolling desks. If you're looking to explore, some of the borough's best neighborhoods—Brooklyn Heights, Cobble Hill, Carroll Gardens, and DUMBO, as well as the Brooklyn Bridge pedestrian path—are just a five-minute walk. If you need to get to Manhattan, major subway lines are a block away or a few short minutes by taxi. **Pros:** near some of New York's hipper neighborhoods; full-service hotel; stylish rooms. **Cons:** on a busy street in downtown Brooklyn. ✉ *333 Adams St., between Johnson and Willoughby Sts., Downtown Brooklyn* ☎ *718/246–7000 or 888/436–3759* ⊕ *www.marriott.com/nycbk* ↘ *666 rooms, 25 suites* ⚲ *In-room: a/c, safe, Internet. In-hotel: restaurant, room service, bar, pool, gym, laundry service, Wi-Fi hotspot, parking (paid)* ⊟ *AE, D, DC, MC, V* Ⓜ *2, 3, 4, 5 to Borough Hall.*

$ 🏨 **Nu Hotel.** Sitting atop Smith Street, one of Brooklyn's main drags for nightlife and shopping, the hip-yet-affordable Nu is perfect for visitors seeking a manageable taste of outer borough New York—and the staff is eager to highlight the neighborhood's charms. Flat-screens, complimentary Wi-Fi, and AV hook-ups for your iPod or laptop make the above-average-size rooms livable, though the minimalist white-and-grey color scheme (punctuated with eco-friendly flourishes like cork floors, organic cotton sheets, and lead-free paint) can feel chilly at times. Just off the small check-in area downstairs, a quiet bar serves small plates of Spanish food at night and free pastries with Starbucks coffee come morning—but more fun can be had outside the front door. **Pros:** great Brooklyn launching pad; knowledgeable staff; fitness center open 24 hours. **Cons:** it's a subway or cab ride to anything in Manhattan; bar area can be a little too quiet; limited in-room amenities. ✉ *85 Smith St., Brooklyn* ☎ *718/852–8585* ⊕ *www.nuhotelbrooklyn.com* ↘ *3 rooms, 16 suites* ⚲ *In-room: a/c, safe, Wi-Fi. In-hotel: bar, gym, Internet terminal, parking (paid)* ⊟ *AE, MC, V* Ⓜ *F to Bergen St.; A, C, G to Hoyt-Schermerhorn.*

LOWER MANHATTAN—BELOW CANAL STREET, INCLUDING TRIBECA

FINANCIAL DISTRICT

$$ 🏨 **Gild Hall.** Captains of Industry, here's a boutique hotel for you. Operated by the owners of the successful, chic 60 Thompson Hotel in SoHo, Gild Hall aggressively courts clientele with a Y chromosome: beds have padded leather headboards and tartan throw blankets. It's manly, but slightly out-of-step with Wall Street's more austere vibe these days—just ask Todd English, who recently pulled out of the hotel restaurant, the Libertine (it's remained under new operators). The rooms are small, but come with custom-made wood desks and tables. The Gold Street

location, though slightly hard to find, is a short walk from downtown's central banks and businesses, as well as two blocks from South Street Seaport and City Hall. **Pros:** central Financial District location; eye-popping lobby; stylish room design. **Cons:** small rooms for the price; untraditional location. ⊠ *15 Gild Hall, at Platt St., Financial District* ☎ *212/232–7700 or 800/268–0700* ⊕ *www.wallstreetdistrict.com* ⊲ *126 rooms* ⌂ *In-room: a/c, safe, Wi-Fi. In-hotel: restaurant, room service, bar, laundry service, Internet terminal, Wi-Fi hotspot* ☱ *AE, D, DC, MC, V* ⌑ *CP* Ⓜ *2, 3, 4, 5, 6, A, C to Fulton St./Broadway-Nassau* ✢ *1:E3.*

> ### WORD OF MOUTH
>
> "I live half a mile from the Brooklyn Marriot. You are near several train stations that can take you to Manhattan in 10 to 15 minutes. Plus, cabs are easily accessible and you are right at the foot of the Brooklyn Bridge. You are also near some nice Brooklyn neighborhoods if you want to see them."
>
> —carol

TRIBECA

$ ⛭ **Cosmopolitan.** Surprisingly, there's no *Sex and the City* affiliation at the Cosmo, but for those saving for Jimmy Choos (or just on a budget) it's a steal. The rooms, with light-wood accents and ceiling fans, are attractive, but be warned: they are sized more for a Carrie than a Mr. Big. The hotel is situated on a busy TriBeCa intersection, and is an ideal launching pad for exploring downtown neighborhoods like Chinatown, Little Italy, and SoHo. The building dates to 1850—Abraham Lincoln slept here. Repeat clientele come for the "miniloft" rooms, with a bed on an upper level and bath downstairs. **Pros:** friendly staff; great location for power shoppers. **Cons:** noisy location; spartan rooms. ⊠ *95 West Broadway, at Chambers St., TriBeCa* ☎ *212/566–1900 or 888/895–9400* ⊕ *www.cosmohotel.com* ⊲ *125 rooms* ⌂ *In-room: a/c, Wi-Fi. In-hotel: Wi-Fi hotspot* ☱ *AE, DC, MC, V* Ⓜ *1, 2, 3, A, C to Chambers St.* ✢ *1:C2.*

$–$$ ⛭ **Duane Street Hotel.** Amid TriBeCa's historic warehouses and trendy art galleries sits the Duane Street Hotel, a fashionable addition to the neighborhood. Comfortable rooms are painted in shades of soft lilac or green apple, and light pours through the loft-like windows. Hardwood floors, flat-screen TVs, and compact fold-up desks give rooms a modern, playful feel, and cashmere throws and fresh flowers add touches of romance. Sophisticated bathrooms have slate floors and "We Live Like This"–brand amenities. Guests can use complimentary passes to work out at a nearby Equinox. Be warned: 'beca, the hotel's equally swanky restaurant, and the rooms facing the street are both loud. **Pros:** great location; in-room spa treatments available through Euphoria Spa TriBeCa; turndown service with Jacques Torres chocolates. **Cons:** noisy; small restaurant. ⊠ *130 Duane St., TriBeCa* ☎ *212/964–6400* ⊕ *www.duanestreethotel.com* ⊲ *45 rooms* ⌂ *In-room: a/c, safe, Wi-Fi. In-hotel: restaurant, room service, bar, Wi-Fi hotspot* ☱ *AE, DC, MC, V* Ⓜ *1, 2, 3 to Chambers St.; A, C to Chambers St.* ✢ *2:D6.*

$$ ⛭ **Embassy Suites New York.** With a convenient downtown location near a waterfront park and the World Financial Center, this flashy Embassy

19

Suites has a lot to offer to families and business travelers. The hotel is part of a complex with a six-screen movie theater and a 20,000-square-foot health club. As the name suggests, every one of the modern rooms here is at least a one-bedroom suite, with a living area that includes a pull-out double-bed sofa, dining table, and microwave oven. The hotel has an attractive lobby, with a 14-story center atrium and a colorful Sol LeWitt mural running down its entire length. You'll have a relatively long walk to the subway, but there is a complimentary evening cocktail reception and the trademark Embassy Suites breakfast bonanza to make up for it. **Pros:** good for families; movie theater downstairs. **Cons:** a schlep to the subway; far from Midtown; nearby construction. ⊠ *102 North End Ave., at Murray St., TriBeCa* ☎ *212/945–0100 or 800/362–2779* ⊕ *www.newyorkcity.embassysuites.com* ↝ *463 suites* ⚲ *In-room: a/c, safe, refrigerator, Wi-Fi. In-hotel: restaurant, room service, bar, laundry service, Internet terminal, Wi-Fi hotspot, parking (paid)* ⊟ *AE, D, DC, MC, V* Ⓜ *R, W to Cortlandt St.; A, C, E to Chambers St.* ✛ *1:A2.*

$$$ ⚇ **Greenwich Hotel.** You talkin' to me? Yes, Robert DeNiro is a financial backer behind the Greenwich Hotel in TriBeCa, DeNiro's backyard. Despite the big name behind it, the Greenwich flies under the radar, with an unmarked entrance leading to a jumbled lobby without a discernable theme. Upstairs, rooms combine Moroccan, French, and Japanese styles, with lots of tile, rugs covering floors made from reclaimed oak, and French doors. No two rooms are decorated alike. Locana Verde, Andrew Carmellini's hotspot, serves rustic Italian, and to maintain the design hodgepodge, the spa is done in a traditional Japanese style, as is the hotel pool. **Pros:** varied yet clever room decoration; great restaurant. **Cons:** odd lobby; price out of sync with quality; can be costly in high season. ⊠ *377 Greenwich St., TriBeCa* ☎ *212/941–8900* ⊕ *www. thegreenwichhotel.com* ↝ *88 rooms, 16 suites* ⚲ *In-room: a/c, safe, DVD, Wi-Fi. In-hotel: restaurant, room service, pool, gym, spa, Internet terminal, parking (paid)* ⊟ *AE, MC, V* Ⓜ *1 to Franklin St.* ✛ *2:C6.*

$$$ ⚇ **Ritz-Carlton New York, Battery Park.** If you're staying this far downtown, the Ritz is your top choice. The hotel provides the classic Ritz-Carlton experience—you'll be greeted by at least one staffer each time you walk into the hotel or enter the lobby from your room—and the big rooms boast sweeping views of the Statue of Liberty and Ellis Island. West-facing Harbor View–rooms come with telescopes. After a $10 million renovation, rooms incorporate HD flat-screens; a gold, teal, gray, and yellow color scheme; and cantilevered desks. The Club Lounge also got a refresh, adding leather chairs, overstuffed couches, and oil paintings. There's steak-house fare at 2 West and a hopping post-work scene at the outdoor Rise Bar on the 14th floor, but neither are exceptional, considering the markup. **Pros:** excellent service; best base for downtown exploring; pet- and kid-friendly; Liberty views. **Cons:** removed from Midtown tourist sights; limited nighttime activities; few neighborhood options for dining and entertainment. ⊠ *2 West St., at Battery Park, TriBeCa* ☎ *212/344–0800 or 800/241–3333* ⊕ *www.ritzcarlton. com* ↝ *254 rooms, 39 suites* ⚲ *In-room: a/c, refrigerator (some), DVD (some), Internet, Wi-Fi. In-hotel: 2 restaurants, room service, bars,*

laundry service, Internet terminal, Wi-Fi hotspot, parking (paid), some pets allowed ▭ *AE, D, DC, MC, V* Ⓜ *1, R, W to Rector St.* ✛ *1:C5.*

$$ 🏨 **Tribeca Grand.** Still popular with the glitterati lo these many years later, the scene at the Tribeca Grand centers around the eight-story atrium's Church Lounge bar and café. Now that things have cooled sufficiently, it's a nice place to hang even if you're not an A-Lister, though it can get noisy for guests upstairs. Comfortable and stylish rooms with a retro nod have low platform beds and podlike bathrooms with aluminum consoles reminiscent of those in airplanes, complete with Malin + Goetz amenities. The special "iStudios" are premium rooms kitted with the latest gadgets from Apple. Pets are welcomed with open arms; you can even request goldfish brought to your room. **Pros:** great dining and bar scene; iPods in each room; fun social atrium; pet-friendly. **Cons:** rooms get noise from restaurant below; bathroom has slightly cold design. ✉ *2 Ave. of the Americas (6th Ave.), between Walker and White Sts., TriBeCa* 🕾 *212/519–6600 or 800/965–3000* ⊕ *www.tribecagrand. com* 🛏 *197 rooms, 6 suites* ⚙ *In-room: a/c, safe, refrigerator, Wi-Fi. In-hotel: restaurant, room service, bar, gym, laundry service, Internet terminal, Wi-Fi hotspot, parking (paid), some pets allowed* ▭ *AE, D, DC, MC, V* Ⓜ *A, C, E to Canal St.* ✛ *2:D5.*

SOHO, NOLITA AND LITTLE ITALY

SOHO

$$$ 🏨 **Crosby Street Hotel.** Here in SoHo's heart sits the Crosby Street Hotel,
Fodor's Choice which in late 2009 became the first branch of the U.K.'s Firmdale Hotels
★ to open in the United States. Hotel design in New York is often a man's world of leather and dark colors; here the pieces, all handpicked by co-owner Kit Kemp, are so colorful, light, and whimsical that it's jarring. Start with the wood-floored lobby, where solicitous staffers in gray suits with ties and vests check guests in, keeping a record of their likes and dislikes for future visits. To one side is the Moroccan-themed Crosby Bar, which has low tables with a Moroccan theme and oversize hanging light fixtures in red and gold. The impressive "cocktail program" here was designed by bartender Marshall Altier. To the other side are the guest-only drawing rooms, chockablock with cushy couches and art that includes two huge oil paintings of Jack Russell terriers. A garden by the bar is open to the public, but guests also have access to a separate back garden. Rooms are expansive, well lit, and splashed with more color than those of just about any other hotel in New York. Each comes with a different set of patterns, though they all have pillows for sitting in the floor-to-ceiling windowsills looking toward SoHo; a sitting area with a fabric couch done in orange, green, or purple; fabric wallpaper; and antique vases and tables sprinkled throughout. The gym could stand to be a little bigger, though, and at this price breakfast should be included in the rate. **Pros:** unique design; big, bright rooms; great bar. **Cons:** breakfast not included; small gym. ✉ *79 Crosby St., between Prince and Spring Sts., SoHo* 🕾 *212/226–6400* ⊕ *www.firmdale.com* 🛏 *86 rooms* ⚙ *In-room: a/c, safe (some), DVD, Wi-Fi. In-hotel: restaurant, room service, bar, gym, laundry service, Wi-Fi, some pets allowed* ▭ *AE, D, MC, V* Ⓜ *6 to Spring St., R, W to Prince St.* ✛ *2:E3.*

19

$$ 🖬 **Holiday Inn SoHo.** "SoHo" and "Holiday Inn" sure don't sound right together, but here they are. Once endangered by developers, SoHo's odd man out is more entrenched than ever thanks to rates dwarfed by other hotels in the vicinity. Oversize arched windows, high ceilings, and a classic exterior are just some of the historical features retained in this former bank building. Rooms are standard-issue chain stuff, but they are well maintained, with touches like in-room coffeemakers and CD players. Bustling Canal Street is on the corner for bargain shopping. **Pros:** cheap SoHo solution; well-trained staff. **Cons:** nothing stylish; closer to Chinatown than to SoHo. ⊠ *138 Lafayette St., near Canal St., SoHo* ☎ *212/966–8898 or 800/465–4329* ⊕ *www.hidowntown-nyc.com* ➫ *215 rooms, 12 suites* ⚒ *In-room: a/c, safe, Wi-Fi. In-hotel: restaurant, room service, bar, gym, laundry service, Internet terminal, Wi-Fi hotspot, parking (paid)* ▤ *AE, D, DC, MC, V* Ⓜ *6, M, N, Q, R, W to Canal St.* ✛ *2:E5.*

$$$ 🖬 **The Mercer.** Owner André Balazs, known for his Chateau Marmont in Hollywood, has a knack for dating Hollywood starlets and channeling a neighborhood sensibility. Here it's SoHo loft all the way, though it's also a favorite crash pad for Tinseltown names. It's superbly situated in the heart of SoHo's myriad name-brand stores, although you wouldn't know it once you're inside the lobby, a minimalist oasis created by acclaimed French designer Christian Liagre. Most guest rooms are generously sized, with long entryways, high ceilings, and walk-in closets, but the lowest-priced rooms are a tight 250 square feet. Dark African woods and custom-designed furniture upholstered in muted solids lend serenity with sophistication. Some bathrooms feature decadent two-person marble tubs surrounded by mirrors. Downstairs is the always happening Mercer Kitchen, and the submercer bar, with a separate entrance, is one of the city's hottest doors. Beware the inconsistent service, which runs from friendly to indifferent. **Pros:** great location; sophisticated design touches; celebrity sightings in lobby. **Cons:** service inconsistent; tiny rooms. ⊠ *147 Mercer St., at Prince St., SoHo* ☎ *212/966–6060 or 888/918–6060* ⊕ *www.mercerhotel.com* ➫ *67 rooms, 8 suites* ⚒ *In-room: a/c, safe, DVD, Wi-Fi. In-hotel: restaurant, room service, bars, Internet terminal, Wi-Fi hotspot, some pets allowed* ▤ *AE, D, DC, MC, V* Ⓜ *R, W to Prince St.* ✛ *2:E3.*

$$ 🖬 **60 Thompson.** This successful hotel has served as the blueprint for the mini-chain's four other hotels in Manhattan, and its set-up has aged well. It's no longer the center of the universe, scene-wise, and that's been a blessing, improving the service and toning down the attitude of hotel staffers. Kittichai, the chic Thai restaurant on the ground floor, has patio dining, a gold-suffused bar and good-looking, if indifferent, servers. The rooftop lounge, A60, remains a guests- and members-only warm-weather haven for hipsters. Thom bar, the second-floor lobby, is a dark space filled with contemporary art, great for whiling away an evening. Rooms feature a dramatic, spare design; the generous use of dark woods and full-wall leather headboards give the rooms welcoming warmth. **Pros:** nightlife central; access to private rooftop club; good gym; some rooms have balconies. **Cons:** not family oriented; no pets allowed. ⊠ *60 Thompson St., between Broome and Spring Sts., SoHo*

☏ 212/431–0400 or 877/431–0400 ⊕ www.thompsonhotels.com ⇥ 82 rooms, 8 suites ⚇ In-room: a/c, safe, DVD, Internet, Wi-Fi. In-hotel: restaurant, room service, bars, Internet terminal, Wi-Fi hotspot, parking (paid) ▭AE, D, DC, MC, V Ⓜ C, E to Spring St. ✛ 2:D4.

$$$ ⌕ **SoHo Grand.** The SoHo Grand defines what SoHo is today—once pioneering, now expensive, and with a vaguely creative vibe. When the Grand opened in 1996 it had been a century since a new hotel debuted in the neighborhood. Today, as new hotels crowd the field, its low-key sophistication stands out more clearly—as do its faults. The Grand Bar & Lounge is sometimes called SoHo's living room for its comfortable, social atmosphere. Public spaces as well as guest rooms use an industrial-chic design to mimic the architecture of the neighborhood, though this can come across as spartan to some. Comfortable contemporary rooms are mainly focused on the view out the ample windows; bathrooms are stark but have deep soaking tubs. A great seasonal pleasure is the Yard—a large outdoor space where you can have a drink or meal and then spread out on the grassy lawn—the only one of its kind in the city. The staff here is professional, polished, and more experienced than you'll find at other fashionable hotels. **Pros:** fashionable, laid-back sophistication; great service; surprisingly discreet setting; diverse eating and drinking options. **Cons:** closer to Canal Street than prime SoHo; rooms on small side. ⊠ 310 West Broadway, at Grand St., SoHo ☏ 212/965–3000 or 800/965–3000 ⊕ www.sohogrand.com ⇥ 365 rooms, 2 suites ⚇ In-room: a/c, safe, refrigerator, Internet, Wi-Fi. In-hotel: restaurant, room service, bars, gym, laundry service, parking (paid), some pets allowed ▭AE, D, DC, MC, V Ⓜ 6, J, M, N, Q, R, W to Canal St. ✛ 2:D4.

19

WORD OF MOUTH

"[The SoHo Grand] is definitely funky, yet nice. The bar is always packed but a good place to people watch. I have found the rooms small but comfortable and the staff helpful. I find it less pretentious that some 'W' hotels at which I have stayed."   —A2

EAST VILLAGE AND LOWER EAST SIDE

EAST VILLAGE

$$ ⌕ **The Cooper Square Hotel.** A jarring, 21-story glass and steel finger rising up in the low-rise East Village, the Cooper Square Hotel was never going to pass under the radar. The addition of the even more futuristic Cooper Union building next door has alleviated the hotel's out-of-character look somewhat, but it's still a focal point—for good and ill, as surrounding neighbors are enmeshed in a fight to close the hotel's noisy outdoor spaces. The lobby goes for casual chic: there are no check-in desks, just reservation agents positioned to meet guests as soon as they walk in the door. (There is a hidden private room for checking in VIPs). The lobby is lined with cushy leather chairs and hundreds of books from the Housing Works and available for purchase, with proceeds going to that charity. Thanks to floor-to-ceiling windows overlooking the eponymous square, rooms are bright, though the sage or slate-blue

carpeting looks cheap. The thoughtful amenities include three different kinds of robes—even one for your dog—as well as a mini-bar stocked with tiny bottles of Hendricks gin and Maker's Mark bourbon, Sferra linens on the beds, flat-screen televisions, iPod docks, and Red Flower bath products. Table 8, a pan-Asian restaurant on the second floor, is pricey for the area. There's no gym in the hotel, but guests can use the New York Health and Racquet across the square for free. **Pros:** stylish rooms; excellent amenities; creative guests. **Cons:** out of character with the area; ugly carpeting; overpriced restaurant. ⊠ *25 Cooper Square, between E. 5th and E. 6th Sts., East Village* ☎ *212/475–5700* ⊕ *www.thecoopersquarehotel.com* ↰ *145 rooms* ♨ *In-room: a/c, safe, Wi-Fi. In-hotel: restaurant, room service, bars, Wi-Fi hotspot, some pets allowed* ⊟ *AE, D, DC, MC, V* Ⓜ *6 to Astor Pl.; R, W to 8th. St./ NYU* ✛ *2:F2.*

LOWER EAST SIDE

$$ ⊡ **The Bowery Hotel**. A stay at the Bowery centers on the lobby, stocked with tabloids for guests, Old World dark wood, and leather chairs. It's an English hunting lodge in Manhattan, warmed by rich floor-to-ceiling tapestries, fireplaces, and chandeliers—the only thing missing is a trusty hound, and there's certainly no shortage of British, who flock to the property. The mood created by the attractive red-coated doormen, the clubby bar, and trendy address makes this one of the hottest hotels—or lobbies, at least—of the moment. Sadly, rooms upstairs don't maintain the richness of the lobby—they're on the minimalist side, with big console desks and old-school windows the only grand flourishes. **Pros:** quirky, fun location; ravishing bar and lobby-lounge area; celebrity sightings; interesting views. **Cons:** gritty neighbors; rooms aren't luxurious; restaurant is crowded but underwhelming. ⊠ *335 Bowery, at 3rd St., Lower East Side* ☎ *212/505–9100* ⊕ *www.theboweryhotel. com* ↰ *117 rooms, 18 suites* ♨ *In-room: a/c, safe, Wi-Fi. In-hotel: restaurant, room service, bar, laundry service, Internet terminal, Wi-Fi hotspot, parking (paid), some pets allowed* ⊟ *AE, D, DC, MC, V* ⑃Ⓞⱡ *CP* Ⓜ *6 to Bleecker; B, D, F, V to Broadway/Lafayette* ✛ *2:F2.*

$$ ⊡ **Hotel on Rivington**. A pioneer when it opened in 2004, THOR is no longer the only glass-walled hotel on the Lower East Side. Furthermore, the years are starting to show, as some fixtures in the room are starting to get tatty. Still, the views of downtown remain breathtaking. The bathrooms aren't for the modest or faint of heart—you'll either want to shower with your glasses on, or you'll blush at being completely naked before the entire city (privacy curtains can be requested). Downstairs, the hotel bar is pure excess—it and the jumping restaurant are velvet-roped mayhem on weekends. (Staying here also gives you access to a small VIP bar next door.) The bar–art library–billiard room on the mezzanine is a hangout you can call your own. **Pros:** superhip location and vibe; huge windows with wonderful New York views; happening bar and restaurant. **Cons:** feels like a club on weekends; spotty service; small rooms and suites. ⊠ *107 Rivington St., between Ludlow and Essex Sts., Lower East Side* ☎ *212/475–2600 or 800/915–1537* ⊕ *www. hotelonrivington.com* ↰ *110 rooms* ♨ *In-room: a/c, safe, refrigerator, Internet, Wi-Fi. In-hotel: restaurant, room service, bar, laundry service,*

parking (paid), some pets allowed ⊟ *AE, D, DC, MC, V* Ⓜ *F, J, M, Z to Delancey/Essex Sts.* ✛ *2:G3.*

$$ Ⓣ **Thompson LES.** The best expression of the Thompson Hotels philosophy, the Thompson LES is a stylish addition to the neighborhood, the smoked glass tower contrasting with the Hotel on Rivington's wide-open views. The two-story lobby, dominated by a hanging black-and-white curtain made of glass, bustles with Europeans, musicians, and others with carefully crafted hair (that includes the too-cool-for-school staff). Shang, a pan-Asian restaurant from Toronto's Susur Lee, shares space on the second floor with the lounge, which has roll-up windows for alfresco drinking in the warmer months. Rooms are stark, black-and-white affairs, with low platform beds whoses headboards are lightboxes displaying works by the photographer Lee Friedlander. The desk space can be cramped, and while the windows are big, come nighttime it's oppressively dark. Bathrooms are stocked with products from New York's own Kiehl's as well as rainfall showerheads; the mini-bar includes snacks from Dean & Deluca, another New York–based company. Suites, on the building's corners, come with balconies with sweeping views of both downtown and Midtown—some of the best in the city. The neighborhood is a nexus for nightlife on the weekends, and it's just a short walk to Chinatown. **Pros:** great amenities; in the heart of downtown; great views from suites. **Cons:** snobby staff; rooms stylish but dark. ⊠ *190 Allen St., between Houston and Stanton Sts., Lower East Side* ☎ *212/460–5300* ⊕ *www.thompsonhotels.com* ⤳ *131 rooms* △ *In-room: a/c, safe, refrigerator, Wi-Fi. In-hotel: restaurant, room service, bars, pool, laundry service, Wi-Fi hotspot* ⊟ *AE, MC, V* Ⓜ *F, J, M, Z to Delancey/Essex Sts.* ✛ *2:G3.*

Fodor's Choice
★

GREENWICH VILLAGE WITH MEATPACKING DISTRICT AND WEST VILLAGE

19

GREENWICH VILLAGE

$ Ⓣ **Washington Square Hotel.** This low-key European-style hotel in Greenwich Village is popular with visiting New York University parents—the location near the renovated Washington Square Park and its magnificent arch is just a bonus. One block from the very central West 4th Street subway station, it's easy to get to the rest of Downtown's sights. Some rooms are cheerfully decorated—deluxe rooms have a snazzy Hollywood Art Deco style and much more natural light than the plainer standard rooms, which have pastel florals and a more limited selection of amenities. Deluxe rooms come with pillow-top mattresses and free high-speed Internet access. The intimate Deco Room has mosaic floors, elegant mirrors, and a wrought-iron-and-glass brass gate from Paris. Daytime guests can sip tea; at night they can pull up a stool at the beautiful bar. North Square restaurant has a jazz brunch and surprisingly sophisticated fare. **Pros:** park-front location; deluxe rooms are charming; great hotel bar. **Cons:** NYU students everywhere; rooms are small. ⊠ *103 Waverly Pl., at MacDougal St., Greenwich Village* ☎ *212/777–9515 or 800/222–0418* ⊕ *www.wshotel.com* ⤳ *160 rooms* △ *In-room: a/c, safe, Internet (some). In-hotel: restaurant, bar, gym,*

Wi-Fi hotspot ☰ AE, MC, V ⍟ CP ⓂA, B, C, D, E, F, V to W. 4th St./ Washington Sq. ✛ 2:D1.

MEATPACKING DISTRICT

$$ 🛏 **Hotel Gansevoort.** Don't you hate it when a younger sibling shows you up? Unfortunately, that's the case at the Gansevoort, which is looking a bit frumpy since the Standard opened a few blocks to the west. Still, there's plenty to like at this chic Meatpacking District pioneer, starting with the sleek rooms that overlook the city or the Hudson River, a rooftop deck with a 45-foot heated pool that remains a draw for locals and tourists alike, and even video-game systems delivered to your room for free. The furnishing themselves are starting to show signs of wear, though the Exhale spa works much better now that it doesn't have to double as a lounge. What was once the high-end restaurant Ono is now the scaled-down Tanuki Tavern, but it's still serving Asian fusion fare. **Pros:** rooftop pool; wonderful art collection; nice amenities. **Cons:** too-trendy location at times; worn rooms; slipshod service. ⊠ 18 9th Ave., at 13th St., Meatpacking District ☎ 212/206–6700 or 877/426–7386 ⊕ www.hotelgansevoort. com ⇱ 166 rooms, 21 suites ⚒ In-room: a/c, safe, Wi-Fi. In-hotel: restaurant, room service, bars, pool, gym, spa, laundry service, Internet terminal, parking (paid), some pets allowed ☰ AE, MC, V ⍟ CP Ⓜ A, C, E, L to 14th St. and 8th Ave. ✛ 3:B4.

¢–$ 🛏 **The Jane.** To some, it's impossibly chic; to others, the rooms are reminiscent of Sing Sing; and to its far West Villge neighbors, it's just a nuisance. Welcome to the Jane Hotel. Off the small lobby, reminiscent of a Correspondent's Club in a former British colony, you'll find the bar and ballroom, a sleek spot that's got the community upset thanks to the crowds it draws on Friday and Saturday nights. The style here is similar to that of the Bowery Hotel, a sister property. Up in the rooms, as Steve Martin might say, let's get small. The intended effect is that of a railway car: the single beds against the wall have storage space above, wood paneling is accented by reds and yellows and an oriental rug; there's also a fan and a/c, but the shared unisex bathroom is down the hall. For more than one person, these rooms would be impossibly cramped. A better option is the "Captain's Cabins" with their own bathrooms and a view of the Hudson along with similar decor at about three times the size (and price). **Pros:** cheap; hot bar scene; convenient neighborhood for downtown sightseeing. **Cons:** impossibly tiny standard rooms; shared bathrooms; hot bar scene. ⊠ 113 Jane Street, at West St. West Village ☎ 212/924–6700 ⊕ www.thejanenyc.com ⇱ 150 rooms, 40 suites ⚒ In-room: a/c, Wi-Fi. In-hotel: bar, Wi-Fi hotspot ☰ AE, D, DC, MC, V Ⓜ A, C, E, L to 14th St. and 8th Ave. ✛ 3:B5.

$ ⌨ **The Standard.** André Balazs's architectural statement on the West Side,
Fodor'sChoice the Standard is New York's hottest hotel (for the moment). It helps to
★ have the High Line, a reclaimed elevated railway turned park, running
underneath it, but the Standard earned much of the buzz itself, with a
lobby full of glamorous types, an authentic beer garden (dig the Ping-
Pong tables), and, guarding the 18th-floor nightclub, one of the toughest
doors in town. Rooms, with low platform beds, flat-screen televisions
(and the occasional banquette) are slightly small, even by New York
standards. They are not for the modest, either: impossibly clear, floor-to-
ceiling windows face the south and west, and some rooms have showers
separated from the bedroom by little more than a glass partition. As
you'd expect in a space (and neighborhood) that's so sceney, it can get
loud at night. The Standard Grill restaurant, which is almost always
packed, handles room service. **Pros:** beautiful building; beautiful people;
impressive restaurant space. **Cons:** noisy at night; tight rooms; sceney.
✉ *848 Washington St., between W. 13th and Little W. 12th Sts., Meatpacking District* ☎ *212/645–4646* ⊕ *www.standardhotels.com* ⇲ *337
rooms* ⚐ *In-room: a/c, Internet, Wi-Fi. In-hotel: 2 restaurants, room
service, bars, gym, spa, Wi-Fi hotspot* ⊟ *AE, MC, V* Ⓜ *A, C, E, L to
14th St. and 8th Ave.* ✛ *3:B4.*

UNION SQUARE WITH FLATIRON DISTRICT, GRAMERCY PARK, AND MURRAY HILL

FLATIRON DISTRICT

$ ⌨ **Ace Hotel.** Step inside the Ace hotel, and any notion of what a hotel
Fodor'sChoice could and should be is left at the door. The eastern outpost of a West
★ Coast hotel chain (locations are already in Seattle, Portland, and Palm
Springs) provides the style and luxury you'd expect to find at five-star
hotel, minus the pretension and price. It almost seems as if you're staying at the pad of your coolest friend, given hipster touches like a young
staff that doesn't have a uniform, a photo booth in the lobby; and some
rooms outfitted with Gibson guitars, turntables, or small Heineken
kegs in the mini-bars. The uniquely designed rooms run from "cheap"
and "bunk," to "super-deluxe" and "loft": from backpackers to bankers, everyone will feel welcome here. Larger rooms have views over
Broadway, clawfoot tubs, and hardwood parquet floors. **Pros:** in-house
restaurant, the Breslin, means you won't have to travel far for trendy
dining; lobby java shop is by the excellent Stumptown Coffee Roast-
ers. **Cons:** caters to a young crowd; may be too sceney for some. ✉ *20
W. 29th St. at Broadway, Flatiron District* ☎ *212/679–2222* ⊕ *www.
acehotel.com* ⇲ *251 rooms, 11 suites* ⚐ *In-room: a/c, safe, refrigerator
(some), Wi-Fi. In-hotel: restaurant, room service, bars, gym, laundry
service, Wi-Fi hotspot, parking (paid), some pets allowed* ⊟ *AE, MC,
V* Ⓜ *N, R, W to 28th St.; 1 to 28th St.* ✛ *3:E1.*

GRAMERCY PARK

$$$ ⌨ **Gramercy Park Hotel.** Like a great comeback album from a favor-
ite singer, Ian Schrager's return to the New York City hotel scene is
much appreciated. The man invented the "boutique hotel" concept
almost two decades ago, and the property reflects some of his hard-

19

Hotel Hot Spots

Some of the city's most stylish bars and lounges are in hotels. These boîtes occasionally require crossing a velvet-roped entrance, but most extend automatic entry to guests of the hotel.

Mega-hotelier Ian Schrager's properties are design temples, with chic lounges favored by jet-setters and locals alike. The new "haute Bohemian" **Gramercy Park Hotel** (⇨ Union Square/Gramercy) is Schrager's latest offering, with its popular—and pricey—Rose Bar and Jade Bar. The hotel also features a private members- and guests-only Roof Club. **The Ace Hotel** (⇨ Union Square/Flatiron) is the sweet spot du jour, with one bar in the eclectic lobby, another at the trendy Breslin restaurant, and also an outpost of Stumptown coffee if you need to sober up. At the **Royalton** (⇨ Midtown West and Chelsea), the immense lobby lounge is a perennial favorite of music and film industry scenesters as well as magazine publishing types.

The Standard (⇨ Greenwich Village/Meatpacking District) has a happening bar scene at the Standard Grill. The 18th-floor lounge is a tough row to hoe unless you're a friend of the owner, but downstairs you can also sip suds in the outdoor beer garden,

which is more egalitarian, and frankly, a lot more fun—they've even got Ping-Pong tables.

Down in SoHo, some of the chicest hotels in the city have rock-star-worthy scenes. Movie stars and their hangers-on imbibe into the wee hours at cool Mercer Bar in the **Mercer Hotel** (⇨ SoHo) or the even trendier and more exclusive submercer—there's a hidden entrance just outside the hotel. **60 Thompson**'s (⇨ SoHo) rooftop lounge is one of the hottest tickets in town on warm evenings; hotel guests get automatic entrance. There's also the less manic Thom bar, just one floor up.

In Midtown the trippy **Dream Hotel** (⇨ Midtown West) has a rooftop bar that swings into action as soon as the weather warms, and three other bars, including a subterranean lounge under the swanky Mediterranean restaurant Amalia. Hotel guests get priority entrance into all the trendy spots.

The **Room Mate Grace** (⇨ Midtown West and Chelsea) in Times Square has a bar that's adjacent to its lobby-level pool; you can see all the underwater action through voyeur windows above the bar. Just make sure to pay attention at the end of the evening, or you might be the hotel's next swimming sensation.

won wisdom. Start with the soaring Medieval Rose Bar, which remains exclusive—unless you're a guest and you've booked a table with the concierge. Meanwhile, the rooftop garden, open year-round, gives you some great city views and Julian Schnabel design. The contemporary art that's scattered throughout includes works by Andy Warhol and Basquiat in the lobby, which has a chic, hushed quality. Upstairs, the rooms go for fabulousness over comfort, with draped velvet, studded leather, and very red drapes. Try for a view overlooking the private Gramercy Park if you can swing it; staffers will also let you into it on request. An Italian restaurant from Danny Meyer is slated to open here by the end of 2010. **Pros:** intensely trendy bar scene; opulent rooms; park-side location. **Cons:** inconsistent service; form-over-function rooms; expensive bar. ⊠ *2 Lexington Ave., at Gramercy Park, Gramercy Park* ☎ *212/920–3300* ⊕ *www.gramercyparkhotel.com* ☞ *140 rooms, 40 suites* ⚿ *In-room: a/c, safe, refrigerator, DVD, Internet. In-hotel: restaurant, room service, bars, gym, laundry service, parking (paid)* ▭ *AE, D, DC, MC, V* Ⓜ *6 to 23rd St.* ✛ *3:F3.*

$$ ⊡ **Inn at Irving Place.** Fantasies of old New York—Manhattan straight
Fodor's Choice   from the pages of Edith Wharton and Henry James, an era of genteel
★   brick town houses and Tiffany lamps—spring to life at this discreet 20-room inn, the city's most romantic. There is no sign outside the 1830 town house, a hint of the somehow small-town qualities of Irving Place, a lightly trafficked street on the south side of Gramercy Park. One of the city's most famous tea salons, Lady Mendl's, is run on the lobby level. Rooms have ornamental fireplaces, four-poster beds with embroidered linens, wood shutters, and glossy cherrywood floors. The room named after Madame Olenska (a lovelorn Wharton character) has a bay window with sitting nook—this is one of the most memorable spots in New York; reserve it for anniversaries. Still, the rooms can sometimes seems like a novel's character who has aged too rapidly—and the street and restaurant noise occasionally spoil the fin-de-siècle fantasy. **Pros:** romantic; quaint; big rooms; excellent breakfast and tea service; Mario Batali's Casa Mono is downstairs. **Cons:** twee; rooms aren't flawless, with imperfections like older grouting; street noise. ⊠ *56 Irving Pl., between E. 17th and E. 18th Sts., Gramercy Park* ☎ *212/533–4600 or 800/685–1447* ⊕ *www.innatirving.com* ☞ *5 rooms, 6 suites* ⚿ *In-room: a/c, refrigerator. In-hotel: restaurant, room service, bar, laundry service, no kids under 8* ▭ *AE, D, DC, MC, V* ⦿|CP Ⓜ *4, 5, 6, L, N, Q, R, W to 14th St./Union Sq.* ✛ *3:G3.*

$ ⊡ **Marcel at Gramercy.** A fall 2008 redesign has transformed the Marcel into a chic, yet affordable stay that gives guests both style and substance in a prime location. The small lobby is outfitted in a dark palette of black, gray, and blue, making it feel like a swanky nightclub; rooms are modernized with flat-screen TVs, iPod docking stations, Frette linens, and Gilchrist & Soames bath amenities. Rooms may still be a bit small for the price point, but the sleek redo added a much-needed zest to the decor. The 10th-floor lounge, where there's complimentary computer and Wi-Fi access, free coffee, and a connecting outdoor patio, offers respite from the bustling city below. The Italian restaurant 'inoteca is on the ground floor, and provides room service. **Pros:** outdoor patio offers great space and spectacular views of the city; good value. **Cons:** elevators are slow; a/c struggles in summer; the wine-and-cheese reception is free but could run longer. ⊠ *201 E. 24th St., Gramercy Park* ☎ *212/696–3800* ⊕ *www.themarcelatgramercy.com* ☞ *133 rooms, 2 suites* ⚿ *In-room: a/c, safe. In-hotel: restaurant, room service, laundry service, Internet terminal, Wi-Fi hotspot* ▭ *AE, D, MC, V* Ⓜ *6 to 23rd St.* ✛ *3:G2.*

19

Crosby Street Hotel

Thompson LES

The Standard

Ace Hotel

Library Hotel,

Inn on 23rd

MURRAY HILL

¢ ⊞ **Carlton Arms.** Europeans and students know about the chipper, winning attitude of this friendly, no-frills hotel. There are some caveats: the unisex bathrooms, two per floor, are shared. Rooms themselves are themed, from an English Cottage to a math classroom, though all the themes exclude a television. Prices remain consistent throughout the year: $130 including tax for a private bath, $110 to share. **Pros:** rock-bottom prices; chipper attitude; quieter residential Murray Hill location. **Cons:** no elevator; few furnishings; many shared baths. ⊠ *160 E. 25th St., at 3rd Ave., Murray Hill* ☎ *212/684–8337; 212/679–0680 for reservations* ⊕ *www.carltonarms.com* ⤵ *54 rooms, 20 with bath* ⌂ *In-room: no phone, a/c, no TV. In-hotel: Internet terminal, some pets allowed* ⊟ *MC, V* Ⓜ *R, W to 28th St.* ✛ *3:G2.*

$$ ⊞ **Carlton on Madison Avenue.** A five-year, $60 million renovation has turned a nearly invisible old dowager into a modern scene-stealer. The Carlton's makeover includes many a happy detail, from the two-story lobby designed by David Rockwell to still-intact, original 1904 Beaux-Arts details such as the stained-glass dome (created by workers from the Tiffany glass factory). Rooms are small for the money—they start at 200 square feet—but make up for it with amenities and flair, including mahogany accents, free Wi-Fi, and docks for iPods plus USB and Ethernet ports. One snafu—the bathrooms, outfitted with swanky Molton Brown products are underlit at best. Country remains a solid, if uninspired, restaurant choice. **Pros:** spectacular lobby; stylish rooms; nice amenities. **Cons:** expensive bar; small rooms; lackluster restaurant. ⊠ *88 Madison Ave., between 28th and 29th Sts., Murray Hill* ☎ *212/532–4100 or 800/601–8500* ⊕ *www.carltonhotelny.com* ⤵ *294 rooms, 22 suites* ⌂ *In-room: a/c, safe, Wi-Fi. In-hotel: 2 restaurants, room service, bar, laundry service, Internet terminal, Wi-Fi hotspot, parking (paid), some pets allowed* ⊟ *AE, D, MC, V* Ⓜ *6 to 28th St.* ✛ *3:F1.*

$–$$ ⊞ **Herald Square Hotel.** The sculpted cherubs on the facade and vintage magazine covers adorning the common areas hint at the Herald's previous incarnation as *Life* magazine's headquarters. The hotel is a great value. Rooms are basic, but all have TVs and phones, and some were renovated to include flat screens. Shabby-chic fixtures and white-on-white bedspreads round out the look, but beware the unrenovated rooms, which verge on just plain shabby. There's no concierge and no room service, but the staff is friendly, and nearby restaurants will deliver. It's a great bargain given the convenient neighborhood. **Pros:** cheap; centrally located. **Cons:** unattractive lobby; readers report inconsistent service. ⊠ *19 W. 31st St., between 5th Ave. and Broadway, Murray Hill* ☎ *212/279–4017 or 800/727–1888* ⊕ *www.heraldsquarehotel. com* ⤵ *120 rooms* ⌂ *In-room: a/c, safe, Wi-Fi. In-hotel: Internet terminal, Wi-Fi hotspot, some pets allowed* ⊟ *AE, D, MC, V* Ⓜ *B, D, F, N, Q, R, V, W to 34th St./Herald Sq.* ✛ *3:E1.*

$$ ⊞ **Hotel Giraffe.** Ensconced just off Park Avenue South for nearly a decade now, the Giraffe remains a consistent property with friendly service, big rooms, and lots of repeat customers, particularly business travelers. The style is Art Deco, right down to the deluxe rooms' red-velvet armchairs and French doors, which open onto private balconies

from which you can survey Park Avenue. Recent upgrades include flat-screen televisions, Egyptian cotton sheets, and iPod docks. Be sure to head to the open-air rooftop bar for a drink in any weather. The civilized service here includes complimentary breakfast, coffee, and a weekday evening champagne reception. **Pros:** high-quality linens: rooftop terrace for guests; quiet hotel. **Cons:** street noise near lower levels; pricey for the quality you get. ✉ *365 Park Ave. S, at E. 26th St., Murray Hill* ☎ *212/685–7700 or 877/296–0009* ⊕ *www.hotelgiraffe.com* ⇱ *52 rooms, 21 suites* ⌂ *In-room: a/c, safe, DVD, Wi-Fi. In-hotel: restaurant, room service, bars, laundry service, Internet terminal, Wi-Fi hotspot, parking (paid)* ⊟ *AE, DC, MC, V* ⌑*CP* Ⓜ *6 to 28th St.* ✛ *3:F2.*

$–$$ ⛨ **Jolly Hotel Madison Towers.** Italians flock to this hotel operated by Jolly Hotels, the largest hotel chain in Italy. In this U.S. flagship you can expect native Italians, or at least Italian-speaking staff at the front desk and the breakfast room. The look is Positano circa 1920, with parquet floors in the Whaler Bar downstairs (plus a fireplace) and a white-and-gold color scheme in the rooms. Deluxe rooms have views of the Empire State Building, and also come outfitted with cherrywood furniture; standard rooms, alas, are sized more like a Fiat than a Ford. A separate concession on the premises offers shiatsu massage and a Japanese sauna. **Pros:** friendly, Italian-style service; good location; attractive bar. **Cons:** no restaurant; no gym; not contemporary in feel; small rooms. ✉ *22 E. 38th St., between Madison and Park Aves., Murray Hill* ☎ *212/802–0600 or 800/225–4340* ⊕ *www.jollymadison. com* ⇱ *238 rooms, 6 suites* ⌂ *In-room: a/c, safe, Wi-Fi. In-hotel: bar, laundry service, Internet terminal, Wi-Fi hotspot, parking (paid), some pets allowed* ⊟ *AE, DC, MC, V* Ⓜ *6 to 33rd St.* ✛ *4:F5.*

$$ ⛨ **The Kitano.** As you might guess from the name, the Kitano imports much of its sensibility from Japan, and such touches include a bilingual concierge and a high-concept Japanese restaurant. Notably, this makes for a service-oriented stay, a welcome change of pace in New York. One thing that's not classically Japanese? The oversize guest rooms, decked out in beige and gold, have an electric tea kettle, Gilchrist & Soames bath amenities, and marble-floored bathrooms. Head downstairs and through the eerily quiet lobby to sample Hakubai, the fantastically high-end restaurant, or just to rub Fernando Botero's rotund sculpture of a dog for good luck—it's the hotel's mascot. **Pros:** extra soundproofing in guest rooms; cute mezzanine bar area; guest pass to great local gym; fairly good value. **Cons:** lower-floor views are limited; very expensive restaurant. ✉ *66 Park Ave., at E. 38th St., Murray Hill* ☎ *212/885–7000 or 800/548–2666* ⊕ *www.kitano.com* ⇱ *149 rooms, 18 suites* ⌂ *In-room: a/c, safe, refrigerator, Internet. In-hotel: 2 restaurants, room service, bar, laundry service, parking (paid)* ⊟ *AE, D, DC, MC, V* Ⓜ *6 to 33rd St.* ✛ *4:F5.*

$ ⛨ **Park South Hotel.** In this beautifully transformed 1906 office building, restful rooms feel smartly contemporary, though they've retained some period details. Watch out for rooms that overlook noisy 27th Street or are too close to the bar on the ground floor; ask instead for a view of the Chrysler Building. Historic New York flavor is the design focus in the mezzanine library, with black-and-white photos of

19

city scenes from the 1880s through 1950s. The Black Duck bar and restaurant warms patrons with its wood-burning fireplace, though the decor is better than the mediocre food. Luckily, several excellent Indian restaurants are just around the corner. The square Murray Hill location may disappoint hipster guests. **Pros:** free breakfast and Internet; turndown service; good value. **Cons:** small elevators; tame location; spotty service. ⊠ *122 E.*

28th St., between Lexington and Park Aves., Murray Hill ☎ *212/448–0888 or 800/315–4642* ⊕ *www.parksouthhotel.com* ↘ *139 rooms, 2 suites* ♿ *In-room: a/c, safe, Internet. In-hotel: restaurant, bar, gym, laundry service, Internet terminal, Wi-Fi hotspot* ⊟ *AE, D, DC, MC, V* ⌾*CP* Ⓜ *6 to 28th St.* ✛ *3:F2.*

$$ ☎ **Hotel Roger Williams.** A colorful choice in a rather plain neighborhood, the Roger Williams continues to have a following among repeat visitors to New York. A lobby styled like a front parlor, with comfy, IKEA-style seats and newspapers is a great place to relax, thanks to the copious light that pours in from the oversize picture windows. Rooms are similarly cheerful and include nice touches like flat-screen televisions, free Wi-Fi, Aveda bath products, and a minibar outfitted with Macallan scotch and snacks. The bathrooms themselves are a little cramped. The hotel's lounge serves American fare at low prices, and the $17 breakfast buffet includes local faves: H&H bagels and Petrossian smoked salmon. **Pros:** colorful room decor; friendly service; good value. **Cons:** no room service; tiny bathrooms. ⊠ *131 Madison Ave., at E. 31st St., Murray Hill* ☎ *212/448–7000 or 877/847–4444* ⊕ *www.rogerwilliamshotel. com* ↘ *193 rooms, 2 suites* ♿ *In-room: a/c, Wi-Fi. In-hotel: restaurant, room service, bar, gym, Internet terminal, Wi-Fi hotspot, parking (paid)* ⊟ *AE, D, MC, V* ⌾*CP* Ⓜ *6 to 33rd St.* ✛ *3:F1.*

$ ☎ **70 Park Avenue.** Branches in the Kimpton hotel chain have something of a cult following with design enthusiasts, but 70 Park is a low-key, slightly disappointing offering that's more for road-warrior business types than style hounds. The lobby, with its limestone fireplace and thick-pillowed couches, looks like a contemporary living room, and you'll find people parked here with their laptops for hours—a couple of laptops are even set out here for guest use. The rest of the hotel simulates a prosperous but rather unexciting home, with a neutral palette, Ultrasuede chairs and couches, and plasma TVs. It all makes for a casual, comfortable, safe choice in this quiet neighborhood a couple of blocks from Grand Central. Some suites have hot tubs and terraces with Empire State Building views. Silverleaf Tavern serves modern-American small plates, and the bar is comfortable even if you're alone. **Pros:** weekday wine reception; polite service; simple, unobtrusive rooms and hotel layout. **Cons:** bland design; no gym. ⊠ *70 Park Ave., at 38th St., Murray Hill* ☎ *212/973–2400 or 800/707–2752* ⊕ *www.70parkave.com* ↘ *201* *rooms, 4 suites ☼ In-room: a/c, safe, DVD, Internet, Wi-Fi. In-hotel: restaurant, room service, bar, laundry service, some pets allowed ▭ AE, D, DC, MC, V Ⓜ 6 to 33rd St. ✛ 4:F5.*

$ 👁 **W New York–The Court and W New York–The Tuscany.** The forgotten children in the family of W's New York City properties, the Court and the Tuscany are separate but close to each other, with a similar vibe and clientele. The lack of "W"-ness here is in many ways a plus: the rooms are bigger than at other Ws in the city, and the residential character of the neighborhood coupled with the older feel of the buildings themselves—former apartments—makes things less frenetic. Even the lobbies are much less of a meat market than elsewhere. The rooms still incorporate plenty of style, though, including dark-wood desks and iPod docks. At the Tuscany you can also sneak a peek at the Empire State or Chrylser building from some of the rooms. Downstairs, skip the restaurant for a drink at Wetbar or a workout at Sweat, the hotel's gym down the street. **Pros:** quiet, residential neighborhood; sleek bar. **Cons:** not for hard-core W guests; 39th Street rooms are noisy; gym not in either hotel building. ✉ *130 E. 39th St., between Lexington and Park Aves., Murray Hill* ☎ *212/685–1100 or 877/946–8357* ⊕ *www. whotels.com* ⤳ *Court: 150 rooms, 39 suites; Tuscany: 122 rooms, 12 suites ☼ In-room: a/c, safe, DVD, Internet. In-hotel: restaurant, room service, bar, gym, spa, laundry service, Internet terminal, Wi-Fi hotspot, some pets allowed ▭ AE, D, DC, MC, V* ✉ *Tuscany, 120 E. 39th St., near Lexington Ave., Murray Hill* ☎ *212/779–7822; 800/223–6725 for reservations* Ⓜ *4, 5, 6, 7, S to 42nd St./Grand Central* ✛ *4:F5.*

UNION SQUARE

$ 👁 **W New York Union Square.** The W chain's iconic New York City property continues to attract a mix of trendsetters and tourists, thanks to the downtown location. Comfortably within the landmarked 1911 Guardian Life building at the end of Park Avenue South, the hotel takes advantage of many original details, including a grand staircase to the Great Room lobby and large picture windows looking out on Union Square. Rooms are of average size, with the classic W look that includes leather headboards, dark furniture, and Bliss bath products. Wi-Fi is a steep $17 a day, so budget accordingly. **Pros:** fashionable location; great restaurant. **Cons:** trendy decor; noisy lobby; expensive Wi-Fi. ✉ *201 Park Ave. S, at E. 17th St., Union Square* ☎ *212/253–9119 or 877/946–8357* ⊕ *www.whotels.com* ⤳ *254 rooms, 16 suites ☼ In-room: a/c, safe, refrigerator, DVD, Wi-Fi. In-hotel: restaurant, room service, bars, gym, spa, laundry service, parking (paid), some pets allowed ▭ AE, D, DC, MC, V* Ⓜ *4, 5, 6, L, N, Q, R, W to 14th St./Union Sq.* ✛ *3:F3.*

19

MIDTOWN WEST AND CHELSEA

CHELSEA

¢ 👁 **Chelsea Lodge.** Popular with Europeans and budget-conscious visitors, the Chelsea Lodge is a great location for guests who don't insist on a lot of amenities. Toilets are shared and down the hall for most rooms, but they do each have their own sink, shower, and TV. In this brownstone that's furnished with wainscoting, wallpaper, and hardwood floors the vibe is decidedly twee. The staff is quite amenable to requests, and best of all, the best of Chelsea, including galleries and Chelsea Market, is right outside your door. **Pros:** on a gorgeous Chelsea block; great bang for the buck; close to subway. **Cons:** not romantic; shared bathrooms not right for everyone. ✉ *318 W. 20th St., between 8th and 9th Aves., Chelsea* ☎ *212/243–4499* ⊕ *www.chelsealodge.com* ⤶ *22 rooms, 2 with bath; 4 suites* ♿ *In-room: no phone, a/c, kitchen (some), Wi-Fi. In-hotel: Wi-Fi hotspot* ═ *AE, D, MC, V* Ⓜ *C, E to 23rd St.; 1 to 18th St.* ✚ *3:C3.*

$ 🖵 **The GEM Hotel Chelsea.** At this stylish, well-priced boutique the modern rooms are small but designed to make the most of the limited space—they come with black-and-white photos on the wall, flat-screen TVs, white linens, iPod docking stations, full-length mirrors, and free Wi-Fi. And since you're in a very handy location near some of the best of New York's culture, bars, and restaurants, you probably won't be spending much time in your room anyway. **Pros:** great Chelsea location; close to several subway lines. **Cons:** gym and business center, both on the lower level, feel like a work in progress; rooms may be too small for some. ✉ *300 W. 22nd St., Chelsea* ☎ *212/675–1911* ⊕ *www.thegemhotel. com* ⤶ *81 rooms* ♿ *In-room: a/c, Wi-Fi. In-hotel: gym, laundry service, Internet terminal* ═ *AE, D, DC, MC, V* Ⓜ *C, E to 23rd St.; 1 to 23rd St.* ✚ *3:C3.*

$ 🖵 **Inn on 23rd.** Friendly innkeepers Annette and Barry Fisherman welcome guests to this five-floor, 19th-century building, which also comes with its own cat/mascot. The uniquely decorated rooms include a "canopy" room with a four-poster bed and a 1940s room with a tube radio and overstuffed lounge chairs. Students from the New School's Culinary Studies program, which holds classes here, prepare the guest breakfasts. **Pros:** charming innkeepers; comfy and relaxed library; affordable given location. **Cons:** few business services; some older amenities; beware if you have cat allergies. ✉ *131 W. 23rd St., between 6th and 7th Aves., Chelsea* ☎ *212/463–0330* ⊕ *www.innon23rd.com* ⤶ *13 rooms, 1 suite* ♿ *In-room: a/c, DVD (some), Internet, Wi-Fi. In-hotel: laundry service, Internet terminal, Wi-Fi hotspot* ═ *AE, D, DC, MC, V* �託 *CP* Ⓜ *F, V to 23rd St.* ✚ *3:D2.*

Fodor's Choice
★
♺

$$ 🖵 **Maritime Hotel.** In just about any other city, the Maritime would be a major entertainment and cultural center. Inside is the Hiro Ballroom nightclub, with room for 800; Matsuri, the cavernous Japanese restaurant below the hotel that's one of the city's most extravagant dining experiences; and La Bottega, a delightful, expansive plaza-level restaurant and bar. You wouldn't need to leave the hotel for a full dose of nightlife. But this is New York, and the Meatpacking District is two blocks away, so you're also near the city's sceniest, priciest clubs and boutiques. The Maritime's white-ceramic tower, the former HQ for the National Maritime Union, was the first luxury hotel to be built in the Chelsea gallery district. The warm, small rooms resemble modern ship's cabins, with burnished teak paneling, sea-blue drapes and bed accents, and 5-foot-tall "portholes" that face the Hudson River skyline. Bonus: the hotel is said to be haunted. **Pros:** nightlife options galore; great restaurants; fun rooms with big porthole windows. **Cons:**

all nightlife all the time; street noise. ✉ *363 W. 16th St., at 9th Ave., Chelsea* ☎ *212/242–4300* ⊕ *www.themaritimehotel.com* ⊷ *120 rooms, 4 suites* ⚷ *In-room: a/c, safe, DVD, Internet, Wi-Fi. In-hotel: 2 restaurants, room service, bars, gym, laundry service, Internet terminal, Wi-Fi hotspot, some pets allowed* ▭ *AE, MC, V* Ⓜ *A, C, E to 14th St.* ⊕ *3:B3.*

MIDTOWN WEST

$$ Ⓣ **Belvedere Hotel.** Guests choose the Belvedere more for the central location, adjacent to Times Square, and less for the rooms, which lack life (and light). The executive rooms are an exception, since they raise the bar considerably with chandeliers, cream-color carpets, and leather chairs. Still, even standard rooms are spacious and come with kitchenettes with microwave, mini-refrigerator, and coffeemakers. The helpful desk staff and location convenient to theaters make this a great affordable choice. **Pros:** good rates available; renovated rooms are good value. **Cons:** can be loud with street noise; slow elevators. ✉ *319 W. 48th St., between 8th and 9th Aves., Midtown West* ☎ *212/245–7000 or 888/468–3558* ⊕ *www.belvederehotelnyc.com* ⊷ *328 rooms, 1 suite* ⚷ *In-room: a/c, safe, kitchen, refrigerator, Wi-Fi. In-hotel: restaurant, laundry facilities, laundry service, Internet terminal, Wi-Fi hotspot, parking (paid)* ▭ *AE, D, DC, MC, V* Ⓜ *C, E to 50th St.* ⊕ *4:B3.*

$$ Ⓣ **The Blakely.** It may be a tried and true design motif, but it's hard to resist the English gentlemen's club when it's done right. The Blakely plays it up, with Chesterfield sofas and wood paneling in the lobby and rooms with flat-screen TVs, large work desks, and Frette robes. The feather-topped beds with Egyptian cotton sheets and duvets are particularly cozy. Room service is provided by Abboccato, a stylish Italian restaurant that gathers a large after-work crowd and that also operates the hotel bar. **Pros:** central location; good-size rooms; quality restaurant. **Cons:** rooms facing 54th Street can be noisy; some rooms have little natural light. ✉ *136 W. 55th St., between 6th and 7th Aves., Midtown West* ☎ *212/245–1800 or 800/735–0710* ⊕ *www.blakelynewyork.com* ⊷ *57 rooms, 54 suites* ⚷ *In-room: a/c, safe, kitchen, refrigerator, DVD, Wi-Fi. In-hotel: restaurant, room service, bar, gym, laundry service, Internet terminal, Wi-Fi hotspot, parking (paid)* ▭ *AE, DC, MC, V* Ⓜ *N, Q, R, W to 57th St.* ⊕ *4:C2.*

$$ Ⓣ **Bryant Park Hotel.** A New York landmark in brown brick towering over the New York Public Library and Bryant Park, this sleekly modern hotel is fashioned from the bones of the former American Radiator Building. Twice a year the hotel is the center of Fashion Week festivities, and the rest of the time a stylish feeling remains. That means lots of over-the-top design elements, like padded leather headboards with a decorative bolster pillow, marble bathrooms with a rainfall showerhead, and "adult toys" available from guest services. Despite the trendiness, the rooms themselves are actually bigger than average, though lower floors tend to be a bit dark and have subpar views. Both the Koi restaurant and Cellar Bar are popular with the after-work crowd, though later in the evening both the restaurants and the neighborhood tend to be overly quiet. Still, during the day, the location can't be beat, with Fifth Avenue and Times Square equidistant from the front door. **Pros:**

19

Romantic Retreats

As the English explorer Sir Walter Raleigh once wrote, "Romance is a love affair in other than domestic surroundings." Indeed, many high-end hotels seem custom-built for romance, with plush feather beds, silky linens, and ultrasoft robes. But some properties go above and beyond in catering to couples, offering services like bath butlers and in-room massage services. Here's our pick of the city's best spots for an intimate getaway.

At the **Ritz-Carlton, Battery Park** (⇨ Lower Manhattan), your wish is their command. Take advantage of lower-than-normal weekend rates to book a Liberty Suite, with sweeping views of the Statue of Liberty. With a quick call to the concierge you can arrange to have Champagne and strawberries waiting in your room when you arrive. A bath butler can then fill your marble tub with a potion of bath oils and flower petals. If you're here in February, don't miss a trip to the penthouse Chocolate Bar, with its aphrodisiac chocolate-and-Champagne buffet.

The Inn at Irving Place (⇨ Union Square/Gramercy) does romance the old-fashioned way, with four-poster beds, fireplaces, fur throws, and plenty of privacy in an elegant 1800s brownstone. The complimentary breakfast is served on fine bone china either in the cozy sitting room or in bed.

The 23,000-square-foot Bliss Spa at **W New York** (⇨ Midtown East and Upper East Side), on Lexington Avenue, is an urban oasis, with men's and women's lounges, a gym, and a full menu of facial and body treatments, massage, waxing, and nail services. Couples can spend a full day being pampered and pedicured in the spa or unwind in their rooms with an in-room massage, offered 24 hours a day.

All the rooms at the **Library Hotel** (⇨ Midtown East and Upper East Side) have an inviting charm that makes them a good choice for a romantic weekend away, but if you're looking for a little mood reading, ask for the Erotic Literature room or the Love Room, curated by Dr. Ruth.

---

gorgeous building; fashionable crowd and setting; across from Bryant Park. **Cons:** expensive; Cellar Bar frequently booked for events. ⊠ *40 W. 40th St., between 5th and 6th Aves., Midtown West* ☎ *212/869–0100 or 877/640–9300* ⊕ *www.bryantparkhotel.com* ↙ *112 rooms, 17 suites* ⌂ *In-room: a/c, safe, Internet, Wi-Fi. In-hotel: restaurant, room service, bars, gym, laundry service, Wi-Fi hotspot, parking (paid)* ▭ *AE, DC, MC, V* Ⓜ *B, D, F, V to 42nd St.; 7 to 5th Ave.* ✛ *4:D5.*

$$ 🎭 **Casablanca Hotel.** Evoking a sultry Mediterranean locale, the Casablanca is outfitted with mirrors and mosaics, ceiling fans, wooden blinds, and dainty little bistro tables in the public spaces. It's all rather theatrical, but then again, so is the neighborhood. Prices have gone up in recent years, which makes a quality stay here dependent on whether or not you find a good rate. Huge tiled bathrooms, many with windows, feature Baroness Cali amenities, and the bedrooms have soundproofed windows to limit noise from the Times Square adjacent location. On the second floor, classical music plays while guests linger in the spacious library-like Rick's Café for the complimentary breakfast buffet

and wine-and-cheese evenings. **Pros:** great access to the Theater District; all rooms are smoke-free. **Cons:** exercise facilities at nearby New York Sports Club, not on premises; heavy tourist foot traffic. ⊠ *147 W. 43rd St., Midtown West* ☎ *212/869–1212* ⊕ *www.casablancahotel.com* ⟆ *48 rooms* ♿ *In-room: a/c, safe, DVD, Wi-Fi. In-hotel: restaurant, room service, bar, laundry facilities, Wi-Fi hotspot* ☰ *AE, MC, V* Ⓜ *1, 2, 3, 7, N, Q, R, W, S to Times Sq./42nd St.* ✛ *4:C4.*

$$$–$$$$ 🖸 **Chambers.** This hotel casts itself as a center for art lovers, with more than 500 contemporary works in public spaces throughout the property. It adds to the sophisticated feel, though the artsy types might be rubbing elbows with foodies soon, as the Chambers is also the site of Má Pêche, David Chang's first Momofuku restaurant north of 14th Street. Whatever your obsession, you'll find sleek rooms designed by David Rockwell, with Bumble & Bumble bath amenities, a beige-and-taupe color scheme, and hardwood floors. The bathrooms, with mosaic tile, are particularly snazzy, though the fixtures as a whole are getting ragged around the edges. The lobby, one of the best in the city, is especially notable for the gigantic, oversize teak doors that separate you from the world outside. **Pros:** artsy, fun, lighthearted style; great art abounds; buzzing restaurant; wonderful central location. **Cons:** no gym; rooms slightly worn. ⊠ *15 W. 56th St., off 5th Ave., Midtown West* ☎ *212/974–5656 or 866/204–5656* ⊕ *www.chambershotel.com* ⟆ *72 rooms, 5 suites* ♿ *In-room: a/c, safe, DVD, Internet, Wi-Fi. In-hotel: restaurant, room service, bar, laundry service, Internet terminal, Wi-Fi hotspot, parking (paid), some pets allowed* ☰ *AE, D, DC, MC, V* Ⓜ *F, V to 57th St.* ✛ *4:E1.*

$$ 🖸 **City Club Hotel.** The City Club's ocean-liner-inspired rooms are brisk, bright, and masculine. They're also about the same size as a room on a cruise ship—that means tight quarters, matey, no matter how much you enjoy sharing space with Jonathan Adler ceramics. All rooms have city-oriented photos from the '50s, Bigalow bathroom products, and "City Club" monogrammed wool blankets. Privacy, not publicity, is the emphasis at this luxe boutique property—the lobby is tiny, and guests who wish to drink are sent across the street to the considerably more spacious Royalton. Top chef Daniel Boulud mans his db bistro moderne downstairs, making for delicious room service. **Pros:** free Wi-Fi; great restaurant; personal service. **Cons:** no gym; some guests find lighting substandard; no real lobby. ⊠ *55 W. 44th St., between 5th and 6th Aves., Midtown West* ☎ *212/921–5500* ⊕ *www.cityclubhotel.com* ⟆ *62 rooms, 3 suites* ♿ *In-room: a/c, safe, DVD, Wi-Fi. In-hotel: restaurant, room service, bar, Internet terminal, Wi-Fi hotspot, parking (paid), some pets allowed* ☰ *AE, D, DC, MC, V* Ⓜ *B, D, F, N, R, V, W, 1, 2, 3, 9 to 42nd St.; 7 to 5th Ave.* ✛ *4:D4.*

$$ 🖸 **DoubleTree Guest Suites Times Square.** A June 2009 renovation of the public spaces in this Fodorite favorite has transformed it into a sleek, modern contender for Times Square top dog. Space is a big draw. Rooms are twice the size of New York City's average, with the one-bedroom suites about 400 square feet; they have double vanities, mini refrigerators, microwaves, and iPod docks. Downstairs, the Wi-Fi is free in the lobby, and guests can sip coffee or martinis in the adjacent

19

lounge, which has gray leather and blue-fringed chandeliers. **Pros:** free 24-hour gym and Wi-Fi in public areas; extremely helpful, informed concierge; convenient to the Theater District. **Cons:** paid Wi-Fi in guest rooms; pricey for a DoubleTree. ✉ *1568 Broadway, at 47th St., Midtown West* ☎ *212/719–1600* ⊕ *doubletree1.hilton.com* ⤵ *460 rooms* ⌂ *In-room: a/c, safe, refrigerator, DVD, Wi-Fi. In-hotel: restaurant, room service, bar, laundry service, Internet terminal, Wi-Fi hotspot, parking (paid), some pets allowed* ▭ *AE, D, DC, MC, V* ❑〇〔 *EP* Ⓜ *B, D, F, V to 42nd St.* ✛ *4:C3.*

$ 🏨 **Dream Hotel.** Part hotel, part Kafkaesque dream, this Midtown experience is brought to you by hotelier Vikram Chatwal, and it specializes in style over comfort. The lobby combines an enormous two-story cylindrical neon-lighted aquarium, an unsettling two-story photograph of a tattooed woman, and a copper sculpture of Catherine the Great. Step off the elevator onto your floor and you'll be met with a jarring neon photograph; rooms are almost as disquieting—stark white walls, black furniture, and light-box desks that glow from within. Stay here if you love things modern: plasma TVs, complimentary iPod use, a Deepak Chopra spa, and a velvet-rope rooftop bar scene. Despite the over-the-top qualities—and noise from the scenesters headed to the rooftop bar—it's quite livable. **Pros:** Ava Lounge penthouse bar; big spa; up-to-the-minute electronics. **Cons:** small rooms; spotty service; trendier-than-thou atmosphere. ✉ *210 W. 55th St., at Broadway, Midtown West* ☎ *212/247–2000 or 866/437–3266* ⊕ *www.dreamny.com* ⤵ *208 rooms, 20 suites* ⌂ *In-room: a/c, safe, refrigerator, Internet, Wi-Fi. In-hotel: restaurant, room service, bars, spa, laundry service, Wi-Fi hotspot, parking (paid), some pets allowed* ▭ *AE, D, DC, MC, V* Ⓜ *N, Q, R, W to 57th St.* ✛ *4:C2.*

$$$ 🏨 **Hilton Times Square.** A glass-and-steel skyscraper atop a 335,000-square-foot retail complex that includes a movie theater and Madame Tussaud's Wax Museum, the Hilton reflects Times Square perfectly. That extends to the interior, which is as homogenous as the Times Square of today. The rooms are above average compared to other sleeps around Midtown at this price, with 37-inch flat-screen TVs, iPod hookups, and LaSource bath amenities. Rooms start on the 23rd floor to keep things quiet; the restaurant, confusingly called Above, is two floors below. Internet access does not, unfortunately, come cheap. **Pros:** immediate access to entertainment; convenient to public transportation; big rooms. **Cons:** impersonal feel; nickel-and-dime charges and overpriced food and drink, including a $26 buffet breakfast. ✉ *234 W. 42nd St., between 7th and 8th Aves., Midtown West* ☎ *212/642–2500 or 800/445–8667* ⊕ *www.hilton.com* ⤵ *444 rooms, 15 suites* ⌂ *In-room: a/c, safe, refrigerator, Internet, Wi-Fi. In-hotel: restaurant, room service, bar, gym, laundry service, parking (paid), some pets allowed* ▭ *AE, D, DC, MC, V* Ⓜ *1, 2, 3, 7, N, Q, R, W, S to 42nd St./Times Sq.* ✛ *4:C4.*

$ 🏨 **Hotel 41.** Bamboo in the window beckons guests to the warmly lighted lobby of the Hotel 41. This stylish hotel is not meant for family visits; rooms are tiny, even for two people. Most standard rooms face a brick wall, but if you can get past the size and not-so-thrilling views, it's a cozy place to stay, with a bed showing off crisp linens and a TV hanging above the closet. Bathrooms are elegant, with half-glass showers and original tile on the floor. Downstairs, Bar 41 is a dark sports bar–like hangout with rock music loudly playing. Find serenity in the intimate back-room wine cellar. **Pros:** DVD player in rooms with DVDs to borrow in the lobby; some rooms have refrigerators; Aveda bath amenities. **Cons:** lack of queen-size beds; small rooms; no view. ✉ *206 W. 41st St., Midtown West* ☎ *212/703–8600* ⊕ *www.hotel41nyc.com* ↪ *47 rooms* ♿ *In-room: a/c, safe, refrigerator (some), DVD, Internet, Wi-Fi. In-hotel: restaurant, room service, bar, laundry facilities, parking (paid)* ⊟ *AE, MC, V* Ⓜ *1, 2, 3, 7, N, Q, R, W, S to Times Sq./42nd St.; A, C, E to 42nd St./Port Authority Bus Terminal* ⊕ *4:C4.*

¢ 🏨 **The Hotel at Times Square.** Yes, there really is a Super 8 in Times Square—though it no longer goes by that name. The rooms are motel-plain with an unfortunate sea-foam color scheme, but most are well maintained. If you're an unfussy traveler who wants to be in the thick of the madness, it's not a bad option. This small prewar hotel shares its block with a plethora of Brazilian restaurants and is near many theaters and Rockefeller Center. The peculiar lobby has a narrow corridor that snakes off around a corner and is decorated with some rather handsome Art Deco Bakelite lamps. **Pros:** free breakfast; free Wi-Fi; free local calls. **Cons:** peremptory, low-frills service; noisy area. ✉ *59 W. 46th St., between 5th and 6th Aves., Midtown West* ☎ *212/719–2300 or 800/848–0020* ⊕ *www.applecorehotels.com* ↪ *209 rooms* ♿ *In-room: a/c, Wi-Fi. In-hotel: bar, gym, Internet terminal, parking (paid)* ⊟ *AE, D, DC, MC, V* Ⓜ *B, D, F, V to 47th–50th Sts./Rockefeller Center* ⊕ *4:D3.*

$–$$ 🏨 **Hotel Metro.** With mirrored columns and elegant black-and-white photos in the lobby, the Hotel Metro feels distinctively retro. Guests tend to hang out in the lounge, where coffee and tea are served all day, or in the adjacent library, a quiet nook with sofas and a desk. Upstairs, restrained, tasteful rooms with leather headboards and cushioned Art Deco chairs include bathrooms with Gilchrist & Soames products and double-height ceilings. In summer the Metro Grill rooftop bar provides outstanding Empire State Building views. **Pros:** renovated exercise room has flat-screen TVs; iPod dock and free Wi-Fi in rooms. **Cons:** noise seeps from outside; rooms are tasteful but spartan. ✉ *45 W. 35th St., between 5th and 6th Aves., Midtown West* ☎ *212/279–1310* ⊕ *www.hotelmetronyc.com* ↪ *179 rooms* ♿ *In-room: a/c, safe, Wi-Fi. In-hotel: restaurant, room service, bar, Wi-Fi hotspot* ⊟ *AE, DC, MC, V* Ⓜ *B, D, F, N, Q, R, V, W to 34th St./Herald Sq.* ⊕ *4:D6.*

$$ 🏨 **Ink48.** The Kimpton chain's first foray onto Manhattan's West Side, the Ink48 (formerly known as the Vu) is all the way west, on 11th Avenue, and a long walk from the nearest subway, three long avenues away. The location makes for a quiet lobby during the day, though things get busier once the bar "cabanas," with buttons to ring servers for drink service, start to fill up. Whatever the state of things downstairs, staffers are eager to please and move you to your room lickety-split. Upstairs, the first thing that impresses are the views, either looking south towards downtown or over the Hudson—and at the Intrepid Sea-Air-Space Museum, a nice bonus for history buffs. The rooms,

19

with iPod docks and big flat-screen TVs, have matching red headboards and duvets, plus gold and orange accents scattered throughout, making them pleasantly bright. (The huge windows help.) Bathrooms are big, and suites have some tubs that are cheekily located in the bedrooms themselves. Though windows are double-paned, some street noise from the West Side Highway can intrude, especially on lower floors. **Pros:** friendly staff; great views; large rooms. **Cons:** strange location; lobby can feel overly quiet at times; street noise. ⊠ *653 11th Avenue, at W. 48th St., Midtown West* ☎ *212/757–0088* ⊕ *www.ink48.com* ⤵ *195 rooms, 27 suites* ⌂ *In-room: a/c, safe, Wi-Fi. In-hotel: restaurant, room service, bar, gym, spa, laundry service, Wi-Fi hotspot, parking (paid), some pets allowed* ☰ *AE, D, DC, MC, V* Ⓜ *C, E to 50th St.* ✛ *4:A3.*

$$$ 🛏 **Jumeirah Essex House.** New managers Jumeirah Hotel Group aimed high with a $90 million refurbishment program for this famed property in 2007, and it still looks spiffy several years on. The lobby of this stately Central Park South property is an Art Deco masterpiece, with inlaid marble floors and bas-relief elevator doors. Dreaming of Central Park? It's across the street. Reproductions of Chippendale or Louis XV antiques decorate guest rooms, all of which have marble bathrooms and luxuriously comfortable beds. Afternoon tea in the lobby lounge is elegantly arranged. Kerry Heffernan's South Gate draws a European crowd to its design-conscious interior with an extensive wine list. **Pros:** great service; amazing views; impressive restaurant. **Cons:** overly complex room gadgetry; very expensive bar. ⊠ *160 Central Park S, between 6th and 7th Aves., Midtown West* ☎ *212/247–0300 or 800/937–8461* ⊕ *www.jumeirahessexhouse.com* ⤵ *515 rooms, 70 suites* ⌂ *In-room: a/c, safe, Internet, Wi-Fi. In-hotel: 2 restaurants, room service, bar, gym, spa, laundry service, Internet terminal, Wi-Fi hotspot, parking (paid), some pets allowed* ☰ *AE, D, DC, MC, V* Ⓜ *F, N, R, Q, W to 57th St.* ✛ *4:C1.*

¢   🛏 **La Quinta Inn.** The name may conjure a cheapie siesta spot, but don't dismiss it: smack in the middle of Koreatown and close to Penn Station, this budget-friendly hotel in a cheerful old Beaux-Arts building may be one of the best deals in town. Never mind the drab green and burgundy decor when your room features treats like free Wi-Fi, an iPod plug-in, and a bathtub. In the morning the free Continental breakfast goes beyond the usual fare by including granola and oatmeal. Perhaps the best part about staying here is access to Mé Bar. In the evening both guests and locals head up to this year-round mellow rooftop bar for a cocktail in the shadow of the Empire State Building. **Pros:** self-check-in machines; gift shop on the premises for necessities. **Cons:** no room service; no frills. ⊠ *17 W. 32nd St., between 5th Ave. and Broadway, Midtown West* ☎ *212/736–1600* ⊕ *www.lq.com* ⤵ *182 rooms* ⌂ *In-room: a/c, safe, Wi-Fi. In-hotel: bar, gym, laundry facilities, Wi-Fi hotspot, parking (paid)* ☰ *AE, D, DC, MC, V* Ⓜ *B, D, F, N, Q, R, V, W to 34th St./Herald Sq.* ✛ *4:E6.*

$$ 🛏 **Le Parker Meridien.** A splash of kookiness in otherwise staid Midtown, ☾ the Parker is a whimsical place to visit, and the little touches shine through. Start with the lobby, where Burger Joint is hiding behind a velvet curtain. This carefully dressed-down fast-food restaurant serves

one of the city's best patties. If you've got more scratch, there's always the $1,000 omelet at Norma's for brunch or breakfast, though the restaurant also serves slightly more cost-effective options. Rooms are modern functionalist, with low platform beds and televisions hidden in recessed, cherry-paneled cabinets that rotate. Views of Central Park are worth asking after, though city views are also impressive. The 15,000-square-foot gym is one of the largest in the city, and especially nice for a hotel. One caveat: the boffo lobby, with marble floors and archways supported by hand-painted columns, can get crowded at peak times. **Pros:** lively, animated spirit; best hotel gym in the city; fun eating options; tech-friendly rooms. **Cons:** lobby is a public space; small bathrooms. ⊠ *118 W. 57th St., between 6th and 7th Aves., Midtown West* ☎ *212/245–5000 or 800/543–4300* ⊕ *www.parkermeridien.com* ⌁ *484 rooms, 249 suites* ⚴ *In-room: a/c, safe, refrigerator, DVD, Internet. In-hotel: 3 restaurants, room service, bar, pool, gym, spa, laundry service, parking (paid)* ▭ *AE, D, DC, MC, V* Ⓜ *B, D, E, N, Q, R, W to 57th St.* ✛ *4:D1.*

$$$ 🛏 **The London NYC.** Boasting the design expertise of David Collins and the cuisine of Gordon Ramsay in his first stateside restaurant, the London NYC merges the style and flair of both of its namesake cities. Each of the spacious, tech-savvy suites has custom furniture, like an embossed-leather desk, and Egyptian-cotton bedding. Bathrooms are equally well styled, with a Waterworks double-head shower and mosaic tiles. For the ultimate splurge, there's the 54th-floor penthouse London Atrium suite, the highest hotel room in New York. The high-end British concierge service, Quintessentially, attends to your every whim with tireless charm. **Pros:** posh atmosphere without prissiness; Gordon Ramsay restaurant; great fitness club. **Cons:** indifferent service; no bathtubs in most rooms; expensive dining options. ⊠ *151 W. 54th St., between 6th and 7th Aves., Midtown West* ☎ *212/307–5000 or 866/690–2029* ⊕ *www.thelondonnyc.com* ⌁ *561 suites* ⚴ *In-room: a/c, safe, Internet, Wi-Fi. In-hotel: restaurant, room service, bar, gym, laundry service, parking (paid), some pets allowed* ▭ *AE, D, DC, MC, V* Ⓜ *B, D, E to 7th Ave.; N, Q, R, W to 57th St.* ✛ *4:C2.*

$$$$
Fodor's Choice
★
🛏 **Mandarin Oriental.** The Mandarin brings some Asian style to a rather staid corner of New York. Its cavernous lobby sizzles with energy from the 35th floor of the Time Warner Center. From two wonderful lounges and the restaurant Asiate you can soak in dramatic views above Columbus Circle and Central Park. On the higher floors silk throws abound on plush beds, and the marble-clad bathrooms prove the Mandarin's commitment to excess. That said, the regular rooms feel small when they're contrasted with the monumental frame created by floor-to-ceiling glass, and the view it presents. Suites are really what set this hotel apart, by creating enough stage space to make the hotel's Asian-influenced decor really dazzle. The swimming pool is one of the city's best in a hotel, with panoramic Hudson River views, and the elaborate spa is also impressive. A caveat: breakfast at Asiate (around $50) is an expensive proposition, so consider a pastry at Bouchon in the Time Warner Center instead. **Pros:** fantastic pool views; all the resources of the Time Warner Center; expansive suites. **Cons:** Trump

19

hotel blocks portion of park views; expensive; mall-like surroundings. ⊠ *80 Columbus Circle, at 60th St., Midtown West* 🖼 *212/805–8800* ⊕ *www.mandarinoriental.com* ⬧ *203 rooms, 46 suites* ⬧ *In-room: a/c, refrigerator, DVD, Internet, Wi-Fi. In-hotel: restaurant, room service, bar, pool, gym, spa, laundry service* ⊟ *AE, D, DC, MC, V* Ⓜ *A, B, C, D, 1 to 59th St./Columbus Circle* ⊹ *5:C6.*

$$ 🖼 **The Mansfield.** They sweat the small stuff at the Mansfield. Wi-Fi is free, bathroom products are from Aveda, and even the key cards are snazzily embossed with scenes of old-timey New York. Built in 1904 as lodging for distinguished bachelors, the small, clubby property has an Edwardian sensibility that shows in the working fireplace in the lounge, the lobby's coffered ceiling, and a marble-and-cast-iron staircase. Small and clubby extends to the "petite" rooms—110 square feet, with microscopic bathrooms. The intimate M Bar, lined with books and leather banquettes, is one of the nicer hotel bars in town. **Pros:** complimentary Wi-Fi; business center; 24-hour gym; great bar. **Cons:** tiny bathrooms; air-conditioners are window units. ⊠ *12 W. 44th St., between 5th and 6th Aves., Midtown West* 🖼 *212/944–6050 or 800/255–5167* ⊕ *www. mansfieldhotel.com* ⬧ *124 rooms, 25 suites* ⬧ *In-room: a/c, safe, Wi-Fi. In-hotel: restaurant, room service, bar, laundry service, Internet terminal, Wi-Fi hotspot, parking (paid), some pets allowed* ⊟ *AE, D, DC, MC, V* Ⓜ *B, D, F, V to 42nd St.* ⊹ *4:E4.*

$$$ 🖼 **The Michelangelo.** Italophiles will feel that they've been transported to the good life in the boot at this deluxe hotel, where the long, wide lobby lounge is clad with multihue marble and Veronese-style oil paintings. Upstairs, rooms are relatively spacious (averaging 475 square feet). You can choose contemporary, neoclassical, Art Deco, or French country styles—all have marble foyers and marble bathrooms equipped with bidets and oversize 55-gallon tubs. (The different styles are mainly manifested in bedspreads and different colored furniture.) Complimentary cappuccino, pastries, and other Italian treats are served each morning in the baroque lobby lounge. The hotel is a few blocks from Rockefeller Center and 5th Avenue shopping. Insieme, an exemplary modern Italian restaurant, is on the ground floor. **Pros:** good location; fantastic restaurant; spacious rooms. **Cons:** noisy air-conditioning units; some rooms have limited views; small closets. ⊠ *152 W. 51st St., at 7th Ave., Midtown West* 🖼 *212/765–1900 or 800/237–0990* ⊕ *www.michelangelohotel.com* ⬧ *123 rooms, 56 suites* ⬧ *In-room: a/c, Internet. In-hotel: restaurant, room service, bar, gym, laundry service, Internet terminal, parking (paid)* ⊟ *AE, D, DC, MC, V* ⦿ *CP* Ⓜ *B, D, E to 7th Ave.; 1 to 50th St.; B, D, F, V to 47th–50th Sts./Rockefeller Center* ⊹ *4:C3.*

$ 🖼 **Muse Hotel.** Fresh off a 2009 renovation, the Muse is a bit more staid than it once was. Yes, the Surrealist prints and busts of Thalia, the muse of comedy, remain, and so do the cheeky robes—now they're zebra print. Rooms, however, are slightly toned down, in black and cream. The new restaurant, Nios, is one of the better contemporary Greek spots in the city, and overall Kimpton has given a nice shine to their property. It's also very pet-friendly—there's even a Pomeranian concierge to greet guests and their furry friends. Six rooms have balconies, and three spa suites have deep hot tubs and separate showers. **Pros:** contemporary interiors; good Midtown location; pet-friendly. **Cons:** street noise; small gym. ⊠ *130 W. 46th St., between 6th and 7th Aves., Midtown West* ☎ *212/485–2400 or 877/692–6873* ⊕ *www.themusehotel.com* ⟿ *200 rooms, 19 suites* ⟳ *In-room: a/c, safe, Wi-Fi. In-hotel: restaurant, room service, bar, gym, laundry service, Internet terminal, Wi-Fi hotspot, parking (paid), some pets allowed* ⊟ *AE, D, DC, MC, V* Ⓜ *Subway: B, D, F, V to 47th–50th Sts./Rockefeller Center* ✛ *4:C4.*

$$$$

Fodor'sChoice

★

🍽 **Plaza Hotel.** Eloise's adopted home on the corner of Central Park, the Plaza is back in the hotel game after a $400 million renovation. Some, but not all, of the rooms were turned into condos, and the hallways are now narrower, as they don't have to accommodate two ladies in full skirts passing each other at the same time anymore. Once again, the hotel is host to all manner of dignitaries, moneymakers, and royalty, as befits one of New York's most storied hotels. Service is a centerpiece, with white-glove butlers for each floor and a portable touch screen in each room for contacting the concierge or just turning down the lights. The rooms themselves strike a balance between old-fashioned and modern: yes, there are flat-screen televisions, iPod docks, and a DVD player, but the design is old school, with opulent gold-leaf fixtures, a faux-fur throw on the bed's Mascioni linens, and big, Beaux-Arts-style headboards. The Oak Room remains a lavish splurge, but the real joy is a drink at the Oak Bar, with its wood filigrees looking better than ever. An Eloise-themed tea is planned for the Palm Court starting in 2010. The expansive Vinothérapie spa includes a hammam (Turkish bath) and a wine lounge. **Pros:** historic property; great hotel bar; lavish rooms. **Cons:** rooms aren't that big for the money; Oak Room restaurant is pricey. ⊠ *768 5th Ave., at Central Park S, Midtown West* ☎ *212/759–3000* ⊕ *www.theplaza.com* ⟿ *282 rooms, 102 suites* ⟳ *In-room: a/c, safe, DVD, Wi-Fi. In-hotel: 2 restaurants, room service, bar, gym, spa, laundry service, Wi-Fi hotspot* ⊟ *AE, D, DC, MC, V* Ⓜ *N, R, W to 59th St.* ✛ *4:E1.*

¢

🍽 **The President.** After a $15 million renovation that transformed it from a ho-hum Best Western, the President is the only politically-themed hotel in the city. It starts with the purple color scheme, a combination of Republican red and Democratic blue. Portraits and other antique presidential gewgaws are scattered throughout the hallways and rooms— suites have Revolutionary War uniforms on freestanding body forms. The lobby fills up at peak times with families and older folks preparing to set off on their day; at the back, Primary, the hotel's bar, is popular with an after-work crowd. Standard rooms have been touched up with white vinyl couches, Lucite furnishings, and flat-screen TVs; they're small, and the moody, colored lighting makes up for the lack of natural light. Bathrooms are even darker, but that can be forgiven for this price. Times Square and the Theater District are at your doorstep here, which makes things convenient, if crowded come nightfall. Guests get free access to the nearby New York Sports Club and, upon request, pre-loaded iPods. **Pros:** sleek rooms for the price; convenient location. **Cons:** cramped lobby; dark bathrooms; poor views. ⊠ *234 W. 48th St., between 8th Ave. and Broadway, Times Square* ☎ *212/246–8800*

19

Kids in Tow

Many New York hotels go out of their way to accommodate families, with special amenities and family-size rooms. However, a hotel claiming that it's child-friendly doesn't always translate to true kid-welcoming style. Ask if cribs come with linens, whether there are high chairs and children's menus in the dining room, and if there are in-house babysitters. Some hotels will even clear out the minibar (for bottle or baby-food storage), baby-proof a room, or provide baby-proofing materials. Here are some of the top picks for traveling with kids.

SUITE LIFE. Space is at a premium in New York hotels, and if you have more than two people in a standard room you'll really start to feel the squeeze. The answer? A suite, where you can spread out in style. The **Embassy Suites New York** (⇨ *Lower Manhattan*), a tried-and-true family option, is even more kid-friendly in New York, since it's in the same building as a multiplex movie theater and several reasonably priced dining options. With renovated, spacious suites, **Affinia 50** (⇨ *Midtown East and Upper East Side*) is the family hotel of choice on the residential East Side.

PURE PAMPERING. Just because you have children in tow doesn't mean your dream of a pampering vacation needs to go down the drain. Several top New York hotels go out of their way to accommodate families. The

Ritz-Carlton's two hotels (⇨ *Lower Manhattan and Midtown West and Chelsea*) offer special healthful children's menus, rubber-duck-filled baths, and toy menus from FAO Schwarz. The Battery Park location has children's etiquette classes the first Saturday of the month; the Central Park branch holds special teddy bear teas.

FUN FLAVOR. Room Mate Grace (⇨ *Midtown West and Chelsea*) might make the perfect respite if you have teens in tow. There's a funky lobby pool; a kiosk that stocks sweets with which to fill the in-room refrigerators; and rooms with bunk beds that levitate out of the walls and have their own plasma TVs. At the hip **Hotel on Rivington** (⇨ *East Village and Lower East Side*) a special family suite has two full bedrooms, one with two sets of bunk beds and a big bin of toys, two full baths, and a Japanese tub. Bonus points: the hotel is across from Economy Candy.

KID KARMA. Family-friendly **Le Parker Meridien** (⇨ *Midtown West and Chelsea*) has a large pool, a restaurant that serves decadent breakfast foods such as chocolate French toast until 3 PM, and a casual dining spot that serves nothing but burgers and shakes. Upon check-in at the **Omni Berkshire Place** (⇨ *Midtown East and Upper East Side*), kids get a goodie bag and a loaner backpack.

⊕ *www.bestwesternnewyork.com* ⟿ *334 rooms* ⚕ *In-room: a/c, safe, Wi-Fi. In-hotel: restaurant, room service, bar, laundry service, Internet terminal, Wi-Fi hotspot* ⊟ *AE, MC, V* Ⓜ *C, E to 50th St.* ✛ *4:C3.*

$ 🗔 **Renaissance Hotel.** After a $26 million refresh headed by designer Jordan Mozer, the Renaissance shifted in fall 2009 from all business to wacky and whimsical, and it's a rather enjoyable move. Rooms are carpeted in wavy orange with blue headboards and mosaic tile showers. Little touches, like flat-screen televisions and elegant metal vases, round out the look. The theme continues in the lobby, with copper wall coverings and space-age light fixtures. The Two Times Square restaurant serves standard American grub, though the space is more about the view than the cuisine. **Pros:** contemporary design; latest in-room technology. **Cons:** in the heart of the Square: pandemonium isn't for everyone; over-the-top design not for everyone. ⊠ *714 7th Ave., between W. 47th and W. 48th Sts., Midtown West* ☎ *212/765–7676 or 800/628–5222* ⊕ *www.renaissancehotels.com* ⇌ *300 rooms, 5 suites* ⚏ *In-room: a/c, safe, Internet, Wi-Fi. In-hotel: restaurant, room service, bars, gym, laundry service, Internet terminal, Wi-Fi hotspot, parking (paid), some pets allowed* ⊟ *AE, D, DC, MC, V* Ⓜ *R, W to 49th St.; 1 to 50th St.* ✢ *4:C3.*

$$$$
Fodor'sChoice
★
☺

Ⓣ **Ritz-Carlton New York, Central Park.** It's all about the park views here. Service aside, the competition among properties near the Park's south side is fierce, and while the Ritz isn't the foremost of the bunch, it does offer some nice perks. Chief among them is the above-and-beyond service, accommodating to a fault, that makes it popular with celebs and other demanding guests. Rooms have typical high-end perks (Frédéric Fekkai bath products, 400 thread count Egyptian cotton bedding) and one that's not so standard: a telescope for viewing park wildlife. The gym is small, however, as is the La Prairie Spa. Laurent Tourondel operates the seasonal BLT Market restaurant on the ground floor. **Pros:** great concierge; personalized service; stellar location; views. **Cons:** pricey; limited common areas. ⊠ *50 Central Park S, at 6th Ave., Midtown West* ☎ *212/308–9100 or 800/241–3333* ⊕ *www.ritzcarlton.com* ⇌ *259 rooms, 47 suites* ⚏ *In-room: a/c, safe, DVD (some), Internet, Wi-Fi. In-hotel: restaurant, room service, bar, gym, spa, laundry service, parking (paid), some pets allowed* ⊟ *AE, D, DC, MC, V* Ⓜ *F, V to 57th St.* ✢ *4:D1.*

$
☺

Ⓣ **Room Mate Grace.** A favorite of European visitors and business travelers in fashion and entertainment, Grace delivers high-design lodgings on a budget. The decor is modern and playful—Jonathan Adler reflective wallpaper, bright geometric patterns, and a check-in desk that doubles as a newsstand. Guests and locals gravitate to the lobby bar and swimming-pool lounge (a real glassed-in pool, with sauna and steam room) for cocktails and eye candy. Rooms are smallish, around 230 square feet to 300 square feet, but smartly designed (comfortable beds are elevated on platforms, so luggage can be stored underneath) and well insulated from street noise. Room capacity varies from two to four people (in a quad bunk-bed layout—each bed with its own TV and headset), convenient for traveling with teenagers or kids. **Pros:** free, ample Continental breakfast; friendly, helpful staff. **Cons:** tiny rooms; little in-room privacy (no door separating shower from main room). ⊠ *125 W. 45th St., Midtown West* ☎ *212/354–2323* ⊕ *www.room-matehotels.com* ⇌ *139 rooms* ⚏ *In-room: a/c, safe, refrigerator, DVD, Wi-Fi. In-hotel: bar, pool, gym, laundry service, parking (paid)* ⊟ *AE, D, DC, MC, V* ❘◎❘ *BP* Ⓜ *B, D, F, V to 42nd St.* ✢ *4:D4.*

$$$–$$$$

Ⓣ **The Royalton.** During the 1990s the Royalton's dramatic lobby started the craze of local A-listers meeting and greeting in hotel bars. The

19

space, after being completely redesigned by Roman and Williams, now attracts a new generation of movers and shakers to congregate around its sumptuous sofas and the warm glow of its massive cast-bronze fireplace. Brasserie 44 is also an excellent locale for a quick bite. Before you can get to your room, you'll have to run the gauntlet of this bustling lounge, but the efficient check-in and helpful staff ensure that things go smoothly. Updated guest rooms, designed by Charlotte Macaux, are all comfortably sleek and elegantly outfitted with atmospheric lighting, fresh flowers, and candles changed daily. Some rooms have working fireplaces, and all have plasma-screen TVs. Bathrooms have been sumptuously renovated with huge circular Roman soaking tubs and rainfall showers. **Pros:** hip lobby scene; luxe beds and bathrooms; helpful service. **Cons:** dark hallways; lighting verges on eye-strainingly dim. ⊠ *44 W. 44th St., between 5th and 6th Aves., Midtown West* ☎ *212/869–4400 or 800/635–9013* ⊕ *www.royaltonhotel.com* ⇗ *141 rooms, 27 suites* ⚘ *In-room: a/c, safe, Internet, Wi-Fi. In-hotel: restaurant, room service, bar, gym, laundry service, Internet terminal, Wi-Fi hotspot, parking (paid)* ▭ *AE, D, DC, MC, V* Ⓜ *B, D, F, V to 42nd St.* ✛ *4:D4.*

$$ ⊡ **The Shoreham.** The Shoreham hopes to attract glamorous types, but the end result is that all the guests feel like they're stars. First, there's a glass of Champagne for you at check-in. In the lobby, you'll see lime-green couches, a small café off to the side, and plenty of people admiring themselves in the mirrored columns. Spring for one of the rooms with massage chairs, which are an inexpensive upgrade. Tech is big here; you can request an Xbox 360 or PS2, and rooms are also equipped with free Wi-Fi and flat-screen televisions. **Pros:** stylish decor; tech-friendly. **Cons:** not designed for families; snooty service. ⊠ *33 W. 55th St., between 5th and 6th Aves., Midtown West* ☎ *212/247–6700 or 877/847–4444* ⊕ *www.shorehamhotel.com* ⇗ *174 rooms, 37 suites* ⚘ *In-room: a/c, safe, DVD, Wi-Fi. In-hotel: restaurant, room service, bar, laundry service, Internet terminal, Wi-Fi hotspot, parking (paid), some pets allowed* ▭ *AE, D, DC, MC, V* ⟊Ⓞⵏ *CP* Ⓜ *E, V to 5th Ave.* ✛ *4:D2.*

$$ ⊡ **Sofitel New York.** This property brings Gallic flair to the neighborhood. In addition to bilingual signage throughout the hotel, there's plenty of velvet in the lobby, along with leather couches and vases of flowers. Guest rooms go the European modern route, with blond-wood headboards, silver wall sconces, and a big work desk. The bathrooms, with tubs and showers in every room, are a nice bonus. Some rooms overlook the Chrysler Building. The hotel's French restaurant, Gaby, is named after a Parisian model from the 1920s, and the food dates from about the same era—it's rich, heavy, and filling. **Pros:** central location; great beds. **Cons:** pricey; room views vary. ⊠ *45 W. 44th St., between 5th and 6th Aves., Midtown West* ☎ *212/354–8844* ⊕ *www.sofitel.com* ⇗ *346 rooms, 52 suites* ⚘ *In-room: a/c, safe, Wi-Fi. In-hotel: restaurant, room service, bar, gym, laundry service, Internet terminal, Wi-Fi hotspot, parking (paid)* ▭ *AE, D, DC, MC, V* Ⓜ *B, D, F, V to 42nd St.* ✛ *4:E4.*

$$ ⊞ **The Time Hotel.** One of the neighborhood's first boutique hotels, this spot half a block from the din of Times Square tempers trendiness with a touch of humor. A ridiculously futuristic glass elevator—eggshells line the bottom of the shaft—transports guests to the second-floor lobby. In the adjoining bar nature videos lighten up the low-slung, serious, gray-scale furnishings, while local DJs spin a fresh selection of music in the trendy Time Lounge. The smallish guest rooms, each themed to one of the primary colors—red, yellow, or blue—have mood lighting and even specific "color" aromas that create a unique, if contrived, hotel experience. Whatever your primary color, they boast iPod docks, large flat-screen TVs, and modern, if not especially comfortable, beds and couches. **Pros:** acclaimed and popular Serafina restaurant downstairs; surprisingly quiet for Times Square location; good turndown service. **Cons:** decor makes the rooms a little dated; service is inconsistent; water pressure is lacking. ⊠ *224 W. 49th St., between Broadway and 8th Ave., Midtown West* ☎ *212/320–2900 or 877/846–3692* ⊕ *www.thetimeny. com* ⤳ *164 rooms, 29 suites* ⌂ *In-room: a/c, safe, Internet. In-hotel: restaurant, room service, bar, gym, laundry service, Internet terminal, parking (paid)* ⊟ *AE, D, DC, MC, V* Ⓜ *1, C, E to 50th St.* ✛ *4:C3.*

$ ⊞ **W Times Square.** First opened at the end of 2001, the W Times Square is looking sleek once again thanks to a recent renovation. One thing they didn't tinker with: the iconic, 57-story exterior, which still stands out among the Times Square craziness. The biggest benefit is in the rooms, with pink and purple accents, hideaway cabinets, a floating platform with a fantastic featherbed, and sleek bathrooms. The more expensive rooms on the higher floors have impressive views to the west over the Hudson River. Blue Fin, the sushi restaurant, and the "Living Room" bar remain popular, if pricey offshoots of the eighth-floor lobby, which is always flooded with activity. **Pros:** bustling nightlife and happy-hour scene; sleek rooms. **Cons:** if you want quiet, head elsewhere; no bathtubs in the smaller rooms. ⊠ *1567 Broadway, at W. 47th St., Midtown West* ☎ *212/930–7400 or 877/946–8357* ⊕ *www.whotels. com* ⤳ *464 rooms, 43 suites* ⌂ *In-room: a/c, safe, DVD, Internet. In-hotel: restaurant, room service, bar, gym, spa, laundry service, Internet terminal, Wi-Fi hotspot, some pets allowed* ⊟ *AE, D, DC, MC, V* Ⓜ *1, 2, 3, 7, N, Q, R, W, S to 42nd St./Times Sq.* ✛ *4:C3.*

19

$$–$$$ ⊞ **Warwick.** This grande dame was built by William Randolph Hearst for his mistress, Hollywood actress Marion Davies. It's hosted many from Tinseltown since then, including Cary Grant in the Presidential Suite for 12 years. Though there are many different room categories, the Premier Suites have benefited from a recent refresh that includes a sea-foam color scheme, flat-screen televisions, and Bulgari bath products. Some of the higher-floor suites have terraces overlooking 6th Avenue. The more standard rooms are a bit tired, however, and some come with "New York-y" views of an airshaft. The Murals on 54 restaurant, which takes up a big portion of the ground floor, serves Italian-influenced American fare under the gaze of 1930s-era murals—try to spot the "obscene" additions that the artist inserted after a disagreement with Hearst. Randolph's Bar remains packed late into the evening. **Pros:** excellent restaurant and bar; historic property; spacious suites. **Cons:**

Mandarin Oriental

Plaza Hotel

Ritz-Carlton New York, Central Park South

Inn at Irving Place

The Peninsula

The St. Regis

not all rooms have been redone; no a/c in the hallways. ✉ *65 W. 54th St., at 6th Ave., Midtown West* ☎ *212/247–2700 or 800/223–4099* ⊕ *www.warwickhotelny.com* ⤴ *359 rooms, 66 suites* ⚘ *In-room: a/c, safe, refrigerator, Wi-Fi. In-hotel: 2 restaurants, room service, bar, gym, laundry service, parking (paid)* ⊟ *AE, DC, MC, V* Ⓜ *E, V to 57th St.; N, Q, R, W to 57th St.* ✛ *4:D2.*

$ 🛎 **Wellington Hotel.** A few blocks south of Central·Park and Columbus
🅒 Circle, the Wellington is a fine jumping-off point for visitors who want to see the sights in Midtown and the Upper West Side. The vibe in the rooms is more classic New York than edgy or modern, with floral patterns and dark-wood headboards and chests. The bathrooms, which are small and dark, don't have much to recommend them. Suites, however, are spacious, and include fold-out couches and extra beds—great for large families. Molyvos, a boisterous Greek restaurant in the hotel, is an excellent dining option, and the breakfast area doubles as a classic diner the rest of the day. The staff is quite amenable to requests. The hotel runs clever themed packages during holidays. **Pros:** central location; chipper staff; good for big families. **Cons:** dark bathrooms; limited breakfast. ✉ *871 7th Ave., at W. 55th St., Midtown West* ☎ *212/247–3900 or 800/652–1212* ⊕ *www.wellingtonhotel.com* ⤴ *600 rooms, 100 suites* ⚘ *In-room: a/c, Wi-Fi. In-hotel: restaurant, bar, laundry facilities, laundry service, Internet terminal, Wi-Fi hotspot, parking (paid)* ⊟ *AE, D, DC, MC, V* Ⓜ *N, Q, R, W to 57th St.* ✛ *4:C2.*

$ 🛎 **Westin New York at Times Square.** Renovations are ongoing at this Westin in the heart of it all, so your experience can vary wildly depending on what type of room you get. Older rooms are a bit tired, though all come with the Heavenly Bed, flat-screen televisions, and Ethernet. For even more comfort, spa-floor rooms come with massage chairs, aromatherapy candles, and other pampering pleasures. Though it costs $10 for entry, the gym is impressive, and it even includes Wii Fit and running tours throughout the city. The huge lobby gets crowded during busy check-in and check-out times; Shula's Steakhouse is a pricey dining option. **Pros:** busy Times Square location; big rooms; great gym. **Cons:** busy Times Square location; small bathroom sinks; some rooms need to be refreshed. ✉ *270 W. 43rd St., at 8th Ave., Midtown West* ☎ *212/201–2700 or 866/837–4183* ⊕ *www.westinny.com* ⤴ *737 rooms, 126 suites* ⚘ *In-room: a/c, safe, refrigerator, Internet, Wi-Fi. In-hotel: restaurant, room service, bars, gym, spa, laundry service, Internet terminal, Wi-Fi hotspot, parking (paid), some pets allowed* ⊟ *AE, D, DC, MC, V* Ⓜ *A, C, E to 42nd St./Times Sq.* ✛ *4:B4.*

MIDTOWN EAST AND UPPER EAST SIDE

MIDTOWN EAST

$$ 🛎 **Affinia 50.** This extremely popular hotel has a businesslike mood, but
🅒 it's also supremely comfortable for families or leisure travelers. Most studios and all suites have plenty of space to stretch out in, with full kitchens and a clean, playful design that incorporates oversize chairs and couches. The second-floor club lounge provides business services and board games for guest use. Those aren't the only quirky amenities, either: there's an "evening cheer" reception with complimentary wine

and cheese Monday through Thursday, fruit and iced tea at reception, and a six-choice pillow menu. All rooms have a mini-refrigerator and microwave, and suites have countertop stoves. **Pros:** apartment-style living; good value; kid- and pet-friendly. **Cons:** ugly lobby; old televisions; pricey Wi-Fi. ⊠ *155 E. 50th St., at 3rd Ave., Midtown East* ☎ *212/751–5710 or 800/637–8483* ⊕ *www.affinia.com* ⤹ *56 rooms, 151 suites* ♿ *In-room: a/c, safe, kitchen (some), refrigerator, Internet. In-hotel: room service, gym, laundry facilities, laundry service, Internet terminal, Wi-Fi hotspot, parking (paid), some pets allowed* ⊟ *AE, D, DC, MC, V* Ⓜ *6 to 51st St./Lexington Ave.; E, V to Lexington–3rd Aves./53rd St.* ✛ *4:G3.*

$$$ 🖼 **The Alex.** Often overlooked in a part of the city that's heavy with office buildings, the Alex is a sleek little oasis of style on Manhattan's East Side. This David Rockwell–designed property is all about the brand names, especially in the suites. You'll see Sub-Zero fridges, Poggenpohl cabinets, and kitchenettes with Gaggenau stove tops and Miele dishwashers. Standard rooms have flat-screen TVs, including one that's mounted in the bathroom mirror, and the posh beds come with Frette linens and hypoallergenic pillows. The end result is a quiet, calm room, and only the sub par views intrude. Award-winning chef Marcus Samuelsson runs the Asian-inflected Riingo restaurant, which also provides room service. **Pros:** most rooms have kitchens; good service; on-site fitness facilities. **Cons:** cramped lobby; small bathrooms; expensive Wi-Fi. ⊠ *205 E. 45th St., between 2nd and 3rd Aves., Midtown East* ☎ *212/867–5100* ⊕ *www.thealexhotel.com* ⤹ *73 rooms, 130 suites* ♿ *In-room: a/c, kitchen (some), refrigerator (some), DVD, Internet. In-hotel: restaurant, room service, bar, gym, laundry service, Internet terminal, Wi-Fi hotspot, parking (paid), some pets allowed* ⊟ *AE, MC, V* Ⓜ *4, 5, 6, 7, S to 42nd St./Grand Central* ✛ *4:G4.*

$$$ 🖼 **The Benjamin.** New York bills itself as the City that Never Sleeps, but of course a good night's rest is essential for visitors who plan to tackle a lot during the day. The Benjamin promotes itself as just the ticket to fight sleeping problems, with a 13-pillow menu to choose from (they include buckwheat, water, and Swedish memory varieties), white-noise machines, and 400-thread-count sheets. While you're awake, you can take advantage of the kitchenettes in some of the rooms, a handy location near Grand Central Terminal, and quality service from a friendly staff. The views—of a neighboring hotel—are a bit blah, however, and the bathrooms could stand to have more style. **Pros:** sleep-friendly; gracious staff; kitchenettes in big rooms. **Cons:** paid Internet and Wi-Fi; boring views; dull neighborhood after dark. ⊠ *125 E. 50th St., at Lexington Ave., Midtown East* ☎ *212/715–2500* ⊕ *www.thebenjamin.com* ⤹ *200 rooms* ♿ *In-room: a/c, safe, kitchen (some), refrigerator, Internet, Wi-Fi. In-hotel: restaurant, room service, bar, gym, spa, laundry service, Internet terminal, parking (paid), some pets allowed* ⊟ *AE, D, DC, MC, V* ⦿*EP* Ⓜ *6 to 51st St./Lexington Ave.; E, V to Lexington–3rd Aves./53rd St.* ✛ *4:F3.*

$$$ 🖼 **The Dylan.** This hotel made a big splash when it opened at the start of the decade, but there haven't been many changes since then, and it's starting to show. Business travelers like the location a block from

19

Grand Central, and the Benjamin, the grand steak house within. The 1903 Beaux-Arts building includes ornate plasterwork on the facade and a stunning marble staircase spiraling up its three floors. The 11-foot ceilings (the lower the floor, the higher the ceilings) give the modern guest rooms a touch of grandeur, and the beakers that serve as glasses in the bathrooms are a clever nod to the building's past as home of the Chemists' Club. Note that some rooms remain small and dark, even after reconstruction. **Pros:** central location; free Internet; new room furnishings. **Cons:** inattentive service; small fitness center; pricey for limited amenities. ✉ *52 E. 41st St., between Park and Madison Aves., Midtown East* ☎ *212/338–0500* ⊕ *www.dylanhotel.com* ☞ *107 rooms, 5 suites* ♿ *In-room: a/c, safe, Internet, Wi-Fi. In-hotel: restaurant, room service, bar, gym, Wi-Fi hotspot* ➡ *AE, D, DC, MC, V* Ⓜ *4, 5, 6, 7, S to 42nd St./Grand Central* ✢ *4:E5.*

$$$$ ☒ **Four Seasons Hotel.** It's the Four Seasons, and for better or worse, it remains the blueprint for what a Manhattan luxury hotel should be. Sure, that also means it's outrageously expensive, but you get a fair amount of bang for your buck: stellar service that goes to the ends of the earth for guests, an imposing lobby done in marble and blond wood; a connected concierge than can get reservations at most of New York's hot tables. The rooms are impressively sized and priced, starting at 600 square feet (and $855 in high season). For that hefty cost you get a mattress custom-designed for the hotel, 10-foot ceilings, flat-screen television, and a marble bathroom with a tub that fills in 60 seconds flat. One complaint is the electronic system for controlling the lights and drapes, which can get confusing; overall, the feel is conservative and perhaps too restrained for the price. Dinner at the counter of esteemed restaurant L'Atelier de Joël Robuchon is a can't-miss splurge. **Pros:** spacious and comfortable rooms; perfect concierge and staff service; afternoon tea in the lobby lounge. **Cons:** pricey; confusing room controls. ✉ *57 E. 57th St., between Park and Madison Aves., Midtown East* ☎ *212/758–5700 or 800/487–3769* ⊕ *www.fourseasons.com* ☞ *300 rooms, 68 suites* ♿ *In-room: a/c, safe, DVD, Internet, Wi-Fi. In-hotel: restaurant, room service, bar, gym, spa, laundry service, Internet terminal, Wi-Fi hotspot, parking (paid), some pets allowed* ➡ *AE, D, DC, MC, V* Ⓜ *4, 5, 6, N, Q, R, W to 59th St./Lexington Ave.* ✢ *4:F1.*

$$
Fodor's Choice
★
☒ **Library Hotel.** Bookishly handsome, this stately landmark brownstone, built in 1900, is inspired by the New York Public Library, a block away. Each of its 10 floors is dedicated to one of the 10 categories of the Dewey Decimal System; modern rooms are stocked with art and books relevant to a subtopic such as erotica, astronomy, or biography— let your interests guide your choice. Either way, many of the rooms are surprisingly big and offer a good value to "check out." The staff is very hospitable, and the whole property is old-leather-armchair comfortable, whether you're unwinding in front of the library fireplace, partaking of the complimentary wine and cheese or Continental breakfast, or relaxing in the roof garden. **Pros:** fun rooftop bar; playful book themes; stylish rooms. **Cons:** rooftop often reserved for events; more books in rooms themselves would be nice. ✉ *299 Madison Ave., at E. 41st St., Midtown East* ☎ *212/983–4500 or 877/793–7323* ⊕ *www.libraryhotel.*

com ↪ *60 rooms* ♻ *In-room: a/c, safe, refrigerator, DVD, Internet, Wi-Fi. In-hotel: restaurant, room service, bar, laundry service, parking (paid)* ⊟ *AE, DC, MC, V* ⏺ *CP* Ⓜ *4, 5, 6, 7, S to 42nd St./Grand Central* ✛ *4:E4.*

$$$ ⬚ **Loews Regency Hotel.** The snazzy lobby sums up the focus of this Park Avenue hotel: service and space. The modern guest rooms have lush details like silk wallpaper and mahogany accents, but more important, are large for the price point and come with flat-screen TVs and high-speed Internet. (That space comes at the expense of the bathrooms, which are on the small side.) Goose-down duvets and ergonomic leather desk chairs reinforce the pleasingly modern feel. Feinstein's at the Regency hosts some of the best (and priciest) cabaret acts in town, and 540 Park has become a destination in its own right among restaurant-savvy locals. **Pros:** friendly and helpful staff; relatively quiet; good for pets. **Cons:** rooms are pretty but not a great value; overpriced room service. ✉ *540 Park Ave., at E. 61st St., Midtown East* ☎ *212/759–4100 or 800/233–2356* ⊕ *www.loewshotels.com* ↪ *266 rooms, 87 suites* ♻ *In-room: a/c, safe, kitchen (some), refrigerator, Internet. In-hotel: restaurant, room service, bar, gym, laundry service, parking (paid), some pets allowed* ⊟ *AE, D, DC, MC, V* Ⓜ *4, 5, 6, N, Q, R, W to 59th St./Lexington Ave.* ✛ *5:F6.*

$$ ⬚ **Millennium UN Plaza.** This sky-high tower near the United Nations begins on the 28th floor. The rooms, which make generous use of warm woods and neutral tones, have breathtaking views—get one facing west, toward Manhattan. The multilingual staff caters to a discerning clientele that includes heads of state. The views also dazzle from the elegant 27th-floor pool and health club, and the indoor rooftop tennis court attracts name players. Service throughout the hotel is first-rate, though the common areas have seen better days. **Pros:** unbeatable East River and city views; good value; great front-door and bell staff. **Cons:** a walk to the subway; pricey Internet access. ✉ *1 United Nations Plaza, at E. 44th St. and 1st Ave., Midtown East* ☎ *212/758–1234 or 866/866–8086* ⊕ *www.millenniumhotels.com* ↪ *382 rooms, 45 suites* ♻ *In-room: a/c, safe, Internet. In-hotel: restaurant, room service, bar, tennis court, pool, gym, laundry service, Internet terminal, Wi-Fi hotspot, parking (paid)* ⊟ *AE, D, DC, MC, V* Ⓜ *4, 5, 6, 7, S to 42nd St./Grand Central* ✛ *4:H4.*

$$$ ⬚ **New York Palace Hotel.** Want the privileged *Gossip Girl* experience? Stay at these connected mansions, built in the 1880s by railroad baron Henry Villard and supposedly populated by Serena van der Woodsen, circa 2009. In the lobby, with its sweeping staircases, golden chandeliers, and arched colonnades, you'll find the acclaimed New American restaurant Gilt. Standard rooms in the main section of the hotel are done up in warming beige and marble, but they are hardly exceptional. The better option is rooms in the tower: either modern or classic, depending on the floor, they have more luxe decor and bathrooms, separate check-in, and more attentive service, with a dedicated concierge and a butler. Many hotel rooms, as well as the 7,000-square-foot health club, have terrific views of St. Patrick's Cathedral. Note that Palace Gate, the alfresco eating and drinking area, is slated for a renovation

19

and will reopen in May 2010. **Pros:** gorgeous courtyard with 15th-century Italian-style motifs; great service; unmatched views of St. Patrick's Cathedral. **Cons:** overpriced; harried service from staff. ⊠ *455 Madison Ave., at E. 50th St., Midtown East* ☎ *212/888–7000 or 800/697–2522* ⊕ *www.newyorkpalace.com* ⤸ *804 rooms, 88 suites* ⏃ *In-room: a/c, safe, refrigerator (some), Internet. In-hotel: 2 restaurants, room service, bars, gym, spa, laundry service, Internet terminal, Wi-Fi hotspot, parking (paid), some pets allowed* ⊟ *AE, D, DC, MC, V* Ⓜ *6 to 51st St./ Lexington Ave.; E, V to Lexington–3rd Aves./53rd St.* ✢ *4:E3.*

$$$$
Fodor's Choice
★
🛏 **The Peninsula.** Stepping through the Peninsula's Beaux-Arts facade onto the grand staircase overhung with a monumental chandelier, you know you're in for a glitzy treat. Service here is world-class, and personalized: expect to be referred to by name as you make your way through the hotel. Rooms have the latest touches in luxury comfort. The views are stunning: see the northward sweep up 5th Avenue to Central Park past church steeples; or look east toward the beautiful St. Regis across the street. The excellent high-tech amenities include a bedside console that controls the lighting, sound, and thermostat for the room as well as a TV mounted over the tub for bath-time viewing (in all but standard rooms). The rooftop health club, with indoor pool, is monumental. The Salon de Ning, a rooftop bar bedecked with chinoiserie, has dazzling views of Midtown. **Pros:** brilliant service; fabulous rooms, with the best lighting of all city hotels (good angles, easy to use); unforgettable rooftop bar. **Cons:** expensive. ⊠ *700 5th Ave., at 55th St., Midtown East* ☎ *212/956–2888 or 800/262–9467* ⊕ *newyork.peninsula.com* ⤸ *185 rooms, 54 suites* ⏃ *In-room: a/c, safe, refrigerator, Internet, Wi-Fi. In-hotel: restaurant, room service, bars, pool, gym, spa, laundry service, parking (paid), some pets allowed* ⊟ *AE, D, DC, MC, V* Ⓜ *E, V to 5th Ave.* ✢ *4:E2.*

¢
🛏 **Pod Hotel.** This is the hotel that made bunk beds cool again—and now they're everywhere. By offering spotless stainless-steel bunks with pull-out flat-screen TVs, the Pod makes tiny, tiny rooms tolerable. If you can handle cramped quarters, this is one of the best deals in Midtown (and it seems spacious compared to the Jane). About half the rooms come with standard queen beds and private bath. The rooms, starting at a meager 100 square feet, borrow space-saving ideas from mass transit, with sink consoles like those in an airplane restroom, and built-in shelves tucked under the beds. In return for the lack of space you get a convenient location and modern amenities like in-room iPod docking stations and free Wi-Fi. Families, take note: five new suites of 336 square feet can give you a little more breathing room. The common areas are cheerful and modern, with an outdoor bar-café and a stylish roof deck. Don't expect luxe linens or fab toiletries. Do expect to book well in advance, as budget-minded hipsters and stylish thrifty folk of all ages keep this hotel hopping. **Pros:** an inexpensive and fun way to save money. **Cons:** many will hate the small rooms; some shared bathrooms. ⊠ *230 E. 51st St., between 2nd and 3rd Aves., Midtown East* ☎ *212/355–0300 or 800/874–0074* ⊕ *www.thepodhotel.com* ⤸ *347 rooms, 195 with bath* ⏃ *In-room: a/c, Wi-Fi* ⊟ *AE, DC, MC, V* Ⓜ *6 to 51st St./Lexington Ave.; E, V to Lexington–3rd Aves./53rd St.* ✢ *4:G2.*

$ ⌑ **Roger Smith**. This quirky choice is one of the better budget buys in the city. The art-filled rooms, matched by the murals in the lobby, are homey and comfortable, with down pillows and quilts on the beds. Some have stocked bookshelves and fireplaces. Suites have kitchenettes. Bathrooms are small, but do have tubs. An eclectic mix of room service is provided by five local restaurants, and guests have access to the nearby New York Sports Club ($10 fee). Rates can drop by as much as $75 per night in winter and summer, so ask when booking. A complimentary Continental breakfast is included. **Pros:** good location near Grand Central; intimate atmosphere; free Wi-Fi. **Cons:** street noise; small bathrooms. ⊠ *501 Lexington Ave., between E. 47th and E. 48th Sts., Midtown East* ☎ *212/755–1400 or 800/445–0277* ⊕ *www. rogersmith.com* ⇆ *102 rooms, 28 suites* ⌂ *In-room: a/c, kitchen (some), refrigerator, Internet, Wi-Fi. In-hotel: restaurant, room service, bar, laundry service, parking (paid), some pets allowed* ⊟ *AE, D, DC, MC, V* ⍩⍣ *CP* Ⓜ *6 to 51st St./Lexington Ave.; E, V to Lexington–3rd Aves./53rd St.* ✛ *4:F3.*

$ ⌑ **Roosevelt Hotel**. Named after Teddy, not Franklin, this Midtown icon steps from Grand Central has plenty of elbow room for stretching out in. An ornate lobby with cushy couches and an old school bar with heavy wood detailing makes the Roosevelt feel like it's from another time, and it should—the property dates from 1924. Happily, the amenities don't hark back to that era, though rooms are a little tired: the carpeting shows some wear, the art on the walls is chain-generic, and the bedding is blah. However, the beds do have pillow-top mattresses, and the bathrooms are nice and big. The rooftop lounge, mad46, serves themed cocktails that include a "Teddy-tini." **Pros:** great public areas; big bathrooms. **Cons:** dated decor; limited in-room amenities. ⊠ *45 E. 45th St., at Madison Ave., Midtown East* ☎ *888/ 833–3969* ⊕ *www. theroosevelthotel.com* ⇆ *1,015 rooms, 24 suites* ⌂ *In-room: a/c, Wi-Fi. In-hotel: restaurant, room service, gym, parking (paid)* ⊟ *AE, MC, V* Ⓜ *4, 5, 6 to Grand Central/42nd St.* ✛ *4:F4.*

$$$$ ⌑ **The St. Regis**. World-class from head to toe, the St. Regis comes as
Fodor's Choice   close to flawless as any hotel in New York. Even without the hive of
★   activity in its unparalleled public spaces, this 5th Avenue Beaux-Arts landmark would rank near the top of any best-of list. You can dine in two dining rooms—including an Alain Ducasse restaurant, Adour—as well as the legendary King Cole Bar, a dimly lighted institution with famously playful Maxfield Parrish murals. In the rooms, easy-to-use bedside consoles (developed by an in-house R&D team) control lighting, audio, and climate; the huge flat-screen TVs rise via remote control from the foot of your bed. Each floor is serviced by its own butler, a touch no other hotel here can match. Rooms have high ceilings, crystal chandeliers, silk wall coverings, Louis XVI antiques—though even at these prices, you're not guaranteed a stellar view or a separate tub in the more basic rooms. Still, if you require the best, the St. Regis delivers. **Pros:** rooms combine true luxury with helpful technology; easy-access butler service; superb in-house dining; prestigious location. **Cons:** expensive; too serious for families seeking fun. ⊠ *2 E. 55th St., at 5th Ave., Midtown East* ☎ *212/753–4500 or 877/787–3447* ⊕ *www.stregis.*

19

comn ↵ *164 rooms, 65 suites* ♿ *In-room: a/c, safe, refrigerator, DVD, Internet. In-hotel: restaurant, room service, gym, laundry service, parking (paid)* ⊟ *AE, D, DC, MC, V* Ⓜ *E, V to 5th Ave.* ✢ *4:E2.*

$$$ ☎ **Sherry-Netherland.** With an iconic sidewalk clock on the southeast corner of Central Park and a captivating finial spire atop its slender form, the Sherry is a stately part of the New York landscape. So it may come as a surprise to learn that it's essentially a tall, luxurious apartment building. The 50 guest rooms on offer come decorated in the fashion of their individual owners, but the standards are kept very high throughout. With a marble-lined lobby, crystal chandeliers, and wall friezes from the Vanderbilt mansion, its historic glamour is undeniable. The luxurious suites—reached via elevator operated by a white-gloved attendant—have separate living and dining areas. Many have decorative fireplaces, antiques, and glorious marble baths. You can use the private hotel entrance to have a complimentary breakfast at Harry Cipriani's. (You might even stay for lunch for some of the best people-watching in town.) **Pros:** gorgeous lobby; commanding, impeccable location; Cipriani access. **Cons:** rooms vary in taste and decor; non-suites are on the small side; interior rooms lack views. ⊠ *781 5th Ave., at E. 59th St., Midtown East* ☏ *212/355–2800 or 800/247–4377* ⊕ *www.sherrynetherland.com* ↵ *30 rooms, 20 suites* ♿ *In-room: a/c, safe, refrigerator, Internet. In-hotel: restaurant, room service, bar, gym, laundry service, parking (paid)* ⊟ *AE, D, DC, MC, V* ⫯Ⓞⵏ *CP* Ⓜ *N, R, Q, W to 5th Ave.* ✢ *5:E6.*

$$$ ☎ **Waldorf=Astoria.** The lobby of this landmark 1931 Art Deco masterpiece, full of murals, mosaics, and elaborate plaster ornamentation, features a grand piano once owned by Cole Porter and still played daily. Standard rooms top out at a cozy 250 square feet, with marble bathrooms and wood headboards to balance the extensive floral patterns. Downstairs, the Bull and Bear Bar is a 1940s throwback complete with miniature soda bottles and no-nonsense barkeeps. The pricier and more luxurious Waldorf Towers (the 28th floor and above) has a separate entrance and management. The Waldorf is famous for its former residents; besides Porter, these have included Herbert Hoover and Nikola Tesla; presidents usually stay here thanks to the security of the drive-in entrance. The new Guerlain spa is an impressive, and much-needed addition. **Pros:** historic Art Deco building filled with NYC's aristocratic, gangster, and jazz histories; best Waldorf salad in town; knowledgeable doormen. **Cons:** rooms not up to date; more about the name than the experience. ⊠ *301 Park Ave., between E. 49th and E. 50th Sts., Midtown East* ☏ *212/355–3000 or 800/925–3673* ⊕ *www.waldorfastoria.com* ↵ *1,176 rooms, 276 suites* ♿ *In-room: a/c, safe, Internet. In-hotel: 4 restaurants, room service, bars, gym, laundry service, Internet terminal, Wi-Fi hotspot, parking (paid), some pets allowed* ⊟ *AE, D, DC, MC, V* Ⓜ *6 to 51st St./Lexington Ave.; E, V to Lexington–3rd Aves./53rd St.* ✢ *4:F3.*

$ ☎ **W Hotel New York.** This was the first of the W hotels to open in New York, and after a decade rooms got a much-needed overhaul in 2008. Window boxes filled with grass, bowls heaped with green apples, flowing curtains, and vast floor-to-ceiling windows that pour sunlight into the airy lobby all conjure up a calming outdoor feeling here—quite a trick considering a hopping bar and a sunken lounge flank the reception area. The rooms hew to the classic W formula: they're small and they look great—especially thanks to the overhaul, which added LED lights around the windows and beds, wooden desks topped with swiveling panes of glass, and amethyst wall coverings in the bathroom. Of course a party-hearty clientele also means you're likely to hear your neighbors partying heartily through the night. Downstairs, Heartbeat Restaurant serves heart-healthy foods; the attached Whiskey Blue

draws a young, hip, and moneyed crowd; and the Bliss Spa flagship draws legions of beauty devotees. **Pros:** central location; great-looking rooms. **Cons:** thin walls; inconsistent service. ⊠ *541 Lexington Ave., between E. 49th and E. 50th Sts., Midtown East* ☎ *212/755–1200 or 877/946–8357* ⊕ *www.whotels.com* ⌁ *629 rooms, 62 suites* ⌂ *In-room: a/c, safe, DVD, Internet. In-hotel: restaurant, room service, bar, gym, spa, laundry service, Internet terminal, Wi-Fi hotspot, some pets allowed* ⊟ *AE, D, DC, MC, V* Ⓜ *6 to 51st St./Lexington Ave.; E, V to Lexington–3rd Aves./53rd St.* ✛ *4:F3.*

UPPER EAST SIDE

$$$$ ⚏ **The Carlyle, A Rosewood Hotel.** On the well-heeled corner of Madison Avenue and 75th Street, this hotel's fusion of venerable elegance and Manhattan swank is like entering a Chanel boutique: walk in chin high, wallet out, and ready to be impressed. As you might expect, everything about this Upper East Side landmark suggests cultivated refinement: rooms decorated with fine antique furniture, vast Central Park views, white-gloved operators working the elevators 24 hours a day. It's all overwhelmingly grand—almost to the point of diminishing comfort. The range of the hotel's dining and entertainment options impresses: Cabaret luminaries take turns holding court at the Café Carlyle (Woody Allen still visits once a week). And Bemelmans Bar is one of the greatest old-school cocktail spots in New York. The polished black slots behind the reception desk, once used to hold room keys, serve as a fashionable reminder of the hotel's storied history as host to presidents and celebrities. **Pros:** perhaps NYC's best Central Park views; refined service; delightful array of dining and bar options. **Cons:** removed from tourist Manhattan; stuffy vibe may not work for families. ⊠ *35 E. 76th St., between Madison and Park Aves., Upper East Side* ☎ *212/744–1600* ⊕ *www.thecarlyle.com* ⌁ *122 rooms, 57 suites* ⌂ *In-room: a/c, safe, refrigerator, DVD, Internet. In-hotel: restaurant, room service, bar, gym, spa, laundry service, parking (paid), some pets allowed* ⊟ *AE, DC, MC, V* Ⓜ *6 to 77th St.* ✛ *5:F3.*

19

$–$$ ☶ **The Franklin.** The Franklin is the best luxury boutique hotel north of 57th Street. And it's way north of 57th Street in spirit, in the residential area of the Upper East Side, where there's nary another hotel to be seen. Though quite small, rooms are well appointed with name-brand knickknacks, including Bulgari toiletries, iHome stations, free wireless, and Frette linens. The lobby of this nine-story town house feels comfortable and lived-in, with newspapers laid out on comfortable couches and a free 24-hour cappuccino machine behind it. The generous complimentary breakfast uses a local bakery for all goods, and the hotel hosts a wine-and-cheese reception on weekday evenings. You can meet (sweaty) locals using a comp pass to New York Sports Club. **Pros:** neighborhood-y location; free Wi-Fi. **Cons:** far from many NYC tourist sights except Museum Mile; small rooms. ⊠ *164 E. 87th St., between Lexington and 3rd Aves., Upper East Side* ☎ *212/369–1000 or 877/847–4444* ⊕ *www.franklinhotel.com* ↬ *50 rooms* ⅙ *In-room: a/c, safe, Wi-Fi. In-hotel: room service, bar, laundry service, Internet terminal, Wi-Fi hotspot, some pets allowed* ▭ *AE, D, DC, MC, V* ⅋❘ *CP* Ⓜ *4, 5, 6 to 86th St.* ⊹ *6:G6.*

$$$$ ☶ **Hôtel Plaza Athénée.** It's easy to be seduced by this luxurious hotel, positioned unobtrusively by Central Park on the Upper East Side. The key is finding the right room—they come in a wide range of layouts and design schemes. Some even have small patios. Service is stellar, with a personal sit-down check-in to the side of the lobby, and extravagant room service. The hotel may seem stuffy to younger visitors. To others, touches like the lobby tapestries depicting forest scenes will be a welcome old-school luxury. The Bar Seine is a dark and secretive hideaway, one of the best bars in the city, and surely the only one with a floor made of leather. Arabelle is a much-touted, if not particularly well-loved restaurant. **Pros:** discerning service; exotic bar. **Cons:** hoity-toity; nonstandarized rooms hit-or-miss. ⊠ *37 E. 64th St., at Madison Ave., Upper East Side* ☎ *212/734–9100 or 800/447–8800* ⊕ *www. plaza-athenee.com* ↬ *115 rooms, 35 suites* ⅙ *In-room: a/c, safe, kitchen (some), refrigerator, Internet. In-hotel: restaurant, room service, bar, gym, laundry service, parking (paid), some pets allowed* ▭ *AE, D, DC, MC, V* Ⓜ *6 to 68th St./Hunter College* ⊹ *5:F5.*

$$ ☶ **Hotel Wales.** Every effort has been made to retain the turn-of-the-
↺ century mood of this 1901 Carnegie Hill landmark—from the cavernous lobby to the Pied Piper parlor, where vintage children's illustrations cover the walls. A complimentary European-style breakfast is served in the parlor; on a nice day you can head up to the rooftop terrace to have it there. Guest rooms are small, but they do have fine oak woodwork, and all come with CD players. Most of the suites face Madison Avenue; unfortunately, the windows aren't soundproof, making for some noisy evenings, especially when coupled with the loud air-conditioning units. The lovely Sarabeth's Restaurant, a local favorite for brunch, is in the hotel. **Pros:** on-site fitness facilities; charming decor. **Cons:** can be noisy; expensive Internet access; cramped rooms. ⊠ *1295 Madison Ave., between E. 92nd and E. 93rd Sts., Upper East Side* ☎ *212/876–6000 or 877/847–4444* ⊕ *www.waleshotel.com* ↬ *46 rooms, 42 suites* ⅙ *In-room: a/c, safe, kitchen (some), refrigerator (some), DVD (some),*

Wi-Fi. *In-hotel: restaurant, room service, bar, gym, laundry service, parking (paid), some pets allowed* ⊟*AE, D, DC, MC, V* ⵙⵏ*CP* Ⓜ*4, 5, 6 to 86th St.* ✛ *6:F5.*

$$$ 🆃 **The Lowell.** This old-money refuge was built as an upscale apartment hotel in the 1920s, and still delivers genteel sophistication and pampering service in an unbeatable location—though expensive, it's a steal for the price category thanks to rooms and service comparable to hotels that are 50 percent more expensive per night. Steps away from Madison Avenue shopping and the Museum Mile, the Lowell is on a leafy residential block. The lobby is small and cramped, but guest rooms have all the civilized comforts of home, including stocked bookshelves, luxe bathrooms, and even umbrellas. Thirty-three of the suites, all decorated in different themes such as the Hollywood Suite and the Garden Suite, have working fireplaces, and 11 have private terraces, the better for spying on posh neighboring abodes. Most of the non-suite rooms have been redecorated in a more modern, streamlined style, with less chintz and no patterns. The Pembroke Room serves a fine afternoon tea, and the Post House serves some of the best steaks in town. The in-room iPods (on request) and *New York Times* delivered to the room are particularly nice touches. **Pros:** great location; service with a personal touch; charming decor. **Cons:** unimpressive, cramped lobby; some rooms need updating. ⊠ *28 E. 63rd St., between Madison and Park Aves., Upper East Side* 🕾 *212/838–1400 or 800/221–4444* ⊕ *www. lowellhotel.com* ⤵*23 rooms, 47 suites* ♿ *In-room: a/c, safe, kitchen, refrigerator, DVD, Internet. In-hotel: 2 restaurants, room service, bar, gym, laundry service, parking (paid), some pets allowed* ⊟*AE, D, DC, MC, V* Ⓜ*4, 5, 6, N, R, W to 59th St./Lexington Ave.; F to 63rd St./ Lexington Ave.* ✛ *5:F6.*

UPPER WEST SIDE

19

$$ 🆃 **The Empire Hotel.** This historic Upper West Side spot, which reopened in 2008 after an extensive redesign, offers a dizzying number of amenities. When you first enter the hotel, you'll be drawn to the sophisticated, bi-level lobby with floor-to-ceiling silk drapes, high-back banquettes, and a dimly lighted bar. That's before you soak up the sun and enjoy the breathtaking views from the rooftop pool and lounge area underneath the hotel's iconic red neon sign. Guest rooms, which are small, provide a comfortable and chic escape from the bustle of the city. A soothing palette of varying shades of brown is complemented with animal-print chairs, dark-wood accents, and luxurious amenities such as flat-screen TVs, iPod docking stations, and Frette linens. **Pros:** prime location next to Lincoln Center and just blocks from Central Park; beautiful rooftop pool and bar; complimentary issues of *Time Out New York* magazine; fresh apples left at your bedside at turndown. **Cons:** elevators are beautifully redecorated but still feel rickety; bathrooms are nicely designed but tiny; pool is also quite small. ⊠ *44 W. 63rd St., at Columbus Ave., Upper West Side* 🕾 *212/265–7400* ⊕ *www.empirehotelnyc.com* ⤵*50 suites, 370 rooms* ♿ *In-room: a/c, safe, refrigerator, Wi-Fi* ⊟*AE, MC, V* Ⓜ*1, A, B, C to 59th St/Columbus Circle* ✛ *5:C5.*

$–$$ ⛄ **Excelsior.** Directly across the street from the American Museum of Natural History, this well-kept spot rubs shoulders with fine prewar apartment buildings (make sure to spring for a room with museum views). The frilly, faux-Victorian rooms with cushy beds have modern comforts like satellite television and Wi-Fi. On the second floor the hotel serves a breakfast that's good but slightly pricey for the neighborhood. The library lounge, with leather sofas, a cozy fireplace, and tables with built-in game boards, is an unexpected plus. On the minus side is a staff that seems to be too busy to focus on customer service. **Pros:** unique Upper West Side location near Central Park and foodie mecca Zabar's; tranquil environment. **Cons:** guests report unfriendly front-desk staff; rooms could use updating. ⊠ *45 W. 81st St., between Central Park W and Columbus Ave., Upper West Side* ☎ *212/362–9200 or 800/368–4575* ⊕ *www.excelsiorhotelny.com* ⟿ *118 rooms, 80 suites* ⛄ *In-room: a/c, safe, Wi-Fi. In-hotel: gym, laundry service, Internet terminal, Wi-Fi hotspot, some pets allowed* ▭ *AE, D, DC, MC, V* Ⓜ *B, C to 81st St.* ✢ *5:C2.*

$–$$ ⛄ **Hotel Beacon.** The Upper West Side's best buy for the price is three blocks from Central Park, ten from Lincoln Center, and footsteps from Zabar's, the gourmet grocery store. All of the generously sized sea-green rooms and suites include marble bathrooms, kitchenettes with coffeemakers, pots and pans, stoves, and microwaves. Closets are huge, and some of the bathrooms have Hollywood dressing room–style mirrors. High floors have views of Central Park, the Hudson River, or the Midtown skyline; the staff here is especially friendly and helpful. In this safe, exciting residential neighborhood, the Hotel Beacon makes a nice choice for exploring a different corner of the city. **Pros:** kitchenettes in all rooms; heart of UWS location; affordable. **Cons:** rooms emphasize comfort over style. ⊠ *2130 Broadway, at W. 75th St., Upper West Side* ☎ *212/787–1100 or 800/572–4969* ⊕ *www.beaconhotel.com* ⟿ *120 rooms, 110 suites* ⛄ *In-room: a/c, safe, kitchen, refrigerator. In-hotel: laundry facilities, parking (paid)* ▭ *AE, D, DC, MC, V* Ⓜ *1, 2, 3 to 72nd St.* ✢ *5:A3.*

$ ⛄ **The Lucerne.** The landmark facade of this exquisite building has more pizzazz than the predictable guest rooms, with their dark-wood reproduction furniture and chintz bedspreads. Health-conscious adults can head to the gym on the top floor, with its city views, and rooms are also stocked with Nintendo systems. Service is the hotel's strong suit, and their popular Mediterranean restaurant Nice Matin is one of the better ones on the Upper West Side. The affluent residential neighborhood is filled with an impressive array of boutiques and gourmet food shops, and the American Museum of Natural History is a short walk away. **Pros:** free Wi-Fi; clean; close to Central Park. **Cons:** inconsistent room size; some guests report uncomfortable pillows. ⊠ *201 W. 79th St., at Amsterdam Ave., Upper West Side* ☎ *212/875–1000 or 800/492–8122* ⊕ *www.thelucernehotel.com* ⟿ *142 rooms, 42 suites* ⛄ *In-room: a/c, kitchen (some), refrigerator (some), Wi-Fi. In-hotel: restaurant, room service, bar, gym, laundry service, Internet terminal, Wi-Fi hotspot, parking (paid)* ▭ *AE, D, DC, MC, V* Ⓜ *1 to 79th St.* ✢ *5:A2.*

Lodging Alternatives

APARTMENT RENTALS VS. SUITE HOTELS

For your trip to New York, you may want a little more space than the city's typically tiny hotel rooms provide. Some travelers consider apartment rentals, but we tend to recommend hotel suites instead. Why? Unfortunately, apartment-rental scams are prevalent. In some published reports, potential guests have arrived to find that the apartment they rented does not exist, or that they are paying for an illegal sublet. In some cases, travelers have lost their deposit money, or their prepaid rent (note: never wire money to an individual's account).

There are a few reputable providers of short-term rentals, noted below. But many Fodorites have turned to suite hotels and B&Bs with apartment-like accommodations to guard themselves from possible scams. We've noted some of their most enthusiastic recommendations.

Local rental agencies: **Abode Limited** (⌂ Box 20022, New York, NY 10028 ☎ 800/835-8880 or 212/472-2000 ⊕ www.abodenyc.com) arranges rentals of furnished apartments. **Manhattan Getaways** (⌂ Box 1994, New York, NY 10022 ☎ 212/956-2010 ⊕ www.manhattangetaways.com).

Suite suggestions from **Fodor's Forums** (⊕ www.fodors.com/forums):

"For a week or less, there's no need to risk being scammed or renting something illegal by renting a private apt. There are LOADS of suite hotels and B&Bs at all price levels that will provide the space and convenience of an apartment, many with the amenities of a hotel including the ability to be able to read reviews of them before you book and know

what you're getting. **Affinia** (⊕ www.Affinia.com) is a group of seven suite hotels at various prices that's well regarded ... **Milburn Hotel** (⊕ www.milburnhotel.com) and **The Salisbury Hotel** (⊕ www.nycsalisbury.com) are some of the more popular independent budget options." —mclaurie

BED-AND-BREAKFASTS

B&Bs booked through a service may be either hosted (you're the guest in someone's quarters) or unhosted (you have full use of someone's vacated apartment, including kitchen privileges). Reservation services: **All Around the Town** (⌂ 270 Lafayette St., Suite 804, New York, NY ☎ 212/675-5600 or 800/443-3800 ⊕ www.newyorkcitybestbb.com). **Bed-and-Breakfast Network of New York** (⌂ 134 W. 32nd St., Suite 602, between 6th and 7th Aves., New York, NY ☎ 212/645-8134 or 800/900-8134 ⊕ www.bedandbreakfastnetny.com). **City Lights Bed-and-Breakfast** (⌂ Box 20355, Cherokee Station, New York, NY 10075 ☎ 212/737-7049 ⊕ www.citylightsbedandbreakfast.com).

"**West Eleventh** (⊕ www.west-eleventh.com) and **Abingdon Guest House** (⊕ www.abingdonguesthouse.com) are two of many B&Bs in the village with some charm, but are only good for two people." —mclaurie

"Also try **B&B Manhattan** (⊕ www.bandbmanhattan.com) which has very nice studio and 1-bed apartments in Chelsea and GV. A friend stayed with them last year and liked it a lot."

—tomassocroccante

19

$ ⌕ **On the Ave Hotel.** This tranquil Upper West Side property is a foodie's delight, as it's home to West Branch, a popular neighborhood brunch, and the Upper West Side branch of the beloved Fatty Crab. Inside, the hotel is tasteful and modern, with the occasional swath of color from a red chair or green drapes. Rooms aren't especially big in relative terms—they start at 240 square feet—but for the price, they are quite spacious. Plus, they're outfitted with Aeron chairs, flat-screen TVs, and Trump-style black-marble bathrooms. Nickel-and-dime charges for Internet, valet parking, and the use of a mini-refrigerator are a bit frustrating, however. Suites and lofts have impressive views of Central Park, and the proximity to Lincoln Center is another plus. **Pros:** great dining options; excellent value. **Cons:** small charges add up; location not ideal for all NYC visitors. ⊠ *2178 Broadway, at W. 77th St., Upper West Side* ☎ *800/509–7598* ⊕ *www.ontheave-nyc.com* ⇨ *250 rooms, 32 suites* ⌂ *In-room: a/c, safe, Internet, Wi-Fi. In-hotel: 2 restaurants, room service, parking (paid)* ⊟ *AE, MC, V* Ⓜ *1 to 79th St.* ✛ *5:A3.*

$$$$ ⌕ **Trump International Hotel and Towers.** Go figure: Donald Trump has created a very discreet hotel. An inconspicuous lobby immediately introduces you to the hotel's fine service, which continues throughout your stay with personal assistants. What is showy is the building, a black skyscraper jutting high above Columbus Circle presenting unobstructed views of Central Park from floor-to-ceiling windows. Suites that corner the park and circle have some of the most compelling urban views in the world. Rooms and suites resemble mini-apartments: all have fully equipped kitchens with dishwashers. Room decor is slightly outdated in that razzle-dazzle Trump style—gold fixtures!—like a luxury apartment from a decade ago. Personalized stationery and business cards are provided on request. The restaurant, Jean Georges, is one of the city's finest, and for a price a Jean Georges sous-chef will prepare a meal in your kitchenette. That's luxury. **Pros:** fine service; stellar views; discerning treatment. **Cons:** somewhat outdated luxury furnishings. ⊠ *1 Central Park W, between W. 59th and W. 60th Sts., Upper West Side* ☎ *212/299–1000 or 888/448–7867* ⊕ *www.trumpintl.com* ⇨ *37 rooms, 130 suites* ⌂ *In-room: a/c, safe, kitchen, refrigerator, DVD, Internet. In-hotel: restaurant, room service, bar, pool, gym, spa, laundry service, parking (paid)* ⊟ *AE, D, DC, MC, V* Ⓜ *1, A, B, C, D to 59th St./Columbus Circle* ✛ *5:C6.*

Travel Smart
New York City

WORD OF MOUTH

"If you are traveling with kids just make sure a parent goes through the [subway] turnstile first and last in case one of the metro cards doesn't work and one of you is stuck on the wrong side from the others."

—richbutnot

GETTING HERE AND AROUND

Made up of five boroughs, New York City packs a staggering range of sights and activities into 322 square mi. You'll probably want to focus most of your visit in Manhattan, a compact island of attractions. To experience the most from the city, you need to think like a New Yorker: explore the city with your eyes open to everything around you; every city block offers new and unexpected sights.

If you're flying into one of three major airports that service New York, pick your mode of transportation for getting to Manhattan before your plane lands. The typical route is to hire a car or wait in the taxi line. Looking to save? Pick from the shuttle or public transportation options we've outlined.

Once you're in Manhattan, getting around can be a breeze when you get the hang of the subway system. You can hop in and out of neighborhoods, each with its own completely different vibe, in minutes. When you're not in a rush, just walk— it's the best way to discover the true New York. Not quite sure where you are or how to get where you're headed? Ask a local. You just may be surprised how friendly the city's inhabitants are, especially when it's not rush hour. In the same getting-there-is-half-the-fun spirit, find water, land, and air journeys to see the city from a whole new perspective.

▮ AIR TRAVEL

Generally, more international flights go in and out of John F. Kennedy Airport, more domestic flights go in and out of LaGuardia Airport, and Newark Airport serves both domestic and international travelers.

Airlines and Airports Airline and Airport Links.com (⊕ *www.airlineandairportlinks.com*) has links to many of the world's airlines and airports.

Airline Security Issues Transportation Security Administration (⊕ *www.tsa.gov*) has answers for almost every question that might come up.

AIRPORTS

The major air gateways to New York City are LaGuardia Airport (LGA) and JFK International Airport (JFK) in the borough of Queens, and Newark Liberty International Airport (EWR) in New Jersey. Cab fares are generally higher to and from Newark. The AirTrain link between Newark Airport and New Jersey transit makes the journey in less than 15 minutes; then you must transfer to a NJ Transit train to Pennsylvania Station in Manhattan.

Airport Information JFK International Airport (☎ *718/244–4444* ⊕ *www.jfkairport. com*). **LaGuardia Airport** (☎ *718/533–3400* ⊕ *www.laguardiaairport.com*). **Newark Liberty International Airport** (☎ *973/961–6000 or 888/397–4636* ⊕ *www.newarkairport.com*).

TRANSFERS—CAR SERVICES

Car services can be a great deal because the driver will often meet you on the concourse or in the baggage-claim area and help you with your luggage. The flat rates and tolls are often comparable to taxi fares, but some car services will charge for parking and waiting time at the airport. To eliminate these expenses, other car services require that you telephone their dispatcher when you land so they can send the next available car to pick you up. New York City Taxi and Limousine Commission rules require that all car services be licensed and pick up riders only by prior arrangement; if possible, call 24 hours in advance for reservations, or at least a half day before your flight's departure. Drivers of nonlicensed vehicles (gypsy cabs) often solicit fares outside the terminal in baggage-claim areas. Don't take them: you run the risk of an unsafe ride, and you'll definitely pay more than the going rate.

For phone numbers, see By Taxi.

TRANSFERS—TAXIS AND SHUTTLES

Outside the baggage-claim area at each of New York's major airports are taxi stands where a uniformed dispatcher helps passengers find taxis (⇨ *By Taxi)*. Cabs are not permitted to pick up fares anywhere else in the arrivals area, so if you want a taxi, take your place in line. Shuttle services generally pick up passengers from a designated spot along the curb.

New York Airport Service runs buses between JFK and LaGuardia airports, and buses from those airports to Grand Central Terminal, Port Authority Bus Terminal, Penn Station, Bryant Park, and hotels between 31st and 60th streets in Manhattan. Fares cost between $12 and $15 one way and $21 to $27 round-trip. Buses operate from 6:05 AM to 11 PM from the airport; between 5 AM and 10 PM going to the airport.

SuperShuttle vans travel to and from Manhattan to JFK, LaGuardia, and Newark. These blue vans will stop at your home, office, or hotel. There are courtesy phones at the airports. For travel to the airport, the company recommends you make your request 24 hours in advance. Fares range from $13 to $22 per person.

Shuttle Service New York Airport Service (☎ *718/875–8200* ⊕ *www.nyairportservice. com)*. **SuperShuttle** (☎ *800/258–3826* ⊕ *www.supershuttle.com)*.

TRANSFERS FROM JFK INTERNATIONAL AIRPORT

Taxis charge a flat fee of $45 plus tolls (which may be as much as $6) to Manhattan only, and take 35–60 minutes. Prices are roughly $20–$55 for trips to most other locations in New York City. You should also tip the driver.

The AirTrain links to the A subway line's Howard Beach station, and to Long Island Railroad's (LIRR) Jamaica Station, which is adjacent to the Sutphin Boulevard/

Archer Avenue E/J/Z subway station, with connections to Manhattan. The monorail system runs 24 hours, leaving from Howard Beach and Jamaica stations every 4 to 8 minutes during peak times and every 12 minutes during off-peak times. From Midtown Manhattan, the longest trip to JFK is via the A train, a trip of less than an hour that costs $2.25 in subway fare in addition to $5 for the AirTrain. The quickest trip is with the Long Island Railroad (about 30 minutes), for a total cost of about $13. When traveling to the Howard Beach station, be sure to take the A train marked FAR ROCKAWAY or ROCKAWAY PARK, not LEFFERTS BOULEVARD.

JFK Transfer Information AirTrain JFK (⊕ *www.airtrainjfk.com)*. **Long Island Railroad** (*Jamaica Station ⊠ 146 Archer Ave., at Sutphin Ave.* ☎ *718/217–5477* ⊕ *www.mta.Info/lirr)*.

TRANSFERS FROM LAGUARDIA AIRPORT

Taxis cost $21–$30 plus tip and tolls (which may be as high as $6) to most destinations in New York City, and take at least 20–40 minutes.

For $2.25 you can ride the M-60 public bus (there are limited luggage facilities on some buses) to 106th Street and Broadway on Manhattan's Upper West Side. From there, you can transfer to the subway to head to your destination. Alternatively, you can take the Q-48 bus to the Main Street subway station in Flushing, where you can transfer to the 7 train. Allow at least 90 minutes for the entire trip to Midtown.

TRANSFERS FROM NEWARK AIRPORT

Taxis to Manhattan cost $50–$70 plus tolls ($8) and take 20 to 45 minutes. "Share and Save" group rates are available for up to four passengers between 8 AM and midnight—make arrangements with the airport's taxi dispatcher. If you're heading to the airport from Manhattan, a $15 surcharge applies to the normal taxi rates and the $5 toll.

AirTrain Newark is an elevated light rail system that connects to New Jersey Transit and Amtrak trains at the Newark

Liberty International Airport Station. Total travel time to Penn Station in Manhattan is approximately 20 minutes and costs $15. AirTrain runs every 3 minutes from 5 AM to midnight and every 15 minutes from midnight to 5 AM.

The AirTrain to Newark's Penn Station takes five minutes. From Newark Penn Station you can catch PATH trains, which run to Manhattan 24 hours a day. PATH trains run every 10 minutes on weekdays, every 15 to 30 minutes on weeknights and weekends. After stopping at Christopher Street, one line travels along 6th Avenue, making stops at West 9th Street, West 14th Street, West 23rd Street, and West 33rd Street. Other PATH trains connect Newark Penn Station with the World Trade Center site. PATH train fare is $1.75.

Coach USA with Olympia Trails buses leave for Grand Central Terminal and Penn Station in Manhattan about every 15 to 30 minutes until midnight. The trip takes roughly 45 minutes, and the fare is $15. Between the Port Authority or Grand Central Terminal and Newark, buses run every 20 to 30 minutes. The trip takes 55 to 65 minutes

Newark Airport Information AirTrain Newark (☎ 888/397–4636 ⊕ www.airtrainnewark. com). **Coach USA** (☎ 877/894–9155 ⊕ www. coachusa.com). **PATH Trains** (☎ 800/234–7284 ⊕ www.pathrail.com).

TRANSFERS BETWEEN AIRPORTS
AirTrain provides detailed, up-to-the-minute recorded information on how to reach your destination from any of New York's airports. Note that if you arrive after midnight at any airport, you may wait a long time for a taxi. Consider calling a car service, as there is no shuttle service at that time.

Contacts AirTrain (☎ 800/247–7433 [800/ AIR–RIDE] ⊕ www.airtrainnewark.com).

■ BOAT TRAVEL

The Staten Island Ferry runs across New York Harbor between Whitehall Street next to Battery Park in Lower Manhattan and St. George terminal in Staten Island. The free 25-minute ride gives you a view of the financial district skyscrapers, the Statue of Liberty, and Ellis Island.

New York Water Taxi, in addition to serving commuters, shuttles tourists to the city's many waterfront attractions between the West and East sides and Lower Manhattan, the South Street Seaport, and Brooklyn's waterfront parks. The hop-on, hop-off one-day pass ticket is $20; the two-day pass is $25.

Information New York Water Taxi (*NYWT* ☎ 212/742–1969 ⊕ newyorkwatertaxi.com). **Staten Island Ferry** (*www.siferry.com*).

■ BUS TRAVEL

Most long-haul and commuter bus lines feed into the Port Authority Bus Terminal, on 8th Avenue between West 40th and 42nd streets. You must purchase your ticket at a ticket counter, not from the bus driver, so give yourself enough time to wait in a line. Several bus lines serving northern New Jersey and Rockland County, New York, make daily stops at the George Washington Bridge Bus Station from 5 AM to 1 AM. The station is connected to the 175th Street Station on the A line of the subway, which travels down the West Side of Manhattan.

A variety of discount bus services, including Bolt Bus and Vamoose Bus, offer direct routes from cities, such as Philadelphia, Boston, and Washington, D.C., with the majority of destinations lying along the East Coast. These budget options, priced from about $20 one way, depart from locations throughout the city.

Most city buses follow easy-to-understand routes along the Manhattan street grid. Routes go up or down the north–south avenues, or east and west on the major two-way crosstown streets: 96th,

86th, 79th, 72nd, 57th, 42nd, 34th, 23rd, and 14th. Usually bus routes operate 24 hours, but service is infrequent late at night. Traffic jams can make rides maddeningly slow, especially along 5th Avenue in Midtown and the Upper East Side. Certain bus routes provide "limited-stop service" during weekday rush hours, which saves travel time by stopping only at major cross streets and transfer points. A sign posted at the front of the bus indicates that it has limited service; ask the driver whether the bus stops near where you want to go before boarding.

To find a bus stop, look for a light-blue sign (green for a limited bus) on a green pole; bus numbers and routes are listed, with the stop's name underneath.

Bus fare is the same as subway fare: $2.25. MetroCards *(⇨ By Public Transportation)* allow you one free transfer between buses or from bus to subway; when using coins on the bus, you can ask the driver for a free transfer coupon, good for one change to an intersecting route. Legal transfer points are listed on the back of the slip. Transfers generally have time limits of two hours. You cannot use the transfer to enter the subway system.

Route maps and schedules are posted at many bus stops in Manhattan and at major stops throughout the other boroughs. Each of the five boroughs of New York has a separate bus map; they're available from some station booths, but rarely on buses. The best places to obtain them are the MTA booth in the Times Square Information Center, or the information kiosks in Grand Central Terminal and Penn Station.

Pay your bus fare when you board, with exact change in coins (no pennies, and no change is given) or with a MetroCard.

Buses in New York Metropolitan Transit Authority (MTA) Travel Information Line (☎ 718/330–1234, 718/330–4847 for non-English speakers ⊕ www.mta.info). **MTA Status information hotline** (☎ 718/243–7777 or 718/330–1234), updated hourly.

Buses to New York Adirondack, Pine Hill & New York Trailways (☎ 800/225–6815 ⊕ www.trailways.com). Coach (☎ 800/631–8405 ⊕ www.coachusa.com/shortlinebus). Greyhound Lines Inc. (☎ 800/231–2222 ⊕ www.greyhound.com). New Jersey Transit (☎ 973/275–5555 ⊕ www.njtransit.com). Peter Pan Trailways (☎ 413/781–2900 or 800/237–8747 ⊕ www.peterpanbus.com). Vermont Transit (☎ 800/552–8737 ⊕ www.vermonttransit.com).

Bus Stations George Washington Bridge Bus Station (✉ 4211 Broadway, between 178th and 179th Sts., Washington Heights ☎ 800/221–9903 ⊕ www.panynj.gov). Port Authority Bus Terminal (✉ 625 8th Ave., at 42nd St., Midtown West ☎ 212/564–8484 ⊕ www.panynj.gov). Bolt Bus ☎ 877/265–8287 ⊕ www.boltbus.com).Vamoose Bus ☎ 877/393–2828 ⊕ www.vamoosebus.com).

■ CAR TRAVEL

If you plan to drive into Manhattan, try to avoid the morning and evening rush hours and lunch hour. The deterioration of the bridges to Manhattan, especially those spanning the East River, means that repairs will be ongoing for the next few years. Listen to traffic reports on the radio before you set off, and don't be surprised if a bridge is partially closed or entirely blocked with traffic.

Driving within Manhattan can be a nightmare of gridlocked streets, obnoxious drivers and bicyclists, and seemingly suicidal jaywalkers. Narrow and one-way streets are common, particularly downtown, and can make driving even more difficult. The most congested streets of the city lie between 14th and 59th streets and 3rd and 8th avenues.

GASOLINE

Gas stations are few and far between in Manhattan. If you can, fill up at stations outside the city, where prices are anywhere from 10¢ to 50¢ cheaper per gallon. The average price of a gallon of regular unleaded gas is between $2.50 and $3, at this writing. In Manhattan, you can refuel at stations along the West Side Highway and 11th Avenue south of West 57th Street and along East Houston Street. Some gas stations in New York require you to pump your own gas; others provide attendants.

PARKING

Free parking is difficult to find in Midtown and on weekday evenings and weekends in other neighborhoods. On the other hand, parking lots charge exorbitant rates—as much as $23 for two hours (this includes an impressive sales tax of 18.625%). If you do drive, use your car sparingly in Manhattan. Instead, park it in a guarded parking garage for at least several hours; hourly rates decrease somewhat if a car is left for a significant amount of time. If you find a spot on the street, check parking signs carefully. Before leaving your car, scour the curb for that bane of every motorist's existence, the painted yellow line that's so faded you had better look twice to ascertain both its existence and range.

CAR RENTALS

When you reserve a car, ask about cancellation penalties, taxes, drop-off charges (if you're planning to pick up the car in one city and leave it in another), and surcharges (for being under or over a certain age, for additional drivers, or for driving across state or country borders or beyond a specific distance from your point of rental). All these things can add substantially to your costs. Request car seats and extras such as GPS when you book.

Rates are sometimes—but not always—better if you book in advance or reserve through a rental agency's Web site. There are other reasons to book ahead, though: for popular destinations, during busy times of the year, or to ensure that you get certain types of cars (vans, SUVs, exotic sports cars).

■**TIP→** Make sure that a confirmed reservation guarantees you a car. Agencies sometimes overbook, particularly for busy weekends and holiday periods.

Rates in New York City are around $75–$125 a day and $250–$400 a week for an economy car with air-conditioning, automatic transmission, and unlimited mileage. This includes the state tax on car rentals, which is 13.62%. Rental costs are lower just outside New York City, specifically in such places as Hoboken, New Jersey, and Yonkers, New York. The Yellow Pages are also filled with a profusion of local car-rental agencies, some renting secondhand vehicles. If you're traveling during a holiday period, make sure that a confirmed reservation guarantees you a car.

CAR-RENTAL INSURANCE

If you own a car and carry comprehensive car insurance for both collision and liability, your personal auto insurance will probably cover a rental, but read your policy's fine print to be sure. If you don't have auto insurance, then you should probably buy the collision- or loss-damage waiver (CDW or LDW) from the rental company. This eliminates your liability for damage to the car. Some credit cards offer CDW coverage, but it's usually supplemental to your own insurance and rarely covers SUVs, minivans, luxury models, and the like. If your coverage is secondary, you may still be liable for loss-of-use costs from the car-rental company (again, read the fine print). But no credit-card insurance is valid unless you use that card for *all* transactions, from reserving to paying the final bill.

You may also be offered supplemental liability coverage; the car-rental company is required to carry a minimal level of liability coverage insuring all renters, but it's rarely enough to cover claims in a really serious accident if you're at fault. Your own auto-insurance policy will protect you if you own a car; if you don't, you have to decide whether you are willing to take the risk.

U.S. rental companies sell CDWs and LDWs for about $15 to $25 a day; supplemental liability is usually more than $10 a day. The car-rental company may offer you all sorts of other policies, but they're rarely worth the cost. Personal accident insurance, which is basic hospitalization coverage, is an especially egregious rip-off if you already have health insurance.

■ **TIP→** You can decline the insurance from the rental company and purchase it through a third-party provider such as Travel Guard (⊕ *www.travelguard.com*)—$9 per day for $35,000 of coverage. That's sometimes just under half the price of the CDW offered by some car-rental companies.

■ PUBLIC TRANSPORTATION TRAVEL

When it comes to getting around New York, you have your pick of transportation in almost every neighborhood. The subway and bus networks are extensive, especially in Manhattan, although getting across town can take some extra maneuvering. If you're not pressed for time, take a public bus (⇨ *By Bus*); they generally are slower than subways, but you can also see the city as you travel. Yellow cabs (⇨ *By Taxi*) are abundant, except during the evening rush hour, when many drivers' shifts change. Like a taxi ride, the subway (⇨ *By Subway*) is a true New York City experience; it's also often the quickest way to get around. But New York is really a walking town, and depending on the time of day and your destination, hoofing it could be the easiest and most enjoyable option.

During weekday rush hours (from 7:30 AM to 9:30 AM and 5 PM to 7 PM) avoid the jammed Midtown area, both in the subways and on the streets—travel time on buses and taxis can easily double.

Subway and bus fares are $2.25, although reduced fares are available for senior citizens and people with disabilities during nonrush hours.

You pay for mass transit with a MetroCard, a plastic card with a magnetic strip. As you swipe the card through a subway turnstile or insert it in a bus's card reader, the cost of the fare is automatically deducted. With the MetroCard, you can transfer free from bus to subway, subway to bus, or bus to bus. You must start with the MetroCard and use it again within two hours to complete your trip.

MetroCards are sold at all subway stations and at some stores—look for an "Authorized Sales Agent" sign. The MTA sells two kinds of MetroCards: unlimited-ride and pay-per-ride. Seven-day unlimited-ride MetroCards ($27) allow bus and subway travel for a week. If you will ride more than 13 times, this is the card to get.

The one-day unlimited-ride Fun Pass ($8.25) is good from the day of purchase through 3 AM the following day. It's sold only by neighborhood MetroCard merchants and MetroCard vending machines at stations (not through the station agent).

When you purchase a pay-per-ride card worth $8 or more, you get a 15% bonus. For example, $20 gives you $23 on your card, which is 10 rides for the price of 9 plus 50¢. Unlike unlimited-ride cards, pay-per-ride MetroCards can be shared between riders. (Unlimited-ride Metro Cards can be used only once at the same station or bus route in an 18-minute period.)

You can buy or add money to an existing MetroCard at a MetroCard vending machine, available at most subway station entrances (usually near the station booth). The machines accept major credit cards and ATM or debit cards. Many also accept cash, but note that the maximum amount of change they will return is $6.

Schedule and Route Information Metropolitan Transit Authority (MTA) Travel Information Line (☎ 718/330–1234, 718/596–8585 travelers with disabilities ⊕ www.mta.info).

■ SUBWAY TRAVEL

The subway system operates on more than 840 mi of track for 24 hours a day and serves nearly all the places you're likely to visit. It's cheaper than a cab, and during the workweek it's often faster than either taxis or buses. The trains are well lighted and air-conditioned. Still, the New York subway is hardly problem-free. Many trains are crowded, the older ones are noisy, the air-conditioning can break, and platforms can be dingy and damp. Homeless people sometimes take refuge from the elements by riding the trains, and panhandlers head there for a captive audience. Although trains usually run frequently, especially during rush hours, you never know when some incident somewhere on the line may stall traffic. In addition, subway construction sometimes causes delays or limitation of service, especially on weekends.

Most subway entrances are at street corners and are marked by lampposts with an illuminated Metropolitan Transit Authority (MTA) logo or globe-shaped green or red lights—green means the station is open 24 hours and red means the station closes at night (though colors don't always correspond to reality). Subway lines are designated by numbers and letters, such as the 3 line or the A line. Some lines run "express" and skip stops, and others are "locals" and make all stops. Each station entrance has a sign indicating the lines that run through the station. Some entrances are also marked "uptown only" or "downtown only." Before entering subway stations, read the signs carefully. One of the most frequent mistakes visitors make is taking the train in the wrong direction. Maps of the full subway system are posted in every train car and usually on the subway platform (though these are sometimes out-of-date). You can usually pick up free maps at station booths.

For the most up-to-date information on subway lines, call the MTA's Travel Information Center or visit its Web site. The Web site Hopstop is a good source for figuring out the best line to take to reach your destination. (You can also call or text Hopstop for directions.) Alternatively, ask a station agent.

Subway fare is the same as bus fare: $2.25. You can transfer between subway lines an unlimited number of times at any of the numerous stations where lines intersect. If you use a MetroCard (⇨ *By Public Transportation*) to pay your fare, you can also transfer to intersecting MTA bus routes for free. Such transfers generally have time limits of two hours.

Pay your subway fare at the turnstile, using a MetroCard bought at the station booth or from a vending machine. **Subway Information Hopstop** (☎ *888/2– HOPSTOP* ⊕ *www.hopstop.com*). **Metropolitan Transportation Authority (MTA) Travel Information Line** (☎ *718/330–1234, 718/330–4847 for non-English speakers* ⊕ *www.mta.info*). **MTA Lost Property Office** (☎ *212/712–4500*). **MTA Status information hotline** (☎ *718/243–7777*), updated hourly.

▮ TAXI TRAVEL

Yellow cabs are in abundance almost everywhere in Manhattan, cruising the streets looking for fares. They are usually easy to hail on the street or from a cab stand in front of major hotels, though finding one at rush hour or in the rain can take some time. Even if you're stuck in a downpour or at the airport, do not accept a ride from a gypsy cab. If a cab is not yellow and does not have a numbered aqua-color plastic medallion riveted to the hood, you could be putting yourself in danger by getting into the car.

You can see whether a taxi is available by checking its rooftop light; if the center panel is lighted and the side panels are dark, the driver is ready to take passengers. Once the meter is engaged (and if it isn't, alert your driver; you'll seldom benefit from negotiating an off-the-record ride), the fare is $2.50 just for entering the vehicle and 40¢ for each unit thereafter. A unit is defined as either 0.20 mi when the cab's cruising at 6 MPH or faster or as 60 seconds when the cab is either not moving or moving at less than 12 MPH. A 50¢ night surcharge is added between 8 PM and 6 AM and a much-maligned $1 weekday surcharge is tacked on to rides after 4 PM and before 8 PM.

One taxi can hold a maximum of four passengers (an additional passenger under the age of 7 is allowed if the child sits on someone's lap). There is no charge for extra passengers. You must pay any bridge or tunnel tolls incurred during your trip (a driver will usually pay the toll himself to keep moving quickly, but that amount will be added to the fare when the ride is over). Taxi drivers expect a 15% to 20% tip.

To avoid unhappy taxi experiences, try to know where you want to go and how to get there before you hail a cab. You should assist your driver, however, by directing him to the specific cross streets of your destination (for instance, "5th Avenue and 42nd Street"), rather than the numerical address, which means nothing to drivers. Also, speak simply and clearly to make sure the driver has heard you correctly. A quick call to your destination will give you cross-street information, as will a glance at a map marked with address numbers. When you leave the cab, remember to take your receipt. It includes the cab's medallion number, which can help you track the cabbie down in the event that you lose your possessions in the cab or if, after the fact, you want to report an unpleasant ride.

Taxis can be extremely difficult (if not impossible) to find in many parts of Brooklyn, Queens, the Bronx, and Staten Island. As a result, you may have no choice but to call a car service. Always determine the fee beforehand when using a car service sedan; a 10%–15% tip is customary above that.

Taxi Companies Carmel Car Service (☎ 212/666–6666 or 866/666–6666 ⊕ www. carmelcarservice.com). **Dial 7 Car Service** (☎ 212/777–7777 ⊕ www.dial7.com).

London Towncars (☎ 212/988–9700 or 800/221–4009 ⊕ www.londontowncars.com).

❚ TRAIN TRAVEL

For information about traveling by subway within New York City, see By Subway.

Metro-North Commuter Railroad trains take passengers from Grand Central Terminal to points north of New York City, both in New York State and Connecticut. Amtrak trains from across the United States arrive at Penn Station. For trains from New York City to Long Island and New Jersey, take the Long Island Railroad and New Jersey Transit, respectively; both operate from Penn Station. The PATH trains offer service to Newark and Jersey City. All of these trains generally run on schedule, although occasional delays occur.

Information Amtrak (☎ 800/872–7245 ⊕ www.amtrak.com). **Long Island Rail Road** (☎ 718/217–5477 ⊕ www.mta.info/ lirr). **Metro-North Commuter Railroad** (☎ 212/532–4900 ⊕ www.mta.info/mnr). **New Jersey Transit** (☎ 973/275-5555 ⊕ www. panynj.gov). **PATH** (☎ 800/234–7284 ⊕ www. pathrail.com).

Train Stations Grand Central Terminal (✉ Park Ave. at E. 42nd St., Midtown East ☎ 212/340.2583 ⊕ www.grandcentralterminal. com). **Penn Station** (✉ W. 31st to W. 33rd Sts., between 7th and 8th Aves., Midtown West ☎ 212/630–6401).

ESSENTIALS

■ COMMUNICATIONS

INTERNET

You can check your e-mail or surf the Internet at cafés, copy centers, libraries, and most hotels. By far the best equipped and probably most convenient is Cyber Café in Times Square, which has dozens of computers plus scanners, color printers, and camera chip readers; it's open from 8 AM to 11 PM on weekdays and 11 AM to 11 PM on weekends. The organization NYCwireless keeps track of free Wi-Fi hot spots in the New York area. The Web site JiWire allows you to find Wi-Fi hot spots in hotels, libraries, parks, and other locations throughout the city.

Contacts JiWire (⊕ www.jiwire.com).

Internet Cafés Cyber Café (✉ 250 W. 49th St., between 8th Ave. and Broadway, Midtown West ☎ 212/333–4109 ⊕ www.cyber-cafe. com). Web 2 Zone (✉ 54 Cooper Sq., East Village ☎ 212/614–7300 ⊕ www.web2zone.com).

Other Internet Locations New York Public Library–Mid-Manhattan Library (✉ 455 5th Ave., at E. 40th St., Midtown East ☎ 212/930–0800 ⊕ www.nypl.org). **NYCwireless** (⊕ www. nycwireless.net).

■ DISABILITIES AND ACCESSIBILITY

New York has come a long way in making life easier for people with disabilities. At most street corners curb cuts allow wheelchairs to roll along unimpeded. Many restaurants, shops, and movie theaters with step-up entrances have wheelchair ramps. And though some New Yorkers may rush past those in need of assistance, you'll find plenty of people who are more than happy to help you get around.

Hospital Audiences maintains a Web site with information on the accessibility of many landmarks and attractions. A similar list, "Tourist and Cultural Information for the Disabled," is available from New York City's Web site. Big Apple Greeters has tours of New York City tailored to visitors' personal preferences. The Andrew Heiskell Braille and Talking Book Library houses an impressive collection of braille, large-print, and recorded books in a layout designed for people with vision impairments.

Local Resources Andrew Heiskell Library (✉ 40 W. 20th St., between 5th and 6th Aves., Flatiron District Ⓜ F, V to 23rd St. ☎ 212/206–5400 ⊕ www.talkingbooks.nypl.org). **Big Apple Greeters** (✉ 1 Centre St., Lower Manhattan ☎ 212/669–8159 ⊕ www.bigapplegreeter. org). **Hospital Audiences** (☎ 212/575–7676 ⊕ www.hospaud.org). **New York City** (☎ 311 in New York City, 212/639–9675 [212/NEW–YORK] outside New York ⊕ www.nyc.gov).

LODGING

Despite the Americans with Disabilities Act, the definition of accessibility seems to differ from hotel to hotel. Some properties may be accessible by ADA standards for people with mobility problems but not for people with hearing or vision impairments, for example.

If you have mobility problems, ask for the lowest floor on which accessible services are offered. If you have a hearing impairment, check whether the hotel has devices to alert you visually to the ring of the telephone, a knock at the door, and a fire/emergency alarm. Some hotels provide these devices without charge. Discuss your needs with hotel personnel if this equipment isn't available, so that a staff member can personally alert you in the event of an emergency.

If you're bringing a guide dog, get authorization ahead of time and write down the name of the person with whom you spoke.

RESERVATIONS

When discussing accessibility with an operator or reservations agent, ask hard questions. Are there any stairs, inside *or* out? Are there grab bars next to the toilet *and* in the shower/tub? How wide is the doorway to the room? To the bathroom? For the most extensive facilities meeting the latest legal specifications, opt for newer accommodations. If you reserve through a toll-free number, consider also calling the hotel's local number to confirm the information from the central reservations office. Get confirmation in writing when you can.

SIGHTS AND ATTRACTIONS

Most public facilities in New York City, whether museums, parks, or theaters, are wheelchair-accessible. Some attractions have tours or programs for people with mobility, sight, or hearing impairments.

TRANSPORTATION

Other than at major subway exchanges, most stations are still all but impossible to navigate; people in wheelchairs should stick to public buses, most of which have wheelchair lifts and "kneelers" at the front to facilitate getting on and off. Bus drivers will provide assistance.

Reduced fares are available to all disabled passengers displaying a Medicare card. Visitors to the city are also eligible for the same Access-a-Ride program benefits as New York City residents. Drivers with disabilities may use windshield cards from their own state or Canadian province to park in designated handicapped spaces.

The U.S. Department of Transportation Aviation Consumer Protection Division's online publication *New Horizons: Information for the Air Traveler with a Disability* offers advice for travelers with a disability, and outlines basic rights. Visit DisabilityInfo.gov for general information.

Information and Complaints Aviation Consumer Protection Division (⊕ airconsumer.ost.dot.gov/publications/horizons. htm for airline travel advice and rights).

Departmental Office of Civil Rights (☎ 202/366-4648, 202/366-8538 TTY ⊕ www. dotcr.ost.dot.gov). **Disability Rights Section** (☎ 202/514-0301 ADA information line, 800/514-0301, 202/514-0383 TTY, 800/514-0383 TTY ⊕ www.ada.gov). **U.S. Department of Transportation Hotline** (☎ 800/778-4838 for disability-related air-travel problems, 800/455-9880 TTY).

∎ GAY AND LESBIAN TRAVEL

Attitudes toward same-sex couples are very tolerant in Manhattan and many parts of Brooklyn. Chelsea, Greenwich Village, and Hell's Kitchen are the most prominently gay neighborhoods, but gay men and lesbians feel right at home almost everywhere. The world's biggest gay-pride parade takes place on 5th Avenue the last Sunday in June.

For details about the gay and lesbian scene, consult *Fodor's Gay Guide to the USA* (available in bookstores everywhere).

PUBLICATIONS

For listings of gay events and places, check out *Next* and the *Gay City News,* both distributed free on the street and in many bars and shops throughout Manhattan. Magazines *Paper* and *Time Out New York* have a gay-friendly take on what's happening in the city.

Local Information Gay & Lesbian Switchboard of NY (☎ 212/989-0999 or 888/843-4564 ⊕ www.glnh.org). **Lesbian, Gay, Bisexual & Transgender Community Center** (✉ 208 W. 13th St., between 7th and 8th Aves., Greenwich Village ☎ 212/620-7310 ⊕ www. gaycenter.org).

Gay Publications Gay City News (⊕ www. gaycitynews.com). **HX** (⊕ www.hx.com). **New York Blade News** (⊕ www.nyblade.com). **Next** (⊕ www.nextmagazine.net).

Gay- and Lesbian-Friendly Travel Agencies Different Roads Travel (☎ 760/325-6964, 800/429-8747 Ext. 14 ⊕ lgernert@tzell.com). **Skylink Travel and Tour/Flying Dutchmen**

Travel (☎ 707/546–9888 or 800/225–5759), serving lesbian travelers.

▌ KIDS IN NEW YORK

For listings of children's events, consult *New York* magazine. The Friday *New York Times* "Weekend" section also includes children's activities. Other good sources on happenings for youngsters are the monthly magazines *New York Family* and *NY Metro Parents,* both available free at toy stores, children's museums, and other places where parents and children are found. The Web site Parents Connect includes listings of what's going on. If you have access to cable television, check the local all-news channel New York 1, where you'll find a spot aired several times daily that covers current and noteworthy children's events. *Fodor's New York City with Kids* (available in bookstores everywhere) can help you plan your days together.

Publications and Web Sites NY Metro Parents (⊕ www.nymetroparents.com). **Parents Connect** (⊕ www.parentsconnect.com).

LODGING

Before you consider using a cot or fold-out couch for your child, ask just how large your hotel room is—New York City rooms tend to be small. Most hotels in New York allow children under a certain age to stay in their parents' room at no extra charge, but others charge for them as extra adults; be sure to find out the cutoff age for children's discounts.

PUBLIC TRANSPORTATION

Children shorter than 44 inches ride for free on MTA buses and subways. If you're pushing a stroller, don't struggle through a subway turnstile; ask the station agent to buzz you through the gate (the attendant will ask you to swipe your MetroCard through the turnstile nearest the gate). Keep a sharp eye on your young ones while on the subway. At some stations there is a gap between the train doors and the platform. Unfortunately, New York riders are not known to give

---

> ### CURB RAMP SAVVY
>
> You will endear yourself to many people with disabilities as well as parents with strollers if you refrain from crowding into the curb ramps that exist at virtually every stoplight. A surprising number of native New Yorkers are still oblivious to this concept.

up their seats for children, for someone carrying a child, or for anyone else.

▌ MONEY

CREDIT CARDS

Throughout this guide, the following abbreviations are used: **AE**, American Express; **D**, Discover; **DC**, Diners Club; **MC**, MasterCard; and **V**, Visa.

Record all your credit-card numbers—as well as the phone numbers to call if your cards are lost or stolen—in a safe place, so you're prepared should something go wrong. Both MasterCard and Visa have general numbers you can call if your card is lost, but you're better off calling the number of your issuing bank, since MasterCard and Visa usually just transfer you to your bank; your bank's number is usually printed on your card.

Reporting Lost Cards American Express (☎ 800/992–3404 in U.S., 336/393–1111 collect from abroad ⊕ www.americanexpress. com). **Diners Club** (☎ 800/234–6377 in U.S., 303/799–1504 collect from abroad ⊕ www. dinersclub.com). **Discover** (☎ 800/347–2683 in U.S., 801/902–3100 collect from abroad ⊕ www.discovercard.com). **MasterCard** (☎ 800/622–7747 in U.S., 636/722–7111 collect from abroad ⊕ www.mastercard.com). **Visa** (☎ 800/847–2911 in U.S., 410/581–9994 collect from abroad ⊕ www.visa.com).

TRAVELER'S CHECKS AND CARDS

Both Citibank (under the Visa brand) and American Express issue traveler's checks in the United States, but Amex is better known and more widely accepted; you can also avoid hefty surcharges by cashing Amex checks at Amex offices. Whatever you do, keep track of all the serial numbers in case the checks are lost or stolen.

Contacts American Express (☎ 888/412-6945 in U.S., 801/945-9450 collect outside of U.S. to add value or speak to customer service ⊕ www.americanexpress.com).

∎ RESTROOMS

Seinfeld fans might recall George Costanza's claim that if you named any given coordinates in New York City, he could instantly name the closest and most worthy public restroom in the vicinity. Regrettably, unless you're traveling with your own George or a potty training–toddler who can drive even the most hardened retailers to share their private bathrooms, public restrooms in New York are few and far between. Plans are in the works to add coin-operated street toilets at several locations. (At press time, the first toilet was operating in Madison Square Park with 20 more on the way).

In the meantime, when looking for a restroom, head for Midtown department stores, museums, or the lobbies of large hotels to find the cleanest bathrooms. Public atriums, such as those at the Citicorp Center and Trump Tower, also provide good public facilities, as do Bryant Park and the many Barnes & Noble bookstores and Starbucks coffee shops in the city. If you're in the area, the Times Square Information Center, on Broadway between 46th and 47th streets, can be a godsend.

Find a Loo The Bathroom Diaries (⊕ www. thebathroomdiaries.com) is flush with unsanitized info on restrooms the world over—each one located, reviewed, and rated.

∎ SAFETY

New York City is one of the safest large cities in the country. However, do not let yourself be lulled into a false sense of security. As in any large city, travelers in New York remain particularly easy marks for pickpockets and hustlers.

After the September 11, 2001, terrorist attacks security was heightened throughout the city. Never leave any bags unattended, and expect to have yourself and your possessions inspected thoroughly in such places as airports, sports stadiums, museums, and city buildings.

Ignore the panhandlers on the streets and subways, people who offer to hail you a cab (they often appear at Penn Station, the Port Authority, and Grand Central), and limousine and gypsy cab drivers who (illegally) offer you a ride.

Keep jewelry out of sight on the street; better yet, leave valuables at home. Men should carry their wallets in their front pants pocket rather than in their back pockets. When in bars or restaurants, never hang your purse or bag on the back of a chair or put it underneath the table.

Avoid deserted blocks in unfamiliar neighborhoods. A brisk, purposeful pace helps deter trouble wherever you go.

The subway runs around the clock and is generally well trafficked until midnight (and until at least 2 AM on Friday and Saturday nights), and overall it is very safe. If you do take the subway late at night, ride in the center car, with the conductor, and wait on the center of the platform. Watch out for unsavory characters lurking around the inside or outside of stations.

When waiting for a train, stand far away from the edge of the subway platform, especially when trains are entering or leaving the station. Once the train pulls into the station, avoid empty cars. While on the train don't engage in verbal exchanges with aggressive riders, who may accuse others of anything from pushing to taking up too much space. If a fellow passenger makes you nervous while on the train, trust your instincts and change cars. When disembarking, stick with the crowd until you reach the street.

Travelers Aid International helps crime victims, stranded travelers, and wayward children, and works closely with the police.

Information Travelers Aid (✉ *JFK International Airport, Terminal 6* ☏ *718/656–4870* ✉ *Newark International Airport, Terminal B* ☏ *973/623–5052* ⊕ *www.travelersaid.org).*

▌SENIOR-CITIZEN TRAVEL

The Metropolitan Transit Authority (MTA) offers lower fares for passengers 65 and over. On the subway, show your Medicare card to the station agent, and for the standard fare ($2.25) you will be issued a MetroCard and a return-trip ticket; on the bus, show your Medicare card to the bus driver and a cash fare of $1.10 can be made. (Payment must be made in coins.)

To qualify for age-related discounts, mention your senior-citizen status up front when booking hotel reservations (not when checking out). Be sure to have identification on hand. When renting a car, ask about promotional car-rental discounts, which can be cheaper than senior-citizen rates.

Educational Programs Elderhostel (☏ *877/426–8056, 978/323–4141 international callers, 877/426–2167 TTY* ⊕ *www.elderhostel. org).*

Information MTA Reduced Fare hotline (☏ *718/243–4999* ⊕ *www.mta.info).*

▌SPORTS AND THE OUTDOORS

The City of New York's Parks & Recreation division lists all of the recreational facilities and activities available through New York's Parks Department. The sports section of *Time Out New York,* sold at most newsstands, lists upcoming events, times, dates, and ticket information.

Contact Information Parks & Recreation division (☏ *311 in New York City, 212/639–*

9675, 212/NEW–YORK outside New York City ⊕ *www.nyc.gov/parks).*

BASEBALL

The subway will get you directly to stadiums of both New York–area major-league teams. A fun alternative, the *Yankee Clipper* cruises from Manhattan's East Side and from New Jersey to Yankee Stadium on game nights. The round-trip cost is $22. The regular baseball season runs from April through September.

In 2009, the New York Mets moved from Shea Stadium to the neighboring, newly constructed CitiField, at the next-to-last stop on the 7 train, in Queens; the New York Yankees also got a new home at the new Yankee Stadium. Founded in 2001, the minor-league Brooklyn Cyclones are named for Coney Island's famous wooden roller coaster. A feeder team for the New York Mets, they play 38 home games at KeySpan Park, next to the boardwalk, with views of the Atlantic over the right-field wall and views of historic Astroland over the left-field wall. Most people make a day of it, with time at the beach and amusement rides before an evening game. Take the D, F, or Q subway to the end of the line, and walk one block to the right of the original Nathan's Famous hot dog stand.

For another fun, family-oriented experience, check out the Staten Island Yankees, one of New York's minor-league teams, which warms up many future New York Yankees players. The stadium, a five-minute walk from the Staten Island Ferry terminal, has magnificent panoramic views of Lower Manhattan and the Statue of Liberty.

Contact Information Brooklyn Cyclones (✉ *1904 Surf Ave., at 19th St., Coney Island* ☏ *718/449–8497* ⊕ *www.brooklyncyclones. com* Ⓜ *D, F, Q to Stillwell Ave.).* **CitiField** (✉ *Roosevelt Ave. off Grand Central Pkwy., Flushing* ☏ *718/507–8499* ⊕ *www.mets. com* Ⓜ *7 to Willets Pt./Shea Stadium).* **Staten Island Yankees** (✉ *Richmond County Bank Ballpark at St. George, Staten Island*

☎ 718/720–9265 ⊕ www.siyanks.com).
Yankee Clipper (✆ 800/533–3779 ⊕ www.
nywaterway.com). **Yankee Stadium** (✉ 161st
St. at River Ave., Bronx ☎ 718/293–6000
⊕ www.yankees.com Ⓜ B, D to 167th St.; 4 to
161st St.–Yankee Stadium).

BASKETBALL

The New York Knicks arouse intense
hometown passions, which means tickets
for home games at Madison Square Garden are hard to come by. The New Jersey
Nets play at the Meadowlands in the Izod
Center but have plans to relocate and possibly become the Brooklyn Nets. Tickets
are generally easy to obtain. The men's
basketball season runs from late October
through April. The New York Liberty,
a member of the Women's NBA, had its
first season in 1997; some of the team's
more high-profile players are already
legendary. The season runs from Memorial Day weekend through August, with
home games played at Madison Square
Garden.

If the professional games are sold out,
try to attend a college game where New
York stalwarts Fordham, Hofstra, and St.
John's compete against national top 25
teams during invitational tournaments.

**Contact Information Madison Square
Garden** (⊕ www.thegarden.com). **New Jersey
Nets** (☎ 201/935–3900 box office, 800/765–
6387 ⊕ www.nba.com/nets). **New York Knicks**
(☎ 212/465–5867 ⊕ www.nba.com/knicks).
New York Liberty (☎ 877/962–2849 tickets,
212/564–9622 fan hotline ⊕ www.wnba.com/
liberty).

BICYCLING

Central Park has a 6-mi circular drive
with a couple of decent climbs. It's closed
to automobile traffic from 10 AM to 3 PM
(except the southeast portion between 6th
Avenue and East 72nd Street) and 7 PM to
7 AM on weekdays, and from 7 PM Friday
to 7 AM Monday. On holidays it's closed
to automobile traffic from 7 PM the night
before until 7 AM the day after.

The bike lane along the Hudson River
Park's esplanade parallels the waterfront
from West 59th Street south to the esplanade of Battery Park City. The lane also
heads north, connecting with the bike
path in Riverside Park, the promenade
between West 72nd and West 110th
streets, and continuing all the way to the
George Washington Bridge. From Battery
Park it's a quick ride to the Wall Street
area, which is deserted on weekends, and
over to South Street and a bike lane along
the East River.

The 3.3-mi circular drive in Brooklyn's
Prospect Park is closed to cars year-round
except from 5 PM to 7 PM on weekends and
7 AM to 9 AM on weekdays except holidays. It has a long, gradual uphill that tops
off near the Grand Army Plaza entrance.
(Biking around Manhattan streets next to
the dense traffic is best left to messengers
and seasoned cyclists.)

**Bike Rentals Bicycle Rentals at Loeb Boat-
house** (✉ Midpark near E. 74th St., Central
Park ☎ 212/517–2233). **BicyclesNYC** (✉ 1400
3rd Ave., between E. 79th and F. 80th Sts.,
Upper East Side ☎ 212/794–2929 Ⓜ 4, 5, 6
to 86th St. ⊕ www.bicyclesnyc.com). **Pedal
Pusher** (✉ 1306 2nd Ave., between E. 68th
and E. 69th Sts., Upper East Side ☎ 212/288–
5592 ⊕ www.pedalpusherbikeshop.com Ⓜ 6
to 68th St./Hunter College). **Toga Bike Shop**
(✉ 110 West End Ave., at W. 64th St., Upper
West Side ☎ 212/799–9625 ⊕ www.togabikes.
com Ⓜ 1 to 66th St.).

GROUP BIKE RIDES

For organized rides with other cyclists,
call or e-mail before you come to New
York. Bike New York runs a five-borough
bike ride in May. The Five Borough Bicycle Club organizes day and weekend rides.
The New York Cycle Club sponsors weekend rides for every level of ability. Time's
Up!, a nonprofit environmental group,
leads free recreational rides at least twice
a month for cyclists as well as skaters; the
Central Park Moonlight Ride, departing
from Columbus Circle at 10 PM the first
Friday of every month, is a favorite.

Contact Information Bike New York (✉ *891 Amsterdam Ave., at W. 103rd St., Upper West Side* ☎ *212/932-2453* ⊕ *www.bikenewyork. org*). **Five Borough Bicycle Club** (✉ *891 Amsterdam Ave., at W. 103rd St., Upper West Side* ☎ *212/932-2300 Ext. 115* ⊕ *www.5bbc. org*). **New York Cycle Club** (📪 *Box 4474, Grand Central Station, 10163* ☎ *212/828-5711* ⊕ *www.nycc.org*). **Time's Up!** (☎ *212/802-8222* ⊕ *www.times-up.org*).

BOATING AND KAYAKING

Central Park has rowboats (plus one Venetian gondola for glides in the moonlight) on the 22-acre Central Park Lake. Rent your rowboat at Loeb Boathouse, near East 74th Street, from March through October; gondola rides are available only in summer. In summer at the Pier 96 Boathouse in Midtown West, you can take a sturdy kayak out for a paddle for free on weekends and weekday evenings from mid-May through mid-October. Beginners learn to paddle in the calmer embayment area closest to shore until they feel ready to venture farther out into open water. More experienced kayakers can partake in the three-hour trips conducted every weekend and on holiday mornings. Sign-ups for these popular tours end at 8 AM. Due to high demand, names are entered into a lottery to see who gets to go out each morning. No reservations are taken in advance. **Manhattan Kayak Company** runs trips (these are not free) and gives lessons for all levels.

Contact Information Loeb Boathouse (✉ *Midpark near E. 74th St., Central Park* ☎ *212/517-2233* ⊕ *www.centralparknyc.org*). **Manhattan Kayak Company** (✉ *Chelsea Piers, Pier 66, W. 26th St. at the Hudson River, Chelsea* ☎ *212/924-1788* ⊕ *www.manhattankayak. com* Ⓜ *C, E to 23rd St.*). **Pier 96 Boathouse** (✉ *56th St. at the Hudson River, Midtown West* ⊕ *www.downtownboathouse.org* Ⓜ *1, A, C, E to 59th St.*).

FOOTBALL

The football season runs from September through December. The enormously popular New York Giants play at Giants Stadium in the Meadowlands Sports Complex. Most seats for Giants games are sold on a season-ticket basis—and there's a long waiting list for those. However, single tickets are occasionally available at the stadium box office. The New York Jets also play at Giants Stadium. Although Jets tickets are not as scarce as those for the Giants, most are snapped up by fans before the season opener.

Contact Information New York Giants (☎ *201/935-8222 for tickets* ⊕ *www.giants. com*). **New York Jets** (☎ *800/469-5387 for tickets* ⊕ *www.newyorkjets.com*).

ICE-SKATING

The outdoor rink in Rockefeller Center, open from October through early April, is much smaller in real life than it appears on TV and in movies. It's also busy, so be prepared to wait—there are no advance ticket sales. Although it's also beautiful, especially when Rock Center's enormous Christmas tree towers above it, you pay for the privilege: rates are $15.50–$19 and skate rentals are $12.

The city's outdoor rinks, open from roughly November through March, all have their own character. Central Park's beautifully situated Wollman Rink offers skating until long after dark beneath the lights of the city. Be prepared for daytime crowds on weekends. The Lasker Rink, at the north end of Central Park, is smaller and usually less crowded than Wollman. Prospect Park's Kate Wollman Rink borders the lake, and has a picture-postcard setting. Chelsea Piers' Sky Rink has two year-round indoor rinks overlooking the Hudson. Rentals are available at all rinks. The Pond at Bryant Park offers free skating, not including the cost of skate rental, from late October through January, from 8 AM to 10 PM from Sunday through Thursday and from 8 AM to midnight Friday and Saturday.

Contact Information Bryant Park (✉ *6th Ave. between 40th and 42nd Sts., Midtown West* ☎ *212/768-4242* ⊕ *www.thepondat-bryantpark.org* Ⓜ *B, D, F, V to 42nd St.*). **Kate**

Wollman Rink (✉ *Ocean and Parkside Aves., Prospect Park, Brooklyn* ☎ *718/287-6431* ⊕ *www.prospectpark.org* Ⓜ *2, 3 to Grand Army Plaza; B, Q to Prospect Park; F to 15th St./ Prospect Park*). **Lasker Rink** (✉ *Midpark near E. 106th St., Central Park* ☎ *917/492-3857* ⊕ *www.wollmanskatingrink.com* Ⓜ *B, C to 103rd St.*). **Rockefeller Center** (✉ *50th St. at 5th Ave., lower plaza, Midtown West* ☎ *212/332-7654* ⊕ *www.therinkatrockcenter. com* Ⓜ *B, D, F, V to 47th–50th Sts./Rockefeller Center; E, V to 5th Ave.–53rd St.*). **Sky Rink** (✉ *Pier 61, W. 23rd St. at the Hudson River, Chelsea* ☎ *212/336-6100* ⊕ *www. chelseapiers.com* Ⓜ *C, E to 23rd St.*). **Wollman Rink** (✉ *North of 6th Ave., between 62nd and 63rd Sts., north of park entrance,* ☎ *212/439-6900* ⊕ *www.wollmanskatingrink.com*).

JOGGING

In Manhattan, Central Park is the busiest spot, specifically along the 1.6-mi path circling the Jacqueline Kennedy Onassis Reservoir, where you jog in a counterclockwise direction. A runners' lane has been designated along the park roads. A good 1.75-mi route starts at the former Tavern on the Green (now closed) along the West Drive, heads south around the bottom of the park to the East Drive, and circles back west on the 72nd Street park road to your starting point; the entire loop road is a hilly 6 mi. Riverside Park, along the Hudson River bank in Manhattan, is glorious at sunset. You can cover 4.5 mi by running from West 72nd to 116th Street and back, and the Greenbelt trail extends 4 more mi north to the George Washington Bridge at 181st Street. Other favorite Manhattan circuits are the Battery Park City esplanade (about 2 mi), which connects to the Hudson River Park (about 1.5 mi), and the East River Esplanade (just over 3 mi from East 59th to East 125th streets).

∎ STUDENTS IN NEW YORK

New York is home to such major schools as Columbia University, New York University, Fordham University, and the City College of New York. With other colleges scattered throughout the five boroughs, as well as a huge population of public and private high-schoolers, it's no wonder the city is rife with student discounts. Wherever you go, especially museums, sightseeing attractions, and performances, identify yourself as a student up front and ask if a discount is available. However, be prepared to show your ID as proof of enrollment and/or age.

A great program for those between the ages of 13 and 18 (or anyone in middle or high school) is High 5 for the Arts. Tickets to all sorts of performances are sold for $5 online or by phone. Write or call to receive a free catalog of events, check it out online, or pick a catalog up at any New York public library or at High 5's offices.

IDs and Services High 5 for the Arts (✉ *520 8th Ave., at 36th St., Midtown* ☎ *212/750-0555* ⊕ *www.highfivetix.org*). **STA Travel** (☎ *212/627-3111, 800/781-4040 24-hr service center* ⊕ *www.sta.com*). **Travel Cuts** (☎ *800/592-2887 in U.S.* ⊕ *www.travelcuts. com*).

∎ TAXES

A sales tax of 8.375% applies to almost everything you can buy retail, including restaurant meals. However, clothing and footwear are exempt as are prescription drugs and nonprepared food bought in grocery stores. For clothing and footwear items over $110, there is no city sales tax, although there is a 4.375% state sales tax.

∎ TIPPING

The customary tipping rate for taxi drivers is 15%–20%, with a minimum of $2; bellhops are usually given $2 per bag in luxury hotels, $1 per bag elsewhere. Hotel maids should be tipped $2 per day of your stay. A doorman who hails or helps you into a cab can be tipped $1–$2. You should also tip your hotel concierge for services rendered; the size of the tip depends on the difficulty of your request, as well as the quality of the concierge's work. Waiters should be tipped 15%–20%, though at higher-end restaurants, a solid 20% is more the norm. Tip $1 per drink you order at the bar.

▮ VISITOR INFORMATION

The Grand Central Partnership (a sort of civic Good Samaritans' group) has installed a number of information booths in and around Grand Central Terminal (there's one near Vanderbilt Avenue and East 43rd Street). They're loaded with maps and helpful brochures on attractions throughout the city and they're staffed by friendly, knowledgeable, multilingual New Yorkers.

NYC & Company's Times Square Visitors Center is decked out with lots of fun and helpful tools like multilingual kiosks. The bureau also has a midtown visitor center on 7th Avenue and runs kiosks in Lower Manhattan at City Hall Park and at Federal Hall National Memorial at 26 Wall Street; in Chinatown at the triangle where Canal, Walker, and Baxter streets meet; and in Harlem at the Apollo Theater at 253 West 125th Street.

The Downtown Alliance has information on the area encompassing City Hall south to Battery Park, and from the East River to West Street. For a free booklet listing New York City attractions and tour packages, contact the New York State Division of Tourism.

CONTACTS

City Information Brooklyn Information & Culture Inc. *(BRIC)* (✉ *647 Fulton St., 2nd fl., Brooklyn* ☎ *718/855-7882* ⊕ *www. bricartsmedia.org).* **Downtown Alliance** (✉ *120 Broadway, Suite 3340, between Pine and Thames Sts., Lower Manhattan* ☎ *212/566-6700* ⊕ *www.downtownny.com).* **Grand Central Partnership** (☎ *212/883-2420* ⊕ *www.grandcentralpartnership.org).* **NYC & Company Convention & Visitors Bureau** (✉ *810 7th Ave., between W. 52nd and W. 53rd*

> ### THE FODORS.COM CONNECTION
>
> Before your trip, be sure to check out what fellow travelers are saying in Talk on www.fodors.com.

Sts., 3rd fl., Midtown West ☎ *212/484-1222* ⊕ *www.nycgo.com).* **Times Square Information Center** (✉ *1560 Broadway, between 46th and 47th Sts., Midtown West* ☎ *212/768-1560* ⊕ *www.timessquarenyc.org).*

Statewide Information New York State Division of Tourism (☎ *518/474-4116 or 800/225-5697* ⊕ *www.iloveny.com).*

> **539**

INDEX

PHOTO CREDITS

1, Bo Zaunders/viestiphoto.com. 2, Kord.com/age fotostock. 5, Liberty Helicopters, Inc. **Chapter 1: Experience New York City:** 8-9, Rudy Sulgan/age fotostock. 10, Luc Novovitch/age fotostock. 11 (left), LHB Photo/Alamy. 11 (right), Oote Boe Photography/Alamy. 14 (top), ACE Stock Limited/Alamy. 14 (bottom), Sharad Haksar/age fotostock. 16 (top), Martha Cooper/viestiphoto.com. 16 (bottom), Photodisc. 18 (left), Ken Ross/viestiphoto.com. 18 (top center), Kord.com/age fotostock. 18 (top right), Doug Scott/age fotostock. 18 (bottom), Ken Ross/viestiphoto.com. 19 (top left), SuperStock/age fotostock. 19 (bottom left), Craig Chesek/AMNH. 19 (right), PictureQuest. 19 (top left), Walter Bibikow/viestiphoto.com. 20 (top left), Walter Bibikow/viestiphoto.com. 20 (bottom left), Frances Roberts/Alamy. 20 (right), Diane Hall/viestiphoto.com. 21, Jeff Greenberg/Alamy. 22, Black Star/Alamy. 23 (left), David H. Wells/age fotostock. 23 (right), Richard Levine/Alamy. 25, Everett Collection. 26, Joe Viesti/viestiphoto.com. 27 (left), Frances M. Roberts/Alamy. 27 (right), adactio/Flickr. 31 (left), emilydickinsonridesabmx/Flickr. 31 (right), David Berkowitz/Flickr. 32, Corbis. 33, Photodisc. 35 (top), Liberty Helicopters, Inc. 35 (bottom), Ken Ross/viestiphoto.com. 37 (top), Corbis. 37 (bottom), Library of Congress Prints and Photographs Division. **Chapter 2: Lower Manhattan:** 39, Ambient Images/Alamy. 41, Kord.com/age fotostock. 42, Chuck Pefley/Alamy. 46, Heeb Christian/age fotostock. 50, Silverstein Properties. 51 (top), SpecialKRB/Flickr. 51 (bottom), Sondra Paulson/iStockphoto. 52 (top left), AP Photo/Marty Lederhandler. 52 (top right), AP Photo/Amy Sancetta. 52 (bottom), RodneyRamsey/Flickr. 53 (left), AP Photo/Mark Lennihan. 53 (center), Peter Comitini/Flickr. 53 (right), Bo Zaunders/viestiphoto.com. 54-55 (top) and 54 (bottom), Silverstein Properties. 55 (bottom left and bottom right), Joe Woolhead/Silverstein Properties. 56 (top left), Keith Reicher/iStockphoto. 56 (bottom left), FaceMePLS/Flickr. 56 (center), jorbasa/Flickr. 56 (top right), p_c w/Flickr. 56 (bottom right), cytech/Flickr. 60, SuperStock. **Chapter 3: SoHo & Little Italy:** 61, Art Kowalsky/Alamy. 63, Ambient Images/Alamy. 64, Yadid Levy/Alamy. 66-67, SIME s.a.s/eStock Photo. 71, OK Harris Works of Art. **Chapter 4: East Village & the Lower East Side:** 73, Jeff Greenberg/Alamy. 75, peyri/Flickr. 76, Ken Ross/viestiphoto.com. 78, Giovanni Simeone/SIME/eStock Photo. **Chapter 5: Greenwich Village & Chelsea:** 83, Kokyat Choong/Alamy. 85, Black Star/Alamy. 86, Frances Roberts/Alamy. 91, Ambient Images Inc./Alamy. 94-95, Kord.com/SuperStock. 98, PCL/Alamy. 99, Frances M. Roberts/Alamy. **Chapter 6: Union Square:** 105, David Shankbone/Wikimedia Commons. 107, Kord.com/age fotostock. 108, Yadid Levy/Alamy. 111, Russell Kord/Alamy. 115, Joe Shlabotnik/Flickr. **Chapter 7: Midtown:** 119, Kord.com/age fotostock. 121, Bruno Perousse/age fotostock. 122, Michel Friang/Alamy. 128-29, Joe Viesti/viestiphoto.com. 131, Renaud Visage/age fotostock. 134, Ken Ross/viestiphoto.com. 135, Rudy Sulgan/age fotostock. 136, Corbis. **Chapter 8: The Upper East Side:** 139, Nicholas Pitt/Alamy. 141, Ken Ross/viestiphoto.com. 142, Janine Wiedel Photolibrary/Alamy. **Chapter 9: Central Park:** 147, Piero Ribelli. 148 (top), Piero Ribelli. 148 (center), Rudy Sulgan/age fotostock. 149 (left), Bo Zaunders/viestiphoto.com. 149 (right), Sandra Baker/Alamy. 150, Worldscapes/age fotostock. 151 (top), Michal Daniel. 151 (bottom), Chris Lee. 152, Peter Arnold. Inc./Alamy. 153 (left), Ken Ross/viestiphoto.com. 153 (right), Agency Jon Arnold Images/age fotostock. 154 (top left), Ken Ross/viestiphoto.com. 154 (top right), Sandra Baker/Alamy. 154 (bottom), Walter Bibikow/age fotostock. 155 (top left), Chuck Pefley/Alamy. 155 (top right), Bo Zaunders/viestiphoto.com. 155 (bottom), Darren Green Photography/Alamy. 156, Piero Ribelli. 157 (left), Sandra Baker/Alamy. 157 (right), Piero Ribelli. 158 (top left), Peter Arnold, Inc./Alamy. 158 (top right), TNT Magazine/Alamy. 158-59 (bottom), Bo Zaunders/viestiphoto.com. 159 (top left), Chuck Pefley/Alamy. 159 (top right), LMR Group/Alamy. 160 (top left), Piero Ribelli. 160 (bottom right), Ken Ross/viestiphoto.com. 161, Jon Arnold/Agency Jon Arnold Images/age fotostock. 162 (top), Lincoln Karim/palemale.com. 162 (center), Piero Ribelli. 162 (bottom images), Lincoln Karim/palemale.com. **Chapter 10: The Upper West Side:** 163, Kord.com/age fotostock. 165, Jeff Greenberg/age fotostock. 166, Kord.com/age fotostock. **Chapter 11: Harlem:** 173, Joe Viesti/viestiphoto.com. 175, Joe Malone/Agency Jon Arnold Images/age fotostock. 176, SuperStock/age fotostock. **Chapter 12: Brooklyn:** 181, Jeff Greenberg/age fotostock. 183, SuperStock/age fotostock. 184, ACE Stock Limited/Alamy. 190-91, Rudy Sulgan/SuperStock. **Chapter 13: Queens, The Bronx, and Staten Island:** 205, Sylvain Grandadam/age fotostock. 207, Michel Friang/Alamy. 208, Siobhan O'Hare. 219, Doug Milner. 223, Johnny Stockshooter/age fotostock. **Chapter 14: Museums:** 227, Bartomeu Amengual/age fotostock. 228, Beverly Logan/age fotostock. 229, Ken Ross/viestiphoto.com. 230-31 and 232 (top left and right), Ken Ross/viestiphoto.com. 232 (bottom), Dennis Finnin/AMNH. 234, Ken Ross/viestiphoto.com. 235 and 236, Dennis Finnin/AMNH. 237 (top), C. Chesek/AMNH. 237 (bottom), Dennis Finnin and C. Chesek/AMNH. 238, Brooks Walker. 239 and 240 (top), Renaud Visage/age fotostock. 240 (center), Metropolitan Museum of Art. 240 (bottom), Ken Ross/viestiphoto.com. 242 (top), Renaud Visage/age fotostock. 242 (bottom), Metropolitan Museum of Art. 243, Wild Bill Studio/Metropolitan Museum of Art. 244 (top and bottom), Metropolitan Museum of Art. 245, Doug Scott/age fotostock.

246, Ken Ross/viestiphoto.com. 247, Geoffrey Clements. **Chapter 15: The Performing Arts:** 261, Joan Marcus. 262, Joe Viesti/viestiphoto.com. 267, Ted Pink/Alamy. 275, Ken Ross/viestiphoto.com. **Chapter 16: Nightlife:** 285, Pictorial Press/Alamy. 286, kriskat£afterglowpix.com. 290, Lebrecht Music and Arts Photo Library/Alamy. 291 (top and bottom), Michael Belardo/Alamy. 292 (top), kriskat£afterglowpix.com. 292 (bottom), Gustavo Andrade/age fotostock. 293 (top), Carlos Davila/age fotostock. 293 (bottom), Happy Valley. 294 (top), Grant Winston. 294 (bottom), foodfolio/Alamy. 295, Mark Molloy. 296, Mike Faivre/Arlene's Grocery. 297 (top), Mike Faivre/Arlene's Grocery. 297 (bottom left), Nicole Fournier. 297 (bottom right), Ted Pink/Alamy. **Chapter 17: Shopping:** 315, Bruno Perousse/age fotostock. 316, Richard Levine/Alamy. 320 and 321 (left), Piero Ribelli. 321 (right), Jonathan Adler. 328 (top), Yadid Levy/Alamy. 328 (bottom), Sigerson Morrison. 329, Yadid Levy/Alamy. 338 (top), Piero Ribelli. 338 (bottom), Louis Vuitton. 339, 348-49, and 356 (top), Piero Ribelli. 356 (bottom), Susan Rosenberg Jones. 357, Piero Ribelli. 364 (top), Las Venus. 364 (bottom), Sugar Sweet Sunshine Bakery. 365 (top), Frock. 365 (bottom), lowereastsideny.com. 372, Frances Roberts/Alamy. 373 (top), Amy's Bread. 373 (bottom), Cynthia Rowley. **Chapter 18: Where to Eat:** 379, Bo Zaunders/viestiphoto.com. 380, ACE Stock Limited/Alamy. 386, Dina Litovsky/Stregoica Photography. 387, Thomas Schauer. 388, Dina Litovsky/Stregoica Photography. 389, pravin.premkumar/Flickr. 390, Dina Litovsky/Stregoica Photography. 391 (top), Noah Kalina. 391 (bottom), Chickpea. 392, Dina Litovsky/Stregoica Photography. 393, Visual Mercenary Group. 394, Frances M. Roberts/Alamy. 395, nicasaurusrex/Flickr. 396, Quality Meats. 397, Kyotofu. 398, The Modern. 399, Rachel from Cupcakes Take the Cake/Flickr. 400, Per Se. 401 (top), Pamela Weekes. 401 (bottom), Frances Roberts/Alamy. **Chapter 19: Where to Stay:** 467, Arcaid/Alamy. 468, On the Ave Hotel. 472, The Carlyle, A Rosewood Hotel. 473, Roy Wright. 486 (top), Simon Brown/Firmdale Hotels. 486 (bottom left), Michael Weber. 486 (bottom right), The Standard. 487 (top), Ace Hotel/Eric Laignel. 487 (bottom left), Library Hotel. 487 (bottom right), Claudia Hehr Photography. 506 (top), Mandarin Oriental. 506 (bottom left), The Plaza. 506 (bottom right), The Ritz-Carlton New York, Central Park. 507 (top), Roy Wright. 507 (bottom left), The Peninsula. 507 (bottom right), St. Regis Hotel, New York.